DISSERTATIONS ON THE APOSTOLIC AGE.

DISSERTATIONS ON THE APOSTOLIC AGE

REPRINTED FROM EDITIONS OF ST PAUL'S EPISTLES.

BY THE LATE

J. B. LIGHTFOOT, D.D., D.C.L., LL.D.,
LORD BISHOP OF DURHAM.

WIPF & STOCK · Eugene, Oregon

Wipf and Stock Publishers
199 W 8th Ave, Suite 3
Eugene, OR 97401

Dissertations on the Apostolic Age
By Lightfoot, Joseph B.
ISBN 13: 978-1-60608-356-7
Publication date 12/19/2008
Previously published by Macmillan and Co., 1892

INTRODUCTORY NOTE.

THE present volume consists of five dissertations reprinted from Dr Lightfoot's published commentaries upon St Paul's Epistles. The Trustees of the Lightfoot Fund feel that there must be a large number of English readers who will be glad to possess in a form separate from the Greek text and commentary such of the late Bishop's valuable excursuses as from the nature of the subjects treated admit of this severance without loss of clearness. This necessary limitation appears to the Trustees to point to the omission of the introductions to the Epistles in question and of one dissertation (*Were the Galatians Celts or Teutons?*) appended to the commentary upon the Epistle to the Galatians.

The dissertations are reprinted just as they stand in the commentaries. No attempt has been made to enlarge the footnotes or references. But at the close of the Essay on the Christian Ministry two short appendices have been added, one giving Dr Lightfoot's final opinion upon the genuineness of the seven Greek Ignatian Epistles, the other consisting of a collection of extracts from his own writings, which was printed by him a year or so before his death to illustrate his view of the Christian Ministry over and above the particular scope of the Essay.

INTRODUCTORY NOTE.

Through the kindness of Prof. J. E. B. Mayor, who placed at the disposal of the Editor a list which he had himself drawn up, the numerous references to the works of Seneca in the fourth dissertation have been made more available to students by the addition, in the Index of Passages, of the number of the section to that of the chapter, thus rendering the quotation more precise. The Trustees take this opportunity of thanking Prof. Mayor for his courtesy, and of expressing their regret that the existence of the list was not known in time to admit of the insertion of the sections in the text of the dissertation.

July, 1892.

EXTRACT FROM THE LAST WILL AND TESTAMENT OF THE LATE
JOSEPH BARBER LIGHTFOOT, LORD BISHOP OF DURHAM.

"I bequeath all my personal Estate not hereinbefore other-
"wise disposed of unto [my Executors] upon trust to pay and
"transfer the same unto the Trustees appointed by me under
"and by virtue of a certain Indenture of Settlement creating a
"Trust to be known by the name of 'The Lightfoot Fund for
"the Diocese of Durham' and bearing even date herewith but
"executed by me immediately before this my Will to be ad-
"ministered and dealt with by them upon the trusts for the
"purposes and in the manner prescribed by such Indenture of
"Settlement."

EXTRACT FROM THE INDENTURE OF SETTLEMENT OF 'THE
LIGHTFOOT FUND FOR THE DIOCESE OF DURHAM.'

"WHEREAS the Bishop is the Author of and is absolutely
"entitled to the Copyright in the several Works mentioned in
"the Schedule hereto, and for the purposes of these presents he
"has assigned or intends forthwith to assign the Copyright in
"all the said Works to the Trustees. Now the Bishop doth
"hereby declare and it is hereby agreed as follows:—

"The Trustees (which term shall hereinafter be taken to
"include the Trustees for the time being of these presents)

viii EXTRACT FROM BISHOP LIGHTFOOT'S WILL.

"shall stand possessed of the said Works and of the Copyright
"therein respectively upon the trusts following (that is to say)
"upon trust to receive all moneys to arise from sales or other-
"wise from the said Works, and at their discretion from time
"to time to bring out new editions of the same Works or any
"of them, or to sell the copyright in the same or any of them,
"or otherwise to deal with the same respectively, it being the
"intention of these presents that the Trustees shall have and
"may exercise all such rights and powers in respect of the said
"Works and the copyright therein respectively, as they could
"or might have or exercise in relation thereto if they were the
"absolute beneficial owners thereof....

"The Trustees shall from time to time, at such discretion as
"aforesaid, pay and apply the income of the Trust funds for or
"towards the erecting, rebuilding, repairing, purchasing, en-
"dowing, supporting, or providing for any Churches, Chapels,
"Schools, Parsonages, and Stipends for Clergy, and other Spiri-
"tual Agents in connection with the Church of England and
"within the Diocese of Durham, and also for or towards such
"other purposes in connection with the said Church of England,
"and within the said Diocese, as the Trustees may in their ab-
"solute discretion think fit, provided always that any payment
"for erecting any building, or in relation to any other works in
"connection with real estate, shall be exercised with due regard
"to the Law of Mortmain; it being declared that nothing here-
"in shall be construed as intended to authorise any act contrary
"to any Statute or other Law....

"In case the Bishop shall at any time assign to the Trustees
"any Works hereafter to be written or published by him, or
"any Copyrights, or any other property, such transfer shall be
"held to be made for the purposes of this Trust, and all the

"provisions of this Deed shall apply to such property, subject
"nevertheless to any direction concerning the same which the
"Bishop may make in writing at the time of such transfer, and
"in case the Bishop shall at any time pay any money, or trans-
"fer any security, stock, or other like property to the Trustees,
"the same shall in like manner be held for the purposes of this
"Trust, subject to any such contemporaneous direction as afore-
"said, and any security, stock or property so transferred, being
"of a nature which can lawfully be held by the Trustees for the
"purposes of these presents, may be retained by the Trustees,
"although the same may not be one of the securities herein-
"after authorised.

"The Bishop of Durham and the Archdeacons of Durham
"and Auckland for the time being shall be *ex-officio* Trustees,
"and accordingly the Bishop and Archdeacons, parties hereto,
"and the succeeding Bishops and Archdeacons, shall cease to be
"Trustees on ceasing to hold their respective offices, and the
"number of the other Trustees may be increased, and the power
"of appointing Trustees in the place of Trustees other than
"Official Trustees, and of appointing extra Trustees, shall be
"exercised by Deed by the Trustees for the time being, pro-
"vided always that the number shall not at any time be less
"than five.

"The Trust premises shall be known by the name of 'The
"Lightfoot Fund for the Diocese of Durham.'"

TABLE OF CONTENTS.

		PAGE
I.	THE BRETHREN OF THE LORD	1—45
II.	ST PAUL AND THE THREE	46—134
III.	THE CHRISTIAN MINISTRY	135—238
	ADDITIONAL NOTES	239—246
IV.	ST PAUL AND SENECA	247—316
	THE LETTERS OF PAUL AND SENECA	317—322
V.	THE ESSENES	323—407
	A. THE NAME ESSENE	325—331
	B. ORIGIN AND AFFINITIES OF THE ESSENES	332—380
	C. ESSENISM AND CHRISTIANITY	381—407
	INDICES.	
	I. INDEX OF SUBJECTS	411—421
	II. INDEX OF PASSAGES	422—435

ERRATA.

Page 52, n. 1, l. 21 read	*Strom.* ii. p. 491.
75, n. 1	*Haer.* xxix. 9.
78, n. 1, l. 3	Hippol. *Haer.* vii. 34.
151, n. 9	Clem. Rom. 42, 44.
176, n. 1	Tertull. *de Praescr.* 36.
177, n. 1, l. 2	iv. p. 687, ed. Delarue.
182, n. 6	Iren. iii. 3. 3.
193, n. 5, l. 12	Augustin. *Op.* iii. P. 2, p. 92.
208, n. 1	*De Unit. Eccl.* 5.

I.

THE BRETHREN OF THE LORD.

I.

THE BRETHREN OF THE LORD[1].

IN the early ages of the Church two conflicting opinions were held regarding the relationship of those who in the Gospels and Apostolic Epistles are termed 'the brethren of the

<small>Two rival theories.</small>

---

[1] The interest in this subject, which was so warmly discussed towards the close of the fourth century, has been revived in more recent times by the publication of Herder's *Briefe zweener Brüder Jesu in unserem Kanon* (1775), in which the Helvidian hypothesis is put forward. Since then it has formed the subject of numberless monographs, dissertations, and incidental comments. The most important later works, with which I am acquainted, are those of Blom, *De τοῖς ἀδελφοῖς et ταῖς ἀδελφαῖς τοῦ Κυρίου* (Leyden, 1839); of Schaf, *Das Verhältniss des Jakobus Bruders des Herrn zu Jakobus Alphäi* (Berlin, 1842); and of Mill, *The accounts of our Lord's Brethren in the New Testament vindicated etc.* (Cambridge, 1843). The two former adopt the Helvidian view; the last is written in support of St Jerome's hypothesis. Blom gives the most satisfactory statement which I have seen of the patristic authorities, and Schaf discusses the Scriptural arguments most carefully. I am also largely indebted to the ability and learning of Mill's treatise, though he seems to me to have mistaken the general tenor of ecclesiastical tradition on this subject. Besides these monographs I have also consulted, with more or less advantage, articles on the subject in works of reference or periodicals, such as those in *Studien u. Kritiken* by Wieseler; *Die Söhne Zebedäi Vettern des Herrn* (1840, p. 648), and *Ueber die Brüder des Herrn*, etc. (1842, p. 71). In preparing for the second edition I looked over the careful investigation in Laurent's *Neutest. Studien* p. 155 sq (1866), where the Helvidian hypothesis is maintained, but saw no reason to make any change in consequence. The works of Arnaud, *Recherches sur l'Epître de Jude*, and of Goy (Mont. 1845), referred to in Bishop Ellicott's *Galatians* i. 19, I have not seen. My object in this dissertation is mainly twofold; (1) To place the Hieronymian hypothesis in its true light, as an effort of pure criticism unsupported by any traditional sanction; and (2) To say a word on behalf of the Epiphanian solution, which seems, at least of late years, to have met with the fate reserved for τὰ μέσα in literature and theology, as well as in politics, ὑπ' ἀμφοτέρων ἢ ὅτι οὐ ξυνηγωνίζοντο ἢ φθόνῳ τοῦ περιεῖναι διεφθείροντο. I suppose it was because he considered it idle to discuss a theory which had no friends, that Prof. Jowett (on Gal. i. 19), while balancing the claims of the other two solutions, does not even mention the existence of this, though in the early centuries it was the received account.

Lord.' On the one hand it was maintained that no blood relationship existed; that these brethren were in fact sons of Joseph by a former wife, before he espoused the Virgin; and that they are therefore called the Lord's brethren only in the same way in which Joseph is called His father, having really no claim to this title but being so designated by an exceptional use of the term adapted to the exceptional fact of the miraculous incarnation. On the other hand certain persons argued that the obvious meaning of the term was the correct meaning, and that these brethren were the Lord's brethren as truly as Mary was the Lord's mother, being her sons by her husband Joseph. The former of these views was held by the vast majority of orthodox believers and by not a few heretics; the latter was the opinion of a father of the Church here and there to whom it occurred as the natural inference from the language of Scripture, as Tertullian for instance, and of certain sects and individuals who set themselves against the incipient worship of the Virgin or the one-sided asceticism of the day, and to whom therefore it was a very serviceable weapon of controversy.

A third propounded by Jerome.

Such was the state of opinion, when towards the close of the fourth century Jerome struck out a novel hypothesis. One Helvidius, who lived in Rome, had attacked the prevailing view of the superiority of virgin over married life, and in doing so had laid great stress on the example of the Lord's mother who had borne children to her husband. In or about the year 383 Jerome, then a young man, at the instigation of 'the brethren' wrote a treatise in reply to Helvidius, in which he put forward his own view[1]. He maintained that the Lord's brethren were His cousins after the flesh, being sons of Mary the wife of Alphæus and sister of the Virgin. Thus, as he boasted, he asserted the virginity not of Mary only but of Joseph also.

Names assigned to these three.

These three accounts are all of sufficient importance either from their real merits or from their wide popularity to deserve

---

[1] *Adv. Helvidium de Perpetua Virginitate B. Mariae*, II. p. 206 (ed. Vall.). Comp. *Comment. ad Gal.* i. 19.

consideration, and I shall therefore investigate their several claims. As it will be convenient to have some short mode of designation, I shall call them respectively the *Epiphanian*, the *Helvidian*, and the *Hieronymian* theories, from the names of their most zealous advocates in the controversies of the fourth century when the question was most warmly debated.

But besides the solutions already mentioned not a few others have been put forward. These however have been for the most part built upon arbitrary assumptions or improbable combinations of known facts, and from their artificial character have failed to secure any wide acceptance. It is assumed for instance, that two persons of the same name, James the son of Alphæus and James the Lord's brother, were leading members of the Church of Jerusalem, though history points to one only[1]; or that James the Lord's brother mentioned in St Paul's Epistles is not the same James whose name occurs among the Lord's brethren in the Gospels, the relationship intended by the term 'brother' being different in the two cases[2]; or that 'brethren' stands for 'foster-brethren,' Joseph having undertaken the charge of his brother Clopas' children after their father's death[3]; or that the Lord's brethren had a double parentage, a legal as well as an actual father, Joseph having raised seed to his deceased brother Clopas by his widow according to the levirate law[4]; or lastly, that the cousins of Jesus were rewarded with the title of His brethren, because they were His steadfast disciples, while His own brothers opposed Him[5].

Arbitrary assumptions

All such assumptions it will be necessary to set aside. In *to be set aside.*

---

[1] e.g. Wieseler *Ueber die Brüder etc.*, l.c., p. 80 sq. According to this writer the James of Gal. ii. 9 and of the Acts is the son of Alphæus, not the Lord's brother, and therefore different from the James of i. 19. See his notes on Gal. i. 19, ii. 9. An ancient writer, the pseudo-Dorotheus (see below, p. 40, note), had represented two of the name as bishops of Jerusalem, making the son of Alphæus the successor of the Lord's brother.

[2] The writers mentioned in Schaf, p. 11.

[3] Lange in *Herzog's Real-Encycl.* in the article 'Jakobus im N.T.'

[4] Theophylact; see below, p. 44.

[5] Renan *Vie de Jésus* p. 24. But in *Saint Paul* p. 285 he inclines to the Epiphanian view.

themselves indeed they can neither be proved nor disproved. But it is safer to aim at the most probable deduction from known facts than to build up a theory on an imaginary foundation. And, where the question is so intricate in itself, there is little temptation to introduce fresh difficulties by giving way to the license of conjecture.

Relation of the three accounts. To confine ourselves then to the three accounts which have the greatest claim to a hearing. It will be seen that the hypothesis which I have called the Epiphanian holds a middle place between the remaining two. With the Helvidian it assigns an intelligible sense to the term 'brethren': with the Hieronymian it preserves the perpetual virginity of the Lord's mother. Whether or not, while uniting in itself the features which have recommended each of these to acceptance, it unites also their difficulties, will be considered in the sequel.

From a critical point of view however, apart from their bearing on Christian doctrine and feeling, the Helvidian and Epiphanian theories hang very closely together, while the Hieronymian stands apart. As well on account of this isolation, as also from the fact which I have hitherto assumed but which I shall endeavour to prove hereafter, that it was the latest born of the three, it will be convenient to consider the last-mentioned theory first.

Jerome's statement. St Jerome then states his view in the treatise against Helvidius somewhat as follows:

The son of Alphæus is the Lord's brother; The list of the Twelve Apostles contains two of the name of James, the son of Zebedee and the son of Alphæus. But elsewhere we read of a James the Lord's brother. What account are we to give of this last James? Either he was an Apostle or he was not. If an Apostle, he must be identified with the son of Alphæus, for the son of Zebedee was no longer living: if not an Apostle, then there were three persons bearing this name. But in this case how can a certain James be called 'the less,' a term which implies only one besides? And how moreover can we account for St Paul's language 'Other of the Apostles saw I none, save James the Lord's brother' (Gal. i. 19)? Clearly therefore James the son of Alphæus and James the Lord's brother are the same person.

And the Gospel narrative explains this identity. Among the Lord's brethren occur the names of James and Joseph. Now it is stated elsewhere that Mary the mother of James the less and of Joseph (or Joses) was present at the crucifixion (Matt. xxvii. 56, Mark xv. 40). This Mary therefore must have been the wife of Alphæus, for Alphæus was the father of James. But again in St John's narrative (xix. 25) the Virgin's sister 'Mary of Cleophas (Clopas)' is represented as standing by the cross. This carries us a step in advance. The last-mentioned Mary is to be identified with the wife of Alphæus and mother of James. Thus James the Lord's brother was in reality the Lord's cousin. *The Virgin's sister being his mother.*

But, if His cousin, how is he called His brother? The following is the explanation. The term 'brethren' is used in four different senses in Holy Scripture: it denotes either (1) actual brotherhood or (2) common nationality, or (3) kinsmanship, or (4) friendship and sympathy. These different senses St Jerome expresses by the four words 'natura, gente, cognatione, affectu.' In the case of the Lord's brethren the third of these senses is to be adopted: brotherhood here denotes mere relationship, just as Abraham calls his nephew Lot brother (Gen. xiii. 8), and as Laban uses the same term of Jacob his sister's son (Gen. xxix. 15). *Meaning of the term Brethren.*

So far St Jerome, who started the theory. But, as worked out by other writers and as generally stated, it involves two particulars besides. *Jerome's theory supplemented.*

(i) *The identity of Alphæus and Clopas.* These two words, it is said, are different renderings of the same Aramaic name חלפי or ساﻟﻔ (Chalphai), the form Clopas being peculiar to St John, the more completely grecized Alphæus taking its place in the other Evangelists. The Aramaic guttural *Cheth*, when the name was reproduced in Greek, might either be omitted as in Alphæus, or replaced by a κ (or χ) as in Clopas. Just in the same way Aloysius and Ludovicus are recognised Latin repre- *Alphæus the same with Clopas.*

sentatives of the Frankish name Clovis (Clodovicus, Hludovicus, Hlouis)[1].

This identification however, though it materially strengthens his theory, was unknown to Jerome himself. In the course of his argument he confesses plainly that he does not know why Mary is called Clopae, (or Cleophae, as he writes it): it may be, he suggests, after her father or from her family surname ('gentilitate familiae') or for some other reason[2]. In his treatise on Hebrew names too he gives an account of the word Alphæus which is scarcely consistent with this identity[3]. Neither have I found any traces of it in any of his other works, though he refers several times to the subject. In Augustine again, who adopts Jerome's hypothesis and his manner of stating it, it does not anywhere appear, so far as I know. It occurs first, I believe, in Chrysostom who incidentally speaks of James the Lord's brother as 'son of Clopas,' and after him in Theodoret who is more explicit (both on Gal. i. 19)[4]. To a Syrian Greek, who, even if he were unable to read the Peshito version, must at all events have known that Chalphai was the Aramæan rendering or rather the Aramæan original of Ἀλφαῖος, it might not unnaturally occur to graft this identification on the original theory of Jerome.

Jude the Lord's brother one of the Twelve,

(ii) *The identity of Judas the Apostle and Judas the Lord's brother.* In St Luke's catalogues of the Twelve (Luke vi. 16, Acts i. 13) the name 'Judas of James' (Ἰούδας Ἰακώβου) occurs. Now we find a Judas also among the four brethren of the Lord (Matt. xiii. 55, Mark vi. 3); and the writer of the epistle, who was doubtless the Judas last mentioned, styles

---

[1] This illustration is taken from Mill, p. 236.

[2] *adv. Helvid.* § 15, II. p. 219.

[3] '*Alphæus*, fugitivus [חלף; the Greek of Origen was doubtless οἰχόμενος, see p. 626], sed melius millesimus [אלף] vel doctus [אלף]'; III. p. 89; and again, '*Alphæus*, millesimus, sive super os [עלפה?] ab ore non ab osse';

ib. p. 98. Thus he deliberately rejects the derivation with a *Cheth*, which is required in order to identify 'Alphæus' with 'Clopas.' Indeed, as he incorrectly wrote Cleopas (or Cleophas) for Clopas with the Latin version, this identification was not likely to occur to him.

[4] See below, p. 44.

himself 'the brother of James' (Jude 1). This coincidence suggests that the ellipsis in 'Judas of James' should be supplied by *brother* as in the English version, not by *son* which would be the more obvious word. Thus Judas the Lord's brother, like James, is made one of the Twelve. I do not know when the Hieronymian theory received this fresh accession, but, though the gain is considerable in apparent strength at least, it does not appear, so far as I have noticed, to have occurred to Jerome himself.

And some have gone a step farther. We find not only a James and a Judas among the Lord's brethren, but also a Symeon or Simon. Now it is remarkable that these three names occur together in St Luke's list of the Twelve: James (the son) of Alphæus, Simon called Zelotes, and Judas (the brother) of James. In the lists of the other Evangelists too these three persons are kept together, though the order is different and Judas appears under another name, Lebbæus or Thaddæus. Can this have been a mere accident? Would the name of a stranger have been inserted by St Luke between two brothers? Is it not therefore highly probable that this Simon also was one of the Lord's brethren? And thus *three* out of the four are included among the Twelve[1]._ *and perhaps Simon also.*

Without these additions the theory is incomplete; and indeed they have been so generally regarded as part of it, that advocates and opponents alike have forgotten or overlooked the fact that Jerome himself nowhere advances them. I shall then consider the theory as involving these two points; for indeed it would never have won its way to such general acceptance, unless presented in this complete form, where its chief recommendation is that it combines a great variety of facts and brings out many striking coincidences.

But before criticizing the theory itself, let me prepare the *Jerome himself*

---

[1] It is found in Sophronius (?), who however confuses him with Jude; 'Simon Cananaeus cognomento Judas, frater Jacobi episcopi, qui et successit illi in episcopatum etc.'; Hieron. *Op.* II. p. 958. Compare the pseudo-Hippolytus (I. App. p. 30, ed. Fabric.). Perhaps the earliest genuine writing in which it occurs is Isidor. Hispal. *de Vit. et Ob. Sanct.* c. 81. See Mill p. 248.

way by divesting it of all fictitious advantages and placing it in its true light. The two points to which attention may be directed, as having been generally overlooked, are these:

(i) claims no traditional sanction for his theory,

(1) *Jerome claims no traditional support for his theory.* This is a remarkable feature in his treatise against Helvidius. He argues the question solely on critical and theological grounds. His opponent had claimed the sanction of two older writers, Tertullian and Victorinus of Pettaw. Jerome in reply is obliged to concede him Tertullian, whose authority he invalidates as 'not a member of the Church,' but denies him Victorinus. Can it be doubted that if he could have produced any names on his own side he would only too gladly have done so? When for instance he is maintaining the virginity of the Lord's mother, a feature possessed by his theory in common with the Epiphanian, he is at no loss for authorities: Ignatius, Polycarp, Irenæus, Justin, and many other 'eloquent apostolic men' occur to him at once[1]. But in support of his own account of the relationship he cannot, or at least does not, name a single writer; he simply offers it as a critical deduction from the statements of Scripture[2]. Again in his later writings, when he refers to the subject, his tone is the same: '*Some* suppose them to have been sons of Joseph: it is *my* opinion, as *I* have maintained in my book against Helvidius, that they were the children of Mary the Virgin's sister[3].' And the whole tenor of patristic evidence, as I shall hope to show, is in accordance with this tone. No decisive instance can be produced of a writer holding Jerome's view, before it was propounded by Jerome himself.

(ii) and does not hold it consistently,

(2) *Jerome does not hold his theory staunchly and consistently.* The references to the subject in his works taken in

[1] See however below, p. 31, note 1.
[2] He sets aside the appeal to authority thus: 'Verum nugas terimus, et fonte veritatis omisso opinionum rivulos consectamur,' *adv. Helvid.* 17.
[3] *de Vir. Illustr.* 2 ' ut *nonnulli* existimant, Joseph ex alia uxore; ut autem *mihi* videtur Mariae sororis matris Domini......filius'; *Comment. in Matth.* xii. 49 (VII. p. 86) '*Quidam* fratres Domini de alia uxore Joseph filios suspicantur...*nos* autem, sicut in libro quem contra Helvidium scripsimus continetur etc.'

chronological order will speak for themselves. The theory is first propounded, as we saw, in the treatise against Helvidius written about 383, when he was a young man. Even here his main point is the perpetual virginity of the Lord's mother, to which his own special solution is quite subordinate: he speaks of himself as not caring to fight hard ('contentiosum funem non traho') for the identity of Mary of Cleophas with Mary the mother of James and Joses, though this is the pivot of his theory. And, as time advances, he seems to hold to his hypothesis more and more loosely. In his commentary on the Epistle to the Galatians (i. 19) written about 387 he speaks very vaguely: he remembers, he says, having when at Rome written a treatise on the subject, with which such as it is he ought to be satisfied ('qualiacunque sunt illa quae scripsimus his contenti esse debemus'); after which he goes on inconsistently enough, 'Suffice it now to say that James was called the Lord's brother on account of his high character, his incomparable faith, and extraordinary wisdom: the other Apostles also are called brothers (John xx. 17; comp. Ps. xxii. 22), but he preeminently so, to whom the Lord at His departure had committed the sons of His mother (i.e. the members of the Church of Jerusalem)'; with more to the same effect: and he concludes by showing that the term Apostle, so far from being confined to the Twelve, has a very wide use, adding that it was 'a monstrous error to identify this James with the Apostle the brother of John[1].' In his Catalogue of Illustrious Men (A.D. 392) and in his Commentary on St Matthew (A.D. 398) he adheres to his earlier opinion, referring in the passages already

but wavers in his view,

---

[1] 'Quod autem exceptis duodecim quidam vocentur apostoli, illud in causa est, omnes qui Dominum viderant et eum postea praedicabant fuisse apostolos appellatos'; and then after giving instances (among others 1 Cor. xv. 7) he adds, 'Unde vehementer erravit qui arbitratus est Jacobum hunc de evangelio esse apostolum fratrem Johannis;... hic autem Jacobus episcopus Hierosolymorum primus fuit cognomento Justus etc.' (VII. p. 396). These are just the arguments which would be brought by one maintaining the Epiphanian account. Altogether Jerome's language here is that of a man who has committed himself to a theory of which he has misgivings, and yet from which he is not bold enough to break loose.

quoted[1] to his treatise against Helvidius, and taunting those who considered the Lord's brethren to be the sons of Joseph by a former wife with 'following the ravings of the apocryphal writings and inventing a wretched creature (mulierculam) Melcha or Escha by name[2].' Yet after all in a still later work, the Epistle to Hedibia (about 406 or 407), enumerating the Maries of the Gospels he mentions Mary of Cleophas the maternal aunt of the Lord and Mary the mother of James and Joses as distinct persons, adding 'although others contend that the mother of James and Joses was His aunt[3].' Yet this identification, of which he here speaks with such indifference, was the keystone of his own theory. Can it be that by his long residence in Bethlehem, having the Palestinian tradition brought more prominently before him, he first relaxed his hold of and finally relinquished his own hypothesis?

and seems at length to abandon it.

If these positions are correct, the Hieronymian view has no claim to any traditional sanction—in other words, there is no reason to believe that time has obliterated any secondary evidence in its favour—and it must therefore be investigated on its own merits.

And compact and plausible as it may seem at first sight, the theory exposes, when examined, many vulnerable parts.

Objections to Jerome's theory. (1) Use of the word Brethren.

(1) The instances alleged notwithstanding, the sense thus assigned to 'brethren' seems to be unsupported by biblical usage. In an affectionate and earnest appeal intended to move the sympathies of the hearer, a speaker might not un-

---

[1] See p. 10, note 3.

[2] 'Sequentes deliramenta apocryphorum et quandam Melcham vel Escham mulierculam confingentes.' *Comm. in Matth.* l. c. 'Nemo non videt,' says Blom, p. 116, 'illud nomen אשה [wife, woman] esse mere fictitium, nec minus posterius [prius] מלכה [queen].' (Comp. Julius Africanus in Routh's *Rel. Sacr.* II. p. 233, 339.) If so, the work must have been the production of some Jewish Christian. But Escha is not a very exact representation of אשה (Ishah). On the other hand, making allowance for the uncertain vocalisation of the Hebrew, the two daughters of Haran (Gen. xi. 29) bear identically the same names: 'the father of Milcah (LXX Μελχά) and the father of Iscah (סכה) (LXX Ἰεσχά).' Doubtless these names were borrowed thence.

[3] *Epist.* cxx. I. p. 826. Comp. Tischendorf's *Evang. Apocr.* p. 104.

naturally address a relation or a friend or even a fellow-countryman as his 'brother.' And even when speaking of such to a third person he might through warmth of feeling and under certain aspects so designate him. But it is scarcely conceivable that the cousins of any one should be commonly and indeed exclusively styled his 'brothers' by indifferent persons; still less, that one cousin in particular should be singled out and described in this loose way, 'James the Lord's brother.'

(2) But again: the Hieronymian theory when completed supposes two, if not three, of the Lord's brethren to be in the number of the Twelve. This is hardly reconcileable with the place they hold in the Evangelical narratives, where they appear sometimes as distinct from, sometimes as antagonistic to the Twelve. Only a short time before the crucifixion they are disbelievers in the Lord's divine mission (John vii. 5). Is it likely that St John would have made this unqualified statement, if it were true of one only or at most of two out of the four? Jerome sees the difficulty and meets it by saying that James was 'not one of those that disbelieved.' But what if Jude and Simon also belong to the Twelve? After the Lord's Ascension, it is true, His brethren appear in company with the Apostles, and apparently by this time their unbelief has been converted into faith. Yet even on this later occasion, though with the Twelve, they are distinguished from the Twelve; for the latter are described as assembling in prayer 'with the women and Mary the mother of Jesus and [with] His brethren' (Acts i. 14). *(2) Relation of the Lord's brethren to the Twelve,*

And scarcely more consistent is this theory with what we know of James and Jude in particular. James, as the resident bishop or presiding elder of the mother Church, held a position hardly compatible with the world-wide duties which devolved on the Twelve. It was the essential feature of his office that he should be stationary; of theirs, that they should move about from place to place. If on the other hand he appears sometimes to be called an Apostle (though not one of the passages *especially James and Jude.*

alleged is free from ambiguity), this term is by no means confined to the Twelve and might therefore be applied to him in its wider sense, as it is to Barnabas[1]. Again, Jude on his part seems to disclaim the title of an Apostle (ver. 17); and if so, he cannot have been one of the Twelve.

(3) Their connexion with Joseph and Mary.

(3) But again: the Lord's brethren are mentioned in the Gospels in connexion with Joseph His reputed father and Mary His mother, never once with Mary of Clopas (the assumed wife of Alphæus). It would surely have been otherwise, if the latter Mary were really their mother.

(4) James the less.

(4) Jerome lays great stress on the epithet *minor* applied to James, as if it implied *two only*, and even those who impugn his theory seem generally to acquiesce in his rendering. But the Greek gives not 'James the less' but 'James the *little*' (ὁ μικρός). Is it not most natural then to explain this epithet of his height[2]? 'There were many of the name of James,' says Hegesippus, and the short stature of one of these might well serve as a distinguishing mark. This interpretation at all events must be regarded as more probable than explaining it either of his comparative youth or of inferior rank and influence. It will be remembered that there is no Scriptural or early sanction for speaking of the son of Zebedee as 'James the Great.'

(5) The mention of Jude in the lists of the Twelve.

(5) The manner in which Jude is mentioned in the lists of the Twelve is on this hypothesis full of perplexities. In the first place it is necessary to translate Ἰακώβου not 'the son' but 'the brother of James,' though the former is the obvious rendering and is supported by two of the earliest versions, the Peshito Syriac and the Thebaic, while two others, the Old Latin and Memphitic, leave the ellipsis unsupplied and thus preserve the ambiguity of the original. But again, if Judas were the brother of James, would not the Evangelist's words have run more naturally, 'James the son of Alphæus and Jude

---

[1] See *Galatians*, p. 95.
[2] As in Xen. *Mem.* I. 4. 2 Ἀριστόδημον τὸν μικρὸν ἐπικαλούμενον, referring to stature, as appears from Plato, *Symp.* 173 B; and in Arist. *Ran.* 708 Κλειγένης ὁ μικρός.

his brother,' or 'James and Jude the sons of Alphæus,' as in the case of the other pairs of brothers? Then again, if Simon Zelotes is not a brother of James, why is he inserted by St Luke between the two? If he also is a brother, why is the designation of brotherhood ('Ιακώβου) attached to the name of Judas only?

Moreover in the different lists of the three Evangelists the Apostle in question is designated in three different ways. In St Matthew (x. 3) he is called Lebbæus (at least according to a well-supported reading); in St Mark (iii. 18) Thaddæus; and in St Luke 'Jude of James.' St John again having occasion to mention him (xiv. 22) distinguishes him by a negative, 'Judas not Iscariot[1].' Is it possible, if he were the Lord's brother Judas, he would in all these places have escaped being so designated, when this designation would have fixed the person meant at once?

(6) Lastly; in order to maintain the Hieronymian theory it is necessary to retain the common punctuation of John xix. 25, thus making 'Mary of Clopas' the Virgin's sister. But it is at least improbable that two sisters should have borne the same name. The case of the Herodian family is scarcely parallel, for

(6) Punctuation of Joh. xix. 25.

---

[1] The perplexity is increased by the Curetonian Syriac, which for 'Ἰούδας οὐχ ὁ Ἰσκαριώτης reads ܪܚܩܪܐ ܬܐܘܡܐ, 'Judas Thomas,' i.e. 'Judas the Twin.' It seems therefore that the translator took the person intended by St John to be not the *Judas Jacobi* in the list of the Twelve, but the *Thomas Didymus*, for Thomas was commonly called Judas in the Syrian Church; e.g. Euseb. *H. E.* i. 13 'Ἰούδας ὁ καὶ Θωμᾶς, and *Acta Thomae* 1 'Ἰούδᾳ Θωμᾷ τῷ καὶ Διδύμῳ (ed. Tisch. p. 190); see Assemani *Bibl. Orient.* I. pp. 100, 318, Cureton's *Syriac Gospels* p. li, *Anc. Syr. Documents* p. 33. As Thomas (Δίδυμος), 'the Twin,' is properly a surname, and this Apostle must have had some other name, there seems no reason for doubting this very early tradition that he also was a Jude. At the same time it is highly improbable that St John should have called the same Apostle elsewhere Thomas (Joh. xi. 16, xiv. 5, xx. 24 etc.) and here Judas, and we may therefore conclude that he is speaking of two different persons. The name of the other brother is supplied in *Clem. Hom.* ii. 1 προσέτι δὲ Θωμᾶς καὶ Ἐλιέζερος οἱ δίδυμοι.

The Thebaic version again for οὐχ ὁ Ἰσκαριώτης substitutes ὁ Κανανίτης. Similarly in Matth. x. 3 for Θαδδαῖος some of the most important mss of the Old Latin have 'Judas Zelotes'; and in the Canon of Gelasius Jude the writer of the epistle is so designated. This points to some connexion or confusion with Simon Zelotes. See p. 9, note.

Heród was a family name, and it is unlikely that a humble Jewish household should have copied a practice which must lead to so much confusion. Here it is not unlikely that a tradition underlies the Peshito rendering which inserts a conjunction: 'His mother and his mother's sister, *and* Mary of Cleophas and Mary Magdalene[1].' The Greek at all events admits, even if it does not favour, this interpretation, for the arrangement of names in couples has a parallel in the lists of the Apostles (e.g. Matt. x. 2—4).

Jerome's hypothesis must be abandoned

I have shown then, if I mistake not, that St Jerome pleaded no traditional authority for his theory, and that therefore the evidence in its favour is to be sought in Scripture alone. I have examined the Scriptural evidence, and the conclusion seems to be, that though this hypothesis, supplemented as it has been by subsequent writers, presents several striking coincidences which attract attention, yet it involves on the other hand a combination of difficulties—many of these arising out of the very elements in the hypothesis which produce the coincidences—which more than counterbalances these secondary arguments in its favour, and in fact must lead to its rejection, if any hypothesis less burdened with difficulties can be found.

and replaced by one of the remaining two.

Thus, as compared with the Hieronymian view, both the Epiphanian and the Helvidian have higher claims to acceptance.

---

[1] See Wieseler *Die Söhne Zebedäi etc.* p. 672. This writer identifies the sister of the Lord's mother (John xix. 25) with Salome (Mark xv. 40, xvi. 1), who again is generally identified with the mother of Zebedee's children (Matt. xxvii. 56); and thus James and John, the sons of Zebedee, are made cousins of our Lord. Compare the pseudo-Papias, (below p. 25, note); and see the various reading Ἰωάννης for Ἰωσήφ in the list of the Lord's brethren in Matt. xiii. 55. But as we are told that there were *many other women* present also (Mark xv. 41, comp. Luke xxiv. 10),—one of whom, Joanna, is mentioned by name—both these identifications must be considered precarious. It would be strange that no hint should be given in the Gospels of the relationship of the sons of Zebedee to our Lord, if it existed.

The Jerusalem Syriac lectionary gives the passage John xix. 25 not less than three times. In two of these places (pp. 387, 541, the exception being p. 445) a stop is put after 'His mother's sister,' thus separating the words from 'Mary of Cleophas' and suggesting by punctuation the same interpretation which the Peshito fixes by inserting a conjunction.

They both assign to the word brethren its natural meaning; they both recognise the main facts related of the Lord's brethren in the Gospels—their unbelief, their distinctness from the Twelve, their connexion with Joseph and Mary—and they both avoid the other difficulties which the Hieronymian theory creates.

And moreover they both exhibit a coincidence which deserves notice. A very short time before the Lord's death His brethren refuse to accept His mission: they are still unbelievers. Immediately after His ascension we find them gathered together with the Apostles, evidently recognising Him as their Master. Whence comes this change? Surely the crucifixion of one who professed to be the Messiah was not likely to bring it about. He had claimed to be King of Israel and He had been condemned as a malefactor: He had promised His followers a triumph and He had left them persecution. Would not all this confirm rather than dissipate their former unbelief? An incidental statement of St Paul explains all; 'Then He was seen of James.' At the time when St Paul wrote, there was but one person eminent enough in the Church to be called James simply without any distinguishing epithet—the Lord's brother, the bishop of Jerusalem. It might therefore reasonably be concluded that this James is here meant. And this view is confirmed by an extant fragment of the Gospel according to the Hebrews, the most important of all the apocryphal gospels, which seems to have preserved more than one true tradition, and which expressly relates the appearance of our Lord to His brother James[1] after His resurrection.

<small>A coincidence common to both.</small>

This interposition, we may suppose, was the turning-point in the religious life of the Lord's brethren; the veil was removed at once and for ever from their hearts. In this way the antagonistic notices in the Gospels—first the disbelief of the Lord's brethren, and then their assembling together with the Apostles—are linked together; and harmony is produced out of discord.

[1] See below, p. 26.

Objections to both.

Two objections however are brought against both these theories, which the Hieronymian escapes.

(1) Repetition of names.

(1) They both, it is objected, assume the existence of two pairs of cousins bearing the same names, James and Joseph the sons of Alphæus, and James and Joseph the Lord's brothers. If moreover we accept the statement of Hegesippus[1] that James was succeeded in the bishopric of Jerusalem by Symeon son of Clopas, and also admit the identification of Clopas with Alphæus, we get a third name Symeon or Simeon common to the two families. Let us see what this objection really amounts to.

Cousinhood on either mothers'

It will be seen that the cousinhood of these persons is represented as a cousinhood on the mothers' side, and that it depends on three assumptions: (1) The identification of James the son of Alphæus in the list of the Twelve with James the Little the son of Mary: (2) The identification of 'Mary of Clopas' in St John with Mary the mother of James and Joses in the other Evangelists: (3) The correctness of the received punctuation of John xix. 25, which makes 'Mary of Clopas' the Virgin's sister. If any one of these be rejected, this cousinhood falls to the ground. Yet of these three assumptions the second alone can safely be pronounced more likely than not[2] (though we are expressly told that 'many other women' were present), for it avoids the unnecessary multiplication of Maries. The first must be considered highly doubtful, seeing that James was a very common name; while the third is most improbable, for it gives two sisters both called Mary—a difficulty far surpassing that of supposing two or even three cousins bearing the same name. On the other hand, if, admitting the second identification and supplying the ellipsis in 'Mary of Clopas' by 'wife[3],'

---

[1] See below, p. 29 sq.

[2] Eusebius however makes 'Mary of Clopas' a different person from Mary the mother of James and Joses; *Quaest. ad Marin.* ii. 5 (*Op.* IV. p. 945, Migne).

[3] As ἡ τοῦ Κλωπᾶ may mean either the *daughter* or the *wife* or the *mother* of Clopas, this expression has been combined with the statement of Hegesippus in various ways. See for instance the apocryphal gospels, *Pseudo-Matth. Evang.* 52 (ed. Tisch. p. 104), *Evang. Inf. Arab.* 29 (ib. p. 186), and the marginal

THE BRETHREN OF THE LORD.

we combine with it the statement of Hegesippus[1] that Clopas the father of Symeon was brother of Joseph, we get three cousins, James, Joses, and Symeon, *on their fathers' side.* Yet this result again must be considered on the whole improbable. [or fathers' side improbable.] I see no reason indeed for doubting the testimony of Hegesippus, who was perhaps born during the lifetime of this Symeon, and is likely to have been well informed. But the chances are against the other hypotheses, on which it depends, being both of them correct. The identification of Clopas and Alphæus will still remain an open question[2].

---

note on the Philoxenian version, Joh. xix. 25, besides other references which will be given in the account of the patristic authorities.

[1] The statement of Hegesippus suggests a solution which would remove the difficulty. We might suppose the two Maries to have been called sisters, as having been married to two brothers; but is there any authority for ascribing to the Jews an extension of the term 'sister' which modern usage scarcely sanctions?

[2] Of the three names *Alphæus* (the father of Levi or Matthew, Mark ii. 14, and the father of James, Matt. x. 3, Mark iii. 18, Luke vi. 15, Acts i. 13), *Clopas* (the husband or father or son of Mary, Joh. xix. 25), and *Cleopas* (the disciple journeying to Emmaus, Luke xxiv. 18), it is considered that the two former are probably identical, and the two latter certainly distinct. Both positions may be disputed with some reason. In forming a judgment, the following points deserve to be considered; (1) In the Greek text there is no variation of reading worth mentioning; Clopas is certainly the reading in St John, and Cleopas in St Luke. (2) The versions however bring them together. Cleopæ (or Cleophæ) is read in the Peshito, Old Latin, Memphitic, Vulgate, and Armenian text of St John. (3) Of these the evidence of the Peshito is particularly important in a matter relating to Aramaic names. While for 'Αλφαῖος in all five places it restores what was doubtless the original Aramaic form ܚܠܦܝ, Chalphai; on the other hand, it gives the same word ܩܠܝܘܦܐ Kleōpha (i. e. Κλεόπας) in Luke xxiv. 18 and in John xix. 25, if the printed texts may be trusted. The Jerusalem Syriac too renders Κλωπᾶς by ܩܠܝܘܦܐ (Kleophas), and 'Αλφαῖος by ܚܠܦܝ (Chalphai). (4) The form Κλωπᾶς, which St John's text gives, is confirmed by Hegesippus (Euseb. *H.E.* iii. 11), and there is every reason to believe that this was a common mode of writing some proper name or other with those acquainted with Aramaic; but it is difficult to see why, if the word intended to be represented were Chalphai, they should not have reproduced it more exactly in Greek. The name Χαλφί in fact does occur in 1 Macc. xi. 70. (5) It is true that Κλεόπας is strictly a Greek name contracted from Κλεόπατρος, like 'Αντίπας from 'Αντίπατρος, etc. But it was a common practice with the Jews to adopt the genuine Greek name which bore the closest resemblance in sound to their own Aramaic name, either side by side with it or in place of it, as Simon for Symeon, Jason for Jesus; and thus a man, whose real Aramaic

THE BRETHREN OF THE LORD.

The names are common.

But, whether they were cousins or not, does the fact of two families having two or three names in common constitute any real difficulty? Is not this a frequent occurrence among ourselves? It must be remembered too that the Jewish names in ordinary use at this time were very few, and that these three, James, Joses, and Symeon, were among the most common, being consecrated in the affections of the Jews from patriarchal times. In the list of the Twelve the name of James appears twice, Symeon twice. In the New Testament no less than twelve persons bear the name of Symeon or Simon, and nearly as many that of Joseph or Joses[1]. In the name was Clopas, might grecize the word and call himself Cleopas. On these grounds it appears to me that, viewing the question as one of names merely, it is quite as reasonable to identify Clopas with Cleopas as with Alphæus. But the identification of names does not carry with it the identification of persons. St Paul's Epaphras for instance is probably a different person from his Epaphroditus.

A Jewish name 'Alfius' occurs in an inscription ALFIVS . IVDA . ARCON . ARCOSINAGOGVS (Inscr. Gudii, p. cclxiii. 5), and possibly this is the Latin substitute for Chalphai or Chalphi, as 'Αλφαῖος is the Greek; Alfius being a not uncommon Latin name. One would be tempted to set down his namesake also, the 'fenerator Alfius' or 'Alphius' of Horace (*Epod.* ii. 67, see Columella I. 7. 2), for a fellow countryman, if his talk were not so pagan.

[1] I am arguing on the supposition that Joses and Joseph are the same name, but this is at least doubtful. In St Matthew, according to the best authorities, the Lord's brother (xiii. 55) is Ἰωσήφ, the son of Mary (xxvii. 56) Ἰωσῆς. In St Mark on the other hand the latter word is found (the genitive being differently written Ἰωσῆτος or Ἰωσῆ, though probably Tregelles is right in preferring the former in all three passages), whether referring to the Lord's brother (vi. 3) or to the son of Mary (xv. 40, 47). Thus if existing authorities in the text of St Mark are to be trusted, there is no distinction between the names. Yet I am disposed to think with Wieseler (*die Söhne Zebedäi etc.* p. 678) that St Matthew's text suggests the real difference, and that the original reading in Mark vi. 3 was Ἰωσήφ; but if so, the corruption was very ancient and very general, for Ἰωσήφ is found in ℵ alone of the uncial manuscripts. A similar confusion of these names appears in the case of Barsabbas, Acts i. 23, and Barnabas, iv. 36; in the former case we find a various reading 'Joses' for 'Joseph,' in the latter we should almost certainly read 'Joseph' for 'Joses' of the received text. I am disposed to think the identification of the names Joses and Joseph improbable for two reasons: (1) It seems unlikely that the same name should be represented in Greek by two such divergent forms as Ἰωσῆς, making a genitive Ἰωσῆτος, and Ἰωσήφ or Ἰώσηπος, which perhaps (replaced by a genuine Greek name) became Ἡγήσιππος. (2) The Peshito in the case of the commoner Hebrew or Aramaic names restores the original form in place of the somewhat disfigured Greek equivalent, e.g. Juchanon for Ἰωάννης, Zabdai for Ζεβε-

THE BRETHREN OF THE LORD. 21

index to Josephus may be counted nineteen Josephs, and twenty-five Simons[1].

And moreover is not the difficulty, if difficulty there be, diminished rather than increased on the supposition of the cousinhood of these two families? The name of a common ancestor or a common relative naturally repeats itself in households connected with each other. And from this point of view it is worthy of notice that the names in question actually occur in the genealogies of our Lord. Joseph's father is Jacob or James in St Matthew (i. 15, 16); and in St Luke's table, exclusively of our Lord's reputed father, the name Joseph or Joses occurs twice at least[2] in a list of thirty-four direct ancestors.

(2) When a certain Mary is described as 'the mother of James,' is it not highly probable that the person intended should be the most celebrated of the name—James the Just, the bishop of Jerusalem, the Lord's brother? This objection to both the Epiphanian and Helvidian theories is at first sight not without force, but it will not bear examination. Why, we may ask, if the best known of all the Jameses were intended here, should it be necessary in some passages to add the name of a brother Joses also, who was a person of no special mark in the Church (Matt. xxvii. 56, Mark xv. 40)? Why again in others should this Mary be designated 'the mother of Joses' alone (Mark xv. 47), the name of his more famous brother being

(2) 'Mary the mother of James.'

δαῖος. Following this rule, it ought, if the names were identical, to have restored ܝܘܣܐ (Joseph) for the Greek Ἰωσῆς, in place of which it has ܝܘܣܐ (Jōsī, Jausī, or Jūsī). In Matt. xxvii. 56, Mark xv. 40, the Memphitic Version separates Μαρία [ἡ τοῦ] Ἰακώβου [τοῦ μικροῦ] and Ἰωσῆ[τος] μήτηρ, making them two different persons. On the other hand, similar instances of abbreviation, e.g. Ashe for Asher, Jochana for Jochanan, Shabba for Shabbath, are produced; see Delitzsch in Laurent *Neutest. Stud.* p. 168.

[1] The popularity of this name is probably due to Simon Maccabæus.

[2] And perhaps not more than twice Ἰωσήφ (vv. 24, 30). In ver. 26 Ἰωσὴχ seems to be the right reading, where the received text has Ἰωσήφ; and in ver. 29 Ἰησοῦ, where it has Ἰωσῆ. Possibly Ἰωσὴχ may be a corruption for Ἰωσήφ through the confusion of ף and ך, which in their older forms resemble each other closely; but if so, it is a corruption not of St Luke's text, but of the Hebrew or Aramaic document from which the genealogy was derived.

suppressed? In only two passages is she called simply 'the mother of James'; in Mark xvi. 1, where it is explained by the fuller description which has gone before 'the mother of James and Joses' (xv. 40); and in Luke xxiv. 10, where no such explanation can be given. It would seem then that this Mary and this James, though not the most famous of their respective names and therefore not at once distinguishable when mentioned alone, were yet sufficiently well known to be discriminated from others, when their names appeared in conjunction.

The two theories compared. The objections then which may be brought against both these theories in common are not very serious; and up to this point in the investigation they present equal claims to acceptance. The next step will be to compare them together, in order to decide which of the two must yield to the other.

(1) Relation of the brethren to Joseph and Mary. 1. The Epiphanian view assumes that the Lord's brethren had really no relationship with Him; and so far the Helvidian has the advantage. But this advantage is rather seeming than real. It is very natural that those who called Joseph His father should call Joseph's sons His brethren. And it must be remembered that this designation is given to Joseph not only by strangers from whom at all events the mystery of the Incarnation was veiled, but by the Lord's mother herself who knew all (Luke ii. 48). Even the Evangelist himself, about whose belief in the miraculous conception of Christ there can be no doubt, allows himself to speak of Joseph and Mary as 'His father and mother' and 'His parents[1].' Nor again is it any argument in favour of the Helvidian account as compared with the Epiphanian, that the Lord's brethren are found in company of Mary rather than of Joseph. Joseph appears in the evangelical history for the last time when Jesus is twelve years old (Luke ii. 43); during the Lord's ministry he is never once seen, though Mary comes forward again and again. There can be little doubt therefore that he had died meanwhile.

---

[1] Luke ii. 33 ὁ πατὴρ αὐτοῦ καὶ ἡ μήτηρ, ii. 41, 43 οἱ γονεῖς αὐτοῦ, the correct reading. Later transcribers have taken offence and substituted 'Joseph and Mary,' 'Joseph and His mother,' in all three places.

2. Certain expressions in the evangelical narratives are said to imply that Mary bore other children besides the Lord, and it is even asserted that no unprejudiced person could interpret them otherwise. The justice of this charge may be fairly questioned. The context in each case seems to suggest another explanation of these expressions, which does not decide anything one way or the other. St Matthew writes that Joseph 'knew not' his wife '*till* (ἕως οὗ) she brought forth a son' (i. 25)[1]; while St Luke speaks of her bringing forth 'her *firstborn* son' (ii. 7). St Matthew's expression however, '*till* she brought forth,' as appears from the context, is intended simply to show that Jesus was not begotten in the course of nature; and thus, while it denies any previous intercourse with her husband, it neither asserts nor implies any subsequent intercourse[2]. Again, the prominent idea conveyed by the term 'firstborn' to a Jew would be not the birth of other children, but the special consecration of this one. The typical reference in fact is foremost in the mind of St Luke, as he himself explains it, '*Every male that openeth the womb* shall be called holy to the Lord' (ii. 23). Thus 'firstborn' does not necessarily suggest 'later-born,' any more than 'son' suggests 'daughter.' The two words together describe the condition under which in obedience to the law a child was consecrated to God. The 'firstborn son' is in fact the Evangelist's equivalent for the 'male that openeth the womb.'

It may indeed be fairly urged that, if the Evangelists had considered the perpetual virginity of the Lord's mother a matter of such paramount importance as it was held to be in the fourth and following centuries, they would have avoided expressions which are at least ambiguous and might be taken to imply the contrary; but these expressions are not in themselves fatal to such a belief.

Whether in itself the sentiment on which this belief was

(2) Virginity of Mary.

---

[1] τὸν πρωτότοκον ought to be rejected from St Matthew's text, having been interpolated from Luke ii. 7.

[2] For parallel instances see Mill, p. 304 sq.

founded be true or false, is a fit subject of enquiry; nor can the present question be considered altogether without reference to it. If it be true, then the Epiphanian theory has an advantage over the Helvidian, as respecting or at least not disregarding it; if false, then it may be thought to have suggested that theory, as it certainly did the Hieronymian, and to this extent the theory itself must lie under suspicion. Into this enquiry however it will not be necessary to enter. Only let me say that it is not altogether correct to represent this belief as suggested solely by the false asceticism of the early Church which exalted virginity at the expense of married life. It appears in fact to be due quite as much to another sentiment which the fathers fantastically expressed by a comparison between the conception and the burial of our Lord. As after death His body was placed in a sepulchre 'wherein never man before was laid,' so it seemed fitting that the womb consecrated by His presence should not thenceforth have borne any offspring of man. It may be added also, that the Epiphanian view prevailed especially in Palestine where there was less disposition than elsewhere to depreciate married life, and prevailed too at a time when extreme ascetic views had not yet mastered the Church at large.

(3) Our Lord's dying words. 3. But one objection has been hurled at the Helvidian theory with great force, and as it seems to me with fatal effect, which is powerless against the Epiphanian[1]. Our Lord in His dying moments commended His mother to the keeping of St John; 'Woman, behold thy son.' The injunction was forthwith obeyed, and 'from that hour that disciple took her unto his own home' (John xix. 26, 27). Yet according to the Helvidian view she had no less than four sons besides daughters living at the time. Is it conceivable that our Lord would thus have snapped asunder the most sacred ties of natural affection? The difficulty is not met by the fact that her own sons were

[1] This argument is brought forward not only by Jerome, but also by Hilary of Poitiers, Ambrose, and Epiphanius, who all held the view which I have designated by the name of the last of the three.

still unbelievers. This fact would scarcely have been allowed to override the paramount duties of filial piety. But even when so explained, what does this hypothesis require us to believe? Though within a few days a special appearance is vouchsafed to one of these brethren, who is destined to rule the mother Church of Jerusalem, and all alike are converted to the faith of Christ; yet she, their mother, living in the same city and joining with them in a common worship (Acts i. 14), is consigned to the care of a stranger of whose house she becomes henceforth the inmate.

Thus it would appear that, taking the scriptural notices alone, the Hieronymian account must be abandoned; while of the remaining two the balance of the argument is against the Helvidian and in favour of the Epiphanian. To what extent the last-mentioned theory can plead the prestige of tradition, will be seen from the following catena of references to the fathers and other early Christian writings[1].

Conclusion.

[1] The testimony of Papias is frequently quoted at the head of the patristic authorities, as favouring the view of Jerome. The passage in question is an extract, to which the name of this very ancient writer is prefixed, in a Bodleian MS, no. 2397, of the date 1302 or 1303. It is given in Grabe's *Spicil.* II. p. 34, Routh's *Rel. Sacr.* I. p. 16, and runs as follows: 'Maria mater Domini: Maria Cleophae, sive Alphei uxor, quae fuit mater Jacobi episcopi et apostoli et Symonis et Thadei et cujusdam Joseph: Maria Salome uxor Zebedei mater Joannis evangelistae et Jacobi. Maria Magdalene: istae quatuor in Evangelio reperiuntur. Jacobus et Judas et Joseph filii erant materterae Domini; Jacobus quoque et Joannes alterius materterae Domini fuerunt filii. Maria Jacobi minoris et Joseph mater, uxor Alphei, soror fuit Mariae matris Domini, quam Cleophae Joannes nominat vel a patre vel a gentilitatis familia vel alia causa. Maria Salome a viro vel a vico dicitur: hanc eandem Cleophae quidam dicunt quod duos viros habuerit. Maria dicitur illuminatrix sive stella maris, genuit enim lumen mundi; sermone autem Syro Domina nuncupatur, quia genuit Dominum.' Grabe's description 'ad marginem expresse adscriptum lego *Papia*' is incorrect; the name is not in the margin but over the passage as a title to it. The authenticity of this fragment is accepted by Mill, p. 238, and by Dean Alford on Matth. xiii. 55. Two writers also in Smith's *Biblical Dictionary* (s. vv. 'Brother' and 'James'), respectively impugning and maintaining the Hieronymian view, refer to it without suspicion. It is strange that able and intelligent critics should not have seen through a fabrication which is so manifestly spurious. Not to mention the difficulties in which we are involved by some of the statements, the following reasons seem conclusive: (1) The last sentence 'Maria dicitur etc.' is evidently

26 THE BRETHREN OF THE LORD.

Hebrew Gospel.

1. The GOSPEL ACCORDING TO THE HEBREWS, one of the earliest and most respectable of the apocryphal narratives, related that the Lord after His resurrection 'went to James and appeared to him; for James had sworn that he would not eat bread from that hour in which the Lord had drunk the cup (biberat calicem Dominus), till he saw Him risen from the dead.' Jesus therefore 'took bread and blessed it and brake it and gave it to James the Just and said to him, My brother, eat thy bread, for the Son of Man has risen from the dead' (Hieron. *de Vir. Illustr.* 2). I have adopted the reading 'Dominus,' as the Greek translation has Κύριος, and it also suits the context better; for the point of time which we should naturally expect is not the institution of the eucharist but the Lord's death[1]. Our Lord had more than once spoken of His sufferings under

very late, and is, as Dr Mill says, 'justly rejected by Grabe.' Grabe says, 'addidit is qui descripsit ex suo'; but the passage is continuous in the MS, and there is neither more nor less authority for assigning this to Papias than the remainder of the extract. (2) The statement about 'Maria uxor Alphei' is taken from Jerome (*adv. Helvid.*) almost word for word, as Dr Mill has seen; and it is purely arbitrary to reject this as spurious and accept the rest as genuine. (3) The writings of Papias were in Jerome's hands, and eager as he was to claim the support of authority, he could not have failed to refer to testimony which was so important and which so entirely confirms his view in the most minute points. Nor is it conceivable that a passage like this, coming from so early a writer, should not have impressed itself very strongly on the ecclesiastical tradition of the early centuries, whereas in fact we discover no traces of it.

For these reasons the extract seemed to be manifestly spurious; but I might have saved myself the trouble of examining the Bodleian MS and writing these remarks, if I had known at the time, that the passage was written by a mediæval namesake of the Bishop of Hierapolis, Papias the author of the 'Elementarium,' who lived in the 11th century. This seems to have been a standard work in its day, and was printed four times in the 15th century under the name of the Lexicon or Vocabulist. I have not had access to a printed copy, but there is a MS of the work (marked Kk. 4. 1) in the Cambridge University Library, the knowledge of which I owe to Mr Bradshaw, the librarian. The variations from the Bodleian extract are unimportant. It is strange that though Grabe actually mentions the later Papias the author of the Dictionary, and Routh copies his note, neither the one nor the other got on the right track. I made the discovery while the first edition of this work was passing through the press [1865].

[1] There might possibly have been an ambiguity in the Hebrew original owing to the absence of case-endings, as Blom suggests (p. 83): but it is more probable that a transcriber of Jerome carelessly wrote down the familiar phrase 'the cup of the Lord.'

the image of draining the cup (Matt. xx. 22, 23, xxvi. 39, 42, Mark x. 38, 39, xiv. 36, Luke xxii. 42)[1]; and He is represented as using this metaphor here. If however we retain 'Domini,' it must be allowed that the writer represented James the Lord's brother as present at the last supper, but it does not follow that he regarded him as one of the Twelve. He may have assigned to him a sort of exceptional position such as he holds in the Clementines, apart from and in some respects superior to the Twelve, and thus his presence at this critical time would be accounted for. At all events this passage confirms the tradition that the James mentioned by St Paul (1 Cor. xv. 7) was the Lord's brother; while at the same time it is characteristic of a Judaic writer whose aim it would be to glorify the head of his Church at all hazards, that an appearance, which seems in reality to have been vouchsafed to this James to win him over from his unbelief, should be represented as a reward for his devotion.

2. The GOSPEL ACCORDING TO PETER was highly esteemed by the Docetæ of the second century. Towards the close of that century, Serapion, bishop of Antioch, found it in circulation at Rhossus a Cilician town, and at first tolerated it: but finding on examination that, though it had much in common with the Gospels recognised by the Catholic Church, there were sentiments in it favourable to the heretical views that were secretly gaining ground there, he forbad its use. In the fragment of Serapion preserved by Eusebius (*H. E.* vi. 12)[2], from which our information is derived, he speaks of this apocryphal work as if it had been long in circulation, so that its date must be about the middle of the second century at the latest, and probably somewhat earlier. To this gospel Origen refers, as stating that the Lord's brethren were Joseph's sons by a former wife and thus maintaining the virginity of the Lord's mother[3].

Gospel of Peter.

---

[1] Comp. *Mart. Polyc.* 14 ἐν τῷ ποτηρίῳ τοῦ Χριστοῦ σου.
[2] For this fragment see Routh's *Rel. Sacr.* I. p. 452, and Westcott *History of the Canon,* p. 385.
[3] See below, p. 35.

28   THE BRETHREN OF THE LORD.

Protevangelium and other apocryphal gospels.

3. PROTEVANGELIUM JACOBI, a purely fictitious but very early narrative, dating probably not later than the middle of the second century, represents Joseph as an old man when the Virgin was espoused to him, having sons of his own (§ 9, ed. Tisch. p. 18) but no daughters (§ 17, p. 31), and James the writer of the account apparently as grown up at the time of Herod's death (§ 25, p. 48). Following in this track, subsequent apocryphal narratives give a similar account with various modifications, in some cases naming Joseph's daughters or his wife. Such are the *Pseudo-Matthæi Evang.* (§ 32, ed. Tisch. p. 104), *Evang. de Nativ. Mar.* (§ 8, *ib.* p. 111), *Historia Joseph.* (§ 2, *ib.* p. 116), *Evang. Thomæ* (§ 16, p. 147), *Evang. Infant. Arab.* (§ 35, p. 191), besides the apocryphal Gospels mentioned by Jerome (*Comm. in Matth.* T. VII. p. 86) which were different from any now extant[1]. Doubtless these accounts, so far as they step beyond the incidents narrated in the Canonical Gospels, are pure fabrications, but the fabrications would scarcely have taken this form, if the Hieronymian view of the Lord's brethren had been received or even known when they were written. It is to these sources that Jerome refers when he taunts the holders of the Epiphanian view with following 'deliramenta apocryphorum.'

Older Versions.

4. The EARLIEST VERSIONS, with the exception of the Old Latin and Memphitic which translate the Greek literally and preserve the same ambiguities, give renderings of certain passages bearing on the subject, which are opposed to the Hieronymian view. The CURETONIAN SYRIAC translates Μαρία Ἰακώβου (Luke xxiv. 10) 'Mary the *daughter* of James.' The PESHITO in John xix. 25 has, 'His mother and His mother's sister *and* Mary of Cleopha and Mary Magdalene'; and in Luke vi. 16, Acts i. 13, it renders 'Judas *son* of James.' One of the old Egyptian versions again, the THEBAIC, in John xix. 25 gives 'Mary *daughter* of Clopas,' and in Luke vi. 16, Acts i. 13 'Judas *son* of James.'

---

[1] As appears from the fact mentioned by Jerome; see above, p. 12, note 2.

5. The CLEMENTINE HOMILIES, written, it would appear, not late in the second century to support a peculiar phase of Ebionism, speak of James as being '*called* the brother of the Lord' (ὁ λεχθεὶς ἀδελφὸς τοῦ Κυρίου, xi. 35), an expression which has been variously interpreted as favouring all three hypotheses (see Blom, p. 88: Schliemann *Clement*. pp. 8, 213), and is indecisive in itself[1]. It is more important to observe that in the Epistle of Clement prefixed to this work and belonging to the same cycle of writings James is styled not Apostle, but Bishop of Bishops, and seems to be distinguished from and in some respects exalted above the Twelve.

6. In the portion of the Clementine Recognitions, which seems to have been founded on the ASCENTS OF JAMES, another very early Ebionite writing[2], the distinction thus implied in the Homilies is explicitly stated. The Twelve Apostles after disputing severally with Caiaphas give an account of their conference to James the chief of Bishops; while James the son of Alphæus is distinctly mentioned among the Twelve as one of the disputants (i. 59).

7. HEGESIPPUS (about 160), a Hebrew Christian of Palestine, writes as follows: 'After the martyrdom of James the Just on the same charge as the Lord, his paternal uncle's child Symeon the son of Clopas is next made bishop, who was put forward by all as the second in succession, being cousin of the Lord' (μετὰ τὸ μαρτυρῆσαι Ἰάκωβον τὸν δίκαιον ὡς καὶ ὁ Κύριος ἐπὶ τῷ αὐτῷ λόγῳ, πάλιν ὁ ἐκ τοῦ θείου αὐτοῦ Συμεὼν ὁ τοῦ Κλωπᾶ καθίσταται ἐπίσκοπος, ὃν προέθεντο πάντες ὄντα ἀνεψιὸν τοῦ Κυρίου δεύτερον[3], Euseb. *H. E.* iv. 22). If the passage be correctly rendered thus (and this rendering alone seems intelligible[4]), Hegesippus distinguishes between the re-

---

[1] The word λεχθείς is most naturally taken, I think, to refer to the *reputed* brotherhood of James, as a consequence of the reputed fatherhood of Joseph, and thus to favour the Epiphanian view. See the expressions of Hegesippus, and of Eusebius, pp. 277, 278.

[2] See the next dissertation.

[3] For δεύτερον comp. Euseb. *H. E.* iii. 14.

[4] A different meaning however has been assigned to the words: πάλιν and δεύτερον being taken to signify '*another* child of his uncle, *another* cousin,' and thus the passage has been represented as favouring the Hieronymian view. So

lationships of James the Lord's brother and Symeon His cousin. So again, referring apparently to this passage, he in another fragment (Euseb. *H. E.* iii. 32) speaks of 'the child of the Lord's paternal uncle, the aforesaid Symeon son of Clopas' (ὁ ἐκ θείου τοῦ Κυρίου ὁ προειρημένος Συμεὼν υἱὸς Κλωπᾶ), to which Eusebius adds, 'for Hegesippus relates that Clopas was the brother of Joseph.' Thus in Hegesippus Symeon is never once called the Lord's brother, while James is always so designated. And this argument powerful in itself is materially strengthened by the fact that, where Hegesippus has occasion to mention Jude, he too like James is styled 'the Lord's brother'; 'There still survived members of the Lord's family *(οἱ ἀπὸ γένους τοῦ Κυρίου)* grandsons of Judas who was called His brother according to the flesh' *(τοῦ κατὰ σάρκα λεγομένου αὐτοῦ ἀδελφοῦ)*; Euseb. *H. E.* iii. 20. In this passage the word 'called' seems to me to point to the Epiphanian rather than the Helvidian view, the brotherhood of these brethren, like the fatherhood of Joseph, being reputed but not real. In yet another passage (Euseb. *H. E.* ii. 23) Hegesippus relates that 'the Church was committed in conjunction with the Apostles[1] to the charge of (διαδέχεται τὴν ἐκκλησίαν μετὰ τῶν ἀποστόλων) the Lord's brother James, who has been entitled Just by all from the Lord's time to our own day; for many bore the name of James.' From this last passage however no inference can be safely drawn; for, supposing the term 'Apostles' to be here restricted

for instance Mill p. 253, Schaf p. 64. On the other hand see Credner *Einl.* p. 575, Neander *Pflanz.* p. 559 (4te aufl.). To this rendering the presence of the definite article alone seems fatal (ὁ ἐκ τοῦ θείου not ἕτερος τῶν ἐκ τοῦ θείου); but indeed the whole passage appears to be framed so as to distinguish the relationships of the two persons; whereas, had the author's object been to represent Symeon as a brother of James, no more circuitous mode could well have been devised for the purpose of stating so very simple a fact. Let me add that

Eusebius (*l.c.*) and Epiphanius (*Haer.* pp. 636, 1039, 1046, ed. Petav.) must have interpreted the words as I have done.

Whether αὐτοῦ should be referred to Ἰάκωβον or to Κύριος is doubtful. If to the former, this alone decides the meaning of the passage. This seems the more natural reference of the two, but the form of expression will admit either.

[1] Jerome (*de Vir. Ill.* § 2) renders it 'post apostolos,' as if μετὰ τοὺς ἀποστόλους; Rufinus correctly 'cum apostolis.'

THE BRETHREN OF THE LORD. 31

to the Twelve, the expression μετὰ τῶν ἀποστόλων may distinguish St James not *from* but *among* the Apostles; as in Acts v. 29, 'Peter and the Apostles answered.'

Thus the testimony of Hegesippus seems distinctly opposed to the Hieronymian view, while of the other two it favours the Epiphanian rather than the Helvidian. If any doubt still remains, the fact that both Eusebius and Epiphanius, who derived their information mainly from Hegesippus, gave this account of the Lord's brethren materially strengthens the position. The testimony of an early Palestinian writer who made it his business to collect such traditions is of the utmost importance.

8. TERTULLIAN's authority was appealed to by Helvidius, and Jerome is content to reply that he was not a member of the Church ('de Tertulliano nihil amplius dico quam ecclesiae hominem non fuisse,' *adv. Helvid.* § 17). It is generally assumed in consequence that Tertullian held the Lord's brethren to be sons of Joseph and Mary. This assumption, though probable, is not absolutely certain. The point at issue in this passage is not the particular opinion of Helvidius respecting the Lord's brethren, but the virginity of the Lord's mother. Accordingly in reply Jerome alleges on his own side the authority of others[1], whose testimony certainly did not go

Tertullian.

---

[1] 'Numquid non possum tibi totam veterum scriptorum seriem commovere: Ignatium, Polycarpum, Irenaeum, Justinum Martyrem, multosque alios apostolicos et eloquentes viros?' (*adv. Helvid.* 17). I have elsewhere (*Galatians* p. 130, note 3) mentioned an instance of the unfair way in which Jerome piles together his authorities. In the present case we are in a position to test him. Jerome did not possess any writings of Ignatius which are not extant now; and in no place does this apostolic father maintain the perpetual virginity of St Mary. In one remarkable passage indeed (*Ephes.* 19), which is several times quoted by subsequent writers, he speaks of the virginity of Mary as a mystery, but this refers distinctly to the time before the birth of our Lord. To this passage which he elsewhere quotes (*Comment. in Matth.* T. VII. p. 12), Jerome is doubtless referring here.

In Cowper's *Syriac Miscell.* p. 61, I find an extract, 'Justin one of the authors who were in the days of Augustus and Tiberius and Gaius wrote in the third discourse: That Mary the Galilean, who was the mother of Christ who was crucified in Jerusalem, had not been with a husband. And Joseph did not repudiate her, but Joseph continued in holiness without a wife, he and his

beyond this one point and had no reference to the relationship of the Lord's brethren. Thus too the more distinct passages in the extant writings of Tertullian relate to the virginity only (*de Carn. Christ.* c. 23 and passim, *de Monog.* c. 8). Elsewhere however, though he does not directly state it, his argument seems to imply that the Lord's brethren were His brothers in the same sense in which Mary was His mother (*adv. Marc.* iv. 19, *de Carn. Christ.* 7). It is therefore highly probable that he held the Helvidian view. Such an admission from one who was so strenuous an advocate of asceticism is worthy of notice.

Clement of Alexandria.

Latin fragment.

9. CLEMENT OF ALEXANDRIA (about A.D. 200) in a passage of the Hypotyposeis preserved in a Latin translation by Cassiodorus (the authorship has been questioned but without sufficient reason[1]) puts forward the Epiphanian solution; 'Jude, who wrote the Catholic Epistle, being one of the sons of Joseph and [the Lord's] brother, a man of deep piety, though he was aware of his relationship to the Lord, nevertheless did not say he was His brother; but what said he? *Jude the servant of*

five sons by a former wife: and Mary continued without a husband.' The editor assigns this passage to Justin Martyr; but not to mention the anachronism, the whole tenor of the passage and the immediate neighbourhood of similar extracts shows that it was intended for the testimony (unquestionably spurious) of some contemporary heathen writer to the facts of the Gospel.

[1] We read in Cassiodorus (*de-Inst. Div. Lit.* 8), 'In epistolas autem canonicas Clemens Alexandrinus presbyter, qui et Stromateus vocatur, id est, in epistola (-am?) S. Petri prima (-am?) S. Johannis prima (-am?) et secunda (-am?) et Jacobi quaedam Attico sermone declaravit. Ubi multa quidem subtiliter sed aliqua incaute loquutus est, quae nos ita transferri fecimus in Latinum, ut exclusis quibusdam offendiculis purificata doctrina ejus securior

possit hauriri.' If . 'Jude' be substituted for 'James,' this description exactly applies to the Latin notes extant under the title *Adumbrationes*. This was a very easy slip of the pen, and I can scarcely doubt that these notes are the same to which Cassiodorus refers as taken from the Hypotyposeis of Clement. Dr Westcott (*Canon*, p. 401) has pointed out in confirmation of this, that while Clement elsewhere directly quotes the Epistle of St Jude, he never refers to the Epistle of St James. Bunsen has included these notes in his collection of fragments of the Hypotyposeis, *Anal. Anten.* I. p. 325. It should be added that the statement about the relationship of Jude must be Clement's own and cannot have been inserted by Cassiodorus, since Cassiodorus in common with the Latin Church would naturally hold the Hieronymian hypothesis.

Jesus Christ, because He was his Lord, *but brother of James;* for this is true; he was his brother, being Joseph's [son][1] (ed. Potter, p. 1007). This statement is explicit. On the other hand, owing to an extract preserved in Eusebius, his authority is generally claimed for the Hieronymian view; 'Clement,' says Eusebius, 'in the sixth book of the Hypotyposeis gives the following account: *Peter and James and John*, he tells us, *after the resurrection of the Saviour were not ambitious of honour, though the preference shown them by the Lord might have entitled them to it, but chose James the Just Bishop of Jerusalem.* The same writer too in the seventh book of the same treatise gives this account also of him (James the Lord's brother); *The Lord after the resurrection delivered the gnosis to James the Just*[2] *and*

<small>Quotations in Eusebius.</small>

---

[1] 'Frater erat ejus [filius] Joseph.' The insertion of 'filius' (with Bunsen) is necessary for the sense, whether Cassiodorus had it or not. Perhaps the Greek words were ἀδελφὸς αὐτοῦ τῶν Ἰωσήφ, which would account for the omission.

[2] Credner, *Einl.* p. 585, condemns the words τῷ δικαίῳ as spurious. Though it might be inferred from the previous extract given by Eusebius that the son of Zebedee is meant here, I believe nevertheless that they are genuine. For (1) They seem to be required as the motive for the explanation which is given afterwards of the different persons bearing the name James. (2) It is natural that a special prominence should be given to the same three Apostles of the Circumcision who are mentioned in Gal. ii. 9 as the pillars of Jewish Christendom. (3) Eusebius introduces the quotation as relating to James the Just (περὶ αὐτοῦ), which would not be a very good description if the other James were the prominent person in the passage. (4) I find from Hippolytus that the Ophite account singled out James the Lord's brother as a possessor of the esoteric gnosis, ταῦτά ἐστιν ἀπὸ πολλῶν πάνυ λόγων τὰ κεφάλαια ἅ φησιν παραδεδωκέναι Μαριάμνῃ τὸν Ἰάκωβον τοῦ Κυρίου τὸν ἀδελφόν, *Haer.* x. 6, p. 95. Clement seems to have derived his information from some work of a Jewish Gnostic complexion, perhaps from the Gospel of the Egyptians with which he was well acquainted (*Strom.* iii. pp. 529 sq, 553, ed. Potter); and as Hippolytus tells us that the Ophites made use of this Gospel (τὰς δὲ ἐξαλλαγὰς ταύτας τὰς ποικίλας ἐν τῷ ἐπιγραφομένῳ κατ' Αἰγυπτίους εὐαγγελίῳ κειμένας ἔχουσιν, *ib.* v. 7, p. 98), it is probable that the account of Clement coincided with that of the Ophites. The words τῳ δικαίῳ are represented in the Syriac translation of Eusebius of which the existing MS (Brit. Mus. add. 14,639) belongs to the 6th century.

I hold τῷ δικαίῳ therefore to be the genuine words of Clement, but I do not feel so sure that the closing explanation δύο δὲ γεγόνασιν Ἰάκωβοι κ.τ.λ. is not an addition of Eusebius. This I suppose to be Bunsen's opinion, for he ends his fragment with the preceding words I. p. 321.

John and Peter. These delivered it to the rest of the Apostles; and the rest of the Apostles to the seventy, of whom Barnabas was one. Now there are two Jameses, one the Just who was thrown down from the pinnacle (of the temple) and beaten to death with a club by a fuller, and another who was beheaded' (*H. E.* ii. 1). This passage however proves nothing. Clement says that there were two of the name of James, but he neither states nor implies that there were two only. His sole object was to distinguish the son of Zebedee from the Lord's brother; and the son of Alphæus, of whom he knew nothing and could tell nothing, did not occur to his mind when he penned this sentence. There is in this passage nothing which contradicts the Latin extract; though indeed in a writer so uncritical in his historical notices[1] such a contradiction would not be surprising[2].

10. ORIGEN († A.D. 253) declares himself very distinctly in favour of the Epiphanian view, stating that the brethren were sons of Joseph by a deceased wife[3]. Elsewhere[4] indeed he says that St Paul 'calls this James the Lord's brother, not so much on account of his kinsmanship or their companionship together, as on account of his character and language,' but this is not inconsistent with the explicit statement already referred to.

---

[1] For instance he distinguished Cephas of Gal. ii. 9 from Peter (see *Galatians*, p. 129), and represented St Paul as a married man (Euseb. *H. E.* iii. 30).

[2] On the supposition that Clement held the Hieronymian theory, as he is represented even by those who themselves reject it, the silence of Origen, who seems never to have heard of this theory, is quite inexplicable. Epiphanius moreover, who appears equally ignorant of it, refers to Clement while writing on this very subject (*Haer.* p. 119, Petav.). Indeed Clement would then stand quite alone before the age of Jerome.

[3] *In Joann.* ii. 12 (*Catena Corder.*

p. 75) ἀδελφοὺς μὲν οὐκ εἶχε φύσει, οὔτε τῆς παρθένου τεκούσης ἕτερον οὐδὲ αὐτὸς ἐκ τοῦ Ἰωσὴφ τυγχάνων· νόμῳ τοιγαροῦν ἐχρημάτισαν αὐτοῦ ἀδελφοί, υἱοὶ Ἰωσὴφ ὄντες ἐκ προτεθνηκυίας γυναικός: *Hom. in Luc.* 7 (III. p. 940, ed. Delarue) 'Hi enim filii qui Joseph dicebantur non erant orti de Maria, neque est ulla scriptura quae ista commemoret.' In this latter passage either the translator has been confused by the order in the original or the words in the translation itself have been displaced accidentally, but the meaning is clear.

[4] *c. Cels.* i. 47 (I. p. 363) οὐ τοσοῦτον διὰ τὸ πρὸς αἵματος συγγενὲς ἢ τὴν κοινὴν αὐτῶν ἀναστροφὴν ὅσον διὰ τὸ ἦθος καὶ τὸν λόγον.

In one passage he writes at some length on the subject; 'Some persons, on the ground of a tradition in the Gospel according to Peter, as it is entitled, or the Book of James (i.e. the Protevangelium), say that the brothers of Jesus were Joseph's sons by a former wife to whom he was married before Mary. Those who hold this view wish to preserve the honour of Mary in virginity throughout...And I think it reasonable that as Jesus was the first-fruit of purity and chastity among men, so Mary was among women: for it is not seemly to ascribe the first-fruit of virginity to any other woman but her' (*in Matt.* xiii. 55, III. p. 462)[1]. This passage shows not only that Origen himself favoured the Epiphanian view which elsewhere he has directly maintained, but that he was wholly unaware of the Hieronymian, the only alternative which presented itself being the denial of the perpetual virginity [2].

---

[1] *Op.* III. p. 462 sq. Mill, pp. 261, 273, has strangely misunderstood the purport of this passage. He speaks of Origen here as 'teaching the opinion of his (James the Just) being the son of Joseph, both as the sentiment of a minority among right-minded Christians and as founded on apocryphal traditions'; and so considers the note on John ii. 12, already referred to, as 'standing strangely contrasted' to Origen's statement here. If Dr Mill's attention however had been directed to the last sentence, καὶ οἶμαι λόγον ἔχειν κ.τ.λ., which, though most important, he has himself omitted in quoting the passage, he could scarcely have failed to see Origen's real meaning.

[2] The authority of Hippolytus of Portus, a contemporary of Origen, has sometimes been alleged in favour of Jerome's hypothesis. In the treatise *De XII Apostolis* ascribed to this author (ed. Fabric. I. app. p. 30) it is said of James the son of Alphæus, κηρύσσων ἐν Ἱερουσαλὴμ ὑπὸ Ἰουδαίων καταλευσθεὶς ἀναιρεῖται καὶ θάπτεται ἐκεῖ παρὰ τῷ ναῷ. He is thus confused or identified with James the Lord's brother. But this blundering treatise was certainly not written by the bishop of Portus: see Le Moyne in Fabricius I. p. 84, and Bunsen's *Hippol.* I. p. 456 (ed. 2). On the other hand in the work *De LXX Apostolis* (Fabricius I. app. p. 41), also ascribed to this writer, we find among the 70 the name of Ἰάκωβος ὁ ἀδελφόθεος ἐπίσκοπος Ἱεροσολύμων, who is thus distinguished from the Twelve. This treatise also is manifestly spurious. Again Nicephorus Callistus, *H. E.* ii. 3, cites as from Hippolytus of Portus an elaborate account of our Lord's brethren following the Epiphanian view (Hippol. *Op.* I. app. 43, ed. Fabric.); but this account seems to be drawn either from Hippolytus the Theban, unless as Bunsen (*l. c.*) supposes this Theban Hippolytus be a mythical personage, or from some forged writings which bore the name of the older Hippolytus.

36 THE BRETHREN OF THE LORD.

Apostolical Constitutions.

11. The APOSTOLICAL CONSTITUTIONS, the main part of which may perhaps be regarded as a work of the third century, though they received considerable additions in later ages, distinguish James the Lord's brother from James the son of Alphæus, making him, like St Paul, a supernumerary apostle, and thus counting fourteen in all (vi. 12, 13, 14; compare ii. 55, vii. 46, viii. 4).

Victorinus of Pettaw.

12. VICTORINUS PETAVIONENSIS (about 300) was claimed by Helvidius as a witness in his own favour. Jerome denied this and put in a counter claim. It may perhaps be inferred from this circumstance that Victorinus did little more than repeat the statements of the evangelists respecting the Lord's brethren (*adv. Helvid.* 17).

Eusebius of Cæsarea.

13. EUSEBIUS OF CÆSAREA († about 340) distinguished James the Lord's brother from the Twelve, representing him as a supernumerary apostle like St Paul (*Comm. in Isai.* in Montfaucon's *Coll. Nov. Patr.* II. p. 422; *Hist. Eccl.* i. 12; comp. vii. 19). Accordingly in another passage he explains that this James 'was called the Lord's brother, because Joseph was His reputed father' (*Hist. Eccl.* ii. 1)[1].

---

[1] Ἰάκωβον τὸν τοῦ Κυρίου λεγόμενον ἀδελφόν, ὅτι δὴ καὶ οὗτος τοῦ Ἰωσὴφ ὠνόμαστο παῖς τοῦ δὲ Χριστοῦ πατὴρ ὁ Ἰωσήφ, ᾧ μνηστευθεῖσα ἡ παρθένος κ.τ.λ. On the whole this passage seems to be best explained by referring οὗτος to Κύριος. But this is not necessary; for ὀνομάζεσθαι (or καλεῖσθαι) παῖς τινὸς is a good Greek phrase to denote real as well as reputed sonship: as Æsch. *Fragm.* 285 αἴδ' ἐπτ' Ἄτλαντος παῖδες ὠνομασμέναι, Soph. *Trach.* 1105 ὁ τῆς ἀρίστης μητρὸς ὠνομασμένος, Eur. *Elect.* 935: comp. Ephes. iii. 15 τὸν πατέρα ἐξ οὗ πᾶσα πατριὰ ὀνομάζεται. The word ὠνόμαστο cannot at all events, as Mill (p. 272) seems disposed to think, imply any doubt on the part of Eusebius about the parentage of James, for the whole drift of the passage is plainly against this. The other reading, ὅτι δὴ καὶ οὗτος τοῦ Ἰωσὴφ τοῦ νομιζομένου οἱονεὶ πατρὸς τοῦ Χριστοῦ, found in some MSS and in the Syriac version, and preferred by Blom p. 98, and Credner *Einl.* p. 585, I cannot but regard as an obvious alteration of some early transcriber for the sake of clearness.

Compare the expressions in i. 12 εἷς δὲ καὶ οὗτος τῶν φερομένων ἀδελφῶν ἦν, and iii. 7 τοῦ Κυρίου χρηματίζων ἀδελφός. He was a *reputed* brother of the Lord, because Joseph was His *reputed* father. See also Eusebius *On the Star*, 'Joseph and Mary and Our Lord with them and the five sons of Hannah (Anna) the first wife of Joseph' (p. 17, Wright's Transl.). The account from which this passage is taken professes to be founded on a document dating A.D. 119.

14. CYRIL OF JERUSALEM († 386) comments on the successive appearances of our Lord related by St Paul, first to Peter, then to the Twelve, then to the five hundred, then to James His own brother, then to Paul His enemy; and his language implies that each appearance was a step in advance of the testimony afforded by the former (*Catech.* xiv. 21, p. 216, ed. Touttée). It may be gathered thence that he distinguished this James from the Twelve. As this however is only an inference from his language, and not a direct statement of his own, too much stress must not be laid on it. In another passage also (*Catech.* iv. 28, p. 65, καὶ τοῖς ἀποστόλοις καὶ Ἰακώβῳ τῷ ταύτης τῆς ἐκκλησίας ἐπισκόπῳ) Cyril seems to make the same distinction, but here again the inference is doubtful.

Cyril of Jerusalem.

15. HILARY OF POITIERS († 368) denounces those who 'claim authority for their opinion (against the virginity of the Lord's mother) from the fact of its being recorded that our Lord had several brothers'; and adds, 'yet if these had been sons of Mary and not rather sons of Joseph, the offspring of a former marriage, she would never at the time of the passion have been transferred to the Apostle John to be his mother' (*Comm. in Matth.* i. 1, p. 671, ed. Bened.). Thus he not only adopts the Epiphanian solution, but shows himself entirely ignorant of the Hieronymian.

Hilary of Poitiers.

16. VICTORINUS THE PHILOSOPHER (about 360) takes εἰ μὴ in Gal. i. 19 as expressing not *exception* but *opposition*, and distinctly states that James was not an Apostle: 'Cum autem fratrem dixit, apostolum negavit.'

Victorinus the Philosopher.

17. The AMBROSIAN HILARY (about 375) comments on Gal. i. 19 as follows; 'The Lord is called the brother of James and the rest in the same way in which He is also designated the son of Joseph. For some in a fit of madness impiously assert and contend that these were true brothers of the Lord, being sons of Mary, allowing at the same time that Joseph, though not His true father, was so-called nevertheless. For if these were His true brothers, then Joseph will be His true father; for he who called Joseph His father also called James

Ambrosiaster.

and the rest His brothers.' Thus his testimony entirely coincides with that of his greater namesake. He sees only the alternative of denying the perpetual virginity as Helvidius did, or accepting the solution of the Protevangelium; and he unhesitatingly adopts the latter.

Basil.

18. BASIL THE GREAT († 379), while allowing that the perpetual virginity is not a necessary article of belief, yet adheres to it himself 'since the lovers of Christ cannot endure to hear that the mother of God ever ceased to be a virgin' (*Hom. in Sanct. Christ. Gen.* II. p. 600, ed. Garn.)[1]. As immediately afterwards he refers, in support of his view, to some apocryphal work which related that Zacharias was slain by the Jews for testifying to the virginity of the mother of Jesus (a story which closely resembles the narrative of his death in the *Protevang.* §§ 23, 24), it may perhaps be inferred that he accepted that account of the Lord's brethren which ran through these apocryphal gospels.

Gregory Nyssen.

19. His brother GREGORY NYSSEN († after 394) certainly adopted the Epiphanian account. At the same time he takes up the very untenable position that the 'Mary who is designated in the other Evangelists (besides St John) the mother of James and Joses is *the mother of God* and none else[2],' being so called because she undertook the education of these her stepsons; and he supposes also that this James is called 'the little' by St Mark to distinguish him from James *the son of Alphæus* who

---

[1] This very moderate expression of opinion is marked by the editors with a *caute legendum* in the margin; and in Garnier's edition the treatise is consigned to an appendix as of doubtful authenticity. The main argument urged against it is the passage here referred to. (See Garnier, II. præf. p. xv.)

[2] Similarly Chrysostom, see below, p. 43, note 1. This identification of the Lord's mother with the mother of James and Joses is adopted and similarly explained also in one of the apocryphal gospels: *Hist. Joseph.* 4 (Tisch. p. 117). Possibly Gregory derived it from some such source. It was also part of the Helvidian hypothesis, where it was less out of place, and gave Jerome an easy triumph over his adversary (*adv. Helvid.* 12 etc.). It is adopted moreover by Cave (Life of St James the Less, § 2), who holds that the Lord's brethren were sons of Joseph, and yet makes James the Lord's brother one of the Twelve, identifying Joseph with Alphæus. Fritzsche also identifies these two Maries (*Matth.* p. 822, *Marc.* p. 697).

was 'great,' because he was in the number of the Twelve Apostles, which the Lord's brother was not (*in Christ. Resurr.* ii. *Op.* III. pp. 412, 413, ed. Paris, 1638).

20. The ANTIDICOMARIANITES, an obscure Arabian sect in the latter half of the fourth century, maintained that the Lord's mother bore children to her husband Joseph. These opinions seem to have produced a reaction, or to have been themselves reactionary, for we read about the same time of a sect called *Collyridians*, likewise in Arabia, who going to the opposite extreme paid divine honours to the Virgin (Epiphan. *Haeres.* lxxviii, lxxix)[1].

Antidicomarianites.

21. EPIPHANIUS a native of Palestine became bishop of Constantia in Cyprus in the year 367. Not very long before Jerome wrote in defence of the perpetual virginity of the Lord's mother against the Helvidians at Rome, Epiphanius came forward as the champion of the same cause against the Antidicomarianites. He denounced them in an elaborate pastoral letter, in which he explains his views at length, and which he has thought fit to incorporate in his subsequently written treatise against Heresies (pp. 1034—1057, ed. Petav.). He moreover discusses the subject incidentally in other parts of his great work (pp. 115, 119, 432, 636), and it is clear that he had devoted much time and attention to it. His account coincides with that of the apocryphal gospels. Joseph, he states, was eighty years old or more when the Virgin was espoused to him; by his former wife he had six children, four sons and two daughters, the names of the daughters were Mary and Salome,

Epiphanius.

---

[1] The names are plainly terms of ridicule invented by their enemies. Augustine supposes the 'Antidicomarianitæ' of Epiphanius (he writes the word 'Antidicomaritæ') to be the same as the Helvidians of Jerome (*adv. Haer.* 84, VIII. p. 24). They held the same tenets, it is true, but there seems to have been otherwise no connexion between the two. Considerations of time and place alike resist this identification.

Epiphanius had heard that these opinions, which he held to be derogatory to the Lord's mother, had been promulgated also by the elder Apollinaris or some of his disciples; but he doubted about this (p. 1034). The report was probably circulated by their opponents in order to bring discredit upon them.

for which names by the way. he alleges the authority of Scripture p. 1041); his sons, St James especially, were called the Lord's brethren because they were brought up with Jesus; the mother of the Lord remained for ever a virgin; as the lioness is said to exhaust her fertility in the production of a single offspring (see Herod. iii. 108), so she who bore the Lion of Judah could not in the nature of things become a mother a second time (pp. 1044, 1045). These particulars with many other besides he gives, quoting as his authority 'the tradition of the Jews' (p. 1039). It is to be observed moreover that, though he thus treats of the subject several times and at great length, he never once alludes to the Hieronymian account; and yet I can scarcely doubt that one who so highly extolled celibacy would have hailed with delight a solution which, as Jerome boasted, saved the virginity not of Mary only but of Joseph also, for whose honour Epiphanius shows himself very jealous (pp. 1040, 1046, 1047).

Helvidius, Bonosus, and Jovinianus.

22. Somewhere about the year 380 HELVIDIUS, who resided in Rome, published a treatise in which he maintained that the Lord's brethren were sons of Joseph and Mary. He seems to have succeeded in convincing a considerable number of persons, for contemporary writers speak of the Helvidians as a party. These views were moreover advocated by BONOSUS, bishop of Sardica in Illyria, about the same time, and apparently also by JOVINIANUS a monk probably of Milan. The former was condemned by a synod assembled at Capua (A.D. 392), and the latter by synods held at Rome and at Milan (about A.D. 390; see Hefele *Conciliengesch.* II. pp. 47, 48)[1].

Motive of the Helvidians.

In earlier times this account of the Lord's brethren, so far as it was the badge of a party, seems to have been held in conjunction with Ebionite views respecting the conception and person of

---

[1] The work ascribed to Dorotheus Tyrius is obviously spurious (see Cave *Hist. Lit.* I. p. 163); and I have therefore not included his testimony in this list. The writer distinguishes James the Lord's brother and James the son of Alphæus, and makes them successive bishops of Jerusalem. See Combefis in Fabricius' *Hippol.* I. app. p. 36.

Christ[1]. For, though not necessarily affecting the belief in the miraculous Incarnation, it was yet a natural accompaniment of the denial thereof. The motive of these latter impugners of the perpetual virginity was very different. They endeavoured to stem the current which had set strongly in the direction of celibacy; and, if their theory was faulty, they still deserve the sympathy due to men who in defiance of public opinion refused to bow their necks to an extravagant and tyrannous superstition.

We have thus arrived at the point of time when Jerome's answer to Helvidius created a new epoch in the history of this controversy. And the following inferences are, if I mistake not, fairly deducible from the evidence produced. *First:* there is not the slightest indication that the Hieronymian solution ever occurred to any individual or sect or church, until it was put forward by Jerome himself. If it had been otherwise, writers like Origen, the two Hilaries, and Epiphanius, who discuss the question, could not have failed to notice it. *Secondly:* the Epiphanian account has the highest claims to the sanction of tradition, whether the value of this sanction be great or small. *Thirdly:* this solution seems especially to represent the Palestinian view.

Evidence summed up.

In the year 382 (or 383) Jerome published his treatise; and the effect of it is visible at once.

Jerome's treatise.

AMBROSE in the year 392 wrote a work *De Institutione Virginis*, in which he especially refutes the impugners of the perpetual virginity of the Lord's mother. In a passage which is perhaps intentionally obscure he speaks to this effect: 'The

Ambrose.

---

[1] [I fear the statement in the text may leave a false impression. Previous writers had spoken of the Ebionites as holding the Helvidian view, and I was betrayed into using similar language. But there is, so far as I am aware, no evidence in favour of this assumption. It would be still more difficult to substantiate the assertions in the following note of Gibbon, *Decline and Fall* c. xvi, 'This appellation ('brethren') was at first understood in the most obvious sense, and it was supposed that the brothers of Jesus were the lawful issue of Joseph and Mary. A devout respect for the virginity of the mother of God suggested to the Gnostics, and afterwards to the Orthodox Greeks, the expedient of bestowing a second wife on Joseph, etc.'] 2nd ed. 1866.

term brothers has a wide application; it is used of members of the same family, the same race, the same country. Witness the Lord's own words *I will declare thy name to my brethren* (Ps. xxii. 22). St Paul too says: *I could wish to be accursed for my brethren* (Rom. ix. 3). Doubtless they might be called brothers as sons of Joseph, not of Mary. And if any one will go into the question carefully, he will find this to be the true account. For myself I do not intend to enter upon this question: it is of no importance to decide what particular relationship is implied; it is sufficient for my purpose that the term "brethren" is used in an extended sense (i.e. of others besides sons of the same mother)[1].' From this I infer that St Ambrose had heard of, though possibly not read, Jerome's tract, in which he discourses on the wide meaning of the term: that, if he had read it, he did not feel inclined to abandon the view with which he was familiar in favour of the novel hypothesis put forward by Jerome: and lastly, that seeing the importance of cooperation against a common enemy he was anxious not to raise dissensions among the champions of the perpetual virginity by the discussion of details.

Pelagius. PELAGIUS, who commented on St Paul a few years after Jerome, adopts his theory and even his language, unless his text has been tampered with here (Gal. i. 19).

Augustine. At the same time Jerome's hypothesis found a much more weighty advocate in ST AUGUSTINE. In his commentary on the Galatians indeed (i. 19), written about 394 while he was still a presbyter, he offers the alternative of the Hieronymian and Epiphanian accounts. But in his later works he consistently maintains the view put forward by Jerome in the

---

[1] The passage, which I have thus paraphrased, is 'Fratres autem gentis, et generis, populi quoque consortium nuncupari docet Dominus ipse qui dicit: *Narrabo nomen tuum fratribus meis; in medio ecclesiae laudabo te.* Paulus quoque ait: *Optabam ego anathema esse pro fratribus meis.* Potuerunt autem fratres esse ex Joseph, non ex Maria. Quod quidem si quis diligentius prosequatur inveniet. Nos ea prosequenda non putavimus, quoniam fraternum nomen liquet pluribus esse commune' (II. p. 260, ed. Ben.). St Ambrose seems to accept so much of Jerome's argument as relates to the wide use of the term 'brothers' and nothing more.

treatise against Helvidius (*In Joh. Evang.* x, III. 2. p. 368, *ib.* xxviii, III. 2. p. 508; *Enarr. in Ps.* cxxvii, IV. 2. p. 1443; *Contr. Faust.* xxii. 35, VIII. p. 383; comp. *Quaest. XVII in Matth.*, III. 2. p. 285).

Thus supported, it won its way to general acceptance in the Latin Church; and the WESTERN SERVICES recognise only one James besides the son of Zebedee, thus identifying the Lord's brother with the son of Alphæus. *Western Church.*

In the East also it met with a certain amount of success, but this was only temporary. CHRYSOSTOM wrote both before and after Jerome's treatise had become generally known, and his expositions of the New Testament mark a period of transition. In his Homilies on the earlier books he takes the Epiphanian view: St James, he says, was at one time an unbeliever with the rest of the Lord's brethren (on Matth. i. 25, VII. p. 77; John vii. 5, VIII. p. 284; see also on 1 Cor. ix. 4, X. p. 181 E); the resurrection was the turning-point in their career; they were called the Lord's brethren, as Joseph himself was reputed the husband of Mary (on Matth. i. 25, l. c.)[1]. Hitherto *Chrysostom.*

---

[1] A comment attributed to Chrysostom in Cramer's *Catena* on 1 Cor. ix. 4—7, but not found in the Homilies, is still more explicit; 'Αδελφοὺς τοῦ Κυρίου λέγει τοὺς νομισθέντας εἶναι αὐτοῦ ἀδελφούς· ἐπειδὴ γὰρ οὗτος ὁ χρηματίζων καὶ αὐτὸς κατὰ τὴν κοινὴν δόξαν εἶπεν αὐτούς· τοὺς δὲ υἱοὺς 'Ιωσὴφ λέγει, οἱ ἀδελφοὶ τοῦ Κυρίου ἐχρημάτισαν διὰ τὴν πρὸς τὴν θεοτόκον μνηστείαν τοῦ 'Ιωσήφ. λέγει δὲ 'Ιάκωβον ἐπίσκοπον 'Ιεροσολύμων καὶ 'Ιωσὴφ ὁμώνυμον τῷ πατέρι καὶ Σίμωνα καὶ 'Ιούδα. I give the passage without attempting to correct the text. This note reappears almost word for word in the Œcumenian catena and in Theophylact. If Chrysostom be not the author, then we gain the testimony of some other ancient writer on the same side. Compare also the pseudo-Chrysostom, *Op.* II. p. 797.

The passages referred to in the text show clearly what was Chrysostom's earlier view. To these may be added the comments on 1 Cor. xv. 7 (x. 355 D), where he evidently regards James as not one of the Twelve; on Matth. x. 2 (VII. pp. 368, 9), where he makes James the son of Alphæus a taxgatherer like Matthew, clearly taking them to be brothers; and on Matth. xxvii. 55 (VII. p. 827 A), where, like Gregory Nyssen, he identifies Μαρία 'Ιακώβου with the Lord's mother. The accounts of Chrysostom's opinion on this subject given by Blom p. 111 sq, and Mill p. 284 note, are unsatisfactory.

The Homilies on the Acts also take the same view (IX. pp. 23 B, 26 A), but though these are generally ascribed to Chrysostom, their genuineness is very questionable. In another spurious work, *Opus imp. in Matth.*, VI. p.

he betrays no knowledge of the Hieronymian account. But in his exposition of the Epistle to the Galatians (i. 19) he not only speaks of James the Lord's brother as if he were an apostle (which proves nothing), but also calls him the son of Clopas[1]. Thus he would appear meanwhile to have accepted the hypothesis of Jerome and to have completed it by the identification of Clopas with Alphæus. And THEODORET, who for the most part closely follows Chrysostom, distinctly repudiates the older view: 'He was not, as some have supposed, a son of Joseph, the offspring of a former marriage, but was son of Clopas and cousin of the Lord; for his mother was the sister of the Lord's mother.'

Theodoret.

But with these exceptions the Epiphanian view maintained its ground in the East. It is found again in CYRIL OF ALEXANDRIA for instance (*Glaphyr. in Gen.* lib. vii. p. 221), and seems to have been held by later Greek writers almost, if not quite, universally. In THEOPHYLACT indeed (on Matth. xiii. 55, Gal. i. 19) we find an attempt to unite the two accounts. James, argues the writer, was the Lord's reputed brother as the son of Joseph and the Lord's cousin as the son of Clopas; the one was his natural, and the other his legal father; Clopas having died childless, Joseph had raised up seed to his brother by his widow according to the law of the levirate[2]. This novel suggestion however found but little favour, and the Eastern Churches continued to distinguish between James the Lord's brother and James the son of Alphæus. The GREEK, SYRIAN, and COPTIC CALENDARS assign a separate day to each.

Cyril of Alexandria.

Theophylact.

Eastern Churches.

The table on the next page gives a conspectus of the patristic and early authorities.

clxxiv E, the Hieronymian view appears; 'Jacobum Alphaei lapidantes: propter quae omnia Jerusalem destructa est a Romanis.'

[1] τὸν τοῦ Κλωπᾶ, ὅπερ καὶ ὁ εὐαγγελιστὴς ἔλεγεν. He is referring, I suppose, to the lists of the Apostles which mention James the son of *Alphæus*. See above, p. 19. This portion of his exposition however is somewhat confused, and it is difficult to resist the suspicion that it has been interpolated.

[2] See the remarks of Mill, p. 228.

A. *Sons of Joseph and Mary.*	{ TERTULLIAN, HELVIDIUS, BONOSUS, JOVINIANUS (?), ANTIDICOMARIANITES. }		
B. *Sons of Joseph by a former wife.*	{ GOSPEL OF PETER, PROTEVANGELIUM etc., CLEMENT OF ALEX., ORIGEN, EUSEBIUS, HILARY OF POITIERS, AMBROSIASTER, GREGORY OF NYSSA, EPIPHANIUS, AMBROSE, [CHRYSOSTOM], CYRIL OF ALEX., EASTERN SERVICES (Greek, Syrian, and Coptic), LATER GREEK WRITERS. }	A. or B. *'Brethren' in a strict sense. James the Just not one of the Twelve.*	{ EARLY VERSIONS, CLEMENTINE HOMILIES (?), ASCENTS OF JAMES, HEGESIPPUS, APOST. CONSTIT., CYRIL OF JERUSALEM (?), VICTORINUS THE PHILOSOPHER. }
		B. or C. *Perpetual virginity of Mary.*	{ BASIL, CATHOLIC WRITERS GENERALLY. }
C. *Sons of the Virgin's sister.*	{ JEROME, PELAGIUS, AUGUSTINE, [CHRYSOSTOM], THEODORET, WESTERN SERVICES, LATER LATIN WRITERS. }		

Uncertain. HEBREW GOSPEL, VICTORINUS PETAVIONENSIS.
Levirate. THEOPHYLACT.

II.

ST PAUL AND THE THREE.

Three Apostles alone besides St Paul prominent.

THREE and three only of the personal disciples and immediate followers of our Lord hold any prominent place in the Apostolic records—James, Peter, and John; the first the Lord's brother, the two latter the foremost members of the Twelve. Apart from an incidental reference to the death of James the son of Zebedee, which is dismissed in a single sentence, the rest of the Twelve are mentioned by name for the last time on the day of the Lord's Ascension. Thenceforward they disappear wholly from the canonical writings.

And this silence also extends to the traditions of succeeding ages. We read indeed of St Thomas in India, of St Andrew in Scythia; but such scanty notices, even if we accept them as trustworthy, show only the more plainly how little the Church could tell of her earliest teachers. Doubtless they laboured zealously and effectively in the spread of the Gospel; but, so far as we know, they have left no impress of their individual mind and character on the Church at large. Occupying the foreground, and indeed covering the whole canvas of early ecclesiastical history, appear four figures alone, St Paul and the three Apostles of the Circumcision.

The four meet together at a great crisis.

Once and, it would appear, not more than once, these four great teachers met together face to face. It was the one great crisis in the history of the Church, on the issue of which was staked her future progress and triumph. Was she to open her doors wide and receive all comers, to declare her legitimate boundaries coextensive with the limits of the human race? Or was she to remain for ever narrow and sectarian, a national institution at best, but most probably a suspected minority even in her own nation?

Not less important, so far as we can see, was the question at issue, when Paul and Barnabas arrived at Jerusalem to confer with the Apostles of the Circumcision on the subject of the Mosaic ritual which then distracted the youthful Church. It must therefore be an intensely interesting study to watch the attitude of the four great leaders of the Church at this crisis, merely as a historical lesson. But the importance of the subject does not rest here. Questions of much wider interest are suggested by the accounts of this conference: What degree of coincidence or antagonism between Jewish and Gentile converts may be discerned in the Church? What were the relations existing between St Paul and the Apostles of the Circumcision? How far do the later sects of Ebionites on the one hand and Marcionites on the other, as they appear in direct antagonism in the second century, represent opposing principles cherished side by side within the bosom of the Church and sheltering themselves under the names, or (as some have ventured to say) sanctioned by the authority, of the leading Apostles? What in fact is the secret history—if there be any secret history—of the origin of Catholic Christianity? *Questions suggested by this meeting.*

On this battle-field the most important of recent theological controversies has been waged: and it is felt by both sides that the Epistle to the Galatians is the true key to the position. In the first place, it is one of the very few documents of the Apostolic ages, whose genuineness has not been seriously challenged by the opponents of revelation. Moreover, as the immediate utterance of one who himself took the chief part in the incidents recorded, it cannot be discredited as having passed through a coloured medium or gathered accretions by lapse of time. And lastly, the very form in which the informa- *Importance of the Galatian Epistle.*

tion is conveyed—by partial and broken allusions rather than by direct and continuous statement—raises it beyond the reach of suspicion, even where suspicion is most active. Here at least both combatants can take their stand on common ground. Nor need the defenders of the Christian faith hesitate to accept the challenge of their opponents and try the question on this issue. If it be only interpreted aright, the Epistle to the Galatians ought to present us with a true, if only a partial, solution of the problem.

Apology for this essay.

Thus the attempt to decipher the relations between Jewish and Gentile Christianity in the first ages of the Church is directly suggested by this epistle; and indeed any commentary would be incomplete which refused to entertain the problem. This must be my excuse for entering upon a subject, about which so much has been written and which involves so many subsidiary questions. It will be impossible within my limits to discuss all these questions in detail. The objections, for instance, which have been urged against the genuineness of a large number of the canonical and other early Christian writings, can only be met indirectly. Reasonable men will hardly be attracted towards a theory which can only be built on an area prepared by this wide clearance of received documents. At all events there is, I think, no unfairness in stating the case thus; that, though they are supported by arguments drawn from other sources, the general starting-point of such objections is the theory itself. If then a fair and reasonable account can be given both of the origin and progress of the Church generally, and of the mutual relations of its more prominent teachers, based on these documents assumed as authentic, a general answer will be supplied to all objections of this class.

Proposed sketch of the relations of Jewish and Gentile Christians.

I purpose therefore to sketch in outline the progressive history of the relations between the Jewish and Gentile converts in the early ages of the Church, as gathered from the Apostolic writings, aided by such scanty information as can be got together from other sources. This will be a fit and indeed a necessary introduction to the subject with which the

Epistle to the Galatians is more directly concerned, the positions occupied by St Paul and the three Apostles of the Circumcision respectively.

This history falls into three periods which mark three distinct stages in its progress: (1) The Extension of the Church to the Gentiles; (2) The Recognition of Gentile Liberty; (3) The Emancipation of the Jewish Churches[1]. *Three main divisions of this subject.*

1. *The Extension of the Church to the Gentiles.*

It appears from the Apostolic history that the believers in the earliest days conformed strictly to Jewish customs in their religious life, retaining the fixed hours of prayer, attending the temple worship and sacrifices, observing the sacred festivals. The Church was still confined to one nation and had not yet broken loose from the national rites and usages. But these swathing bands, which were perhaps needed to support its infancy, would only cripple its later growth, and must be thrown off, if it was ever to attain to a healthy maturity. This emancipation then was the great problem which the Apostles had to work out. The Master Himself had left no express instructions. He had charged them, it is true, to preach the Gospel to all nations, but how this injunction was to be carried out, by what changes a national Church must expand into an universal Church, they had not been told. He had indeed asserted the sovereignty of the spirit over the letter; He had enunciated the great principle—as wide in its application as the law itself *The early Church of Jerusalem.*

Our Lord's teaching.

---

[1] Important works treating of the relation between the Jewish and Gentile Christians are Lechler's *Apostolisches und Nachapostolisches Zeitalter* (2te aufl. 1857), and Ritschl's *Entstehung der Altkatholischen Kirche* (2te aufl. 1857). I am indebted to both these works, but to the latter especially, which is very able and suggestive. Ritschl should be read in his second edition, in which with a noble sacrifice of consistency to truth he has abandoned many of his former positions, and placed himself in more direct antagonism to the Tübingen school in which he was educated. The historical speculations of that school are developed in Baur's *Paulus* and *Christenthum und die Christliche Kirche der drei ersten Jahrhunderte*, and in Schwegler's *Nachapostolisches Zeitalter*.

—that 'Man was not made for the sabbath, but the sabbath for man'; He had pointed to the fulfilment of the law in the Gospel. So far He had discredited the law, but He had not deposed or abolished it. It was left to the Apostles themselves under the guidance of the Spirit, moulded by circumstances and moulding them in turn, to work out this great change.

Jews of the Dispersion.

And soon enough the pressure of events began to be felt. The dispersion was the link which connected the Hebrews of Palestine with the outer world. Led captive by the power of Greek philosophy at Athens and Tarsus and Alexandria, attracted by the fascinations of Oriental mysticism in Asia, swept along with the busy whirl of social life in the city and court of the Cæsars, these outlying members of the chosen race had inhaled a freer spirit and contracted wider interests than their fellow-countrymen at home. By a series of insensible gradations—proselytes of the covenant—proselytes of the gate[1]—superstitious devotees who observed the rites without accepting the faith of the Mosaic dispensation—curious lookers-on who interested themselves in the Jewish ritual as they would in the worship of Isis or of Astarte—the most stubborn zealot of the law was linked to the idolatrous heathen whom he abhorred and who despised him in turn. Thus the train was unconsciously laid, when the spark fell from heaven and fired it.

First day of Pentecost.

The very baptism of the Christian Church opened the path for its extension to the Gentile world. On the first day of Pentecost were gathered together Hellenist Jews from all the principal centres of the dispersion. With them were assembled also numbers of incorporated Israelites, proselytes of the covenant. The former of these by contact with Gentile thought

---

[1] The distinction between proselytes of the covenant or of righteousness and proselytes of the gate is found in the Gemara: the former were circumcised, and observed the whole law; the latter acknowledged the God of Israel and conformed to Jewish worship in some respects, but stood without the covenant, not having been incorporated by the initiatory rite. The former alone, it would appear, are called προσήλυτοι in the New Testament; the latter, who hardly form a distinct class, are οἱ σεβόμενοι τὸν Θεόν, οἱ εὐσεβεῖς etc. In speaking therefore of 'proselytes of the gate' I am using a convenient anachronism.

and life, the latter by the force of early habits and associations[1], would accept and interpret the new revelation in a less rigorous spirit than the Hebrew zealot of Jerusalem. Each successive festival must have been followed by similar though less striking results. The stream of Hellenists and proselytes, constantly ebbing and flowing, must have swept away fragments at least of the new truth, purging it of some local encumbrances which would gather about it in the mother country, and carrying it thus purged to far distant shores.

Meanwhile at Jerusalem some years passed away before the barrier of Judaism was assailed. The Apostles still observed the Mosaic ritual; they still confined their preaching to Jews by birth, or Jews by adoption, the proselytes of the covenant. At length a breach was made, and the assailants as might be expected were Hellenists. The first step towards the creation of an organised ministry was also the first step towards the emancipation of the Church. The Jews of Judæa, 'Hebrews of the Hebrews,' had ever regarded their Hellenist brethren with suspicion and distrust; and this estrangement reproduced itself in the Christian Church. The interests of the Hellenist widows had been neglected in the daily distribution of alms. Hence 'arose a murmuring of the Hellenists against the Hebrews' (Acts vi. 1), which was met by the appointment of seven persons specially charged with providing for the wants of these neglected poor. If the selection was made, as St Luke's language seems to imply, not by the Hellenists themselves but by the Church at large (vi. 2), the concession when granted was carried out in a liberal spirit. All the names of the seven are Greek, pointing to a Hellenist rather than a Hebrew extraction, and one is especially described as a proselyte, being doubtless chosen to represent a hitherto small but growing section of the community.

Appointment of Hellenist officers.

By this appointment the Hellenist members obtained a *Effects of this measure.*

[1] 'Trust not a proselyte,' said one of the rabbis, 'till twenty-four generations; for he holds his leaven.' Yalkut (Shimoni) on Ruth i. 11, 12, § 601. See also the passages given by Danz in Meuschen *Test. Illustr.* p. 651.

status in the Church; and the effects of this measure soon became visible. Two out of the seven stand prominently forward as the champions of emancipation, Stephen the preacher and martyr of liberty, and Philip the practical worker[1].

Stephen's testimony. STEPHEN is the acknowledged forerunner of the Apostle of the Gentiles. He was the first to 'look steadfastly to the end of that which is abolished,' to sound the death-knell of the Mosaic ordinances and the temple worship, and to claim for the Gospel unfettered liberty and universal rights. 'This man,' said his accusers, 'ceaseth not to speak words against the holy place and the law; for we have heard him say that this Jesus of Nazareth shall destroy this place and shall change the customs which Moses delivered us' (vi. 13, 14). The charge was only false as misrepresenting the spirit which animated his teaching. The accused attempts no denial, but pleads justification. To seal this testimony the first blood of the noble army of martyrs is shed.

---

[1] In Nicolas, the only one of the remaining five whose name reappears in history, liberty is degraded into licence. I see no valid reason for doubting the very early tradition that the Nicolaitans (Apoc. ii. 6, 15) derived their name from him. If there was a traitor among the Twelve, there might well be a heresiarch among the Seven. Nor is it likely that an account so discreditable to one who in the New Testament is named only in connexion with his appointment to an honourable office would have been circulated unless there were some foundation in fact. At the same time the Nicolaitans may have exaggerated and perverted the teaching of Nicolas. Irenæus (i. 26, 3) and Hippolytus (*Haer.* vii. 36) believe him to have been the founder of the sect; while Clement of Alexandria (*Strom.* ii. p. 411, iii. p. 522, Potter) attributes to him an ambiguous saying that 'the flesh must be abused (δεῖν παραχρῆσθαι τῇ σαρκί),' of which these Nicolaitans perverted the meaning; and in attempting to clear his reputation relates a highly improbable story, which, if true, would be far from creditable. In another passage of Hippolytus, a fragment preserved in Syriac (Lagarde's *Anec. Syr.* p. 87, Cowper's *Syr. Miscell.* p. 55) and taken from the 'Discourse on the Resurrection' addressed to Mammæa, this writer again represents Nicolas as the founder of the sect, speaking of him as 'stirred by a strange spirit' and teaching that the resurrection is past (2 Tim. ii. 18), but not attributing to him any directly immoral doctrines. A common interpretation, which makes Nicolaus a Greek rendering of Balaam, is not very happy; for Νικόλαος does not altogether correspond with any possible derivation of Balaam, least of all with בלע עם 'the destroyer of the people,' generally adopted by those who so explain Νικόλαος. See below, p. 64, with the notes.

ST PAUL AND THE THREE. 53

The indirect consequences of his martyrdom extend far *Indirect conse-*
beyond the immediate effect of his dying words. A persecution *quences.*
'arose about Stephen.' The disciples of the mother Church
'were scattered abroad throughout the regions of Judæa and
Samaria' (viii. 1). Some of the refugees even 'travelled as far
as Phenice and Cyprus and Antioch' (xi. 19). This dispersion
was, as we shall see, the parent of the first Gentile congregation.
The Church of the Gentiles, it may be truly said, was baptized
in the blood of Stephen.

The doctrine, which Stephen preached and for which he *Philip*
died, was carried into practice by PHILIP. The sacred narra- *converts*
tive mentions two incidents in his career, each marking an
onward stride in the free development of the Church. It is
therefore not without significance that years afterwards we find
him styled '*the* Evangelist' (xxi. 8), as if he had earned this
honourable title by some signal service rendered to the Gospel.

1. The Samaritan occupied the border land between the *(1) The*
Jew and the Gentile. Theologically, as geographically, he was the *Samari-*
connecting link between the one and the other. Half Hebrew *tans;*
by race, half Israelite in his acceptance of a portion of the
sacred canon, he held an anomalous position, shunning and
shunned by the Jew, yet clinging to the same promises and
looking forward to the same hopes. With a bold venture of
faith Philip offers the Gospel to this mongrel people. His
overtures are welcomed with joy, and 'Samaria receives the
word of God.' The sacred historian relates moreover, that his
labours were sanctioned by the presence of the chief Apostles
Peter and John, and confirmed by an outpouring of the Holy
Spirit (viii. 14—17). 'He who eats the bread of a Samaritan,'
said the Jewish doctor, 'is as one who eats swine's flesh[1].' 'No
Samaritan shall ever be made a proselyte. They have no share
in the resurrection of the dead[2].' In opening her treasures to

---

[1] *Mishnah Shebiith* viii. 10.
[2] *Pirke Rabbi Elieser* 38. The passage so well illustrates the statement in the text, that I give it in full: 'What did Ezra and Zerubbabel the son of Shealtiel and Jehoshua the son of Jehozadak? (They went) and they gathered together all the congregation into the temple of

this hated race, the Church had surmounted the first barrier of prejudice behind which the exclusiveness of the nation had entrenched itself. To be a Samaritan was to have a devil, in the eyes of a rigid Jew (John viii. 48, comp. iv. 9).

(2) The Ethiopian eunuch.

2. Nor was it long before Philip broke through a second and more formidable line of defence. The blood of the patriarchs, though diluted, still flowed in the veins of the Samaritans. His next convert had no such claim to respect. A descendant of the accursed race of Ham[1], shut out from the congregation by his physical defect (Deut. xxiii. 1), the Ethiopian chamberlain laboured under a twofold disability. This double line is assailed by the Hellenist preacher and taken by storm. The desire of the Ethiopian to know and to do God's will is held by Philip to be a sufficient claim. He acts boldly and without hesitation. He accosts him, instructs him, baptizes him then and there.

Conversion of Cornelius.

The venture of the subordinate minister however still wanted the sanction of the leaders of the Church. At length this sanction was given in a signal way. The Apostles of the Circumcision, even St Peter himself, had failed hitherto to comprehend the wide purpose of God. With their fellow-

the Lord, and they brought 300 priests and 300 children and 300 trumpets and 300 scrolls of the law in their hands, and they blew, and the Levites sang and played, and they banned the Cuthæans (Samaritans) by the mystery of the ineffable name and by the writing which is written on the tables and by the anathema of the upper (heavenly) court of justice and by the anathema of the nether (earthly) court of justice, that no one of Israel should eat the bread of a Cuthæan for ever. Hence they (the elders) said: Whosoever eats the bread of a Cuthæan is as if he ate swine's flesh; and no Cuthæan shall ever be made a proselyte: and they have no share in the resurrection of the dead; for it is said (Ezra iv. 3), *Ye have nothing to do with us to build an house unto our God,* (that is) neither in this world nor in the future. And that they should have neither portion nor inheritance in Jerusalem, as it is said (Neh. ii. 20), *But ye had no portion nor right nor memorial in Jerusalem.* And they communicated the anathema to Israel which is in Babylon. And they put upon them anathema upon anathema. And king Cyrus also decreed upon them an everlasting anathema, as it is said (Ezra vi. 12), *And the God that has caused His name to dwell there etc.*' Several passages bearing on this subject are collected in the article 'Samaritan Pentateuch,' by Mr E. Deutsch, in Smith's *Dictionary of the Bible.*

[1] Amos ix. 7, 'Are ye not as the children of the Ethiopians unto me, O children of Israel?'

ST PAUL AND THE THREE. 55

countrymen they still 'held it unlawful for a Jew to keep company with or to come near an alien' (Acts x. 28). The time when the Gospel should be preached to the Gentiles seemed not yet to have arrived: the manner in which it should be preached was still hidden from them. At length a divine vision scatters the dark scruples of Peter, teaching him to call no man 'common or unclean.' He goes himself and seeks out the devout Roman centurion Cornelius, whose household he instructs in the faith. The Gentile Church, thus founded on the same 'rock' with the Jewish, receives also the same divine confirmation. As Peter began to speak, 'the Holy Ghost fell on them, as it did' on the Jewish disciples on the first day of Pentecost (xi. 15). As if the approval of God could not be too prompt or too manifest, the usual sequence is reversed and the outpouring of the Spirit precedes the rite of baptism (x. 44—48).

The case of Cornelius does not, I think, differ essentially from the case of the Ethiopian eunuch. There is no ground for assuming that the latter was a proselyte of the covenant. His mutilation excluded him from the congregation by a Mosaic ordinance, and it is an arbitrary conjecture that the definite enactment of the law was overruled by the spiritual promise of the prophet (Is. lvi. 3—5). This liberal interpretation at all events accords little with the narrow and formal spirit of the age. Both converts alike had the inward qualification of 'fearing God and working righteousness' (x. 35); both alike were disabled by external circumstances, and the disabilities of the Ethiopian eunuch were even greater than those of the Roman centurion. If so, the significance of the conversion of the latter consists in this, that now in the case of the Gentile, as before in the case of the Samaritan, the principle asserted by the Hellenist Philip is confirmed by the Apostles of the Circumcision in the person of their chief and sealed by the outpouring of the Spirit. *Significance of this event.*

Meanwhile others were asserting the universality of the Church elsewhere, if not with the same sanction of authority, at all events with a larger measure of success. With the dying *Preaching to Gentiles at Antioch.*

words of Stephen, the martyr of Christian liberty, still ringing in their ears, the persecuted brethren had fled from Jerusalem and carried the tidings of the Gospel to distant lands. At first they 'preached the word to none but to the Jews only' (xi. 19). At length others bolder than the rest, 'when they were come to Antioch, spake unto the Gentiles[1], preaching the Lord Jesus.' Probably this was an advance even on the conversion of the Ethiopian eunuch and of Cornelius. These two converts at all events recognised the God of the old covenant. Now for the first time, it would seem, the Gospel was offered to heathen idolaters. Here, as before, the innovators were not Hebrews but Hellenists, 'men of Cyprus and Cyrene' (xi. 20). Their success was signal: crowds flocked to hear them; and at Antioch first the brethren were called by a new name—a term of ridicule and contempt then, now the pride and glory of the civilized world. Hitherto the believers had been known as 'Galileans' or 'Nazarenes'; now they were called 'Christians.' The transition from a Jewish to a heathen term marks the point of time when the Church of the Gentiles first threatens to supersede the Church of the Circumcision.

The name Christians.

Thus the first stage in the emancipation of the Church was gained. The principle was broadly asserted that the Gospel received all comers, asking no questions, allowing no impediments, insisting on no preliminary conditions, if only it were found that the petitioner 'feared God and worked righteousness.'

The first step gained.

2. *The Recognition of Gentile Liberty.*

It is plain that the principle, which had thus been asserted, involved consequences very much wider than were hitherto clearly foreseen and acknowledged. But between asserting a principle and carrying it out to its legitimate results a long interval must necessarily elapse, for many misgivings have to be dissipated and many impediments to be overcome.

---

[1] xi. 20. I cannot doubt that Ἕλληνας is correct, as the preceding Ἰουδαίους requires it; but external authority preponderates in favour of Ἑλληνιστάς.

So it was with the growth of Gentile Christendom. The Gentiles were no longer refused admission into the Church unless first incorporated with Israel by the initiatory rite. But many questions remained still unsettled. What was their exact position, when thus received? What submission, if any, must they yield to the Mosaic law? Should they be treated as in all respects on an equality with the true Israelite? Was it right for the Jewish Christian so far to lay aside the traditions of his race, as to associate freely with his Gentile brother? These must necessarily in time become practical questions, and press for a solution.

Questions yet unsettled.

At this point in the history of the Church a new character appears on the scene. The mantle of Stephen has fallen on the persecutor of Stephen. SAUL has been called to bear the name of Christ to the Gentiles. Descended of pure Hebrew ancestry and schooled in the law by the most famous of living teachers, born and residing in a great university town second to none in its reputation for Greek wisdom and learning, inheriting the privileges and the bearing of a Roman citizen, he seemed to combine in himself all those varied qualifications which would best fit him for this work. These wide experiences, which had lain dormant before, were quickened into thought and life by the lightning flash on the way to Damascus; and stubborn zeal was melted and fused into large-hearted and comprehensive charity. From his conversion to the present time we read only of his preaching in the synagogues at Damascus (ix. 20, 22) and to the Hellenists at Jerusalem (ix. 29). But now the moment was ripe, when he must enter upon that wider sphere of action for which he had been specially designed. The Gentile Church, founded on the 'rock,' must be handed over to the 'wise master-builder' to enlarge and complete. So at the bidding of the Apostles, Barnabas seeks out Saul in his retirement at Tarsus and brings him to Antioch. Doubtless he seemed to all to be the fittest instrument for carrying out the work so auspiciously begun.

Saul of Tarsus

goes to Antioch.

Meanwhile events at Jerusalem were clearing the way for *Circum-*

stances affecting the mother Church.

his great work. The star of Jewish Christendom was already on the wane, while the independence of the Gentiles was gradually asserting itself. Two circumstances especially were instrumental in reversing the positions hitherto held by these two branches of the Church.

(1) Withdrawal of the Apostles.

1. It has been seen that the martyrdom of Stephen marked an epoch in the emancipation of the Church. The martyrdom of James the son of Zebedee is scarcely less important in its influence on her progressive career. The former persecution had sown the disciples broad-cast over heathen lands; the latter seems to have been the signal for the withdrawal of the Apostles themselves from Jerusalem. The twelve years, which according to an old tradition our Lord had assigned as the limit of their fixed residence there, had drawn to a close[1]. So, consigning the direction of the mother Church to James the Lord's brother and the presbytery, they depart thence to enter upon a wider field of action. Their withdrawal must have deprived the Church of Jerusalem of half her prestige and more than half her influence. Henceforth she remained indeed the mother Church of the nation, but she was no longer the mother Church of the world.

(2) Famine relieved by Gentile alms.

2. About the same time another incident also contributed to lessen her influence. A severe famine devastated Palestine and reduced the Christian population to extreme want. Collections were made at Antioch, and relief was sent to the brethren in Judæa. By this exercise of liberality the Gentile Churches were made to feel their own importance: while the recipients, thus practically confessing their dependence, were deposed from the level of proud isolation which many of them would gladly have maintained. This famine seems to have ranged over many years, or at all events its attacks were several times repeated. Again and again the alms of the Gentile Christians were conveyed by the hands of the Gentile Apostles, and the Churches of Judæa laid themselves under fresh obligations to the heathen converts.

---

[1] See *Galatians*, p. 127, n. 1.

Events being thus ripe, Saul still residing at Antioch is set *New stage of the Gospel.* apart by the Spirit for the Apostleship of the Gentiles to which he had been called years before.

The Gospel thus enters upon a new career of triumph. The primacy of the Church passes from Peter to Paul—from the Apostle of the Circumcision to the Apostle of the Gentiles. The centre of evangelical work is transferred from Jerusalem to Antioch. Paul and Barnabas set forth on their first missionary tour.

Though they give precedence everywhere to the Jews, their *St Paul's first missionary journey.* mission is emphatically to the Gentiles. In Cyprus, the first country visited, its character is signally manifested in the conversion of the Roman proconsul, Sergius Paulus. And soon it becomes evident that the younger Church must supplant the elder. At Antioch in Pisidia matters are brought to a crisis: the Jews reject the offer of the Gospel: the Gentiles entreat to hear the message. Thereupon the doom is pronounced: 'It was necessary that the word of God should first have been spoken to you; but seeing ye put it from you and judge yourselves unworthy of everlasting life, lo we turn to the Gentiles' (xiii. 46). The incidents at Pisidian Antioch foreshadow the destiny which awaits the Gospel throughout the world. Everywhere the Apostles deliver their message to the Jews first, and everywhere the offer rejected by them is welcomed by the heathen. The mission of Paul and Barnabas is successful, but its success is confined almost wholly to the Gentiles. They return to Antioch.

Hitherto no attempt had been made to define the mutual *The question of circumcision raised.* relations of Jewish and Gentile converts. All such questions, it would seem, had been tacitly passed over, neither side perhaps being desirous of provoking discussion. But the inevitable crisis at length arrives. Certain converts, who had imported into the Church of Christ the rigid and exclusive spirit of Pharisaism, stir up the slumbering feud at Antioch, starting the question in its most trenchant form. They desire to impose circumcision on the Gentiles, not only as a condition of equality, but as necessary to salvation (xv. 1). The imposition of this burden is resisted by Paul and Barnabas, who go on a mission to Jerusalem to confer with the Apostles and elders.

Accounts of the conference.

I have given elsewhere what seems to me the probable account of the part taken by the leading Apostles in these controversies[1], and shall have to return to the subject later. Our difficulty in reading this page of history arises not so much from the absence of light as from the perplexity of cross lights. The narratives of St Luke and St Paul only then cease to conflict, when we take into account the different positions of the writers and the different objects they had in view.

Twofold results.

At present we are concerned only with the results of this conference. These are twofold: *First*, the settlement of the points of dispute between the Jewish and Gentile converts: *Secondly*, the recognition of the authority and commission of Paul and Barnabas by the Apostles of the Circumcision. It will be necessary, as briefly as possible, to point out the significance of these two conclusions and to examine how far they were recognised and acted upon subsequently.

The decree a compromise.

1. The arrangement of the disputed points was effected by a mutual compromise. On the one hand it was decided once and for ever that the rite of circumcision should not be imposed on the Gentiles. On the other, concessions were demanded of them in turn; they were asked to 'abstain from meats offered to idols, and from blood, and from things strangled, and from fornication.'

Emancipating clause.

The first of these decisions was a question of principle. If the initiatory rite of the old dispensation were imposed on all members of the Christian Church, this would be in effect to deny that the Gospel was a new covenant; in other words to deny its essential character[2]. It was thus the vital point on which the whole controversy turned. And the liberal decision

---

[1] See *Galatians*, p. 126 sq, and the notes on Gal. ii. 1—10.
[2] See Ritschl, p. 127.

of the council was not only the charter of Gentile freedom but the assertion of the supremacy of the Gospel.

On the other hand it is not so easy to understand the bearing of the restrictions imposed on the Gentile converts. Their significance in fact seems to be relative rather than absolute. There were certain practices into which, though most abhorrent to the feelings of their Jewish brethren, the Gentile Christians from early habit and constant association would easily be betrayed. These were of different kinds: some were grave moral offences, others only violations of time-honoured observances, inwrought in the conscience of the Israelite. After the large concession of principle made to the Gentiles in the matter of circumcision, it was not unreasonable that they should be required in turn to abstain from practices which gave so much offence to the Jews. Hence the prohibitions in question. It is strange indeed that offences so heterogeneous should be thrown together and brought under one prohibition; but this is perhaps sufficiently explained by supposing the decree framed to meet some definite complaint of the Jewish brethren. If, in the course of the hot dispute which preceded the speeches of the leading Apostles, attention had been specially called by the Pharisaic party to these detested practices, St James would not unnaturally take up the subject and propose to satisfy them by a direct condemnation of the offences in question[1].

Restrictive clauses.

It would betray great ignorance of human nature to suppose that a decision thus authoritatively pronounced must have silenced all opposition. If therefore we should find its provisions constantly disregarded hereafter, it is no argument against the genuineness of the decree itself. The bigoted

The decree disregarded by some.

---

[1] This seems to me much simpler than explaining the clauses as enforcing the conditions under which proselytes of the gate were received by the Jews. In this latter case πορνεία will perhaps refer to unlawful marriage, e.g. within the prohibited degrees of kindred (Levit. xviii. 18), as it is interpreted by Ritschl p. 129 sq, who ably maintains this view. These difficulties of interpretation are to my mind a very strong evidence of the genuineness of the decree.

minority was little likely to make an absolute surrender of its most stubborn prejudices to any external influence. Many even of those, who at the time were persuaded by the leading Apostles into acquiescence, would find their misgivings return, when they saw that the effect of the decree was to wrest the sceptre from their grasp and place it in the hands of the Gentile Church.

Circumcision still insisted on.

Even the question of circumcision, on which an absolute decision had been pronounced, was revived again and again. Long after, the Judaizing antagonists of St Paul in Galatia attempted to force this rite on his Gentile converts. Perhaps however they rather evaded than defied the decree. They may for instance have no longer insisted upon it as a condition of salvation, but urged it as a title to preference. But however this may be, there is nothing startling in the fact itself.

The restrictive clauses not uniformly enforced.

But while the *emancipating* clause of the decree, though express and definite, was thus parried or resisted, the *restrictive* clauses were with much greater reason interpreted with latitude. The miscellaneous character of these prohibitions showed that, taken as a whole, they had no binding force independently of the circumstances which dictated them. They were a temporary expedient framed to meet a temporary emergency. Their object was the avoidance of offence in mixed communities of Jew and Gentile converts. Beyond this recognised aim and the general understanding implied therein the limits of their application were not defined. Hence there was room for much latitude in individual cases.

St James.

St James, as the head of the mother Church where the difficulties which it was framed to meet were most felt, naturally refers to the decree seven years after as still regulating the intercourse between Jewish and Gentile converts (xxi. 25).

Antioch and the neighbouring churches.

At Antioch too and in the neighbouring Churches of Syria and Cilicia, to which alone the Apostolic letter was addressed and on which alone therefore the enactments were directly binding (xv. 23), it was doubtless long observed. The close communication between these churches and Jerusalem would at once justify and secure its strict observance. We read also of its being delivered to the brotherhoods of Lycaonia and Pisidia, already founded when the council was held, and near enough to Palestine to feel the pressure of Jewish feelings (xvi. 4). But as the circle widens, its influence becomes feebler. In strictly Gentile churches it seems never to have been enforced. St Paul, writing to the Corinthians, discusses two of the four practices which it prohibits without any reference to its enactments. Fornication he condemns absolutely as defiling the body which is the temple of God (1 Cor. v. 1—13, vi. 18—20). Of eating meats sacrificed to idols he speaks as a thing indifferent in itself, only to be avoided in so far as it implies participation in idol worship or is offensive to the consciences of others. His rule therefore is this: 'Do not sit down to a banquet celebrated in an idol's temple. You may say that in itself an idol is nothing, that neither the abstaining from meat nor the partaking of meat commends us to God. All this I grant is true: but such knowledge is dangerous. You are running the risk of falling into idolatry yourself, you are certainly by your example leading others astray; you are in fact committing an overt act of treason to God, you are a partaker of the tables of devils. On the other hand do not officiously inquire when you make a purchase at the shambles or when you dine in a private house: but if in such cases you are plainly told that the meat has been offered in sacrifice, then abstain at all hazards. Lay down this rule, to give no offence either to Jews or Gentiles or to the churches of God' (1 Cor. viii. 1—13, x. 14—22). This wise counsel, if it disregards the letter, preserves the spirit of the decree, which was framed for the avoidance of offence. But St Paul's language shows that the decree itself was not held binding, perhaps was unknown at Corinth: otherwise the discussion would have been foreclosed. Once again we come across the same topics in the apocalyptic message to the Churches of Pergamos and Thyatira. The same irregularities prevailed here as at Corinth: there was the temptation on the one hand to impure living, on the other to acts of conformity

<small>St Paul to the Corinthians.</small>

<small>St John to the Asiatic churches.</small>

with heathen worship which compromised their allegiance to the one true God. Our Lord in St John's vision denounces them through the symbolism of the Old Testament history. In the Church of Pergamos were certain Nicolaitans 'holding the doctrine of Balaam who taught Balac to cast a stumblingblock before the children of Israel, to eat things sacrificed to idols and to commit fornication' (ii. 14). At Thyatira the evil had struck its roots deeper. The angel of that Church is rebuked because he 'suffers his wife Jezebel who calls herself a prophetess, and she teacheth and seduceth God's servants to commit fornication and to eat things sacrificed to idols.' I see no reason for assuming a reference here to the Apostolic decree. The two offences singled out are those to which Gentile churches would be most liable, and which at the same time are illustrated by the Old Testament parallels. If St Paul denounces them independently of the decree, St John may have done so likewise[1]. In the matter of sacrificial meats indeed the condemnation of the latter is more absolute and uncompromising. But this is owing partly to the epigrammatic terseness and symbolic reference of the passage, partly, also, we may suppose, to the more definite form which the evil itself had assumed[2]. In both cases the practice was justified by a vaunted knowledge which held itself superior to any such restrictions[3]. But at Corinth

---

[1] Yet the expression οὐ βάλλω ἐφ' ὑμᾶς ἄλλο βάρος (ii. 24) looks like a reference to the decree.

[2] The coincidence of the two Apostles extends also to their language. (1) If St John denounces the offence as a following of Balaam, St Paul uses the same Old Testament illustration, 1 Cor. x. 7, 8, 'Neither be ye idolaters, as were some of them; as it is written, The people sat down to eat and drink, and rose up to play: neither let us commit fornication, as some of them committed, and fell in one day three and twenty thousand.' (2) If St John speaks of 'casting a stumblingblock (σκάνδαλον) before the children of Israel,' the whole purport of St Paul's warning is 'to give no offence' (μὴ σκανδαλίζειν, viii. 13, ἀπρόσκοποι γίνεσθαι, x. 32). With all these coincidences of matter and language, it is a strange phenomenon that any critic should maintain, as Baur, Zeller, and Schwegler have done, that the denunciations in the Apocalypse are directed against St Paul himself.

[3] Comp. Apoc. ii. 24 ὅσοι οὐκ ἔχουσιν τὴν διδαχὴν ταύτην, οἵτινες οὐκ ἔγνωσαν τὰ βαθέα τοῦ Σατανᾶ, ὡς λέγουσιν. The false teachers boasted a knowledge of the deep things of God;

this temper was still immature and under restraint: while in the Asiatic churches it had outgrown shame and broken out into the wildest excesses[1].

Thus then the decree was neither permanently nor universally binding. But there was also another point which admitted much latitude of interpretation. What was understood to be the design of these enactments? They were articles of peace indeed, but of what nature was this peace to be? Was it to effect an entire union between the Jewish and Gentile churches, a complete identity of interest; or only to secure a strict neutrality, a condition of mutual toleration? Were the Gentiles to be welcomed as brothers and admitted at once to all the privileges of sons of Israel: or was the Church hereafter to be composed of two separate nationalities, as it were, equal and independent; or lastly, were the heathen converts to be recognised indeed, but only as holding a subordinate position like proselytes under the old covenant? The first interpretation is alone consistent with the spirit of the Gospel: but either of the others might honestly be maintained without any direct violation of the letter of the decree. The Church of Antioch, influenced doubtless by St Paul, took the

Object of the enactments not defined.

they possessed only a knowledge of the deep things of Satan. St John's meaning is illustrated by a passage in Hippolytus (*Haer.* v. 6, p. 94) relating to the Ophites, who offer other striking resemblances to the heretics of the Apostolic age; ἐπεκάλεσαν ἑαυτοὺς γνωστικούς, φάσκοντες μόνοι τὰ βάθη γινώσκειν: see also Iren. ii. 28. 9. St Paul's rebuke is very different in form, but the same in effect. He begins each time in a strain of noble irony. 'We all have knowledge'; 'I speak as to wise men': he appears to concede, to defer, to sympathize, even to encourage: and then he turns round upon the laxity of this vaunted wisdom and condemns and crushes it: 'I will eat no flesh while the world standeth, lest I make my brother to offend';

'I would not that ye should have fellowship with devils.'

[1] The subject of εἰδωλόθυτα does not disappear with the Apostolic age: it turns up again for instance in the middle of the second century, in Agrippa Castor (Euseb. *H. E.* iv. 7) writing against Basilides, and in Justin (*Dial.* 35, p. 253 D) who mentions the Basilideans among other Gnostic sects as 'participating in lawless and godless rites': comp. *Orac. Sib.* ii. 96. Both these writers condemn the practice, the latter with great severity. When the persecution began, and the Christians were required to deny their faith by participating in the sacrifices, it became a matter of extreme importance to avoid any act of conformity, however slight.

larger and truer view; Jewish and Gentile converts lived freely together as members of one brotherhood. A portion at least of the Church of Jerusalem, 'certain who came from James,' adopted a narrower interpretation and still clung to the old distinctions, regarding their Gentile brethren as unclean and refusing to eat with them. This was not the Truth of the Gospel, it was not the Spirit of Christ; but neither was it a direct breach of compact.

St Paul's authority recognised. 2. Scarcely less important than the settlement of the disputed points was the other result of these conferences, the recognition of St Paul's office and mission by the Apostles of the Circumcision. This recognition is recorded in similar language in the narrative of the Acts and in the Epistle to the Galatians. In the Apostolic circular inserted in the former Paul and Barnabas are commended as 'men who have hazarded their lives for the name of our Lord Jesus Christ' (xv. 26). In the conferences, as related in the latter, the three Apostles, James, Peter, and John, seeing that 'the Gospel of the uncircumcision was committed unto him,' and 'perceiving the grace that was given unto him, gave to him and Barnabas the right hand of fellowship, that they should go unto the heathen' (ii. 7—10).

Continued opposition to St Paul. This ample recognition would doubtless carry weight with a large number of Jewish converts: but no sanction of authority could overcome in others the deep repugnance felt to one who, himself a 'Hebrew of the Hebrews,' had systematically opposed the law of Moses and triumphed in his opposition. Henceforth St Paul's career was one life-long conflict with Judaizing antagonists. Setting aside the Epistles to the Thessalonians, which were written too early to be affected by this struggle, all his letters addressed to churches, with but one exception[1], refer more or less directly to such opposition. It assumed different forms in different places: in Galatia it was purely

---

[1] This exception, the Epistle to the Ephesians, may be explained by its character as a circular letter to the Asiatic churches, in which special references would be out of place.

Pharisaic; in Phrygia and Asia it was strongly tinged with speculative mysticism; but everywhere and under all circumstances zeal for the law was its ruling passion. The systematic hatred of St Paul is an important fact, which we are too apt to overlook, but without which the whole history of the Apostolic ages will be misread and misunderstood.

3. *The Emancipation of the Jewish Churches.*

We have seen hitherto no signs of waning affection for the law in the Jewish converts to Christianity as a body. On the contrary the danger which threatened it from a quarter so unexpected seems to have fanned their zeal to a red heat. Even in the churches of St Paul's own founding his name and authority were not powerful enough to check the encroachments of the Judaizing party. Only here and there, in mixed communities, the softening influences of daily intercourse must have been felt, and the true spirit of the Gospel insensibly diffused, inculcating the truth that 'in Christ was neither Jew nor Greek.' Zeal for the law.

But the mother Church of Jerusalem, being composed entirely of Jewish converts, lacked these valuable lessons of daily experience. Moreover the law had claims on a Hebrew of Palestine wholly independent of his religious obligations. To him it was a national institution, as well as a divine covenant. Under the Gospel he might consider his relations to it in this latter character altered, but as embodying the decrees and usages of his country it still demanded his allegiance. To be a good Christian he was not required to be a bad citizen. On these grounds the more enlightened members of the mother church would justify their continued adhesion to the law. Nor is there any reason to suppose that St Paul himself took a different view of their obligations. The Apostles of the Circumcision meanwhile, if conscious themselves that the law was fulfilled in the Gospel they strove nevertheless by strict conformity to conciliate the zealots both within and without the Reasons for its observance in the mother Church.

5—2

Church, were only acting upon St Paul's own maxim, who 'became to the Jews a Jew that he might gain the Jews.' Meanwhile they felt that a catastrophe was impending, that a deliverance was at hand. Though they were left in uncertainty as to the time and manner of this divine event, the mysterious warnings of the Lord had placed the fact itself beyond a doubt. They might well therefore leave all perplexing questions to the solution of time, devoting themselves meanwhile to the practical work which lay at their doors.

Fall of Jerusalem.
A.D. 70.

And soon the catastrophe came which solved the difficult problem. The storm which had long been gathering burst over the devoted city. Jerusalem was razed to the ground, and the Temple-worship ceased, never again to be revived. The Christians foreseeing the calamity had fled before the tempest; and at Pella, a city of the Decapolis, in the midst of a population chiefly Gentile the Church of the Circumcision was reconstituted. They were warned to flee, said the story, by an oracle[1]: but no special message from heaven was needed at this juncture; the signs of the times, in themselves full of warning, interpreted by the light of the Master's prophecies plainly foretold the approaching doom. Before the crisis came, they had been deprived of the counsel and guidance of the leading Apostles. Peter had fallen a martyr at Rome; John had retired to Asia Minor; James the Lord's brother was slain not long before the great catastrophe; and some thought that the horrors of the Flavian war were the just vengeance of an offended God for the murder of so holy a man[2]. He was succeeded by his cousin Symeon, the son of Clopas and nephew of Joseph.

The Church at Pella.

Under these circumstances the Church was reformed at Pella. Its history in the ages following is a hopeless blank[3];

---

[1] Euseb. *H. E.* iii. 5 κατά τινα χρησμὸν τοῖς αὐτόθι δοκίμοις δι' ἀποκαλύψεως ἐκδοθέντα κ.τ.λ.

[2] Hegesippus in Euseb. *H. E.* ii. 23 καὶ εὐθὺς Οὐεσπασιανὸς πολιορκεῖ αὐτούς, and the pseudo-Josephus also quoted there, ταῦτα δὲ συμβέβηκεν Ἰουδαίοις κατ' ἐκδίκησιν Ἰακώβου τοῦ δικαίου κ.τ.λ.

[3] The Church of Pella however contributed one author at least to the ranks of early Christian literature in Ariston, the writer of an apology in

and it would be vain to attempt to fill in the picture from conjecture. We cannot doubt however that the consequences of the fall of Jerusalem, direct or indirect, were very great. In two points especially its effects would be powerfully felt, in the change of opinion produced within the Church itself and in the altered relations between the converted and unconverted Jews. *Effects of the change.*

(1) The loss of their great leader at this critical moment was compensated to the Church of the Circumcision by the stern teaching of facts. In the obliteration of the Temple services they were brought at length to see that all other sacrifices were transitory shadows, faint emblems of the one Paschal Lamb, slain once and for ever for the sins of the world. In the impossibility of observing the Mosaic ordinances except in part, they must have been led to question the efficacy of the whole. And besides all this, those who had hitherto maintained their allegiance to the law purely as a national institution were by the overthrow of the nation set free henceforth from any such obligation. We need not suppose that these inferences were drawn at once or drawn by all alike; but slowly and surely the fall of the city must have produced this effect. *(1) The law loses its power.*

(2) At the same time it wholly changed their relations *(2) Jews and*

the form of a dialogue between Jason a Hebrew Christian and Papiscus an Alexandrian Jew: see Routh I. p. 93. One of his works however was written after the Bar-cochba rebellion, to which it alludes (Euseb. *H. E.* iv. 6); and from the purport of the allusion we may infer that it was this very dialogue. The expulsion of the Jews by Hadrian was a powerful common-place in the treatises of the Apologists; see e.g. Justin Martyr *Apol.* i. 47. On the other hand it cannot have been written long after, for it was quoted by Celsus (Orig. *c. Cels.* iv. 52, p. 544, Delarue). The shade of doubt which rests on the authorship of this dialogue is very slight. Undue weight seems to be attributed to the fact of its being quoted anonymously; e.g. in Westcott's *Canon*, p. 93, Donaldson's *Christian Literature etc.* II. p. 58. If I am right in conjecturing that the reference to the banishment of the Jews was taken from this dialogue, Eusebius himself directly attributes it to Ariston. The name of the author however is of little consequence, for the work was clearly written by a Hebrew Christian not later than the middle of the second century. Whoever he may have been, the writer was no Ebionite, for he explained Gen. i. 1, 'In filio fecit Deus caelum et terram' (Hieron. *Quaest. Hebr. in Gen.*, III. p. 305, ed. Vall.); and the fact is important, as this is the earliest known expression of Hebrew Christian doctrine after the canonical writings, except perhaps the Testaments of the Twelve Patriarchs.

Christians in antagonism. with their unconverted countrymen. Hitherto they had maintained such close intercourse that in the eyes of the Roman the Christians were as one of the many Jewish sects. Henceforth they stood in a position of direct antagonism. The sayings ascribed to the Jewish rabbis of this period are charged with the bitterest reproaches of the Christians, who are denounced as more dangerous than the heathen, and anathemas against the hated sect were introduced into their daily prayers[1]. The probable cause of this change is not far to seek. While the catastrophe was still impending, the Christians seem to have stood forward and denounced the national sins which had brought down the chastisement of God on their country. In the traditional notices at least this feature may be discerned. Nor could they fail to connect together as cause and effect the stubborn rejection of Messiah and the coming doom which He Himself had foretold. And when at length the blow fell, by withdrawing from the city and refusing to share the fate of their countrymen they declared by an overt act that henceforth they were strangers, that now at length their hopes and interests were separate.

Difficulties and dissensions. These altered relations both to the Mosaic law and to the Jewish people must have worked as leaven in the minds of the Christians of the Circumcision. Questions were asked now, which from their nature could not have been asked before. Difficulties hitherto unfelt seemed to start up on all sides. The relations of the Church to the synagogue, of the Gospel to the law, must now be settled in some way or other. Thus diversities of opinion, which had hitherto been lulled in a broken and fitful slumber, suddenly woke up into dangerous activity. The Apostles, who at an earlier date had moderated extreme tendencies and to whom all would have looked instinctively for counsel and instruction, had passed away from the scene.

---

[1] See especially Graetz *Geschichte der Juden* IV. p. 112 sq. The antagonism between the Jews and Christians at this period is strongly insisted upon by this writer, whose account is the more striking as given from a Jewish point of view.

One personal follower of the Lord however still remained, Symeon the aged bishop, who had succeeded James[1]. At length he too was removed. After a long tenure of office he was martyred at a very advanced age in the ninth year of Trajan. His death, according to Hegesippus, was the signal for a shameless outbreak of multitudinous heresies which had hitherto worked underground, the Church having as yet preserved her virgin purity undefiled[2]. Though this early historian has interwoven many fabulous details in his account, there seems no reason to doubt the truth of the broad statement, confirmed as it is from another source[3], that this epoch was the birth-time of many forms of dissent in the Church of the Circumcision.

Symeon son of Clopas.
A.D. 106.

How far these dissensions and diversities of opinion had ripened meanwhile into open schism, to what extent the majority still conformed to the Mosaic ordinances (as for instance in the practice of circumcision and the observance of the sabbath), we have no data to determine. But the work begun by the fall of Jerusalem was only at length completed by the advent of another crisis. By this second catastrophe the Church and the law were finally divorced; and the malcontents who had hitherto remained within the pale of the Church became declared separatists.

A revolution of the Jews broke out in all the principal centres of the dispersion. The flame thus kindled in the dependencies spread later to the mother country. In Palestine a leader started up, professing himself to be the long promised Messiah, and in reference to the prophecy of Balaam styling himself 'Bar-cochba,' 'the son of the Star.' We have the testimony of one who wrote while these scenes of bloodshed were still fresh in men's memories, that the Christians were the

Rebellion of Bar-cochba.
A.D. 132–135.

---

[1] Hegesippus in Euseb. *H. E.* iv. 22. This writer also mentions grandsons of Jude the Lord's brother as ruling over the Churches and surviving till the time of Trajan; *H. E.* iii. 32.

[2] Euseb. *H. E.* iii. 32 ἐπιλέγει ὡς ἄρα μέχρι τῶν τότε χρόνων παρθένος καθαρὰ καὶ ἀδιάφθορος ἔμεινεν ἡ ἐκκλησία, ἐν ἀδήλῳ πού σκότει φωλευόντων εἰσέτι τότε τῶν, εἰ καί τινες ὑπῆρχον, παραφθείρειν ἐπιχειρούντων κ.τ.λ.: comp. iv. 22.

[3] See below, p. 82, note 3.

chief sufferers from this rebel chieftain[1]. Even without such testimony this might have been safely inferred. Their very existence was a protest against his claims: they must be denounced and extirpated, if his pretensions were to be made good. The cause of Bar-cochba was taken up as the cause of the whole Jewish nation, and thus the antagonism between Judaism and Christianity was brought to a head. After a desperate struggle the rebellion was trampled out and the severest vengeance taken on the insurgents. The practice of circumcision and the observance of the sabbath—indeed all the distinguishing marks of Judaism—were visited with the severest penalties. On the other hand the Christians, as the avowed enemies of the rebel chief, seem to have been favourably received. On the ruins of Jerusalem Hadrian had built his new city Ælia Capitolina. Though no Jew was admitted within sight of its walls, the Christians were allowed to settle there freely[2]. Now for the first time a Gentile bishop was appointed, and the Church of Jerusalem ceased to be the Church of the Circumcision[3].

Ælia Capitolina.

The church reconstituted.

The account of Eusebius seems to imply that long before this disastrous outbreak of the Jews the main part of the Christians had left their retirement in Pella and returned to their original home. At all events he traces the succession of bishops of Jerusalem in an unbroken line from James the Lord's brother until the foundation of the new city[4]. If so, we must imagine the Church once more scattered by this second

---

[1] Justin *Apol.* i. 31, p. 72 E, ἐν τῷ νῦν γεγενημένῳ Ἰουδαϊκῷ πολέμῳ Βαρχωχέβας ὁ τῆς Ἰουδαίων ἀποστάσεως ἀρχηγέτης Χριστιανοὺς μόνους εἰς τιμωρίας δεινάς, εἰ μὴ ἀρνοῖντο Ἰησοῦν τὸν Χριστὸν καὶ βλασφημοῖεν, ἐκέλευεν ἀπάγεσθαι.

[2] Justin *Apol.* i. 47, p. 84 B, *Dial.* 110, p. 337 D; Ariston of Pella in Euseb. *H. E.* iv. 6; Celsus in Orig. c. *Cels.* viii. 69.

[3] Sulpicius Severus (*H. S.* ii. 31) speaking of Hadrian's decree says, 'Quod quidem Christianae fidei proficiebat, quia tum pene omnes Christum Deum sub legis observatione credebant; nimirum id Domino ordinante dispositum, ut legis servitus a libertate fidei atque ecclesiae tolleretur.'

[4] *H. E.* iii. 32, 35, iv. 5. Eusebius seems to narrate all the incidents affecting the Church of the Circumcision during this period, as taking place not at Pella but at Jerusalem.

catastrophe, and once more reformed when the terror was passed. But the Church of Ælia Capitolina was very differently constituted from the Church of Pella or the Church of Jerusalem; a large proportion of its members at least were Gentiles[1]. Of the Christians of the Circumcision not a few doubtless accepted the conqueror's terms, content to live henceforth as Gentiles, and settled down in the new city of Hadrian. But there were others who clung to the law of their forefathers with a stubborn grasp which no force of circumstances could loosen: and henceforward we read of two distinct sects of Judaizing Christians, observing the law with equal rigour but observing it on different grounds[2]. *Judaizing sects.*

---

[1] Euseb. *H. E.* iv. 6 τῆς αὐτόθι ἐκκλησίας ἐξ ἐθνῶν συγκροτηθείσης.

[2] As early as the middle of the second century Justin Martyr distinguishes two classes of Judaizers; those who retaining the Mosaic law themselves did not wish to impose it on their Gentile brethren, and those who insisted upon conformity in all Christians alike as a condition of communion and a means of salvation (*Dial. c. Tryph.* § 47; see Schliemann *Clement*. p. 553 sq). In the next chapter Justin alludes with disapprobation to *some* Jewish converts who held that our Lord was a mere man; and it seems not unreasonable to connect this opinion with the second of the two classes before mentioned. We thus obtain a tolerably clear view of their distinctive tenets. But the first direct and definite account of both sects is given by the fathers of the fourth century, especially Epiphanius and Jerome, who distinguish them by the respective names of 'Nazarenes' and 'Ebionites.' Irenæus (i. 26. 2), Tertullian (*de Praescr.* 33), and Hippolytus (*Haer.* vii. 34, p. 257), contemplate only the second, whom they call Ebionites. The Nazarenes in fact, being for the most part orthodox in their creed and holding communion with Catholic Christians, would not generally be included in the category of heretics: and moreover, being few in number and living in an obscure region, they would easily escape notice. Origen (*c. Cels.* v. 61) mentions two classes of Christians who observe the Mosaic law, the one holding with the Catholics that Jesus was born of a Virgin, the other that He was conceived like other men; and both these he calls Ebionites. In another passage he says that both classes of Ebionites ('Εβιωναῖοι ἀμφότεροι) reject St Paul's Epistles (v. 65). If these two classes correspond to the 'Nazarenes' and 'Ebionites' of Jerome, Origen's information would seem to be incorrect. On the other hand it is very possible that he entirely overlooks the Nazarenes and alludes to some differences of opinion among the Ebionites properly so called; but in this case it is not easy to identify his two classes with the Pharisaic and Essene Ebionites of whom I shall have to speak later. Eusebius, who also describes two classes of Ebionites (*H. E.* iii. 27), seems to have taken his account wholly from Irenæus and Origen. If, as appears probable, both names 'Nazarenes' and 'Ebionites' were originally applied to the

Nazarenes.

1. The NAZARENES appear at the close of the fourth century as a small and insignificant sect dwelling beyond the Jordan in Pella and the neighbouring places[1]. Indications of their existence however occur in Justin two centuries and a half earlier; and both their locality and their name carry us back to the primitive ages of Jewish Christianity. Can we doubt that they were the remnant of the fugitive Church, which refused to return from their exile with the majority to the now Gentile city, some because they were too indolent or too satisfied to move, others because the abandonment of the law seemed too heavy a price to pay for Roman forbearance?

Their tenets.

The account of their tenets is at all events favourable to this inference[2]. They held themselves bound to the Mosaic ordinances, rejecting however all Pharisaic interpretations and additions. Nevertheless they did not consider the Gentile Christians under the same obligations or refuse to hold communion with them; and in the like spirit, in this distinguished from all other Judaizing sectarians, they fully recognised the work and mission of St Paul[3]. It is stated moreover that they mourned over the unbelief of their fellow-countrymen, praying for and looking forward to the time when they too should be brought to confess Christ. Their doctrine of the person of

---

whole body of Jewish Christians indiscriminately, the confusion of Origen and others is easily explained. In recent times, since Gieseler published his treatise *Ueber die Nazaräer und Ebioniten* (Stäudlin u. Tzschirner *Archiv für Kirchengesch.* iv. p. 279 sq, 1819), the distinction has been generally recognised. A succinct and good account of these sects of Judaizers will be found in Schliemann *Clement*. p. 449 sq, where the authorities are given; but the discovery of the work of Hippolytus has since thrown fresh light on the Essene Ebionites. The portion of Ritschl's work (p. 152 sq) relating to these sects should be consulted.

[1] Epiphan. *Haer*. xxix. 7; comp. Hieron. *de Vir. Ill.* § 3.

[2] See the account in Schliemann, p. 445 sq, with the authorities there given and compare Ritschl p. 152 sq.

[3] Hieron. *in Is.* ix. 1 (IV. p. 130), 'Nazaraei...hunc locum ita explanare conantur: Adveniente Christo et praedicatione illius coruscante prima terra Zabulon et terra Nephthali scribarum et Pharisaeorum est erroribus liberata et gravissimum traditionum Judaicarum jugum excussit de cervicibus suis. Postea autem per evangelium apostoli Pauli, qui novissimus apostolorum omnium fuit, ingravata est, id est, multiplicata praedicatio; et in terminos gentium et viam universi maris Christi evangelium splenduit.'

Christ has been variously represented; but this seems at all events clear that, if it fell short of the Catholic standard, it rose above the level of other Judaic sects. The fierce and indiscriminate verdict of Epiphanius indeed pronounces these Nazarenes 'Jews and nothing else[1]': but his contemporary Jerome, himself no lenient judge of heresy, whose opinion was founded on personal intercourse, regards them more favourably. In his eyes they seem to be separated from the creeds and usages of Catholic Christendom chiefly by their retention of the Mosaic law.

Thus they were distinguished from other Judaizing sects by a loftier conception of the person of Christ and by a frank recognition of the liberty of the Gentile Churches and the commission of the Gentile Apostle. These distinguishing features may be traced to the lingering influence of the teaching of the Apostles of the Circumcision. To the example of these same Apostles also they might have appealed in defending their rigid observance of the Mosaic law. But herein, while copying the letter, they did not copy the spirit of their model; for they took no account of altered circumstances. *Their relation to the Twelve.*

Of this type of belief, if not of this very Nazarene sect, an early document still extant furnishes an example. The book called the 'Testaments of the Twelve Patriarchs[2]' was certainly *Testaments of the Twelve Patriarchs.*

---

[1] *Haer.* xxx. 9.

[2] It is printed in Grabe's *Spicil. SS. Patr.* I. p. 145 sq (ed. 2, 1700), and in Fabricius *Cod. Pseudepigr. Vet. Test.* I. p. 519 sq (ed. 2, 1722), and has recently been edited with an introductory essay by Sinker (Cambridge, 1869). Ritschl in his first edition had assigned this work to a writer of the Pauline school. His opinion was controverted by Kayser in the *Strassburg. Beitr. z. den Theol. Wissensch.* III. p. 107 (1851), and with characteristic honesty he withdrew it in his second edition, attributing the work to a Nazarene author (p. 172 sq). Meanwhile Ritschl's first view had been adopted in a monograph by Vorstman *Disquis. de Test. xii. Patr.* (Roterod. 1857), and defended against Kayser. The whole tone and colouring of the book however seem to show very plainly that the writer was a Jewish Christian, and the opposite view would probably never have been entertained but for the preconceived theory that a believer of the Circumcision could not have written so liberally of the Gentile Christians and so honourably of St Paul. Some writers again who have maintained the Judaic authorship (Kayser for instance, whose treatise I only know at second hand) have got over this assumed difficulty by rejecting certain passages as interpolations. On the other hand Ewald pronounces it 'mere

written after the capture of Jerusalem by Titus and probably before the rebellion of Bar-cochba, but may be later[1]. With some alien features, perhaps stamped upon it by the individual writer, it exhibits generally the characteristics of this Nazarene sect. In this respect at least it offers a remarkable parallel, that to a strong Israelite feeling it unites the fullest recognition of the Gentile Churches. Our Lord is represented as the renovator of the law[2]: the imagery and illustrations are all Hebrew: certain virtues are strongly commended and certain vices strongly denounced by a Hebrew standard: many incidents in the lives of the patriarchs are derived from some unknown legendary Hebrew source[3]. Nay more; the sympathies of the writer are not only Judaic but Levitical. The Messiah is represented as a descendant not of Judah only but of Levi also; thus he is high priest as well as king[4]; but his priestly office

Hebrew sympathies

---

folly to assert that *Benj.* c. 11 (the prophecy about St Paul) was a later addition to the work' (*Gesch. d. Volks Isr.* VII. p. 329), and certainly such arbitrary assumptions would render criticism hopeless.

Whether Ritschl is right or not in supposing that the author was actually a Nazarene, it is difficult and not very important to decide. The really important feature in the work is the complexion of the opinions. I do not think however that the mere fact of its having been written in Greek proves the author to have been a Hellenist (Ewald *ib.* p. 333).

[1] The following dates have been assigned to it by recent critics; A.D. 100–135 (Dorner), 100–120 (Wieseler), 133–163 (Kayser), 100–153 (Nitzsch, Lücke), 117–193 (Gieseler), 100–200 (Hase), about 150 (Reuss), 90–110 (Ewald). These dates except the last are taken from Vorstman p. 19 sq, who himself places it soon after the fall of Jerusalem (A.D. 70). The frequent references to this event fix the earliest possible date, while the absence of any allusion to the rebellion of Bar-cochba seems to show that it was written before that time. It is directly named by Origen (*Hom. in Jos.* xv. 6), and probably was known to Tertullian (*c. Marc.* v. 1, *Scorpiace* 13), and (as I believe) even earlier to Irenæus (*Fragm.* 17, p. 836 sq Stieren).

[2] *Levi* 10, ἀνακαινοποιοῦντα τὸν νόμον ἐν δυνάμει ὑψίστου. 'The law of God, the law of the Lord,' are constant phrases with this writer; *Levi* 13, 19, *Judas* 18, 26, *Issach.* 5, *Zabul.* 10, *Dan* 6, *Gad* 3, *Aser* 2, 6, 7, *Joseph* 11, *Benj.* 10: see also *Nepht.* 8. His language in this respect is formed on the model of the Epistle of St James, as Ewald remarks (p. 329). Thus the Law of God with him 'is one with the revealed will of God, and he never therefore understands it in the narrow sense of a Jew or even of an Ebionite.'

[3] See Ewald *Gesch.* I. p. 490.

[4] *Simeon* 5, 7, *Issach.* 5, *Dan* 5, *Nepht.* 6, 8, *Gad* 8, *Joseph* 19, besides the passages referred to in the next note.

is higher than his kingly, as Levi is greater than Judah[1]: the dying patriarchs one after another enjoin obedience to Levi: to the Testament of Levi are consigned the most important prophecies of all: the character of Levi is justified and partially cleansed of the stain which in the Old Testament narrative attaches to it[2]. Yet notwithstanding all this, the admission of the Gentiles into the privileges of the covenant is a constant theme of thanksgiving with the writer, who mourns over the falling away of the Jews but looks forward to their final restitution. And into the mouth of the dying Benjamin he puts a prophecy foretelling an illustrious descendant who is to 'arise in after days, beloved of the Lord, listening to His voice, enlightening all the Gentiles with new knowledge'; who is to be 'in the synagogues of the Gentiles until the completion of the ages, and among their rulers as a musical strain in the mouth of all'; who shall 'be written in the holy books, he and his work and his word, and shall be the elect of God for ever[3].' *united with liberal principles.*

2. But besides these Nazarenes, there were other Judaizing sects, narrow and uncompromising, to whose principles or prejudices language such as I have just quoted would be most abhorrent. *Ebionites.*

The EBIONITES were a much larger and more important body than the Nazarenes. They were not confined to the neighbourhood of Pella or even to Palestine and the surrounding countries, but were found in Rome and probably also in all the great centres of the dispersion[4]. Not content with observing *Their tenets.*

---

[1] *Reuben* 6 πρὸς τὸν Λευΐ ἐγγίσατε... αὐτὸς γὰρ εὐλογήσει τὸν Ἰσραὴλ καὶ τὸν Ἰούδαν, *Judas* 21 καὶ νῦν τέκνα μου ἀγαπήσατε τὸν Λευΐ...ἐμοὶ γὰρ ἔδωκε Κύριος τὴν βασιλείαν κἀκείνῳ τὴν ἱερατείαν καὶ ὑπέταξε τὴν βασιλείαν τῇ ἱερωσύνῃ· ἐμοὶ ἔδωκε τὰ ἐπὶ τῆς γῆς κἀκείνῳ τὰ ἐν οὐρανοῖς, *ib.* 25 Λευΐ πρῶτος, δεύτερος ἐγώ, *Nepht.* 5 Λευΐ ἐκράτησε τὸν ἥλιον καὶ Ἰούδας φθάσας ἐπίασε τὴν σελήνην.

[2] *Levi* 6, 7.

[3] *Benj.* 11. Besides this prophecy the work presents several coincidences of language with St Paul (see Vorstman p. 115 sq), and at least one quotation, *Levi* 6 ἔφθασε δὲ ἡ ὀργὴ Κυρίου ἐπ' αὐτοὺς εἰς τέλος, from 1 Thess. ii. 16. On the whole however the language in the moral and didactic portions takes its colour from the Epistle of St James, and in the prophetic and apocalyptic from the Revelation of St John.

[4] Epiphan. *Haer.* xxx. 18.

the Mosaic ordinances themselves, they maintained that the law was binding on all Christians alike, and regarded Gentile believers as impure because they refused to conform. As a necessary consequence they rejected the authority and the writings of St Paul, branding him as an apostate and pursuing his memory with bitter reproaches. In their theology also they were far removed from the Catholic Church, holding our Lord to be a mere man, the son of Joseph and Mary, who was justified, as any of themselves might be justified, by his rigorous performance of the law[1].

Relation to the Judaizers of the Apostolic age.

If the Nazarenes might have claimed some affinity to the Apostles of the Circumcision, the Ebionites were the direct spiritual descendants of those false brethren, the Judaizers of the Apostolic age, who first disturbed the peace of the Antiochene Church and then dogged St Paul's footsteps from city to city, everywhere thwarting his efforts and undermining his authority. If Ebionism was not primitive Christianity, neither was it a creation of the second century. As an organization, a distinct sect, it first made itself known, we may suppose, in the reign of Trajan: but as a sentiment, it had been harboured within the Church from the very earliest days. Moderated by the personal influence of the Apostles, soothed by the general practice of their church, not yet forced into declaring themselves by the turn of events, though scarcely tolerant of others these Judaizers were tolerated for a time themselves. The beginning of the second century was a winnowing season in the Church of the Circumcision.

Another type of Ebionism,

The form of Ebionism[2], which is most prominent in early

---

[1] For the opinions of these Ebionites see the references in Schliemann p. 481 sq, and add Hippol. *Haer.* vii. 3 εἰ γὰρ καὶ ἕτερός τις πεποιήκει τὰ ἐν νόμῳ προστεταγμένα, ἦν ἂν ἐκεῖνος ὁ Χριστός· δύνασθαι δὲ καὶ ἑαυτοὺς ὁμοίως ποιήσαντας Χριστοὺς γενέσθαι· καὶ γὰρ καὶ αὐτὸν ὁμοίως ἄνθρωπον εἶναι πᾶσιν λέγουσιν.

[2] The following opinions were shared by all Ebionites alike: (1) The recognition of Jesus as Messiah; (2) The denial of His divinity; (3) The universal obligation of the law; (4) The rejection and hatred of St Paul. Their differences consisted in (1) Their view of what constituted the law, and (2) Their conception of the Person of Christ; e.g. whether He was born of a Virgin or in the course of nature;

writers and which I have hitherto had in view, is purely Pharisaic; but we meet also with another type, agreeing with the former up to a certain point but introducing at the same time a new element, half ascetic, half mystical.

This foreign element was probably due to Essene influences. The doctrines of the Christian school bear so close a resemblance to the characteristic features of the Jewish sect as to place their parentage almost beyond a doubt[1]: and moreover the head-quarters of these heretics—the countries bordering on the Dead Sea—coincide roughly with the head-quarters of their prototype. This view however does not exclude the working of other influences more directly Gnostic or Oriental: and as this type of Ebionism seems to have passed through different phases at different times, and indeed to have comprehended several species at the same time, such modifications ought probably to be attributed to forces external to Judaism. Having regard then to its probable origin as well as to its typical character, we can hardly do wrong in adopting the name *Essene* or *Gnostic Ebionism* to distinguish it from the common type, *Pharisaic Ebionism* or *Ebionism proper*.

derived from the Essenes.

If Pharisaic Ebionism was a disease inherent in the Church of the Circumcision from the first, Essene Ebionism seems to have been a later infection caught by external contact. In the Palestinian Church at all events we see no symptoms of it during the Apostolic age. It is a probable conjecture, that after the destruction of Jerusalem the fugitive Christians, living in their retirement in the neighbourhood of the Essene settlements, received large accessions to their numbers from this sect, which thus inoculated the Church with its peculiar views[2]. It is at least worthy of notice, that in a religious work

Its later origin,

---

what supernatural endowments He had and at what time they were bestowed on Him, whether at His birth or at His baptism, etc.

The Ebionites of earlier writers, as Irenæus and Hippolytus, belong to the Pharisaic type; while those of Epipha-nius are strongly Essene.

[1] See especially the careful investigation of Ritschl p. 204 sq.

[2] Ritschl (p. 223), who adopts this view, suggests that this sect, which had stood aloof from the temple-worship and abhorred sacrifices, would be led to

emanating from this school of Ebionites the 'true Gospel' is reported to have been first propagated 'after the destruction of the holy place[1].'

This younger form of Judaic Christianity seems soon to have eclipsed the elder. In the account of Ebionism given by Epiphanius the Pharisaic characteristics are almost entirely absorbed in the Essene. This prominence is probably due in some measure to their greater literary capacity, a remarkable feature doubtless derived from the speculative tendencies and studious habits of the Jewish sect[2] to which they traced their parentage. Besides the Clementine writings which we possess whole, and the book of Elchasai of which a few fragmentary notices are preserved, a vast number of works which, though no longer extant, have yet moulded the traditions of the early Church, emanated from these Christian Essenes. Hence doubtless are derived the ascetic portraits of James the Lord's brother in Hegesippus and of Matthew the Apostle in Clement of Alexandria[3], to which the account of St Peter in the extant Clementines presents a close parallel[4].

but greater literary activity,

And with greater literary activity they seem also to have united greater missionary zeal. To this spirit of proselytism we owe much important information relating to the tenets of the sect.

and zealous proselytism.

One of their missionaries early in the third century brought to Rome a sacred book bearing the name of Elchasai or Elxai, whence also the sect were called Elchasaites. This book fell into the hands of Hippolytus the writer on heresies[5], from

Book of Elchasai.

welcome Christ as the true prophet, when they saw the fulfilment of His predictions against the temple. In *Clem. Hom.* iii. 15 great stress is laid on the fulfilment of these prophecies: comp. also *Clem. Recogn.* i. 37 (especially in the Syriac).

[1] *Clem. Hom.* ii. 17 μετὰ καθαίρεσιν τοῦ ἁγίου τόπου εὐαγγέλιον ἀληθὲς κρύφα διαπεμφθῆναι εἰς ἐπανόρθωσιν τῶν ἐσομένων αἱρέσεων: comp. *Clem. Recogn.*

i. 37, 64, iii. 61 (in the Syriac, as below, p. 86, note 5). See also Epiphan. *Haer.* xxx. 2.

[2] Joseph. *B. J.* ii. 8. 6.

[3] *Paedag.* ii. 1 (p. 174 Potter), where St Matthew is said to have lived on seeds, berries, and herbs, abstaining from animal food. See Ritschl p. 224.

[4] *Clem. Hom.* xii. 6, comp. viii. 15, xv. 7.

[5] *Haer.* ix. 13. See a valuable

whom our knowledge of it is chiefly derived. It professed to have been obtained from the Seres, a Parthian tribe, and to contain a revelation which had been first made in the third year of Trajan (A.D. 100). These Seres hold the same place in the fictions of Essene Ebionism, as the Hyperboreans in Greek legend: they are a mythical race, perfectly pure and therefore perfectly happy, long-lived and free from pain, scrupulous in the performance of all ceremonial rites and thus exempt from the penalties attaching to their neglect[1]. Elchasai, an Aramaic word signifying the 'hidden power[2],' seems to be the name of the divine messenger who communicated the revelation, and probably the title of the book itself: Hippolytus understands it of the person who received the revelation, the founder of the sect. 'Elchasai,' adds this father, 'delivered it to a certain person called Sobiai.' Here again he was led astray by his ignorance of Aramaic: Sobiai is not the name of an individual but signifies 'the sworn members[3],' to whom alone the revelation was to be communicated and who,

---

paper on the Elchasaites by Ritschl in Niedner's *Zeitschrift* IV. p. 573 sq (1853), the substance of which is given also in the second edition of his *Altkatholische Kirche*. Hilgenfeld has edited the fragments of the book of Elxai in his *Novum Testamentum extra Canonem Receptum*, fasc. III. p. 153 sq (1866). The use made of it by Epiphanius is investigated by Lipsius, *Quellenkritik des Epiphan.* p. 143 sq.

[1] *Clem. Recogn.* viii. 48, ix. 19. Even in classical writers the Seres or Chinese are invested with something of an ideal character: e.g. Plin. vi. 24, Strabo xv. p. 701, Mela iii. 7. But in the passage which most strikingly illustrates this fact (*Geogr. Graec. Min.* II. p. 514, ed. Müller), the name disappears when the text is correctly read ('se regentes,' and not 'Serae gentes').

[2] חיל כסי. Epiphanius correctly explains it δύναμις κεκαλυμμένη, Haer. xix. 2. See Ritschl l. c. p. 581, and *Altkath. Kirche* p. 245. Other explanations of the word, given in Hilgenfeld l. c. p. 156, in M. Nicolas *Évangiles Apocryphes* p. 108 (1866), and by Geiger *Zeitsch. der Deutsch. Morgenl. Gesellsch.* XVIII. p. 824 (1864), do not recommend themselves. The name is differently written in Greek, Ηλχασαι, Ελκεσαι and Ηλξαι. The first, which is most correct, is found in Hippolytus, who had seen the book.

[3] From שבע. Accordingly Hippolytus (ix. 17) relates that the Elchasaite missionary Alcibiades made a mystery of his teaching, forbidding it to be divulged except to the faithful; see Ritschl l. c. p. 589. Ewald however (*Gesch.* VII. p. 159) derives Sobiai from ܨܒܐ i.e. βαπτισταί. See also Chwolson *die Ssabier* etc. I. p. 111.

perhaps, like their Essene prototypes[1], took an oath to divulge it only to the brotherhood. I need not follow this strange but instructive notice farther. Whether this was the sacred book of the whole sect or of a part only, whether the name Elchasaism is coextensive with Essene Ebionism or not, it is unimportant for my purpose to enquire. The pretended era of this revelation is of more consequence. Whether the book itself was really as early as the reign of Trajan or whether the date was part of the dramatic fiction, it is impossible to decide[2]. Even in the latter case, it will still show that according to their own tradition this epoch marked some striking development in the opinions or history of the sect; and the date given corresponds, it will be remembered, very nearly with the epoch mentioned by Hegesippus as the birthtime of a numerous brood of heresies[3].

Its pretended date.

Without attempting to discriminate the different forms of doctrine which this Essene Ebionism comprised in itself—to point out for instance the distinctive features of the book of Elchasai, of the Homilies, and of the Recognitions respectively —it will be sufficient to observe the broad line of demarcation which separates the Essene from the Pharisaic type[4]. Laying almost equal stress with the others on the observance of the law as an essential part of Christianity, the Essene Ebionites undertook to settle by arbitrary criticism what the law was[5].

Essene Ebionites distinguished from Pharisaic,

---

[1] Joseph. *B. J.* ii. 8. 7.

[2] Hilgenfeld (p. xxi) maintains the early date very positively against Ritschl. Lipsius (l. c.) will not pronounce an opinion.

[3] See above, p. 71 sq. In the passage there quoted Hegesippus speaks of these heresies 'as living underground, burrowing (φωλευόντων)' until the reign of Trajan. This agrees with the statement in the Homilies (ii. 17) already referred to (p. 80, note 1) that the true Gospel (i.e. Essene Ebionism) was first 'secretly propagated' after the destruction of the temple. The opinions which had thus been progressing stealthily now showed a bold front; but whether the actual organization of the sect or sects took place now or at a still later date (after the rebellion of Bar-cochba), it is impossible to say.

[4] The chief authorities for the Essene Ebionites are Epiphanius (*Haer.* xix, xxx); Hippolytus (*Haer.* ix. 13—17) and Origen (Euseb. *H. E.* vi. 38), whose accounts refer especially to the book of Elchasai; and the Clementine writings.

[5] See *Colossians* p. 372.

By this capricious process they eliminated from the Old Testament all elements distasteful to them—the doctrine of sacrifices especially, which was abhorrent to Essene principles —cutting down the law to their own standard and rejecting the prophets wholly. As a compensation, they introduced certain ritual observances of their own, on which they laid great stress; more especially lustral washings and abstinence from wine and from animal food. In their Christology also they differed widely from the Pharisaic Ebionites, maintaining that the Word or Wisdom of God had been incarnate more than once, and that thus there had been more Christs than one, of whom Adam was the first and Jesus the last. Christianity in fact was regarded by them merely as the restoration of the primeval religion: in other words, of pure Mosaism before it had been corrupted by foreign accretions. Thus equally with the Pharisaic Ebionites they denied the Gospel the character of a new covenant; and, as a natural consequence, equally with them they rejected the authority and reviled the name of St Paul[1].

If the Pharisaic Ebionites are the direct lineal descendants of the 'false brethren' who seduced St Paul's Galatian converts from their allegiance, the Essene Ebionites bear a striking family likeness to those other Judaizers against whom he raises his voice as endangering the safety of the Church at Colossae[2]. *and allied to the Colossian heretics.*

Of the hostility of these Christian Essenes to St Paul, as of their other typical features, a striking example is extant in the fictitious writings attributed to the Roman bishop Clement. These are preserved in two forms: the *Homilies*, extant in the Greek, apparently an uniform work, which perhaps may be assigned to the middle or latter half of the second century; and the *Recognitions*, a composite production probably later than the Homilies, founded, it would appear, partly on them or some earlier work which was the common basis of both and partly on other documents, and known to us through the Latin *Clementine writings.*

---

[1] See Epiphan. *Haer.* xxx. 16, 25, Orig. ap. Euseb. l. c. τὸν ἀπόστολον τέλεον ἀθετεῖ; besides the passages in the Clementine writings quoted in the text.

[2] See *Colossians* p. 73 sq.

6—2

translation of Rufinus, who avowedly altered his original with great freedom[1].

Attack on St Paul in the Homilies,
In the Homilies Simon Magus is the impersonation of manifold heresy, and as such is refuted and condemned by St Peter. Among other false teachers, who are covertly denounced in his person, we cannot fail to recognise the lineaments of St Paul[2]. Thus St Peter charges his hearers, 'Shun any apostle, or teacher, or prophet, who does not first compare his preaching with James called the brother of my Lord and entrusted with the care of the Church of the Hebrews in Jerusalem, and has not come to you with witnesses[3]; lest the wickedness, which contended with the Lord forty days and prevailed not, should afterwards fall upon the earth as lightning

---

[1] The only complete editions of the Homilies are those of Dressel, *Clementis Romani quae feruntur Homiliae Viginti* (1853), and of Lagarde, *Clementina* (1865); the end of the 19th and the whole of the 20th homily having been published for the first time by Dressel. The Recognitions, which have been printed several times, may be read most conveniently in Gersdorf's edition (Lips. 1838). A Syriac Version lately published by Lagarde (*Clementis Romani Recognitiones Syriace*, Lips. et Lond. 1861) is made up partly of the Recognitions (i, ii, iii, iv), and partly of the Homilies (x, xi, xii, xiii, xiv, the xth book being imperfect). The older of the two extant MSS of this version was actually written A.D. 411, the year after the death of Rufinus; but the errors of transcription, which it exhibits, show that it was taken from an earlier MS. We are thus carried back to a very remote date. The first part, containing the early books of the Recognitions, is extremely valuable, for it enables us to measure the liberties which Rufinus took with his original. An important instance of his arbitrary treatment will be given below, p. 86, note 5. Two abridgments of the Homilies are extant. These have been edited by Dressel, *Clementinorum Epitomae duae* (Lips. 1859), one of them for the first time. Of those monographs which I have read on the relations between the different Clementine writings, the treatise of Uhlhorn, *Die Homilien und Recognitionen* etc. (Göttingen, 1854), seems to me on the whole the most satisfactory. It is dangerous to express an opinion where able critics are so divided; and the remarks in the text are not hazarded without some hesitation. Baur, Schliemann, Schwegler, and Uhlhorn, give the priority to the Homilies, Hilgenfeld and Ritschl to the Recognitions, Lehmann partly to the one and partly to the other, while Reuss and others decline to pronounce a decided opinion.

[2] See on this subject Schliemann *Clement.* pp. 96 sq, 534 sq : comp. Stanley's *Corinthians*, p. 366 sq.

[3] καὶ μετὰ μαρτύρων προσεληλυθότα. It is needless to insert μή with Schliemann and Schwegler: the negative is carried on from the former clause μὴ πρότερον ἀντιβάλλοντα.

from heaven and send forth a preacher against you, just as he suborned Simon against us, preaching in the name of our Lord and sowing error under the pretence of truth; wherefore He that sent us said, *Many shall come to me in sheep's clothing, but within they are ravening wolves* (xi. 35).' The allusions here to St Paul's rejection of 'commendatory letters' (2 Cor. iii. 1) and to the scene on the way to Damascus (Acts ix. 3) are clear. In another passage St Peter, after explaining that Christ must be preceded by Antichrist, the true prophet by the false, and applying this law to the preaching of Simon and himself, adds: 'If he had been known ($εἰ ἐγινώσκετο$) he would not have been believed, but now being not known ($ἀγνοούμενος$) he is wrongly believed...being death, he has been desired as if he were a saviour...and being a deceiver he is heard as if he spake the truth (ii. 17, 18).' The writer seems to be playing with St Paul's own words, 'as deceivers and yet true, as unknown and yet well known, as dying and behold we live (2 Cor. vi. 8, 9).' In a third passage there is a very distinct allusion to the Apostle's account of the conflict at Antioch in the Galatian Epistle: 'If then,' says St Peter to Simon, 'our Jesus was made known to thee also and conversed with thee being seen in a vision, He was angry with thee as an adversary, and therefore He spake with thee by visions and dreams, or even by outward revelations. Can any one be made wise unto doctrine by visions? If thou sayest he can, then why did the Teacher abide and converse with us a whole year when we were awake?- And how shall we ever believe thee in this, that He was seen of thee? Nay, how could He have been seen of thee, when thy thoughts are contrary to His teaching? If having been seen and instructed of Him for a single hour thou wast made an Apostle, then preach His words, expound His teaching, love His Apostles, do not fight against me His companion. For thou hast withstood and opposed me ($ἐναντίος ἀνθέστηκάς μοι$), the firm rock, the foundation of the Church. If thou hadst not been an adversary, thou wouldest not have calumniated and reviled my preaching, that I might not be believed when I told what I had heard myself in person from the Lord, as though forsooth I were condemned (καταγνωσθέντος) and thou wert highly regarded[1]. Nay, if thou callest me condemned (κατεγνωσμένον), thou accusest God who revealed Christ to me and assailest Him that called me blessed in my revelation[2] (xvii. 19).' In this same bitter spirit the writer would rob him of all his missionary triumphs and transfer them to his supposed rival: the Apostleship of the Gentiles, according to the Homilies, belongs not to St Paul but to St Peter: Barnabas is no more the companion nor Clement the disciple of St Paul but of St Peter[3].

in the Letter of Peter,

Again, in the letter of Peter to James prefixed to the Homilies, emanating from the same school though perhaps not part of the work itself, and if so, furnishing another example of this bitterness of feeling, St Peter is made to denounce those Gentile converts who repudiate his lawful preaching, welcoming a certain lawless and foolish doctrine of the enemy (τοῦ ἐχθροῦ ἀνθρώπου ἄνομόν τινα καὶ φλυαρώδη διδασκαλίαν), complaining also that 'certain persons attempted by crafty interpretations to wrest his words to the abolishing of the law, pretending that this was his opinion, but that he did not openly preach it,' with more to the same effect (§ 2).

in the Recognitions,

In the Recognitions, probably a later patch-work[4], the harsher features of the Essene-Ebionite doctrine, as it appears in the Homilies, are softened down, and these bitter though indirect attacks on St Paul omitted; whether by the original redactor or by his translator Rufinus, it is not easy to say[5].

---

[1] The existing text has καὶ ἐμοῦ εὐδοκιμοῦντος, for which some have proposed to read καὶ μὴ εὐδοκιμοῦντος. It is better perhaps to substitute σοῦ or οὐδαμοῦ for ἐμοῦ, though neither is a neat emendation. Some change however is absolutely needed.

[2] τοῦ ἐπὶ ἀποκαλύψει μακαρίσαντός με. The allusion is to Matt. xvi. 17, μακάριος εἶ κ.τ.λ.

[3] See also other references to St Paul noted elsewhere, *Galatians*, p. 61.

[4] Not much earlier than the middle of the third century; for a portion of the treatise *de Fato*, written probably by a disciple of Bardesanes, is worked up in the later books; unless indeed this is itself borrowed from the Recognitions.

[5] In one instance at least the change is due to Rufinus himself. His translation of *Clem. Recogn.* iii. 61 contains a distinct recognition of St Paul's

ST PAUL AND THE THREE. 87

Thus in the portions corresponding to and probably taken from the Homilies no traces of this hostility remain. But in one passage adapted from another work, probably the 'Ascents of James[1],' it can still be discerned, the allusion having either escaped notice or been spared because it was too covert to give offence. It is there related that a certain enemy (homo quidam inimicus) raised a tumult against the Apostles and with his own hands assaulted James and threw him down from the steps of the temple, ceasing then to maltreat him, only because he believed him to be dead; and that after this the Apostles received secret information from Gamaliel, that this enemy (inimicus ille homo) had been sent by Caiaphas on a mission to Damascus to persecute and slay the disciples, and more especially to take Peter, who was supposed to have fled thither (i. 70, 71)[2]. The original work, from which this portion of the Recognitions seems to have been borrowed, was much more violent and unscrupulous in its attacks on St Paul; for in the 'Ascents of James' Epiphanius read the story, that he was of Gentile parentage, but coming to Jerusalem and wishing to marry the high-priest's daughter he became a proselyte and was circumcised: then, being disappointed of his hope, he turned round and furiously attacked the Mosaic ordinances (*Haer.* xxx. 16).

and in the Ascents of James.

Apostleship, '*Nonum (par) omnium gentium et illius qui mittetur seminare verbum inter gentes.*' (On these συζυγίαι of the false and the true see above, p. 85.) But the corresponding passage in the Syriac version (p. 115, l. 20, Lagarde) is wholly different, and translated back into Greek will run thus: ἡ δὲ ἐννάτη (συζυγία) τοῦ σπέρματος τῶν ζιζανίων καὶ τοῦ εὐαγγελίου τοῦ πεμπομένου εἰς ἐπιστροφήν, ὅταν ἐκριζωθῇ τὸ ἅγιον καὶ εἰς τὴν ἐρήμωσιν αὐτοῦ θήσουσι τὸ βδέλυγμα: see Dan. ix. 27, and compare *Clem. Hom.* ii. 17 (quoted above, p. 80, note 1). Thus the commendation of St Paul, which is wholly alien to the spirit of these Clementine writings, disappears.

[1] Uhlhorn, p. 366. Epiphanius mentions this book, ἀναβαθμοὶ Ἰακώβου, as being in circulation among the Ebionites (xxx. 16). It was so called doubtless as describing the *ascents* of James up the temple-stairs, whence he harangued the people. The name and the description of its contents in Epiphanius alike favour the view that it was the original of this portion of the Recognitions. But if so, the redactor of the Recognitions must have taken the same liberties with it as he has done with the Homilies.

[2] This passage is substantially the same in the Syriac.

88 ST PAUL AND THE THREE.

Activity of the sect

In the earlier part of the third century these Gnostic Ebionites seem to have made some futile efforts to propagate their views. An emissary of the sect, one Alcibiades of Apamea in Syria, appeared in Rome with the pretended revelation of Elchasai, and (thinking himself the better juggler of the two, says Hippolytus) half succeeded in cajoling the pope Callistus, but was exposed and defeated by the zealous bishop of Portus who tells the story (*Haer.* ix. 13—17). Not many years after another emissary, if it was not this same Alcibiades, appears to have visited Cæsarea, where he was confronted and denounced by Origen[1].

at Rome, A.D. 219—223,

and Cæsarea, A.D. 247?

The Churches of Palestine not Ebionite.

This display of activity might lead to an exaggerated estimate of the influence of these Judaizing sects. It is not probable that they left any wide or lasting impression west of Syria. In Palestine itself they would appear to have been confined to certain localities lying for the most part about the Jordan and the Dead Sea. After the reconstitution of the mother Church at Ælia Capitolina the Christianity of Palestine seems to have been for the most part neither Ebionite nor Nazarene. It is a significant fact, implying more than appears at first sight, that in the Paschal controversy which raged in the middle and later half of the second century the bishops of Cæsarea and Jerusalem, of Tyre and Ptolemais, ranged themselves, not with the Churches of Asia Minor which regulated their Easter festival by the Jewish passover without regard to the day of the week, but with those of Rome and Alexandria and Gaul which observed another rule; thus avoiding even the semblance of Judaism[2]. But we have more direct testimony to the main features of Palestinian doctrine about the middle of the second century in the known opinions of two writers who lived at the time—Justin as representative of the Samaritan, and Hegesippus of the Hebrew Christianity of their day. The

Paschal controversy.

---

[1] Euseb. *H. E.* vi. 38. This extract is taken from Origen's Homily on the 82nd Psalm, which appears to have been delivered in Cæsarea about A.D. 247. See Redepenning *Origenes* II. p. 72.

[2] Euseb. *H. E.* v. 23, 24. See below, p. 101, note 2.

ST PAUL AND THE THREE. 89

former of these declares himself distinctly against the two characteristic tenets of Ebionism. Against their humanitarian Justin. views he expressly argues, maintaining the divinity of Christ[1]. On the universal obligation of the law he declares, not only that those who maintain this opinion are wrong, but that he himself will hold no communion with them, for he doubts whether they can be saved[2]. If, as an apologist for the Gospel against Gentile and Jew, he is precluded by the nature of his writings from quoting St Paul[3], whose name would be received by the one with indifference and by the other with hatred, he still shows by his manner of citing and applying the Old Testament that he is not unfamiliar with this Apostle's writings[4]. The testimony of Hegesippus is still more im- Hegesippus, portant, for his extant fragments prove him to have been a thorough Hebrew in all his thoughts and feelings. This writer made a journey to Rome, calling on the way at Corinth among other places; he expresses himself entirely satisfied with the teaching of the Churches which he thus visited; 'Under each successive bishop,' he says, 'and in each city it is so as the law and the prophets and the Lord preach[5].' Was the doctrine of

---

[1] *Dial.* cc. 48, 127.
[2] *Dial.* cc. 47, 48.
[3] See Westcott's argument (*Canon* p. 117 sq) drawn from the usage of other apologists, Tertullian for instance, who does not quote even the Gospels in his Apology.
[4] See *Galatians*, p. 60, and the notes on Gal. iii. 28, iv. 27.
[5] In Euseb. *H. E.* iv. 22. The extract ends, γενόμενος δὲ ἐν Ῥώμῃ διαδοχὴν ἐποιησάμην μέχρις Ἀνικήτου οὗ διάκονος ἦν Ἐλεύθερος· καὶ παρὰ Ἀνικήτου διαδέχεται Σωτήρ, μεθ᾽ ὃν Ἐλεύθερος· ἐν ἑκάστῃ δὲ διαδοχῇ καὶ ἐν ἑκάστῃ πόλει οὕτως ἔχει ὡς ὁ νόμος κηρύττει καὶ οἱ προφῆται καὶ ὁ Κύριος. If the text be correct, διαδοχὴν ἐποιησάμην must mean 'I drew up a list or an account of the successive bishops' (see Pearson in Routh I. p. 268 sq); and in this case Hegesippus would seem to be referring to some earlier work or earlier portion of this work, which he now supplements. Possibly however the conjectural reading διατριβὴν ἐποιησάμην, 'I continued to reside,' may be correct: but the translation of Rufinus, 'permansi inibi (i.e. Romae) donec Aniceto Soter et Soteri successit Eleutherus,' is of little or no weight on this side; for he constantly uses his fluency in Latin to gloze over his imperfect knowledge of Greek, and the evasion of a real difficulty is with him the rule rather than the exception. If we retain διαδοχήν, the words of Hegesippus would still seem to imply that he left Rome during the episcopate of Anicetus. Eusebius indeed (*H. E.* iv. 11) infers, apparently from this passage, that he remained there till Eleutherus

the whole Christian world at this time (A.D. 150) Ebionite, or was the doctrine of Hegesippus Catholic? There is no other alternative. We happen to possess information which leaves no doubt as to the true answer. Eusebius speaks of Hegesippus as 'having recorded the unerring tradition of the apostolic preaching' (*H. E.* iv. 8); and classes him with Dionysius of Corinth, Melito, Irenæus, and others, as one of those in whose writings 'the orthodoxy of sound faith derived from the apostolic tradition had been handed down[1].' In this Eusebius could not have been mistaken, for he himself states that Hegesippus 'left the *fullest record* of his own opinions in five books of memoirs' which were in his hands (*H. E.* iv. 22). It is surely a bold effort of recent criticism in the face of these plain facts to set down Hegesippus as an Ebionite and to infer thence that a great part of Christendom was Ebionite also. True, this writer gives a traditional account of St James which represents him as a severe and rigorous ascetic[2]; but between this stern view of life and Ebionite doctrine the interval may be wide enough; and on this showing how many fathers of the Church, Jerome and Basil for instance in the fourth century, Bernard and Dominic and Francis of Assisi in later ages, must plead guilty of Ebionism. True, he used the Hebrew Gospel; but what authority he attributed to it, or whether it was otherwise than orthodox, does not appear. True also, he appeals in a passage already quoted to the authority of 'the law and the

not an Ebionite.

---

became bishop; and Jerome (*de Vir. Ill.* 22), as usual, repeats Eusebius. This inference, though intelligible, seems hardly correct; but it shows almost conclusively that Eusebius did not read διατριβήν. The early Syriac translator of Eusebius (see above, p. 33, note 2) certainly read διαδοχήν. The dates of the accession of the successive bishops as determined by Lipsius are, Pius 141 (at the latest), Anicetus 154—156, Soter 166 or 167, Eleutherus 174 or 175, Victor 189, Zephyrinus 198 or 199, Callistus 217, Urbanus 222; *Chron. der Röm. Bisch.* p. 263. But there is considerable variation in the authorities, the accession of Anicetus being placed by some as early as A.D. 150; see the lists in Clinton's *Fasti Romani* II. p. 534 sq.

[1] *H. E.* iv. 21 ὧν καὶ εἰς ἡμᾶς τῆς ἀποστολικῆς παραδόσεως ἡ τῆς ὑγιοῦς πίστεως ἔγγραφος κατῆλθεν ὀρθοδοξία.

[2] Euseb. *H. E.* ii. 23. See the account of St James below.

prophets and the Lord[1]'; but this is a natural equivalent for 'the Old and New Testament,' and corresponding expressions would not appear out of place even in our own age. True lastly, he condemns the use made of the text, 'Eye hath not seen nor ear heard' etc.[2], as contradicting our Lord's words,

[1] See the passage quoted above, p. 89, note 5. For the inferences of the Tübingen school see Schwegler *Nachapost. Zeitalter* I. p. 355, Baur *Christenthum* etc. p. 78. A parallel instance will serve the purpose better than much argument. In a poem by the late Prof. Selwyn (*Winfrid, afterwards called Boniface*, Camb. 1864) the hero is spoken of as 'Printing heaven's message deeper in his soul, By reading holy writ, Prophet and Law, And fourfold Gospel.' Here, as in Hegesippus, the law is mentioned and 'the Apostle' is not. Yet who would say that this passage savours of Ebionism? Comp. Irenæus *Haer*. ii. 30. 6 'Relinquentes eloquia Domini et Moysen et reliquos prophetas,' and again in *Spicil. Solesm.* I. p. 3, and the Clementine *Epistles to Virgins* i. 12 'Sicut ex lege ac prophetis et a Domino nostro Jesu Christo didicimus' (Westcott *Canon* p. 187, 6th ed.). So too *Apost. Const.* ii. 39 μετὰ τὴν ἀνάγνωσιν τοῦ νόμου καὶ τῶν προφητῶν καὶ τοῦ εὐαγγελίου, Hippol. *Haer*. viii. 19 πλεῖόν τι δι' αὐτῶν...μεμαθηκέναι ἢ ἐκ νόμου καὶ προφητῶν καὶ εὐαγγελίων.

[2] The fragment to which I refer is preserved in an extract from Stephanus Gobarus given in Photius *Bibl.* 232. After quoting the words τὰ ἡτοιμασμένα τοῖς δικαίοις ἀγαθὰ οὔτε ὀφθαλμὸς εἶδεν οὔτε οὓς ἤκουσεν οὔτε ἐπὶ καρδίαν ἀνθρώπου ἀνέβη, Stephanus proceeds, 'Ηγήσιππος μέντοι, ἀρχαῖός τε ἀνὴρ καὶ ἀποστολικός, ἐν τῷ πέμπτῳ τῶν ὑπομνημάτων, οὐκ οἶδ' ὅ τι καὶ παθών, μάτην μὲν εἰρῆσθαι ταῦτα λέγει καὶ καταψεύδεσθαι τοὺς ταῦτα φαμένους τῶν τε θείων γραφῶν καὶ τοῦ Κυρίου λέγοντος

Μακάριοι οἱ ὀφθαλμοὶ ὑμῶν κ.τ.λ. It is not surprising that this writer, who lived when Gnosticism had passed out of memory, should be puzzled to 'know what had come to Hegesippus': but modern critics ought not to have gone astray. Hegesippus can hardly be objecting to the passage itself, which is probably a quotation from Is. lxiv. 4. His objection therefore must be to some *application* of it. But whose application? Even had there been no direct evidence, it might have been gathered from the argument which follows that he referred to the esoteric teaching of the Gnostics; but the lately discovered treatise of Hippolytus establishes the fact that it was a favourite text of these heretics, being introduced into the form of initiation: see v. 24, 26, 27 (of Justin the Gnostic), vi. 24 (of Valentinus). This is the opinion of Lechler p. 463, Ritschl p. 267, Westcott *Canon* pp. 208, 284, Bunsen *Hippolytus* I. p. 132 (2nd ed.), and Hilgenfeld *Apost. Väter* p. 102, but otherwise *Zeitschr. f. Wiss. Theol.* 1876, p. 203 sq. Yet Baur (*Christenthum* p. 77, *Paulus* p. 221), and Schwegler (I. p. 352), forcing an unnatural meaning on the words, contend that Hegesippus is directly denying St Paul's claim to a revelation and asserting that this privilege belongs only to those who have seen and heard Christ in the flesh. It is worth noticing that the same quotation, 'eye hath not seen etc.,' is found in the Epistle of Clement (c. 34) [where see note]; and this epistle was referred to by Hegesippus, as the notice of Eusebius seems to imply (*H. E.* iv. 22),

'Blessed are your eyes for ye see, etc.'; but he is here protesting against its perverted application by the Gnostics, who employed it of the initiated few, and whom elsewhere he severely denounces; and it is a mere accident that the words are quoted also by St Paul (1 Cor. ii. 9). Many of the facts mentioned point him out as a Hebrew, but not one brands him as an Ebionite. The decisive evidence on the other side is fatal to this inference. If Hegesippus may be taken as a type of the Hebrew Church in his day, then the doctrine of that Church was Catholic.

<small>Ebionism not prevalent in other Churches.</small> And if the Palestinian Churches of the second century held Catholic doctrine, we shall see little or no reason to fix the charge of Ebionism on other communities farther removed from the focus of Judaic influences. Here and there indeed Judaism seems to have made a desperate struggle, but only to sustain a signal defeat. At Antioch this conflict began earlier and probably continued longer than elsewhere; yet the names of her bishops Ignatius, Theophilus, and Serapion vouch for the doctrine and practice of the Antiochene Church in the second century. In Asia Minor the influence first of St Paul and then of St John must have been fatal to the ascendancy of Ebionism. A disproportionate share indeed of the faint light which glimmers over the Church of the second century is concentrated on this region: and the notices, though occasional and fragmentary, are sufficient to establish this general fact. The same is true with regard to Greece: similar influences were at work and with similar results. The Churches of Gaul took their colour from Asia Minor, which furnished their greatest teachers: Irenæus bears witness to the Catholicity of their faith. In Alexandria, when at length the curtain rises, Christianity is seen enthroned between Greek philosophy and Gnostic speculation, while Judaism is far in the background. The infancy of the African Church is wrapt in hopeless darkness: but when she too emerges from her obscurity, she comes

<small>with approval. This very mention of Clement's epistle is in itself a secondary evidence that Hegesippus recognised the authority of St Paul.</small>

forward in no uncertain attitude, with no deep scars as of a recent conflict, offering neither a mutilated canon nor a dwarfed theology. The African Bible, as it appears in the old Latin version, contains all the books which were received without dispute for two centuries after. The African theology, as represented by Tertullian, in no way falls short of the standard of Catholic doctrine maintained in other parts of Christendom.

But the Church of the metropolis demands special attention. At Rome, if anywhere, we should expect to see very distinct traces of these successive phenomena, which are supposed to have extended throughout or almost throughout the Christian Church—first, the supremacy of Ebionism—then the conflict of the Judaic with the Pauline Gospel—lastly, towards the close of the second century, the triumph of a modified Paulinism and the consequent birth of Catholic Christianity[1]. Yet, even if this were the history of Catholicity at Rome, it would still be an unfounded assumption to extend the phenomenon to other parts of Christendom. Rome had not yet learnt to dictate to the Church at large. At this early period she appears for the most part unstable and pliant, the easy prey of designing or enthusiastic adventurers in theology, not the originator of a policy and a creed of her own. The prerogative of Christian doctrine and practice rests hitherto with the Churches of Antioch and Asia Minor.

The Church of Rome.

But the evidence lends no countenance to the idea that the tendencies of the Roman Church during this period were towards Ebionism. Her early history indeed is wrapt in obscurity. If the veil were raised, the spectacle would probably not be very edifying, but there is no reason to imagine that Judaism was her characteristic taint. As late heathen Rome

Heretics congregate there.

[1] The episcopate of Victor (about A.D. 190—200) is fixed by the Tübingen critics (see Schwegler II. p. 206 sq) as the epoch of the antijudaic revolution in the Roman Church. This date follows necessarily from their assumption that Hegesippus was an Ebionite; for his approval of this Church extends to the episcopate of Eleutherus, the immediate predecessor of Victor; see above, p. 89, note 5. They suppose however that the current had been setting in this direction some time before.

had been the sink of all Pagan superstitions, so early Christian Rome was the meeting-point of all heretical creeds and philosophies. If the presence of Simon Magus in the metropolis be not a historical fact, it is still a carrying out of the typical character with which he is invested in early tradition, as the father of heresy. Most of the great heresiarchs—among others Valentinus, Marcion, Praxeas, Theodotus, Sabellius—taught in Rome. Ebionism alone would not be idle, where all other heresies were active. But the great battle with this form of error seems to have been fought out at an early date, in the lifetime of the Apostles themselves and in the age immediately following.

Secession of Judaizers.

The last notice of the Roman Church in the Apostolic writings seems to point to two separate communities, a Judaizing Church and a Pauline Church. The arrival of the Gentile Apostle in the metropolis, it would appear, was the signal for the separation of the Judaizers, who had hitherto associated with their Gentile brethren coldly and distrustfully. The presence of St Paul must have vastly strengthened the numbers and influence of the more liberal and Catholic party; while the Judaizers provoked by rivalry redoubled their efforts, that in making converts to the Gospel they might also gain proselytes to the law[1]. Thus 'in every way Christ was preached.'

St Peter in Rome.

If St Peter ever visited Rome, it must have been at a later date than these notices. Of this visit, far from improbable in itself, there is fair if not conclusive evidence; and once admitted, we may reasonably assume that important consequences flowed from it. Where all is obscurity, conjecture on one side is fairly answered by conjecture on the other. We may venture therefore to suggest this, as a not unlikely result of the presence of both Apostles in Rome. As they had done before in the world at large, so they would agree to do now in

---

[1] The inferences in the text are drawn from Phil. i. 15—18, compared with Col. iv. 11 'These only (i.e. of the circumcision) are my fellow-workers etc.'

the metropolis: they would exchange the right hand of fellowship, devoting themselves the one more especially to the Jewish, the other to the Gentile converts. Christian Rome was large enough to admit two communities or two sections in one community, until the time was ripe for their more complete amalgamation. Thus either as separate bodies with separate governments, or as a confederation of distinct interests represented each by their own officers in a common presbytery, we may suppose that the Jewish and Gentile brotherhoods at Rome were organized by the combined action of the two Apostles. This fact possibly underlies the tradition that St Peter and St Paul were joint founders of the Roman Church: and it may explain the discrepancies in the lists of the early bishops, which perhaps point to a double succession. At all events, the presence of the two Apostles must have tended to tone down antipathies and to draw parties closer together. The Judaizers seeing that the Apostle of the Circumcision, whose name they had venerated at a distance but whose principles they had hitherto imperfectly understood, was associating on terms of equality with the 'hated one,' the subverter of the law, would be led to follow his example slowly and suspiciously: and advances on the one side would be met eagerly by advances on the other. Hence at the close of the first century we see no more traces of a twofold Church. The work of the Apostles, now withdrawn from the scene, has passed into the hands of no unworthy disciple. The liberal and catholic spirit of Clement eminently fitted him for the task of conciliation; and he appears as the first bishop or presiding elder of the one Roman Church. This amalgamation however could not be effected without some opposition; the extreme Judaizers must necessarily have been embittered and alienated: and, if a little later we discern traces of Ebionite sectarianism in Rome, this is not only no surprise, but the most natural consequence of a severe but short-lived struggle.

A twofold Church,

united under Clement.

The Epistle to the Corinthians written by Clement in the name of the Roman Church cannot well be placed after the

Clement's Epistle.

close of the first century and may possibly date some years earlier. It is not unreasonable to regard this as a typical document, reflecting the comprehensive principles and large sympathies which had been impressed upon the united Church of Rome, in great measure perhaps by the influence of the distinguished writer. There is no early Christian writing which combines more fully than this the distinctive features of all the Apostolic Epistles, now asserting the supremacy of faith with St Paul, now urging the necessity of works with St James, at one time echoing the language of St Peter, at another repeating the very words of the Epistle to the Hebrews[1]. Not without some show of truth, the authority of Clement was claimed in after generations for writings of very different tendencies. Belonging to no party, he seemed to belong to all.

Not many years after this Epistle was written, Ignatius now on his way to martyrdom addresses a letter to the Roman brethren. It contains no indications of any division in the Church of the metropolis or of the prevalence of Ebionite views among his readers. On the contrary, he lavishes epithets of praise on them in the opening salutation; and throughout the letter there is not the faintest shadow of blame. His only fear is that they may be too kind to him and deprive him of the honour of martyrdom by their intercessions. To the Ephesians, and even to Polycarp, he offers words of advice and warning; but to the Romans he utters only the language of joyful satisfaction[2].

But in a Church thus formed we might expect to meet with

---

[1] See Westcott *History of the Canon* p. 24 sq.

[2] This is the case, even though we should accept only the parts preserved in the Syriac as genuine; but the Greek (Vossian) Epistles are still more explicit. They distinctly acquit the Romans of any participation in heresy; speaking of them as 'united in flesh and spirit with every commandment of Christ, filled with the grace of God inseparably, and strained clear of every foreign colour ($\dot{a}\pi o\delta\iota\upsilon\lambda\iota\sigma\mu\acute{e}\nu o\iota\varsigma$ $\dot{a}\pi\grave{o}$ $\pi a\nu\tau\grave{o}\varsigma$ $\dot{a}\lambda\lambda o\tau\rho\acute{\iota}o\upsilon$ $\chi\rho\acute{\omega}\mu a\tau o\varsigma$).' At the same time the writer appears in other passages as a stubborn opponent of Judaism, *Magn.* 8, 10, *Philad.* 6.

other and narrower types of doctrine than the Epistle of Clement exhibits. Traditional principles and habits of thought would still linger on, modified indeed but not wholly transformed by the predominance of a Catholicity which comprehended all elements in due proportion. One such type is represented by an extant work which emanated from the Roman Church during the first half of the second century[1].

In its general tone the Shepherd of Hermas confessedly differs from the Epistle of Clement; but on the other hand the writer was certainly no Ebionite, as he has been sometimes represented. If he dwells almost exclusively on works, he yet states that the 'elect of God will be saved through faith[2]': if he rarely quotes the New Testament, his references to the Old Testament are still fainter and scantier: if he speaks seldom of our Lord and never mentions Him by name, he yet asserts that the Son of God was present with His Father in counsel at the founding of creation[3], and holds that the world is 'sustained by Him[4].' Such expressions no Ebionite could have used. Of all the New Testament writings the Shepherd most resembles in tone the Epistle of St James, whose language it sometimes reflects: but the teaching of St James appears here in an exaggerated and perverted form. The author lays great stress on works, and so far he copies his model: but his interpretation of works is often formal and ritualistic, and in one passage he even states the doctrine of supererogation[5]. Whether the tone of this writing is to be ascribed to the traditional

Shepherd of Hermas not Ebionite.

c. A.D. 145.

[1] On the date of the Shepherd see *Galatians*, p. 99, note 3.
[2] *Vis.* iii. 8 : comp. *Mand.* viii.
[3] *Sim.* ix. 12. The whole passage is striking: Πρῶτον, φημί, πάντων, κύριε, τοῦτό μοι δήλωσον· ἡ πέτρα καὶ ἡ πύλη τίς ἐστιν; Ἡ πέτρα, φησίν, αὕτη καὶ ἡ πύλη ὁ υἱὸς τοῦ Θεοῦ ἐστί. Πῶς, φημί, κύριε, ἡ πέτρα παλαιά ἐστιν, ἡ δὲ πύλη καινή; Ἄκουε, φησί, καὶ σύνιε, ἀσύνετε. ὁ μὲν υἱὸς τοῦ Θεοῦ πάσης τῆς κτίσεως αὐτοῦ προγενέστερός ἐστιν, ὥστε σύμβουλον αὐτὸν γενέσθαι τῷ πατρὶ τῆς κτίσεως αὐτοῦ· διὰ τοῦτο καὶ παλαιός ἐστιν. Ἡ δὲ πύλη διὰ τί καινή, φημί, κύριε; Ὅτι, φησίν, ἐπ' ἐσχάτων τῶν ἡμερῶν τῆς συντελείας φανερὸς ἐγένετο, διὰ τοῦτο καινὴ ἐγένετο ἡ πύλη, ἵνα οἱ μέλλοντες σώζεσθαι δι' αὐτῆς εἰς τὴν βασιλείαν εἰσέλθωσι τοῦ Θεοῦ.
[4] *Sim.* ix. 14 τὸ ὄνομα τοῦ υἱοῦ τοῦ Θεοῦ μέγα ἐστὶ καὶ ἀχώρητον καὶ τὸν κόσμον ὅλον βαστάζει. On the whole subject see Dorner *Lehre* etc. I. p. 186 sq, Westcott *Canon* p. 202 sq.
[5] *Sim.* v. 3 : comp. *Mand.* iv. 4.

feelings of Judaism yet lingering in the Church, or to the influence of a Judaic section still tolerated, or to the constitution of the author's own mind, it is impossible to say. The view of Christian ethics here presented deviates considerably, it is true, from St Paul's teaching; but the deviation is the same in kind and not greater in degree than marks a vast number of mediæval writings, and may in fact be said to characterize more or less distinctly the whole mediæval Church. Thus it affords no ground for the charge of Ebionism. Hermas speaks of law indeed, as St James speaks of it; yet by law he means not the Mosaic ordinances but the rule introduced by Christ. On the other hand his very silence is eloquent. There is not a word in favour of Judaic observances properly so called, not a word of denunciation direct or indirect against either the doctrine or the person of St Paul or his disciples. In this respect the Shepherd presents a marked contrast to the truly Ebionite work, which must be taken next in order.

Roman origin of the Clementines questioned.

The Clementine writings have been assigned with great confidence by most recent critics of ability to a Roman authorship[1]. Of the truth of this view I am very far from convinced. The great argument—indeed almost the only argument—in its favour is the fact that the plot of the romance turns upon the wanderings of this illustrious bishop of Rome, who is at once the narrator and the hero of the story. But the fame of Clement reached far beyond the limits of his own jurisdiction. To him, we are specially told by a contemporary writer, was assigned the task of corresponding with foreign churches[2]. His rank and position, his acknowledged wisdom and piety, would point him out as the best typical representative of the Gentile converts: and an Ebionite writer, designing by a religious fiction to impress his views on Gentile Christendom, would

---

[1] So for instance Baur, Schliemann, Ritschl, Hilgenfeld: and this view is adopted by Dean Milman *Latin Christianity* I. p. 31, who speaks of it as 'the unanimous opinion of those who in later days have critically examined the Clementina.' Uhlhorn is almost alone among recent critics in raising his voice against this general verdict: p. 370 sq.

[2] Hermas *Vis.* ii. 4 πέμψει οὖν Κλήμης εἰς τὰς ἔξω πόλεις· ἐκείνῳ γὰρ ἐπιτέτραπται.

naturally single out Clement for his hero, and by his example enforce the duty of obedience to the Church of the Circumcision, as the prerogative Church and the true standard of orthodoxy. At all events it is to be noticed that, beyond the use made of Clement's name, these writings do not betray any familiarity with or make any reference to the Roman Church in particular[1]. On the contrary, the scenes are all laid in the East; and the supreme arbiter, the ultimate referee in all that relates to Christian doctrine and practice, is not Peter, the Clementine Apostle of the Gentiles, the reputed founder of the Roman Church, but James the Lord's brother, the bishop of bishops, the ruler of the mother Church of the Circumcision.

If the Roman origin of these works is more than doubtful, the time of writing also is open to much question. The dates assigned to the Homilies by the ablest critics range over the whole of the second century, and some place them even later. If the Roman authorship be abandoned, many reasons for a very early date will fall to the ground also. Whenever they were written, the Homilies are among the most interesting and important of early Christian writings; but they have no right to the place assigned them in the system of a modern critical school, as the missing link between the Judaism of the Christian era and the Catholicism of the close of the second century, as representing in fact the phase of Christianity taught at Rome and generally throughout the Church during the early ages. The very complexion of the writer's opinions is such, that they can hardly have been maintained by any large and important community, at least in the West. Had they presented a purer form of Judaism, founded on the Old Testament Scriptures, a

Their importance exaggerated.

They cannot represent the doctrine

---

[1] The Epistle of Clement to James, prefixed to the work, is an exception; for it gives an elaborate account of the writer's appointment by St Peter as his successor. The purpose of this letter, which is to glorify the see of Rome, shows that it was no part of and probably is later than the Homilies themselves.

If the Homilies had really been written by a Roman Christian, the slight and incidental mention of St Peter's sojourn in Rome (i. 16, comp. *Recogn.* i. 74) would have thrown considerable doubt on the fact. But if they emanated from the East, from Syria for instance, no explanation of this silence is needed.

7—2

of the Roman Church.

more plausible case might have been made out. But the theology of the Clementines does not lie in a direct line between the Old Testament and Catholic Christianity: it deviates equally from the one and the other. In its rejection of half the Mosaic law and much more than half of the Old Testament, and in its doctrine of successive avatars of the Christ, it must have been as repugnant to the religious sentiments of a Jew trained in the school of Hillel, as it could possibly be to a disciple of St Paul in the first century or to a Catholic Christian in the third. Moreover the tone of the writer is not at all the tone of one who addresses a sympathetic audience. His attacks on St Paul are covert and indirect; he makes St Peter complain that he has been misrepresented and libelled. Altogether there is an air of deprecation and apology in the Homilies. If they were really written by a Roman Christian, they cannot represent the main body of the Church, but must have emanated from one of the many heresies with which the metropolis swarmed in the second century, when all promulgators of new doctrine gathered there, as the largest and therefore the most favourable market for their spiritual wares.

Notice in Hippolytus.

There is another reason also for thinking that this Gnostic Ebionism cannot have obtained any wide or lasting influence in the Church of Rome. During the episcopate of Callistus (A.D. 219—223) a heretical teacher appears in the metropolis, promulgating Elchasaite doctrines substantially, though not identically, the same with the creed of the Clementines, and at first seems likely to attain some measure of success, but is denounced and foiled by Hippolytus. It is clear that this learned writer on heresies regarded the Elchasaite doctrine as a novelty, against which therefore it was the more necessary to warn the faithful Christian. If the Ebionism of the Clementines had ever prevailed at Rome, it had passed into oblivion when Hippolytus wrote.

No Ebionite leanings in the Roman Church.

The few notices of the Roman Church in the second century point to other than Ebionite leanings. In their ecclesiastical ordinances the Romans seem anxious to separate themselves as widely as possible from Jewish practices. Thus they extended the Friday's fast over the Saturday, showing thereby a marked disregard of the sabbatical festival[1]. Thus again they observed Easter on a different day from the Jewish passover; and so zealous were they in favour of their own traditional usage in this respect, that in the Paschal controversy their bishop Victor resorted to the extreme measure of renouncing communion with those churches which differed from it[2]. This controversy affords a valuable testimony to the Catholicity of Christianity at Rome in another way. It is clear that the churches ranged on different sides on this question of ritual are nevertheless substantially agreed on all important points of doctrine and practice. This fact appears when Anicetus of Rome permits Polycarp of Smyrna, who had visited the metropolis in order to settle some disputed points and had failed in arranging the Paschal question, to celebrate the eucharist in his stead. It is distinctly stated by Irenæus when he remonstrates with Victor for disturbing the peace of the Church by insisting on non-essentials[3]. In its creed the Roman Church was one with the Gallic and Asiatic Churches; and that this creed was not Ebionite, the names of Polycarp and Irenæus are guarantees. Nor is it only in the Paschal controversy that the Catholicity of the Romans may be inferred from their intercourse with other Christian communities.

Evidence of the Paschal controversy.

---

[1] Tertull. *de Jejun.* 14; see Neander *Ch. Hist.* I. p. 410 (Bohn).

[2] On the Paschal controversy see Euseb. *H. E.* v. 23—25. Polycrates on behalf of the Asiatic Churches claimed the sanction of St John; and there seems no reason to doubt the validity of this claim. On the other hand a different rule had been observed in the Roman Church at least as far back as the episcopate of Xystus (about 120—129) and perhaps earlier. It seems probable then that the Easter festival had been established independently by the Romans and those who followed the Roman practice. Thus in the first instance the difference of usage was no index of Judaic or antijudaic leanings: but when once attention was called to its existence, and it became a matter of controversy, the observance of the Christian anniversary on the same day with the Jewish festival would afford a handle for the charge of Judaism; and where it was a matter of policy or of principle to stand clear of any sympathy with Jewish customs (as for instance in Palestine after the collision of the Jews with the Romans), the Roman usage would be adopted in preference to the Asiatic.

[3] In Euseb. *H. E.* v. 24 ἡ διαφωνία τῆς νηστείας τὴν ὁμόνοιαν τῆς πίστεως συνίστησιν, and the whole extract.

Other communications with foreign churches.

The remains of ecclesiastical literature, though sparse and fragmentary, are yet sufficient to reveal a wide network of intercommunication between the churches of the second century; and herein Rome naturally holds a central position. The visit of Hegesippus to the metropolis has been mentioned already. Not very long after we find Dionysius bishop of Corinth, whose 'orthodoxy' is praised by Eusebius, among other letters addressed to foreign churches, writing also to the Romans in terms of cordial sympathy and respect[1]. On the Catholicity of the African Church I have already remarked: and the African Church was a daughter of the Roman, from whom therefore it may be assumed she derived her doctrine[2].

Internal condition of the Roman Church.

The gleams of light which break in upon the internal history of the Roman Church at the close of the second and beginning of the third century exhibit her assailed by rival heresies, compromised by the weakness and worldliness of her rulers, altogether distracted and unsteady, but in no way Ebionite. One bishop, whose name is not given, first dallies with the fanatical spiritualism of Montanus; then suddenly turning round, surrenders himself to the patripassian speculations of Praxeas[3]. Later than this two successive bishops, Zephyrinus and Callistus, are stated, by no friendly critic indeed but yet a contemporary writer, the one from stupidity and avarice, the other from craft and ambition, to have listened favourably to the heresies of Noetus and Sabellius[4]. It was at this point in her history that the Church of Rome was surprised by the novel doctrines of the Elchasaite teacher, whom I have already mentioned more than once. But no one would maintain that at this

---

[1] In Euseb. *H. E.* iv. 23.

[2] Tertull. *de Praescr.* 36. Cyprian *Epist.* 48 (ed. Fell) writing to Cornelius speaks of Rome as 'Ecclesiae catholicae radicem et matricem,' in reference to the African Churches.

[3] Tertull. *adv. Prax.* 1. Tertullian, now a Montanist, writes of Praxeas who had persuaded this nameless bishop of Rome to revoke his concessions to Montanism, 'Ita duo negotia diaboli Praxeas Romae procuravit, prophetiam expulit et haeresim intulit, paracletum fugavit et patrem crucifixit.' For speculations as to the name of this bishop see Wordsworth's *Hippolytus* pp. 131, 132.

[4] Hippol. *Haer.* ix. 7 sq.

late date Ebionism predominated either at Rome or in Christendom generally.

Ebionites indeed there were at this time and very much later. Even at the close of the fourth century, they seem to have mustered in considerable numbers in the east of Palestine, and were scattered through the great cities of the empire. But their existence was not prolonged much later. About the middle of the fifth century they had almost disappeared[1]. They would gradually be absorbed either into the Catholic Church or into the Jewish synagogue: into the latter probably, for their attachment to the law seems all along to have been stronger than their attachment to Christ. *Ebionism dies out.*

Thus then a comprehensive survey of the Church in the second century seems to reveal a substantial unity of doctrine and a general recognition of Jewish and Gentile Apostles alike throughout the greater part of Christendom. At the same time it could hardly happen, that the influence of both should be equally felt or the authority of both estimated alike in all branches of the Church. St Paul and the Twelve had by mutual consent occupied distinct spheres of labour; and this distribution of provinces must necessarily have produced some effect on the subsequent history of the Church[2]. The communities founded by St Paul would collect and preserve the letters of their founder with special care; while the brotherhoods evangelized by the Apostles of the Circumcision would attribute a superior, if not an exclusive, value to the writings of these 'pillars' of the Church. It would therefore be no great surprise if we should find that in individual writers of the second century and in different parts of the early Church, the Epistles of St Paul on the one hand, the Apocalypse of St John or the letter of St James on the other, were seldom or never appealed to as authorities[3]. The equable circulation of all the apostolic writings was necessarily the work of time.

---

[1] Theodoret, *Haer. Fab.* ii. 11, mentions the Ebionites and the Elchasaites among those of whom οὐδὲ βραχὺ διέμεινε λείψανον.

[2] Gal. ii. 9; see Westcott's *History of the Canon* p. 78 sq.

[3] Many false inferences however, affecting the history of the Canonical

Use of the foregoing account.

THE foregoing account of the conflict of the Church with Judaism has been necessarily imperfect, and in some points conjectural; but it will prepare the way for a more correct estimate of the relations between St Paul and the leading Apostles of the Circumcision. We shall be in a position to view these relations no longer as an isolated chapter in history, but in connexion with events before and after: and we shall be furnished also with means of estimating the value of later traditional accounts of these first preachers of the Gospel.

St Paul.

ST PAUL himself is so clearly reflected in his own writings, that a distorted image of his life and doctrine would seem to be due only to defective vision. Yet our first impressions require to be corrected or rather supplemented by an after consideration. Seeing him chiefly as the champion of Gentile liberty, the constant antagonist of Jew and Judaizer, we are apt to forget that his character has another side also. By birth and education he was a Hebrew of the Hebrews: and the traditions and feelings of his race held him in honourable captivity to the very last.

His portrait in the Acts.

Of this fact the narrative of the Acts affords many striking examples. It exhibits him associating with the Apostles of the Circumcision on terms of mutual respect and love, celebrating the festivals and observing the rites of his countrymen, everywhere giving the precedence to the Jew over the Gentile.

Its truth questioned,

But the character of the witness has been called in question. This narrative, it is said, is neither contemporary nor trustworthy. It was written long after the events recorded, with

writings, have been drawn from the silence of Eusebius, which has been entirely misapprehended: see *Contemporary Review*, January, 1875, p. 169 sq, *Colossians* p. 52 sq.

The phenomenon exhibited in the *Ancient Syriac Documents* (edited by Cureton, 1864) is remarkable. Though they refer more than once to the Acts of the Apostles (pp. 15, 27, 35) as the work of St Luke and as possessing canonical authority, and though they allude incidentally to St Paul's labours (pp. 35, 61, 62), there is yet no reference to the epistles of this Apostle, where the omission cannot have been accidental (p. 32), and the most important churches founded by him, as Ephesus, Thessalonica, Corinth, etc., are stated to have received 'the Apostles' Hand of Priesthood from John the Evangelist' (p. 34).

the definite purpose of uniting the two parties in the Church. Thus the incidents are forged or wrested to subserve the purpose of the writer. It was part of his plan to represent St Peter and St Paul as living on friendly terms, in order to reconcile the Petrine and Pauline factions.

The Acts of the Apostles in the multiplicity and variety of its details probably affords greater means of testing its general character for truth than any other ancient narrative in existence; and in my opinion it satisfies the tests fully. But this is not the place for such an investigation. Neither shall I start from the assumption that it has any historical value. Taking common ground with those whose views I am considering, I shall draw my proofs from St Paul's Epistles alone in the first instance, nor from all of these, but from such only as are allowed even by the extreme critics of the Tübingen school to be genuine, the Epistles to the Romans, Corinthians, and Galatians[1]. It so happens that they are the most important for my purpose. If they contain the severest denunciations of the Judaizers, if they display the most uncompromising antagonism to Judaism, they also exhibit more strongly than any others St Paul's sympathies with his fellow-countrymen. *but established by his own writings.*

These then are the facts for which we have St Paul's direct personal testimony in the epistles allowed by all to be genuine. (1) *The position of the Jews.* He assigns to them the prerogative over the Gentiles; a prior right to the privileges of the Gospel, involving a prior reward if they are accepted and, according to an universal rule in things spiritual, a prior retribution if they are spurned (Rom. i. 16, ii. 9, 10). In the same spirit he declares that the advantage is on the side of the Jew, and that this advantage is 'much every way' (Rom. iii. 1, 2). (2) *His* *(1) Position of the Jews.*

(2) His affection for them.

---

[1] These four epistles alone were accepted as genuine by Baur and Schwegler. Hilgenfeld, who may now be regarded as the chief of the Tübingen school, has in this, as in many other points, deserted the extreme position of Baur whom he calls the 'great master.' He accepts as genuine 1 Thessalonians, Philippians, and Philemon: thus substituting, as he expresses it, the sacred number Seven for the heathen Tetractys of his master: see *Zeitsch. für wissensch. Theol.* v. p. 226 (1862).

affection for his countrymen. His earnestness and depth of feeling are nowhere more striking than when he is speaking of the Jews: 'Brethren, my heart's desire and prayer to God for Israel is, that they might be saved: for I bear them record that they have a zeal of God, but not according to knowledge' (Rom. x. 1, 2). Thus in spite of their present stubborn apostasy he will not allow that they have been cast away (xi. 1), but looks forward to the time when 'all Israel shall be saved' (xi. 26). So strong indeed is his language in one passage, that commentators regarding the letter rather than the spirit of the Apostle's prayer, have striven to explain it away by feeble apologies and unnatural interpretations: 'I say the truth in Christ, I lie not, my conscience also bearing me witness in the Holy Ghost, that I have great heaviness and continual sorrow in my heart: for I could wish that myself were accursed from Christ ($ἀνάθεμα\ εἶναι\ αὐτὸς\ ἐγὼ\ ἀπὸ\ τοῦ\ Χριστοῦ$) for my brethren, my kinsmen according to the flesh' (Rom. ix. 1—3). (3) *His practical care for his countrymen.* The collection of alms for the poor brethren of Judæa occupies much of his attention and suggests messages to various churches (Rom. xv. 25, 26; 1 Cor. xvi. 1—6; 2 Cor. viii, ix; Gal. ii. 10). It is clear not only that he is very solicitous himself on behalf of the Christians of the Circumcision, but that he is anxious also to inspire his Gentile converts with the same interest. (4) *His conformity to Jewish habits and usages.* St Paul lays down this rule, to 'become all things to all men that he may by all means save some' (1 Cor. ix. 22). This is the key to all seeming inconsistencies in different representations of his conduct. In his epistles we see him chiefly as a Gentile among Gentiles; but this powerful moral weapon has another edge. Applying this maxim, he himself tells us emphatically that 'unto the Jews he became as a Jew, that he might gain the Jews; unto them that are under the law as under the law, that he might gain them that are under the law' (1 Cor. ix. 20). The charges of his Judaizing opponents are a witness that he did carry out his maxim in this direction, as in the other. With a semblance of truth they taunt him with inconsistency, urging that in his

---

(3) His practical care for them.

(4) His conformity to their usages.

own practice he had virtually admitted their principles, that in fact he had himself preached circumcision[1]. (5) *His reverence for the Old Testament Scriptures.* This is a strongly marked feature in the four epistles which I am considering. They teem with quotations, while there are comparatively few in his remaining letters. For metaphor, allegory, example, argument, confirmation, he draws upon this inexhaustible store. However widely he may have differed from his rabbinical teachers in other respects, he at least did not yield to them in reverence for 'the law and the prophets and the psalms.'

These facts being borne in mind (and they are indisputable) the portrait of St Paul in the Acts ought not to present any difficulties. It records no one fact of the Apostle, it attributes no sentiment to him, which is not either covered by some comprehensive maxim or supported by some practical instance in his acknowledged letters. On the other hand the tone of the history confessedly differs somewhat from the tone of the epistles. Nor could it possibly have been otherwise. Written in the heat of the conflict, written to confute unscrupulous antagonists and to guard against dangerous errors, St Paul's language could not give a complete picture of his relations with the Apostles and the Church of the Circumcision. Arguments directed against men, who disparaged his authority by undue exaltation of the Twelve, offered the least favourable opportunity of expressing his sympathy with the Twelve. Denunciations of Judaizing teachers, who would force their national rites on the Gentile Churches, were no fit vehicle for acknowledging his respect for and conformity with those rites. The fairness of this line of argument will be seen by comparing the differences observable in his own epistles. His tone may be said to be graduated according to the temper and character of his hearers. The opposition of the Galatian letter to the Mosaic ritual is stern and uncompromising. It was written to correct a virulent form of Judaism. On the other hand the remonstrances in the Epistle to the Romans are much more moderate, guarded by

_{(5) His use of the Old Testament.}

_{Difference in tone between the Acts and Epistles.}

---

[1] See *Galatians* p. 28 sq, and notes on Gal. i. 10, ii. 3, v. 2, 11.

constant explanations and counterpoised by expressions of deep sympathy. Here he was writing to a mixed church of Jews and Gentiles, where there had been no direct opposition to his authority, no violent outbreak of Judaism. If then we picture him in his intercourse with his own countrymen at Jerusalem, where the claims of his nation were paramount and where the cause of Gentile liberty could not be compromised, it seems most natural that he should have spoken and acted as he is represented in the Acts. Luther denouncing the pope for idolatry and Luther rebuking Carlstadt for iconoclasm writes like two different persons. He bids the timid and gentle Melanchthon 'sin and sin boldly': he would have cut his right hand off sooner than pen such words to the antinomian rioters of Munster. It is not that the man or his principles were changed: but the same words addressed to persons of opposite tempers would have conveyed a directly opposite meaning.

St Paul's relations with the Three as described in this epistle.
St Paul's language then, when in this epistle he describes his relations with the Three, must be interpreted with this caution, that it necessarily exhibits those relations in a partial aspect. The purport of this language, as I understand it, is explained in the notes: and I shall content myself here with gathering up the results.

(1) There is a general recognition of the position and authority of the elder Apostles, both in the earlier visit to Jerusalem when he seeks Peter apparently for the purpose of obtaining instruction in the facts of the Gospel, staying with him a fortnight, and in the later visit which is undertaken for the purpose, if I may use the phrase, of comparing notes with the other Apostles and obtaining their sanction for the freedom of the Gentile Churches. (2) On the other hand there is an uncompromising resistance to the extravagant and exclusive claims set up on their behalf by the Judaizers. (3) In contrast to these claims, St Paul's language leaves the impression (though the inference cannot be regarded as certain), that they had not offered a prompt resistance to the Judaizers in the first instance, hoping perhaps to conciliate them, and that the brunt

of the contest had been borne by himself and Barnabas. (4) At the same time they are distinctly separated from the policy and principles of the Judaizers, who are termed false brethren, spies in the Christian camp. (5) The Apostles of the Circumcision find no fault with St Paul's Gospel, and have nothing to add to it. (6) Their recognition of his office is most complete. The language is decisive in two respects: it represents this recognition *first* as thoroughly mutual, and *secondly* as admitting a perfect equality and independent position. (7) At the same time a separate sphere of labour is assigned to each: the one are to preach to the heathen, the other to the Circumcision. There is no implication, as some have represented, that the Gospel preached to the Gentile would differ from the Gospel preached to the Jew. Such an idea is alien to the whole spirit of the passage. Lastly, (8) Notwithstanding their distinct spheres of work, St Paul is requested by the Apostles of the Circumcision to collect the alms of the Gentiles for the poor brethren of Judæa, and to this request he responds cordially.

With the exception of the incident at Antioch, which will be considered presently, the Epistle to the Galatians contains nothing more bearing directly on the relations between St Paul and the Apostles of the Circumcision. Other special references are found in the Epistles to the Corinthians, but none elsewhere. These notices, slight though they are, accord with the view presented by the Galatian letter. St Paul indeed says more than once that he is 'not a whit behind the very chiefest Apostles' (τῶν ὑπερλίαν ἀποστόλων, 2 Cor. xi. 5, xii. 11), and there is in the original a slight touch of irony which disappears in the translation: but the irony loses its point unless the exclusive preference of the elder Apostles is regarded as an exaggeration of substantial claims. Elsewhere St Paul speaks of Cephas and the Lord's brethren as exercising an apostolic privilege which belonged also to himself and Barnabas (1 Cor. ix. 5), of Cephas and James as witnesses of the Lord's resurrection like himself (1 Cor. xv. 5, 7). In the last passage he calls himself (with evident reference to the elder Apostles who are

References to them in other epistles.

mentioned immediately before) 'the least of the Apostles, who is not worthy to be called an Apostle.' In rebuking the dissensions at Corinth, he treats the name of Cephas with a delicate courtesy and respect which has almost escaped notice. When he comes to argue the question, he at once drops the name of St Peter; 'While one saith, I am of Paul, and another, I am of Apóllos, are ye not carnal? What then is Apollos, and what is Paul?' Apollos was so closely connected with him (1 Cor. xvi. 12), that he could use his name without fear of misapprehension. But in speaking of Cephas he had to observe more caution: certain persons persisted in regarding St Peter as the head of a rival party, and therefore he is careful to avoid any seeming depreciation of his brother Apostle.

No antagonism between St Paul and the other Apostles.

In all this there is nothing inconsistent with the character of St Paul as drawn in the Acts, nothing certainly which represents him as he was represented by extreme partisans in ancient times, by Ebionites on the one hand and Marcionites on the other, and as he has been represented of late by a certain school of critics, in a position of antagonism to the chief Apostles of the Circumcision. I shall next examine the scriptural notices and traditional representations of these three.

St Peter claimed by Ebionites

1. The author of the Clementine Homilies makes ST PETER the mouth-piece of his own Ebionite views. In the prefatory letter of Peter to James which, though possibly the work of another author, represents the same sentiments, the Apostle complains that he has been misrepresented as holding that the law was abolished but fearing to preach this doctrine openly. 'Far be it,' he adds, 'for to act so is to oppose the law of God which was spoken by Moses and to which our Lord bare witness that it should abide for ever. For thus He said, *Heaven and earth shall pass away: one jot or one tittle shall in no wise pass away from the law.* And this He said that all things might be fulfilled. Yet these persons professing to give my sentiments (τὸν ἐμὸν νοῦν ἐπαγγελλόμενοι) I know not how, attempt to interpret the words that they have heard from me more

cleverly (φρονιμώτερον) than myself who spoke them, telling their pupils that this is my meaning (φρόνημα), though it never once entered into my mind (ὃ ἐγὼ οὐδὲ ἐνεθυμήθην). But if they dare to tell such falsehoods of me while I am still alive, how much more will those who come after me venture to do it when I am gone (§ 2).' It has been held by some modern critics that the words thus put into the Apostle's mouth are quite in character; that St Peter did maintain the perpetuity of the law; and that therefore the traditional account which has pervaded Catholic Christendom from the writing of the Acts to the present day gives an essentially false view of the Apostle.

I think the words quoted will strike most readers as betraying a consciousness on the part of the writer that he is treading on hollow and dangerous ground. But without insisting on this, it is important to observe that the sanction of this venerated name was claimed by other sectarians of opposite opinions. and also by opposite sects. Basilides (about A.D. 130), the famous Gnostic teacher, announced that he had been instructed by one Glaucias an 'interpreter' of St Peter[1]. An early apocryphal writing moreover, which should probably be assigned to the beginning of the second century and which expressed strong antijudaic views[2], was

[1] Clem. Alex. *Strom.* vii. p. 898, Potter.

[2] On this work, the κήρυγμα Πέτρου, see Schwegler *Nachap. Zeit.* II. p. 30 sq. Its opposition to Judaism appears in an extant fragment preserved in Clem. Alex. *Strom.* vi. p. 760, μηδὲ κατὰ Ἰουδαίους σέβεσθε...ὥστε καὶ ὑμεῖς ὁσίως καὶ δικαίως μανθάνοντες ἃ παραδίδομεν ὑμῖν φυλάσσεσθε, καινῶς τὸν Θεὸν διὰ τοῦ Χριστοῦ σεβόμενοι· εὕρομεν γὰρ ἐν ταῖς γραφαῖς καθὼς ὁ Κύριος λέγει· Ἰδοὺ διατίθεμαι ὑμῖν καινὴν διαθήκην κ.τ.λ. The fragments of this work are collected by Grabe, *Spicil.* I. p. 62 sq. It was made use of by Heracleon the Valentinian, and is quoted more than once, apparently as genuine, by Clement of Alexandria.

The identity of this work with the *Praedicatio Pauli* quoted in the treatise *De Baptismo Haereticorum* printed among Cyprian's works (App. p. 30, Fell) seems to me very doubtful, though maintained by several able critics. The passage there quoted is strangely misinterpreted by Baur (*Christenthum* p. 53). I give his words, lest I should have misunderstood him: 'Auch die kirchliche Sage, welche die Apostel wieder zusammenbrachte, lässt erst am Ende nach einer langen Zeit der Trennung die gegenseitige Anerkennung zu Stande kommen. Post tanta tempora, hiess es in der Prædicatio Pauli in der Stelle, welche sich in der Cyprian's Werken angehängten

entitled the 'Preaching of Peter.' I do not see why these assertions have not as great a claim to a hearing as the opposite statement of the Ebionite writer. They are probably earlier; and in one case at least we have more tangible evidence than the irresponsible venture of an anonymous romance writer. The probable inference however from such conflicting statements would be, that St Peter's true position was somewhere between the two extremes.

But we are not to look for trustworthy information from such sources as these. If we wish to learn the Apostle's real attitude in the conflict between Jewish and Gentile converts, the one fragmentary notice in the Epistle to the Galatians will reveal more than all the distorted and interested accounts of later ages: 'But when Cephas came to Antioch I withstood him to the face, for he was condemned (his conduct condemned itself). For before that certain came from James, he did eat with the Gentiles, but when they came, he withdrew and separated himself, fearing those of the circumcision: and the rest of the Jews also dissembled with him, so that even Barnabas was carried away with their dissimulation ($\sigma\upsilon\nu\alpha\pi\acute{\eta}\chi\theta\eta$ $\alpha\grave{\upsilon}\tau\hat{\omega}\nu$ $\tau\hat{\eta}$ $\dot{\upsilon}\pi\omicron\kappa\rho\acute{\iota}\sigma\epsilon\iota$). But when I saw that they walked not straight according to the truth of the Gospel, I said unto Cephas before all, If thou, being born a Jew ('Ἰουδαῖος ὑπάρχων), livest after the manner of the Gentiles and not after the

St Paul's notice of the occurrence at Antioch.

Schrift de rebaptismate erhalten hat (Cypr. *Opp.* ed. Baluz. s. 365 f.), Petrum et Paulum post conlationem evangelii in Jerusalem et mutuam cogitationem [?] et altercationem et rerum agendarum dispositionem postremo in urbe, quasi tunc primum, invicem sibi esse cognitos.' Baur thus treats the comment of the writer as if it were part of the quotation. In this treatise the writer denounces the *Praedicatio Pauli* as maintaining 'adulterinum, imo internecinum baptisma'; in order to invalidate its authority, he proceeds to show its thoroughly unhistorical character; and among other instances he alleges the fact that it makes St Peter and St Paul meet in Rome as if for the first time, forgetting all about the congress at Jerusalem, the collision at Antioch, and so forth. Schwegler takes the correct view of the passage, II. p. 32.

Other early apocryphal works attributed to the chief Apostle of the Circumcision are the Gospel, the Acts, and the Apocalypse of Peter; but our information respecting these is too scanty to throw much light on the present question: on the Gospel of Peter see above, p. 27.

manner of the Jews, how compellest thou the Gentiles to live like the Jews?' etc.' (ii. 11—14).

Now the point of St Paul's rebuke is plainly this: that in sanctioning the Jewish feeling which regarded eating with the Gentiles as an unclean thing, St Peter was *untrue to his principles*, was acting hypocritically and from fear. In the argument which follows he assumes that it was the normal practice of Peter to live as a Gentile (ἐθνικῶς ζῆς and not ἐθνικῶς ἔζης), in other words, to mix freely with the Gentiles, to eat with them, and therefore to disregard the distinction of things clean and unclean: and he argues on the glaring inconsistency and unfairness that Cephas should claim this liberty himself though not born to it, and yet by hypocritical compliance with the Jews should practically force the ritual law on the Gentiles and deprive them of a freedom which was their natural right[1].

How St Peter came to hold these liberal principles, so entirely opposed to the narrow traditions of his age and country, is explained by an incident narrated in the Acts. He was at one time as rigid and as scrupulous as the most bigoted of his countrymen: 'nothing common or unclean had at any time entered into his mouth' (x. 14, xi. 8). Suddenly a light bursts in upon the darkness of his religious convictions. He is taught by a vision 'not to call any man common or unclean' (x. 28). His sudden change scandalizes the Jewish

It accords with an incident related in the Acts

---

[1] I do not see how this conclusion can be resisted. According to the Tübingen view of St Peter's position, his hypocrisy or dissimulation must have consisted not in withdrawing from, but in holding intercourse with the Gentiles; but this is not the view of St Paul on any natural interpretation of his words; and certainly the Ebionite writer already quoted (p. 110) did not so understand his meaning. Schwegler (I. p. 129) explains συνυπεκρίθησαν αὐτῷ 'were hypocritical enough to side with him,' thus forcing the expression itself and severing it from the context; but even then he is obliged to acquit the other Jewish Christians at Antioch of Ebionism. Hilgenfeld (*Galater* p. 61 sq) discards Schwegler's interpretation and explains ὑπόκρισις of the self-contradiction, the unconscious inconsistency of Jewish Christian or Ebionite principles: but inconsistency is not dissimulation or hypocrisy, and this interpretation, like the former, loses sight of the context which denounces St Peter for abandoning a certain line of conduct *from timidity*.

L. 8

brethren: but he explains and for the moment at least convinces (xi. 18).

and with his character as given in the Gospels.

And if his normal principles are explained by the narrative of the Acts, his exceptional departure from them is illustrated by his character as it appears in the Gospels. The occasional timidity and weakness of St Peter will be judged most harshly by those who have never themselves felt the agony of a great moral crisis, when not their own ease and comfort only, which is a small thing, but the spiritual welfare of others seems to clamour for a surrender of their principles. His true nobleness—his fiery zeal and overflowing love and abandoned self-devotion—will be appreciated most fully by spirits which can claim some kindred however remote with his spirit.

Thus the fragmentary notices in the Gospels, the Acts, and the Epistles of St Paul, combine to form a harmonious portrait of a character, not consistent indeed, but—to use Aristotle's significant phrase—consistently inconsistent (ὁμαλῶς ἀνώμαλον);

The First Epistle of St Peter

and this is a much safer criterion of truth. But there is yet another source of information to be considered—his own letters. If the deficiency of external evidence forbids the use of the Second Epistle in controversy, the First labours under no such disabilities; for very few of the apostolical writings are better attested.

shows the influence of St Paul,

To this epistle indeed it has been objected that it bears too manifest traces of Pauline influence to be the genuine writing of St Peter. The objection however seems to overlook two important considerations. *First.* If we consider the prominent part borne by St Paul as the chief preacher of Christianity in countries Hellenic by race or by adoption; if we remember further that his writings were probably the first which clothed the truths of the Gospel and the aspirations of the Church in the language of Greece; we shall hardly hesitate to allow that he 'had a great influence in moulding this language for Christian purposes, and that those who afterwards trod in his footsteps could hardly depart much from the idiom thus moulded[1].'

[1] Schleiermacher, *Einl. ins N. T.* p. 402 sq.

ST PAUL AND THE THREE. 115

Secondly. It is begging the whole question to assume that St Peter derived nothing from the influence of the Apostle of the Gentiles. The one was essentially a character to impress, the other to be impressed. His superior in intellectual culture, in breadth of sympathy, and in knowledge of men, his equal in love and zeal for Christ, St Paul must have made his influence felt on the frank and enthusiastic temperament of the elder Apostle. The weighty spiritual maxims thrown out during the dispute at Antioch for instance would sink deep into his heart[1]; and taking into account the many occasions when either by his writings or by personal intercourse St Paul's influence would be communicated, we can hardly doubt that the whole effect was great.

But after all the epistle bears the stamp of an individual mind quite independent of this foreign element. The substratum of the thoughts is the writer's own. Its individuality indeed appears more in the contemplation of the life and sufferings of Christ, in the view taken of the relations between the believer and the world around, in the realisation of the promises made to the chosen people of old, in the pervading sense of a regenerate life and the reiterated hope of a glorious advent, than in any special development of doctrine: but it would be difficult to give any reason why, prior to experience, we should have expected it to be otherwise. *but bears the individual stamp*

Altogether the epistle is anything but Ebionite. Not only is the 'law' never once named, but there is no allusion to formal ordinances of any kind. The writer indeed is essentially an Israelite, but he is an Israelite after a Christian type. When he speaks of the truths of the Gospel, he speaks of them through the forms of the older dispensation: he alludes again and again to the ransom of Christ's death, but the image present to his *of a mind Hebrew but not Ebionite.*

---

[1] See 1 Pet. ii. 24 τὰς ἁμαρτίας ἡμῶν αὐτὸς ἀνήνεγκεν ἐν τῷ σώματι αὐτοῦ ἐπὶ τὸ ξύλον, ἵνα ταῖς ἁμαρτίαις ἀπογενόμενοι τῇ δικαιοσύνῃ ζήσωμεν. This is the most striking instance which the epistle exhibits of coincidence with St Paul's doctrinal teaching (though there are occasionally strong resemblances of language). With it compare Gal. ii. 20 Χριστῷ συνεσταύρωμαι· ζῶ δὲ οὐκέτι ἐγώ, ζῇ δὲ ἐν ἐμοὶ Χριστὸς κ.τ.λ.

8—2

mind is the paschal lamb without spot or blemish; he addresses himself to Gentile converts, but he transfers to them the cherished titles of the covenant race; they are the true 'dispersion' (i. 1); they are 'a chosen generation, a royal priesthood, a holy nation, a peculiar people' (ii. 9). The believer in Christ is the Israelite; the unbeliever the Gentile (ii. 12).

Its relation to St Paul and St James. Corresponding to the position of St Peter as he appears in the Apostolic history, this epistle in its language and tone occupies a place midway between the writings of St James and St Paul. With St James it dwells earnestly on the old: with St Paul it expands to the comprehension of the new. In its denunciation of luxurious wealth, in its commendation of the simple and homely virtues, in its fond reference to past examples in Jewish history for imitation or warning, it recalls the tone of the head of the Hebrew Church: in its conception of the grace of God, of the ransom of Christ's death, of the wide purpose of the Gospel, it approaches to the language of the Apostle of the Gentiles.

Mark and Silvanus. With St Paul too the writer links himself by the mention of two names, both Christians of the Circumcision, and both companions of the Gentile Apostle; Mark who, having accompanied him on his first missionary tour, after some years of alienation is found by his side once more (Col. iv. 10), and Silvanus who shared with him the labours and perils of planting the Gospel in Europe. Silvanus is the bearer or the amanuensis of St Peter's letter; Mark joins in the salutations (v. 12, 13).

St Peter and St Paul associated in early tradition. Thus the Churches of the next generation, which were likely to be well informed, delighted to unite the names of the two leading Apostles as the greatest teachers of the Gospel, the brightest examples of Christian life. At Rome probably, at Antioch certainly, both these Apostles were personally known. We have the witness of the one Church in Clement; of the *Rome.* other in Ignatius. The former classes them together as the two 'noble ensamples of his own generation,' 'the greatest and most righteous pillars' of the Church, who 'for hatred and envy *Antioch.* were persecuted even unto death' (§ 5). The latter will not venture to command the Christians of Rome, 'as Peter and Paul did; they were Apostles, he a convict; they were free, he a slave to that very hour[1].' Clement wrote before the close of the first century, Ignatius at the beginning of the second. It seems probable that both these fathers had conversed with one or other of the two Apostles. Besides Antioch and Rome, the names of St Peter and St Paul appear together also in connexion with the Church of Corinth (1 Cor. iii. 22). This church again has not withheld her voice, though here the later date of her testimony detracts somewhat from its value[2], Dionysius bishop of Corinth, writing to the Romans during the episcopate of Soter (c. 166—174), claims kindred with them on the ground that both churches alike had profited by the joint instruction of St Peter and St Paul[3].

Corinth.

But though the essential unity of these two Apostles is thus recognised by different branches of the Catholic Church, a disposition to sever them seems early to have manifested itself in some quarters. Even during their own lifetime the religious agitators at Corinth would have placed them in spite of themselves at the head of rival parties. And when death had removed all fear of contradiction, extreme partisans boldly claimed the sanction of the one or the other for their own views. The precursors of the Ebionites misrepresented the Israelite sympathies of St Peter, as if he had himself striven to put a yoke upon the neck of the Gentiles which neither their

Misrepresentations of extreme parties.

---

[1] *Rom.* 4. The words οὐχ ὡς Πέτρος καὶ Παῦλος διατάσσομαι ὑμῖν gain force, as addressed to the Romans, if we suppose both Apostles to have preached in Rome.

[2] The language of Clement however implicitly contains the testimony of this church at an earlier date: for he assumes the acquiescence of the Corinthians when he mentions both Apostles as of equal authority (§§ 5, 47).

[3] In Euseb. *H. E.* ii. 25 τὴν ἀπὸ Πέτρου καὶ Παύλου φυτείαν γενηθεῖσαν Ῥωμαίων τε καὶ Κορινθίων συνεκεράσατε.

καὶ γὰρ ἄμφω καὶ εἰς τὴν ἡμετέραν Κόρινθον φοιτήσαντες ἡμᾶς ὁμοίως ἐδίδαξαν, ὁμοίως δὲ καὶ εἰς τὴν Ἰταλίαν ὁμόσε διδάξαντες ἐμαρτύρησαν κατὰ τὸν αὐτὸν καιρόν. All the MSS and the Syriac version here have φυτεύσαντες; but φοιτήσαντες is read by Georgius Syncellus, and Rufinus has 'adventantes'; the sense too seems to require it. In any case it is hardly a safe inference that Dionysius erroneously supposed the Churches of Rome and Corinth to have been *founded* by both Apostles jointly.

fathers nor they were able to bear. The precursors of Marcionism exaggerated the antagonism of St Paul to the Mosaic ritual, as if he had indeed held the law to be sin and the commandment neither holy nor just nor good. It seems to have been a subsidiary aim of St Luke's narrative, which must have been written not many years after the martyrdom of both Apostles, to show that this growing tendency was false, and that in their life, as in their death, they were not divided. A rough parallelism between the career of the two reveals itself in the narrative when carefully examined. Recent criticism has laid much stress on this 'conciliatory' purpose of the Acts, as if it were fatal to the credit of the narrative. But denying the inference we may concede the fact, and the very concession draws its sting. Such a purpose is at least as likely to have been entertained by a writer, if the two Apostles were essentially united, as if they were not. The truth or falsehood of the account must be determined on other grounds.

Conciliatory aim of the Acts.

2. While St Peter was claimed as their leader by the Judaizers, no such liberty seems to have been taken with the name of ST JOHN[1]. Long settled in an important Gentile city, surrounded by a numerous school of disciples, still living at the dawn of the second century, he must have secured for his teaching such notoriety as protected it from gross misrepresentation.

St John not claimed by Ebionites.

His last act recorded in St Luke's narrative is a visit to the newly founded Churches of Samaria, in company with St Peter (viii. 14). He thus stamps with his approval the first move-

His position in the apostolic history.

[1] In the portion of the first book of the Recognitions, which seems to have been taken from the 'Ascents of James,' the sons of Zebedee are introduced with the rest of the Twelve confuting heresies, but the sentiments attributed to them are in no way Ebionite (i. 57). It is this work perhaps to which Epiphanius refers (xxx. 23), for his notice does not imply anything more than a casual introduction of St John's name in their writings. In another passage Epiphanius attributes to the sons of Zebedee the same ascetic practices which distinguished James the Lord's brother (*Haer*. lxxviii. 13); and this account he perhaps derived from some Essene Ebionite source. But I do not know that they ever claimed St John in the same way as they claimed St Peter and St James.

ment of the Church in its liberal progress. From the silence of both St Paul and St Luke it may be inferred that he took no very prominent part in the disputes about the Mosaic law. Only at the close of the conferences we find him together with St Peter and St James recognising the authority and work of St Paul, and thus giving another guarantee of his desire to advance the liberties of the Church. This is the only passage where he is mentioned in St Paul's Epistles. Yet it seems probable that though he did not actually participate in the public discussions, his unseen influence was exerted to promote the result. As in the earliest days of the Church, so now we may imagine him ever at St Peter's side, his faithful colleague and wise counsellor, not forward and demonstrative, but most powerful in private, pouring into the receptive heart of the elder Apostle the lessons of his own inward experience, drawn from close personal intercourse and constant spiritual communion with his Lord.

At length the hidden fires of his nature burst out into flame. When St Peter and St Paul have ended their labours, the more active career of St John is just beginning. If it had been their task to organize and extend the Church, to remove her barriers and to advance her liberties, it is his special province to build up and complete her theology. The most probable chronology makes his withdrawal from Palestine to Asia Minor coincide very nearly with the martyrdom of these two Apostles, who have guided the Church through her first storms and led her to her earliest victories. This epoch divides his life into two distinct periods: hitherto he has lived as a Jew among Jews; henceforth he will be as a Gentile among Gentiles. The writings of St John in the Canon probably mark the close of each period. The Apocalypse winds up his career in the Church of the Circumcision; the Gospel and the Epistles are the crowning result of a long residence in the heart of Gentile Christendom. *His life in relation to his writings.*

Both the one and the other contrast strongly with the leading features of Ebionite doctrine; and this fact alone would

120   ST PAUL AND THE THREE.

deter the Judaizers from claiming the sanction of a name so revered.

The Apocalypse Hebrew in its imagery,   Of all the writings of the New Testament the APOCALYPSE is most thoroughly Jewish in its language and imagery. The whole book is saturated with illustrations from the Old Testament. It speaks not the language of Paul, but of Isaiah and Ezekiel and Daniel. Its tone may be well described by an expression borrowed from the book itself; 'the testimony of Jesus is the spirit of prophecy' (xix. 10). The doctrine of Balaam, the whoredoms of Jezebel, the song of Moses, the lion of Judah, the key of David, the great river Euphrates, the great city Babylon, Sodom and Egypt, Gog and Magog, these and similar expressions are but the more striking instances of an imagery with which the Apocalypse teems. Nor are the symbols derived solely from the canonical Scriptures; in the picture of the New Jerusalem the inspired Apostle has borrowed many touches from the creations of rabbinical fancy. Up to this point the Apocalypse is completely Jewish and might have been Ebionite.

but not Ebionite in doctrine.   But the same framing serves only to bring out more strongly the contrast between the pictures themselves. The two distinctive features of Ebionism, its mean estimate of the person of Christ and its extravagant exaltation of the Mosaic law, are opposed alike to the spirit and language of St John.

The Christ.   It might have been expected that the beloved disciple, who had leaned on his Master's bosom, would have dwelt with fond preference on the humanity of our Lord: yet in none of the New Testament writings, not even in the Epistles of St Paul, do we find a more express recognition of His divine power and majesty. He is 'the Amen, the faithful and true witness, the beginning (the source) of the creation of God' (iii. 14). 'Blessing, honour, glory, and power' are ascribed not 'to Him that sitteth on the throne' only, but 'to the Lamb for ever and ever' (v. 13). His name is 'the Word of God' (xix. 13). Therefore He claims the titles and attributes of Deity. He declares Himself 'the Alpha and Omega, the first and last, the beginning and the end' (xxii. 13; comp. i. 8). He is 'the Lord of lords and the King of kings' (xvii. 14, xix. 16). And so too the Ebionite reverence for the law as still binding has no place in the Apocalypse. The word does not occur from beginning to end, nor is there a single allusion to its ceremonial as an abiding ordinance. The Paschal Lamb indeed is ever present to St John's thought; but with him it signifies not the sacrifice offered in every Jewish home year by year, but the Christ who once 'was slain, and hath redeemed us to God by His blood out of every kindred and tongue and people and nation' (v. 9). All this is very remarkable, since there is every reason to believe that up to this time St John had in practice observed the Jewish law[1]. To him however it was only a national custom

The law.

---

[1] Certain traditions of St John's residence at Ephesus, illustrating his relation to the Mosaic law, deserve notice here. They are given by Polycrates who was himself bishop of Ephesus (Euseb. *H. E.* v. 24). Writing to pope Victor, probably in the last decade of the second century, he mentions that he 'numbers (ἔχων) sixty-five years in the Lord' (whether he refers to the date of his birth or of his conversion, is uncertain, but the former seems more probable), and that he has had seven relations bishops, whose tradition he follows. We are thus carried back to a very early date. The two statements with which we are concerned are these. (1) St John celebrated the Paschal day on the 14th of the month, coinciding with the Jewish passover. It seems to me, as I have said already (see p. 101), that there is no good ground for questioning this tradition. The institution of such an annual celebration by this Apostle derives light from the many references to the Paschal Lamb in the Apocalypse; and in the first instance it would seem most natural to celebrate it on the exact anniversary of the Passover. It is more questionable whether the Roman and other Churches, whose usage has passed into the law of Christendom, had really the apostolic sanction which they vaguely asserted for celebrating it always on the Friday. This usage, if not quite so obvious as the other, was not unnatural and probably was found much more convenient. (2) Polycrates says incidentally of St John that he was 'a priest wearing the mitre and a martyr and teacher (ὃς ἐγενήθη ἱερεὺς τὸ πέταλον πεφορεκὼς καὶ μάρτυς καὶ διδάσκαλος).' The reference in the πέταλον is doubtless to the metal plate on the high-priest's mitre, cf. Exod. xxviii. 36 πέταλον χρυσοῦν καθαρόν, comp. *Protevang.* c. 5 τὸ πέταλον τοῦ ἱερέως; but the meaning of Polycrates is far from clear. He has perhaps mistaken metaphor for matter of fact (see Stanley *Apostolical Age* p. 285); in like manner as the name Theophorus assumed by Ignatius gave rise to the later story that he was the child whom our Lord took in His arms and blessed. I think it probable however that the words as they stand in Polycrates are intended for a metaphor, since the short fragment which contains them has several figurative expressions almost, if not quite, as violent; e.g. μεγάλα στοιχεῖα κεκοίμηται (where στοιχεῖα means 'luminaries,' being used of the heavenly bodies); Μελίτωνα τὸν εὐνοῦχον (proba-

and not an universal obligation, only one of the many garbs in which religious worship might clothe itself, and not the essence of religious life. In itself circumcision is nothing, as uncircumcision also is nothing; and therefore he passes it over as if it were not. The distinction between Jew and Gentile has ceased; the middle wall of partition is broken down in Christ. If preserving the Jewish imagery which pervades the book, he records the sealing of twelve thousand from each tribe of Israel, his range of vision expands at once, and he sees before the throne 'a great multitude, which no man could number, of all nations and kindreds and peoples and tongues' (vii. 9). If he denounces the errors of heathen speculation, taking up their own watchword 'knowledge ($\gamma\nu\hat{\omega}\sigma\iota\varsigma$)' and retorting upon them that they *know* only 'the depths of Satan' (ii. 24)[1], on the other hand he condemns in similar language the bigotry of Jewish prejudice, denouncing the blasphemy of those 'who say they are Jews and are not, but are a synagogue of Satan' (ii. 9; comp. iii. 9).

bly a metaphor, as Rufinus translates it, 'propter regnum dei eunuchum'; see Matt. xix. 12 and comp. Athenag. *Suppl.* 33, 34, Clem. Alex. *Paed.* iii. 4, p. 269, *Strom.* iii. 1. p. 509 sq); τὸν μικρόν μου ἄνθρωπον ('my insignificance'; comp. Rom. vi. 6 ὁ παλαιὸς ἡμῶν ἄνθρωπος, 2 Cor. iv. 16 ὁ ἔξω ἡμῶν ἄνθρωπος, 1 Pet. iii. 4 ὁ κρυπτὸς τῆς καρδίας ἄνθρωπος). The whole passage is a very rude specimen of the florid 'Asiatic' style, which even in its higher forms Cicero condemns as suited only to the ears of a people wanting in polish and good taste ('minime politae minimeque elegantes,' *Orator*, 25) and which is described by another writer as κομπώδης καὶ φρυαγματίας καὶ κενοῦ γαυριάματος καὶ φιλοτιμίας ἀνωμάλου μεστός, Plut. *Vit. Anton.* 2; see Bernhardy *Griech. Litt.* i. p. 465. On the other hand it is possible—I think not probable—that St John did wear this decoration as an emblem of his Christian privileges; nor ought this view to cause any offence, as inconsistent with the spirituality of his character. If in Christ the use of external symbols is nothing, the avoidance of them is nothing also. But whether the statement of Polycrates be metaphor or matter of fact, its significance, as in the case of the Paschal celebration, is to be learnt from the Apostle's own language in the Apocalypse, where not only is great stress laid on the *priesthood* of the believers generally (i. 6, v. 10, xx. 6), but even the special privileges of the *highpriest* are bestowed on the victorious Christian (Rev. ii. 17, as explained by Züllig, Trench, and others: see Stanley l. c. p. 285; comp. Justin *Dial.* 116 ἀρχιερατικὸν τὸ ἀληθινὸν γένος ἐσμὲν τοῦ Θεοῦ, and see below, p. 218). The expression is a striking example of the lingering power not of Ebionite tenets but of Hebrew imagery.

[1] See above, p. 64, note 3.

A lapse of more than thirty years spent in the midst of a Gentile population will explain the contrasts of language and imagery between the Apocalypse and the later writings of St John, due allowance being made for the difference of subject[1]. The language and colouring of the Gospel and Epistles are no longer Hebrew; but so far as a Hebrew mind was capable of the transformation, Greek or rather Greco-Asiatic. The teaching of these latter writings it will be unnecessary to examine; for all, I believe, will allow their general agreement with the theology of St Paul; and it were a bold criticism which should discover in them any Ebionite tendencies. Only it seems to be often overlooked that the leading doctrinal ideas which they contain are anticipated in the Apocalypse. The passages which I have quoted from the latter relating to the divinity of Christ are a case in point: not only do they ascribe to our Lord the same majesty and power; but the very title 'the Word,' with which both the Gospel and the first Epistle open, is found here, though it occurs nowhere else in the New Testament. On the other hand, if the Apocalypse seems to assign a certain prerogative to the Jews, this is expressed equally in the sayings of the Gospel that Christ 'came to his own' (i. 11), and that 'Salvation is of the Jews' (iv. 22), as it is involved also in St Paul's maxim 'to the Jew first and then to the Gentile.' It is indeed rather a historical fact than a theological dogma. The difference between the earlier and the later writings of St John is not in the fundamental conception of the Gospel, but in the subject and treatment and language. The Apocalypse is not Ebionite, unless the Gospel and Epistles are Ebionite also.

The Gospel and Epistles contrasted and compared with the Apocalypse.

3. ST JAMES occupies a position very different from St

ST JAMES holds a local office.

---

[1] Owing to the difference of style, many critics have seen only the alternative of denying the apostolic authorship either of the Apocalypse or of the Gospel and Epistles. The considerations urged in the text seem sufficient to meet the difficulties, which are greatly increased if a late date is assigned to the Apocalypse. Writers of the Tübingen school reject the Gospel and Epistles but accept the Apocalypse. This book alone, if its apostolical authorship is conceded, seems to me to furnish an ample refutation of their peculiar views.

Peter or St John. If his importance to the brotherhood of Jerusalem was greater than theirs, it was far less to the world at large. In a foregoing essay I have attempted to show that he was not one of the Twelve. This result seems to me to have much more than a critical interest. Only when we have learnt to regard his office as purely local, shall we appreciate the traditional notices of his life or estimate truly his position in the conflict between Jewish and Gentile Christians.

Reasons for his appointment. A disbeliever in the Lord's mission to the very close of His earthly life, he was convinced, it would seem, by the appearance of the risen Jesus[1]. This interposition marked him out for some special work. Among a people who set a high value on advantages of race and blood, the Lord's brother would be more likely to win his way than a teacher who would claim no such connexion. In a state of religious feeling where scrupulous attention to outward forms was held to be a condition of favour with God, one who was a strict observer of the law, if not a rigid ascetic, might hope to obtain a hearing which would be denied to men of less austere lives and wider experiences. These considerations would lead to his selection as the ruler of the mother Church. The persecution of Herod which obliged the Twelve to seek safety in flight would naturally be the signal for the appointment of a resident head. At all events it is at this crisis that James appears for the first time with his presbytery in a position though not identical with, yet so far resembling, the 'bishop' of later times, that we may without much violence to language give him this title (Acts xii. 17, xxi. 18).

His allegiance to the law. As the local representative then of the Church of the Circumcision we must consider him. To one holding this position the law must have worn a very different aspect from that which it wore to St Peter or St John or St Paul. While they were required to become 'all things to all men,' he was required only to be 'a Jew to the Jews.' No troublesome questions of conflicting duties, such as entangled St Peter at

[1] See above, p. 17.

Antioch, need perplex him. Under the law he must live and die. His surname of the Just[1] is a witness to his rigid observance of the Mosaic ritual. A remarkable notice in the Acts shows how he identified himself in all external usages with those 'many thousands of Jews which believed and were all zealous of the law' (xxi. 20). And a later tradition, somewhat distorted indeed but perhaps in this one point substantially true, related how by his rigid life and strict integrity he had won the respect of the whole Jewish people[2].

A strict observer of the law he doubtless was; but whether to this he added a rigorous asceticism, may fairly be questioned. The account to which I have just referred, the tradition preserved in Hegesippus, represents him as observing many formalities not enjoined in the Mosaic ritual. 'He was holy,' says the writer, 'from his mother's womb. He drank no wine nor strong drink, neither did he eat flesh. No razor ever touched his head; he did not anoint himself with oil; he did not use the bath. He alone was allowed to enter into the holy place (εἰς τὰ ἅγια). For he wore no wool, but only fine linen. And he would enter into the temple (ναόν) alone, and be found there kneeling on his knees and asking forgiveness for the people, so that his knees grew hard like a camel's knees, because he was ever upon them worshipping God and asking forgiveness for the people.' There is much in this account which cannot be true: the assigning to him a privilege which was confined to the high-priest alone, while it is entangled with the rest of the narrative, is plainly false, and can only have been started when a new generation had grown up which knew nothing of the temple services[3]. Moreover the account of his

The account of Hegesippus not trustworthy.

---

[1] In the account of Hegesippus, referred to in the following note, ὁ δίκαιος 'Justus' is used almost as a proper name. Two later bishops of Jerusalem in the early part of the second century also bear the name 'Justus' (Euseb. *H. E.* iv. 5), either in memory of their predecessor or in token of their own rigid lives: compare also Acts i. 23, xviii. 7, Col. iv. 11 (with the note).

[2] Hegesippus in Euseb. *H. E.* ii. 23.

[3] It is perhaps to be explained like the similar account of St John: see above, p. 121, note 1. Compare Stanley *Apostolical Age* p. 324. Epiphanius

testimony and death, which follows, not only contradicts the brief contemporary notice of Josephus[1], but is in itself so melodramatic and so full of high improbabilities, that it must throw discredit on the whole context[2].

(*Haer.* lxxviii. 14) makes the same statement of St James which Polycrates does of St John, πέταλον ἐπὶ τῆς κεφαλῆς ἐφόρεσε.

[1] Josephus (*Antiq.* xx. 9. 1) relates that in the interregnum between the death of Festus and the arrival of Albinus, the high-priest Ananus the younger, who belonged to the sect of the Sadducees (notorious for their severity in judicial matters), considering this a favourable opportunity καθίζει συνέδριον κριτῶν, καὶ παραγαγὼν εἰς αὐτὸ τὸν ἀδελφὸν Ἰησοῦ τοῦ λεγομένου Χριστοῦ, Ἰάκωβος ὄνομα αὐτῷ, καί τινας ἑτέρους, ὡς παρανομησάντων κατηγορίαν ποιησάμενος παρέδωκε λευσθησομένους. This notice is wholly irreconcilable with the account of Hegesippus. Yet it is probable in itself (which the account of Hegesippus is not), and is such as Josephus might be expected to write if he alluded to the matter at all. His stolid silence about Christianity elsewhere cannot be owing to ignorance, for a sect which had been singled out years before he wrote as a mark for imperial vengeance at Rome must have been only too well known in Judæa. On the other hand, if the passage had been a Christian interpolation, the notice of James would have been more laudatory, as is actually the case in the spurious passage of Josephus read by Origen and Eusebius (*H. E.* ii. 23, see above, p. 68, note 2), but not found in existing copies. On these grounds I do not hesitate to prefer the account in Josephus to that of Hegesippus. This is the opinion of Neander (*Planting* I. p. 367, Eng. Trans.), of Ewald (*Geschichte* VI. p. 547), and of some few writers besides (so recently Gerlach *Römische Statthalter*

etc. p. 81, 1865): but the majority take the opposite view.

[2] The account is briefly this. Certain of the seven sects being brought by the preaching of James to confess Christ, the whole Jewish people are alarmed. To counteract the spread of the new doctrine, the scribes and Pharisees request James, as a man of acknowledged probity, to 'persuade the multitude not to go astray concerning Jesus.' In order that he may do this to more effect, on the day of the Passover they place him on the pinnacle (πτερύγιον) of the temple. Instead of denouncing Jesus however, he preaches Him. Finding their mistake, the scribes and Pharisees throw him down from the height; and as he is not killed by the fall, they stone him. Finally he is despatched by a fuller's club, praying meanwhile for his murderers. The improbability of the narrative will appear in this outline, but it is much increased by the details. The points of resemblance with the portion of the Recognitions conjectured to be taken from the 'Ascents of James' (see above, p. 87) are striking, and recent writers have called attention to these as showing that the narrative of Hegesippus was derived from a similar source (Uhlhorn *Clement.* p. 367, Ritschl p. 226 sq). May we not go a step farther and hazard the conjecture that the story of the martyrdom, to which Hegesippus is indebted, was the grand *finale* of these 'Ascents,' of which the earlier portions are preserved in the Recognitions? The Recognitions record how James with the Twelve refuted the Jewish sects: the account of Hegesippus makes the conversion of certain of these sects the starting-point of the persecution which

We are not therefore justified in laying much stress on this tradition. It is interesting as a phenomenon, but not trustworthy as a history. Still it is possible that James may have been a Nazarite, may have been a strict ascetic. Such a representation perhaps some will view with impatience, as unworthy an Apostle of Christ. But this is unreasonable. Christian devotion does not assume the same outward garb in all persons, and at all times; not the same in James as in Paul; not the same in mediæval as in protestant Christianity. In James, the Lord's brother, if this account be true, we have the prototype of those later saints, whose rigid life and formal devotion elicits, it may be, only the contempt of the world, but of whom nevertheless the world was not and is not worthy. *He was perhaps an ascetic.*

But to retrace our steps from this slippery path of tradition to firmer ground. The difference of position between St James and the other Apostles appears plainly in the narrative of the so-called Apostolic council in the Acts. It is Peter who proposes the emancipation of the Gentile converts from the law; James who suggests the restrictive clauses of the decree. It is *St James stands apart from the Twelve in the Acts,*

led to his martyrdom. In the Recognitions James is represented ascending the stairs which led up to the temple and addressing the people from these: in Hegesippus he is placed on the pinnacle of the temple whence he delivers his testimony. In the Recognitions he is thrown down the flight of steps and left as dead by his persecutors, but is taken up alive by the brethren; in Hegesippus he is hurled from the still loftier station, and this time his death is made sure. Thus the narrative of Hegesippus seems to preserve the consummation of his testimony and his sufferings, as treated in this romance, the last of a series of 'Ascents,' the first of these being embodied in the Recognitions.

If Hegesippus, himself no Ebionite, has borrowed these incidents (whether directly or indirectly, we cannot say) from an Ebionite source, he has done no more than Clement of Alexandria did after him (see above, p. 80), than Epiphanius, the scourge of heretics, does repeatedly. The religious romance seems to have been a favourite style of composition with the Essene Ebionites: and in the lack of authentic information relating to the Apostles, Catholic writers eagerly and unsuspiciously gathered incidents from writings of which they repudiated the doctrines. It is worthy of notice that though the *Essenes* are named among the sects in Hegesippus, they are not mentioned in the Recognitions; and that, while the Recognitions lay much stress on baptisms and washings (a cardinal doctrine of Essene Ebionism), this feature entirely disappears in the account of James given by Hegesippus.

Peter who echoes St Paul's sentiment that Jew and Gentile alike can hope to be saved only 'by the grace of the Lord Jesus'; James who speaks of Moses having them that preach him and being read in the synagogue every sabbath day. I cannot but regard this appropriateness of sentiment as a subsidiary proof of the authenticity of these speeches recorded by St Luke.

and in the Catholic Epistles.

And the same distinction extends also to their own writings. St Peter and St John, with a larger sphere of action and wider obligations, necessarily took up a neutral position with regard to the law, now carefully observing it at Jerusalem, now relaxing their observance among the Gentile converts. To St James on the other hand, mixing only with those to whom the Mosaic ordinances were the rule of life, the word and the thing have a higher importance. The neutrality of the former is reflected in the silence which pervades their writings, where 'law' is not once mentioned[1]. The respect of the latter appears in his differential use of the term, which he employs almost as a synonyme for 'Gospel[2].'

The Gospel a higher law.

But while so using the term 'law,' he nowhere implies that the Mosaic ritual is identical with or even a necessary part of Christianity. On the contrary he distinguishes the new dispensation as the perfect law, the law of liberty (i. 25, ii. 12), thus tacitly implying imperfection and bondage in the old. He assumes indeed that his readers pay allegiance to the Mosaic law (ii. 9, 10, iv. 11), and he accepts this condition without commenting upon it. But the mere ritual has no value in his eyes. When he refers to the Mosaic law, he refers to its moral, not to its ceremonial ordinances (ii. 8—11). The external service of the religionist who puts no moral restraint on himself, who will not exert himself for others, is pronounced deceitful and vain. The external service, the outward garb,

---

[1] As regards St John this is true only of the Epistles and the Apocalypse: in the Gospel the law is necessarily mentioned by way of narrative. In 1 Joh. iii. 4 it is said significantly ἡ ἁμαρτία ἐστὶν ἡ ἀνομία. In St Peter neither νόμος nor ἀνομία occurs.

[2] The words εὐαγγέλιον, εὐαγγελίζεσθαι, do not occur in St James.

the very ritual, of Christianity is a life of purity and love and self-devotion[1]. What its true essence, its inmost spirit, may be, the writer does not say, but leaves this to be inferred.

Thus, though with St Paul the new dispensation is the negation of law, with St James the perfection of law, the ideas underlying these contradictory forms of expression need not be essentially different. And this leads to the consideration of the language held by both Apostles on the subject of faith and works. *St James and St Paul.*

The real significance of St James's language, its true relation to the doctrine of St Paul, is determined by the view taken of the persons to whom the epistle is addressed. If it is intended to counteract any modification or perversion of St Paul's teaching, then there is, though not a plain contradiction, yet at all events a considerable divergency in the mode of dealing with the question by the two Apostles. I say the mode of dealing with the question, for antinomian inferences from his teaching are rebuked with even greater severity by St Paul himself than they are by St James[2]. If on the other hand the epistle is directed against an arrogant and barren orthodoxy, a Pharisaic self-satisfaction, to which the Churches of the Circumcision would be most exposed, then the case is considerably altered. The language of the Epistles to the Romans and Galatians at once suggests the former as the true account. But further consideration leads us to question our first rapid inference. Justification and faith seem to have been common terms, Abraham's faith a common example, in the Jewish schools[3]. This fact, if allowed, counteracts the *prima facie* evidence on the other side, and leaves us free to judge from the tenour of the epistle itself. Now, since in this very passage St James mentions as the object of their vaunted faith, not the funda- *Faith and works.*

---

[1] James i. 26, 27. Coleridge directs attention to the meaning of θρησκεία, and the consequent bearing of the text, in a well-known passage in *Aids to Reflection*, Introd. Aphor. 23. For the signification of θρησκεία both in the New Testament and elsewhere, as the 'cultus exterior,' see Trench *Synon.* § xlviii.

[2] e.g. Rom. vi. 15—23, 1 Cor. vi. 9—20, Gal. v. 13 sq.

[3] See *Galatians*, p. 164.

mental fact of the Gospel 'Thou believest that God raised Christ from the dead[1],' but the fundamental axiom of the law 'Thou believest that God is one[2]'; since moreover he elsewhere denounces the mere ritualist, telling him that his ritualism is nothing worth; since lastly the whole tone of the epistle recalls our Lord's denunciations of the scribes and Pharisees, and seems directed against a kindred spirit; it is reasonable to conclude that St James is denouncing not the moral aberrations of the professed disciple of St Paul (for with such he was not likely to be brought into close contact), but the self-complacent orthodoxy of the Pharisaic Christian, who, satisfied with the possession of a pure monotheism and vaunting his descent from Abraham, needed to be reminded not to neglect the still 'weightier matters' of a self-denying love. If this view be correct, the expressions of the two Apostles can hardly be compared, for they are speaking, as it were, a different language. But in either case we may acquiesce in the verdict of a recent able writer, more free than most men both from traditional and from reactionary prejudices, that in the teaching of the two Apostles 'there exists certainly a striking difference in the whole bent of mind, but no opposition of doctrine[3].'

Ebionite misrepresentations of St James explained. Thus the representation of St James in the canonical Scriptures differs from its Ebionite counterpart as the true portrait from the caricature. The James of the Clementines could not have acquiesced in the apostolic decree, nor could he have held out the right hand of fellowship to St Paul. On the other hand, the Ebionite picture was not drawn entirely from imagination. A scrupulous observer of the law, perhaps a rigid ascetic, partly from temper and habit, partly from the requirements of his position, he might, without any very direct or conscious falsification, appear to interested partisans of a later age to represent their own tenets, from which he differed less in the external forms of worship than in the vital principles of religion. More-

---

[1] Rom. x. 9.
[2] ii. 19. Comp. *Clem. Hom.* iii. 6 sq.
[3] Bleek (*Einl. in das N. T.* p. 550), who however considers that St James is writing against perversions of St Paul's teaching.

over during his lifetime he was compromised by those with whom his office associated him. In all revolutionary periods, whether of political or religious history, the leaders of the movement have found themselves unable to control the extravagances of their bigoted and short-sighted followers: and this great crisis of all was certainly not exempt from the common rule. St Paul is constantly checking and rebuking the excesses of those who professed to honour his name and to adopt his teaching: if we cannot state this of St James with equal confidence, it is because the sources of information are scantier.

Of the Judaizers who are denounced in St Paul's Epistles this much is certain; that they exalted the authority of the Apostles of the Circumcision: and that in some instances at least, as members of the mother Church, they had direct relations with James the Lord's brother. But when we attempt to define these relations, we are lost in a maze of conjecture. *His relations with the Judaizers.*

The Hebrew Christians whose arrival at Antioch caused the rupture between the Jewish and Gentile converts are related to have 'come from James' (Gal. ii. 12). Did they bear any commission from him? If so, did it relate to independent matters, or to this very question of eating with the Gentiles? It seems most natural to interpret this notice by the parallel case of the Pharisaic brethren, who had before troubled this same Antiochene Church, 'going forth' from the Apostles and insisting on circumcision and the observance of the law, though they 'gave them no orders' (Acts xv. 24). But on the least favourable supposition it amounts to this, that St James, though he had sanctioned the emancipation of the Gentiles from the law, was not prepared to welcome them as Israelites and admit them as such to full communion: that in fact he had not yet overcome scruples which even St Peter had only relinquished after many years and by a special revelation; in this, as in his recognition of Jesus as the Christ, moving more slowly than the Twelve. *Antioch.*

Turning from Antioch to Galatia, we meet with Judaic teachers who urged circumcision on the Gentile converts and, *Galatia.*

9—2

as the best means of weakening the authority of St Paul, asserted for the Apostles of the Circumcision the exclusive right of dictating to the Church. How great an abuse was thus made of the names of the Three, I trust the foregoing account has shown: yet here again the observance of the law by the Apostles of the Circumcision, especially by St James, would furnish a plausible argument to men who were unscrupulous enough to turn the occasional concessions of St Paul himself to the same account. But we are led to ask, Did these false teachers belong to the mother Church? had they any relation with James? is it possible that they had ever been personal disciples of the Lord Himself? There are some faint indications that such was the case; and, remembering that there was a Judas among the Twelve, we cannot set aside this supposition as impossible.

Corinth. In Corinth again we meet with false teachers of a similar stamp; whose opinions are less marked indeed than those of St Paul's Galatian antagonists, but whose connexion with the mother Church is more clearly indicated. It is doubtless among those who said 'I am of Peter, and I of Christ,' among the latter especially, that we are to seek the counterpart of the Galatian Judaizers[1]. To the latter class St Paul alludes again in the Second Epistle: these must have been the men who 'trusted to themselves that they were *of Christ*' (x. 7), who invaded another's sphere of labour and boasted of work which was ready to hand (x. 13—16), who were 'false apostles, crafty workers,

The two Judaizing parties.

---

[1] Several writers representing different schools have agreed in denying the existence of a 'Christ party.' Possibly the word 'party' may be too strong to describe what was rather a sentiment than an organization. But if admissible at all, I cannot see how, allowing that there were three parties, the existence of the fourth can be questioned. For (1) the four watchwords are co-ordinated, and there is no indication that ἐγὼ δὲ Χριστοῦ is to be isolated from the others and differently interpreted. (2) The remonstrance immediately following (μεμέρισται ὁ Χριστός) shows that the name of Christ, which ought to be common to all, had been made the badge of a party. (3) In 2 Cor. x. 7 the words εἴ τις πέποιθεν ἑαυτῷ Χριστοῦ εἶναι and the description which follows gain force and definiteness on this supposition. There is in fact more evidence for the existence of a party of Christ than there is of a party of Peter.

transforming themselves into apostles of Christ' (xi. 13), who 'commended themselves' (x. 12, 18), who vaunted their pure Israelite descent (xi. 21—23). It is noteworthy that this party of extreme Judaizers call themselves by the name not of James, but of Christ. This may perhaps be taken as a token that his concessions to Gentile liberty had shaken their confidence in his fidelity to the law. The leaders of this extreme party would appear to have seen Christ in the flesh: hence their watchword 'I am of Christ'; hence also St Paul's counter-claim that 'he was of Christ' also, and his unwilling boast that he had himself had visions and revelations of the Lord in abundance (xii. 1 sq). On the other hand, of the party of Cephas no distinct features are preserved; but the passage itself implies that they differed from the extreme Judaizers, and we may therefore conjecture that they took up a middle position with regard to the law, similar to that which was occupied later by the Nazarenes. In claiming Cephas as the head of their party they had probably neither more nor less ground than their rivals who sheltered themselves under the names of Apollos and of Paul.

Is it to these extreme Judaizers that St Paul alludes when he mentions 'certain persons' as 'needing letters of recommendation to the Corinthians and of recommendation from them' (2 Cor. iii. 1)? If so, by whom were these letters to Corinth given? By some half-Judaic, half-Christian brotherhood of the dispersion? By the mother Church of Jerusalem? By any of the primitive disciples? By James the Lord's brother himself? It is wisest to confess plainly that the facts are too scanty to supply an answer. We may well be content to rest on the broad and direct statements in the Acts and Epistles, which declare the relations between St James and St Paul. A habit of suspicious interpretation, which neglects plain facts and dwells on doubtful allusions, is as unhealthy in theological criticism as in social life, and not more conducive to truth. *Letters of commendation.*

Such incidental notices then, though they throw much light on the practical difficulties and entanglements of his position, reveal nothing or next to nothing of the true principles of *Inferences from these notices.*

St James. Only so long as we picture to ourselves an ideal standard of obedience, where the will of the ruler is the law of the subject, will such notices cause us perplexity. But, whether this be a healthy condition for any society or not, it is very far from representing the state of Christendom in the apostolic ages. If the Church had been a religious machine, if the Apostles had possessed absolute control over its working, if the manifold passions of men had been for once annihilated, if there had been no place for misgiving, prejudice, treachery, hatred, superstition, then the picture would have been very different. But then also the history of the first ages of the Gospel would have had no lessons for us. As it is, we may well take courage from the study. However great may be the theological differences and religious animosities of our own time, they are far surpassed in magnitude by the distractions of an age which, closing our eyes to facts, we are apt to invest with an ideal excellence. In the early Church was fulfilled, in its inward dissensions no less than in its outward sufferings, the Master's sad warning that He came 'not to send peace on earth, but a sword.'

III.

THE CHRISTIAN MINISTRY.

III.

THE CHRISTIAN MINISTRY.

THE kingdom of Christ, not being a kingdom of this world, is *Ideal of the Christian Church.* not limited by the restrictions which fetter other societies, political or religious. It is in the fullest sense free, comprehensive, universal. It displays this character, not only in the acceptance of all comers who seek admission, irrespective of race or caste or sex, but also in the instruction and treatment of those who are already its members. It has no sacred days or seasons, no special sanctuaries, because every time and every place alike are holy. Above all it has no sacerdotal system. It interposes no sacrificial tribe or class between God and man, by whose intervention alone God is reconciled and man forgiven. Each individual member holds personal communion with the Divine Head. To Him immediately he is responsible, and from Him directly he obtains pardon and draws strength.

It is most important that we should keep this ideal *Necessary qualification.* definitely in view, and I have therefore stated it as broadly as possible. Yet the broad statement, if allowed to stand alone, would suggest a false impression, or at least would convey only a half truth. It must be evident that no society of men could hold together without officers, without rules, without institutions of any kind; and the Church of Christ is not exempt from this universal law. The conception in short is strictly an *ideal*, which we must ever hold before our eyes,

The idea and the realization.

which should inspire and interpret ecclesiastical polity, but which nevertheless cannot supersede the necessary wants of human society, and, if crudely and hastily applied, will lead only to signal failure. As appointed days and set places are indispensable to her efficiency, so also the Church could not fulfil the purposes for which she exists, without rulers and teachers, without a ministry of reconciliation, in short, without an order of men who may in some sense be designated a priesthood. In this respect the ethics of Christianity present an analogy to the politics. Here also the ideal conception and the actual realization are incommensurate and in a manner contradictory. The Gospel is contrasted with the Law, as the spirit with the letter. Its ethical principle is not a code of positive ordinances, but conformity to a perfect exemplar, incorporation into a divine life. The distinction is most important and eminently fertile in practical results. Yet no man would dare to live without laying down more or less definite rules for his own guidance, without yielding obedience to law in some sense; and those who discard or attempt to discard all such aids are often farthest from the attainment of Christian perfection.

Special characteristic of Christianity.

This qualification is introduced here to deprecate any misunderstanding to which the opening statement, if left without compensation, would fairly be exposed. It will be time to enquire hereafter in what sense the Christian ministry may or may not be called a priesthood. But in attempting to investigate the historical development of this divine institution, no better starting-point suggested itself than the characteristic distinction of Christianity, as declared occasionally by the direct language but more frequently by the eloquent silence of the apostolic writings.

The Jewish priesthood.

For in this respect Christianity stands apart from all the older religions of the world. So far at least, the Mosaic dispensation did not differ from the religions of Egypt or Asia or Greece. Yet the sacerdotal system of the Old Testament possessed one important characteristic, which separated it from

THE CHRISTIAN MINISTRY. 139

heathen priesthoods and which deserves especial notice. The priestly tribe held this peculiar relation to God only as the *representatives* of the whole nation. As *delegates* of the people, they offered sacrifice and made atonement. The whole community is regarded as 'a kingdom of priests,' 'a holy nation.' When the sons of Levi are set apart, their consecration is distinctly stated to be due under the divine guidance not to any inherent sanctity or to any caste privilege, but to an act of delegation on the part of the entire people. The Levites are, so to speak, ordained by the whole congregation. 'The children of Israel,' it is said, 'shall put their hands upon the Levites[1].' The nation thus deputes to a single tribe the priestly functions which belong properly to itself as a whole.

The Christian idea therefore was the restitution of this immediate and direct relation with God, which was partly suspended but not abolished by the appointment of a sacerdotal tribe. The Levitical priesthood, like the Mosaic law, had served its temporary purpose. The period of childhood had passed, and the Church of God was now arrived at mature age. The covenant people resumed their sacerdotal functions. But the privileges of the covenant were no longer confined to the limits of a single nation. Every member of the human family was *potentially* a member of the Church, and, as such, a priest of God. *Its relation to the Christian priesthood.*

The influence of this idea on the moral and spiritual growth of the individual believer is too plain to require any comment; but its social effects may call for a passing remark. It will hardly be denied, I think, by those who have studied the history of modern civilization with attention, that this conception of the Christian Church has been mainly instrumental in the emancipation of the degraded and oppressed, in the removal of artificial barriers between class and class, and in the diffusion of a general philanthropy untrammelled by the fetters of party or race; in short, that to it mainly must be attributed the most important advantages which constitute the superiority of *Influence of the Christian ideal.*

[1] Num. viii. 10.

modern societies over ancient. Consciously or unconsciously, the idea of an universal priesthood, of the religious equality of all men, which, though not untaught before, was first embodied in the Church of Christ, has worked and is working untold blessings in political institutions and in social life. But the careful student will also observe that this idea has hitherto been very imperfectly apprehended; that throughout the history of the Church it has been struggling for recognition, at most times discerned in some of its aspects but at all times wholly ignored in others; and that therefore the actual results are a very inadequate measure of its efficacy, if only it could assume due prominence and were allowed free scope in action.

This then is the Christian ideal; a holy season extending the whole year round—a temple confined only by the limits of the habitable world—a priesthood coextensive with the human race.

Practical organization. Strict loyalty to this conception was not held incompatible with practical measures of organization. As the Church grew in numbers, as new and heterogeneous elements were added, as the early fervour of devotion cooled and strange forms of disorder sprang up, it became necessary to provide for the emergency by fixed rules and definite officers. The community of goods, by which the infant Church had attempted to give effect to the idea of an universal brotherhood, must very soon have been abandoned under the pressure of circumstances. The *Fixed days and places of worship;* celebration of the first day in the week at once, the institution of annual festivals afterwards, were seen to be necessary to stimulate and direct the devotion of the believers. The appointment of definite places of meeting in the earliest days, the erection of special buildings for worship at a later date, were found indispensable to the working of the Church. But the *but the idea kept in view.* Apostles never lost sight of the idea in their teaching. They proclaimed loudly that 'God dwelleth not in temples made by hands.' They indignantly denounced those who, 'observed days and months and seasons and years.' This language is not satisfied by supposing that they condemned only the temple-worship in the one case, that they reprobated only Jewish sabbaths and new moons in the other. It was against the false principle that they waged war; the principle which exalted the means into an end, and gave an absolute intrinsic value to subordinate aids and expedients. These aids and expedients, for his own sake and for the good of the society to which he belonged, a Christian could not afford to hold lightly or neglect. But they were no part of the *essence* of God's message to man in the Gospel: they must not be allowed to obscure the idea of Christian worship.

So it was also with the Christian priesthood. For communicating instruction and for preserving public order, for conducting religious worship and for dispensing social charities, it became necessary to appoint special officers. But the priestly functions and privileges of the Christian people are never regarded as transferred or even delegated to these officers. They are called stewards or messengers of God, servants or ministers of the Church, and the like: but the sacerdotal title is never once conferred upon them. The only priests under the Gospel, designated as such in the New Testament, are the saints, the members of the Christian brotherhood[1]. *Appointment of a ministry.*

As individuals, all Christians are priests alike. As members of a corporation, they have their several and distinct offices. The similitude of the human body, where each limb or organ performs its own functions, and the health and growth of the whole frame are promoted by the harmonious but separate working of every part, was chosen by St Paul to represent the progress and operation of the Church. In two passages, written at two different stages in his apostolic career, he briefly sums up the offices in the Church with reference to this image. *Two passages in St Paul relating thereto.*

---

[1] 1 Pet. ii. 5, 9, Apoc. i. 6, v. 10, xx. 6. The commentator Hilary has expressed this truth with much distinctness: 'In lege nascebantur sacerdotes ex genere Aaron Levitae: nunc autem omnes ex genere sunt sacerdotali, dicente Petro Apostolo, Quia estis genus regale et sacerdotale etc.' (Ambrosiast. on Ephes. iv. 12). The whole passage, to which I shall have occasion to refer again, contains a singularly appreciative account of the relation of the ministry to the congregation.

In the earlier[1] he enumerates 'first apostles, secondly prophets, thirdly teachers, then powers, then gifts of healing, helps, governments, kinds of tongues.' In the second passage[2] the list is briefer; 'some apostles, and some prophets, and some evangelists, and some pastors and teachers.' The earlier enumeration differs chiefly from the later in specifying distinctly certain miraculous powers, this being required by the Apostle's argument which is directed against an exaggerated estimate and abuse of such gifts. Neither list can have been intended to be exhaustive. In both alike the work of converting unbelievers and founding congregations holds the foremost place, while the permanent government and instruction of the several churches is kept in the background. This prominence was necessary in the earliest age of the Gospel. The apostles, prophets, evangelists, all range under the former head. But the permanent ministry, though lightly touched upon, is not forgotten; for under the designation of 'teachers, helps, governments' in the one passage, of 'pastors and teachers' in the other, these officers must be intended. Again in both passages alike it will be seen that great stress is laid on the work of the Spirit. The faculty of governing not less than the utterance of prophecy, the gift of healing not less than the gift of tongues, is an inspiration of the Holy Ghost. But on the other hand in both alike there is an entire silence about priestly functions: for the most exalted office in the Church, the highest gift of the Spirit, conveyed no sacerdotal right which was not enjoyed by the humblest member of the Christian community.

<small>They refer chiefly to the temporary ministry.</small>

<small>Growing importance of the permanent ministry.</small>

From the subordinate place, which it thus occupies in the notices of St Paul, the permanent ministry gradually emerged, as the Church assumed a more settled form, and the higher but temporary offices, such as the apostolate, fell away. This progressive growth and development of the ministry, until it arrived at its mature and normal state, it will be the object of the following pages to trace.

<small>Definition of terms necessary.</small>

But before proceeding further, some definition of terms is

[1] 1 Cor. xii. 28.   [2] Ephes. iv. 11.

necessary. On no subject has more serious error arisen from the confusion of language. The word 'priest' has two different senses. In the one it is a synonyme for presbyter or elder, and designates the minister who presides over and instructs a Christian congregation: in the other it is equivalent to the Latin sacerdos, the Greek ἱερεύς, or the Hebrew כהן, the offerer of sacrifices, who also performs other mediatorial offices between God and man. How the confusion between these two meanings has affected the history and theology of the Church, it will be instructive to consider in the sequel. At present it is sufficient to say that the word will be used throughout this essay, as it has been used hitherto, in the latter sense only, so that priestly will be equivalent to 'sacerdotal' or 'hieratic.' Etymologically indeed the other meaning is alone correct (for the words priest and presbyter are the same); but convenience will justify its restriction to this secondary and imported sense, since the English language supplies no other rendering of sacerdos or ἱερεύς. On the other hand, when the Christian elder is meant, the longer form 'presbyter' will be employed throughout. 'Priest' and 'presbyter.'

History seems to show decisively that before the middle of the second century each church or organized Christian community had its three orders of ministers, its bishop, its presbyters, and its deacons. On this point there cannot reasonably be two opinions. But at what time and under what circumstances this organization was matured, and to what extent our allegiance is due to it as an authoritative ordinance, are more difficult questions. Some have recognized in episcopacy an institution of divine origin, absolute and indispensable; others have represented it as destitute of all apostolic sanction and authority. Some again have sought for the archetype of the threefold ministry in the Aaronic priesthood; others in the arrangements of synagogue worship. In this clamour of antagonistic opinions history is obviously the sole upright, impartial referee; and the historical mode of treatment will Different views on the origin of the threefold ministry.

144   THE CHRISTIAN MINISTRY.

therefore be strictly adhered to in the following investigation. The doctrine in this instance at all events is involved in the history[1].

Ministry appointed to relieve the Apostles.

St Luke's narrative represents the Twelve Apostles in the earliest days as the sole directors and administrators of the Church. For the financial business of the infant community, not less than for its spiritual guidance, they alone are responsible. This state of things could not last long. By the rapid accession of numbers, and still more by the admission of heterogeneous classes into the Church, the work became too vast and too various for them to discharge unaided. To relieve them from the increasing pressure, the inferior and less important functions passed successively into other hands: and thus each grade of the ministry, beginning from the lowest, was created in order.

1. Deacons. Appointment of the Seven.

1. The establishment of the diaconate came first. Complaints had reached the ears of the Apostles from an outlying portion of the community. The Hellenist widows had been overlooked in the daily distribution of food and alms. To remedy this neglect a new office was created. Seven men were appointed whose duty it was to superintend the public messes[2], and, as we may suppose, to provide in other ways for the bodily wants of the helpless poor. Thus relieved, the Twelve were enabled to devote themselves without interruption 'to prayer and to the ministry of the word.' The Apostles suggested the creation of this new office, but the persons were chosen by popular election and afterwards ordained by the Twelve with imposition of hands. Though the complaint came from the Hellenists, it must not be supposed that the ministrations of the Seven were confined to this class[3]. The object in creating

---

[1] The origin of the Christian ministry is ably investigated in Rothe's *Anfänge der Christlichen Kirche etc.* (1837), and Ritschl's *Entstehung der Altkatholischen Kirche* (2nd ed. 1857). These are the most important of the more recent works on the subject with which I am acquainted, and to both of them I wish to acknowledge my obligations, though in many respects I have arrived at results different from either.

[2] Acts vi. 2 διακονεῖν τραπέζαις.

[3] So for instance Vitringa *de Synag.* III. 2. 5, p. 928 sq, and Mosheim *de*

this new office is stated to be not the partial but the entire relief of the Apostles from the serving of tables. This being the case, the appointment of Hellenists (for such they would appear to have been from their names[1]) is a token of the liberal and loving spirit which prompted the Hebrew members of the Church in the selection of persons to fill the office.

I have assumed that the office thus established represents the later diaconate; for though this point has been much disputed, I do not see how the identity of the two can reasonably be called in question[2]. If the word 'deacon' does not occur in the passage, yet the corresponding verb and substantive, διακονεῖν and διακονία, are repeated more than once. The functions moreover are substantially those which devolved on the deacons of the earliest ages, and which still in theory, though not altogether in practice, form the primary duties of the office. Again, it seems clear from the emphasis with which St Luke dwells on the new institution, that he looks on the establishment of this office, not as an isolated incident, but as the initiation of a new order of things in the Church. It is in short one of those representative facts, of which the earlier part of his narrative is almost wholly made up. Lastly, the tradition of the identity of the two offices has been unanimous from the earliest times. Irenæus, the first writer who alludes to the appointment of the Seven, distinctly holds them to have been deacons[3]. The Roman Church some centuries later, though

The Seven were deacons.

Reb. Christ. p. 119, followed by many later writers.

[1] This inference however is far from certain, since many Hebrews bore Greek names, e.g. the Apostles Andrew and Philip.

[2] It is maintained by Vitringa III. 2. 5, p. 920 sq., that the office of the Seven was different from the later diaconate. He quotes Chrysost. *Hom.* 14 *in Act.* (IX. p. 115, ed. Montf.) and Can. 10 of the Quinisextine Council (comp. p. 146, note 2) as favouring his view. With strange perversity Böhmer (*Diss. Jur. Eccl.* p. 349 sq.) supposes them to be presbyters, and this account has been adopted even by Ritschl, p. 355 sq. According to another view the office of the Seven branched out into the two later orders of the diaconate and the presbyterate, Lange *Apost. Zeit.* II. i. p. 75.

[3] Iren. i. 26. 3, iii. 12. 10, iv. 15. 1.

the presbytery had largely increased meanwhile, still restricted the number of deacons to seven, thus preserving the memory of the first institution of this office[1]. And in like manner a canon of the Council of Neocæsarea (A.D. 315) enacted that there should be no more than seven deacons in any city however great[2], alleging the apostolic model. This rule, it is true, was only partially observed; but the tradition was at all events so far respected, that the creation of an order of subdeacons was found necessary in order to remedy the inconvenience arising from the limitation[3].

The office was a new institution

The narrative in the Acts, if I mistake not, implies that the office thus created was entirely new. Some writers however have explained the incident as an extension to the Hellenists of an institution which already existed among the Hebrew Christians and is implied in the 'younger men' mentioned in an earlier part of St Luke's history[4]. This view seems not only to be groundless in itself, but also to contradict the general tenour of the narrative. It would appear moreover, that the institution was not merely new within the Christian Church, but novel absolutely. There is no reason for connecting it with any prototype existing in the Jewish community. The narrative offers no hint that it was either a continuation of the order of Levites or an adaptation of an office in the synagogue. The philanthropic purpose for which it was established presents no direct point of contact with the known duties of either. The Levite, whose function it was to keep the beasts for slaughter, to cleanse away the blood and offal of the

not borrowed from the Levitical order,

[1] In the middle of the third century, when Cornelius writes to Fabius, Rome has 46 presbyters but only 7 deacons, Euseb. *H. E.* vi. 43; see Routh's *Rel. Sacr.* III. p. 23, with his note p. 61. Even in the fourth and fifth centuries the number of Roman deacons still remained constant: see Ambrosiast. on 1 Tim. iii. 13, Sozom. vii. 19 διάκονοι δὲ παρὰ 'Ρωμαίοις εἰσέτι νῦν εἰσὶν ἑπτά... παρὰ δὲ τοῖς ἄλλοις ἀδιάφορος ὁ τούτων ἀριθμός.

[2] Concil. Neocæs. c. 14 (Routh *Rel. Sacr.* IV. p. 185): see Bingham's *Antiq.* II. 20. 19. At the Quinisextine or 2nd Trullan council (A.D. 692) this Neocæsarean canon was refuted and rejected: see Hefele *Consiliengesch.* III. p. 304, and Vitringa p. 922.

[3] See Bingham III. 1. 3.

[4] Acts v. 6, 10. This is the view of Mosheim *de Reb. Christ.* p. 114.

sacrifices, to serve as porter at the temple gates, and to swell the chorus of sacred psalmody, bears no strong resemblance to the Christian deacon, whose ministrations lay among the widows and orphans, and whose time was almost wholly spent in works of charity. And again, the Chazan or attendant in the synagogue, whose duties were confined to the care of the building and the preparation for service, has more in common with the modern parish clerk than with the deacon in the infant Church of Christ[1]. It is therefore a baseless, though a very common, assumption that the Christian diaconate was copied from the arrangements of the synagogue. The Hebrew Chazan is not rendered by 'deacon' in the Greek Testament; but a different word is used instead[2]. We may fairly presume that St Luke dwells at such length on the establishment of the diaconate, because he regards it as a novel creation.

nor from the synagogue.

Thus the work primarily assigned to the deacons was the relief of the poor. Their office was essentially a 'serving of tables,' as distinguished from the higher function of preaching and instruction. But partly from the circumstances of their position, partly from the personal character of those first appointed, the deacons at once assumed a prominence which is not indicated in the original creation of the office. Moving about freely among the poorer brethren and charged with the relief of their material wants, they would find opportunities of influence which were denied to the higher officers of the Church who necessarily kept themselves more aloof. The devout zeal of a Stephen or a Philip would turn these opportunities to the best account; and thus, without ceasing to be dispensers of alms, they became also ministers of the Word. The Apostles themselves had directed that the persons chosen should be not only 'men of honest report,' but also 'full of the Holy Ghost and wisdom': and this careful foresight, to which

Teaching only incidental to the office.

---

[1] Vitringa (III. 2. 4, p. 914 sq., III. 2. 22, p. 1130 sq.) derives the Christian deacon from the Chazan of the synagogue. Among other objections to this view, the fact that as a rule there was only one Chazan to each synagogue must not be overlooked.

[2] ὑπηρέτης, Luke iv. 20.

the extended influence of the diaconate may be ascribed, proved also the security against its abuse. But still the work of teaching must be traced rather to the capacity of the individual officer than to the direct functions of the office. St Paul, writing thirty years later, and stating the requirements of the diaconate, lays the stress mainly on those qualifications which would be most important in persons moving about from house to house and entrusted with the distribution of alms. While he requires that they shall 'hold the mystery of the faith in a pure conscience,' in other words, that they shall be sincere believers, he is not anxious, as in the case of the presbyters, to secure 'aptness to teach,' but demands especially that they shall be free from certain vicious habits, such as a love of gossiping, and a greed of paltry gain, into which they might easily fall from the nature of their duties[1].

Spread of the diaconate to Gentile churches.
From the mother Church of Jerusalem the institution spread to Gentile Christian brotherhoods. By the 'helps[2]' in the First Epistle to the Corinthians (A.D. 57), and by the 'ministration[3]' in the Epistle to the Romans (A.D. 58), the diaconate solely or chiefly seems to be intended; but besides these incidental allusions, the latter epistle bears more significant testimony to the general extension of the office. The strict seclusion of the female sex in Greece and in some Oriental countries necessarily debarred them from the ministrations of men: and to meet the want thus felt, it was found necessary at an early date to admit women to the diaconate. A woman-deacon belonging to the Church of Cenchreæ is mentioned in the Epistle to the Romans[4]. As time advances, the diaconate becomes still more prominent. In the Philippian Church a few years later (about A.D. 62) the deacons take their rank after the presbyters, the two orders together constituting the recognised ministry of the Christian society there[5]. Again, passing over another interval of some years, we find St Paul in

---

[1] 1 Tim. iii. 8 sq.
[2] 1 Cor. xii. 28.
[3] Rom. xii. 7.
[4] Rom. xvi. 1.
[5] Phil. i. 1.

THE CHRISTIAN MINISTRY. 149

the First Epistle to Timothy (about A.D. 66) giving express directions as to the qualifications of men-deacons and women-deacons alike¹. From the tenour of his language it seems clear that in the Christian communities of proconsular Asia at all events the institution was so common that ministerial organization would be considered incomplete without it. On the other hand we may perhaps infer from the instructions which he sends about the same time to Titus in Crete, that he did not consider it indispensable; for while he mentions having given direct orders to his delegate to appoint presbyters in every city, he is silent about a diaconate².

2. While the diaconate was thus an entirely new creation, called forth by a special emergency and developed by the progress of events, the early history of the presbyterate was different. If the sacred historian dwells at length on the institution of the lower office but is silent about the first beginnings of the higher, the explanation seems to be that the latter had not the claim of novelty like the former. The Christian Church in its earliest stage was regarded by the body of the Jewish people as nothing more than a new sect springing up by the side of the old. This was not unnatural: for the first disciples conformed to the religion of their fathers in all essential points, practising circumcision, observing the sabbaths, and attending the temple-worship. The sects in the Jewish commonwealth were not, properly speaking, nonconformists. They only superadded their own special organization to the established religion of their country, which for the most part they were careful to observe. The institution of synagogues was flexible enough to allow free scope for wide divergences of creed and practice. Different races as the Cyrenians and Alexandrians, different classes of society as the freedmen³, perhaps also different sects as the Sadducees or the Essenes, each had or could have their own special synagogue⁴, where

2. PRES-
BYTERS,

not a new office,

but adopted from the synagogue.

---

¹ 1 Tim. iii. 8 sq.
² Tit. i. 5 sq.
³ Acts vi. 9.

⁴ It is stated, that there were no less than 480 synagogues in Jerusalem. The number is doubtless greatly ex-

150   THE CHRISTIAN MINISTRY.

they might indulge their peculiarities without hindrance. As soon as the expansion of the Church rendered some organization necessary, it would form a 'synagogue' of its own. The Christian congregations in Palestine long continued to be designated by this name[1], though the term 'ecclesia' took its place from the very first in heathen countries. With the synagogue itself they would naturally, if not necessarily, adopt the normal government of a synagogue, and a body of elders or presbyters would be chosen to direct the religious worship and partly also to watch over the temporal well-being of the society.

<small>Occasion of its adoption.</small> Hence the silence of St Luke. When he first mentions the presbyters, he introduces them without preface, as though the institution were a matter of course. But the moment of their introduction is significant. I have pointed out elsewhere[2] that the two persecutions, of which St Stephen and St James were respectively the chief victims, mark two important stages in the diffusion of the Gospel. Their connexion with the internal organization of the Church is not less remarkable. The first results directly from the establishment of the lowest order in the ministry, the diaconate. To the second may probably be ascribed the adoption of the next higher grade, the presbytery. This later persecution was the signal for the dispersion of the Twelve on a wider mission. Since Jerusalem would no longer be their home as hitherto, it became necessary to provide for the permanent direction of the Church there; and for this purpose the usual government of the synagogue would be adopted. Now at all events for the first time we read of 'presbyters' in connexion with the Christian brotherhood at Jerusalem[3].

aggerated, but must have been very considerable: see Vitringa prol. 4, p. 28, and I. 1. 14, p. 253.

[1] James ii. 2. Epiphanius (xxx. 18, p. 142) says of the Ebionites συναγωγὴν οὗτοι καλοῦσι τὴν ἑαυτῶν ἐκκλησίαν, καὶ οὐχὶ ἐκκλησίαν. See also Hieron.

Epist. cxii. 13 (I. p. 746, ed. Vall.) 'per totas orientis synagogas,' speaking of the Nazaræans; though his meaning is not altogether clear. Comp. Test. xii Patr. Benj. 11.

[2] See above, pp. 53, 58.

[3] Acts xi. 30. On the sequence of

THE CHRISTIAN MINISTRY.   151

From this time forward all official communications with the mother Church are carried on through their intervention. To the presbyters Barnabas and Saul bear the alms contributed by the Gentile Churches[1]. The presbyters are persistently associated with the Apostles, in convening the congress, in the superscription of the decree, and in the general settlement of the dispute between the Jewish and Gentile Christians[2]. By the presbyters St Paul is received many years later on his last visit to Jerusalem, and to them he gives an account of his missionary labours and triumphs[3]. *Presbytery of Jerusalem.*

But the office was not confined to the mother Church alone. Jewish presbyteries existed already in all the principal cities of the dispersion, and Christian presbyteries would early occupy a not less wide area. On their very first missionary journey the Apostles Paul and Barnabas are described as appointing presbyters in every church[4]. The same rule was doubtless carried out in all the brotherhoods founded later; but it is mentioned here and here only, because the mode of procedure on this occasion would suffice as a type of the Apostles' dealings elsewhere under similar circumstances. *Extension of the office to Gentile Churches.*

The name of the presbyter then presents no difficulty. But what must be said of the term 'bishop'? It has been shown that in the apostolic writings the two are only different designations of one and the same office[5]. How and where was this second name originated? *Presbyters called also bishops,*

To the officers of Gentile Churches alone is the term applied, as a synonyme for presbyter. At Philippi[6], in Asia Minor[7], in Crete[8], the presbyter is so called. In the next generation the title is employed in a letter written by the Greek Church of Rome to the Greek Church of Corinth[9]. Thus the word would seem to be especially Hellenic. Beyond this we are left to *but only in Gentile Churches.*

Possible origin of the term.

events at this time see *Galatians* p. 124.
[1] Acts xi. 30.
[2] Acts xv. 2, 4, 6, 22, 23, xvi. 4.
[3] Acts xxi. 18.
[4] Acts xiv. 23.
[5] See *Philippians* p. 96 sq.
[6] Phil. i. 1.
[7] Acts xx. 28, 1 Tim. iii. 1, 2; comp. 1 Pet. ii. 25, v. 2.
[8] Tit. i. 7.
[9] Clem. Rom. 42, 44.

152   THE CHRISTIAN MINISTRY.

conjecture. But if we may assume that the directors of religious and social clubs among the heathen were commonly so called[1], it would naturally occur, if not to the Gentile Christians themselves, at all events to their heathen associates, as a fit designation for the presiding members of the new society. The infant Church of Christ, which appeared to the Jew as a synagogue, would be regarded by the heathen as a confraternity[2]. But whatever may have been the origin of the term, it did not altogether dispossess the earlier name 'presbyter,' which still held its place as a synonym even in Gentile congregations[3]. And, when at length the term bishop was appropriated to a higher office in the Church, the latter became again, as it had been at first, the sole designation of the Christian elder[4].

Twofold duties of the presbyter.

The duties of the presbyters were twofold. They were both rulers and instructors of the congregation. This double function appears in St Paul's expression 'pastors and teachers[5],' where, as the form of the original seems to show, the two words describe the same office under different aspects. Though *government* was probably the first conception of the office, yet the work of *teaching* must have fallen to the presbyters from the very first and have assumed greater prominence as time went on. With the growth of the Church, the visits of the apostles and evangelists to any individual community must

The function of teaching.

have become less and less frequent, so that the burden of instruction would be gradually transferred from these missionary

---

[1] The evidence however is slight: see *Philippians* p. 95, note 2. Some light is thrown on this subject by the fact that the Roman government seems first to have recognised the Christian brotherhoods in their corporate capacity, as burial clubs: see de Rossi *Rom. Sotterr.* I. p. 371.

[2] On these clubs or confraternities see Renan *Les Apôtres* p. 351 sq.; comp. *Saint Paul* p. 239.

[3] Acts xx. 17, 1 Tim. v. 17, Tit. i. 5, 1 Pet. v. 1, Clem. Rom. 21, 44.

[4] Other more general designations in the New Testament are οἱ προιστάμενοι (1 Thess. v. 12, Rom. xii. 8: comp. 1 Tim. v. 17), or οἱ ἡγούμενοι (Hebr. xiii. 7, 17, 24). For the former comp. Hermas *Vis.* ii. 4, Justin. *Apol.* i. 67 (ὁ προεστώς); for the latter, Clem. Rom. 1, 21, Hermas *Vis.* ii. 2, iii. 9 (οἱ προηγούμενοι).

[5] Ephes. iv. 11 τοὺς δὲ ποιμένας καὶ διδασκάλους. For ποιμαίνειν applied to the ἐπίσκοπος or πρεσβύτερος see Acts xx. 28, 1 Pet. v. 2; comp. 1 Pet. ii. 25.

THE CHRISTIAN MINISTRY. 153

preachers to the local officers of the congregation. Hence St Paul in two passages, where he gives directions relating to bishops or presbyters, insists specially on the faculty of teaching as a qualification for the position[1]. Yet even here this work seems to be regarded rather as incidental to than as inherent in the office. In the one epistle he directs that double honour shall be paid to those presbyters who have ruled well, but *especially* to such as 'labour in word and doctrine[2],' as though one holding this office might decline the work of instruction. In the other, he closes the list of qualifications with the requirement that the bishop (or presbyter) hold fast the faithful word in accordance with the apostolic teaching, 'that he may be able both to exhort in the healthy doctrine and to confute gainsayers,' alleging as a reason the pernicious activity and growing numbers of the false teachers. Nevertheless there is no ground for supposing that the work of teaching and the work of governing pertained to separate members of the presbyteral college[3]. As each had his special gift, so would he devote himself more or less exclusively to the one or the other of these sacred functions.

3. It is clear then that at the close of the apostolic age, the two lower orders of the threefold ministry were firmly and widely established; but traces of the third and highest order, the episcopate properly so called, are few and indistinct.

3. BISHOPS.

For the opinion hazarded by Theodoret and adopted by many later writers[4], that the same officers in the Church who

The office not a continuation

---

[1] 1 Tim. iii. 2, Tit. i. 9.
[2] 1 Tim. v. 17 μάλιστα οἱ κοπιῶντες ἐν λόγῳ καὶ διδασκαλίᾳ. At a much later date we read of 'presbyteri doctores,' whence it may perhaps be inferred that even then the work of teaching was not absolutely indispensable to the presbyteral office; Act. Perp. et Fel. 13, Cyprian. Epist. 29: see Ritschl p. 352.
[3] The distinction of lay or ruling elders, and ministers proper or teaching elders, was laid down by Calvin and has been adopted as the constitution of several presbyterian Churches. This interpretation of St Paul's language is refuted by Rothe p. 224, Ritschl p. 352 sq., and Schaff *Hist. of Apost. Ch.* II. p. 312, besides older writers such as Vitringa and Mosheim.
[4] On 1 Tim. iii. 1, τοὺς δὲ νῦν καλουμένους ἐπισκόπους ἀποστόλους ὠνόμαζον· τοῦ δὲ χρόνου προϊόντος τὸ μὲν τῆς ἀποστολῆς ὄνομα τοῖς ἀληθῶς ἀποστόλοις

were first called apostles came afterwards to be designated bishops, is baseless. If the two offices had been identical, the substitution of the one name for the other would have required some explanation. But in fact the functions of the Apostle and the bishop differed widely. The Apostle, like the prophet or the evangelist, held no *local* office. He was essentially, as his name denotes, a missionary, moving about from place to place, founding and confirming new brotherhoods. The only ground on which Theodoret builds his theory is a false interpretation of a passage in St Paul. At the opening of the Epistle to Philippi the presbyters (here called bishops) and deacons are saluted, while in the body of the letter one Epaphroditus is mentioned as an 'apostle' of the Philippians. If 'apostle' here had the meaning which is thus assigned to it, all the three orders of the ministry would be found at Philippi. But this interpretation will not stand. The true Apostle, like St Peter or St John, bears this title as the messenger, the delegate, of Christ Himself: while Epaphroditus is only so styled as the messenger of the Philippian brotherhood; and in the very next clause the expression is explained by the statement that he carried their alms to St Paul[1]. The use of the word here has a parallel in another passage[2], where messengers (or apostles) of the churches are mentioned. It is not therefore to the apostle that we must look for the prototype of the bishop. How far indeed and in what sense the bishop may be called a successor of the Apostles, will be a proper subject for consideration: but the succession at least does not consist in an identity of office.

of the apostolate.

Phil. ii. 25 wrongly explained.

κατέλιπον, τὸ δὲ τῆς ἐπισκοπῆς τοῖς πάλαι καλουμένοις ἀποστόλοις ἐπέθεσαν. See also his note on Phil. i. 1. Comp. Wordsworth *Theoph. Angl.* c. x, Blunt *First Three Centuries* p. 81. Theodoret, as usual, has borrowed from Theodore of Mopsuestia on 1 Tim. iii. 1, 'Qui vero nunc episcopi nominantur, illi tunc apostoli dicebantur...Beatis vero apostolis decedentibus, illi qui post illos ordinati sunt...grave existimaverunt apostolorum sibi vindicare nuncupationem; diviserunt ergo ipsa nomina etc.' (Raban. Maur. vi. p. 604 D, ed. Migne). Theodore however makes a distinction between the two offices: nor does he, like Theodoret, misinterpret Phil. ii. 25. The commentator Hilary also, on Ephes. iv. 11, says 'apostoli episcopi sunt.'

[1] Phil. ii. 25, see *Philippians* p. 123.
[2] 2 Cor. viii. 23, see *Galatians* p. 95, note 3.

The history of the name itself suggests a different account *The episcopate developed out of the presbytery.* of the origin of the episcopate. If bishop was at first used as a synonym for presbyter and afterwards came to designate the higher officer under whom the presbyters served, the episcopate properly so called would seem to have been developed from the subordinate office. In other words, the episcopate was formed not out of the apostolic order by localisation but out of the presbyteral by elevation: and the title, which originally was common to all, came at length to be appropriated to the chief among them[1].

If this account be true, we might expect to find in the mother Church of Jerusalem, which as the earliest founded would soonest ripen into maturity, the first traces of this developed form of the ministry. Nor is this expectation disappointed. James the Lord's brother alone, within the period compassed by the apostolic writings, can claim to be regarded as a bishop in the later and more special sense of the term. In the language of St Paul he takes precedence even of the earliest and greatest preachers of the Gospel, St Peter and St John[2], where the affairs of the Jewish Church specially are concerned. In St Luke's narrative he appears as the local representative of the brotherhood in Jerusalem, presiding at the congress, whose decision he suggests and whose decree he appears to have framed[3], receiving the missionary preachers as they revisit the mother Church[4], acting generally as the referee in communications with foreign brotherhoods. The place assigned to him in the spurious Clementines, where he is

St James was the earliest bishop,

---

[1] A parallel instance from Athenian institutions will illustrate this usage. The ἐπιστάτης was chairman of a body of ten πρόεδροι, who themselves were appointed in turn by lot to serve from a larger body of fifty πρυτάνεις. Yet we find the ἐπιστάτης not only designated πρύτανις par excellence (Demosth. *Timocr.* § 157), but even addressed by this name in the presence of the other πρόεδροι (Thuc. vi. 14).

[2] Gal. ii. 9; see the note.

[3] Acts xv. 13 sq. St James speaks last and apparently with some degree of authority (ἐγὼ κρίνω ver. 19). The decree is clearly framed on his recommendations, and some indecisive coincidences of style with his epistle have been pointed out.

[4] Acts xxi. 18; comp. xii. 17. See also Gal. i. 19, ii. 12.

represented as supreme arbiter over the Church universal in matters of doctrine, must be treated as a gross exaggeration. This kind of authority is nowhere conferred upon him in the apostolic writings: but his social and ecclesiastical position, as it appears in St Luke and St Paul, explains how the exaggeration was possible. And this position is the more remarkable if, as seems to have been the case, he was not one of the Twelve[1].

but yet not isolated from his presbytery.

On the other hand, though especially prominent, he appears in the Acts as a member of a body. When St Peter, after his escape from prison, is about to leave Jerusalem, he desires that his deliverance shall be reported to 'James and the brethren[2].' When again St Paul on his last visit to the Holy City goes to see James, we are told that all the presbyters were present[3]. If in some passages St James is named by himself, in others he is omitted and the presbyters alone are mentioned[4]. From this it may be inferred that though holding a position superior to the rest, he was still considered as a member of the presbytery; that he was in fact the head or president of the college. What power this presidency conferred, how far it was recognised as an independent official position, and to what degree it was due to the ascendancy of his personal gifts, are questions, which in the absence of direct information can only be answered by conjecture. But his close relationship with the Lord, his rare energy of character, and his rigid sanctity of life which won the respect even of the unconverted Jews[5], would react upon his office, and may perhaps have elevated it to a level which was not definitely contemplated in its origin.

No bishops as yet in the Gentile Churches.

But while the episcopal office thus existed in the mother Church of Jerusalem from very early days, at least in a rudimentary form, the New Testament presents no distinct traces of such organization in the Gentile congregations. The government of the Gentile churches, as there represented, exhibits two successive stages of development tending in this direction; but

Two stages of development:

---

[1] See above, p. 1 sq.
[2] Acts xii. 17.
[3] Acts xxi. 18.
[4] Acts xi. 30; comp. xv. 4, 23, xvi. 4.
[5] See above, p. 12 sq.

the third stage, in which episcopacy definitely appears, still lies beyond the horizon.

(1) We have first of all the Apostles themselves exercising the superintendence of the churches under their care, sometimes in person and on the spot, sometimes at a distance by letter or by message. The imaginary picture drawn by St Paul, when he directs the punishment of the Corinthian offender, vividly represents his position in this respect. The members of the church are gathered together, the elders, we may suppose, being seated apart on a dais or tribune; he himself, as president, directs their deliberations, collects their votes, pronounces sentence on the guilty man[1]. How the absence of the apostolic president was actually supplied in this instance, we do not know. But a council was held; he did direct their verdict 'in spirit though not in person'; and 'the majority' condemned the offender[2]. In the same way St Peter, giving directions to the elders, claims a place among them. The title 'fellow-presbyter,' which he applies to himself[3], would doubtless recal to the memory of his readers the occasions when he himself had presided with the elders and guided their deliberations.

(1) Occasional supervision by the Apostles themselves.

(2) As the first stage then, the Apostles themselves were the superintendents of each individual church. But the wider spread of the Gospel would diminish the frequency of their visits and impair the efficiency of such supervision. In the second stage therefore we find them, at critical seasons and in important congregations, delegating some trustworthy disciple who should fix his abode in a given place for a time and direct the affairs of the church there. The Pastoral Epistles present this second stage to our view. It is the conception of a later age which represents Timothy as bishop of Ephesus and Titus as bishop of Crete[4]. St Paul's own language implies that the position which they held was temporary. In both cases their

(2) Residence of apostolic delegates.

---

[1] 1 Cor. v. 3 sq.
[2] 2 Cor. ii. 6 ἡ ἐπιτιμία αὕτη ἡ ὑπὸ τῶν πλειόνων.
[3] 1 Pet. v. 1.
[4] *Const. Apost.* vii. 46, Euseb. *H. E.* iii. 4, and later writers.

158   THE CHRISTIAN MINISTRY.

term of office is drawing to a close, when the Apostle writes[1]. But the conception is not altogether without foundation. With less permanence but perhaps greater authority, the position occupied by these apostolic delegates nevertheless fairly represents the functions of the bishop early in the second century. They were in fact the link between the Apostle whose superintendence was occasional and general and the bishop who exercised a permanent supervision over an individual congregation.

The angels in the Apocalypse not bishops. Beyond this second stage the notices in the apostolic writings do not carry us. The angels of the seven churches indeed are frequently alleged as an exception[2]. But neither does the name 'angel' itself suggest such an explanation[3], nor is this view in keeping with the highly figurative style of this wonderful book. Its sublime imagery seems to be seriously impaired by this interpretation. On the other hand St John's own language gives the true key to the symbolism. 'The seven stars,' so it is explained, 'are the seven angels of the seven churches, and the seven candlesticks are the seven churches[4].' This contrast between the heavenly and the earthly fires—the star shining steadily by its own inherent

---

[1] See 1 Tim. i. 3, iii. 14, 2 Tim. iv. 9, 21, Tit. i. 5, iii. 12.

[2] See for instance among recent writers Thiersch *Gesch. der Apost. Kirche* p. 278, Trench *Epistles to the Seven Churches* p. 47 sq., with others. This explanation is as old as the earliest commentators. Rothe supposes that the word *anticipates* the establishment of episcopacy, being a kind of prophetic symbol, p. 423 sq. Others again take the angel to designate the collective ministry, i.e. the whole body of priests and deacons. For various explanations see Schaff *Hist. of Apost. Ch.* II. p. 223.

Rothe (p. 426) supposes that Diotrephes ὁ φιλοπρωτεύων αὐτῶν (3 Joh. 9) was a bishop. This cannot be pronounced impossible, but the language is far too indefinite to encourage such an inference.

[3] It is conceivable indeed that a bishop or chief pastor should be called an angel or messenger of God or of Christ (comp. Hag. i. 13, Mal. ii. 7), but he would hardly be styled an angel of the church over which he presides. See the parallel case of ἀπόστολος above, p. 154. Vitringa (II. 9, p. 550), and others after him, explain ἄγγελος in the Apocalypse by the שְׁלִיחַ, the messenger or deputy of the synagogue. These however were only inferior officers, and could not be compared to stars or made responsible for the well-being of the churches; see Rothe p. 504.

[4] Rev. i. 20

eternal light, and the lamp flickering and uncertain, requiring to be fed with fuel and tended with care—cannot be devoid of meaning. The star is the suprasensual counterpart, the heavenly representative; the lamp, the earthly realisation, the outward embodiment. Whether the angel is here conceived as an actual person, the celestial guardian, or only as a personification, the idea or spirit of the church, it is unnecessary for my present purpose to consider. But whatever may be the exact conception, he is identified with and made responsible for it to a degree wholly unsuited to any human officer. Nothing is predicated of him, which may not be predicated of it. To him are imputed all its hopes, its fears, its graces, its shortcomings. He is punished with it, and he is rewarded with it. In one passage especially the language applied to the angel seems to exclude the common interpretation. In the message to Thyatira the angel is blamed, because he suffers himself to be led astray by 'his wife Jezebel[1].' In this image of Ahab's idolatrous queen some dangerous and immoral teaching must be personified; for it does violence alike to the general tenour and to the individual expressions in the passage to suppose that an actual woman is meant. Thus the symbolism of the passage is entirely in keeping. Nor again is this mode of representation new. The 'princes' in the prophecy of Daniel[2] present a very near if not an exact parallel to the angels of the Revelation. Here, as elsewhere, St John seems to adapt the imagery of this earliest apocalyptic book.

True explanation.

Indeed, if with most recent writers we adopt the early date of the Apocalypse of St John, it is scarcely possible that the episcopal organization should have been so mature when it was written. In this case probably not more than two or three years have elapsed from the date of the Pastoral Epistles[3], and

---

[1] Rev. ii. 20 τὴν γυναῖκά σου 'Ιεζάβελ. The word σου should probably be retained in the text: or at least, if not a correct reading, it seems to be a correct gloss.

[2] Dan. x. 13, 20, 21.

[3] The date of the Pastoral Epistles may be and probably is as late as A.D. 66 or 67; while the Apocalypse on this hypothesis was written not later than A.D. 70.

160   THE CHRISTIAN MINISTRY.

this interval seems quite insufficient to account for so great a change in the administration of the Asiatic churches.

Episcopacy established in Gentile churches before the close of the century.   As late therefore as the year 70 no distinct signs of episcopal government have hitherto appeared in Gentile Christendom. Yet unless we have recourse to a sweeping condemnation of received documents, it seems vain to deny that early in the second century the episcopal office was firmly and widely established. Thus during the last three decades of the first century, and consequently during the lifetime of the latest surviving Apostle, this change must have been brought about. But the circumstances under which it was effected are shrouded in darkness; and various attempts have been made to read the obscure enigma. Of several solutions offered one at least deserves special notice. If Rothe's view cannot be accepted as final, its examination will at least serve to bring out the conditions of the problem: and for this reason I shall state and discuss it as briefly as possible[1]. For the words in which the theory is stated I am myself responsible.

Rothe's solution.

Importance of the crisis.   'The epoch to which we last adverted marks an important crisis in the history of Christianity. The Church was distracted and dismayed by the growing dissensions between the Jewish and Gentile brethren and by the menacing apparition of Gnostic heresy. So long as its three most prominent leaders were living, there had been some security against the extravagance of parties, some guarantee of harmonious combination among diverse churches. But St Peter, St Paul, and St James, were carried away by death almost at the same time and in the face of this great emergency. Another blow too had fallen: the long-delayed judgment of God on the once Holy City was delayed no more. With the overthrow of Jerusalem the visible centre of the Church was removed. The keystone of the fabric was withdrawn, and the whole edifice

---

[1] See Rothe's *Anfänge etc.* pp. 354—392. Rothe's account of the origin of episcopacy is assailed (on grounds in many respects differing from those which I have urged) by Baur *Ursprung des Episcopats* p. 39 sq., and Ritschl p. 410 sq.

threatened with ruin. There was a crying need for some organization which should cement together the diverse elements of Christian society and preserve it from disintegration.'

'Out of this need the Catholic Church arose. Christendom had hitherto existed as a number of distinct isolated congregations, drawn in the same direction by a common faith and common sympathies, accidentally linked one with another by the personal influence and apostolic authority of their common teachers, but not bound together in a harmonious whole by any permanent external organization. Now at length this great result was brought about. The magnitude of the change effected during this period may be measured by the difference in the constitution and conception of the Christian Church as presented in the Pastoral Epistles of St Paul and the letters of St Ignatius respectively.' *Origin of the Catholic Church.*

'By whom then was the new constitution organized? To this question only one answer can be given. This great work must be ascribed to the surviving Apostles. St John especially, who built up the speculative theology of the Church, was mainly instrumental in completing its external constitution also; for Asia Minor was the centre from which the new movement spread. St John however was not the only Apostle or early disciple who lived in this province. St Philip is known to have settled in Hierapolis[1]. St Andrew also seems to have dwelt in these parts[2]. The silence of history clearly proclaims the fact which the voice of history but faintly suggests. If we hear nothing more of the Apostles' missionary labours, it is because they had organized an united Church, to which they had transferred the work of evangelization.' *Agency of the surviving Apostles.*

'Of such a combined effort on the part of the Apostles, resulting in a definite ecclesiastical polity, in an united Catholic Church, no direct account is preserved: but incidental notices are not wanting; and in the general paucity of informa- *Evidence of a second Apostolic Council.*

---

[1] Papias in Euseb. *H. E.* iii. 39; Polycrates and Caius in Euseb. *H. E.* iii. 31.

[2] Muratorian Canon (circ. 170 A.D.) Routh *Rel. Sacr.* I. p. 394.

tion respecting the whole period more than this was not to be expected¹.'

Hegesippus.

'(1) Eusebius relates that after the martyrdom of St James and the fall of Jerusalem, the remaining Apostles and personal disciples of the Lord, with his surviving relations, met together and after consultation unanimously appointed Symeon the son of Clopas to the vacant see². It can hardly be doubted, that Eusebius in this passage quotes from the earlier historian Hegesippus, from whom he has derived the other incidents in the lives of James and Symeon: and we may well believe that this council discussed larger questions than the appointment of a single bishop, and that the constitution and prospects of the Church generally came under deliberation. It may have been on this occasion that the surviving Apostles partitioned out the world among them, and 'Asia was assigned to John³.'

Irenæus.

'(2) A fragment of Irenæus points in the same direction. Writing of the holy eucharist he says, 'They who have paid attention to the second ordinances of the Apostles know that the Lord appointed a new offering in the new covenant⁴.' By these 'second ordinances' must be understood some later decrees or injunctions than those contained in the apostolic epistles: and these would naturally be framed and promulgated by such a council as the notice of Eusebius suggests.'

Clement of Rome.

'(3) To the same effect St Clement of Rome writes, that the Apostles, having appointed elders in every church and foreseeing the disputes which would arise, 'afterwards added a codicil (supplementary direction) that if they should fall asleep,

---

¹ Besides the evidence which I have stated and discussed in the text, Rothe also brings forward a fragment of the *Praedicatio Pauli* (preserved in the tract *de Baptismo Haereticorum*, which is included among Cyprian's works, app. p. 30, ed. Fell; see above, p. 111, note 2), where the writer mentions a meeting of St Peter and St Paul in Rome. The main question however is so slightly affected thereby, that I have not thought it necessary to investigate the value and bearing of this fragment.

² Euseb. *H. E.* iii. 11.

³ According to the tradition reported by Origen as quoted in Euseb. *H. E.* iii. 1.

⁴ One of the Pfaffian fragments, no. xxxviii, p. 854 in Stieren's edition of Irenæus (vol. I.).

other approved men should succeed to their office[1].' Here the pronouns 'they,' 'their,' must refer, not to the first appointed presbyters, but to the Apostles themselves. Thus interpreted, the passage contains a distinct notice of the institution of bishops as successors of the Apostles; while in the word 'afterwards' is involved an allusion to the later council to which the 'second ordinances' of Irenæus also refer[2].'

'These notices seem to justify the conclusion that immediately after the fall of Jerusalem a council of the apostles and first teachers of the Gospel was held to deliberate on the crisis, and to frame measures for the well-being of the Church. The centre of the system then organized was episcopacy, which at once secured the compact and harmonious working of each individual congregation, and as the link of communication between separate brotherhoods formed the whole into one undivided Catholic Church. Recommended by this high authority, the new constitution was immediately and generally adopted.' *Results of the Council.*

This theory, which is maintained with much ability and vigour, attracted considerable notice, as being a new defence of episcopacy advanced by a member of a presbyterian Church. On the other hand, its intrinsic value seems to have been unduly depreciated; for, if it fails to give a satisfactory solution, it has at least the merit of stating the conditions of the problem with great distinctness, and of pointing out the direction to be followed. On this account it seemed worthy of attention. *Value of Rothe's theory.*

---

[1] Clem. Rom. § 44 κατέστησαν τοὺς προειρημένους (sc. πρευβυτέρους) καὶ μεταξὺ † ἐπινομὴν † δεδώκασιν, ὅπως, ἐὰν κοιμηθῶσιν, διαδέξωνται ἕτεροι δεδοκιμασμένοι ἄνδρες τὴν λειτουργίαν αὐτῶν. The interpretation of the passage depends on the persons intended in κοιμηθῶσιν and αὐτῶν (see the notes on the passage).

[2] A much more explicit though somewhat later authority may be quoted in favour of his view. The Ambrosian Hilary on Ephes. iv. 12, speaking of the change from the presbyteral to the episcopal form of government, says 'immutata est ratio, *prospiciente concilio*, ut non ordo etc.' If the reading be correct, I suppose he was thinking of the Apostolic Constitutions. See also the expression of St Jerome on Tit. i. 5 (quoted below, p. 166) 'in toto orbe decretum est.'

The evidence examined.

Hegesippus.

It must indeed be confessed that the historical notices will not bear the weight of the inference built upon them. (1) The account of Hegesippus (for to Hegesippus the statement in Eusebius may fairly be ascribed) confines the object of this gathering to the appointment of a successor to St James. If its deliberations had exerted that vast and permanent influence on the future of the Church which Rothe's theory supposes, it is scarcely possible that this early historian should have been ignorant of the fact or knowing it should have passed it over in silence. (2) The genuineness of the Pfaffian fragments of

Irenæus.

Irenæus must always remain doubtful[1]. Independently of the mystery which hangs over their publication, the very passage quoted throws great suspicion on their authorship; for the expression in question[2] seems naturally to refer to the so-called Apostolic Constitutions, which have been swelled to their present size by the accretions of successive generations, but can hardly have existed even in a rudimentary form in the age of Irenæus, or if existing have been regarded by him as genuine. If he had been acquainted with such later ordinances issued by the authority of an apostolic council, is it conceivable that in his great work on heresies he should have omitted to quote a sanction so unquestionable, where his main object is to show that the doctrine of the Catholic Church in his day represented the true teaching of the Apostles, and his main argument the fact that the Catholic bishops of his time derived their office

Clement.

by direct succession from the Apostles? (3) The passage in the epistle of St Clement cannot be correctly interpreted by Rothe: for his explanation, though elaborately defended, disregards the purpose of the letter. The Corinthian Church is disturbed by a spirit of insubordination. Presbyters, who have

---

[1] The controversial treatises on either side are printed in Stieren's Irenæus II. p. 381 sq. It is sufficient here to state that shortly after the transcription of these fragments by Pfaff, the Turin MS from which they were taken disappeared; so that there was no means of testing the accuracy of the transcriber or ascertaining the character of the MS.

[2] The expression αἱ δεύτεραι τῶν ἀποστόλων διατάξεις closely resembles the language of these Constitutions; see Hippol. p. 74, 82 (Lagarde).

faithfully discharged their duties, have nevertheless been ruthlessly expelled from office. St Clement writes in the name of the Roman Church to correct these irregularities. He reminds the Corinthians that the presbyteral office was established by the Apostles, who not only themselves appointed elders, but also gave directions that the vacancies caused from time to time by death should be filled up by other men of character, thus providing for a succession in the ministry. Consequently in these unworthy feuds they were setting themselves in opposition to officers of repute either actually nominated by Apostles, or appointed by those so nominated in accordance with the apostolic injunctions. There is no mention of episcopacy, properly so called, throughout the epistle; for in the language of St Clement, 'bishop' and 'presbyter' are still synonymous terms[1]. Thus the pronouns 'they,' 'their,' refer naturally to the presbyters first appointed by the Apostles themselves. Whether (supposing the reading to be correct[2]) Rothe has rightly translated ἐπινομήν 'a codicil,' it is unnecessary to enquire, as the rendering does not materially affect the question.

Nor again does it appear that the rise of episcopacy was so sudden and so immediate, that an authoritative order issuing from an apostolic council alone can explain the phenomenon. In the mysterious period which comprises the last thirty years of the first century, and on which history is almost wholly silent, episcopacy must, it is true, have been mainly developed. But before this period its beginnings may be traced, and after the close it is not yet fully matured. It seems vain to deny with Rothe[3] that the position of St James in the mother Church furnished the precedent and the pattern of the later episcopate. It appears equally mistaken to maintain, as this theory requires, that at the close of the first and the beginning of the second century the organization of all churches alike had arrived at the same stage of development and exhibited the episcopate in an equally perfect form.

Episcopacy not a sudden creation,

[1] See *Philippians* pp. 97, 98.
[2] The right reading is probably ἐπι- μονήν; see the notes on the passage.
[3] p. 264 sq.

166 THE CHRISTIAN MINISTRY.

but matured by a critical emergency

On the other hand, the emergency which consolidated the episcopal form of government is correctly and forcibly stated. It was remarked long ago by Jerome, that 'before factions were introduced into religion by the prompting of the devil,' the churches were governed by a council of elders, 'but as soon as each man began to consider those whom he had baptized to belong to himself and not to Christ, it was decided throughout the world that one elected from among the elders should be placed over the rest, so that the care of the church should devolve on him, and the seeds of schism be removed[1].' And again in another passage he writes to the same effect; 'When afterwards one presbyter was elected that he might be placed over the rest, this was done as a remedy against schism, that each man might not drag to himself and thus break up the Church of Christ[2].' To the dissensions of Jew and Gentile converts, and to the disputes of Gnostic false teachers, the development of episcopacy may be mainly ascribed.

and in Asia Minor under the influence of St John.

Nor again is Rothe probably wrong as to the authority mainly instrumental in effecting the change. Asia Minor was the adopted home of more than one Apostle after the fall of Jerusalem. Asia Minor too was the nurse, if not the mother, of episcopacy in the Gentile Churches. So important an institution, developed in a Christian community of which St John was the living centre and guide, could hardly have grown up without his sanction: and, as will be seen presently, early tradition very distinctly connects his name with the appointment of bishops in these parts.

Manner of its development.

But to the question how this change was brought about, a somewhat different answer must be given. We have seen that the needs of the Church and the ascendancy of his personal character placed St James at the head of the Christian brotherhood in Jerusalem. Though remaining a member of the presbyteral council, he was singled out from the rest and placed in a position of superior responsibility. His exact power it

---

[1] On Tit. i. 5 (VII. p. 694, ed. Vall.).
[2] *Epist.* cxlvi *ad Evang.* (I. p. 1082).

would be impossible, and it is unnecessary, to define. When therefore after the fall of the city St John with other surviving Apostles removed to Asia Minor and found there manifold irregularities and threatening symptoms of disruption, he would not unnaturally encourage an approach in these Gentile Churches to the same organization, which had been signally blessed, and proved effectual in holding together the mother Church amid dangers not less serious. The existence of a council or college necessarily supposes a presidency of some kind, whether this presidency be assumed by each member in turn, or lodged in the hands of a single person[1]. It was only necessary therefore for him to give permanence, definiteness, stability, to an office which already existed in germ. There is no reason however for supposing that any direct ordinance was issued to the churches. The evident utility and even pressing need of such an office, sanctioned by the most venerated name in Christendom, would be sufficient to secure its wide though gradual reception. Such a reception, it is true, supposes a substantial harmony and freedom of intercourse among the churches, which remained undisturbed by the troubles of the times; but the silence of history is not at all unfavourable to this supposition. In this way, during the historical blank which extends over half a century after the fall of Jerusalem, episcopacy was matured and the Catholic Church consolidated[2].

---

[1] The Ambrosian Hilary on Ephes. iv. 12 seems to say that the senior member was president; but this may be mere conjecture. The constitution of the synagogue does not aid materially in settling this question. In the New Testament at all events ἀρχισυνάγωγος is only another name for an *elder* of the synagogue (Mark v. 22, Acts xiii. 15, xviii. 8, 17; comp. Justin *Dial. c. Tryph.* § 137), and therefore corresponds not to the bishop but to the presbyter of the Christian Church. Sometimes however ἀρχισυνάγωγος appears to denote the president of the council of elders: see Vitringa II. 2. p. 586 sq., III. 1. p. 610 sq. The opinions of Vitringa must be received with caution, as his tendency to press the resemblance between the government of the Jewish synagogue and the Christian Church is strong. The real likeness consists in the council of presbyters; but the threefold order of the Christian ministry as a whole seems to have no counterpart in the synagogue.

[2] The expression 'Catholic Church' is found first in the Ignatian letter to the Smyrnæans § 8. In the Martyrdom of Polycarp it occurs several

This view supported by the notices of individual churches.

At all events, when we come to trace the early history of the office in the principal churches of Christendom in succession, we shall find all the facts consistent with the account adopted here, while some of them are hardly reconcileable with any other. In this review it will be convenient to commence with the mother Church, and to take the others in order, as they are connected either by neighbourhood or by political or religious sympathy.

JERUSALEM.

1. The Church of JERUSALEM, as I have already pointed out, presents the earliest instance of a bishop. A certain

St James. official prominence is assigned to James the Lord's brother, both in the Epistles of St Paul and in the Acts of the Apostles. And the inference drawn from the notices in the canonical Scriptures is borne out by the tradition of the next ages. As early as the middle of the second century all parties concur in representing him as a bishop in the strict sense of the term¹. In this respect Catholic Christians and Ebionite Christians hold the same language: the testimony of Hegesippus on the one hand is matched by the testimony of the Clementine writings on the other. On his death, which is recorded as

Symeon. taking place immediately before the war of Vespasian, Symeon was appointed in his place². Hegesippus, who is our authority for this statement, distinctly regards Symeon as holding the same office with James, and no less distinctly calls him a bishop. This same historian also mentions the circumstance that one Thebuthis (apparently on this occasion), being disappointed of the bishopric, raised a schism and attempted to corrupt the virgin purity of the Church with false doctrine. As Symeon died in the reign of Trajan at an advanced age, it is not im-

Later bishops. probable that Hegesippus was born during his lifetime. Of the successors of Symeon a complete list is preserved by Eusebius³.

times, inscr. and §§ 8, 16, 19. On its meaning see Westcott *Canon* p. 28, note (4th ed.).

¹ Hegesipp. in Euseb. *H. E.* ii. 23, iv. 22; *Clem. Hom.* xi. 35, Ep. Petr. init., and Ep. Clem. init.; *Clem.*

Recogn. i. 43, 68, 73; Clem. Alex. in Euseb. ii. 1; *Const. Apost.* v. 8, vi. 14, viii. 35, 46.

² Hegesipp. in Euseb. *H. E.* iv. 22.

³ *H. E.* iv. 5. The episcopate of Justus the successor of Symeon com-

THE CHRISTIAN MINISTRY. 169

The fact however that it comprises thirteen names within a period of less than thirty years must throw suspicion on its accuracy. A succession so rapid is hardly consistent with the known tenure of life offices in ordinary cases: and if the list be correct, the frequent changes must be attributed to the troubles and uncertainties of the times[1]. If Eusebius here also had derived his information from Hegesippus, it must at least have had some solid foundation in fact; but even then the alternation between Jerusalem and Pella, and the possible confusion of the bishops with other prominent members of the presbytery, might introduce much error. It appears however that in this instance he was indebted to less trustworthy sources of information[2]. The statement that after the foundation of Aelia Capitolina (A.D. 136) Marcus presided over the mother Church, as its first Gentile bishop, need not be questioned; and beyond this point it is unnecessary to carry the investigation[3].

Of other bishops in PALESTINE and the neighbourhood, before the latter half of the second century, no trustworthy notice is preserved, so far as I know. During the Roman episcopate of Victor however (about A.D. 190), we find three bishops, Theophilus of Cæsarea, Cassius of Tyre, and Clarus of Ptolemais, in conjunction with Narcissus of Jerusalem, writing an encyclical letter in favour of the western view in the Paschal

Other sees in Palestine and neighbouring countries.

---

mences about A.D. 108: that of Marcus the first Gentile bishop, A.D. 136. Thus thirteen bishops occupy only about twenty-eight years. Even after the foundation of Ælia Capitolina the succession is very rapid. In the period from Marcus (A.D. 136) to Narcissus (A.D. 190) we count fifteen bishops. The repetition of the same names however suggests that some conflict was going on during this interval.

[1] Parallels nevertheless may be found in the annals of the papacy. Thus from A.D. 882 to A.D. 904 there were thirteen popes: and in other times of trouble the succession has been almost as rapid.

[2] This may be inferred from a comparison of *H. E.* iv. 5 τοσοῦτον ἐξ ἐγγράφων παρείληφα with *H. E.* v. 12 αἱ τῶν αὐτόθι διαδοχαὶ περιέχουσι. His information was probably taken from a list kept at Jerusalem; but the case of the spurious correspondence with Abgarus preserved in the archives of Edessa (*H. E.* i. 13) shows how treacherous such sources of information were.

[3] Narcissus, who became bishop of Jerusalem in 190 A.D., might well have preserved the memory of much earlier times. His successor Alexander, in whose favour he resigned A.D. 214, speaks of him as still living at the advanced age of 116 (Euseb. *H. E.* vi. 11).

controversy[1]. If indeed any reliance could be placed on the Clementine writings, the episcopate of Palestine was matured at a very early date: for St Peter is there represented as appointing bishops in every city which he visits, in Cæsarea, Tyre, Sidon, Berytus, Tripolis, and Laodicea[2]. And though the fictions of this theological romance have no direct historical value, it is hardly probable that the writer would have indulged in such statements, unless an early development of the episcopate in these parts had invested his narrative with an air of probability. The institution would naturally spread from the Church of Jerusalem to the more important communities in the neighbourhood, even without the direct intervention of the Apostles.

ANTIOCH.

2. From the mother Church of the Hebrews we pass naturally to the metropolis of Gentile Christendom. ANTIOCH is traditionally reported to have received its first bishop

Evodius.

Evodius from St Peter[3]. The story may perhaps rest on some basis of truth, though no confidence can be placed in this class of statements, unless they are known to have been derived from

Ignatius.

some early authority. But of Ignatius, who stands second in the traditional catalogue of Antiochene bishops, we can speak with more confidence. He is designated a bishop by very early authors, and he himself speaks as such. He writes to one bishop, Polycarp; and he mentions several others. Again and again he urges the duty of obedience to their bishops on his correspondents. And, lest it should be supposed that he uses the term in its earlier sense as a synonyme for presbyter, he names in conjunction the three orders of the ministry, the bishop, the presbyter, and the deacons[4]. Altogether it is plain that he looks upon the episcopal system as the one recognised and authoritative form of government in all those churches

---

[1] Euseb. *H. E.* v. 25.
[2] *Clem. Hom.* iii. 68 sq. (Cæsarea), vii. 5 (Tyre), vii. 8 (Sidon), vii. 12 (Berytus), xi. 36 (Tripolis), xx. 23 (Laodicea): comp. *Clem. Recogn.* iii. 65, 66, 74, vi. 15, x. 68.

[3] *Const. Apost.* vii. 46, Euseb. *H. E.* iii. 22.
[4] *e.g. Polyc.* 6. I single out this passage from several which might be alleged, because it is found in the Syriac. See below, p. 198.

THE CHRISTIAN MINISTRY. 171

with which he is most directly concerned. It may be suggested indeed that he would hardly have enforced the claims of episcopacy, unless it were an object of attack, and its comparatively recent origin might therefore be inferred: but still some years would be required before it could have assumed that mature and definite form which it has in his letters. It seems impossible to decide, and it is needless to investigate, the exact date of the epistles of St Ignatius: but we cannot do wrong in placing them during the earliest years of the second century. The immediate successor of Ignatius is reported to have been Hero[1]: and from his time onward the list of Antiochene bishops is complete[2]. If the authenticity of the list, as a whole, is questionable, two bishops of Antioch at least during the second century, Theophilus and Serapion, are known as historical persons. *Later bishops.*

If the Clementine writings emanated, as seems probable, from Syria or Palestine[3], this will be the proper place to state their attitude with regard to episcopacy. Whether the opinions there advanced exhibit the recognised tenets of a sect or congregation, or the private views of the individual writer or writers, will probably never be ascertained; but, whatever may be said on this point, these heretical books outstrip the most rigid orthodoxy in their reverence for the episcopal office. Monarchy is represented as necessary to the peace of the Church[4]. The bishop occupies the seat of Christ and must be honoured as the image of God[5]. And hence St Peter, as he moves from place to place, ordains bishops everywhere, as though this were the crowning act of his missionary labours[6]. The divergence of the Clementine doctrine from the tenets of Catholic Christianity only renders this phenomenon more remarkable, when we remember the very early date of these writings; for the Homilies cannot well be placed later than the *Clementine writings.*

---

[1] Euseb. *H. E.* iii. 36.
[2] Euseb. *H. E.* iv. 20.
[3] See above, pp. 98 sq.
[4] *Clem. Hom.* iii. 62.
[5] *Clem. Hom.* iii. 62, 66, 70. See below, p. 202.
[6] See the references given above, p. 170, note 2.

172   THE CHRISTIAN MINISTRY.

end, and should perhaps be placed before the middle of the second century.

SYRIAN CHURCH.

3. We have hitherto been concerned only with the Greek Church of Syria. Of the early history of the SYRIAN CHURCH, strictly so called, no trustworthy account is preserved. The documents which profess to give information respecting it are comparatively late: and while their violent anachronisms discredit them as a whole, it is impossible to separate the fabulous from the historic[1]. It should be remarked however, that they exhibit a high sacerdotal view of the episcopate as prevailing in these churches from the earliest times of which any record is preserved[2].

ASIA MINOR.

4. ASIA MINOR follows next in order; and here we find the widest and most unequivocal traces of episcopacy at an early date. Clement of Alexandria distinctly states that St John went about from city to city, his purpose being 'in some places

Activity of St John in proconsular Asia.

to establish bishops, in others to consolidate whole churches, in others again to appoint to the clerical office some one of those who had been signified by the Spirit[3].' 'The sequence of bishops,' writes Tertullian in like manner of Asia Minor, 'traced back to its origin will be found to rest on the authority of John[4].' And a writer earlier than either speaks of St John's 'fellow-disciples and bishops[5]' as gathered about him. The conclusiveness even of such testimony might perhaps be doubted, if it were not supported by other more direct evidence. At the

---

[1] *Ancient Syriac Documents* (ed. Cureton). The *Doctrine of Addai* has recently been published complete by Dr Phillips, London 1876. This work at all events must be old, for it was found by Eusebius in the archives of Edessa (*H. E.* i. 13); but it abounds in gross anachronisms and probably is not earlier than the middle of the 3rd century: see Zahn *Gött. Gel. Anz.* 1877, p. 161 sq.

[2] See for instance pp. 13, 16, 18, 21, 23, 24, 26, 29, 30, 33, 34, 35, 42, 71 (Cureton). The succession to the episcopate is conferred by the 'Hand of Priesthood' through the Apostles, who received it from our Lord, and is derived ultimately from Moses and Aaron (p. 24).

[3] *Quis Div. Salv.* 42 (p. 959).

[4] *Adv. Marc.* iv. 5.

[5] Muratorian Fragment, Routh *Rel. Sacr.* I. p. 394. Irenæus too, whose experience was drawn chiefly from Asia Minor, more than once speaks of bishops appointed by the Apostles, iii. 3. 1, v. 20. 1.

beginning of the second century the letters of Ignatius, even if we accept as genuine only the part contained in the Syriac, mention by name two bishops in these parts, Onesimus of Ephesus and Polycarp of Smyrna[1]. Of the former nothing more is known: the latter evidently writes as a bishop, for he distinguishes himself from his presbyters[2], and is expressly so called by other writers besides Ignatius. His pupil Irenæus says of him, that he had 'not only been instructed by Apostles and conversed with many who had seen Christ, but had also been established by Apostles in Asia as bishop in the Church at Smyrna[3].' Polycrates also, a younger contemporary of Polycarp and himself bishop of Ephesus, designates him by this title[4]; and again in the letter written by his own church and giving an account of his martyrdom he is styled 'bishop of the Church in Smyrna[5].' As Polycarp survived the middle of the second century, dying at a very advanced age (A.D. 155 or 156), the possibility of error on this point seems to be excluded: and indeed all historical evidence must be thrown aside as worthless, if testimony so strong can be disregarded.

Onesimus. Polycarp.

It is probable however, that we should receive as genuine not only those portions of the Ignatian letters which are represented in the Syriac, but also the Greek text in its shorter form. Under any circumstances, this text can hardly have been made later than the middle of the second century[6], and its witness would still be highly valuable, even if it were a forgery. The staunch advocacy of the episcopate which distinguishes these writings is well known and will be considered hereafter. At present we are only concerned with the historical testimony which they bear to the wide extension and authoritative claims of the episcopal office. Besides Polycarp and Onesimus, mentioned in the Syriac, the writer names also

Ignatian letters.

---

[1] *Polyc.* inscr., *Ephes.* 1.
[2] Polyc. *Phil.* init.
[3] Iren. iii. 3. 4. Comp. Tertull. *de Praescr.* 32.
[4] In Euseb. v. 24.
[5] *Mart. Polyc.* 16. Polycarp is called 'bishop of Smyrna' also in *Mart. Ignat. Ant.* 3.
[6] See below, p. 198, note.

Damas bishop of Magnesia[1] and Polybius bishop of Tralles[2]; and he urges on the Philadelphians also the duty of obedience to their bishop[3], though the name is not given. Under any circumstances it seems probable that these were not fictitious personages, for, even if he were a forger, he would be anxious to give an air of reality to his writings: but whether or not we regard his testimony as indirectly affecting the age of Ignatius, for his own time at least it must be regarded as valid.

But the evidence is not confined to the persons and the churches already mentioned. Papias, who was a friend of Polycarp and had conversed with personal disciples of the Lord, is commonly designated bishop of Hierapolis[4]; and we learn from a younger contemporary Serapion[5], that Claudius Apollinaris, known as a writer against the Montanists, also held this see in the reign of M. Aurelius. Again Sagaris the martyr, who seems to have perished in the early years of M. Aurelius, about A.D. 165[6], is designated bishop of Laodicea by an author writing towards the close of the same century, who also alludes to Melito the contemporary of Sagaris as holding the see of Sardis[7]. The authority just quoted, Polycrates of Ephesus, who flourished in the last decade of the century, says moreover that he had had seven relations bishops before him, himself being the eighth, and that he followed their tradition[8]. When he wrote he had been 'sixty-five years in the Lord'; so that even if this period date from the time of his birth and not of his conversion or baptism, he must have been born scarcely a quarter of a century after the death of the last surviving Apostle, whose latest years were spent in the very Church over which Polycrates himself presided. It

Side notes: Bishops of Hierapolis. Sagaris. Melito. Polycrates and his relations.

---

[1] *Magn.* 2.
[2] *Trall.* 1.
[3] *Philad.* 1.
[4] Euseb. *H. E.* iii. 36.
[5] In Euseb. *H. E.* v. 19.
[6] On the authority of his contemporary Melito in Euseb. *H. E.* iv. 26: see *Colossians* p. 63.

[7] Polycrates in Euseb. *H. E.* v. 24. Melito's office may be inferred from the contrast implied in περιμένων τὴν ἀπὸ τῶν οὐρανῶν ἐπισκοπήν.

[8] In Euseb. *H. E.* v. 24. See above, p. 121, note.

THE CHRISTIAN MINISTRY. 175

appears moreover from his language that none of these relations to whom he refers were surviving when he wrote.

Thus the evidence for the early and wide extension of episcopacy throughout proconsular Asia, the scene of St John's latest labours, may be considered irrefragable. And when we pass to other districts of Asia Minor, examples are not wanting though these are neither so early nor so frequent. Marcion a native of Sinope is related to have been the son of a Christian bishop[1]: and Marcion himself had elaborated his theological system before the middle of the second century. Again, a bishop of Eumenia, Thraseas by name, is stated by Polycrates to have been martyred and buried at Smyrna[2]; and, as he is mentioned in connexion with Polycarp, it may fairly be supposed that the two suffered in the same persecution. Dionysius of Corinth moreover, writing to Amastris and the other churches of Pontus (about A.D. 170), mentions Palmas the bishop of this city[3]: and when the Paschal controversy breaks out afresh under Victor of Rome, we find this same Palmas putting his signature first to a circular letter, as the senior of the bishops of Pontus[4]. An anonymous writer also, who took part in the Montanist controversy, speaks of two bishops of repute, Zoticus of Comana and Julianus of Apamea, as having resisted the impostures of the false prophetesses[5]. But indeed the frequent notices of encyclical letters written and synods held towards the close of the second century are a much more powerful testimony to the wide extension of episcopacy throughout the provinces of Asia Minor than the incidental mention of individual names. On one such occasion Polycrates speaks of the 'crowds' of bishops whom he had summoned to confer with him on the Paschal question[6].

Bishops in other parts of Asia Minor.

Episcopal synods.

5. As we turn from Asia Minor to MACEDONIA and *MACEDONIA and GREECE.*

---

[1] [Tertull.] *adv. omn. haeres.* 6.
[2] In Euseb. *H. E.* v. 24.
[3] In Euseb. *H. E.* iv. 23.
[4] Euseb. *H. E.* v. 23.
[5] In Euseb. *H. E.* v. 16. As Apamea on the Mæander is mentioned at the end of the chapter, probably this is the place meant.
[6] In Euseb. *H. E.* v. 24 πολλὰ πλήθη.

176   THE CHRISTIAN MINISTRY.

GREECE, the evidence becomes fainter and scantier. This circumstance is no doubt due partly to the fact that these churches were much less active and important during the second century than the Christian communities of Asia Minor, but the phenomena cannot perhaps be wholly explained by this consideration. When Tertullian in one of his rhetorical flights challenges the heretical teachers to consult the apostolic churches, where 'the very sees of the Apostles still preside,' adding, 'If Achaia is nearest to you, then you have Corinth; if you are not far from Macedonia, you have Philippi, you have the Thessalonians; if you can reach Asia, you have Ephesus[1]': his main argument was doubtless just, and even the language would commend itself to its own age, for episcopacy was the only form of government known or remembered in the church when he wrote: but a careful investigation scarcely allows, and certainly does not encourage us, to place Corinth and Philippi and Thessalonica in the same category with Ephesus as regards episcopacy. The term 'apostolic see' was appropriate to the latter; but so far as we know, it cannot be strictly applied to the former. During the early years of the second century, when episcopacy was firmly established in the principal churches of Asia Minor, Polycarp sends a letter to the Philippians. He writes in the name of himself and his presbyters; he gives advice to the Philippians respecting the obligations and the authority of presbyters and deacons; he is minute in his instructions respecting one individual presbyter, Valens by name, who had been guilty of some crime; but throughout the letter he never once refers to their bishop; and indeed its whole tone is hardly consistent with the supposition that they had any chief officer holding the same prominent position at Philippi which he himself held at Smyrna. We are thus led to the inference that episcopacy did not exist at all among the Philippians at this time, or existed only in an elementary form, so that the bishop was a mere president of the presbyteral council. At Thessalonica indeed, according to a tradition

Later development of episcopacy.

Philippi.

Thessalonica.

[1] Tertull. *de Praescr.* 37.

mentioned by Origen[1], the same Caius whom St Paul describes as his host at Corinth was afterwards appointed bishop; but with so common a name the possibilities of error are great, even if the testimony were earlier in date and expressed in more distinct terms. When from Macedonia we pass to Achaia, the same phenomena present themselves. At the close of the first century Clement writes to Corinth, as at the beginning of the second century Polycarp writes to Philippi. As in the latter epistle, so in the former, there is no allusion to the episcopal office: yet the main subject of Clement's letter is the expulsion and ill-treatment of certain presbyters, whose authority he maintains as holding an office instituted by and handed down from the Apostles themselves. If Corinth however was without a bishop in the strict sense at the close of the first century, she cannot long have remained so. When some fifty years later Hegesippus stayed here on his way to Rome, Primus was bishop of this Church; and it is clear moreover from this writer's language that Primus had been preceded by several occupants of the see[2]. Indeed the order of his narrative, so far as we can piece it together from the broken fragments preserved in Eusebius, might suggest the inference, not at all improbable in itself, that episcopacy had been established at Corinth as a corrective of the dissensions and feuds which had called forth Clement's letter[3]. Again Dionysius, one of the immediate successors of Primus, was the writer of several letters of which fragments are extant[4]; and at the close of the century we meet

Corinth.

---

[1] On Rom. xvi. 23; 'Fertur sane traditione majorum' (IV. p. 86, ed. Delarue).

[2] In Euseb. *H. E.* iv. 22, καὶ ἐπέμενεν ἡ ἐκκλησία ἡ Κορινθίων ἐν τῷ ὀρθῷ λόγῳ μέχρι Πρίμου ἐπισκοπεύοντος ἐν Κορίνθῳ κ.τ.λ. A little later he speaks of ἑκάστη διαδοχή, referring apparently to Corinth among other churches.

[3] Hegesippus mentioned the feuds in the Church of Corinth during the reign of Domitian, which had occasioned the writing of this letter (*H. E.* iii. 16);

and then after some account of Clement's epistle (μετά τινα περὶ τῆς Κλήμεντος πρὸς Κορινθίους ἐπιστολῆς αὐτῷ εἰρημένα, *H. E.* iv. 22) he continued in the words which are quoted in the last note (ἐπιλέγοντος ταῦτα, Καὶ ἐπέμενεν ἡ ἐκκλησία κ.τ.λ.). On the probable tenor of Hegesippus' work see below, p. 182.

[4] The fragments of Dionysius are found in Euseb. *H. E.* iv. 23. See also Routh *Rel. Sacr.* I. p. 177 sq.

178   THE CHRISTIAN MINISTRY.

Athens.

with a later bishop of Corinth, Bacchyllus, who takes an active part in the Paschal controversy[1]. When from Corinth we pass on to Athens, a very early instance of a bishop confronts us, on authority which seems at first sight good. Eusebius represents Dionysius of Corinth, who wrote apparently about the year 170, as stating that his namesake the Areopagite, 'having been brought to the faith by the Apostle Paul according to the account in the Acts, was the first to be entrusted with the bishopric (or supervision) of the diocese (in the language of those times, the parish) of the Athenians[2].' Now, if we could be sure that Eusebius was here reporting the exact words of Dionysius, the testimony though not conclusive would be entitled to great deference. In this case the easiest solution would be, that this ancient writer had not unnaturally confounded the earlier and later usage of the word bishop. But it seems not improbable that Eusebius (for he does not profess to be giving a direct quotation) has unintentionally paraphrased and interpreted the statement of Dionysius by the light of later ecclesiastical usages. However Athens, like Corinth, did not long remain without a bishop. The same Dionysius, writing to the Athenians, reminds them how, after the martyrdom of Publius their ruler (τὸν προεστῶτα), Quadratus becoming bishop sustained the courage and stimulated the faith of the Athenian brotherhood[3]. If, as seems more probable than not, this was the famous Quadratus who presented his apology to Hadrian during that emperor's visit to Athens, the existence of episcopacy in this city is thrown back early in the century; even though Quadratus were not already bishop when Hadrian paid his visit.

CRETE.

6. The same writer, from whom we learn these particulars about episcopacy at Athens, also furnishes information on the Church in CRETE. He writes letters to two different communities in this island, the one to Gortyna commending Philip who held this see, the other to the Cnossians offering words of advice to their bishop Pinytus[3]. The first was author of a

[1] Euseb. *H. E.* v. 22, 23.   [2] In Euseb. *H. E.* iv. 23.   [3] Euseb. *H. E.* iv. 23.

treatise against Marcion[1]; the latter wrote a reply to Dionysius, of which Eusebius has preserved a brief notice[2].

7. Of episcopacy in THRACE, and indeed of the Thracian Church generally, we read nothing till the close of the second century, when one Ælius Publius Julius bishop of Debeltum, a colony in this province, signs an encyclical letter[2]. The existence of a see at a place so unimportant implies the wide spread of episcopacy in these regions. *THRACE.*

8. As we turn to ROME, we are confronted by a far more perplexing problem than any encountered hitherto. The attempt to decipher the early history of episcopacy here seems almost hopeless, where the evidence is at once scanty and conflicting. It has been often assumed that in the metropolis of the world, the seat of imperial rule, the spirit which dominated in the State must by natural predisposition and sympathy have infused itself into the Church also, so that a monarchical form of government would be developed more rapidly here than in other parts of Christendom. This supposition seems to overlook the fact that the influences which prevailed in the early church of the metropolis were more Greek than Roman[3], and that therefore the tendency would be rather towards individual liberty than towards compact and rigorous government. But indeed such presumptions, however attractive and specious, are valueless against the slightest evidence of facts. And the most trustworthy sources of information which we possess do not countenance the idea. The earliest authentic document bearing on the subject is the Epistle from the Romans to the Corinthians, probably written in the last decade of the first century. I have already considered the bearing of this letter on episcopacy in the Church of Corinth, and it is now time to ask what light *ROME.* *The prevailing spirit not monarchical.* *Bearing of Clement's Epistle.*

---

[1] Euseb. *H. E.* iv. 25.

[2] Euseb. *H. E.* v. 19. The combination of three gentile names in 'Ælius Publius Julius' is possible at this late epoch; but, being a gross violation of Roman usage, suggests the suspicion that the signatures of three distinct persons have got confused. The error however, if error it be, does not affect the inference in the text.

[3] See *Philippians*, p. 20 sq.

180   THE CHRISTIAN MINISTRY.

it throws on the same institution at Rome. Now we cannot hesitate to accept the universal testimony of antiquity that it was written by Clement, the reputed bishop of Rome: and it is therefore the more surprising that, if he held this high office, the writer should not only not distinguish himself in any way from the rest of the church (as Polycarp does for instance), but that even his name should be suppressed[1]. It is still more important to observe that, though he has occasion to speak of the ministry as an institution of the Apostles, he mentions only two orders and is silent about the episcopal office. Moreover he still uses the word 'bishop' in the older sense in which it occurs in the apostolic writings, as a synonyme for presbyter[2], and it may be argued that the recognition of the episcopate as a higher and distinct office would oblige the adoption of a special name and therefore must have synchronized roughly with the separation of meaning between 'bishop' and 'presbyter.'

Testimony of Ignatius Again, not many years after the date of Clement's letter, St Ignatius on his way to martyrdom writes to the Romans. Though this saint is the recognised champion of episcopacy, though the remaining six of the Ignatian letters all contain direct injunctions of obedience to bishops, in this epistle alone there is no allusion to the episcopal office as existing among his correspondents. The lapse of a few years carries us from the *and Hermas.* letters of Ignatius to the *Shepherd* of Hermas. And here the indications are equivocal. Hermas receives directions in a vision to impart the revelation to the presbyters and also to make two copies, the one for Clement who shall communicate with the foreign churches (such being his duty), the other for Grapte who shall instruct the widows. Hermas himself is charged to 'read it to this city with the elders who preside over the church[3].' Elsewhere mention is made of the 'rulers' of the

---

[1] See *S. Clement of Rome* p. 252 sq. Appendix [and *Apostolic Fathers*, Part 1, *S. Clement of Rome*, I. p. 69 sq.].

[2] See *Philippians* p. 96 sq.

[3] *Vis.* ii. 4 γράψεις οὖν δύο βιβλιδάρια καὶ πέμψεις ἐν Κλήμεντι καὶ ἐν Γραπτῇ. πέμψει οὖν Κλήμης εἰς τὰς ἔξω πόλεις· ἐκείνῳ γὰρ ἐπιτέτραπται· Γραπτὴ δὲ νουθετήσει τὰς χήρας καὶ τοὺς ὀρφανούς· σὺ δὲ ἀναγνώσεις εἰς ταύτην τὴν πόλιν μετὰ τῶν πρεσβυτέρων τῶν προϊσταμένων τῆς ἐκκλησίας.

THE CHRISTIAN MINISTRY. 181

church[1]. And again, in an enumeration of the faithful officers of the churches past and present, he speaks of the 'apostles and bishops and teachers and deacons[2].' Here most probably the word 'bishop' is used in its later sense, and the presbyters are designated by the term 'teachers.' Yet this interpretation cannot be regarded as certain, for the 'bishops and teachers' in Hermas, like the 'pastors and teachers' in St Paul, might possibly refer to the one presbyteral office in its twofold aspect. Other passages in which Hermas uses the same terms are indecisive. Thus he speaks of 'apostles and teachers who preached to the whole world and taught with reverence and purity the word of the Lord[3]'; of 'deacons who exercised their diaconate ill and plundered the life ($\tau\dot{\eta}\nu$ $\zeta\omega\dot{\eta}\nu$) of widows and orphans[4]'; of 'hospitable bishops who at all times received the servants of God into their homes cheerfully and without hypocrisy,' 'who protected the bereaved and the widows in their ministrations without ceasing[5].' From these passages it seems impossible to arrive at a safe conclusion respecting the ministry at the time when Hermas wrote. In other places he condemns the false prophet 'who, seeming to have the Spirit, exalts himself and would fain have the first seat[6]'; or he warns 'those who rule over the church and those who hold the chief-seat,' bidding them give up their dissensions and live at peace among themselves[7]; or he denounces those who have 'emulation one with another for the first place or for some honour[8].' If we could accept the suggestion that in this last class of passages the writer condemns the ambition which aimed at transforming the presbyterian into the episcopal form of government[9], we should have arrived at a solution of the difficulty: but the rebukes are couched in the most general terms and apply at least as well

Unwarranted inference.

---

[1] *Vis.* ii. 2, iii. 9.
[2] *Vis.* iii. 5.
[3] *Sim.* ix. 25.
[4] *Sim.* ix. 26.
[5] *Sim.* ix. 27.
[6] *Mand.* xi.
[7] *Vis.* iii. 9 ὑμῖν λέγω τοῖς προηγουμένοις τῆς ἐκκλησίας καὶ τοῖς πρωτοκαθεδρίταις, κ.τ.λ. For the form πρωτοκαθεδρίτης see the note on συνδιδασκαλίταις, Ignat. *Ephes.* 3.
[8] *Sim.* viii. 7.
[9] So Ritschl pp. 403, 535.

to the ambitious pursuit of existing offices as to the arrogant assertion of a hitherto unrecognized power[1]. This clue failing us, the notices in the *Shepherd* are in themselves too vague to lead to any result. Were it not known that the writer's own brother was bishop of Rome, we should be at a loss what to say about the constitution of the Roman Church in his day[2].

But while the testimony of these early writers appears at first sight and on the whole unfavourable to the existence of episcopacy in Rome when they wrote, the impression needs to be corrected by important considerations on the other side. Hegesippus, who visited Rome about the middle of the second century during the papacy of Anicetus, has left it on record that he drew up a list of the Roman bishops to his own time[3]. As the list is not preserved[4], we can only conjecture its contents; but if we may judge from the sentence immediately following, in which he praises the orthodoxy of this and other churches under each succession, his object was probably to show that the teachings of the Apostles had been carefully preserved and handed down, and he would therefore trace the episcopal succession back to apostolic times[5]. Such at all events is the aim and method of Irenæus, who, writing somewhat later than Hegesippus and combating Gnostic heresies, appeals especially to the bishops of Rome, as depositaries of the apostolic tradition[6]. The list of Irenæus commences with Linus, whom he identifies

Testimony of Hegesippus

and of Irenæus.

Lists of Roman bishops.

---

[1] Comp. Matt. xxiii. 6, etc. When Irenæus wrote, episcopacy was certainly a venerable institution: yet his language closely resembles the reproachful expressions of Hermas: 'Contumeliis agunt reliquos et principalis consessionis (MSS concessionis) tumore elati sunt' (iv. 26. 3).

[2] See *Philippians* p. 168, note 9, and *S. Clement of Rome* p. 316, *Appendix* [*Apostolic Fathers*, Part I. *S. Clement of Rome* I. p. 359 sq.].

[3] In Euseb. *H. E.* iv. 22.

[4] [It is probably preserved in Epiphanius, see *Apostolic Fathers*, Part I. *S. Clement of Rome* I. p. 327 sq.]

[5] The words of Hegesippus ἐν ἑκάστῃ διαδοχῇ καὶ ἐν ἑκάστῃ πόλει κ.τ.λ. have a parallel in those of Irenæus (iii. 3. 3) τῇ αὐτῇ τάξει καὶ τῇ αὐτῇ διδαχῇ (Lat. 'hac ordinatione et successione') ἥ τε ἀπὸ τῶν ἀποστόλων ἐν τῇ ἐκκλησίᾳ παράδοσις καὶ τὸ τῆς ἀληθείας κήρυγμα κατήντηκεν εἰς ἡμᾶς. May not Irenæus have derived his information from the διαδοχή of Roman bishops which Hegesippus drew up? See below, p. 204 [and *Apostolic Fathers*, Part I. *S. Clement of Rome* I. pp. 63 sq., 204 sq., 327 sq.].

[6] Iren. iii. 33.

THE CHRISTIAN MINISTRY.   183

with the person of this name mentioned by St Paul, and whom he states to have been 'entrusted with the office of the bishopric' by the Apostles. The second in succession is Anencletus of whom he relates nothing, the third Clemens whom he describes as a hearer of the Apostles and as writer of the letter to the Corinthians. The others in order are Evarestus, Alexander, Xystus, Telesphorus, Hyginus, Pius, Anicetus, Soter, and Eleutherus during whose episcopacy Irenæus writes. Eusebius in different works gives two lists, both agreeing in the order with Irenæus, though not according with each other in the dates. Catalogues are also found in writers later than Irenæus, transposing the sequence of the earliest bishops, and adding the name Cletus or substituting it for Anencletus[1]. These discrepancies may be explained by assuming two distinct churches in Rome— a Jewish and a Gentile community—in the first age; or they may have arisen from a confusion of the earlier and later senses of ἐπίσκοπος; or the names may have been transposed in the later lists owing to the influence of the *Clementine Homilies*, in which romance Clement is represented as the immediate disciple and successor of St Peter[2]. With the many possibilities of error, no more can safely be assumed of LINUS and ANENCLETUS than that they held some prominent position in the Roman Church. But the reason for supposing CLEMENT to have been a bishop is as strong as the universal tradition of the next ages can make it. Yet, while calling him a bishop, we need not suppose him to have attained the same distinct isolated position

Linus, A.D. 68.
Anencletus, A.D. 80.
Clement, A.D. 92.

---

[1] On this subject see Pearson's *Dissertationes duae de serie et successione primorum Romae episcoporum* in his *Minor Theological Works* II. p. 296 sq. (ed. Churton), and especially the recent work of Lipsius, *Chronologie der römischen Bischöfe*, Kiel 1869. The earliest list which places Clement's name first belongs to the age of Hippolytus. The omission of his name in a recently discovered Syriac list (*Ancient Syriac Documents* p. 71) is doubtless due to the fact that the names Cletus, Clemens, begin with the same letters. In the margin I have for convenience given the dates of the Roman bishops from the Ecclesiastical History of Eusebius, without however attaching any weight to them in the case of the earlier names. See *Philippians* p. 169 [and *Apostolic Fathers*, Part I. *S. Clement of Rome* I. p. 201 sq.].

[2] See above, p. 99.

of authority which was occupied by his successors Eleutherus and Victor for instance at the close of the second century, or even by his contemporaries Ignatius of Antioch and Polycarp of Smyrna. He was rather the chief of the presbyters than the chief over the presbyters. Only when thus limited, can the episcopacy of St Clement be reconciled with the language of his own epistle or with the notice in his younger contemporary Hermas. At the same time the allusion in the *Shepherd*, though inconsistent with any exalted conception of his office, does assign to him as his special province the duty of communicating with foreign churches[1], which in the early ages was essentially the bishop's function, as may be seen by the instances of Polycarp, of Dionysius, of Irenæus, and of Polycrates. Of the two succeeding bishops, EVARESTUS and ALEXANDER, no authentic notices are preserved. XYSTUS, who follows, is the reputed author of a collection of proverbs, which a recent distinguished critic has not hesitated to accept as genuine[2]. He is also the earliest of those Roman prelates whom Irenæus, writing to Victor in the name of the Gallican Churches, mentions as having observed Easter after the western reckoning and yet maintained peace with those who kept it otherwise[3]. The next two, TELESPHORUS and HYGINUS, are described in the same terms. The former is likewise distinguished as the sole martyr among the early bishops of the metropolis[4]; the latter is mentioned as being in office when the peace of the Roman Church was disturbed by the presence of the heretics Valentinus and Cerdon[5]. With PIUS, the next in order, the office, if not the man, emerges into daylight. An anonymous writer, treating on the canon of Scripture, says that the *Shepherd* was written by Hermas 'quite lately while his brother Pius held the

Evarestus, A.D. 100.
Alexander, A.D. 109.
Xystus, A.D. 119.

Telesphorus, A.D. 128.
Hyginus, A.D. 139.

Pius, A.D. 142.

---

[1] See above, p. 180, note 3.

[2] Ewald, *Gesch. des V. I.* VII. p. 321 sq. On the other hand see Zeller *Philos. der Griechen* III. 1, p. 601 note, and Sänger in the *Jüdische Zeitschrift* (1867) p. 29 sq. It has recently been edited by Gildemeister, *Sexti Sententiæ*, 1873.

[3] Iren. in Euseb. *H. E.* v. 24.

[4] Iren. iii. 3. 3. At least Irenæus mentions him alone as a martyr. Later stories confer the glory of martyrdom on others also.

[5] Iren. iii. 4. 3.

see of the Church of Rome¹.' This passage, written by a contemporary, besides the testimony which it bears to the date and authorship of the *Shepherd* (with which we are not here concerned), is valuable in its bearing on this investigation; for the use of the 'chair' or 'see' as a recognised phrase points to a more or less prolonged existence of episcopacy in Rome, when this writer lived. To Pius succeeds ANICETUS. And now Rome becomes for the moment the centre of interest and activity in the Christian world². During this episcopate Hegesippus, visiting the metropolis for the purpose of ascertaining and recording the doctrines of the Roman Church, is welcomed by the bishop³. About the same time also another more illustrious visitor, Polycarp the venerable bishop of Smyrna, arrives in Rome to confer with the head of the Roman Church on the Paschal dispute⁴ and there falls in with and denounces the heretic Marcion⁵. These facts are stated on contemporary authority. Of SOTER also, the next in succession, a contemporary record is preserved. Dionysius of Corinth, writing to the Romans, praises the zeal of their bishop, who in his fatherly care for the suffering poor and for the prisoners working in the mines had maintained and extended the hereditary fame of his church for zeal in all charitable and good works⁶. In ELEUTHERUS, who succeeds Soter, we have the earliest recorded instance of an archdeacon. When Hegesippus paid his visit to the metropolis, he found Eleutherus standing in this relation to the bishop Anicetus, and seems to have made his acquaintance while acting in this capacity⁷. Eleutherus however was a contemporary, not only of Hegesippus, but also of the great writers Irenæus and Tertullian⁸, who speak of the episcopal succession in the churches generally, and in Rome especially, as

Anicetus, A.D. 157.

Soter, A.D. 168.

Eleutherus, A.D. 177.

---

¹ See *Philippians* p. 168, note 9, where the passage is quoted.
² See Westcott *Canon* p. 191, ed. 4.
³ Hegesipp. in Euseb. *H. E.* iv. 22.
⁴ Iren. in Euseb. *H. E.* v. 24.
⁵ Iren. iii. 3. 4; comp. iii. 4. 4.
⁶ In Euseb. *H. E.* iv. 23.

⁷ In Euseb. *H. E.* iv. 22 μέχρις Ἀνικήτου οὗ διάκονος ἦν Ἐλεύθερος.
⁸ He is mentioned by Irenæus iii. 3. 3 νῦν δωδεκάτῳ τόπῳ τὸν τῆς ἐπισκοπῆς ἀπὸ τῶν ἀποστόλων κατέχει κλῆρον Ἐλεύθερος, and by Tertullian, *Praescr.* 30 'sub episcopatu Eleutheri benedicti.'

186   THE CHRISTIAN MINISTRY.

Victor, A.D. 189.

the best safeguard for the transmission of the true faith from apostolic times[1]. With VICTOR, the successor of Eleutherus, a new era begins. Apparently the first Latin prelate who held the metropolitan see of Latin Christendom[2], he was moreover the first Roman bishop who is known to have had intimate relations with the imperial court[3], and the first also who advanced those claims to universal dominion which his successors in later ages have always consistently and often successfully maintained[4]. 'I hear,' writes Tertullian scornfully, 'that an edict has gone forth, aye and that a peremptory edict; the chief pontiff, forsooth, I mean the bishop of bishops, has issued his commands[5].' At the end of the first century the Roman Church was swayed by the mild and peaceful counsels of the presbyter-bishop Clement; the close of the second witnessed the autocratic pretensions of the haughty pope Victor, the prototype of a Hildebrand or an Innocent.

GAUL.

9. The Churches of GAUL were closely connected with and probably descended from the Churches of Asia Minor. If so, the episcopal form of government would probably be coeval with

[1] Iren. iii. 3. 2, Tertull. de Praescr. 32, 36, adv. Marc. iv. 5.

[2] All the predecessors of Victor bear Greek names with two exceptions, Clemens and Pius; and even these appear not to have been Latin. Clement writes in Greek, and his style is wholly unlike what might be expected from a Roman. Hermas, the brother of Pius, not only employs the Greek language in writing, but bears a Greek name also. It is worth observing also that Tertullian (de Praescr. 30), speaking of the episcopate of Eleutherus, designates the church of the metropolis not 'ecclesia Romana,' but 'ecclesia Romanensis,' i.e. not the Church of Rome, but the Church in Rome. The transition from a Greek to a Latin Church was of course gradual; but, if a definite epoch must be named, the episcopate of Victor serves better than any other. The two immediate successors of Victor, Zephyrinus (202—219) and Callistus (219—223), bear Greek names, and it may be inferred from the account in Hippolytus that they were Greeks; but from this time forward the Roman bishops, with scarcely an exception, seem to have been Latins.

[3] Hippol. Haer. ix. 12, pp. 287, 288.

[4] See the account of his attitude in the Paschal controversy, Euseb. H. E. v. 24.

[5] Tertull. de Pudic. 1. The bishop here mentioned will be either Victor or Zephyrinus; and the passage points to the assumption of extraordinary titles by the Roman bishops about this time. See also Cyprian in the opening of the Concil. Carth. p. 158 (ed. Fell) 'neque enim quisquam nostrum episcopum se episcoporum constituit etc.,' doubtless in allusion to the arrogance of the Roman prelates.

the foundation of Christian brotherhoods in this country. It is true we do not meet with any earlier bishop than the immediate predecessor of Irenæus at Lyons, the aged Pothinus, of whose martyrdom an account is given in the letter of the Gallican Churches[1]. But this is also the first distinct historical notice of any kind relating to Christianity in Gaul.

10. AFRICA again was evangelized from Rome at a compa- AFRICA. ratively late date. Of the African Church before the close of the second century, when a flood of light is suddenly thrown upon it by the writings of Tertullian, we know absolutely nothing. But we need not doubt that this father represents the traditions and sentiments of his church, when he lays stress on episcopacy as an apostolic institution and on the episcopate as the depositary of pure Christian doctrine. If we may judge by the large number of prelates assembled in the African councils of a later generation, it would appear that the extension of the episcopate was far more rapid here than in most parts of Christendom[2].

11. The Church of ALEXANDRIA, on the other hand, was ALEXANDRIA. probably founded in apostolic times[3]. Nor is there any reason to doubt the tradition which connects it with the name of St Mark, though the authorities for the statement are comparatively recent. Nevertheless of its early history we have no

---

[1] The Epistle of the Gallican Churches in Euseb. *H. E.* v. 1.

[2] At the African council convoked by Cyprian about 50 years later, the opinions of as many as 87 bishops are recorded; and allusion is made in one of his letters (*Epist.* 59) to a council held before his time, when 90 bishops assembled. For a list of the African bishoprics at this time see Münter *Primord. Eccl. Afric.* p. 31 sq. The enormous number of African bishops a few centuries later would seem incredible, were it not reported on the best authority. Dupin (Optat. Milev. p. lix) counts up as many as 690 African sees: compare also the Notitia in Ruinart's Victor Vitensis p. 117 sq., with the notes p. 215 sq. These last references I owe to Gibbon, c. xxxvii. and c. xli.

[3] Independently of the tradition relating to St Mark, this may be inferred from extant canonical and uncanonical writings which appear to have emanated from Alexandria. The Epistle to the Hebrews, even if we may not ascribe it to the learned Alexandrian Apollos (Acts xviii. 24), at least bears obvious marks of Alexandrian culture. The so-called Epistle of Barnabas again, which may have been written as early as the reign of Vespasian and can hardly date later than Nerva, must be referred to the Alexandrian school of theology.

188   THE CHRISTIAN MINISTRY.

Hadrian's letter.

authentic record. Eusebius indeed gives a list of bishops beginning with St Mark, which here, as in the case of the Roman see, is accompanied by dates[1]; but from what source he derived his information is unknown. The first contemporary notice of church officers in Alexandria is found in a heathen writer. The emperor Hadrian, writing to the consul Servianus, thus describes the state of religion in this city: 'I have become perfectly familiar with Egypt, which you praised to me; it is fickle, uncertain, blown about by every gust of rumour. Those who worship Serapis are Christians, and those are devoted to Serapis who call themselves bishops of Christ. There is no ruler of a synagogue there, no Samaritan, no Christian presbyter, who is not an astrologer, a soothsayer, a quack. The patriarch himself whenever he comes to Egypt is compelled by some to worship Serapis, by others to worship Christ[2].' In this letter, which seems to have been written in the year 134, Hadrian shows more knowledge of Jewish ecclesiastical polity than of Christian: but, apparently without knowing the exact value of terms, he seems to

---

[1] Euseb. *H. E.* ii. 24, iii. 14, etc. See Clinton's *Fasti Romani* II. p. 544.

[2] Preserved in Vopiscus *Vit. Saturn.* 8. The Jewish patriarch (who resided at Tiberias) is doubtless intended; for it would be no hardship to the Christian bishop of Alexandria to be 'compelled to worship Christ.' Otherwise the anachronism involved in such a title would alone have sufficed to condemn the letter as spurious. Yet Salmasius, Casaubon, and the older commentators generally, agree in the supposition that the bishop of Alexandria is styled patriarch here. The manner in which the document is stated by Vopiscus to have been preserved ('Hadriani epistolam ex libris Phlegontis liberti ejus proditam') is favourable to its genuineness; nor does the mention of Verus as the emperor's 'son' in another part of the letter present any real chronological difficulty. Hadrian paid his visit to Egypt in the autumn of 130, but the letter is not stated to have been written there. The date of the third consulship of Servianus is A.D. 134, and the account of Spartianus (*Ver.* 3) easily admits of the adoption of Verus before or during this year, though Clinton (*Fast. Rom.* I. p. 124) places it as late as A.D. 135. Gregorovius (*Kaiser Hadrian* p. 71) suggests that 'filium meum' may have been added by Phlegon or by some one else. The prominence of the Christians in this letter is not surprising, when we remember how Hadrian interested himself in their tenets on another occasion (at Athens). This document is considered genuine by such opposite authorities as Tillemont (*Hist. des Emp.* II. p. 265) and Gregorovius (l. c. p. 41), and may be accepted without hesitation.

distinguish the bishop and the presbyter in the Christian community[1]. From the age of Hadrian to the age of Clement no contemporary or nearly contemporary notices are found, bearing on the government of the Alexandrian Church. The language of Clement is significant; he speaks sometimes of two orders of the ministry, the presbyters and deacons[2]; sometimes of three, the bishops, presbyters, and deacons[3]. Thus it would appear that even as late as the close of the second century the bishop of Alexandria was regarded as distinct and yet not distinct from the presbytery[4]. And the language of Clement is further illustrated by the fact, which will have to be considered at length presently, that at Alexandria the bishop was nominated and apparently ordained by the twelve presbyters out of their own number[5]. The episcopal office in this Church during the second century gives no presage of the world-wide influence to which under the prouder name of patriarchate it was destined in later ages to attain. The Alexandrian succession, in which history is hitherto most interested, is not the succession of the bishops but of the heads of the catechetical school. The first bishop of Alexandria, of whom any distinct incident is recorded on trustworthy authority, was a contemporary of Origen.

Clement of Alexandria.

The notices thus collected[6] present a large body of evidence

Inferences

---

[1] At this time there appears to have been only one bishop in Egypt (see below, p. 196). But Hadrian, who would have heard of numerous bishops elsewhere, and perhaps had no very precise knowledge of the Egyptian Church, might well indulge in this rhetorical flourish. At all events he seems to mean different offices, when speaking of the bishop and the presbyter.

[2] *Strom.* vii. 1 (p. 830, Potter) ὁμοίως δὲ καὶ κατὰ τὴν ἐκκλησίαν, τὴν μὲν βελτιωτικὴν οἱ πρεσβύτεροι σώζουσιν εἰκόνα, τὴν ὑπηρετικὴν δὲ οἱ διάκονοι.

[3] *Strom.* vi. 13 (p. 793) αἱ ἐνταῦθα κατὰ τὴν ἐκκλησίαν προκοπαί, ἐπισκόπων, πρεσβυτέρων, διακόνων, μιμήματα οἶμαι ἀγγελικῆς δόξης, *Strom.* iii. 12 (p. 552), *Paed.* iii. 12 (see the next note): see Kaye's *Clement of Alexandria* p. 463 sq.

[4] Yet in one passage he, like Irenæus (see *Philippians* p. 98), betrays his ignorance that in the language of the New Testament bishop and presbyter are synonymes; see *Paed.* iii. 12 (p. 309) μυρίαι δὲ ὅσαι ὑποθῆκαι εἰς πρόσωπα ἐκλεκτὰ διατείνουσαι ἐγγεγράφαται ταῖς βίβλοις ταῖς ἁγίαις, αἱ μὲν πρεσβυτέροις αἱ δὲ ἐπισκόποις αἱ δὲ διακόνοις, ἄλλαι χήραις κ.τ.λ.

[5] See below, p. 194.

[6] In this sketch of the episcopate in the different churches I have not thought it necessary to carry the lists later than

190 THE CHRISTIAN MINISTRY.

The general prevalence of episcopacy.

establishing the fact of the early and extensive adoption of episcopacy in the Christian Church. The investigation however would not be complete, unless attention were called to such indirect testimony as is furnished by the tacit assumptions of writers living towards and at the close of the second century. Episcopacy is so inseparably interwoven with all the traditions and beliefs of men like Irenæus and Tertullian, that they betray no knowledge of a time when it was not. Even Irenæus, the earlier of these, who was certainly born and probably grown up before the middle of the century, seems to be wholly ignorant that the word bishop had passed from a lower to a higher value since the apostolic times[1]. Nor is it important only to observe the positive though indirect testimony which they afford. Their silence suggests a strong negative presumption, that while every other point of doctrine or practice was eagerly canvassed, the form of Church government alone scarcely came under discussion.

Gradual and uneven development of the office.

But these notices, besides establishing the general prevalence of episcopacy, also throw considerable light on its origin. They indicate that the solution suggested by the history of the word 'bishop' and its transference from the lower to the higher office is the true solution, and that the episcopate was created out of the presbytery. They shew that this creation was not so much an isolated act as a progressive development, not advancing everywhere at an uniform rate but exhibiting at one and the same time different stages of growth in different churches. They seem to hint also that, so far as this development was affected at all by national temper and characteristics, it was slower where the prevailing influences were more purely Greek, as at Corinth and Philippi and Rome, and more rapid where an oriental spirit predominated, as at Jerusalem and

---

the second century. Nor (except in a very few cases) has any testimony been accepted, unless the writer himself flourished before the close of this century. The Apostolic Constitutions would add several names to the list; but this evidence is not trustworthy, though in many cases the statements doubtless rested on some traditional basis.

[1] See *Philippians* p. 98. The same is true of Clement of Alexandria: see above, p. 189, note 4.

Antioch and Ephesus. Above all, they establish this result clearly, that its maturer forms are seen first in those regions where the latest surviving Apostles (more especially St John) fixed their abode, and at a time when its prevalence cannot be dissociated from their influence or their sanction.

The original relation of the bishop to the presbyter, which this investigation reveals, was not forgotten even after the lapse of centuries. Though set over the presbyters, he was still regarded as in some sense one of them. Irenæus indicates this position of the episcopate very clearly. In his language a presbyter is never designated a bishop, while on the other hand he very frequently speaks of a bishop as a presbyter. In other words, though he views the episcopate as a distinct office from the presbytery, he does not regard it as a distinct order in the same sense in which the diaconate is a distinct order. Thus, arguing against the heretics he says, 'But when again we appeal against them to that tradition which is derived from the Apostles, which is preserved in the churches by successions of *presbyters*, they place themselves in opposition to it, saying that they, being wiser not only than the *presbyters* but even than the Apostles, have discovered the genuine truth[1].' Yet just below, after again mentioning the apostolic tradition, he adds, 'We are able to enumerate those who have been appointed by the Apostles *bishops* in the churches and their successors down to our own time[2]'; and still further, after saying that it would take up too much space if he were to trace the succession in all the churches, he declares that he will confound his opponents by singling out the ancient and renowned Church of Rome founded by the Apostles Peter and Paul and will point out the tradition handed down to his own time 'by the succession of *bishops*,' after which he gives a list from Linus to Eleutherus[3]. So again in another passage he writes, 'Therefore obedience ought to be rendered to the *presbyters* who are in the churches, who have the succession from the Apostles as we have shown, who with the succession

Original relation of the two offices not forgotten.

A bishop still called a presbyter by Irenæus

---

[1] Iren. iii. 2. 2.   [2] Iren. iii. 3. 1.   [3] Iren. iii. 3. 2, 3.

of the *episcopate* have also received the sure grace of truth according to the pleasure of the Father'; after which he mentions some 'who are believed by many to be *presbyters*, but serve their own lusts and are elated with the pomp of the *chief seat*,' and bids his readers shun these and seek such as 'together with the rank of the *presbytery* show their speech sound and their conversation void of offence,' adding of these latter, 'Such *presbyters* the Church nurtures and rears, concerning whom also the prophet saith, "I will give thy rulers in peace and thy *bishops* in righteousness[1]"'. Thus also writing to Victor of Rome in the name of the Gallican churches, he says, 'It was not so observed by the *presbyters* before Soter, who ruled the Church which thou now guidest, we mean Anicetus and Pius, Hyginus and Telesphorus and Xystus[2].'

and Clement of Alexandria. And the same estimate of the office appears in Clement of Alexandria: for, while he speaks elsewhere of the three offices in the ministry, mentioning them by name, he in one passage puts forward a twofold division, the presbyters whose duty it is to *improve*, and the deacons whose duty it is to *serve*, the Church[3]. The functions of the bishop and presbyter are thus regarded as substantially the same in kind, though different in degree, while the functions of the diaconate are separate *Testimony of Ambrosiaster,* from both. More than a century and a half later, this view is put forward with the greatest distinctness by the most learned and most illustrious of the Latin fathers. 'There is

---

[1] Iren. iv. 26. 2, 3, 4, 5.

[2] In Euseb. *H. E.* v. 24. In other places Irenæus apparently uses πρεσβύτεροι to denote antiquity and not office, as in the letter to Florinus, Euseb. *H. E.* v. 20 οἱ πρὸ ἡμῶν πρεσβύτεροι οἱ καὶ τοῖς ἀποστόλοις συμφοιτήσαντες (comp. ii. 22. 5); in which sense the word occurs also in Papias (Euseb. *H. E.* iii. 39; see *Contemporary Review*, Aug. 1875, p. 379 sq. [*Essays on Supernatural Religion* p. 143 sq.]); but the passages quoted in the text are decisive, nor is there any reason (as Rothe assumes, p. 414 sq.) why the usage of Irenæus should throughout be uniform in this matter.

[3] See the passage quoted above, p. 189, note 2. So also in the anecdote of St John (*Quis div. salv.* 42, p. 959) we read τῷ καθεστῶτι προσβλέψας ἐπισκόπῳ, but immediately afterwards ὁ δὲ πρεσβύτερος ἀναλαβών κ.τ.λ., and then again ἄγε δή, ἔφη, ὦ ἐπίσκοπε, of the same person. Thus he too, like Irenæus, regards the bishop as a presbyter, though the converse would not be true.

one ordination,' writes the commentator Hilary, 'of the bishop and the presbyter; for either is a priest, but the bishop is first. Every bishop is a presbyter, but every presbyter is not a bishop: for he is bishop who is first among the presbyters[1].' The language of St Jerome to the same effect has been quoted elsewhere[2]. To the passages there given may be added the following: 'This has been said to show that with the ancients presbyters were the same as bishops: but gradually all the responsibility was deferred to a single person, that the thickets of heresies might be rooted out. Therefore, as presbyters know that by *the custom of the Church* they are subject to him who shall have been set over them, so let bishops also be aware that they are superior to presbyters *more owing to custom than to any actual ordinance of the Lord*, etc.: Let us see therefore what sort of person ought to be ordained presbyter or bishop[3].' In the same spirit too the great Augustine writing to Jerome says, 'Although according to titles of honour which *the practice of the Church has now made valid*, the episcopate is greater than the presbytery, yet in many things Augustine is less than Jerome[4].' To these fathers this view seemed to be an obvious deduction from the identity of the terms 'bishop' and 'presbyter' in the apostolic writings; nor indeed, when they wrote, had usage entirely effaced the original connexion between the two offices. Even in the fourth and fifth centuries, when the independence and power of the episcopate had reached its maximum, it was still customary for a bishop in writing to a presbyter to address him as 'fellow-presbyter[5],' thus bearing testimony to a substantial identity of

Jerome,
and Augustine.
Bishops styled themselves fellow-presbyters.

---

[1] Ambrosiast. on 1 Tim. iii. 10.
[2] See *Philippians* p. 98.
[3] On Tit. i. 5 (VII. p. 696).
[4] *Epist.* lxxxii. 33 (II. p. 202, ed. Ben.).
[5] So for instance Cyprian, *Epist.* 14, writes 'compresbyteri nostri Donatus et Fortunatus'; and addressing Cornelius bishop of Rome (*Epist.* 45) he says 'cum ad me talia de te et compresbyteris tecum considentibus scripta venissent.' Compare also *Epist.* 44, 45, 71, 76. Augustine writes to Jerome in the same terms, and in fact this seems to have been the recognised form of address. See the *Quaest. Vet. et Nov. Test.* ci. (in Augustin. *Op.* III. P. 2, p. 93) 'Quid est enim episcopus nisi primus presbyter, hoc est summus sacerdos?

order. Nor does it appear that this view was ever questioned until the era of the Reformation. In the western Church at all events it carried the sanction of the highest ecclesiastical authorities and was maintained even by popes and councils[1].

The bishop of Alexandria chosen and created by the presbytery.

Nor was it only in the *language* of the later Church that the memory of this fact was preserved. Even in her practice indications might here and there be traced, which pointed to a time when the bishop was still only the chief member of the presbytery. The case of the Alexandrian Church, which has already been mentioned casually, deserves special notice. St Jerome, after denouncing the audacity of certain persons who 'would give to deacons the precedence over presbyters, that is over bishops,' and alleging scriptural proofs of the identity of the two, gives the following fact in illustration: 'At Alexandria, from Mark the Evangelist down to the times of the bishops Heraclas (A.D. 233—249) and Dionysius (A.D. 249—265), the presbyters always nominated as bishop one chosen out of their own body and placed in a higher grade: just as if an army were to appoint a general, or deacons were to choose from their own body one whom they knew to be diligent and call him archdeacon[2].' Though the direct statement of this father refers only to the *appointment* of the bishop, still it may be inferred that the function of the presbyters extended also to the *consecration*. And this inference is borne out by other evidence. 'In Egypt,' writes an older contemporary of St Jerome, the commentator Hilary, 'the presbyters seal (i.e. ordain or consecrate), if the bishop be not present[3].' This however might refer only to the ordination of presbyters, and not

---

Denique non aliter quam compresbyteros hic vocat et consacerdotes suos. Numquid et ministros condiaconos suos dicit episcopus?', where the writer is arguing against the arrogance of the Roman deacons. See *Philippians* p. 96.

[1] See the references collected by Gieseler, I. p. 105 sq.

[2] *Epist.* cxlvi. *ad Evang.* (I. p. 1082).

[3] Ambrosiast. on Ephes. iv. 12. So too in the *Quaest. Vet. et Nov. Test.* ci. (falsely ascribed to St Augustine), August. *Op.* III. P. 2, p. 93, 'Nam in Alexandria et per totam Ægyptum, si desit episcopus, consecrat (v. l. consignat) presbyter.'

THE CHRISTIAN MINISTRY. 195

to the consecration of a bishop. But even the latter is supported by direct evidence, which though comparatively late deserves consideration, inasmuch as it comes from one who was himself a patriarch of Alexandria. Eutychius, who held the patriarchal see from A.D. 933 to A.D. 940, writes as follows: *Testimony of Eutychius.*
'The Evangelist Mark appointed along with the patriarch Hananias twelve presbyters who should remain with the patriarch, to the end that, when the patriarchate was vacant, they might choose one of the twelve presbyters, on whose head the remaining eleven laying their hands should bless him and create him patriarch.' The vacant place in the presbytery was then to be filled up, that the number twelve might be constant[1]. 'This custom,' adds this writer, 'did not cease till the time of Alexander (A.D. 313—326), patriarch of Alexandria. He however forbad that henceforth the presbyters should create the patriarch, and decreed that on the death of the patriarch the bishops should meet to ordain the (new) patriarch, etc.[2]' It is clear from this passage that Eutychius considered the functions of nomination and ordination to rest with the same persons.

If this view however be correct, the practice of the

---

[1] Eutychii Patr. Alexandr. *Annales* I. p. 331 (Pococke, Oxon. 1656). The inferences in the text are resisted by Abraham Ecchellensis *Eutychius vindicatus* p. 22 sq. (in answer to Selden the translator of Eutychius), and by Le Quien *Oriens Christianus* II. p. 342, who urge all that can be said on the opposite side. The authority of a writer so inaccurate as Eutychius, if it had been unsupported, would have had no weight; but, as we have seen, this is not the case.

[2] Between Dionysius and Alexander four bishops of Alexandria intervene, Maximus (A.D. 265), Theonas (A.D. 283), Peter I. (A.D. 301), and Achillas (A.D. 312). It will therefore be seen that there is a considerable discrepancy between the accounts of Jerome and Eutychius as to the time when the change was effected. But we may reasonably conjecture (with Ritschl, p. 432) that the transition from the old state of things to the new would be the result of a prolonged conflict between the Alexandrian presbytery who had hitherto held these functions, and the bishops of the recently created Egyptian sees to whom it was proposed to transfer them.

Somewhat later one Ischyras was deprived of his orders by an Alexandrian synod, because he had been ordained by a presbyter only: Athan. *Apol. c. Arian.* 75 (I. p. 152). From this time at all events the Alexandrian Church insisted as strictly as any other on episcopal ordination.

13—2

196   THE CHRISTIAN MINISTRY.

Alexandrian Church was exceptional; for at this time the formal act of the bishop was considered generally necessary to give validity to ordination. Nor is the exception difficult to account for. At the close of the second century, when every considerable church in Europe and Asia appears to have had its bishop, the only representative of the episcopal order in Egypt was the bishop of Alexandria. It was Demetrius first (A.D. 190—233), as Eutychius informs us[1], who appointed three other bishops, to which number his successor Heraclas (A.D. 233—249) added twenty more. This extension of episcopacy to the provincial towns of Egypt paved the way for a change in the mode of appointing and ordaining the patriarch of Alexandria. But before this time it was a matter of convenience and almost of necessity that the Alexandrian presbyters should themselves ordain their chief.

Increase of the Egyptian episcopate.

Nor is it only in Alexandria that we meet with this peculiarity. Where the same urgent reason existed, the same exceptional practice seems to have been tolerated. A decree of the Council of Ancyra (A.D. 314) ordains that 'it be not allowed to country-bishops (χωρεπισκόποις) to ordain presbyters or deacons, nor even to city-presbyters, except permission be given in each parish by the bishop in writing[2].' Thus while

Decree of the Council of Ancyra.

---

[1] Eutych. *Ann.* l. c. p. 332. Heraclas, we are informed on the same authority (p. 335), was the first Alexandrian prelate who bore the title of patriarch; this designation being equivalent to metropolitan or bishop of bishops.

[2] *Concil. Ancyr.* can. 13 (Routh *Rel. Sacr.* IV. p. 121) χωρεπισκόποις μὴ ἐξεῖναι πρεσβυτέρους ἢ διακόνους χειροτονεῖν, ἀλλὰ [μὴν] μηδὲ πρεσβυτέροις πόλεως χωρὶς τοῦ ἐπιτραπῆναι ὑπὸ τοῦ ἐπισκόπου μετὰ γραμμάτων ἐν ἑκάστῃ παροικίᾳ. The various readings and interpretations of this canon will be found in Routh's note, p. 144 sq. Routh himself reads ἀλλὰ μὴν μηδὲ πρεσβυτέρους πόλεως, making πρεσβυτέρους πόλεως the object of χειροτονεῖν, but to this there is a twofold objection: (1) he necessarily understands the former πρεσβυτέρους to mean πρεσβυτέρους χώρας, though this is not expressed: (2) he interprets ἀλλὰ μὴν μηδέ 'much less,' a sense which μηδέ seems to exclude and which is not borne out by his examples.

The name and office of the χωρεπίσκοπος appear to be reliques of the time when ἐπίσκοπος and πρεσβύτερος were synonymes. While the large cities had their college of presbyters, for the villages a single πρεσβύτερος (or ἐπίσκοπος) would suffice; but from his isolated position he would be tempted, even if he were not obliged, to perform on his

restraining the existing license, the framers of the decree still allow very considerable latitude. And it is especially important to observe that they lay more stress on episcopal sanction than on episcopal ordination. Provided that the former is secured, they are content to dispense with the latter.

As a general rule however, even those writers who maintain a substantial identity in the offices of the bishop and presbyter reserve the power of ordaining to the former[1]. This distinction in fact may be regarded as a settled maxim of Church polity in the fourth and later centuries. And when Aerius maintained the equality of the bishop and presbyter and denied the necessity of episcopal ordination, his opinion was condemned as heretical, and is stigmatized as 'frantic' by Epiphanius[2].

It has been seen that the institution of an episcopate must be placed as far back as the closing years of the first

Ordination confined to the bishops.

own responsibility certain acts which in the city would only be performed by the bishop properly so called, or at least would not be performed without his consent. Out of this position the office of the later χωρεπίσκοπος would gradually be developed; but the rate of progression would not be uniform, and the regulations affecting it would be determined by the circumstances of the particular locality. Hence, at a later date, it seems in some places to have been presbyteral, in others episcopal. In the Ancyran canon just quoted a chorepiscopus is evidently placed below the city presbytery; but in other notices he occupies a higher position. For the conflicting accounts of the χωρεπίσκοπος see Bingham II. xiv.

Baur's account of the origin of the episcopate supposes that each Christian congregation was presided over, not by a college of presbyters, but by a single πρεσβύτερος or ἐπίσκοπος, i.e. that the constitution of the Church was from the first monarchical: see *Pastoralbriefe* p. 81 sq., *Ursprung des Episcopats* p. 84 sq. This view is inconsistent alike with the analogy of the synagogue and with the notices in the apostolic and early ecclesiastical writings. But the practice which he considers to have been the general rule would probably hold in small country congregations, where a college of presbyters would be unnecessary as well as impossible.

[1] St Jerome himself (*Epist.* cxlvi.), in the context of the passage in which he maintains the identity of the two orders and alleges the tradition of the Alexandrian Church (see above, p. 194), adds, 'Quid enim facit *excepta ordinatione* episcopus quod presbyter non faciat?' So also *Const. Apost.* viii. 28 ἐπίσκοπος χειροθετεῖ χειροτονεῖ...πρεσβύτερος χειροθετεῖ οὐ χειροτονεῖ, Chrysost. *Hom.* xi. on 1 Tim. iii. 8 τῇ χειροτονίᾳ μόνῃ ὑπερβεβήκασι καὶ τούτῳ μόνον δοκοῦσι πλεονεκτεῖν πρεσβυτέρους. See Bingham II. iii. 5, 6, 7, for other references.

[2] *Haer.* lxxv. 3; comp. Augustine *Haer.* § 53. See Wordsworth *Theoph. Angl.* c. x.

198   THE CHRISTIAN MINISTRY.

<small>Causes of the development of episcopacy.</small>
century, and that it cannot, without violence to historical testimony, be dissevered from the name of St John. But it has been seen also that the earliest bishops did not hold the same independent position of supremacy which was and is occupied by their later representatives. It will therefore be instructive to trace the successive stages by which the power of the office was developed during the second and third centuries. Though something must be attributed to the frailty of human pride and love of power, it will nevertheless appear that the pressing needs of the Church were mainly instrumental in bringing about the result, and that this development of the episcopal office was a providential safeguard amid the confusion of speculative opinion, the distracting effects of persecution, and the growing anarchy of social life, which threatened not only the extension but the very existence of the Church of Christ. Ambition of office in a society where prominence of rank involved prominence of risk was at least no vulgar and selfish passion.

<small>Three names connected with its progress.</small>
This development will be conveniently connected with three great names, each separated from the other by an interval of more than half a century, and each marking a distinct stage in its progress. Ignatius, Irenæus, and Cyprian, represent three successive advances towards the supremacy which was ultimately attained.

<small>1. Ignatius.</small>
1. IGNATIUS of Antioch is commonly recognized as the staunchest advocate of episcopacy in the early ages. Even,

<small>The Syriac Version.</small>
though we should refuse to accept as genuine any portions which are not contained in the Syriac Version[1], this view would nevertheless be amply justified. Confining our attention for the moment to the Syriac letters we find that to this father the chief value of episcopacy lies in the fact that it constitutes

---

[1] In the earlier editions of this work I assumed that the Syriac Version published by Cureton represented the Epistles of Ignatius in their original form. I am now convinced that this is only an abridgment and that the shorter Greek form is genuine; but for the sake of argument I have kept the two apart in the text. I hope before long to give reasons for this change of opinion in my edition of this father. [See p. 239 sq., *Additional Note A.*]

a visible *centre of unity* in the congregation. He seems in the development of the office to keep in view the same purpose which we may suppose to have influenced the last surviving Apostles in its institution. The withdrawal of the authoritative preachers of the Gospel, the personal disciples of the Lord, had severed one bond of union. The destruction of the original abode of Christendom, the scene of the life and passion of the Saviour and of the earliest triumphs of the Church, had removed another. Thus deprived at once of the personal and the local ties which had hitherto bound individual to individual and church to church, the Christian brotherhood was threatened with schism, disunion, dissolution. 'Vindicate thine office with all diligence,' writes Ignatius to the bishop of Smyrna, 'in things temporal as well as spiritual. Have a care of unity, than which nothing is better[1].' 'The crisis requires thee, as the pilot requires the winds or the storm-tossed mariner a haven, so as to attain unto God[2].' 'Let not those who seem to be plausible and teach falsehoods dismay thee; but stand thou firm as an anvil under the hammer: 'tis the part of a great athlete to be bruised and to conquer[3].' 'Let nothing be done without thy consent, and do thou nothing without the consent of God[4].' He adds directions also, that those who decide on a life of virginity shall disclose their intention to the bishop only, and those who marry shall obtain his consent to their union, that 'their marriage may be according to the Lord and not according to lust[5].' And turning from the bishop to the people he adds, 'Give heed to your bishop, that God also may give heed to you. I give my life for those who are obedient to the bishop, to presbyters, to deacons. With them may I have my portion in the presence of God[6].' Writing to the Ephesians also he says that in receiving their bishop Onesimus he is receiving their whole body, and he charges them to love him, and one and all to be in his likeness[7], adding, 'Since love does

The bishop regarded as a centre of unity.

[1] *Polyc.* 1.
[2] *Polyc.* 2.
[3] *Polyc.* 3.
[4] *Polyc.* 4.
[5] *Polyc.* 5.
[6] *Polyc.* 6.
[7] *Ephes.* 1.

200   THE CHRISTIAN MINISTRY.

not permit me to be silent, therefore I have been forward in exhorting you to conform to the will of God[1].'

From these passages it will be seen that St Ignatius values the episcopate chiefly as a security for good discipline and harmonious working in the Church. And, when we pass from the Syriac letters to the Short Greek, the standing ground is still unchanged. At the same time, though the point of view is unaltered, the Greek letters contain far stronger expressions than are found in the Syriac. Throughout the whole range of Christian literature, no more uncompromising advocacy of the episcopate can be found than appears in these writings. This championship indeed is extended to the two lower orders of the ministry[2], more especially to the presbyters[3]. But it is when asserting the claims of the episcopal office to obedience and respect, that the language is strained to the utmost. 'The bishops established in the farthest parts of the world are in the counsels of Jesus Christ[4].' 'Every one whom the Master of the house sendeth to govern His own household we ought to receive, as Him that sent him; clearly therefore we ought to regard the bishop as the Lord Himself[5].' Those 'live a life after Christ,' who 'obey the bishop as Jesus Christ[6].' 'It is good to know God and the bishop; he that honoureth the bishop is honoured of God; he that doeth anything without the knowledge of the bishop serveth the devil[7].' He that obeys his bishop, obeys 'not him, but the Father of Jesus Christ, the Bishop of all.' On the other hand, he that practises hypocrisy towards his bishop, 'not only deceiveth the visible one, but cheateth the Unseen[8].' 'As many as are of God and of Jesus Christ, are with the bishop[9].' Those are approved who are 'inseparate [from God], from Jesus Christ, and from the bishop, and from the ordinances of the Apostles[10].' 'Do ye all,' says this writer

---

[1] *Ephes.* 3.
[2] *Magn.* 13, *Trall.* 3, 7, *Philad.* 4, 7, *Smyrn.* 8, 12.
[3] *Ephes.* 2, 20, *Magn.* 2, 6, *Trall.* 13.
[4] *Ephes.* 3.
[5] *Ephes.* 6.
[6] *Trall.* 2.
[7] *Smyrn.* 9.
[8] *Magn.* 3.
[9] *Philad.* 3.
[10] *Trall.* 7.

THE CHRISTIAN MINISTRY. 201

again, 'follow the bishop, as Jesus Christ followed the Father[1].' The Ephesians are commended accordingly, because they are so united with their bishop 'as the Church with Jesus Christ and as Jesus Christ with the Father.' 'If,' it is added, 'the prayer of one or two hath so much power, how much more the prayer of the bishop and of the whole Church[2].' 'Wherever the bishop may appear, there let the multitude be, just as where Jesus Christ may be, there is the universal Church[3].' Therefore 'let no man do anything pertaining to the Church without the bishop[4].' 'It is not allowable either to baptize or to hold a love-feast without the bishop: but whatsoever he may approve, this also is well pleasing to God, that everything which is done may be safe and valid[5].' 'Unity of God,' according to this writer, consists in harmonious co-operation with the bishop[6].

And yet with all this extravagant exaltation of the episcopal office, the presbyters are not put out of sight. They form a council[7], a 'worthy spiritual coronal[8]' round the bishop. It is the duty of every individual, but especially of them, 'to refresh the bishop unto the honour of the Father and of Jesus Christ and of the Apostles[9].' They stand in the same relation to him, 'as the chords to the lyre[10].' If the bishop occupies the place of God or of Jesus Christ, the presbyters are as the Apostles, as the council of God[11]. If obedience is due to the bishop as the grace of God, it is due to the presbytery as the law of Jesus Christ[12]. *The presbytery however not forgotten.*

It need hardly be remarked how subversive of the true spirit of Christianity, in the negation of individual freedom and the consequent suppression of direct responsibility to God in Christ, is the crushing despotism with which this language, if *Considerations suggested by this language.*

---

[1] *Smyrn.* 8, comp. *Magn.* 7.
[2] *Ephes.* 5.
[3] *Smyrn.* 8.
[4] *ib.*; comp. *Magn.* 4, *Philad.* 7.
[5] *Smyrn.* 8.
[6] *Polyc.* 8 ἐν ἑνότητι Θεοῦ καὶ ἐπισκόπου (v. l. ἐπισκοπῇ): comp. *Philad.* 3, 8.
[7] The word πρεσβυτέριον, which occurs 1 Tim. iv. 14, is very frequent in the Ignatian Epistles.
[8] *Magn.* 13.
[9] *Trall.* 12.
[10] *Ephes.* 4; comp. the metaphor in *Philad.* 1.
[11] *Trall.* 2, 3, *Magn.* 6, *Smyrn.* 8.
[12] *Magn.* 2.

taken literally, would invest the episcopal office. It is more important to bear in mind the extenuating fact, that the needs and distractions of the age seemed to call for a greater concentration of authority in the episcopate; and we might well be surprised, if at a great crisis the defence of an all-important institution were expressed in words carefully weighed and guarded.

The same views advanced in the interests of Ebionism. Strangely-enough, not many years after Ignatius thus asserted the claims of the episcopate as a safeguard of orthodoxy, another writer used the same instrument to advance a very different form of Christianity. The organization, which is thus employed to consolidate and advance the Catholic Church, might serve equally well to establish a compact Ebionite community. I have already mentioned the author of the *Clementine Homilies* as a staunch advocate of episcopacy[1]. His view of the sanctions and privileges of the office does not differ materially from that of Ignatius. 'The multitude of the faithful,' he says, 'must obey a single person, that so it may be able to continue in harmony.' Monarchy is a necessary condition of peace; this may be seen from the aspect of the world around: at present there are many kings, and the result is discord and war; in the world to come God has appointed one King only, that 'by reason of monarchy an indestructible peace may be established: therefore all ought to follow some one person as guide, preferring him in honour as the image of God; and this guide must show the way that leadeth to the Holy City[2].' Accordingly he delights to speak of the bishop as occupying the place or the seat of Christ[3]. Every insult, he says, and every honour offered to a bishop is carried to Christ and from Christ is taken up to the presence of the Father; and thus it is requited manifold[4]. Similarly another writer of the Clementine cycle, if he be not the same, compares Christ to the captain, the bishop to the mate, and the presbyters to the sailors, while the lower orders

---

[1] See above, p. 171.
[2] *Clem. Hom.* iii. 61, 62.
[3] *ib.* iii. 60, 66, 70.
[4] *ib.* iii. 66, 70.

and the laity have each their proper place in the ship of the Church[1].

It is no surprise that such extravagant claims should not have been allowed to pass unchallenged. In opposition to the lofty hierarchical pretensions thus advanced on the one hand in the Ignatian letters on behalf of Catholicism and on the other by the Clementine writer in the interests of Ebionism, a strong spiritualist reaction set in. If in its mental aspect the heresy of Montanus must be regarded as a protest against the speculative subtleties of Gnosticism, on its practical side it was equally a rebound from the aggressive tyranny of hierarchical assumption. Montanus taught that the true succession of the Spirit, the authorized channel of Divine grace, must be sought not in the hierarchical but in the prophetic order. For a rigid outward system he substituted the free inward impulse. Wildly fanatical as were its manifestations, this reaction nevertheless issued from a true instinct which rebelled against the oppressive yoke of external tradition and did battle for the freedom of the individual spirit. Montanus was excommunicated and Montanism died out; but though dead, it yet spake; for a portion of its better spirit was infused into the Catholic Church, which it leavened and refreshed and invigorated. *Montanism, a reaction against this extravagance.*

2. IRENÆUS followed Ignatius after an interval of about two generations. With the altered circumstances of the Church, the aspect of the episcopal office has also undergone a change. The religious atmosphere is now charged with heretical speculations of all kinds. Amidst the competition of rival teachers, all eagerly bidding for support, the perplexed believer asks for some decisive test by which he may try the claims of the disputants. To this question Irenæus supplies an answer. 'If you wish,' he argues, 'to ascertain the doctrine of the Apostles, apply to the Church of the Apostles. In the succession of bishops tracing their descent from the primitive age and appointed by the Apostles themselves, you have a guarantee for the trans- *2. IRENÆUS. The bishop the depositary of primitive truth.*

---

[1] *Clem. Hom.* Ep. Clem. 15.

204   THE CHRISTIAN MINISTRY.

mission of the pure faith, which no isolated, upstart, self-constituted teacher can furnish. There is the Church of Rome for instance, whose episcopal pedigree is perfect in all its links, and whose earliest bishops, Linus and Clement, associated with the Apostles themselves: there is the Church of Smyrna again, whose bishop Polycarp, the disciple of St John, died only the other day[1].' Thus the episcopate is regarded now not so much as the *centre of ecclesiastical unity* but rather as the *depositary of apostolic tradition*.

The same view held by Hegesippus and Tertullian.

This view is not peculiar to Irenæus. It seems to have been advanced earlier by Hegesippus, for in a detached fragment he lays stress on the succession of the bishops at Rome and at Corinth, adding that in each church and in each succession the pure faith was preserved[2]; so that he seems here to be controverting that 'gnosis falsely so called' which elsewhere he denounces[3]. It is distinctly maintained by Tertullian, the younger contemporary of Irenæus, who refers, if not with the same frequency, at least with equal emphasis, to the tradition of the apostolic churches as preserved by the succession of the episcopate[4].

3. CYPRIAN.

3. As two generations intervened between Ignatius and Irenæus, so the same period roughly speaking separates Irenæus from CYPRIAN. If with Ignatius the bishop is the centre of Christian unity, if with Irenæus he is the depositary of the apostolic tradition, with Cyprian he is the *absolute vicegerent of Christ* in things spiritual. In mere strength of language indeed it would be difficult to surpass Ignatius, who lived about a century and a half earlier. With the single exception of the sacerdotal view of the ministry which had grown up meanwhile, Cyprian puts forward no assumption which this father had not advanced either literally or substantially long before. This one exception however is all important, for it raised the sanctions of the episcopate to a higher level and put new force into old

The bishop the vicegerent of Christ.

---

[1] See especially iii. cc. 2, 3, 4, iv. 26. 2 sq., iv. 32, 1, v. præf., v. 20, 1, 2.

[2] In Euseb. *H. E.* iv. 22. See above,

p. 182.

[3] Euseb. *H. E.* iii. 32.

[4] Tertull. *de Praescr.* 32.

titles of respect. Theoretically therefore it may be said that Cyprian took his stand on the combination of the ecclesiastical authority as asserted by Ignatius with the sacerdotal claim which had been developed in the half century just past. But the real influence which he exercised in the elevation of the episcopate consisted not in the novelty of his theoretical views, but in his practical energy and success. The absolute supremacy of the bishop had remained hitherto a lofty title or at least a vague ill-defined assumption: it became through his exertions a substantial and patent and world-wide fact. The first prelate whose force of character vibrated throughout the whole of Christendom, he was driven not less by the circumstances of his position than by his own temperament and conviction to throw all his energy into this scale. And the permanent result was much vaster than he could have anticipated beforehand or realized after the fact. Forced into the episcopate against his will, he raised it to a position of absolute independence, from which it has never since been deposed. The two great controversies in which Cyprian engaged, though immediately arising out of questions of discipline, combined from opposite sides to consolidate and enhance the power of the bishops[1].

Influence of Cyprian on the episcopate.

The first question of dispute concerned the treatment of such as had lapsed during the recent persecution under Decius. Cyprian found himself on this occasion doing battle for the episcopate against a twofold opposition, against the confessors who claimed the right of absolving and restoring these fallen brethren, and against his own presbyters who in the absence of their bishop supported the claims of the confessors. From his retirement he launched his shafts against this combined array, where an aristocracy of moral influence was leagued with an aristocracy of official position. With signal determination and

First controversy.

Treatment of the lapsed.

---

[1] The influence of Cyprian on the episcopate is ably stated in two vigorous articles by Kayser entitled *Cyprien ou l'Autonomie de l'Épiscopat* in the *Revue de Théologie* xv. pp. 138 sq., 242 sq. (1857). See also Rettberg *Thascius Cäcilius Cyprianus* p. 367 sq., Huther *Cyprian's Lehre von der Kirche* p. 59 sq. For Cyprian's work generally see *Smith's Dict. of Christ. Biogr.* s. v.

courage in pursuing his aim, and with not less sagacity and address in discerning the means for carrying it out, Cyprian had on this occasion the further advantage, that he was defending the cause of order and right. He succeeded moreover in enlisting in his cause the rulers of the most powerful church in Christendom. The Roman clergy declared for the bishop and against the presbyters of Carthage. Of Cyprian's sincerity no reasonable question can be entertained. In maintaining the authority of his office he believed himself to be fighting his Master's battle, and he sought success as the only safeguard of the integrity of the Church of Christ. In this lofty and disinterested spirit, and with these advantages of position, he entered upon the contest.

It is unnecessary for my purpose to follow out the conflict in detail: to show how ultimately the positions of the two combatants were shifted, so that from maintaining discipline against the champions of too great laxity Cyprian found himself protecting the fallen against the advocates of too great severity; to trace the progress of the schism and the attempt to establish a rival episcopate; or to unravel the entanglements of the Novatian controversy and lay open the intricate relations between Rome and Carthage[1]. It is sufficient to say that Cyprian's victory was complete. He triumphed over the confessors, triumphed over his own presbyters, triumphed over the schismatic bishop and his party. It was the most signal success hitherto achieved for the episcopate, because the battle had been fought and the victory won on this definite issue. The absolute supremacy of the episcopal office was thus established against the two antagonists from which it had most to fear, against a recognised aristocracy of ecclesiastical office and an irregular but not less powerful aristocracy of moral weight.

Power of the bishop in his own church defined.

---

[1] The intricacy of the whole proceeding is a strong evidence of the genuineness of the letters and other documents which contain the account of the controversy. The situations of the antagonists, varying and even interchanged with the change of circumstances, are very natural, but very unlike the invention of a forger who has a distinct side to maintain.

The position of the bishop with respect to the individual church over which he ruled was thus defined by the first contest in which Cyprian engaged. The second conflict resulted in determining his relation to the Church universal. The schism which had grown up during the first conflict created the difficulty which gave occasion to the second. A question arose whether baptism by heretics and schismatics should be held valid or not. Stephen the Roman bishop, pleading the immemorial custom of his church, recognised its validity. Cyprian insisted on rebaptism in such cases. Hitherto the bishop of Carthage had acted in cordial harmony with Rome: but now there was a collision. Stephen, inheriting the haughty temper and aggressive policy of his earlier predecessor Victor, excommunicated those who differed from the Roman usage in this matter. These arrogant assumptions were directly met by Cyprian. He summoned first one and then another synod of African bishops, who declared in his favour. He had on his side also the churches of Asia Minor, which had been included in Stephen's edict of excommunication. Thus the bolt hurled by Stephen fell innocuous, and the churches of Africa and Asia retained their practice. The principle asserted in the struggle was not unimportant. As in the former conflict Cyprian had maintained the independent supremacy of the bishop over the officers and members of his own congregation, so now he contended successfully for his immunity from any interference from without. At a later period indeed Rome carried the victory, but the immediate result of this controversy was to establish the independence and enhance the power of the episcopate. Moreover this struggle had the further and not less important consequence of defining and exhibiting the relations of the episcopate to the Church in another way. As the individual bishop had been pronounced indispensable to the existence of the individual community, so the episcopal order was now put forward as the absolute indefeasible representative of the universal Church. Synods of bishops indeed had been held frequently before; but under Cyprian's guidance they assumed

Second controversy. Re-baptism of heretics.

Relations of the bishops to the Universal Church defined.

a prominence which threw all existing precedents into the shade. A 'one undivided episcopate' was his watchword. The unity of the Church, he maintained, consists in the unanimity of the bishops[1]. In this controversy, as in the former, he acted throughout on the principle, distinctly asserted, that the existence of the episcopal office was not a matter of practical advantage or ecclesiastical rule or even of apostolic sanction, but an absolute incontrovertible decree of God. The triumph of Cyprian therefore was the triumph of this principle.

Cyprian's view of the episcopate.

The greatness of Cyprian's influence on the episcopate is indeed due to this fact, that with him the statement of the principle precedes and necessitates the practical measures. Of the sharpness and distinctness of his sacerdotal views it will be time to speak presently; but of his conception of the episcopal office generally thus much may be said here, that he regards the bishop as exclusively the representative of God to the congregation and hardly, if at all, as the representative of the congregation before God. The bishop is the indispensable channel of divine grace, the indispensable bond of Christian brotherhood. The episcopate is not so much the roof as the foundation-stone of the ecclesiastical edifice; not so much the legitimate development as the primary condition of a church[2]. The bishop is appointed directly by God, is responsible directly

---

[1] *De Unit. Eccl.* 2 'Quam unitatem firmiter tenere et vindicare debemus maxime episcopi qui in ecclesia praesidemus, ut episcopatum quoque ipsum unum atque indivisum probemus'; and again 'Episcopatus unus est, cujus a singulis in solidum pars tenetur: ecclesia quoque una est etc.' So again he argues (*Epist.* 43) that, as there is one Church, there must be only 'unum altare et unum sacerdotium (i.e. one episcopate).' Comp. also *Epist.* 46, 55, 67.

[2] *Epist.* 66 'Scire debes episcopum in ecclesia esse et ecclesiam in episcopo, et si quis cum episcopo non sit, in ecclesia non esse'; *Epist.* 33 'Ut ecclesia super episcopos constituatur et omnis actus ecclesiae per eosdem praepositos gubernetur.' Hence the expression 'nec episcopum nec ecclesiam cogitans,' *Epist.* 41; hence also 'honor episcopi' is associated not only with 'ecclesiae ratio' (*Epist.* 33) but even with 'timor Dei' (*Epist.* 15). Compare also the language (*Epist.* 59) 'Nec ecclesia istic cuiquam clauditur nec episcopus alicui denegatur,' and again (*Epist.* 43) 'Soli cum episcopis non sint, qui contra episcopos rebellarunt.'

to God, is inspired directly from God[1]. This last point deserves especial notice. Though in words he frequently defers to the established usage of consulting the presbyters and even the laity in the appointment of officers and in other matters affecting the well-being of the community, yet he only makes the concession to nullify it immediately. He pleads a direct official inspiration[2] which enables him to dispense with ecclesiastical custom and to act on his own responsibility. Though the presbyters may still have retained the shadow of a controlling power over the acts of the bishop, though the courtesy of language by which they were recognised as fellow-presbyters[3] was not laid aside, yet for all practical ends the independent supremacy of the episcopate was completely established by the principles and the measures of Cyprian.

The power of the bishops a question of practical convenience,

In the investigation just concluded I have endeavoured to trace the changes in the relative position of the first and second orders of the ministry, by which the power was gradually concentrated in the hands of the former. Such a development involves no new principle and must be regarded chiefly in its practical bearings. It is plainly competent for the Church at any given time to entrust a particular office with larger powers, as the emergency may require. And, though the grounds on which the independent authority of the episcopate was at times defended may have been false or exaggerated, no reasonable objection can be taken to later forms of ecclesiastical polity because the measure of power accorded to the bishop does not remain exactly the same as in the Church of the subapostolic ages. Nay, to many thoughtful and dispassionate minds even the gigantic power wielded by the popes during the middle ages will appear justifiable in itself (though they will repudiate

---

[1] See esp. *Epist.* 3, 43, 55, 59, 73, and above all 66 (*Ad Pupianum*).

[2] *Epist.* 38 'Expectanda non sunt testimonia humana, cum praecedunt divina suffragia'; *Epist.* 39 'Non humana suffragatione sed divina dignatione conjunctum'; *Epist.* 40 'Admonitos nos et instructos sciatis dignatione divina ut Numidicus presbyter adscribatur presbyterorum etc.'

[3] See above, p. 193, note 5.

L. 14

the false pretensions on which it was founded, and the false opinions which were associated with it), since only by such a providential concentration of authority could the Church, humanly speaking, have braved the storms of those ages of anarchy and violence. Now however it is my purpose to investigate the origin and growth of a new principle, which is nowhere enunciated in the New Testament, but which notwithstanding has worked its way into general recognition and seriously modified the character of later Christianity. The progress of the *sacerdotal* view of the ministry is one of the most striking and important phenomena in the history of the Church.

and unconnected with sacerdotalism.

It has been pointed out already that the sacerdotal functions and privileges, which alone are mentioned in the apostolic writings, pertain to all believers alike and do not refer solely or specially to the ministerial office. If to this statement it be objected that the inference is built upon the *silence* of the Apostles and Evangelists, and that such reasoning is always precarious, the reply is that an exclusive sacerdotalism (as the word is commonly understood)[1] contradicts the general tenour of the Gospel. But indeed the strength or weakness of an argument drawn from silence depends wholly on the circumstance under which the silence is maintained. And in this case it cannot be considered devoid of weight. In the Pastoral Epistles for instance, which are largely occupied with questions relating to the Christian ministry, it seems scarcely possible that this aspect should have been overlooked, if it had any place in St Paul's teaching. The Apostle discusses at length the requirements, the responsibilities, the sanctions, of the

No sacerdotalism in the New Testament.

---

[1] In speaking of sacerdotalism, I assume the term to have essentially the same force as when applied to the Jewish priesthood. In a certain sense (to be considered hereafter) all officers appointed to minister 'for men in things pertaining to God' may be called priests; and sacerdotal phraseology, when first applied to the Christian ministry, may have borne this innocent meaning. But at a later date it was certainly so used as to imply a substantial identity of character with the Jewish priesthood, i.e. to designate the Christian minister as one who offers sacrifices and makes atonement for the sins of others.

ministerial office: he regards the presbyter as an example, as a teacher, as a philanthropist, as a ruler. How then, it may well be asked, are the sacerdotal functions, the sacerdotal privileges, of the office wholly set aside? If these claims were recognised by him at all, they must necessarily have taken a foremost place. The same argument again applies with not less force to those passages in the Epistles to the Corinthians, where St Paul asserts his apostolic authority against his detractors. Nevertheless, so entirely had the primitive conception of the Christian Church been supplanted by this sacerdotal view of the ministry, before the northern races were converted to the Gospel, and the dialects derived from the Latin took the place of the ancient tongue, that the languages of modern Europe very generally supply only one word to represent alike the priest of the Jewish or heathen ceremonial and the presbyter of the Christian ministry[1].

Its rapid spread at a later date.

For, though no distinct traces of sacerdotalism are visible in the ages immediately after the Apostles, yet having once taken root in the Church it shot up rapidly into maturity. Towards

---

[1] It is a significant fact that in those languages which have only one word to express the two ideas, this word etymologically represents 'presbyterus' and not 'sacerdos,' e.g. the French *prêtre*, the German *priester*, and the English *priest;* thus showing that the sacerdotal idea was imported and not original. In the Italian, where two words *prete* and *sacerdote* exist side by side, there is no marked difference in usage, except that *prete* is the more common. If the latter brings out the sacerdotal idea more prominently, the former is also applied to Jewish and Heathen priests and therefore distinctly involves this idea. Wiclif's version of the New Testament naturally conforms to the Vulgate, in which it seems to be the rule to translate πρεσβύτεροι by 'presbyteri' (in Wiclif 'preestes') where it obviously denotes the second order in the ministry (e.g. Acts xiv. 23, 1 Tim. v. 17, 19, Tit. i. 5, James v. 14), and by 'seniores' (in Wiclif 'eldres' or 'elder men') in other passages: but if so, this rule is not always successfully applied (e.g. Acts xi. 30, xxi. 18, 1 Pet. v. 1). A doubt about the meaning may explain the anomaly that the word is translated 'presbyteri,' 'preestes,' Acts xv. 2, and 'seniores,' 'elder men,' Acts xv. 4, 6, 22, xvi. 4; though the persons intended are the same. In Acts xx. 17, it is rendered in Wiclif's version 'the grettist men of birthe,' a misunderstanding of the Vulgate 'majores natu.' The English versions of the reformers and the reformed Church from Tyndale downward translate πρεσβύτεροι uniformly by 'elders.'

212   THE CHRISTIAN MINISTRY.

the close of the second century we discern the first germs appearing above the surface: yet, shortly after the middle of the third, the plant has all but attained its full growth. The origin of this idea, the progress of its development, and the conditions favourable to its spread, will be considered in the present section of this essay.

Distinction of the clergy from the laity

A separation of orders, it is true, appeared at a much earlier date, and was in some sense involved in the appointment of a special ministry. This, and not more than this, was originally contained in the distinction of clergy and laity. If the sacerdotal view of the ministry engrafted itself on this distinction, it nevertheless was not necessarily implied or even indirectly suggested thereby. The term 'clerus,' as a designation of the ministerial office, did not owing to any existing associations convey the idea of sacerdotal functions.

not derived from the Levitical priesthood.

The word is not used of the Aaronic priesthood in any special sense which would explain its transference to the Christian ministry. It is indeed said of the Levites, that they have no 'clerus' in the land, the Lord Himself being their 'clerus'[1]. But the Jewish priesthood is never described conversely as the special 'clerus' of Jehovah: while on the other hand the metaphor thus inverted is more than once applied to the whole Israelite people[2]. Up to this point therefore the analogy of Old Testament usage would have suggested 'clerus' as a name rather for the entire body of the faithful than for the ministry specially or exclusively. Nor do other references to the clerus or lot in connexion with the Levitical priesthood countenance its special application. The tithes, it is true, were assigned to the sons of Levi as their 'clerus'[3]; but in this there is nothing distinctive, and in fact the word is employed much more prominently in describing the

---

[1] Deut. x. 9, xviii. 1, 2; comp. Num. xxvi. 62, Deut. xii. 12, xiv. 27, 29, Josh. xiv. 3. Jerome (*Epist.* lii. 5, I. p. 258) says, 'Propterea vocantur clerici, vel quia de sorte sunt Domini, vel quia ipse Dominus sors, id est pars, clericorum est.' The former explanation would be reasonable, if it were supported by the language of the Old Testament: the latter is plainly inadequate.

[2] Deut. iv. 20 εἶναι αὐτῷ λαὸν ἔγκληρον: comp. ix. 29 οὗτοι λαός σου καὶ κλῆρός σου.

[3] Num. xviii. 21, 24, 26.

THE CHRISTIAN MINISTRY.   213

lands allotted to the whole people. Again the courses of priests and Levites selected to conduct the temple-service were appointed by lot[1]; but the mode adopted in distributing a particular set of duties is far too special to have supplied a distinctive name for the whole order. If indeed it were an established fact that the Aaronic priesthood at the time of the Christian era commonly bore the name of 'clergy,' we might be driven to explain the designation in this or in some similar way; but apparently no evidence of any such usage exists[2], and it is therefore needless to cast about for an explanation of a fact which itself is only conjectural. The origin of the term clergy, as applied to the Christian ministry, must be sought elsewhere.

And the record of the earliest appointment made by the Christian Church after the Ascension of the Lord seems to supply the clue. Exhorting the assembled brethren to elect a successor in place of Judas, St Peter tells them that the traitor 'had been numbered among them and had received the *lot* ($κλῆρον$) of the ministry': while in the account of the subsequent proceedings it is recorded that the Apostles 'distributed *lots*' to the brethren, and that 'the *lot* fell on Matthias and he was added to the eleven Apostles[3].' The following therefore seems to be the sequence of meanings, by which the word $κλῆρος$ arrived at this peculiar sense: (1) the lot by which the office was assigned; (2) the office thus assigned by lot; (3) the body of persons holding the office. The first two senses are illustrated by the passages quoted from the Acts; and from the second to the third the transition is easy and natural. It must not be

Origin of 'Clerus' as a name for the Christian ministry.

---

[1] 1 Chron. xxiv. 5, 7, 31, xxv. 8, 9.

[2] On the other hand λαός is used of the people, as contrasted either with the rulers or with the priests. From this latter contrast comes λαϊκός, 'laic' or 'profane,' and λαϊκόω 'to profane'; which, though not found in the LXX, occur frequently in the versions of Aquila, Symmachus, and Theodotion (λαϊκός, 1 Sam. xxi. 4, Ezek. xlviii. 15; λαϊκόω, Deut. xx. 6, xxviii. 30, Ruth i. 12, Ezek. vii. 22); comp. Clem. Rom. 40.

[3] Acts i. 17 ἔλαχεν τὸν κλῆρον, 26 ἔδωκαν κλήρους αὐτοῖς καὶ ἔπεσεν ὁ κλῆρος ἐπὶ Ματθίαν. In ver. 25 κλῆρον is a false reading. The use of the word in 1 Pet. v. 3 κατακυριεύοντες τῶν κλήρων (i.e. the flocks assigned to them) does not illustrate this meaning.

214   THE CHRISTIAN MINISTRY.

supposed however that the mode of appointing officers by lot prevailed generally in the early Church. Besides the case of Matthias no other instance is recorded in the New Testament; nor is this procedure likely to have been commonly adopted. But just as in the passage quoted the word is used to describe the office of Judas, though Judas was certainly not selected by lot, so generally from signifying one special mode of appointment to office it got to signify office in the Church generally[1]. If this account of the application of 'clerus' to the Christian ministry be correct, we should expect to find it illustrated by a corresponding progress in the actual usage of the word. And this is in fact the case. The sense 'clerical appointment or office' chronologically precedes the sense 'clergy.' The former meaning occurs several times in Irenæus. He speaks of Hyginus as 'holding the ninth clerus of the episcopal succession from the Apostles[2]'; and of Eleutherus in like manner he says, 'He now occupies the clerus of the episcopate in the tenth place from the Apostles[3].' On the other hand the earliest instance of 'clerus,' meaning clergy, seems to occur in Tertullian[4], who belongs to the next generation.

No sacerdotal idea conveyed by the term.

It will thus be seen that the use of 'clerus' to denote the ministry cannot be traced to the Jewish priesthood, and is therefore wholly unconnected with any sacerdotal views. The term

---

[1] See Clem. Alex. *Quis div. salv.* 42, where κληροῦν is 'to appoint to the ministry'; and Iren. iii. 3. 3 κληροῦσθαι τὴν ἐπισκοπήν. A similar extension of meaning is seen in this same word κλῆρος applied to land. Signifying originally a piece of ground assigned by lot, it gets to mean landed property generally, whether obtained by assignment or by inheritance or in any other way.

[2] Iren. i. 27. 1.

[3] Iren. iii. 3. 3. In this passage however, as in the preceding, the word is explained by a qualifying genitive. In Hippol. *Haer.* ix. 12 (p. 290), ἤρξαντο ἐπίσκοποι καὶ πρεσβύτεροι καὶ διάκονοι δίγαμοι καὶ τρίγαμοι καθίστασθαι εἰς κλή- ρους, it is used absolutely of 'clerical offices.' The Epistle of the Gallican Churches (Euseb. *H. E.* v. 1) speaks more than once of the κλῆρος τῶν μαρτύρων, i.e. the order or rank of martyrs: comp. *Test. xii Patr.* Levi 8. See Ritschl p. 390 sq., to whom I am indebted for several of the passages which are quoted in this investigation.

[4] e.g. *de Monog.* 12 'Unde enim episcopi et clerus?' and again 'Extollimur et inflamur adversus clerum.' Perhaps however earlier instances may have escaped notice. In Clem. Alex. *Quis div. salv.* 42 the word seems not to be used in this sense.

does indeed recognise the clergy as an order distinct from the laity; but this is a mere question of ecclesiastical rule or polity, and involves no doctrinal bearings. The origin of sacerdotal phraseology and ideas must be sought elsewhere.

Attention has been already directed to the absence of any appeal to sacerdotal claims in the Pastoral Epistles. The silence of the apostolic fathers deserves also to be noticed. Though the genuine letters of all three may be truly said to hinge on questions relating to the ministry, no distinct traces of this influence are visible. St Clement, as the representative of the Roman Church, writes to the Christian brotherhood at Corinth, offering friendly counsel in their disputes and rebuking their factious and unworthy conduct towards certain presbyters whom, though blameless, they had ejected from office. He appeals to motives of Christian love, to principles of Christian order. He adduces a large number of examples from biblical history condemnatory of jealousy and insubordination. He urges that men, who had been appointed directly by the Apostles or by persons themselves so appointed, ought to have received better treatment. Dwelling at great length on the subject, he nevertheless advances no sacerdotal claims or immunities on behalf of the ejected ministers. He does, it is true, adduce the Aaronic priesthood and the Temple service as showing that God has appointed set persons and set places and will have all things done in order. He had before illustrated this lesson by the subordination of ranks in an army, and by the relation of the different members of the human body: he had insisted on the duties of the strong towards the weak, of the rich towards the poor, of the wise towards the ignorant, and so forth: he had enforced the appeal by reminding his readers of the utter feebleness and insignificance of man in the sight of God, as represented in the Scriptures of the Old Testament; and then follows the passage which contains the allusion in question: 'He hath not commanded (the offerings and ministrations) to be performed at random or in disorder, but at fixed times and seasons; and where and through whom He willeth them to be

Silence of the apostolic fathers on sacerdotalism.

Clement.

Import of his comparison with the Aaronic priesthood.

performed, He hath ordained by His supreme will. They therefore who make their offerings at the appointed seasons are acceptable and blessed, since following the ordinances of the Master they do not go wrong. For to the high priest peculiar services are entrusted, and the priests have their peculiar office assigned to them, and on Levites peculiar ministrations are imposed: the layman is bound by lay ordinances. Let each of you, brethren, in his own rank give thanks to God, retaining a good conscience, not transgressing the appointed rule of his service (λειτουργίας) etc.[1]' Here it is clear that in St Clement's conception the sanction possessed in common by the Aaronic priesthood and the Christian ministry is not the sacerdotal consecration, but the divinely appointed order. He passes over in silence the numerous passages in the Old Testament which enjoin obedience to the priests; while the only sentence (§ 42) which he puts forward as anticipating and enforcing the authority of the Christian ministry is a misquoted and misinterpreted verse from Isaiah; 'I will establish their overseers (bishops) in righteousness and their ministers (deacons) in faith[2].' Again a little later he mentions in illustration the murmuring of the Israelites which was rebuked by the budding of Aaron's rod[3]. But here too he makes it clear how far he considers the analogy to extend. He calls the sedition in the one case 'jealousy concerning the priesthood,' in the other 'strife concerning the honour of the episcopate[4].' He keeps the names

---

[1] Clem. Rom. 40, 41. Neander (*Church History*, I. p. 272 note, Bohn's translation) conjectures that this passage is an 'interpolation from a hierarchical interest,' and Dean Milman (*Hist. of Christianity*, III. p. 259) says that it is 'rejected by all judicious and impartial scholars.' At the risk of forfeiting all claim to judiciousness and impartiality one may venture to demur to this arbitrary criticism. Indeed the recent discovery of a second independent MS and of a Syriac Version, both containing the suspected passage, may be regarded as decisive on this point.

[2] Is. lx. 17, where the A. V. correctly renders the original, 'I will also make thy officers (lit. magistrates) peace and thine exactors (i.e. task-masters) righteousness'; i.e. there shall be no tyranny or oppression. The LXX departs from the original, and Clement has altered the LXX. By this double divergence a reference to the two orders of the ministry is obtained.

[3] Clem. Rom. 43.

[4] Contrast § 43 ζῆλου ἐμπεσόντος περὶ τῆς ἱερωσύνης with § 44 ἔρις ἔσται

and the offices distinct. The significance of this fact will be felt at once by comparing his language with the expressions used by any later writer, such as Cyprian, who was penetrated with the spirit of sacerdotalism¹.

Of St Ignatius, as the champion of episcopacy, much has *Ignatius.* been said already. It is sufficient to add here, that he never regards the ministry as a sacerdotal office. This is equally true, whether we accept as genuine the whole of the seven letters in the short Greek, or only those portions contained in the Syriac version. While these letters teem with passages enjoining the strictest obedience to bishops, while their language is frequently so strong as to sound almost profane, this father never once appeals to sacerdotal claims², though such an appeal would have made his case more than doubly strong. If it be ever safe to take the sentiments of an individual writer as expressing the belief of his age, we may infer from the silence which pervades these letters, that the sacerdotal view of the ministry had not yet found its way into the Christian Church.

When we pass on to the third apostolic father, the same phenomenon is repeated. Polycarp, like Clement and Ignatius, *Polycarp.* occupies much space in discussing the duties and the claims of Christian ministers. He takes occasion especially to give his correspondents advice as to a certain presbyter who had disgraced his office by a grave offence³. Yet he again knows nothing, or at least says nothing, of any sacerdotal privileges

ἐπὶ τοῦ ὀνόματος τῆς ἐπισκοπῆς. The common feature which connects the two offices together is stated in the words, § 43 ἵνα μὴ ἀκαταστασία γένηται.

¹ See below, p. 226 sq.

² Some passages are quoted in Greenwood *Cathedra Petri* I. p. 73 as tending in this direction, e.g. *Philad.* 9 καλοὶ καὶ οἱ ἱερεῖς, κρεῖσσον δὲ ὁ ἀρχιερεύς κ.τ.λ. But rightly interpreted they do not favour this view. In the passage quoted for instance, the writer seems to be maintaining the superiority of the new covenant, as represented by the great High-Priest (ἀρχιερεύς) in and through whom the whole Church has access to God, over the old dispensation of the Levitical priesthood (ἱερεῖς). If this interpretation be correct, the passage echoes the teaching of the Epistle to the Hebrews, and is opposed to exclusive sacerdotalism. On the meaning of θυσιαστήριον in the Ignatian Epistles see below, p. 234, note 1.

³ See *Philippians* p. 63 sq.

which claimed respect, or of any sacerdotal sanctity which has been violated.

<small>Justin Martyr</small>

Justin Martyr writes about a generation later. He speaks at length and with emphasis on the eucharistic offerings. Here at least we might expect to find sacerdotal views of the Christian ministry propounded. Yet this is far from being the case. He does indeed lay stress on sacerdotal functions, but these belong to the whole body of the Church, and are not in any way the exclusive right of the clergy. 'So we,' he writes, when arguing against Trypho the Jew, 'who through the name of Jesus have believed as one man in God the maker of the universe, having divested ourselves of our filthy garments, that is our sins, through the name of His first-born Son, and having been refined (πυρωθέντες) by the word of His calling, are the true high-priestly race of God, as God Himself also beareth witness, saying that in every place among the Gentiles are men offering sacrifices well-pleasing unto Him and pure (Mal. i. 11). Yet God doth not receive sacrifices from any one, except through His priests. Therefore God anticipating all sacrifices through this name, which Jesus Christ ordained to be offered, I mean those offered by the Christians in every region of the earth with (ἐπὶ) the thanksgiving (the eucharist) of the bread and of the cup, beareth witness that they are well-pleasing to Him; but the sacrifices offered by you and through those your priests He rejecteth, saying, "And your sacrifices I will not accept from your hands etc. (Mal. i. 10)"[1].' The whole Christian people therefore (such is Justin's conception) have not only taken the place of the Aaronic priesthood, but have become a nation of *high-priests*, being made one with the great High-Priest of the new covenant and presenting their eucharistic offerings in His name.

<small>maintains an universal priesthood.</small>

<small>Irenæus</small>

Another generation leads us from Justin Martyr to Irenæus. When Irenæus writes, the second century is very far advanced. Yet still the silence which has accompanied us hitherto remains

---

[1] *Dial. c. Tryph.* c. 116, 117, p. 344.

unbroken. And here again it is important to observe that Irenæus, if he held the sacerdotal view, had every motive for urging it, since the importance and authority of the episcopate occupy a large space in his teaching. Nevertheless he not only withholds this title as a special designation of the Christian ministry, but advances an entirely different view of the priestly office. He recognises only the priesthood of moral holiness, the priesthood of apostolic self-denial. Thus commenting on the reference made by our Lord to the incident in David's life where the king and his followers eat the shew-bread, 'which it is not lawful to eat save for the priests alone,' Irenæus remarks[1]; 'He excuseth His disciples by the words of the law, and signifieth that it is lawful for priests to act freely. For David had been called to be a priest in the sight of God, although Saul carried on a persecution against him; for all just men belong to the sacerdotal order[2]. Now all apostles of the Lord are priests, for they inherit neither lands nor houses here, but ever attend on the altar and on God': 'Who are they,' he goes on, 'that have left father and mother and have renounced all their kindred for the sake of the word of God and His covenant, but the disciples of the Lord? Of these Moses saith again, "But they shall have no inheritance; for the Lord Himself shall be their inheritance"; and again, "The priests, the Levites, in the whole tribe of Levi shall have no part nor inheritance with Israel: the first-fruits (fructificationes) of the Lord are their inheritance; they shall eat them." For this reason also Paul saith, "I require not the gift, but I require the fruit." The disciples of the Lord, he would say, were allowed when hungry to take food of the seeds (they had sown): for "The labourer is worthy of his food."' Again, striking upon the same topic in a

acknowledges only a moral priesthood.

---

[1] *Haer.* iv. 8. 3.

[2] This sentence is cited by John Damascene and Antonius πᾶς βασιλεὺς δίκαιος ἱερατικὴν ἔχει τάξιν; but the words were quoted doubtless from memory by the one writer and borrowed by the other from him. βασιλεὺς is not represented in the Latin and does not suit the context. The close conformity of their quotations from the Ignatian letters is a sufficient proof that these two writers are not independent authorities; see the passages in Cureton's *Corp. Ignat.* p. 180 sq.

later passage¹ and commenting on the words of Jeremiah (xxxi. 14), "I will intoxicate the soul of the priests the sons of Levi, and my people shall be filled with my good things," he adds, 'we have shown in a former book, that all disciples of the Lord are priests and Levites: who also profaned the Sabbath in the temple and are blameless.' Thus Irenæus too recognises the whole body of the faithful under the new dispensation as the counterparts of the sons of Levi under the old. The position of the Apostles and Evangelists has not yet been abandoned.

Explanation of a passage in Polycrates.

A few years later, but still before the close of the century, Polycrates of Ephesus writes to Victor of Rome. Incidentally he speaks of St John as 'having been made a priest' and 'wearing the mitre'²; and this might seem to be a distinct expression of sacerdotal views, for the 'mitre' to which he alludes is doubtless the tiara of the Jewish high-priest. But it may very reasonably be questioned if this is the correct meaning of the passage. Whether St John did actually wear this decoration of the high-priestly office, or whether Polycrates has mistaken a symbolical expression in some earlier writer for an actual fact, or whether lastly his language itself should be treated as a violent metaphor, I have had occasion to discuss above³. But in any case the notice is explained by the language of St John himself, who regards the whole body of believers as high-priests of the new covenant⁴; and it is certain that the contemporaries of Polycrates still continued to hold similar language⁵. As a figurative expression or as a literal fact, the notice points to St John as the veteran teacher, the

---

¹ *Haer.* v. 34. 3.
² In Euseb. *H. E.* v. 24 ὃς ἐγενήθη ἱερεὺς τὸ πέταλον πεφορεκώς. Comp. Tertull. *adv. Jud.* 14 'exornatus podere et mitra,' *Test. xii Patr.* Levi 8 ἀναστὰς ἔνδυσαι τὴν στολὴν τῆς ἱερατείας... τὸν ποδήρη τῆς ἀληθείας καὶ τὸ πέταλον τῆς πίστεως κ.τ.λ. See also, as an illustration of the metaphor, Tertull. *Monog.* 12 'Cum ad peraequationem disciplinae sacerdotalis provocamur, *deponimus infulas*.'
³ See above, p. 121 note.
⁴ Rev. ii. 17; see the commentators.
⁵ So Justin in the words already quoted (p. 218), *Dial. c. Tryph.* § 116 ἀρχιερατικὸν τὸ ἀληθινὸν γένος ἐσμὲν τοῦ Θεοῦ. See also the passage of Origen quoted below, p. 224.

chief representative, of a pontifical race. On the other hand, it is possible that this was not the sense which Polycrates himself attached to the figure or the fact: and if so, we have here perhaps the earliest passage in any extant Christian writing where the sacerdotal view of the ministry is distinctly put forward.

Clement of Alexandria was a contemporary of Polycrates. Though his extant writings are considerable in extent and though they are largely occupied with questions of Christian ethics and social life, the ministry does not hold a prominent place in them. In the few passages where he mentions it, he does not betray any tendency to sacerdotal or even to hierarchical views. The bias of his mind indeed lay in an opposite direction. He would be much more inclined to maintain an aristocracy of intellectual contemplation than of sacerdotal office. And in Alexandria generally, as we have seen, the development of the hierarchy was slower than in other churches. How far he is from maintaining a sacerdotal view of the ministry and how substantially he coincides with Irenæus in this respect, will appear from the following passage. 'It is possible for men even now, by exercising themselves in the commandments of the Lord and by living a perfect gnostic life in obedience to the Gospel, to be inscribed in the roll of the Apostles. Such men are genuine presbyters of the Church and true deacons of the will of God, if they practise and teach the things of the Lord, being not indeed ordained by men nor considered righteous because they are presbyters, but enrolled in the presbytery because they are righteous: and though here on earth they may not be honoured with a chief seat, yet shall they sit on the four and twenty thrones judging the people[1].' It is quite consistent with this truly spiritual view, that he should elsewhere recognise the presbyter, the deacon, and the layman, as distinct orders[2]. But on the other hand he never uses the words 'priest,' 'priestly,' 'priesthood,' of the Christian

Clement of Alexandria.

His 'gnostic' priesthood.

---

[1] *Strom.* vi. 13, p. 793. [2] *Strom.* iii. 90, p. 552.

ministry. In one passage indeed he contrasts laity and priesthood, but without any such reference. Speaking of the veil of the temple and assigning to it a symbolical meaning, he describes it as 'a barrier against laic unbelief,' behind which 'the priestly ministration is hidden[1].' Here the laymen and the priests are respectively those who reject and those who appropriate the spiritual mysteries of the Gospel. Accordingly in the context St Clement, following up the hint thrown out in the Epistle to the Hebrews, gives a spiritual meaning to all the furniture of the holy place.

Tertullian holds a sacerdotal view of the ministry,

His younger contemporary Tertullian is the first to assert direct sacerdotal claims on behalf of the Christian ministry. Of the heretics he complains that they impose sacerdotal functions on laymen[2]. 'The right of giving baptism,' he says elsewhere, 'belongs to the chief priest (summus sacerdos), that is, the bishop[3].' 'No woman,' he asserts, 'ought to teach, baptize, celebrate the eucharist, or arrogate to herself the performance of any duty pertaining to males, much less of the sacerdotal office[4].' And generally he uses the words sacerdos, sacerdotium, sacerdotalis, of the Christian ministry. It seems plain moreover from his mode of speaking, that such language was not peculiar to himself but passed current in the churches among which he moved. Yet he himself supplies the true counterpoise to this special sacerdotalism in his strong assertion of the universal priesthood of all true believers. 'We should be foolish,' so he writes when arguing against second marriages, 'to suppose that a latitude is allowed to laymen which is denied to priests. Are not we laymen also priests? It is written, "He hath also made us a kingdom and priests to God and His Father." It is the authority of the Church which makes a difference between the order (the clergy) and the

yet qualifies it by his assertion of an universal priesthood.

---

[1] *Strom.* v. 33 sq., p. 665 sq. Bp. Kaye (*Clement of Alexandria* p. 464) incorrectly adduces this passage as an express mention of 'the distinction between the clergy and laity.'

[2] *de Praescr. Haer.* 41 'Nam et laicis sacerdotalia munera injungunt.'

[3] *de Baptismo* 17.

[4] *de Virg. vel.* 9.

THE CHRISTIAN MINISTRY. 223

people—this authority and the consecration of their rank by the assignment of special benches to the clergy. Thus where there is no bench of clergy, you present the eucharistic offerings and baptize and are your own sole priest. For where three are gathered together, there is a church, even though they be laymen. Therefore if you exercise the rights of a priest in cases of necessity, it is your duty also to observe the discipline enjoined on a priest, where of necessity you exercise the rights of a priest[1].' And in another treatise he writes in bitter irony, 'When we begin to exalt and inflame ourselves against the clergy, then we are all one; then we are all priests, because "He made us priests to God and His Father": but when we are required to submit ourselves equally to the priestly discipline, we throw off our fillets and are no longer equal[2].' These passages, it is true, occur in treatises probably written after Tertullian had become wholly or in part a Montanist: but this consideration is of little consequence, for they bear witness to the fact that the scriptural doctrine of an universal priesthood was common ground to himself and his opponents, and had not yet been obscured by the sacerdotal view of the Christian ministry[3].

An incidental expression in Hippolytus serves to show that a few years later than Tertullian sacerdotal terms were commonly used to designate the different orders of the clergy. 'We,' says the zealous bishop of Portus, 'being successors of the Apostles and partaking of the same grace both of *high-priesthood* and of teaching and accounted guardians of the

Sacerdotal language in Hippolytus.

---

[1] *de Exh. Cast.* 7. See Kaye's *Tertullian* p. 211, whose interpretation of 'honor per ordinis consessum sanctificatus' I have adopted.

[2] *de Monog.* 12. I have taken the reading 'impares' for 'pares,' as required by the context.

[3] Tertullian regards Christ, our great High-Priest, as the counterpart under the new dispensation of the priest under the old, and so interprets the text 'Show thyself to the priest'; *adv. Marc.* iv. 9, *adv. Jud.* 14. Again, he uses 'sacerdos' in a moral sense, *de Spectac.* 16 'sacerdotes pacis,' *de Cult. Fem.* ii. 12 'sacerdotes pudicitiae,' *ad Uxor.* i. 6 (comp. 7) 'virginitatis et viduitatis sacerdotia.' On the other hand in *de Pall.* 4 he seems to compare the Christian minister with the heathen priests, but too much stress must not be laid on a rhetorical image.

224   THE CHRISTIAN MINISTRY.

Church, do not close our eyes drowsily or tacitly suppress the true word, etc¹.'

Origen interprets the priesthood spiritually,   The march of sacerdotal ideas was probably slower at Alexandria than at Carthage or Rome. Though belonging to the next generation, Origen's views are hardly so advanced as those of Tertullian. In the temple of the Church, he says, there are two sanctuaries: the heavenly, accessible only to Jesus Christ, our great High-Priest; the earthly, open to all priests of the new covenant, that is, to all faithful believers. For Christians are a sacerdotal race and therefore have access to the outer sanctuary. There they must present their offerings, their holocausts of love and self-denial. From this outer sanctuary our High-Priest takes the fire, as He enters the Holy of Holies to offer incense to the Father (see Lev. xvi. 12)². Very many professed Christians, he writes elsewhere (I am here abridging his words), occupied chiefly with the concerns of this world and dedicating few of their actions to God, are represented by the tribes, who merely present their tithes and first-fruits. On the other hand 'those who are devoted to the divine word, and are dedicated sincerely to the sole worship of God, may not unreasonably be called priests and Levites according to the difference in this respect of their impulses tending thereto.' Lastly 'those who excel the men of their own generation perchance will be high-priests.' They are only high-priests however after the order of Aaron, our Lord Himself being High-Priest after the order of Melchisedek³. Again in a third place he says, 'The Apostles and they that are made like unto the Apostles, being priests after the order of the great High-Priest, having received the knowledge of the worship of God and being instructed by the Spirit, know for what sins they ought to offer sacrifices, etc.⁴.' In all these passages Origen has taken spiritual enlightenment and not sacerdotal office to be the Christian counterpart to the Aaronic priesthood.

¹ *Haer.* prooem. p. 3.
² *Hom. ix in Lev.* 9, 10 (II. p. 243 Delarue).
³ *In Joann.* i. § 3 (IV. p. 3).
⁴ *de Orat.* 28 (I. p. 255). See also *Hom. iv in Num.* 3 (II. p. 283).

Elsewhere however he makes use of sacerdotal terms to describe the ministry of the Church[1]; and in one place distinguishes the priests and the Levites as representing the presbyters and deacons respectively[2].

but applies sacerdotal terms to the ministry.

Hitherto the sacerdotal view of the Christian ministry has not been held apart from a distinct recognition of the sacerdotal functions of the whole Christian body. The minister is thus regarded as a priest, because he is the mouthpiece, the representative, of a priestly race. Such appears to be the conception of Tertullian, who speaks of the clergy as separate from the laity only because the Church in the exercise of her prerogative has for convenience entrusted to them the performance of certain sacerdotal functions belonging properly to the whole congregation, and of Origen, who, giving a moral and spiritual interpretation to the sacerdotal office, considers the priesthood of the clergy to differ from the priesthood of the laity only in degree, in so far as the former devote their time and their thoughts more entirely to God than the latter. So long as this important aspect is kept in view, so long as the priesthood of the ministry is regarded as springing from the priesthood of the whole body, the teaching of the Apostles has not been directly violated. But still it was not a safe nomenclature which assigned the terms sacerdos, ἱερεύς, and the like, to the ministry, as a *special* designation. The appearance of this phenomenon marks the period of transition from the universal sacerdotalism of the New Testament to the particular sacerdotalism of a later age.

The priesthood of the ministry springs from the priesthood of the congregation.

[1] *Hom. v in Lev.* 4 (II. p. 208 sq.) 'Discant sacerdotes Domini qui ecclesiis praesunt,' and also ib. *Hom.* ii. 4 (II. p. 191) 'Cum non erubescit sacerdoti Domini indicare peccatum suum et quaerere medicinam' (he quotes James v. 14 in illustration). But *Hom. x in Num.* 1, 2 (II. p. 302), quoted by Redepenning (*Origenes* II. p. 417), hardly bears this sense, for the 'pontifex' applies to our Lord; and it is clear from *Hom. in Ps.* xxxvii. § 6 (II. p. 688) that in Origen's opinion the confessor to the penitent need not be an ordained minister. The passages in Redepenning's *Origenes* bearing on this subject are I. p. 357, II. pp. 250, 417, 436 sq.

[2] *Hom. xii in Jerem.* 3 (III. p. 196) 'If any one therefore among these priests (I mean us the presbyters) or among these Levites who stand about the people (I mean the deacons) etc.'

L.

226   THE CHRISTIAN MINISTRY.

Cyprian the champion of undisguised sacerdotalism.

If Tertullian and Origen are still hovering on the border, Cyprian has boldly transferred himself into the new domain. It is not only that he uses the terms sacerdos, sacerdotium, sacerdotalis, of the ministry with a frequency hitherto without parallel. But he treats all the passages in the Old Testament which refer to the privileges, the sanctions, the duties, and the responsibilities of the Aaronic priesthood, as applying to the officers of the Christian Church. His opponents are profane and sacrilegious; they have passed sentence of death on themselves by disobeying the command of the Lord in Deuteronomy to 'hear the priest[1]'; they have forgotten the injunction of Solomon to honour and reverence God's priests[2]; they have despised the example of St Paul who regretted that he 'did not know it was the high priest[3]'; they have been guilty of the sin of Korah, Dathan, and Abiram[4]. These passages are urged again and again. They are urged moreover, as applying not by parity of reasoning, not by analogy of circumstance, but as absolute and immediate and unquestionable. As Cyprian crowned the edifice of episcopal power, so also was he the first to put forward without relief or disguise the sacerdotal assumptions; and so uncompromising was the tone in which he asserted them, that nothing was left to his successors but to enforce his principles and reiterate his language[5].

After thus tracing the gradual departure from the Apostolic teaching in the encroachment of the sacerdotal on the pastoral and ministerial view of the clergy, it will be instructive to investigate the causes to which this divergence from primitive truth may be ascribed. To the question whether the change was due to Jewish or Gentile influences, opposite answers have been given. To some it has appeared as a reproduction of the

Were sacerdotal views due to Jewish

---

[1] Deut. xvii. 12; see *Epist.* 3, 4, 43, 59, 66.

[2] Though the words are ascribed to Solomon, the quotation comes from Ecclus. vii. 29, 31; see *Epist.* 3.

[3] Acts xxiii. 4; see *Epist.* 3, 59, 66.

[4] *De Unit. Eccl.* p. 83 (Fell), *Epist.* 3, 67, 69, 73.

[5] The sacerdotal language in the *Apostolical Constitutions* is hardly less strong, while it is more systematic; but their date is uncertain and cannot well be placed earlier than Cyprian.

Aaronic priesthood, due to Pharisaic tendencies, such as we find among St Paul's converts in Galatia and at Corinth, still lingering in the Church: to others, as imported into Christianity by the ever-increasing mass of heathen converts who were incapable of shaking off their sacerdotal prejudices and appreciating the free spirit of the Gospel. The latter view seems correct in the main, but requires some modification.

or Gentile influences?

At all events so far as the evidence of extant writings goes, there is no reason for supposing that sacerdotalism was especially rife among the Jewish converts. The Testaments of the Twelve Patriarchs may be taken to represent one phase of Judaic Christianity; the Clementine writings exhibit another. In both alike there is an entire absence of sacerdotal views of the ministry. The former work indeed dwells at length on our Lord's office, as the descendant and heir of Levi[1], and alludes more than once to His institution of a new priesthood; but this priesthood is spiritual and comprehensive. Christ Himself is the High-Priest[2], and the sacerdotal office is described as being "after the type of the Gentiles, extending to all the Gentiles[3]." On the Christian ministry the writer is silent. In the *Clementine Homilies* the case is somewhat different, but the inference is still more obvious. Though the episcopate is regarded as the backbone of the Church, though the claims of the ministry are urged with great distinctness, no appeal is ever made to priestly sanctity as the ground of this exalted estimate[4]. Indeed the hold of the Levitical priesthood on the mind of the pious Jew must have been materially weakened at the Christian era by the development of the synagogue organization on the one hand, and by the ever-growing influence of the learned and literary classes, the scribes and rabbis, on the other. The points on which the Judaizers of the apostolic age insist are the rite of circumcision, the distinction of meats, the observance of sabbaths, and the like. The necessity of the priesthood was not, or at least is not known to have been, part of their

The earliest Jewish Christian writings contain no traces of sacerdotalism.

---

[1] See above, p. 76.
[2] Ruben 6, Symeon 7, Levi 18.
[3] Levi 8.
[4] See the next note.

programme. Among the Essene Jews especially, who went so far as to repudiate the temple sacrifices, no great importance could have been attached to the Aaronic priesthood[1]: and after the Apostolic age at all events, the most active Judaizers of the Dispersion seem to have belonged to the Essene type. But indeed the overwhelming argument against ascribing the growth of sacerdotal views to Jewish influence lies in the fact, that there is a singular absence of distinct sacerdotalism during the first century and a half, when alone on any showing Judaism was powerful enough to impress itself on the belief of the Church at large.

Sacerdotalism was due to Gentile influences,

It is therefore to Gentile feeling that this development must be ascribed. For the heathen, familiar with auguries, lustrations, sacrifices, and depending on the intervention of some priest for all the manifold religious rites of the state, the club, and the family, the sacerdotal functions must have occupied a far larger space in the affairs of every-day life, than for the Jew of the Dispersion who of necessity dispensed, and had no scruple at dispensing, with priestly ministrations from one year's end to the other. With this presumption drawn from probability the evidence of fact accords. In Latin Christendom, as represented by the Church of Carthage, the germs of the sacerdotal idea appear first and soonest ripen to maturity. If we could satisfy ourselves of the early date of the Ancient Syriac Documents lately published, we should have discovered another centre from which this idea was propagated. And so far their testimony may perhaps be accepted. Syria was at least a soil where such a plant would thrive and luxuriate. In no country of the civilized world was sacerdotal authority among the heathen greater. The most important

---

[1] See above, pp. 79, 82 sq.; below, p. 350; *Colossians* p. 89. In the syzygies of the Clementine Homilies (ii. 16, 33) Aaron is opposed to Moses, the highpriest to the lawgiver, as the bad to the good, the false to the true, like Cain to Abel, Ishmael to Isaac, etc. In the Recognitions the estimate of the highpriest's position is still unfavourable (I. 46, 48). Compare the statement in Justin, *Dial. c. Tryph.* 117.

centres of Syrian Christianity, Antioch and Emesa, were also the cradles of strongly-marked sacerdotal religions which at different times made their influence felt throughout the Roman empire[1]. This being so, it is a significant fact that the first instance of the term 'priest,' applied to a Christian minister, occurs in a heathen writer. At least I have not found any example of this application earlier than Lucian[2].

But though the spirit, which imported the idea into the Church of Christ and sustained it there, was chiefly due to Gentile education, yet its form was almost as certainly derived from the Old Testament. And this is the modification which needs to be made in the statement, in itself substantially true, that sacerdotalism must be traced to the influence of Heathen rather than of Jewish converts. *but sought support in Old Testament analogies.*

In the Apostolic writings we find the terms 'offering,' 'sacrifice,' applied to certain conditions and actions of the Christian life. These sacrifices or offerings are described as spiritual[3]; they consist of praise[4], of faith[5], of almsgiving[6], of the devotion of the body[7], of the conversion of unbelievers[8], and the like. Thus whatever is dedicated to God's service may be included under this metaphor. In one passage also the image is so far extended, that the Apostolic writer speaks of an *altar*[9] pertaining to the spiritual service of the Christian Church. If on this noble Scriptural language a false superstructure has been reared, we have here only one instance out of many, where the truth has been impaired by transferring statements from the region of metaphor to the region of fact. *(1) Metaphor of 'sacrifices.'*

---

[1] The worship of the Syrian goddess of Antioch was among the most popular of oriental superstitions under the earlier Cæsars; the rites of the Sungod of Emesa became fashionable under Elagabalus.

[2] *de Mort. Peregr.* 11 τὴν θαυμαστὴν σοφίαν τῶν Χριστιανῶν ἐξέμαθε περὶ τὴν Παλαιστίνην τοῖς ἱερεῦσι καὶ γραμματεῦσιν αὐτῶν ξυγγενόμενος.

[3] 1 Pet. ii. 5.
[4] Heb. xiii. 15.
[5] Phil. ii. 17.
[6] Acts xxiv. 17, Phil. iv. 18; comp. Heb. xiii. 16.
[7] Rom. xii. 1.
[8] Rom. xv. 16.
[9] Heb. xiii. 10. See below, p. 234, note 1.

230   THE CHRISTIAN MINISTRY.

Offerings presented by the ministers.

These 'sacrifices' were very frequently the acts not of the individual Christian, but of the whole congregation. Such for instance were the offerings of public prayer and thanksgiving, or the collection of alms on the first day of the week, or the contribution of food for the agape, and the like. In such cases the congregation was represented by its minister, who thus acted as its mouthpiece and was said to 'present the offerings' to God. So the expression is used in the Epistle of St Clement of Rome[1]. But in itself it involves no sacerdotal view. This ancient father regards the sacrifice or offering as the act of the whole Church performed through its presbyters. The minister is a priest in the same sense only in which each individual member of the congregation is a priest. When St Clement denounces those who usurp the functions of the presbyters, he reprobates their conduct not as an act of sacrilege but as a violation of order. He views the presbytery as an Apostolic ordinance, not as a sacerdotal caste.

Thus when this father speaks of the presbytery as 'presenting the offerings,' he uses an expression which, if not directly scriptural, is at least accordant with the tenour of Scripture. But from such language the transition to sacerdotal views was easy, where the sacerdotal spirit was rife. From being the act of the whole congregation, the sacrifice came to be regarded as the act of the minister who officiated on its behalf.

Special

And this transition was moreover facilitated by the growing

---

[1] Clem. Rom. 44 τοὺς ἀμέμπτως καὶ ὁσίως προσενεγκόντας τὰ δῶρα. What sort of offerings are meant, may be gathered from other passages in Clement's Epistle; e.g. § 35 θυσία αἰνέσεως δοξάσει με, § 52 θῦσον τῷ Θεῷ θυσίαν αἰνέσεως καὶ ἀπόδος τῷ ὑψίστῳ τὰς εὐχάς σου, § 36 εὕρομεν τὸ σωτήριον ἡμῶν Ἰησοῦν Χριστὸν τὸν ἀρχιερέα τῶν προσφορῶν ἡμῶν τὸν προστάτην καὶ βοηθὸν τῆς ἀσθενείας ἡμῶν, and § 41 ἕκαστος ὑμῶν, ἀδελφοί, ἐν τῷ ἰδίῳ τάγματι εὐχαριστείτω τῷ Θεῷ ἐν ἀγαθῇ συνειδήσει ὑπάρχων, μὴ παρεκβαίνων τὸν ὡρισμένον τῆς λειτουργίας αὐτοῦ κανόνα. Compare especially Heb. xiii. 10, 15, 16 ἔχομεν θυσιαστήριον ἐξ οὗ φαγεῖν οὐκ ἔχουσιν [ἐξουσίαν] οἱ τῇ σκηνῇ λατρεύοντες...Δι' αὐτοῦ οὖν ἀναφέρωμεν θυσίαν αἰνέσεως διὰ παντὸς τῷ Θεῷ, τουτέστιν, καρπὸν χειλέων ὁμολογούντων τῷ ὀνόματι αὐτοῦ· τῆς δὲ εὐποιΐας καὶ κοινωνίας μὴ ἐπιλανθάνεσθε, τοιαύταις γὰρ θυσίαις εὐαρεστεῖται ὁ Θεός.

The doctrine of the early Church respecting 'sacrifice' is investigated by Höfling *die Lehre der ältesten Kirche vom Opfer* (Erlangen 1851).

tendency to apply the terms 'sacrifice' and 'offering' exclusively or chiefly to the eucharistic service. It may be doubted whether, even as used by St Clement, the expression may not have a special reference to this chief act of Christian dedication[1]. It is quite certain that writers belonging to the generations next following, Justin Martyr and Irenæus for instance[2], employ the terms very frequently with this reference. We may here reserve the question in what sense the celebration of the Lord's supper may or may not be truly called a sacrifice. The point to be noticed at present is this; that the offering of the eucharist, being regarded as the one special act of sacrifice and appearing externally to the eye as the act of the officiating minister, might well lead to the minister being called a priest and then being thought a priest in some exclusive sense, where the religious bias was in this direction and as soon as the true position of the minister as the representative of the congregation was lost sight of.

reference of the metaphor to the eucharist.

But besides the metaphor or the analogy of the sacrifice, there was another point of resemblance also between the Jewish priesthood and the Christian ministry, which favoured the sacerdotal view of the latter. As soon as the episcopate and presbytery ceased to be regarded as sub-orders and were looked

(2) Analogy of the three orders and the Levitical priesthood.

---

[1] On the whole however the passage from the Epistle to the Hebrews alluded to in the last note seems to be the best exponent of St Clement's meaning, as he very frequently follows this Apostolic writer. If εὐχαριστείτω has any special reference to the holy eucharist, as it may have, δῶρα will nevertheless be the alms and prayers and thanksgivings which accompanied the celebration of it. Compare *Const. Apost.* ii. 25 αἱ τότε θυσίαι νῦν εὐχαὶ καὶ δεήσεις καὶ εὐχαριστίαι, αἱ τότε ἀπαρχαὶ καὶ δεκάται καὶ ἀφαιρέματα καὶ δῶρα νῦν προσφοραὶ αἱ διὰ τῶν ὁσίων ἐπισκόπων προσφερόμεναι Κυρίῳ κ.τ.λ., § 27 προσήκει οὖν καὶ ὑμᾶς, ἀδελφοί, τὰς θυσίας ὑμῶν ἤτοι προσφορὰς τῷ ἐπισκόπῳ προσ-φέρειν ὡς ἀρχιερεῖ κ.τ.λ., § 34 τοὺς καρποὺς ὑμῶν καὶ τὰ ἔργα τῶν χειρῶν ὑμῶν εἰς εὐλογίαν ὑμῶν προσφέροντες αὐτῷ (sc. τῷ ἐπισκόπῳ)...τὰ δῶρα ὑμῶν διδόντες αὐτῷ ὡς ἱερεῖ Θεοῦ, § 53 δῶρον δέ ἐστι Θεῷ ἡ ἑκάστου προσευχὴ καὶ εὐχαριστία: comp. also § 35. These passages are quoted in Höfling, p. 27 sq.

[2] The chief passages in these fathers relating to Christian oblations are, Justin. *Apol.* i. 13 (p. 60), i. 65, 66, 67 (p. 97 sq.), *Dial.* 28, 29 (p. 246), 41 (p. 259 sq.), 116, 117 (p. 344 sq.), Iren. *Haer.* iv. cc. 17, 18, 19, v. 2. 3 *Fragm.* 38 (Stieren). The place occupied by the eucharistic elements in their view of sacrifice will only be appreciated by reading the passages continuously.

upon as distinct orders, the correspondence of the threefold ministry with the three ranks of the Levitical priesthood could not fail to suggest itself. The solitary bishop represented the solitary high-priest; the principal acts of Christian sacrifice were performed by the presbyters, as the principal acts of Jewish sacrifice by the priests; and the attendant ministrations were assigned in the one case to the deacon, as in the other to the Levite. Thus the analogy seemed complete. To this correspondence however there was one grave impediment. The only High-Priest under the Gospel recognised by the apostolic writings, is our Lord Himself. Accordingly in the Christian remains of the ages next succeeding this title is reserved as by right to Him[1]; and though belonging to various schools, all writers alike abstain from applying it to the bishop. Yet the scruple was at length set aside. When it had become usual to speak of the presbyters as 'sacerdotes,' the designation of 'pontifex' or 'summus sacerdos' for the bishop was far too convenient and too appropriate to be neglected.

Thus the analogy of the sacrifices and the correspondence of the threefold order supplied the material on which the sacerdotal feeling worked. And in this way, by the union of Gentile sentiment with the ordinances of the Old Dispensation, the doctrine of an exclusive priesthood found its way into the Church of Christ.

Question suggested. How far is the language of the later Church justifiable? Can the Christian ministry be called a priesthood in any sense? and if so, in what sense? The historical investigation, which has suggested this question as its proper corollary, has also supplied the means of answering it.

Silence of the Apostolic writers. Though different interpretations may be put upon the fact that the sacred writers throughout refrain from applying sacerdotal terms to the Christian ministry, I think it must be taken

---

[1] See Clem. Rom. 36, 58, Polyc. Phil. 12, Ignat. Philad. 9, Test. xii Patr. Rub. 6, Sym. 7, etc., Clem. Recogn. i. 48.

to signify this much at least, that this ministry, if a priesthood at all, is a priesthood of a type essentially different from the Jewish. Otherwise we shall be perplexed to explain why the earliest Christian teachers should have abstained from using those terms which alone would adequately express to their hearers the one most important aspect of the ministerial office. It is often said in reply, that we have here a question not of words, but of things. This is undeniable: but words express things; and the silence of the Apostles still requires an explanation.

However the interpretation of this fact is not far to seek. The Epistle to the Hebrews speaks at great length on priests and sacrifices in their Jewish and their Christian bearing. It is plain from this epistle, as it may be gathered also from other notices Jewish and Heathen, that the one prominent idea of the priestly office at this time was the function of *offering sacrifice* and thereby making atonement. Now this Apostolic writer teaches that all sacrifices had been consummated in the one Sacrifice, all priesthoods absorbed in the one Priest. The offering had been made once for all: and, as there were no more victims, there could be no more priests[1]. All former priesthoods had borne witness to the necessity of a human mediator, and this sentiment had its satisfaction in the Person and Office of the Son of Man. All past sacrifices had proclaimed the need of an atoning death, and had their antitype, their realisation, their annulment, in the Cross of Christ. This explicit statement supplements and interprets the silence elsewhere noticed in the Apostolic writings.

Epistle to the Hebrews;

its doctrinal teaching,

---

[1] The epistle deals mainly with the office of Christ as the antitype of the *High-Priest* offering the *annual* sacrifice of atonement: and it has been urged that there is still room for a sacrificial priesthood under the High Priest. The whole argument however is equally applicable to the inferior priests: and in one passage at least it is directly so applied (x. 11, 12), 'And every priest standeth daily (καθ' ἡμέραν) ministering and offering the same sacrifices, etc.'; where the v. l. ἀρχιερεὺς for ἱερεὺς seems to have arisen from the desire to bring the verse into more exact conformity with what has gone before. This passage, it should be remembered, is the summing-up and generalisation of the previous argument.

234   THE CHRISTIAN MINISTRY.

and spiritual analogies. Strictly accordant too with the general tenour of his argument is the language used throughout by the writer of this epistle. He speaks of Christian sacrifices, of a Christian altar; but the sacrifices are praise and thanksgiving and well-doing, the altar is apparently the Cross of Christ[1]. If the Christian

---

[1] It is surprising that some should have interpreted θυσιαστήριον in Heb. xiii. 10 of the Lord's table. There may be a doubt as to the exact significance of the term in this passage, but an actual altar is plainly not intended. This is shown by the context both before and after: e.g. ver. 9 the opposition of χάρις and βρώματα, ver. 15 the contrast implied in the mention of θυσία αἰνέσεως and καρπὸς χειλέων, and ver. 16 the naming εὐποιΐα καὶ κοινωνία as the kind of sacrifice with which God is well pleased. In my former editions I interpreted the θυσιαστήριον of the congregation assembled for worship, having been led to this interpretation by the Christian phraseology of succeeding ages. So Clem. Alex. *Strom.* vii. 6, p. 848, ἔστι γοῦν τὸ παρ' ἡμῖν θυσιαστήριον ἐνταῦθα τὸ ἐπίγειον τὸ ἄθροισμα τῶν ταῖς εὐχαῖς ἀνακειμένων. The use of the word in Ignatius also, though less obvious, appears to be substantially the same, *Ephes.* 5, *Trall.* 7, *Philad.* 4 (but in *Magn.* 7 it seems to be a metaphor for our Lord Himself); see Höfling *Opfer* etc. p. 32 sq. Similarly too Polycarp (§ 4) speaks of the body of widows as θυσιαστήριον Θεοῦ. [See notes on these passages in *Apostolic Fathers* Part II., *S. Ignatius, S. Polycarp.*] But I have since been convinced that the context points to the Cross of Christ spiritually regarded, as the true interpretation.

Since my first edition appeared, a wholly different interpretation of the passage has been advocated by more than one writer. It is maintained that ἔχομεν θυσιαστήριον should be understood 'we Jews have an altar,' and that the writer of the epistle is here bringing an example from the Old Dispensation itself (the sin-offering on the day of atonement) in which the sacrifices were not eaten. This interpretation is attractive, but it seems to me inadequate to explain the *whole* context (though it suits parts well enough), and is ill adapted to individual expressions (e.g. θυσιαστήριον where θυσία would be expected, and οἱ τῇ σκηνῇ λατρεύοντες which thus becomes needlessly emphatic), not to mention that the first person plural and the present tense ἔχομεν seem unnatural where the author and his readers are spoken of, not as actual Christians, but as former Jews. In fact the analogy of the sacrifice on the day of atonement appears not to be introduced till the next verse, ὧν γὰρ εἰσφέρεται ζῴων κ.τ.λ.

Some interpreters again, from a comparison of 1 Cor. ix. 13 with 1 Cor. x. 18, have inferred that St Paul recognises the designation of the Lord's table as an altar. On the contrary it is a speaking fact, that in both passages he avoids using this term of the Lord's table, though the language of the context might readily have suggested it to him, if he had considered it appropriate. Nor does the argument in either case require or encourage such an inference. In 1 Cor. ix. 13, 14, the Apostle writes 'Know ye not that they which wait at the altar are partakers with the altar? Even so hath the Lord ordained that they which preach the gospel should

ministry were a sacerdotal office, if the holy eucharist were a sacerdotal act, in the same sense in which the Jewish priesthood and the Jewish sacrifice were sacerdotal, then his argument is faulty and his language misleading. Though dwelling at great length on the Christian counterparts to the Jewish priest, the Jewish altar, the Jewish sacrifice, he omits to mention the one office, the one place, the one act, which on this showing would be their truest and liveliest counterparts in the every-day worship of the Church of Christ. He has rejected these, and he has chosen instead moral and spiritual analogies for all these sacred types[1]. Thus in what he has said and in what he has left unsaid alike, his language points to one and the same result.

If therefore the sacerdotal office be understood to imply the offering of sacrifices, then the Epistle to the Hebrews leaves no place for a Christian priesthood. If on the other hand the word be taken in a wider and looser acceptation, it cannot well be withheld from the ministry of the Church of Christ. Only in this case the meaning of the term should be clearly apprehended: and it might have been better if the later Christian vocabulary had conformed to the silence of the Apostolic writers, so that the possibility of confusion would have been avoided. *Christian ministers are priests in another sense;*

According to this broader meaning, the priest may be defined as one who represents God to man and man to God. It is moreover indispensable that he should be called by God, for no man 'taketh this honour to himself.' The Christian ministry satisfies both these conditions.

Of the fulfilment of the latter the only evidence within our cognisance is the fact that the minister is called according to a divinely appointed order. If the preceding investigation be *as having a divine appointment,*

---

live of the gospel.' The point of resemblance in the two cases is the holding a sacred office; but the ministering on the altar is predicated only of the former. So also in 1 Cor. x. 18 sq., the *altar* is named as common to Jews and Heathens, but the *table* only as common to Christians and Heathens; i.e. the holy eucharist is a banquet but it is not a sacrifice (in the Jewish or Heathen sense of sacrifice).

[1] For the passages see above, pp. 229, 230.

substantially correct, the three-fold ministry can be traced to Apostolic direction; and short of an express statement we can possess no better assurance of a Divine appointment or at least a Divine sanction. If the facts do not allow us to unchurch other Christian communities differently organized, they may at least justify our jealous adhesion to a polity derived from this source.

And while the mode of appointment satisfies the one condition, the nature of the office itself satisfies the other; for it exhibits the doubly representative character which is there laid down.

<small>as representing God to man,</small>
The Christian minister is God's ambassador to men: he is charged with the ministry of reconciliation; he unfolds the will of heaven; he declares in God's name the terms on which pardon is offered; and he pronounces in God's name the absolution of the penitent. This last mentioned function has been thought to invest the ministry with a distinctly sacerdotal character. Yet it is very closely connected with the magisterial and pastoral duties of the office, and is only priestly in the same sense in which they are priestly. As empowered to declare the conditions of God's grace, he is empowered also to proclaim the consequences of their acceptance. But throughout his office is representative and not vicarial[1]. He does not interpose between God and man in such a way that direct communion with God is superseded on the one hand, or that his own mediation becomes indispensable on the other.

<small>and as representing man to God.</small>
Again, the Christian minister is the representative of man to God—of the congregation primarily, of the individual indirectly as a member of the congregation. The alms, the prayers, the thanksgivings of the community are offered through him. Some representation is as necessary in the Church as it is in a popular government: and the nature of the representation is not affected by the fact that the form of the ministry has been handed down from Apostolic times and may well be

---

[1] The distinction is made in Maurice's *Kingdom of Christ* II. p. 216.

presumed to have a Divine sanction. For here again it must be borne in mind that the minister's function is *representative* without being *vicarial*. He is a priest, as the mouthpiece, the delegate, of a priestly race. His acts are not his own, but the acts of the congregation. Hence too it will follow that, viewed on this side as on the other, his function cannot be absolute and indispensable. It may be a general rule, it may be under ordinary circumstances a practically universal law, that the highest acts of congregational worship shall be performed through the principal officers of the congregation. But an emergency may arise when the spirit and not the letter must decide. The Christian ideal will then interpose and interpret our duty. The higher ordinance of the universal priesthood will overrule all special limitations. The layman will assume functions which are otherwise restricted to the ordained minister[1].

Yet it would be vain to deny that a very different conception prevailed for many centuries in the Church of Christ. The Apostolic ideal was set forth, and within a few generations forgotten. The vision was only for a time and then vanished. A strictly sacerdotal view of the ministry superseded the broader and more spiritual conception of their priestly functions. From being the representatives, the ambassadors, of God, they came to be regarded His vicars. Nor is this the only instance where a false conception has seemed to maintain a long-lived domination over the Church. For some centuries the idea of the Holy Roman Empire enthralled the minds of men. For a still longer period the idea of the Holy Roman See held undisturbed sway over Western Christendom. To those who take a comprehensive view of the progress of Christianity, even these more lasting obscurations of the truth will present no serious difficulty. They will not suffer themselves to be blinded thereby to the true nobility of Ecclesiastical History: they will not fail to see

The prevalence of sacerdotalism considered.

---

[1] For the opinion of the early Church on this subject see especially the passage of Tertullian quoted above, p. 223.

that, even in the seasons of her deepest degradation, the Church was still the regenerator of society, the upholder of right principle against selfish interest, the visible witness of the Invisible God; they will thankfully confess that, notwithstanding the pride and selfishness and dishonour of individual rulers, notwithstanding the imperfections and errors of special institutions and developments, yet in her continuous history the Divine promise has been signally realised, 'Lo I am with you always, even unto the end of the world.'

ADDITIONAL NOTES TO THE DISSERTATION UPON THE
CHRISTIAN MINISTRY.

A.

In the following passage in his later work, The Apostolic Fathers Part II., S. Ignatius, S. Polycarp I. p. 407 sq. (*1st edit.* 1885), I. p. 422 sq. (*2nd edit.* 1889), *Dr Lightfoot sums up his reasons for the change of opinion upon the Ignatian question announced above, p.* 198, *note* 1.

The facts then are these:

(1) No Christian writings of the second century, and very few writings of antiquity, whether Christian or pagan, are so well authenticated as the Epistles of Ignatius. If the Epistle of Polycarp be accepted as genuine, the authentication is perfect[1].

(2) The main ground of objection against the genuineness of the Epistle of Polycarp is its authentication of the Ignatian Epistles. Otherwise there is every reason to believe that it would have passed unquestioned.

(3) The Epistle of Polycarp itself is exceptionally well authenticated by the testimony of his disciple Irenæus.

(4) All attempts to explain the phenomena of the Epistle of Polycarp, as forged or interpolated to give colour to the Ignatian Epistles, have signally failed.

(5) The external testimony to the Ignatian Epistles being so strong, only the most decisive marks of spuriousness in the epistles themselves, as for instance proved anachronisms, would justify us in suspecting them as interpolated or rejecting them as spurious.

(6) But so far is this from being the case that one after another

---

[1] 'If the Epistle of Polycarp be accepted as genuine' (2nd edit.).

the anachronisms urged against these letters have vanished in the light of further knowledge. Thus the alleged refutation of the Valentinian doctrine of æons in *Magn.* 8 depends on a false reading which recently discovered materials for the text have corrected. The supposed anachronism of 'the leopards' (*Rom.* 5) has been refuted by the production of passages overlooked by the objector. The argument from the mention of the 'Catholic Church' (*Smyrn.* 8) has been shown to rest on a false interpretation which disregards the context.

(7) As regards the argument which Daillé calls 'palmary'—the prevalence of episcopacy as a recognized institution—we may say boldly that all the facts point the other way. If the writer of these letters had represented the Churches of Asia Minor as under presbyteral government, he would have contradicted all the evidence, which without one dissentient voice points to episcopacy as the established form of Church government in these districts from the close of the first century.

(8) The circumstances of the condemnation, captivity, and journey of Ignatius, which have been a stumbling-block to some modern critics, did not present any difficulty to those who lived near the time and therefore knew best what might be expected under the circumstances; and they are sufficiently borne out by examples, more or less analogous, to establish their credibility.

(9) The objections to the style and language of the epistles are beside the purpose. In some cases they arise from a misunderstanding of the writer's meaning. Generally they may be said to rest on the assumption that an apostolic father could not use exaggerated expressions, overstrained images, and the like—certainly a sandy foundation on which to build an argument.

(10) A like answer holds with regard to any extravagances in sentiment or opinion or character. Why should Ignatius not have exceeded the bounds of sober reason or correct taste? Other men in his own and immediately succeeding ages did both. As an apostolic father he was not exempt from the failings, if failings they were, of his age and position.

(11) While the investigation of the contents of these epistles has yielded this negative result, in dissipating the objections, it has at the same time had a high positive value, as revealing indications of a very early date, and therefore presumably of genuineness, in the surrounding circumstances, more especially in the types of false doctrine which it combats, in the ecclesiastical status which it

presents, and in the manner in which it deals with the evangelical and apostolic documents.

(12) Moreover we discover in the personal environments of the assumed writer, and more especially in the notices of his route, many subtle coincidences which we are constrained to regard as undesigned, and which seem altogether beyond the reach of a forger.

(13) So likewise the peculiarities in style and diction of the epistles, as also in the representation of the writer's character, are much more capable of explanation in a genuine writing than in a forgery.

(14) While external and internal evidence thus combine to assert the genuineness of these writings, no satisfactory account has been or apparently can be given of them as a forgery of a later date than Ignatius. They would be quite purposeless as such; for they entirely omit all topics which would especially interest any subsequent age.

On these grounds we are constrained to accept the Seven Epistles of the Middle Form as the genuine work of Ignatius.

B.

The following extracts from Bishop Lightfoot's works illustrate his view of the Christian Ministry over and above the particular scope of the Essay in his Commentary on the Philippians. He felt that unfair use had been made of that special line of thought which he there pursued, and soon after the close of the Lambeth Conference of 1888 he had this collection of passages printed.

It is felt by those who have the best means of knowing that he would himself have wished the collection to stand together simply as his reply to the constant imputation to him of opinions for which writers wished to claim his support without any justification.

1. Commentary on the Epistle to the Philippians (Essay on the Christian Ministry, 1868).

(i) p. 199, ed. 1; p. 201, later edd. (See above, p. 160.)

'Unless we have recourse to a sweeping condemnation of received documents, it seems vain to deny that early in the second century the episcopal office was firmly and widely established. Thus during the last three decades of the first century, and consequently during the lifetime of the latest surviving Apostle, this change must have been brought about.'

(ii) p. 212, ed. 1; p. 214, later edd. (See above, p. 175.)

'The evidence for the early and wide extension of episcopacy throughout proconsular Asia, the scene of St John's latest labours, may be considered irrefragable.'

(iii) p. 225, ed. 1; p. 227, later edd. (See above, pp. 190, 191.)

'But these notices, besides establishing the general prevalence of episcopacy, also throw considerable light on its origin...Above all, they establish this result clearly, that its maturer forms are seen first in those regions where the latest surviving Apostles (more especially St John) fixed their abode, and at a time when its prevalence cannot be dissociated from their influence or their sanction.'

(iv) p. 232, ed. 1; p. 234, later edd. (See above, pp. 197, 198.)

'It has been seen that the institution of an episcopate must be placed as far back as the closing years of the first century, and that it cannot, without violence to historical testimony, be dissociated from the name of St John.'

(v) p. 265, ed. 1; p. 267, later edd. (See above, pp. 235, 236.)

'If the preceding investigation be substantially correct, the threefold ministry can be traced to Apostolic direction; and short of an express statement we can possess no better assurance of a Divine appointment or at least a Divine sanction. If the facts do not allow us to unchurch other Christian communities differently organized, they may at least justify our jealous adhesion to a polity derived from this source.'

2. Commentary on the Epistle to the Philippians (Preface to the Sixth Edition), 1881.

'The present edition is an exact reprint of the preceding one. This statement applies as well to the Essay on the Threefold Ministry as to the rest of the work. I should not have thought it necessary to be thus explicit, had I not been informed of a rumour that I had found reason to abandon the main opinions expressed in that Essay. There is no foundation for any such report. The only point of importance on which I have modified my views, since the Essay was first written, is the authentic form of the letters of St Ignatius. Whereas in the earlier editions of this work I had accepted the three Curetonian letters, I have since been convinced (as stated in later editions) that the seven letters of the Short Greek are genuine. This divergence however does not materially affect the main point at issue, since even the Curetonian letters afford abundant evidence of the spread of episcopacy in the earliest years of the second century.

But on the other hand, while disclaiming any change in my opinions, I desire equally to disclaim the representations of those opinions which have been put forward in some quarters. The object of the Essay was an investigation into the origin of the Christian Ministry. The result has been a confirmation of the statement in the English Ordinal, "It is evident unto all men diligently reading the Holy Scripture and ancient authors that from the Apostles' time there have been these orders of Ministers in Christ's Church, Bishops, Priests, and Deacons." But I was scrupulously anxious not to overstate the evidence in any case; and it would seem that partial and qualifying statements, prompted by this anxiety, have assumed undue proportions in the minds of some readers, who have emphasized them to the neglect of the general drift of the Essay.'

3. Sermon preached before the Representative Council of the Scottish Episcopal Church in St Mary's Church at Glasgow, October 10, 1882. ('Sermons preached on Special Occasions', p. 182 sq.)

'When I spoke of unity as St Paul's charge to the Church of Corinth, the thoughts of all present must, I imagine, have fastened on one application of the Apostolic rule which closely concerns yourselves. Episcopal communities in Scotland outside the organization of the Scottish Episcopal Church—this is a spectacle which no one, I imagine, would view with satisfaction in itself, and which only a very urgent necessity could justify. Can such a necessity be pleaded? "One body" as well as "one Spirit," this is the Apostolic rule. No natural interpretation can be put on these words which does not recognize the obligation of external, corporate union. Circumstances may prevent the realisation of the Apostle's conception, but the ideal must be ever present to our aspirations and our prayers. I have reason to believe that this matter lies very near to the hearts of all Scottish Episcopalians. May God grant you a speedy accomplishment of your desire. You have the same doctrinal formularies: you acknowledge the same episcopal polity: you respect the same liturgical forms. "Sirs, ye are brethren." Do not strain the conditions of reunion too tightly. I cannot say, for I do not know, what faults or what misunderstandings there may have been on either side in the past. If there have been any faults, forget them. If there exist any misunderstandings, clear them up. "Let the dead past bury its dead."

* * * * * * * *

While you seek unity among yourselves, you will pray likewise that unity may be restored to your Presbyterian brothers. Not insensible to the special blessings which you yourselves enjoy, clinging tenaciously to the threefold ministry as the completeness of the Apostolic ordinance and the historical backbone of the Church, valuing highly all those sanctities of liturgical office and ecclesiastical season, which, modified from age to age, you have inherited from an almost immemorial past, thanking GOD, but not thanking Him in any Pharisaic spirit, that these so many and great privileges are continued to you which others have lost, you will nevertheless shrink, as from the venom of a serpent's fang, from any mean desire that their divisions may be perpetuated in the hope of profiting by their troubles. *Divide et impera* may be a shrewd worldly motto; but coming in contact with spiritual things, it defiles them like pitch. *Pacifica et impera* is the true watchword of the Christian and the Churchman.'

4. The Apostolic Fathers, Part II., St Ignatius: St Polycarp, Vol. I. pp. 376, 377, 1885 (pp. 390, 391, 1889).

'The whole subject has been investigated by me in an Essay on "The Christian Ministry"; and to this I venture to refer my readers for fuller information. It is there shown, if I mistake not, that though the New Testament itself contains as yet no direct and indisputable notices of a localized episcopate in the Gentile Churches, as distinguished from the moveable episcopate exercised by Timothy in Ephesus and by Titus in Crete, yet there is satisfactory evidence of its development in the later years of the Apostolic age; that this development was not simultaneous and equal in all parts of Christendom; that it is more especially connected with the name of St John; and that in the early years of the second century the episcopate was widely spread and had taken firm root, more especially in Asia Minor and in Syria. If the evidence on which its extension in the regions east of the Ægean at this epoch be resisted, I am at a loss to understand what single fact relating to the history of the Christian Church during the first half of the second century can be regarded as established; for the testimony in favour of this spread of the episcopate is more abundant and more varied than for any other institution or event during this period, so far as I recollect.'

5. Sermon preached before the Church Congress at Wolverhampton, October 3, 1887. ('Sermons preached on Special Occasions', p. 259 sq.)

'But if this charge fails, what shall we say of her isolation? Is not this isolation, so far as it is true, much more her misfortune than her fault? Is she to be blamed because she retained a form of Church government which had been handed down in unbroken continuity from the Apostolic times, and thus a line was drawn between her and the reformed Churches of other countries? Is it a reproach to her that she asserted her liberty to cast off the accretions which had gathered about the Apostolic doctrine and practice through long ages, and for this act was repudiated by the Roman Church? But this very position,—call it isolation if you will—which was her reproach in the past, is her hope for the future. She was isolated because she could not consort with either extreme. She was isolated because she stood midway between the two. This central position is her vantage ground, which fits her to be a mediator, wheresoever an occasion of mediation may arise.

But this charge of isolation, if it had any appearance of truth seventy years ago, has lost its force now.'

6. Durham Diocesan Conference. Inaugural Address, October, 1887.

'When I speak of her religious position I refer alike to polity and to doctrine. In both respects the negative, as well as the positive, bearing of her position has to be considered. She has retained the form of Church government inherited from the Apostolic times, while she has shaken off a yoke, which even in medieval times our fathers found too heavy to bear, and which subsequent developments have rendered tenfold more oppressive. She has remained stedfast in the faith of Nicaea, but she has never compromised herself by any declaration which may entangle her in the meshes of science. The doctrinal inheritance of the past is hers, and the scientific hopes of the future are hers. She is intermediate and she may become mediatorial, when the opportunity occurs. It was this twofold inheritance of doctrine and polity which I had in view, when I spoke of the essentials which could under no circumstances be abandoned. Beyond this, it seems to me that large concessions might be made. Unity is not uniformity......On the other hand it would be very short-sighted policy—even if it were not traitorous to the truth—to tamper with essentials and thus to imperil our mediatorial vantage ground, for the sake of snatching an immediate increase of numbers.'

7. Address on the Reopening of the Chapel, Auckland Castle, August 1st, 1888. ('Leaders in the Northern Church,' p. 145.)

'But, while we "lengthen our cords," we must "strengthen our stakes" likewise. Indeed this strengthening of our stakes will alone enable us to lengthen our cords with safety, when the storms are howling around us. We cannot afford to sacrifice any portion of the faith once delivered to the saints; we cannot surrender for any immediate advantages the threefold ministry which we have inherited from Apostolic times, and which is the historic backbone of the Church. But neither can we on the other hand return to the fables of medievalism or submit to a yoke which our fathers found too grievous to be borne—a yoke now rendered a hundredfold more oppressive to the mind and conscience, weighted as it is by recent and unwarranted impositions of doctrine.'

IV.

ST PAUL AND SENECA.

IV.

ST PAUL AND SENECA.

THE earliest of the Latin fathers, Tertullian, writing about a century and a half after the death of Seneca, speaks of this philosopher as 'often our own[1].' Some two hundred years later St Jerome, having occasion to quote him, omits the qualifying adverb and calls him broadly 'our own Seneca[2].' Living midway between these two writers, Lactantius points out several coincidences with the teaching of the Gospel in the writings of Seneca, whom nevertheless he styles 'the most determined of the Roman Stoics[3].' From the age of St Jerome, Seneca was commonly regarded as standing on the very threshold of the Christian Church, even if he had not actually passed within its portals. In one Ecclesiastical Council at least, held at Tours in the year 567, his authority is quoted with a deference generally accorded only to fathers of the Church[4]. And even to the present day in the marionette plays of his native Spain St Seneca takes his place by the side of St Peter and St Paul in the representations of our Lord's passion[5].

Comparing the language of Tertullian and Jerome, we are

Seneca traditionally accounted a Christian.

---

[1] Tertull. *de Anim.* 20 'Seneca saepe noster.'

[2] *Adv. Jovin.* i. 49 (II. p. 318) 'Scripserunt Aristoteles et Plutarchus et noster Seneca de matrimonio libros etc.'

[3] *Div. Inst.* i. 5 'Annaeus Seneca qui ex Romanis vel acerrimus Stoicus fuit': comp. ii. 9, vi. 24, etc.

[4] Labbæi *Concilia* v. p. 856 (Paris, 1671) 'Sicut ait Seneca pessimum in eo vitium esse qui in id quo insanit caeteros putat furere.' See Fleury *Saint Paul et Sénèque* I. p. 14.

[5] So Fleury states, I. p. 289.

The forged correspondence of Paul and Seneca. able to measure the growth of this idea in the interval of time which separates the two. One important impulse however, which it received meanwhile, must not be overlooked. When St Jerome wrote, the Christianity of Seneca seemed to be established on a sounder basis than mere critical inference. A correspondence, purporting to have passed between the heathen philosopher and the Apostle of the Gentiles, was then in general circulation; and, without either affirming or denying its genuineness, this father was thereby induced to give a place to Seneca in his catalogue of Christian writers[1]. If the letters of Paul and Seneca, which have come down to us, are the same with those read by him (and there is no sufficient reason for doubting the identity[2]), it is strange that he could for a moment have entertained the question of their authenticity. The poverty of thought and style, the errors in chronology and history, and the whole conception of the relative positions of the Stoic philosopher and the Christian Apostle, betray clearly the hand of a forger. Yet this correspondence has without doubt been mainly instrumental in fixing the belief on the mind of the later Church, as it was even sufficient to induce some hesitation in St Jerome himself. How far the known history and the extant writings of either favour this idea, it will be the object of the present essay to examine. The enquiry into the historical connexion between these two great contemporaries will naturally expand into an investigation of the relations, whether of coincidence or of contrast, between the systems of which they were the respective exponents. And, as Stoicism was the only philosophy which could even pretend to rival Christianity in the earlier ages of the Church, such an investigation ought not to be uninstructive[3].

---

[1] *Vir. Illustr.* 12 'Quem non ponerem in catalogo sanctorum, nisi me illae epistolae provocarent quae leguntur a plurimis, Pauli ad Senecam et Senecae ad Paulum.'

[2] See the note at the end of this dissertation.

[3] In the sketch, which I have given, of the relation of Stoicism to the circumstances of the time and to other earlier and contemporary systems of philosophy, I am greatly indebted to the account in Zeller's *Philosophie der Griechen* Th. III. Abth. 1 *Die nach-*

Like all the later systems of Greek philosophy, Stoicism was the offspring of despair. Of despair in religion: for the old mythologies had ceased to command the belief or influence the conduct of men. Of despair in politics: for the Macedonian conquest had broken the independence of the Hellenic states and stamped out the last sparks of corporate life. Of despair even in philosophy itself: for the older thinkers, though they devoted their lives to forging a golden chain which should link earth to heaven, appeared now to have spent their strength in weaving ropes of sand. The sublime intuitions of Plato had been found too vague and unsubstantial, and the subtle analyses of Aristotle too hard and cold, to satisfy the natural craving of man for some guidance which should teach him how to live and to die.

Later philosophies the children of despair.

Thus the soil of Greece had been prepared by the uprootal of past interests and associations for fresh developments of religious and philosophic thought. When political life became impossible, the moral faculties of man were turned inward upon himself and concentrated on the discipline of the individual soul. When speculation had been cast aside as barren and unprofitable, the search was directed towards some practical rule or rules which might take its place. When the gods of Hellas had been deposed and dishonoured, some new powers must be created or discovered to occupy their vacant throne.

Greece prepared for new systems of philosophy.

Stimulated by the same need, Epicurus and Zeno strove in different ways to solve the problem which the perplexities of their age presented. Both alike, avoiding philosophy in the proper sense of the term, concentrated their energies on ethics: but the one took happiness, the other virtue, as his supreme good, and made it the starting-point of his ethical teaching. Both alike contrasted with the older masters in building their systems on the needs of the individual and not of the state: but the one strove to satisfy the cravings of man, as a being intended

Coincidences and contrasts of the Epicurean and Stoic philosophies.

aristotelische Philosophie (2nd ed. 1865), which it is impossible to praise too highly. See also the instructive essay of Sir A. Grant on 'The Ancient Stoics' in his edition of *Aristotle's Ethics* I. p. 243 sq. (2nd ed.).

by nature for social life, by laying stress on the claims and privileges of friendship, the other by expanding his sphere of duty and representing him as a citizen of the world or even of the universe. Both alike paid a certain respect to the waning beliefs of their day: but the one without denying the existence of the gods banished them from all concern in the affairs of men, while the other, transforming and utilising the creations of Hellenic mythology, identified them with the powers of the physical world. Both alike took conformity to nature as their guiding maxim: but nature with the one was interpreted to mean the equable balance of all the impulses and faculties of man, with the other the absolute supremacy of the reason, as the ruling principle of his being. And lastly; both alike sought refuge from the turmoil and confusion of the age in the inward calm and composure of the soul. If Serenity (ἀταραξία) was the supreme virtue of the one, her twin sister Passionlessness (ἀπαθία) was the sovereign principle of the other.

Oriental origin of Stoicism.

These two later developments of Greek philosophy both took root and grew to maturity in Greek soil. But, while the seed of the one was strictly Hellenic, the other was derived from an Oriental stock. Epicurus was a Greek of the Greeks, a child of Athenian parents. Zeno on the other hand, a native of Citium, a Phœnician colony in Crete, was probably of Shemitic race, for he is commonly styled 'the Phœnician[1].' Babylon, Tyre, Sidon, Carthage, reared some of his most illustrious successors. Cilicia, Phrygia, Rhodes, were the homes of others. Not a single Stoic of any name was a native of Greece proper[2].

Its moral earnestness derived thence.

To Eastern affinities Stoicism was without doubt largely indebted for the features which distinguished it from other schools of Greek philosophy. To this fact may be ascribed the intense moral earnestness which was its most honourable characteristic. If the later philosophers generally, as distin-

---

[1] See Diog. Laert. vii. 3, where Crates addresses him τί φεύγεις, ὦ Φοινικίδιον; comp. § 15 Φοίνισσαν; § 25 Φοινικικῶς; § 30 εἰ δὲ πάτρα Φοίνισσα, τίς ὁ φθόνος; We are told also § 7 ἀντεποιοῦντο δ' αὐτοῦ καὶ οἱ ἐν Σιδῶνι Κιτιεῖς. So again ii. 114 Ζήνωνα τὸν Φοίνικα.

[2] See below, pp. 282, 288.

guished from the earlier, busied themselves with ethics rather than metaphysics, with the Stoics this was the one absorbing passion. The contrast between the light, reckless gaiety of the Hellenic spirit and the stern, unbending, almost fanatical moralism of the followers of Zeno is as complete as could well be imagined. The ever-active conscience which is the glory, and the proud self-consciousness which is the reproach, of the Stoic school are alike alien to the temper of ancient Greece. Stoicism breathes rather the religious atmosphere of the East, which fostered on the one hand the inspired devotion of a David or an Isaiah, and on the other the self-mortification and self-righteousness of an Egyptian therapeute or an Indian fakir. A recent writer, to whom we are indebted for a highly appreciative account of the Stoic school, describes this new phase of Greek philosophy, which we have been reviewing and of which Stoicism was the truest exponent, as 'the transition to *modernism*[1].' It might with greater truth be described as the contact of Oriental influences with the world of classical thought. Stoicism was in fact the earliest offspring of the union between the religious consciousness of the East and the intellectual culture of the West. The recognition of the claims of the individual soul, the sense of personal responsibility, the habit of judicial introspection, in short the subjective view of ethics, were in no sense new, for they are known to have held sway over the mind of the chosen people from the earliest dawn of their history as a nation. But now for the first time they presented themselves at the doors of Western civilization and demanded admission. The occasion was eminently favourable. The conquests of Alexander, which rendered the fusion of the East and West for the first time possible, also evoked the moral need which they had thus supplied the means of satisfying. By the overthrow of the state the importance of the individual was enhanced. In the failure of political relations, men were thrown

Union of oriental with classical thought.

---

[1] Grant, *l. c.* p. 243. Sir A. Grant however fully recognises the Eastern element in Stoicism (p. 246).

back on their inward resources and led to examine their moral wants and to educate their moral faculties.

Exclusive attention to ethics. It was in this way that the Eastern origin of Stoicism combined with the circumstances and requirements of the age to give it an exclusively *ethical* character. The Stoics did, it is true, pay some little attention to physical questions: and one or two leading representatives of the school also contributed towards the systematic treatment of logic. But consciously and expressly they held these branches of study to be valueless except in their bearing on moral questions. Representing philosophy under the image of a field, they compared physics to the trees, ethics to the fruit for which the trees exist, and logic to the wall or fence which protects the enclosure[1]. Or again, adopting another comparison, they likened logic to the shell of an egg, physics to the white, and ethics to the yolk[2].

Practical neglect of physics As the fundamental maxim of Stoical ethics was conformity to nature, and as therefore it was of signal importance to ascertain man's relation to the world around, it might have been supposed that the study of physics would have made great progress in the hands of Zeno's disciples. But, pursuing it for the most part without any love for the study itself and pursuing it moreover only to support certain foregone ethical conclusions, they instituted few independent researches and discovered no *and depreciation of logic.* hidden truths. To logic they assigned a still meaner part. The place which it occupies in the images already mentioned clearly points to their conception of its functions. It was not so much a means of arriving at truth, as an expedient for protecting

---

[1] Diog. Laert. vii. 40, Philo *de Agric.* 3, p. 302 M. See also *de Mut. Nom.* § 10, p. 589 M, where Philo after giving this comparison says οὕτως οὖν ἔφασαν καὶ ἐν φιλοσοφίᾳ δεῖν τήν τε φυσικὴν καὶ λογικὴν πραγματείαν ἐπὶ τὴν ἠθικὴν ἀναφέρεσθαι κ.τ.λ.

[2] Sext. Emp. vii. 17. On the other hand Diog. Laert. *l.c.* makes ethics the white and physics the yolk. See Zeller *l.c.* p. 57, and Ritter and Preller *Hist. Phil.* § 396. But this is a matter of little moment; for, whichever form of the metaphor be adopted, the ethical bearing of physics is put prominently forward. Indeed as ancient naturalists were not agreed about the respective functions of the yolk and the white, the application of the metaphor must have been influenced by this uncertainty. The inferiority of logic appears in all the comparisons.

truth already attained from external assaults. An extreme representative of the school went so far as to say that 'Of subjects of philosophical investigation some pertain to us, some have no relation to us, and some are beyond us: ethical questions belong to the first class; dialectics to the second, for they contribute nothing towards the amendment of life; and physics to the third, for they are beyond the reach of knowledge and are profitless withal[1].' This was the genuine spirit of the school[2], though other adherents were more guarded in their statements. Physical science is conversant in *experiment*; logical science in *argumentation*. But the Stoic was impatient alike of the one and the other; for he was essentially a philosopher of *intuitions*.

And here again the Oriental spirit manifested itself. The Greek moralist was a reasoner: the Oriental for the most part, whether inspired or uninspired, a prophet. Though they might clothe their systems of morality in a dialectical garb, the Stoic teachers belonged essentially to this latter class. Even Chrysippus, the great logician and controversialist of the sect, is reported to have told his master Cleanthes, that 'he only wanted the doctrines, and would himself find out the proofs[3].' This saying has been condemned as 'betraying a want of earnestness as to the truth[4]'; but I can hardly think that it ought to be regarded in this light. Flippant though it would appear at first sight, it may well express the intense faith in intuition, or what I have called the prophetic[5] spirit, which distinguishes the school. Like the other Stoics, Chrysippus

Prophetic spirit of the school.

---

[1] Ariston in Diog. Laert. vii. 160, Stob. *Flor.* lxxx. 7. See Zeller *l.c.* p. 50.
[2] 'Quicquid legeris *ad mores* statim referas,' says Seneca *Ep. Mor.* lxxxix. See the whole of the preceding epistle.
[3] Diog. Laert. vii. 179 πολλάκις ἔλεγε μόνης τῆς τῶν δογμάτων διδασκαλίας χρῄζειν τὰς δ' ἀποδείξεις αὐτὸς εὑρήσειν.
[4] Grant *l.c.* p. 253.
[5] Perhaps the use of this term needs some apology; but I could not find a better. I meant to express by it the characteristic of enunciating moral truths as authoritative, independently of processes of reasoning. The Stoic, being a pantheist and having no distinct belief in a personal God, was not a prophet in the ordinary sense, but only as being the exponent of his own inner consciousness, which was his supreme authority.

had no belief in argumentation, but welcomed the highest truths as intuitively apprehended. Logic was to him, as to them, only the egg-shell which protected the germ of future life, the fence which guarded the fruitful garden. As a useful weapon of defence against assailants, and nothing more, it was regarded by the most perfect master of the science which the school produced. The doctrines did not derive their validity from logical reasoning: they were absolute and self-contained. Once stated, they must commend themselves to the innate faculty, when not clouded by ignoble prejudices of education or degrading habits of life.

Parallel to Christianity in the westward progress of Stoicism.

But though the germ of Stoicism was derived from the East, its systematic development and its practical successes were attained by transplantation into a western soil. In this respect its career, as it travelled westward, presents a rough but instructive parallel to the progress of the Christian Church. The fundamental ideas, derived from Oriental parentage, were reduced to a system and placed on an intellectual basis by the instrumentality of Greek thought. The schools of Athens and of Tarsus did for Stoicism the same work which was accomplished for the doctrines of the Gospel by the controversial writings of the Greek fathers and the authoritative decrees of the Greek councils. Zeno and Chrysippus and Panætius are the counterparts of an Origen, an Athanasius, or a Basil. But, while the systematic expositions of the Stoic tenets were directly or indirectly the products of Hellenic thought and were matured on Greek soil, the scene of its greatest practical manifestations was elsewhere. It must be allowed that the Roman representatives of the school were very inadequate exponents of the Stoic philosophy regarded as a speculative system: but just as Latin Christianity adopted from her Greek sister the creeds which she herself was incapable of framing, and built thereupon an edifice of moral influence and social organization far more stately and enduring, so also when naturalised in its Latin home Stoicism became a motive power in the world, and exhibited those practical results to which its renown is chiefly due. This

Influence of Greece

and of Rome.

comparison is instituted between movements hardly comparable in their character or their effects; and it necessarily stops short of the incorporation of the Teutonic nations. But the distinctive feature of Christianity as a Divine revelation and of the Church as a Divine institution does not exempt them from the ordinary laws of progress: and the contrasts between the doctrines of the Porch and the Gospel, to which I shall have to call attention later, are rendered only the more instructive by observing this parallelism in their outward career.

It is this latest or Roman period of Stoic philosophy which has chiefly attracted attention, not only because its practical influence then became most manifest, but also because this stage of its history alone is adequately illustrated by extant writings of the school. On the Christian student moreover it has a special claim; for he will learn an instructive lesson in the conflicts or coincidences of Stoicism with the doctrines of the Gospel and the progress of the Church. And of this stage in its history Seneca is without doubt the most striking representative. *Attention directed to the Roman period.*

Seneca was strictly a contemporary of St Paul. Born probably within a few years of each other, the Christian Apostle and the Stoic philosopher both died about the same time and both fell victims of the same tyrant's rage. Here, it would have seemed, the parallelism must end. One might indeed indulge in an interesting speculation whether Seneca, like so many other Stoics, had not Shemitic blood in his veins. The whole district from which he came was thickly populated with Phœnician settlers either from the mother country or from her great African colony. The name of his native province Bætica, the name of his native city Corduba, are both said to be Phœnician. Even his own name, though commonly derived from the Latin, may perhaps have a Shemitic origin; for it is borne by a Jew of Palestine early in the second century[1]. *Seneca*

---

[1] The name Σεννεκᾶς or Σενεκᾶς occurs in the list of the early bishops of Jerusalem, Euseb. *H. E.* iv. 5. The word is usually connected with 'senex.' Curtius *Griech. Etym.* § 428.

contrasted with St Paul.

This however is thrown out merely as a conjecture. Otherwise the Stoic philosopher from the extreme West and the Christian Apostle from the extreme East of the Roman dominions would seem very unlikely to present any features in common. The one a wealthy courtier and statesman settled in the metropolis, the other a poor and homeless preacher wandering in distant provinces, they were separated not less by the manifold influences of daily life than by the circumstances of their birth and early education.

Coincidences of thought and language.

Yet the coincidences of thought and even of language between the two are at first sight so striking, that many writers have been at a loss to account for them, except on the supposition of personal intercourse, if not of direct plagiarism[1]. The inference indeed appears unnecessary: but

---

[1] The connexion of St Paul and Seneca has been a favourite subject with French writers. The most elaborate of recent works is A. Fleury's *Saint Paul et Sénèque* (Paris 1853), in which the author attempts to show that Seneca was a disciple of St Paul. It is interesting and full of materials, but extravagant and unsatisfactory. Far more critical is C. Aubertin's *Étude Critique sur les rapports supposés entre Sénèque et Saint Paul* (Paris 1857), which appears intended as an answer to Fleury. Aubertin shows that many of the parallels are fallacious, and that many others prove nothing, since the same sentiments occur in earlier writers. At the same time he fails to account for other more striking coincidences. It must be added also that he is sometimes very careless in his statements. For instance (p. 186) he fixes an epoch by coupling together the names of Celsus and Julian, though they are separated by nearly two centuries. Fleury's opinion is combated also in Baur's articles *Seneca und Paulus*, republished in *Drei Abhandlungen etc.* p. 377 sq. (ed. Zeller, 1876). Among other recent French works in which Seneca's obligations to Christianity are maintained, may be named those of Troplong, *De l'influence du Christianisme sur le droit civil des Romains* p. 76 (Paris 1843), and C. Schmidt *Essai historique sur la société civile dans le monde Romain et sur sa transformation par le Christianisme* (Paris 1853). The opposite view is taken by C. Martha *Les Moralistes sous l'Empire Romain* (2ᵐᵉ éd. Paris 1866). *Le Stoicisme à Rome*, by P. Montée (Paris 1865), is a readable little book, but does not throw any fresh light on the subject. *Seekers after God*, a popular and instructive work by the Rev. F. W. Farrar, appeared about the same time as my first edition. Still later are the discussions of G. Boissier *La Religion Romaine* II. p. 52 sq. (Paris 1874) and K. Franke *Stoicismus u. Christenthum* (Breslau 1876). The older literature of the subject will be found in Fleury I. p. 2 sq. In reading through Seneca I have been able to add some striking coincidences to those collected by Fleury and others, while at the same time I have rejected a vast number as insufficient or illusory.

the facts are remarkable enough to challenge investigation, and I propose now to consider their bearing.

Though general resemblances of sentiment and teaching will carry less weight, as compared with the more special coincidences of language and illustration, yet the data would be incomplete without taking the former into account[1]. Thus we might imagine ourselves listening to a Christian divine, when we read in the pages of Seneca that 'God made the world because He is good,' and that 'as the good never grudges anything good, He therefore made everything the best possible[2].' Yet if we are tempted to draw a hasty inference from this parallel, we are checked by remembering that it is a quotation from Plato. Again Seneca maintains that 'in worshipping the gods, the first thing is to believe in the gods,' and that 'he who has copied them has worshipped them adequately[3]'; and on this duty of imitating the gods he insists frequently and emphatically[4]. But here too his sentiment is common to Plato and many other

Goodness of God.

Relation of man to God.

---

[1] No account is here taken of certain direct reproductions of Christian teaching which some writers have found in Seneca. Thus the doctrine of the Trinity is supposed to be enunciated by these words 'Quisquis formator universi fuit, sive ille *Deus* est *potens omnium*, sive incorporalis *ratio* ingentium operum artifex, sive *divinus spiritus* per omnia maxima ac minima aequali intentione diffusus, sive fatum et inmutabilis causarum inter se cohaerentium series' (*ad Helv. matr.* 8). Fleury (I. p. 97), who holds this view, significantly ends his quotation with 'diffusus,' omitting the clause 'sive fatum, etc.' Thus again some writers have found an allusion to the Christian sacraments in Seneca's language, 'Ad hoc sacramentum adacti sumus ferre mortalia,' *de Vit. beat.* 15 (comp. *Ep. Mor.* lxv). Such criticisms are mere plays on words and do not even deserve credit for ingenuity. On the other hand Seneca does mention the doctrine of guardian angels or demons; 'Sepone in praesentia quae quibusdam placent, unicuique nostrum paedagogum dari deum,' *Ep. Mor.* cx; but, as Aubertin shows (p. 284 sq.), this was a tenet common to many earlier philosophers; and in the very passage quoted Seneca himself adds, 'Ita tamen hoc seponas volo, ut memineris majores nostros, qui crediderunt, Stoicos fuisse, singulis enim et Genium et Junonem dederunt.' See Zeller p. 297 sq.

[2] *Ep. Mor.* lxv. 10.

[3] *Ep. Mor.* xcv. 50.

[4] *de Vit. beat.* 15 'Habebit illud in animo vetus praeceptum: deum sequere'; *de Benef.* iv. 25 'Propositum est nobis secundum rerum naturam vivere et deorum exemplum sequi'; *ib.* i. 1 'Hos sequamur duces quantum humana imbecillitas patitur'; *Ep. Mor.* cxxiv. 23 'Animus emendatus ac purus, aemulator dei.'

of the older philosophers. 'No man,' he says elsewhere, 'is good without God[1].' 'Between good men and the gods there exists a friendship—a friendship do I say? nay, rather a relationship and a resemblance[2]'; and using still stronger language he speaks of men as the children of God[3]. But here again he is treading in the footsteps of the older Stoic teachers, and his very language is anticipated in the words quoted by St Paul from Cleanthes or Aratus, 'We too His offspring are[4].'

Fatherly chastisement of God.

From the recognition of God's fatherly relation to man important consequences flow. In almost Apostolic language Seneca describes the trials and sufferings of good men as the chastisements of a wise and beneficent parent: 'God has a fatherly mind towards good men and loves them stoutly; and, saith He, Let them be harassed with toils, with pains, with losses, that they may gather true strength[5].' 'Those therefore whom God approves, whom He loves, them He hardens, He chastises, He disciplines[6].' Hence the 'sweet uses of adversity' find in him an eloquent exponent. 'Nothing,' he says, quoting his friend Demetrius, 'seems to me more unhappy than the man whom no adversity has ever befallen[7].' 'The life free from care and from any buffetings of fortune is a dead sea[8].' Hence too it follows that resignation under adversity becomes a plain duty. 'It is best to endure what you cannot mend, and without murmuring to attend upon God, by whose ordering all things come to pass. He is a bad soldier who follows his captain complaining[9].'

The indwelling spirit of God.

Still more strikingly Christian is his language, when he speaks of God, who 'is near us, is with us, is within,' of 'a holy spirit residing in us, the guardian and observer of our good and evil deeds[10].' 'By what other name,' he asks, 'can we call an

---

[1] *Ep. Mor.* xli ; comp. lxxiii.
[2] *de Prov.*1; comp. *Nat. Quaest.* prol., etc.
[3] *de Prov.* 1, *de Benef.* ii. 29.
[4] Acts xvii. 28.
[5] *de Prov.* 2.
[6] *de Prov.* 4 ; comp. *ib.* § 1.
[7] *de Prov.* 3.
[8] *Ep. Mor.* lxvii. This again is a saying of Demetrius.
[9] *Ep. Mor.* cvii ; comp. *ib.* lxxvi.
[10] *Ep. Mor.* xli ; comp. *ib.* lxxiii.

upright and good and great mind except (a) god lodging in a human body¹?' The spark of a heavenly flame has alighted on the hearts of men². They are associates with, are members of God. The mind came from God and yearns towards God³.

From this doctrine of the abiding presence of a divine spirit the practical inferences are not less weighty. 'So live with men, as if God saw you; so speak with God, as if men heard you⁴.' 'What profits it, if any matter is kept secret from men? nothing is hidden from God⁵.' 'The gods are witnesses of everything⁶.'

But even more remarkable perhaps, than this devoutness of tone in which the duties of man to God arising out of his filial relation are set forth, is the energy of Seneca's language, when he paints the internal struggle of the human soul and prescribes the discipline needed for its release. The soul is bound in a prison-house, is weighed down by a heavy burden⁷. Life is a continual warfare⁸. From the terrors of this struggle none escape unscathed. The Apostolic doctrine that all have sinned has an apparent counterpart in the teaching of Seneca; 'We shall ever be obliged to pronounce the same sentence upon ourselves, that we are evil, that we have been evil, and (I will add it unwillingly) that we shall be evil⁹.' 'Every vice exists in every man, though every vice is not prominent in each¹⁰.' 'If we would be upright judges of all things, let us first persuade ourselves of this, that not one of us is without fault¹¹.' 'These are vices of mankind and not of the times. No age has been free from fault¹².' 'Capital punishment is appointed for all, and

Universal dominion of sin.

---

¹ *Ep. Mor.* xxxi. The want of the definite article in Latin leaves the exact meaning uncertain; but this uncertainty is suited to the vagueness of Stoic theology. In *Ep. Mor.* xli Seneca quotes the words 'Quis deus, incertum est; habitat Deus' (Virg. *Æn.* viii. 352), and applies them to this inward monitor.
² *de Otio* 5.
³ *Ep. Mor.* xcii.
⁴ *Ep. Mor.* x.
⁵ *Ep. Mor.* lxxxiii; comp. *Fragm.* 14 (in Lactant. vi. 24).
⁶ *Ep. Mor.* cii.
⁷ *ad Helv. matr.* 11, *Ep. Mor.* lxv, cii.
⁸ See below, p. 269, note 5.
⁹ *de Benef.* i. 10.
¹⁰ *de Benef.* iv. 27.
¹¹ *de Ira* ii. 28; comp. *ad Polyb.* 11, *Ep. Mor.* xlii.
¹² *Ep. Mor.* xcvii.

262   ST PAUL AND SENECA.

this by a most righteous ordinance[1].' 'No one will be found who can acquit himself; and any man calling himself innocent has regard to the witness, not to his own conscience[2].' 'Every day, every hour,' he exclaims, 'shows us our nothingness, and reminds us by some new token, when we forget our frailty[3].'

Office of the conscience. Thus Seneca, in common with the Stoic school generally, lays great stress on the office of the conscience, as 'making cowards of us all.' 'It reproaches them,' he says, 'and shows them to themselves[4].' 'The first and greatest punishment of sinners is the fact of having sinned[5].' 'The beginning of safety is the knowledge of sin.' 'I think this,' he adds, 'an admirable saying of Epicurus[6].'

Self-examination and confession. Hence also follows the duty of strict self-examination. 'As far as thou canst, accuse thyself, try thyself: discharge the office, first of a prosecutor, then of a judge, lastly of an intercessor[7].' Accordingly he relates at some length how, on lying down to rest every night, he follows the example of Sextius and reviews his shortcomings during the day: 'When the light is removed out of sight, and my wife, who is by this time aware of my practice, is now silent, I pass the whole of my day under examination, and I review my deeds and words. I hide nothing from myself, I pass over nothing[8].' Similarly he describes the good man as one who 'has opened out his conscience to the gods, and always lives as if in public, fearing himself more than others[9].' In the same spirit too he enlarges on the advantage of having a faithful friend, 'a ready heart into which your every

---

[1] *Qu. Nat.* ii. 59.
[2] *de Ira* i. 14.
[3] *Ep. Mor.* ci.
[4] *Ep. Mor.* xcvii. 15.
[5] *ib.* 14.
[6] *Ep. Mor.* xxviii. 9 'Initium est salutis notitia peccati.' For convenience I have translated *peccatum* here as elsewhere by 'sin'; but it will be evident at once that in a saying of Epicurus, whose gods were indifferent to the doings of men, the associations connected with the word must be very different. See the remarks below, p. 279. Fleury (I. p. 111) is eloquent on this coincidence, but omits to mention that it occurs in a saying of Epicurus. His argument crumbles into dust before our eyes, when the light of this fact is admitted.
[7] *ib.* 10.
[8] *de Ira* iii. 36.
[9] *de Benef.* vii. 1.

secret can be safely deposited, whose privity you need fear less than your own[1]'; and urges again and again the duty of meditation and self-converse[2], quoting on this head the saying of Epicurus, 'Then retire within thyself most, when thou art forced to be in a crowd[3].'

Nor, when we pass from the duty of individual self-discipline to the social relations of man, does the Stoic philosophy, as represented by Seneca, hold a less lofty tone. He acknowledges in almost Scriptural language the obligation of breaking bread with the hungry[4]. 'You must live for another,' he writes, 'if you would live for yourself[5].' 'For what purpose do I get myself a friend?' he exclaims with all the extravagance of Stoic self-renunciation, 'That I may have one for whom I can die, one whom I can follow into exile, one whom I can shield from death at the cost of my own life[6].' 'I will so live,' he says elsewhere, 'as if I knew that I was born for others, and will give thanks to nature on this score[7].'

Moreover these duties of humanity extend to all classes and ranks in the social scale. The slave has claims equally with the freeman, the base-born equally with the noble. 'They are slaves, you urge; nay, they are men. They are slaves; nay, they are comrades. They are slaves; nay, they are humble friends. They are slaves; nay, they are fellow-slaves, if you reflect that fortune has the same power over both.' 'Let some of them,' he adds, 'dine with you, because they are worthy; others, that they may become worthy.' 'He is a slave, you say. Yet perchance he is free in spirit. He is a slave. Will this harm him? Show me who is not. One is a slave to lust, another to avarice, a third to ambition, all alike to fear[8].'

Duties towards others.

---

[1] *de Tranq. Anim.* 7. Comp. *Ep. Mor.* xi.

[2] *Ep. Mor.* vii 'Recede in teipsum quantum potes,' *de Otio* 28 (1) 'Proderit tamen per se ipsum secedere; meliores erimus singuli': comp. *ad Marc.* 23.

[3] *Ep. Mor.* xxv.

[4] *Ep. Mor.* xcv 'Cum esuriente panem suum dividat': comp. Is. lviii. 7 (Vulg.) 'Frange esurienti panem tuum, Ezek. xviii. 7, 16.

[5] *Ep. Mor.* xlviii.

[6] *Ep. Mor.* ix.

[7] *de Vit. beat.* 20: comp. *de Otio* 30 (3).

[8] *Ep. Mor.* xlvii. 15, 17.

264   ST PAUL AND SENECA.

Parallels to the Sermon on the Mount.

But the moral teaching of Seneca will be brought out more clearly, while at the same time the conditions of the problem before us will be better understood, by collecting the parallels, which are scattered up and down his writings, to the sentiments and images in the Sermon on the Mount.

Matt. v. 8. 'The mind, unless it is pure and holy, comprehends not God[1].'

v. 21 sq. 'A man is a robber even before he stains his hands; for he is already armed to slay, and has the desire to spoil and to kill[2].' 'The deed will not be upright, unless the will be upright[3].'

v. 29. 'Cast out whatsoever things rend thy heart: nay, if they could not be extracted otherwise, thou shouldst have plucked out thy heart itself with them[4].'

v. 39. 'What will the wise man do when he is buffeted (colaphis percussus)? He will do as Cato did when he was smitten on the mouth. He did not burst into a passion, did not avenge himself, did not even forgive it, but denied its having been done[5].'

v. 44. 'I will be agreeable to friends, gentle and yielding to enemies[6].' 'Give aid even to enemies[7].'

v. 45. 'Let us follow the gods as leaders, so far as human weakness allows: let us give our good services and not lend them on usury...How many are unworthy of the light: and yet the day arises...This is characteristic of a great and good mind, to

---

[1] *Ep. Mor.* lxxxvii. 21.

[2] *de Benef.* v. 14. So also *de Const. Sap.* 7 he teaches that the sin consists in the intent, not the act, and instances adultery, theft, and murder.

[3] *Ep. Mor.* xcv 'Actio recta non erit, nisi recta fuerit voluntas,' *de Benef.* v. 19 'Mens spectanda est dantis.'

[4] *Ep. Mor.* li. 13.

[5] *de Const. Sap.* 14.

[6] *de Vit. beat.* 20 'Ero amicis jucundus, inimicis mitis et facilis.'

[7] *de Otio* 28 (1) 'Non desinemus communi bono operam dare, adjuvare singulos, opem ferre etiam inimicis miti (*v.l.* senili) manu': comp. also *de Benef.* v. 1 (fin.), vii. 31, *de Ira* i. 14. Such however is not always Seneca's tone with regard to enemies: comp. *Ep. Mor.* lxxxi 'Hoc certe, inquis, justitiae convenit, suum cuique reddere, beneficio gratiam, injuriae talionem aut certe malam gratiam. Verum erit istud, cum alius injuriam fecerit, alius beneficium dederit etc.' This passage shows that Seneca's doctrine was a very feeble and imperfect recognition of the Christian maxim 'Love your enemies.'

pursue not the fruits of a kind deed but the deeds themselves[1].'

'We propose to ourselves...to follow the example of the gods... See what great things they bring to pass daily, what great gifts they bestow, with what abundant fruits they fill the earth...with what suddenly falling showers they soften the ground...All these things they do without reward, without any advantage accruing to themselves...Let us be ashamed to hold out any benefit for sale: we find the gods giving gratuitously. If you imitate the gods, confer benefits even on the unthankful: for the sun rises even on the wicked, and the seas are open to pirates[2].' [Luke vi. 35.]

'One ought so to give that another may receive. It is not giving or receiving to transfer to the right hand from the left[3].' [Matt. vi. 3 sq.]
'This is the law of a good deed between two: the one ought at once to forget that it was conferred, the other never to forget that it was received[4].'

'Let whatsoever has been pleasing to God, be pleasing to man[5].' [vi. 10.]

'Do not, like those whose desire is not to make progress but to be seen, do anything to attract notice in your demeanour or mode of life. Avoid a rough exterior and unshorn hair and a carelessly kept beard and professed hatred of money and a bed laid on the ground and whatever else affects ambitious display by a perverse path...Let everything within us be unlike, but let our outward appearance (frons) resemble the common people[6].' [vi. 16.]

---

[1] *de Benef.* i. 1. See the whole context.
[2] *de Benef.* iv. 25, 26. See the context. Compare also *de Benef.* vii. 31.
[3] *de Benef.* v. 8.
[4] *de Benef.* ii. 10.
[5] *Ep. Mor.* lxxiv. 20.
[6] *Ep. Mor.* v. 1, 2. Other writers are equally severe on the insincere professors of Stoic principles. 'Like their Jewish counterpart, the Pharisees, they were formal, austere, pretentious, and not unfrequently hypocritical'; Grant p. 281. Of the villain P. Egnatius Tacitus writes (*Ann.* xvi. 32), 'Auctoritatem Stoicae sectae praeferebat habitu et ore ad exprimendam imaginem honesti exercitus.' Egnatius, like so many other Stoics, was an Oriental, a native of Beyrout (Juv. iii. 116). If the philosopher's busts may be trusted, the language of Tacitus would well describe Seneca's own appearance: but probably with him this austerity was not affected.

vi. 19.   'Apply thyself rather to the true riches. It is shameful to depend for a happy life on silver and gold[1].' 'Let thy good deeds be invested like a treasure deep-buried in the ground, which thou canst not bring to light,. except it be necessary[2].'

vii. 3 sq.   'Do ye mark the pimples of others, being covered with countless ulcers? This is as if a man should mock at the moles or warts on the most beautiful persons, when he himself is devoured by a fierce scab[3].'

vii. 12.   'Expect from others what you have done to another[4].' 'Let us so give as we would wish to receive[5].'

vii. 16, 17.   'Therefore good things cannot spring of evil...good does not grow of evil, any more than a fig of an olive tree. The fruits correspond to the seed[6].'

vii. 26.   'Not otherwise than some rock standing alone in a shallow sea, which the waves cease not from whichever side they are driven to beat upon, and yet do not either stir it from its place, etc....Seek some soft and yielding material in which to fix your darts[7].'

Other coincidences with our Lord's language.

Nor are these coincidences of thought and imagery confined to the Sermon on the Mount. If our Lord compares the hypocritical Pharisees to whited walls, and contrasts the scrupulously clean outside of the cup and platter with the inward corruption, Seneca also adopts the same images: 'Within is no good: if thou shouldest see them, not where they are exposed to view but where they are concealed, they are miserable, filthy, vile, adorned without like their own walls...Then it appears how much real foulness beneath the surface this borrowed glitter has concealed[8].' If our Lord declares that the branches must perish unless they abide in the vine, the language of Seneca presents an eminently instructive parallel: 'As the leaves cannot flourish by themselves, but want a branch

---

[1] *Ep. Mor.* cx. 18.
[2] *de Vit. beat.* 24.
[3] *de Vit. beat.* 27.
[4] *Ep. Mor.* xciv. 43. This is a quotation.
[5] *de Benef.* ii. 1.
[6] *Ep. Mor.* lxxxvii. 24, 25.
[7] *de Vit. beat.* 27.
[8] *de Provid.* 6.

wherein they may grow and whence they may draw sap, so those precepts wither if they are alone: they need to be grafted in a sect¹.' Again the parables of the sower, of the mustard-seed, of the debtor forgiven, of the talents placed out at usury, of the rich fool, have all their echoes in the writings of the Roman Stoic: 'Words must be sown like seed which, though it be small, yet when it has found a suitable place unfolds its strength and from being the least spreads into the largest growth...They are few things which are spoken: yet if the mind has received them well, they gain strength and grow. The same, I say, is the case with precepts as with seeds. They produce much and yet they are scanty².' 'Divine seeds are sown in human bodies. If a good husbandman receives them, they spring up like their origin...; if a bad one, they are killed as by barren and marshy ground, and then weeds are produced in place of grain³.' 'We have received our good things as a loan. The use and advantage are ours, and the duration thereof the Divine disposer of his own bounty regulates. We ought to have in readiness what He has given us for an uncertain period, and to restore it, when summoned to do so, without complaint. He is the worst debtor, who reproaches his creditor⁴.' 'As the money-lender does not summon some creditors whom he knows to be bankrupt...so I will openly and persistently pass over some ungrateful persons nor demand any benefit from them in turn⁵.' 'O how great is the madness of those who embark on distant hopes: I will buy, I will build, I will lend out, I will demand payment, I will bear honours: then at length I will resign my old age wearied and sated to rest. Believe me, all things are uncertain even to the prosperous. No man ought to promise himself anything out of the future. Even what we hold slips through our hands, and fortune assails the very hour on which we are pressing⁶.' If

---

[1] *Ep. Mor.* xcv. 59. See the remarks below, p. 313, on this parallel.
[2] *Ep. Mor.* xxxviii. 2.
[3] *Ep. Mor.* lxxiii. 16.
[4] *ad Marc.* 10.
[5] *de Benef.* v. 21.
[6] *Ep. Mor.* ci. 4.

our Master declares that 'it is more blessed to give than to receive,' the Stoic philosopher tells his readers that he 'would rather not receive benefits, than not confer them[1],' and that 'it is more wretched to the good man to do an injury than to receive one[2].' If our Lord reminds His hearers of the Scriptural warning 'I will have mercy and not sacrifice,' if He commends the poor widow's mite thrown into the treasury as a richer gift than the most lavish offerings of the wealthy, if His whole life is a comment on the prophet's declaration to the Jews that God 'cannot away with their sabbaths and new moons,' so also Seneca writes: 'Not even in victims, though they be fat and their brows glitter with gold, is honour paid to the gods, but in the pious and upright intent of the worshippers[3].' The gods are 'worshipped not by the wholesale slaughter of fat carcasses of bulls nor by votive offerings of gold or silver, nor by money poured into their treasuries, but by the pious and upright intent[4].' 'Let us forbid any one to light lamps on sabbath-days, since the gods do not want light, and even men take no pleasure in smoke...he worships God, who knows Him[5].' And lastly, if the dying prayer of the Redeemer is 'Father, forgive them, for they know not what they do,' some have discovered a striking counterpart (I can only see a mean caricature) of this expression of triumphant self-sacrifice in the language of Seneca: 'There is no reason why thou shouldest be angry: pardon them; they are all mad[6].'

Coincidences with the Apostolic Epistles,

Nor are the coincidences confined to the Gospel narratives. The writings of Seneca present several points of resemblance also to the Apostolic Epistles. The declaration of St John that 'perfect love casteth out fear[7]' has its echo in the philosopher's words, 'Love cannot be mingled with fear[8].' The metaphor of St Peter, also, 'Girding up the loins of your mind be watchful

---

[1] *de Benef.* i. 1.
[2] *Ep. Mor.* xcv. 52: comp. *de Benef.* iv. 12, vii. 31, 32.
[3] *de Benef.* i. 6.
[4] *Ep. Mor.* cxv. 5.
[5] *Ep. Mor.* xcv. 47.
[6] *de Benef.* v. 17. See the remarks below, p. 280.
[7] 1 Joh. iv. 18.
[8] *Ep. Mor.* xlvii. 18.

and hope[1],' reappears in the same connexion in Seneca, 'Let the mind stand ready-girt, and let it never fear what is necessary but ever expect what is uncertain[2].' And again, if St James rebukes the presumption of those who say, 'To-day or to-morrow we will go into such a city, when they ought to say, If the Lord will, we shall live and do this or that[3],' Seneca in a similar spirit says that the wise man will 'never promise himself anything on the security of fortune, but will say, I will sail unless anything happen, and, I will become prætor unless anything happen, and, My business will turn out well for me unless anything happen[4].'

The coincidences with St Paul are even more numerous and not less striking. It is not only that Seneca, like the Apostle of the Gentiles, compares life to a warfare[5], or describes the struggle after good as a 'contest with the flesh[6],' or speaks of this present existence as a pilgrimage in a strange land and of our mortal bodies as tabernacles of the soul[7]. Though some of these metaphors are more Oriental than Greek or Roman, they are too common to suggest any immediate historical connexion. It is more to the purpose to note special coincidences of thought and diction. The hateful flattery, first of Claudius and then of

and especially with St Paul.

---

[1] 1 Pet. i. 13.

[2] *ad Polyb.* 11 'In procinctu stet animus etc.'

[3] James iv. 13.

[4] *de Tranq. Anim.* 13.

[5] *Ep. Mor.* xcvi 'Vivere, Lucili, militare est'; *ib.* li 'Nobis quoque militandum est et quidem genere militiae quo numquam quies, numquam otium, datur'; *ib.* lxv 'Hoc quod vivit stipendium putat'; *ib.* cxx. 12 'Civem se esse universi et militem credens.' The comparison is at least as old as the Book of Job, vii. 1.

[6] *ad Marc.* 24 'Omne illi cum hac carne grave certamen est.' The flesh is not unfrequently used for the carnal desires and repulsions, e.g. *Ep. Mor.* lxxiv 'Non est summa felicitatis nostrae in carne ponenda.' This use of $\sigma\grave{\alpha}\rho\xi$ has been traced to Epicurus.

[7] *Ep. Mor.* cxx 'Nec domum esse hoc corpus sed hospitium et quidem breve hospitium,' and again 'Magnus animus...nihil horum quae circa sunt suum judicat, sed ut commodatis utitur peregrinus et properans.' So also *Ep. Mor.* cii. 24 'Quicquid circa te jacet rerum tamquam hospitalis loci sarcinas specta.' In this last letter (§ 23) he speaks of advancing age as a 'ripening to another birth (in alium maturescimus partum),' and designates death by the term since consecrated in the language of the Christian Church, as the birth-day of eternity: 'Dies iste, quem tamquam supremum reformidas, aeterni natalis est' (§ 26).

Nero, to which the expressions are prostituted by Seneca, does not conceal the resemblance of the following passages to the language of St Paul where they occur in a truer and nobler application. Of the former emperor he writes to a friend at court, 'In him are all things and he is instead of all things to thee[1]': to the latter he says, 'The gentleness of thy spirit will spread by degrees through the whole body of the empire, and all things will be formed after thy likeness: health passes from the head to all the members[2].' Nor are still closer parallels wanting. Thus, while St Paul professes that he will 'gladly spend and be spent' for his Corinthian converts, Seneca repeats the same striking expression, 'Good men toil, they spend and are spent[3].' While the Apostle declares that 'unto the pure all things are pure, but unto the defiled and unbelieving nothing is pure,' it is the Roman philosopher's dictum that 'the evil man turns all things to evil[4].' While St Paul in a well-remembered passage compares and contrasts the training for the mortal and the immortal crown, a strikingly similar use is made of the same comparison in the following words of Seneca; 'What blows do athletes receive in their face, what blows all over their body. Yet they bear all the torture from thirst of glory. Let us also overcome all things, for our reward is not a crown or a palm branch or the trumpeter proclaiming silence for the announcement of our name, but virtue and strength of mind and peace acquired ever after[5].'

2 Cor. xii. 15.
Tit. i. 15.
1 Cor. ix. 25.

The coincidence will be further illustrated by the following passages of Seneca, to which the corresponding references in St Paul are given in the margin.

Rom. i. 23. 'They consecrate the holy and immortal and inviolable gods in motionless matter of the vilest kind: they clothe them with the forms of men, and beasts, and fishes[6].'

Rom. i. 28, 32. 'They are even enamoured of their own ill deeds, which is

---

[1] ad Polyb. 7.
[2] de Clem. ii. 2.
[3] de Provid. 5.
[4] Ep. Mor. xcviii. 3.
[5] Ep. Mor. lxxviii. 16.
[6] de Superst. (Fragm. 31) in August. Civ. Dei vi. 10.

'the last ill of all: and then is their wretchedness complete, when shameful things not only delight them but are even approved by them[1].'

'The tyrant is angry with the homicide, and the sacrilegious man punishes thefts[2].' Rom. ii. 21, 22.

'Hope is the name for an uncertain good[3].' Rom. viii. 24.

'Pertinacious goodness overcomes evil men[4].' Rom. xii. 21.

'I have a better and a surer light whereby I can discern the true from the false. The mind discovers the good of the mind[5].' 1 Cor. ii. 11.

'Let us use them, let us not boast of them: and let us use them sparingly, as a loan deposited with us, which will soon depart[6].' 1 Cor. vii. 31.

'To obey God is liberty[7].' 2 Cor. iii. 17.

'Not only corrected but transfigured[8].' 2 Cor. iii. 18.

'A man is not yet wise, unless his mind is transfigured into those things which he has learnt[9].'

'What is man? A cracked vessel which will break at the least fall[10].' 2 Cor. iv. 7.

'This is salutary; not to associate with those unlike ourselves and having different desires[11].' 2 Cor. vi. 14.

'That gift is far more welcome which is given with a ready than that which is given with a full hand[12].' 2 Cor. ix. 7 (Prov. xxii. 9.)

'Gather up and preserve the time[13].' Eph. v. 16.

'I confess that love of our own body is natural to us[14].' Eph. v. 28, 29.

'Which comes or passes away very quickly, destined to perish in the very using (in ipso usu sui periturum)[15].' Col. ii. 22.

---

[1] *Ep. Mor.* xxxix. 6.
[2] *de Ira* ii. 28.
[3] *Ep. Mor.* x. § 2.
[4] *de Benef.* vii. 31.
[5] *de Vit. beat.* 2.
[6] *Ep. Mor.* lxxiv. 18.
[7] *de Vit. beat.* 15. Compare the language of our Liturgy, 'Whose service is perfect freedom.' Elsewhere (*Ep. Mor.* viii) he quotes a saying of Epicurus, 'Thou must be the slave of philosophy, that true liberty may fall to thy lot.'
[8] *Ep. Mor.* vi. 1.
[9] *Ep. Mor.* xciv. 48.
[10] *ad Marc.* 11. So Ps. xxxi. 12 'I am become like a broken vessel.'
[11] *Ep. Mor.* xxxii. 2.
[12] *de Benef.* i. 7.
[13] *Ep. Mor.* i. 1. So also he speaks elsewhere (*de Brev. Vit.* 1) of 'investing' time (conlocaretur).
[14] *Ep. Mor.* xiv. 1. The word used for love is 'caritas.'
[15] *de Vit. beat.* 7.

1 Tim. ii. 9. 'Neither jewels nor pearls turned thee aside[1].'

1 Tim. iv. 8. 'I reflect how many exercise their bodies, how few their minds[2].' 'It is a foolish occupation to exercise the muscles of the arms...Return quickly from the body to the mind: exercise this, night and day[3].'

1 Tim. v. 6. 'Do these men fear death, into which while living they have buried themselves[4]?' 'He is sick: nay, he is dead[5].'

2 Tim. iii. 7. 'They live ill, who are always learning to live[6].' 'How long wilt thou learn? begin to teach[7].'

In the opening sentences of our Burial Service two passages of Scripture are combined: 'We brought nothing into this world and it is certain we can carry nothing out. The Lord gave and the Lord hath taken away: blessed be the name of the Lord.' Both passages have parallels in Seneca: 'Non licet plus efferre quam intuleris[8];' 'Abstulit (fortuna) sed dedit[9].'

1 Tim. vi. 7.
Job i. 21.

In the speech on the Areopagus again, which was addressed partly to a Stoic audience, we should naturally expect to find parallels. The following passages justify this expectation.

Acts xvii. 24 sq. 'The whole world is the temple of the immortal gods[10].' 'Temples are not to be built to God of stones piled on high: He must be consecrated in the heart of each man[11].'

xvii. 25. 'God wants not ministers. How so? He Himself ministereth to the human race. He is at hand everywhere and to all men[12].'

xvii. 27. 'God is near thee: He is with thee; He is within[13].'

xvii. 29. 'Thou shalt not form Him of silver and gold: a true likeness of God cannot be moulded of this material[14].'

The first impression from these The first impression made by this series of parallels is striking. They seem to show a general coincidence in the

---

[1] *ad Helv. matr.* 16.
[2] *Ep. Mor.* lxxx. 2.
[3] *Ep. Mor.* xv. 2, 5.
[4] *Ep. Mor.* cxxii. 3.
[5] *de Brev. Vit.* 12.
[6] *Ep. Mor.* xxiii. 9.
[7] *Ep. Mor.* xxxiii. 9.
[8] *Ep. Mor.* cii. 25.
[9] *Ep. Mor.* lxiii. 7.
[10] *de Benef.* vii. 7.
[11] *Fragm.* 123, in Lactant. *Div. Inst.* vi. 25.
[12] *Ep. Mor.* xcv. 47.
[13] *Ep. Mor.* xli. 1.
[14] *Ep. Mor.* xxxi. 11.

fundamental principles of theology and the leading maxims in ethics: they exhibit moreover special resemblances in imagery and expression, which, it would seem, cannot be explained as the result of accident, but must point to some historical connexion. *parallels needs to be modified.*

Nevertheless a nearer examination very materially diminishes the force of this impression. In many cases, where the parallels are most close, the theory of a direct historical connexion is impossible; in many others it can be shown to be quite unnecessary; while in not a few instances the resemblance, however striking, must be condemned as illusory and fallacious. After deductions made on all these heads, we shall still have to consider whether the remaining coincidences are such as to require or to suggest this mode of solution.

1. In investigating the reasonableness of explaining coincidences between two different authors by direct obligation on the one hand or the other, the dates of the several writings are obviously a most important element in the decision. In the present instance the relative chronology is involved in considerable difficulty. It is roughly true that the literary activity of Seneca comprises about the same period over which (with such exceptions as the Gospel and Epistles of St John) the writings of the Apostles and Evangelists extend. But in some cases of parallelism it is difficult, and in others wholly impossible, to say which writing can claim priority of time. If the Epistles of St Paul may for the most part be dated within narrow limits, this is not the case with the Gospels: and on the other hand the chronology of Seneca's writings is with some few exceptions vague and uncertain. In many cases however it seems impossible that the Stoic philosopher can have derived his thoughts or his language from the New Testament. Though the most numerous and most striking parallels are found in his latest writings, yet some coincidences occur in works which must be assigned to his earlier years, and these were composed certainly before the first Gospels could have been circulated in Rome, and perhaps before they were *Difficulty of establishing the relative chronology.*

The priority sometimes belongs to Seneca.

even written. Again, several strong resemblances occur in Seneca to those books of the New Testament which were written after his death. Thus the passage which dwells on the fatherly chastisement of God[1] presents a coincidence, as remarkable as any, to the language of the Epistle to the Hebrews. Thus again in tracing the portrait of the perfect man (which has been thought to reflect many features of the life of Christ, delineated in the Gospels) he describes him as 'shining like a light in the darkness[2]'; an expression which at once recalls the language applied to the Divine Word in the prologue of St John's Gospel. And again in the series of parallels given above many resemblances will have been noticed to the Pastoral Epistles, which can hardly have been written before Seneca's death. These facts, if they do not prove much, are at least so far valid as to show that the simple theory of direct borrowing from the Apostolic writings will not meet all the facts of the case.

Seneca's obligations to previous writers.

2. Again; it is not sufficient to examine Seneca's writings by themselves, but we must enquire how far he was anticipated by the older philosophers in those brilliant flashes of theological truth or of ethical sentiment, which from time to time dazzle us in his writings. If after all they should prove to be only lights reflected from the noblest thoughts and sayings of former days, or at best old fires rekindled and fanned into a brighter flame, we have found a solution more simple and natural, than if we were to ascribe them to direct intercourse with Christian teachers or immediate acquaintance with Christian writings. We shall not cease in this case to regard them as true promptings of the Word of God which was from the beginning, bright rays of the Divine Light which 'was in the world' though 'the world knew it not,' which 'shineth in the darkness' though 'the darkness comprehended it not': but we shall no longer confound them with the direct effulgence of

---

[1] See above, p. 260 sq. Compare Hebrews xii. 5 sq., and see Prov. iii. 11, 12, which is quoted there.

[2] *Ep. Mor.* cxx. 13 'Non aliter quam in tenebris lumen effulsit.'

the same Word made flesh, the Shechinah at length tabernacled among men, 'whose glory we beheld, the glory as of the only-begotten of the Father.'

And this is manifestly the solution of many coincidences which have been adduced above. Though Seneca was essentially a Stoic, yet he read widely and borrowed freely from all existing schools of philosophy[1]. To the Pythagoreans and the Platonists he is largely indebted; and even of Epicurus, the founder of the rival school, he speaks with the deepest respect[2]. It will have been noticed that several of the most striking passages cited above are direct quotations from earlier writers, and therefore can have no immediate connexion with Christian ethics. The sentiment for instance, which approaches most nearly to the Christian maxim 'Love your enemies,' is avowedly based on the teaching of his Stoic predecessors[3]. And where this is not the case, recent research has shown that (with some exceptions) passages not only as profound in feeling and truthful in sentiment, but often very similar in expression and not less striking in their resemblance to the Apostolic writings, can be produced from the older philosophers and poets of Greece and Rome[4]. One instance will suffice. Seneca's picture of the perfect man has been already mentioned as reflecting some features of the 'Son of Man' delineated in the Gospels. Yet the earlier portrait drawn by Plato in its minute touches reproduces the likeness with a fidelity so striking, that the chronological impossibility alone has rescued him from the charge of plagiarism: 'Though doing no wrong,' Socrates is represented saying, 'he will have the greatest reputation for

Parallels as striking found in earlier authors.

---

[1] See what he says of himself, *de Vit. beat.* 3, *de Otio* 2 (29).

[2] *de Vit. beat.* 13 'In ea quidem ipsa sententia sum, invitis hoc nostris popularibus dicam, sancta Epicurum et recta praecipere et, si propius accesseris, tristia': comp. *Ep. Mor.* ii. 5, vi. 6, viii. 8, xx. 9.

[3] *de Otio* 1 (28). See above, p. 264, note 7. See also R. Schneider *Christ-liche Klänge aus den Griechischen und Römischen Klassikern* (Gotha, 1865), p. 327 sq.

[4] Such parallels are produced from older writers by Aubertin (*Sénèque et Saint Paul*), who has worked out this line of argument. See also the large collection of passages in R. Schneider *Christliche Klänge*.

wrong-doing,' 'he will go forward immovable even to death, appearing to be unjust throughout life but being just,' 'he will be scourged,' 'last of all after suffering every kind of evil he will be crucified ($ἀνασχινδυλευθήσεται$)[1].' Not unnaturally Clement of Alexandria, quoting this passage, describes Plato as 'all but foretelling the dispensation of salvation[2].'

<small>Many coincidences are fallacious.</small>

3. Lastly: the proverbial suspicion which attaches to statistics ought to be extended to coincidences of language, for they may be, and often are, equally fallacious. An expression or a maxim, which detached from its context offers a striking resemblance to the theology or the ethics of the Gospel, is found to have a wholly different bearing when considered in its proper relations.

<small>Stoicism and Christianity are opposed.</small>

This consideration is especially important in the case before us. Stoicism and Christianity are founded on widely different theological conceptions; and the ethical teaching of the two in many respects presents a direct contrast. St Jerome was led astray either by his ignorance of philosophy or by his partiality for a stern asceticism, when he said that 'the Stoic dogmas in very many points coincide with our own[3].' It is in the doctrines of the Platonist and the Pythagorean that the truer resemblances to the teaching of the Bible are to be sought. It was not the Porch but the Academy that so many famous teachers, like Justin Martyr and Augustine, found to be the vestibule to the Church of Christ. Again and again the Platonic philosophy comes in contact with the Gospel; but Stoicism moves in another line, running parallel indeed and impressive by its parallelism, but for this very reason precluded from any approximation. Only when he deserts the Stoic platform, does Seneca really approach the level of Christianity. Struck by their beauty, he adopts and embodies the maxims of other schools: but they betray their foreign origin, and refuse to be incorporated into his system.

---

[1] Plato *Resp.* ii. pp. 361, 362. See Aubertin p. 254 sq.

[2] *Strom.* v. 14 $μονονουχὶ\ προφητεύων\ τὴν\ σωτήριον\ οἰκονομίαν.$

[3] Hieron. *Comm. in Isai.* iv. c. 11 'Stoici qui nostro dogmati in plerisque concordant' (*Op.* IV. p. 159, Vallarsi).

For on the whole Lactantius was right, when he called *Seneca was a true Stoic.* Seneca a most determined follower of the Stoics[1]. It can only excite our marvel that any one, after reading a few pages of this writer, should entertain a suspicion of his having been in any sense a Christian. If the superficial colouring is not seldom deceptive, we cannot penetrate skindeep without encountering some rigid and inflexible dogma of the Stoic school. In his fundamental principles he is a disciple of Zeno; and, being a disciple of Zeno, he could not possibly be a disciple of Christ.

Interpreted by this fact, those passages which at first sight strike us by their resemblance to the language of the Apostles and Evangelists assume a wholly different meaning. The basis of Stoic theology is gross materialism, though it is more or less relieved and compensated in different writers of the school by a vague mysticism. The supreme God of the Stoic had no existence distinct from external nature. Seneca himself identifies Him with fate, with necessity, with nature, with the world as a living whole[2]. The different elements of the universe, such as the planetary bodies, were inferior gods, members of the Universal Being[3]. With a bold consistency the Stoic assigned a corporeal existence even to moral abstractions. Here also Seneca manifests his adherence to the tenets of his school. Courage, prudence, reverence, cheerfulness, wisdom, he says, are all bodily substances, for otherwise they could not affect bodies, as they manifestly do[4]. *His pantheistic materialism.*

Viewed by the light of this material pantheism, the injunction to be 'followers of God' cannot mean the same to him as *His language must be in-*

---

[1] See above, p. 249.

[2] See especially *de Benef.* iv. 7, 8 'Natura, inquit, hoc mihi praestat. Non intellegis te, cum hoc dicis, mutare nomen deo? quid enim aliud est natura quam deus et divina ratio toti mundo partibusque ejus inserta?...Hunc eundem et fatum si dixeris, non mentieris ...Sic nunc naturam voca, fatum, fortunam, omnia ejusdem dei nomina sunt varie utentis sua potestate'; *de Vit. beat.* 8 'Mundus cuncta complectens rectorque universi deus.' Occasionally a more personal conception of deity appears: e.g. *ad Helv. Matr.* 8.

[3] *de Clem.* i. 8.

[4] *Ep. Mor.* cvi: comp. *Ep. Mor.* cxvii.

278   ST PAUL AND SENECA.

terpreted by his tenets. it does even to the Platonic philosopher, still less to the Christian Apostle. In Stoic phraseology 'imitation of God' signifies nothing deeper than a due recognition of physical laws on the part of man, and a conformity thereto in his own actions. It is merely a synonyme for the favourite Stoic formula of 'accordance with nature.' This may be a useful precept; but so interpreted the expression is emptied of its religious significance. In fact to follow the world and to follow God are equivalent phrases with Seneca[1]. Again, in like manner, the lesson drawn from the rain and the sunshine freely bestowed upon all[2], though in form it coincides so nearly with the language of the Gospel, loses its theological meaning and becomes merely an appeal to a physical fact, when interpreted by Stoic doctrine.

Consistent blasphemies in speaking of God. Hence also language, which must strike the ear of a Christian as shocking blasphemy, was consistent and natural on the lips of a Stoic. Seneca quotes with approbation the saying of his revered Sextius, that Jupiter is not better than a good man; he is richer, but riches do not constitute superior goodness; he is longer-lived, but greater longevity does not ensure greater happiness[3]. 'The good man,' he says elsewhere, 'differs from God only in length of time[4].' 'He is like God, excepting his mortality[5].' In the same spirit an earlier Stoic, Chrysippus, had boldly argued that the wise man is as useful to Zeus, as Zeus is to the wise man[6]. Such language is the legitimate consequence of Stoic pantheism.

He has no consciousness of sin. Hence also the Stoic, so long as he was true to the tenets of his school, could have no real consciousness of sin. Only where there is a distinct belief in a personal God, can this

---

[1] *de Ira* ii. 16 'Quid est autem cur hominem ad tam infelicia exempla revoces, cum habeas *mundum deumque*, quem ex omnibus animalibus ut solus imitetur, solus intellegit.'

[2] See the passages quoted above, p. 264 sq.

[3] *Ep. Mor.* lxxiii. 12, 13.

[4] *de Prov.* 1.

[5] *de Const. Sap.* 8: comp. *Ep. Mor.* xxxi. 'Par deo surges.' Nay, in one respect good men excel God, 'Ille extra patientiam malorum est, vos supra patientiam,' *de Prov.* 6.

[6] Plut. *adv. Stoic.* 33 (*Op. Mor.* p. 1078).

consciousness find a resting-place. Seneca and Tertullian might use the same word *peccatum*, but its value and significance to the two writers cannot be compared. The Christian Apostle and the Stoic philosopher alike can say, and do say, that 'All men have erred[1]'; but the moral key in which the saying is pitched is wholly different. With Seneca error or sin is nothing more than the failure in attaining to the ideal of the perfect man which he sets before him, the running counter to the law of the universe in which he finds himself placed. He does not view it as an offence done to the will of an all-holy all-righteous Being, an unfilial act of defiance towards a loving and gracious Father. The Stoic conception of error or sin is not referred at all to the idea of God[2]. His pantheism had so obscured the personality of the Divine Being, that such reference was, if not impossible, at least unnatural.

And the influence of this pantheism necessarily pervades the Stoic vocabulary. The 'sacer spiritus' of Seneca may be translated literally by the Holy Spirit, the πνεῦμα ἅγιον, of Scriptural language; but it signifies something quite different. His declaration, that we are 'members of God,' is in words almost identical with certain expressions of the Apostle; but its meaning has nothing in common. Both the one and the other are modes of stating the Stoic dogma, that the Universe is one great animal pervaded by one soul or principle of life, and that into men, as fractions of this whole, as limbs of this body, is transfused a portion of the universal spirit[3]. It is almost purely a physical conception, and has no strictly theological value. *Meaning of the holy spirit in Seneca.*

Again, though the sterner colours of Stoic morality are frequently toned down in Seneca, still the foundation of his ethical system betrays the repulsive features of his school. His fundamental maxim is not to guide and train nature, but to *overcome* *His moral teaching has all the repulsive features of Stoicism.*

---

[1] See the passages quoted above, p. 261 sq.

[2] See the remarks of Baur *l. c.* p. 190 sq., on this subject.

[3] Compare the well-known passage in Virgil, *Æn.* vi. 726 sq. 'Spiritus intus alit totamque infusa per artus mens agitat molem et magno se corpore miscet.'

it[1]. The passions and affections are not to be directed, but to be crushed. The wise man, he says, will be clement and gentle, but he will not feel pity, for only old women and girls will be moved by tears; he will not pardon, for pardon is the remission of a deserved penalty; he will be strictly and inexorably just[2].

It is obvious that this tone leaves no place for repentance, for forgiveness, for restitution, on which the theological ethics of the Gospel are built. The very passage[3], which has often been quoted as a parallel to the Saviour's dying words, 'Father, forgive them, for they know not what they do,' really stands in direct contrast to the spirit of those words: for it is not dictated by tenderness and love, but expresses a contemptuous pity, if not a withering scorn.

In the same spirit Seneca commits himself to the impassive calm which forms the moral ideal of his school[4]. He has no sympathy with a righteous indignation, which Aristotle called 'the spur of virtue'; for it would disturb the serenity of the mind[5]. He could only have regarded with a lofty disdain (unless for the moment the man triumphed over the philosopher) the grand outburst of passionate sympathy which in the Apostle of the Gentiles has wrung a tribute of admiration even from unbelievers, 'Who is weak, and I am not weak? Who is offended, and I burn not[6]?' He would neither have appreciated nor respected the spirit which dictated those touching words, 'I say the truth...I lie not...I have great heaviness and continual sorrow of heart...for my brethren, my kinsmen according to the flesh[7].' He must have spurned the precept which bids the Christian 'rejoice with them that do rejoice, and weep with

Its impassiveness contrasts with the ethics of the Gospel.

---

[1] *de Brev. Vit.* 14 'Hominis naturam cum Stoicis vincere.'

[2] *de Clem.* ii. 5—7, where he makes a curious attempt to vindicate the Stoics.

[3] It is quoted above, p. 268.

[4] *Ep. Mor.* lxxiv. 30 'Non adfligitur sapiens liberorum amissione, non amicorum: eodem enim animo fert illorum mortem quo suam exspectat. Non magis hanc timet quam illam dolet... Inhonesta est omnis trepidatio et sollicitudo.' And see especially *Ep. Mor.* cxvi.

[5] *de Ira* iii. 3.

[6] 2 Cor. xi. 29.

[7] Rom. ix. 1, 2, 3.

them that weep[1],' as giving the direct lie to a sovereign maxim of Stoic philosophy. To the consistent disciple of Zeno the agony of Gethsemane could not have appeared, as to the Christian it ever will appear, the most sublime spectacle of moral sympathy, the proper consummation of a Divine life: for insensibility to the sorrows and sufferings of others was the only passport to perfection, as conceived in the Stoic ideal.

These considerations will have shown that many even of the most obvious parallels in Seneca's language are really no parallels at all. They will have served moreover to reveal the wide gulf which separates him from Christianity. It must be added however, that his humanity frequently triumphs over his philosophy; that he often writes with a kindliness and a sympathy which, if little creditable to his consistency, is highly honourable to his heart. In this respect however he does not stand alone. Stoicism is in fact the most incongruous, the most self-contradictory, of all philosophic systems. With a gross and material pantheism it unites the most vivid expressions of the fatherly love and providence of God: with the sheerest fatalism it combines the most exaggerated statements of the independence and self-sufficiency of the human soul: with the hardest and most uncompromising isolation of the individual it proclaims the most expansive view of his relations to all around. The inconsistencies of Stoicism were a favourite taunt with the teachers of rival schools[2]. The human heart in fact refused to be silenced by the dictation of a rigorous and artificial system, and was constantly bursting its philosophical fetters.

Inconsistencies of Seneca and of Stoicism.

But after all allowance made for the considerations just urged, some facts remain which still require explanation. It appears that the Christian parallels in Seneca's writings become more frequent as he advances in life[3]. It is not less true that

Coincidences still remain to be explained.

---

[1] Rom. xii. 15.
[2] See for instance the treatise of Plutarch *de Repugnantiis Stoicorum* (*Op. Mor.* p. 1033 sq.).

[3] Among his more Christian works are the *de Providentia, de Otio, de Vita beata, de Beneficiis,* and the *Epistolae Morales;* among his less Christian, the

they are much more striking and more numerous than in the other great Stoics of the Roman period, Epictetus and M. Aurelius; for though in character these later writers approached much nearer to the Christian ideal than the minister of Nero, though their fundamental doctrines are as little inconsistent with Christian theology and ethics as his, yet the closer resemblances of sentiment and expression, which alone would suggest any direct obligations to Christianity, are, I believe, decidedly more frequent in Seneca[1]. Lastly: after all deductions made, a class of coincidences still remains, of which the expression 'spend and be spent' may be taken as a type[2], and which can hardly be considered accidental. If any historical connexion (direct or indirect) can be traced with a fair degree of probability, we may reasonably look to this for the solution of such coincidences. I shall content myself here with stating the different ways in which such a connexion was possible or probable, without venturing to affirm what was actually the case, for the data are not sufficient to justify any definite theory.

Historical connexion.

1. The fact already mentioned is not unimportant, that the principal Stoic teachers all came from the East, and that therefore their language and thought must in a greater or less degree have borne the stamp of their Oriental origin. We advance a step further towards the object of our search, if we remember that the most famous of them were not only Oriental but Shemitic. Babylonia, Phœnicia, Syria, Palestine, are their homes. One comes from Scythopolis, a second from Apamea, a third from Ascalon, a fourth from Ptolemais, two others from

(1) The Eastern origin of Stoicism.

---

de *Constantia Sapientis* and *de Ira*. In some cases the date is uncertain; but what I have said in the text will, I think, be found substantially true.

[1] I have read Epictetus and M. Aurelius through with a view to such coincidences, and believe the statement in the text to be correct. Several of the more remarkable parallels in the former writer occur in the passages quoted below, p. 299 sq., and seem to warrant the belief that he was acquainted with the language of the Gospel.

[2] See above, p. 270. Aubertin has attacked this very instance (p. 360 sq.), but without success. He only shows (what did not need showing) that 'impendere' is used elsewhere in this same sense. The important feature in the coincidence is the combination of the active and passive voices.

Hierapolis, besides several from Tyre and Sidon or their colonies, such as Citium and Carthage[1]. What religious systems they had the opportunity of studying, and how far they were indebted to any of these, it is impossible to say. But it would indeed be strange if, living on the confines and even within the borders of the home of Judaism, the Stoic teachers escaped all influence from the One religion which, it would seem, must have attracted the attention of the thoughtful and earnest mind, which even then was making rapid progress through the Roman Empire, and which afterwards through the Gospel has made itself far more widely felt than any other throughout the civilised world. I have already ventured to ascribe the intense moral earnestness of the Stoics to their Eastern origin. It would be no extravagant assumption that they also owed some ethical maxims and some theological terms (though certainly not their main doctrines) directly or indirectly to the flourishing Jewish schools of their age, founded on the teaching of the Old Testament. The exaggerations of the early Christian fathers, who set down all the loftier sentiments of the Greek philosophers as plagiarisms from the lawgiver or the prophets, have cast suspicion on any such affiliation: but we should not allow ourselves to be blinded by reactionary prejudices to the possibilities or rather the probabilities in the case before us.

Its possible obligations to Judaism.

2. The consideration which I have just advanced will

(2) Seneca's possible know-

---

[1] I have noted down the following homes of more or less distinguished Stoic teachers from the East; *Seleucia*, Diogenes (p. 41); *Epiphania*, Euphrates (p. 613); *Scythopolis*, Basilides (p. 614); *Ascalon*, Antibius, Eubius (p. 615); *Hierapolis in Syria* (?), Serapio (p. 612); Publius (p. 615); *Tyre*, Antipater, Apollonius (p. 520); *Sidon*, Zeno (p. 36), Boethus? (p. 40); *Ptolemais*, Diogenes (p. 43); *Apamea in Syria*, Posidonius (p. 509); *Citium*, Zeno (p. 27), Persæus (p. 34); *Carthage*, Herillus (p. 33);

Cyrene, Eratosthenes (p. 39). The Cilician Stoics are enumerated below p. 288. Of the other famous teachers belonging to the School, Cleanthes came from Assos (p. 31), Ariston from Chios (p. 32), Dionysius from Heraclea (p. 35), Sphærus from Bosporus (p. 35), Panætius from Rhodes (p. 500), Epictetus from Hierapolis in Phrygia (p. 660). The references are to the pages of Zeller's work, where the authorities for the statements will be found.

ledge of Christianity.

explain many coincidences: but we may proceed a step further. Is it impossible, or rather is it improbable, that Seneca was acquainted with the teaching of the Gospel in some rudimentary form? His silence about Christianity proves nothing, because it proves too much. If an appreciable part of the lower population of Rome had become Christians some few years before Seneca's death[1], if the Gospel claimed converts within the very palace walls[2], if a few (probably not more than a few) even in the higher grades of society, like Pomponia Græcina[3], had adopted the new faith, his acquaintance with its main facts is at least a very tenable supposition. If his own account may be trusted, he made a practice of dining with his slaves and engaging them in familiar conversation[4]; so that the avenues of information open to him were manifold[5]. His acquaintance with any written documents of Christianity is less probable; but of the oral Gospel, as repeated from the lips of slaves and others, he might at least have had an accidental and fragmentary knowledge. This supposition would explain the coincidences with the Sermon on the Mount and with the parables of our Lord, if they are clear and numerous enough to demand an explanation.

(3) His supposed connexion with St Paul.

3. But the legend goes beyond this, and connects Seneca directly with St Paul. The Stoic philosopher is supposed to be included among the 'members of Cæsar's household' mentioned in one of the Apostle's letters from Rome. The legend itself however has no value as independent evidence. The coincidences noted above would suggest it, and the forged correspondence would fix and substantiate it. We are therefore thrown back on the probabilities of the case; and it must be confessed that, when we examine the Apostle's history with a

---

[1] See *Philippians* pp. 17 sq., 25 sq.
[2] Phil. iv. 22; see *Philippians* p. 171 sq.
[3] See *Philippians* p. 21.
[4] *Ep. Mor.* xlvii.
[5] An early inscription at Ostia (de Rossi *Bull. di Archeol. Crist.* 1867, p 6, quoted by Friedländer, III. p. 535) mentions one M. Anneus Paulus Petrus, obviously a Christian. Was he descended from some freedman of Seneca's house?

view to tracing a historical connexion, the result is not very encouraging. St Paul, it is true, when at Corinth, was brought before Seneca's brother Gallio, to whom the philosopher dedicates more than one work and of whom he speaks in tenderly affectionate language[1]; but Gallio, who 'cared for none of these things,' to whom the questions at issue between St Paul and his accusers were merely idle and frivolous disputes about obscure national customs[2], would be little likely to bestow a serious thought upon a case apparently so unimportant, still less likely to communicate his experiences to his brother in Rome. Again, it may be urged that as St Paul on his arrival in Rome was delivered to Burrus the prefect of the prætorian guards[3], the intimate friend of Seneca, it might be expected that some communication between the Apostle and the philosopher would be established in this way. Yet, if we reflect that the prætorian prefect must yearly have been receiving hundreds of prisoners from the different provinces, that St Paul himself was only one of several committed to his guardianship at the same time, that the interview of this supreme magistrate with any individual prisoner must have been purely formal, that from his position and character Burrus was little likely to discriminate between St Paul's case and any other, and finally that he appears to have died not very long after the Apostle's arrival in Rome[4], we shall see very little cause to lay stress on such a supposition. Lastly; it is said that, when St Paul was brought before Nero for trial, Seneca must have been present as the emperor's adviser, and being present must have interested himself in the religious opinions of so remarkable a prisoner. But here again we have only a series of assumptions more or less probable. It is not known under what circumstances and in whose presence

---

[1] *Nat. Qu.* iv. præf. § 10 'Gallionem fratrem meum quem nemo non parum amat, etiam qui amare plus non potest,' and again § 11 'Nemo mortalium uni tam dulcis est, quam hic omnibus': comp. *Ep. Mor.* civ. 'domini mei Gallionis.'

[2] Acts xviii. 14 sq.

[3] See *Philippians* p. 7 sq.

[4] See *Philippians* pp. 5, 8, 39.

such a trial would take place; it is very far from certain that St Paul's case came on before Seneca had retired from the court; and it is questionable whether amid the formalities of the trial there would have been the opportunity, even if there were the will, to enter into questions of religious or philosophical interest. On the whole therefore it must be confessed that no great stress can be laid on the direct historical links which might connect Seneca with the Apostle of the Gentiles.

Summary of results.

I have hitherto investigated the historical circumstances which might explain any coincidences of language or thought as arising out of obligations on the part of Seneca or of his Stoic predecessors. It has been seen that the teachers of this school generally were in all likelihood indebted to Oriental, if not to Jewish, sources for their religious vocabulary; that Seneca himself not improbably had a vague and partial acquaintance with Christianity, though he was certainly anything but a Christian himself; and that his personal intercourse with the Apostle of the Gentiles, though not substantiated, is at least not an impossibility. How far the coincidences may be ascribed to one or other of these causes, I shall not attempt to discriminate: but there is also another aspect of the question which must not be put out of sight. In some instances at least, if any obligation exist at all, it cannot be on the side of the philosopher, for the chronology resists this inference: and for these cases some other solution must be found.

Stoicism, like Alexandrian Judaism, a preparation for the Gospel.

As the speculations of Alexandrian Judaism had elaborated a new and important theological vocabulary, so also to the language of Stoicism, which itself likewise had sprung from the union of the religious sentiment of the East with the philosophical thought of the West, was due an equally remarkable development of moral terms and images. To the Gospel, which was announced to the world in 'the fulness of time,' both the one and the other paid their tribute. As St John (nor St John alone) adopted the terms of Alexandrian theosophy as the least inadequate to express the highest doctrines of Christianity, so St Paul (nor St Paul alone) found in the ethical language of the Stoics expressions more fit than he could find elsewhere to describe in certain aspects the duties and privileges, the struggles and the triumphs, of the Christian life. But though the words and symbols remained substantially the same, yet in their application they became instinct with new force and meaning. This change in either case they owed to their being placed in relation to the central fact of Christianity, the Incarnation of the Son. The Alexandrian terms, expressing the attributes and operations of the Divine Word, which in their origin had a purely metaphysical bearing, were translated into the sphere of practical theology, when God had descended among men to lift up men to God. The Stoic expressions, describing the independence of the individual spirit, the subjugation of the unruly passions, the universal empire of a triumphant self-control, the cosmopolitan relations of the wise man, were quickened into new life, when an unfailing source of strength and a boundless hope of victory had been revealed in the Gospel, when all men were proclaimed to be brothers, and each and every man united with God in Christ.

It is difficult to estimate, and perhaps not very easy to overrate, the extent to which Stoic philosophy had leavened the moral vocabulary of the civilised world at the time of the Christian era. To take a single instance; the most important of moral terms, the crowning triumph of ethical nomenclature, συνείδησις, conscientia, the internal, absolute, supreme judge of individual action, if not struck in the mint of the Stoics, at all events became current coin through their influence. To a great extent therefore the general diffusion of Stoic language would lead to its adoption by the first teachers of Christianity; while at the same time in St Paul's own case personal circumstances might have led to a closer acquaintance with the diction of this school. *Wide influence of the ethical language of Stoicism.*

Tarsus, the birth-place and constant home of St Paul, was at this time a most important, if not the foremost, seat of *Stoicism at Tarsus.*

Greek learning. Of all the philosophical schools, the Stoic was the most numerously and ably represented at this great centre. Its geographical position, as a half-way house, had doubtless some influence in recommending it to a philosophy which had its birth-place in the East and grew into maturity in the West. At all events we may count up six or more[1] well-known Stoic teachers whose home was at Tarsus, besides Chrysippus and Aratus who came from the neighbouring Soli[2], and three others who resided at Mallos, also a Cilician town[3]. If St Paul's early education was Jewish, he was at least instructed by the most liberal teacher of the day, who, unlike his stricter countrymen and contemporaries, had no dread of Greek learning; and during his repeated and lengthened sojourns in Tarsus, he must have come in contact with Stoic maxims and dogmas. But indeed it is not mere conjecture, that St Paul had some acquaintance with the teachers or the writings of this school. The speech on the Areopagus, addressed partly to Stoics, shows a clear appreciation of the elements of truth contained in their philosophy, and a studied coincidence with their modes of expression[4]. Its one quotation moreover is taken from a Stoic writing, the hymn of Cleanthes, the noblest expression of heathen devotion which Greek literature has preserved to us[5].

St Paul's acquaintance with Stoic teaching.

---

[1] Strabo (xiv. 13, 14. p. 673 sq.) mentions five by name, Antipater, Archedemus, Nestor, Athenodorus surnamed Cordylion, and Athenodorus son of Sandon. To these may be added Zeno (Zeller, p. 40: Diog. Laert. vii. 35 enumerates eight of the name), and Heracleides (Zeller, p. 43). Of Athenodorus son of Sandon, Strabo adds ὃν καὶ Κανανίτην φασὶν ἀπὸ κώμης τινός. If Strabo's explanation of Κανανίτης be correct, the coincidence with a surname of one of the Twelve Apostles is accidental. But one is tempted to suspect that the word had a Shemitic origin.

[2] The fathers of both these famous men appear to have migrated from Tarsus. For Chrysippus see Strabo xiv. 8, p. 671; of Aratus we are told that Asclepiades Ταρσέα φησὶν αὐτὸν γεγονέναι ἀλλ' οὐ Σολέα (Arati Opera II. p. 429 ed. Buhle).

[3] Crates (Zeller, p. 42), the two Procluses (*ib.* p. 615).

[4] See above, p. 272.

[5] Acts xvii. 28. The words in Cleanthes are ἐκ σοῦ γὰρ γένος ἐσμέν. The quotation of St Paul agrees exactly with a half-line in Aratus another Stoic poet, connected with his native Tarsus, τοῦ γὰρ καὶ γένος ἐσμέν. Since the Apostle introduces the words as quoted

And I think we may find occasionally also in St Paul's epistles sufficiently distinct traces of the influence of Stoic diction. A few instances are set down in my notes to this epistle. Many more might be gathered from his other letters, especially the Pastoral Epistles. But I will content myself with giving two broad examples, where the characteristic common-places of Stoic morality seem to be adopted and transfigured in the language of the Christian Apostle. *Two instances given.*

1. The portrait of the wise man, the ideal of Stoic aspiration, has very distinct and peculiar features—so peculiar that they presented an easy butt for the ridicule of antagonists. It is his prominent characteristic that he is sufficient in himself, that he wants nothing, that he possesses everything. This topic is expanded with a fervour and energy which often oversteps the proper bounds of Stoic calm. The wise man alone is free: he alone is happy: he alone is beautiful. He and he only possesses absolute wealth. He is the true king and the true priest[1]. *1. The portrait of the wise man.*

Now may we not say that this image has suggested many expressions to the Apostle of the Gentiles? 'Even now are ye full,' he exclaims in impassioned irony to the Corinthians, 'even now are ye rich, even now are ye made kings without us': 'we are fools for Christ, but ye are wise in Christ: we are weak, but ye are strong: ye are glorious, but we are dishonoured.' 'All things are yours,' he says elsewhere, 'all things are yours, and ye are Christ's, and Christ is God's.' So too he describes himself and the other Apostles, 'As being grieved, yet always rejoicing; as beggars, yet making many rich; as having nothing, and yet possessing all things.' 'In every thing at every time having every self-sufficiency (αὐτάρκειαν)...in every thing being enriched.' 'I have learnt,' he says again, 'in *1 Cor. iv. 8. 1 Cor. iv. 10. 1 Cor. iii. 22, 23. 2 Cor. vi. 10. 2 Cor. ix. 8, 11. Phil. iv. 11, 13, 18.*

---

from *some* of their own poets, he would seem to have both passages in view. By οἱ καθ' ὑμᾶς ποιηταί he probably means the poets belonging to the same school as his Stoic audience.

[1] See esp. Seneca *de Benef.* vii. 3, 4, 6, 10, *Ep. Mor.* ix. Compare Zeller p. 231. The ridicule of Horace (*Sat.* i. 3. 124 sq.) will be remembered. See also the passages from Plutarch quoted in Orelli's Excursus (II. p. 67).

whatsoever circumstances I am, to be self-sufficing. I have all strength in Him that giveth me power. I have all things to the full and to overflowing.'

Coincidence and contrast with Stoicism in St Paul's conception.

If the coincidence of imagery in these passages is remarkable, the contrast of sentiment is not less striking. This universal dominion, this boundless inheritance, is promised alike by the Stoic philosopher to the wise man and by the Christian Apostle to the believer. But the one must attain it by self-isolation, the other by incorporation. The essential requisite in the former case is a proud independence; in the latter an entire reliance on, and intimate union with, an unseen power. It is ἐν τῷ ἐνδυναμοῦντι that the faithful becomes all-sufficient, all-powerful; it is ἐν Χριστῷ that he is crowned a king and consecrated a priest. All things are his, but they are only his, in so far as he is Christ's and because Christ is God's. Here and here only the Apostle found the realisation of the proud ideal which the chief philosophers of his native Tarsus had sketched in such bold outline and painted in these brilliant colours.

2. The cosmopolitan teaching of the Stoics

2. The instance just given relates to the development of the individual man. The example which I shall next take expresses his widest relations to others. The cosmopolitan tenets of the Stoics have been already mentioned. They grew out of the history of one age and were interpreted by the history of another. Negatively they were suggested by the hopeless state of politics under the successors of Alexander. Positively they were realised, or rather represented, by the condition of the world under the Roman Empire[1]. In the age

---

[1] Plutarch (*Op. Mor.* p. 329 B) says that Alexander himself realised this ideal of a world-wide polity, which Zeno only 'delineated as a dream or a phantom (ὥσπερ ὄναρ ἢ εἴδωλον ἀνατυπωσάμενος).' If Plutarch's statement be correct that Alexander looked upon himself as entrusted with a divine mission to 'reconcile the whole world,' he certainly had the conception in his mind; but his actual work was only the beginning of the end, and the realisation of the idea (so far as it was destined to be realised) was reserved for the Romans. 'Fecisti patriam diversis gentibus unam,' 'Urbem fecisti quod prius orbis erat,' says a later poet addressing the emperor of his day; Rutil. *de Red.* i. 63, 66.

of the Seleucids and Ptolemies, when the old national barriers had been overthrown, and petty states with all their interests and ambitions had crumbled into the dust, the longing eye of the Greek philosopher wandered over the ruinous waste, until his range of view expanded to the ideal of a world-wide state, which for the first time became a possibility to his intellectual vision, when it became also a want to his social instincts. A few generations passed, and the wide extension of the Roman Empire, the far-reaching protectorate of the Roman franchise[1], seemed to give a definite meaning, a concrete form, in some sense a local habitation, to this idea which the Stoic philosopher of Greece had meanwhile transmitted to the Stoic moralist of Rome.

The language of Seneca well illustrates the nature of this cosmopolitan ideal. 'All this, which thou seest, in which are comprised things human and divine, is one. We are members of a vast body. Nature made us kin, when she produced us from the same things and to the same ends[2].' 'I will look upon all lands as belonging to me, and my own lands as belonging to all. I will so live as if I knew that I am born for others, and on this account I will give thanks to nature...She gave me alone to all men and all men to me alone[3].' 'I well know that the world is my country and the gods its rulers; that they stand above me and about me, the censors of my deeds and words[4].' 'Seeing that we assigned to the wise man a commonwealth worthy of him, I mean the world, he is not beyond the borders of his commonwealth, even though he has gone into retirement. Nay, perhaps he has left one corner of it and passed into a larger and ampler region; and raised above the heavens he understands (at length) how lowly he was seated when he mounted the chair of state or the bench of justice[5].' 'Let us embrace in our thoughts two commonwealths, the one

illustrated by the language of Seneca.

[1] See Cicero *pro Balb.* 13, *Verr.* v. 57, 65.
[2] *Ep. Mor.* xcv. 52.
[3] *de Vit. beat.* 20.
[4] *ibid.*
[5] *Ep. Mor.* lxviii.

vast and truly named common, in which are comprised gods and men, in which we look not to this corner or to that, but we measure the boundaries of our state with the sun; the other, to which the circumstances of our birth have assigned us[1].' 'Virtue is barred to none: she is open to all, she receives all, she invites all, gentlefolk, freedmen, slaves, kings, exiles alike[2].' 'Nature bids me assist *men*; and whether they be bond or free, whether gentlefolk or freedmen, whether they enjoy liberty as a right or as a friendly gift, what matter? Wherever a *man* is, there is room for doing good[3].' 'This mind may belong as well to a Roman knight, as to a freedman, as to slave: for what is a Roman knight or a freedman or a slave? Names which had their origin in ambition or injustice[4].'

Its Christian counterpart in the heavenly citizenship of St Paul.

Did St Paul speak quite independently of this Stoic imagery, when the vision of a nobler polity rose before him, the revelation of a 'city not made with hands, eternal in the heavens?' Is there not a strange coincidence in his language—a coincidence only the more striking because it clothes an idea in many respects very different? 'Our citizenship is in heaven.' 'God raised us with Him, and seated us with Him in the heavenly places in Christ Jesus.' 'Therefore ye are no more strangers and sojourners, but fellow-citizens with the saints and members of God's household.' 'Fulfil your duties as citizens worthily of the Gospel of Christ.' 'We being many are one body in Christ, and members one of another.' 'For as the body is one and hath many members, and all the members of the body being many are one body, so also is Christ: for we all are baptized in one Spirit into one body, whether Jews or Greeks, whether bond or free. Ye are the body of Christ and members in particular.' 'There is neither Jew nor Greek; there is neither bond nor free; there is no male and female: for ye all are one in Christ Jesus.' 'Not Greek and Jew, circumcision and uncircumcision,

Phil. iii. 20.
Ephes. ii. 6.
Ephes. ii. 19.
Phil. i. 27.
Rom. xii. 5.
1 Cor. xii. 12, 13, 27.
[Ephes. iv. 25, v. 30.]
Gal. iii. 28.
Col. iii. 11.

---

[1] *de Otio* 4 (31). 'Glaubt man hier nicht,' asks Zeller (p. 275), 'fast Augustin De Civitate Dei zu hören?'
[2] *de Benef.* iii. 18.
[3] *de Vit. beat.* 24.
[4] *Ep. Mor.* xxxi. 11.

barbarian, Scythian, bond, free: but Christ is all things and in all[1].'

Here again, though the images are the same, the idea is transfigured and glorified. At length the bond of coherence, the missing principle of universal brotherhood, has been found. As in the former case, so here the magic words ἐν Χριστῷ have produced the change and realised the conception. A living soul has been breathed into the marble statue by Christianity; and thus from the 'much admired polity of Zeno[2]' arises the Civitas Dei of St Augustine.

It has been the aim of the investigation just concluded to point out how far the coincidences between Seneca and St Paul are real, and how far fallacious; to show that these coincidences may in some cases be explained by the natural and independent development of religious thought, while in others a historical connexion seems to be required; and to indicate generally the different ways in which this historical connexion was probable or possible, without however attempting to decide by which of several channels the resemblance in each individual instance was derived. *Summary.*

In conclusion it may be useful to pass from the special connexion between St Paul and Seneca to the more general relation between Christianity and Stoicism, and to compare *Christianity and Stoicism compared.*

---

[1] *Ecce Homo* p. 136 'The city of God, of which the Stoics doubtfully and feebly spoke, was now set up before the eyes of men. It was no unsubstantial city such as we fancy in the clouds, no invisible pattern such as Plato thought might be laid up in heaven, but a visible corporation whose members met together to eat bread and drink wine, and into which they were initiated by bodily immersion in water. Here the Gentile met the Jew whom he had been accustomed to regard as an enemy of the human race: the Roman met the lying Greek sophist, the Syrian slave, the gladiator born beside the Danube. In brotherhood they met, the natural birth and kindred of each forgotten, the baptism alone remembered in which they have been born again to God and to each other.' See the whole context.

[2] Plut. *Op. Mor.* p. 329 ἡ πολὺ θαυμαζομένη πολιτεία τοῦ τὴν Στωϊκὴν αἵρεσιν καταβαλομένου Ζήνωνος. It is remarkable that this ideal is described in the context under a Scriptural image, εἷς δὲ βίος ᾖ καὶ κόσμος, ὥσπερ ἀγέλης συννόμου νομῷ κοινῷ συντρεφομένης: comp. Joh. x. 16 καὶ γενήσονται μία ποίμνη, εἷς ποιμήν.

them very briefly in their principles, their operations, and their results. Stoicism has died out, having produced during its short lifetime only very transient and partial effects; Christianity has become the dominant religion of the civilised world, and leavened society through its whole mass. The very coincidences, on which we have been dwelling so long, throw into relief the contrast between the failure of the one and the triumph of the other, and stimulate enquiry into the causes of this difference.

The question at issue stated. To some it may seem sufficient to reply that the one is a mere human philosophy, the other a Divine revelation. But this answer shelves without solving the problem; for it is equivalent to saying that the one is partial, defective, and fallacious, while the other is absolutely true. The question, therefore, to which an answer is sought, may be stated thus: What are those theological and ethical principles, ignored or denied by Stoicism, and enforced by the Gospel, in which the Divine power of the latter lies, and to which it owes its empire over the hearts and actions of men? This is a very wide subject of discussion; and I shall only attempt to indicate a few more striking points of contrast. Yet even when treated thus imperfectly, such an investigation ought not to be useless. In an age when the distinctive characteristics of Christianity are regarded as a stumblingblock by a few, and more or less consciously ignored as of little moment by others, it is a matter of vast importance to enquire whether the secret of its strength does or does not lie in these; and the points at issue cannot be better suggested, than by comparing it with an abstract system of philosophy so imposing as the Stoic.

Meagre results of Stoicism. Indeed our first wonder is, that from a system so rigorous and unflinching in its principles and so heroic in its proportions the direct results should have been marvellously little. It produced, or at least attracted, a few isolated great men: but on the life of the masses, and on the policy of states, it was almost wholly powerless.

The older Stoics. Of the founder and his immediate successors not very much is known; but we are warranted in believing that they were men of earnest aspirations, of rare self-denial, and for the most part (though the grossness of their language seems hardly reconcilable with this view[1]) of moral and upright lives. Zeno himself indeed cannot be set down to the credit of the school. He made the philosophy and was not made by it. But Cleanthes was directly moulded by the influence of his master's teaching: and for calm perseverance, for rigorous self-discipline, and for unwavering devotion to a noble ideal, few characters in the history of Greek philosophy are comparable to him. Yet Cleanthes, like Zeno, died a suicide. The example, not less than the precept, of the first teachers of the sect created a fatal passion for self-murder, which was the most indelible, if not the darkest, blot on Stoic morality.

It was not however among the Greeks, to whose national temper the genius of Stoicism was alien, that this school achieved its proudest triumphs. The stern and practical spirit of the Romans offered a more congenial sphere for its influence. And here again it is worth observing, that their principal instructors were almost all Easterns. Posidonius for instance, the familiar friend of many famous Romans and the most influential missionary of Stoic doctrine in Rome, was a native of the Syrian Apamea. From this time forward it became a common custom for the Roman noble to maintain in his house some eminent philosopher, as the instructor of his children and the religious director of himself and his family[2]; and in this

Stoicism in Rome.

Its obligations to the East.

---

[1] It is impossible to speak with any confidence on this point. The language held by Zeno and Chrysippus was grossly licentious, and might be taken to show that they viewed with indifference and even complacency the most hateful forms of heathen impurity (see Plutarch *Op. Mor.* p. 1044, *Clem. Hom.* v. 18, Sext. Emp. *Pyrrh.* iii. 200 sq.). But it is due to the known character and teaching of these men, that we should put the most favourable construction on such expressions; and they may perhaps be regarded as theoretical extravagances of language, illustrating the Stoic doctrine that externals are indifferent (see Zeller, p. 261 sq.). Yet this mode of speaking must have been highly dangerous to morals; and the danger would only be increased by the fact that such language was held by men whose characters were justly admired in other respects.

[2] Seneca *ad Marc.* 4 'Consol[atori se] Areo *philosopho viri sui* praebuit et multum eam rem profuisse sibi confessa est,' where he is speaking of Livia after the death of her son Drusus. This philo-

capacity we meet with several Oriental Stoics. Thus Cato the younger had at different times two professors of this sect domesticated in his household, both of Eastern origin, Antipater of Tyre and Athenodorus of Tarsus[1]. In Cato himself, whom his contemporaries regarded as the 'most perfect Stoic[2],' and in whom the sect at large would probably have recognised its most illustrious representative, we have a signal example alike of the virtues and of the defects of the school. Honest, earnest, and courageous even to death, but hard, stolid, impracticable, and almost inhuman, he paralysed the higher qualities of his nature by his unamiable philosophy, so that they were rendered almost useless to his generation and country. A recent Roman historian has described him as 'one of the most melancholy phenomena in an age so abounding in political caricatures.' 'There was more nobility,' he writes bitterly, 'and above all more judgment in the death of Cato than there had been in his life.' 'It only elevates the tragic significance of his death that he was himself a fool[3].' Exaggerated as this language may be, it is yet not wholly without truth; and, were the direct social and political results of Cato's life alone to be regarded, his career must be pronounced a failure. But in fact his importance lies, not in what he did, but in what he was. It was a vast gain to humanity, that in an age of worldly self-seeking, of crooked and fraudulent policy, of scepticism and infidelity to all right principle, one man held his ground, stern, unbending, upright to the last. Such a man may fail, as Cato failed, in all the practical aims of life: but he has left a valuable legacy to after ages in the staunch assertion of principle; he has bequeathed to them a fructifying estate, not the less productive because its richest harvests must be reaped by generations yet unborn.

Cato the younger.

His excellences and defects.

sopher is represented as using the following words in his reply to her: 'Ego adsiduus viri tui comes, cui non tantum quae in publicum emittuntur nota, sed omnes sunt secretiores animorum vestrorum motus.' For another allusion to these domestic chaplains of heathendom see *de Tranq. Anim.* 14 'Prosequebatur illum *philosophus suus.*'

[1] Plutarch *Vit. Cat.* 4, 10, 16.
[2] Cicero *Brut.* xxxi, *Parad.* proœm. 2.
[3] Mommsen's *History of Rome,* IV. pp. 156, 448 sq. (Eng. trans.).

Cato was the true type of Stoicism in its striking excellence, as in its hopeless weakness. The later Roman Stoics are feeble copies, more or less conscious, of Cato. Like him, they were hard, impracticable, perverse, studiously antagonistic to the prevailing spirit or the dominant power of their age: but, like him also, they were living protests, when protests were most needed, against the dishonesty and corruption of the times; and their fearless demeanour was felt as a standing reproach alike to the profligate despotism of the ruler and to the mean and cringing flattery of the subject. Yet it is mournful to reflect how much greater might have been the influence of men like Thrasea Pætus and Helvidius Priscus on their generation, if their strict integrity had been allied to a more sympathetic creed. *Later Roman Stoics.*

In these men however there was an earnest singleness of purpose, which may condone many faults. Unhappily the same cannot be said of Seneca. We may reject as calumnies the grosser charges with which the malignity of his enemies had laden his memory; but enough remains in the admissions of his admirers, and more than enough in the testimony of his own writings, to forfeit his character as a high-minded and sincere man. No words are too strong to condemn the baseness of one who could overwhelm the emperor Claudius, while living, with the most fulsome and slavish flattery, and then, when his ashes were scarcely cold, turn upon him and poison his memory with the venom of malicious satire[1]. From this charge there is no escape; for his extant writings convict him. We may well refuse to believe, as his enemies asserted, that he counselled the murder of Agrippina; but it seems that he was in some way implicated with the matricide, and it is quite certain that he connived at other iniquities of his imperial pupil. We may indignantly repudiate, as we are probably justified in doing, the *Seneca.* *His faults.*

---

[1] The treatise *ad Polybium de Consolatione* would be disgraceful, if it stood alone; but contrasted with the *Ludus de Morte Claudii* it becomes odious. To complete his shame, he was the author of the extravagant panegyric pronounced by Nero over his predecessor (Tac. *Ann.* xiii. 3).

grave charges of moral profligacy which were brought against him in his lifetime and after his death; but the man who, while condemning, can describe at length the grossest forms of impurity (as Seneca does occasionally) had surely no very sensitive shrinking from sins 'of which it is a shame even to speak.' We may demur to accepting the account of his enemies, that his wealth was amassed by fraud and violence; but there is no doubt that, while preaching a lofty indifference to worldly advantages, he consented to be enriched by a profligate and unscrupulous tyrant, and that the enormous property thus accumulated exposed him to the reproaches of his contemporaries. A portrait which combines all these features will command no great respect. Yet, notwithstanding a somewhat obtrusive rhetoric, there is in Seneca's writings an earnestness of purpose, a yearning after moral perfection, and a constant reference to an ideal standard, which cannot be mere affectation. He seems to have been a rigorous ascetic in early life, and to the last to have maintained a severe self-discipline. Such at least is his own statement; nor is it unsupported by less partial testimony[1].

His own confessions of weakness. For all this inconsistency however we must blame not the creed but the man. He would probably have been much worse, if his philosophy had not held up to him a stern ideal for imitation. Is it genuine or affected humility—a palliative or an aggravation of his offence—that he himself confesses how far he falls short of this ideal? To those taunting enemies of philosophy, who pointing to his luxury and wealth ask, 'Why do you speak more bravely than you live?', he replies, 'I will add to your reproaches just now, and I will bring more charges against myself than you think. For the present I give you this answer: I am not wise, and (to feed your malevolence) I shall not be wise. Therefore require of me, not that I should equal the best men, but that I should be better than the bad. It is enough for me daily to diminish my vices in some degree and to chide my errors.' 'These things,' he adds, 'I say not in

---

[1] See *Ep. Mor.* lxxxvii. 2, cviii. 14; comp. Tac. *Ann.* xiv. 53, xv. 45, 63.

my own defence, for I am sunk deep in all vices, but in defence of him who has made some progress[1].' 'The wise man,' he writes apologetically, 'does not think himself unworthy of any advantages of fortune. He does not love riches but he prefers them. He receives them not into his soul but into his house. Nor does he spurn them when he has them in his possession, but retains them and desires ampler material for his virtue to be furnished thereby[2].' 'I am not now speaking to you of myself,' he writes to Lucilius, 'for I fall far short of a moderate, not to say a perfect man, but of one over whom fortune has lost her power[3].' Seneca, more than any man, must have felt the truth of the saying, 'How hardly shall they that have riches enter into the kingdom of God[4].'

From Seneca it is refreshing to turn to Epictetus. The lame slave of Epaphroditus is a far nobler type of Stoic discipline than the wealthy courtier of Epaphroditus' master. Here at all events, we feel instinctively that we have to do with genuine earnestness. His motto 'bear and forbear[5]' inspires his discourses throughout, as it appears also to have been the guide of his life. But more striking still is the spirit of piety which pervades his thoughts. 'When ye have shut the doors,' he says, 'and have made all dark within, remember never to say that ye are alone, for ye are not; but God is within and so is your angel ($\delta\alpha\iota\mu\omega\nu$); and what need of light have these to see what ye do? To this God ye also ought to swear allegiance, as soldiers do to Cæsar[6].' 'If we had sense, ought we to do anything else both in public and in private but praise and honour the divine being ($\tau\grave{o}$ $\theta\epsilon\hat{\iota}ov$) and recount his favours?... ...What then? Since ye, the many, are blinded, should there

Epictetus.

Expressions of piety in his writings.

---

[1] *de Vit. beat.* 17; comp. *ad Helv. Matr.* 5.
[2] *de Vit. beat.* 21.
[3] *Ep. Mor.* lvii. 3.
[4] The account of Seneca in Martha's *Moralistes* p. 1 sq. is well worth reading, though the idea of the spiritual direction in the letters to Lucilius seems exaggerated. I wish I could take as favourable a view of Seneca's character as this writer does.
[5] ἀνέχου καὶ ἀπέχου, Aul. Gell. xvii. 19, where the words are explained.
[6] *Diss.* i. 14. 13 sq.; comp. Matt. xxii. 21.

not be some one to fill this station and to sing for all men the hymn to God? For what else can I, a lame old man, do but sing hymns to God? Nay, if I were a nightingale, I had done the work of a nightingale; if a swan, the work of a swan. So being what I am, a rational creature, I must sing hymns to God. This is my task, and I perform it; nor will I ever desert this post, so far as it is vouchsafed me: and you I exhort to join in this same song[1].' 'How then dost thou appear? As a witness called by God: *Come thou and bear witness to me...* What witness dost thou bear to God? *I am in wretched plight, O Lord, and I am miserable; no one cares for me, no one gives me anything; all men blame me, all men speak ill of me.* Wilt thou bear this witness, and disgrace the calling wherewith He hath called thee, for that He honoured thee and held thee worthy to be brought forward as a witness in this great cause[2]?' 'When thou goest to visit any great person, remember that Another also above seeth what is done, and that thou oughtest to please Him rather than this one[3].' 'Thou art an offshoot (ἀπόσπασμα) of God; thou hast some part of Him in thyself. Why therefore dost thou not perceive thy noble birth? Why dost thou not know whence thou art come? Thou bearest God about with thee, wretched man, and thou dost not perceive it. Thinkest thou that I mean some god of silver or gold, without thee? Within thyself thou bearest Him, and thou dost not feel that thou art defiling Him with thy impure thoughts and thy filthy deeds. If an image of God were present, thou wouldest not dare to do any of these things which thou doest: but, God Himself being present within thee, and overlooking

---

[1] *Diss.* i. 16. 15 sq.

[2] *Diss.* i. 29. 46 sq. The words τὴν κλῆσιν ἣν κέκληκεν appear from the context to refer to citing witnesses, but they recall a familiar expression of St Paul; 1 Cor. vii. 20, Ephes. iv. 1, comp. 2 Tim. i. 9. The address Κύριε, used in prayer to God, is frequent in Epictetus, but does not occur (so far as I am aware) in any heathen writing before the Apostolic times. Sometimes we find Κύριε ὁ Θεός, and once he writes Κύριε ἐλέησον (ii. 7. 12). It is worth noting that all the three cities where Epictetus is known to have lived—Hierapolis, Rome, Nicopolis—occur in the history of St Paul.

[3] *Diss.* i. 30. 1.

and overhearing all, thou art not ashamed to think and to do these things, O man, insensible of thine own nature, and visited with the wrath of God[1].' 'Remember that thou art a son. What profession is due to this character? To consider all that belongs to Him as belonging to a father, to obey Him in all things, never to complain of Him to any one, nor to say or do anything hurtful to Him, to yield and give way to Him in all things, working with Him to the utmost of thy power[2].' 'Dare to look up to God and say, Use me henceforth whereunto thou wilt, I consent unto Thee, I am Thine. I shrink from nothing that seemeth good to Thee. Lead me where Thou wilt: clothe me with what garments Thou wilt. Wouldest Thou that I should be in office or out of office, should live at home or in exile, should be rich or poor? I will defend Thee for all these things before men[3].' 'These (vices) thou canst not cast out otherwise than by looking to God alone, by setting thine affections ($\pi\rho\sigma\pi\epsilon\pi\sigma\nu\theta\acute{o}\tau\alpha$) on Him alone, by being consecrated to His commands[4].' 'When thou hast heard these words, O young man, go thy way and say to thyself, It is not Epictetus who has told me these things (for whence did *he* come by them?), but some kind God speaking through him. For it would never have entered into the heart of Epictetus to say these things, seeing it is not his wont to speak (so) to any man. Come then, let us obey God, lest God's wrath fall upon us ($\emph{\'{i}}\nu\alpha$ $\mu\grave{\eta}$ $\theta\epsilon\sigma\chi\acute{o}\lambda\omega\tau\sigma\iota$ $\check{\omega}\mu\epsilon\nu$[5]).' 'Thus much I can tell thee now, that he, who setteth his hand to so great a matter without God, calls down God's wrath and does but desire to behave himself unseemly in public. For neither in a well-ordered household does any one come forward and say to himself *I must be steward.* Else the master, observing him and seeing him giving his orders insolently, drags him off to be scourged. So it happens also in this great city (of the world); for here too there is a house-

---

[1] *Diss.* ii. 8. 11 sq. We are reminded of the surname θεοφόρος, borne by a Christian contemporary of Epictetus; see the notes on Ignat. *Ephes.* inscr., 9.

[2] *Diss.* ii. 10. 7.
[3] *Diss.* ii. 16. 42.
[4] *Diss.* ii. 16. 46.
[5] *Diss.* iii. 1. 36 sq.

holder, who ordereth everything[1].' 'The cynic (i.e. the true philosopher) ought to know that he is sent a messenger from God to men, to show them concerning good and evil[2].' 'He must be wholly given without distraction to the service of God, free to converse with mankind, not tied down by private duties, nor entangled in relations, which if he transgresses, he will no longer keep the character of a noble and good man, and if he observes, he will fail in his part as the messenger and watchman and herald of the gods[3].'

Improved tone of Stoic theology.

The genuine piety of these passages is a remarkable contrast to the arrogance and blasphemy in which the older Stoics sometimes indulged and which even Seneca repeats with approval[4]. Stoic theology, as represented by Epictetus, is fast wiping away its reproach; but in so doing it has almost ceased to be Stoic. The pantheistic creed, which identifies God with the world, is kept in the background; and by this subordination greater room is left for the expansion of true reverence. On the other hand (to pass over graver defects in his system) he has not yet emancipated himself from the austerity and isolation of Stoical

---

[1] *Diss.* iii. 22. 2 sq. The passage bears a strong resemblance to our Lord's parable in Matt. xxiv. 45 sq., Luke xii. 41 sq. The expressions, ὁ οἰκονόμος, ὁ κύριος, ὁ οἰκοδεσπότης, occur in both the philosopher and the Evangelists. Moreover the word ἔτεμεν in Epictetus corresponds to διχοτομήσει in the Gospels, and in both words the difficulty of interpretation is the same. I can hardly believe that so strange a coincidence is quite accidental. Combined with the numerous parallels in Seneca's writings collected above (p. 281 sq.), it favours the supposition that our Lord's discourses in some form or other were early known to heathen writers. For other coincidences more' or less close see i. 9. 19, i. 25. 10, i. 29. 31, iii. 21. 16, iii. 22. 35, iv. 1. 79 (ἂν δ' ἀγγαρεία ᾖ κ.τ.λ., comp. Matt. v. 41), iv. 8. 36.

[2] *Diss.* iii. 22, 23.

[3] *Diss.* iii. 22. 69. I have only been able to give short extracts, but the whole passage should be read. Epictetus appears throughout to be treading in the footsteps of St Paul. His words, ἀπερίσπαστον εἶναι δεῖ ὅλον πρὸς τῇ διακονίᾳ τοῦ Θεοῦ, correspond to the Apostle's expression, εὐπάρεδρον τῷ Κυρίῳ ἀπερισπάστως (1 Cor. vii. 35), and the reason given for remaining unmarried is the same. Another close coincidence with St Paul is ὁ μὲν θέλει οὐ ποιεῖ (ii. 26. 1). Again, such phrases as νομίμως ἀθλεῖν (iii. 10. 8), γράμματα συστατικά (ii. 3. 1), ταῦτα μελέτα (iv. 1. 170), οὐκ εἰμὶ ἐλεύθερος; (iii. 22. 48), recall the Apostle's language. Other Scriptural expressions also occur, such as Θεοῦ ζηλωτής (ii. 14. 13), τροφὴ στερεωτέρα (ii. 16, 39), etc.

[4] See above, p. 278.

ethics. There still remains a hardness and want of sympathy about his moral teaching, which betrays its parentage. But enough has been said to account for the fact that the remains of Epictetus have found a place in the library of the Church, and that the most pious and thoughtful Christian divines have listened with admiration to his devout utterances[1].

As Epictetus gives a higher tone to the theology of the school, so the writings of M. Aurelius manifest an improvement in its ethical teaching. The manifold opportunities of his position would cherish in an emperor naturally humane and sensitive wider sympathies, than were possible to a lame old man born and bred a slave, whom cruel treatment had estranged from his kind and who was still further isolated by his bodily infirmity. At all events it is in this point, and perhaps in this alone, that the meditations of M. Aurelius impress us more favourably than the discourses of Epictetus. As a conscious witness of God and a stern preacher of righteousness, the Phrygian slave holds a higher place: but as a kindly philanthropist, conscientiously alive to the claims of all men far and near, the Roman emperor commands deeper respect. In him, for the first and last time in the history of the school, the cosmopolitan sympathies, with which the Stoic invested his wise man, become more than a mere empty form of rhetoric. His natural disposition softened the harsher features of Stoical ethics. The brooding melancholy and the almost feminine tenderness, which appear in his meditations, are a marked contrast to the hard outlines in the portraiture of the older Stoics. Cato was the most perfect type of the school: but

M. Aurelius.

Improved tone of Stoic morality.

---

[1] 'Epictetus seems as if he had come after or before his time; too late for philosophy, too early for religion. We are tempted continually to apply to his system the hackneyed phrase: It is all very magnificent, but it is not philosophy—it is too one-sided and careless of knowledge for its own sake; and it is not religion—it is inadequate and wants a basis. Yet for all this, as long as men appreciate elevated thought, in direct and genuine language, about human duties and human improvement, Epictetus will have much to teach those who know more than he did both of philosophy and religion. It is no wonder that he kindled the enthusiasm of Pascal or fed the thought of Butler. *Saturday Review*, Vol. XXII. p. 580.

M. Aurelius was the better man, because he was the worse Stoic. Altogether there is a true beauty and nobleness of character in this emperor, which the accidents of his position throw into stronger relief. Beset by all the temptations which unlimited power could create, and sorely tried in the most intimate and sacred relations of life—with a profligate wife and an inhuman son—he neither sullied nor hardened his heart, but remained pure and upright and amiable to the end, the model of a conscientious if not a wise ruler, and the best type which heathendom could give of a high-minded gentleman. With all this it is a more than 'tragical fact,' that his justice and his humanity alike broke down in one essential point, and that by his bigotry or through his connivance the Christians suffered more widely and cruelly during his reign than at any other epoch in the first century and a half of their existence[1]. Moreover the inherent and vital defects of the school, after all the modifications it had undergone and despite the amiable character of its latest representative, are still patent. 'The Stoicism of M. Aurelius gives many of the moral precepts of the Gospel, but without their foundation, which can find no place in his system. It is impossible to read his reflections without emotion, but they have no creative energy. They are the last strain of a dying creed[2].'

Persecution of the Christians.

It is interesting to note the language in which these two latest and noblest representatives of Stoicism refer to the Christians. Once and once only is the now numerous and rapidly growing sect mentioned by either philosopher, and in each case dismissed curtly with an expression of contempt.

References to Christianity in Epictetus and M. Aurelius.

---

[1] Martha, *Moralistes* p. 212, attempts to defend M. Aurelius against this charge; but the evidence of a wide persecution is irresistible. For the motives which might lead M. Aurelius, both as a ruler and as a philosopher, to sanction these cruelties, see Zeller *Marcus Aurelius Antoninus* in his *Vorträge* p. 101 sq. If it were established that this emperor had intimate relations with a Jewish rabbi, as has been recently maintained (*M. Aurelius Antoninus als Freund u. Zeitgenosse des Rabbi Jehuda ha-Nasi* by A. Bodek, Leipzig 1868), he would have an additional motive for his treatment of the Christians; but, to say the least, the identification of the emperor is very uncertain.

[2] Westcott in Smith's *Dictionary of the Bible* II. p. 857, s. v. *Philosophy*.

'Is it possible,' asks Epictetus, 'that a man may be so disposed under these circumstances from madness, or from habit like the Galileans, and can no one learn by reason and demonstration that God has made all things which are in the world[1]?' 'This readiness to die,' writes M. Aurelius, 'should follow from individual judgment, not from sheer obstinacy as with the Christians, but after due consideration and with dignity and without scenic display (ἀτραγῴδως), so as to convince others also[2].' The justice of such contemptuous allusions may be tested by the simple and touching narrative of the deaths of this very emperor's victims, of the Gallic martyrs at Vienne and Lyons: and the appeal may confidently be made to the impartial judgment of mankind to decide whether there was more scenic display or more genuine obstinacy in their last moments, than in the much vaunted suicide of Cato and Cato's imitators.

I have spoken of Epictetus and M. Aurelius as Stoics, for so they regarded themselves; nor indeed could they be assigned to any other school of philosophy. But their teaching belongs to a type, which in many respects would hardly have been recognised by Zeno or Chrysippus. Stoicism during the Roman period had been first attaching to itself, and then assimilating, diverse foreign elements, Platonic, Pythagorean, even Jewish and Christian. In Seneca these appear side by side, but distinct; in Epictetus and M. Aurelius they are more or less fused and blended. Roman Stoicism in fact presents to us not a picture with clear and definite outlines, but a dissolving view. It becomes more and more eclectic. The materialism of its earlier theology gradually recedes; and the mystical element appears in the foreground[3]. At length Stoicism fades away; and a new eclectic system, in which mysticism has still greater predominance, emerges and takes its place. Stoicism has fought the battle of heathen philosophy against the Gospel, and been vanquished. Under the banner of Neoplatonism, and with

Eclecticism of the later Stoics.

Stoicism succeeded by Neoplatonism.

---

[1] *Diss.* iv. 7. 6.
[2] M. Anton. xi. 3.
[3] On the approximation of the later Stoics, and more especially of M. Aurelius, to Neoplatonism, see Zeller's *Nacharistotelische Philosophie* II. p. 201 sq.

weapons forged in the armoury of Christianity itself, the contest is renewed. But the day of heathendom is past. This new champion also retires from the conflict in confusion, and the Gospel remains in possession of the field.

The masses unaffected by Stoicism.

In this attempt to sketch the progress and results of this school, I have not travelled beyond a few great names. Nor has any injustice been done to it by this course, for Stoicism has no other history, except the history of its leaders. It consisted of isolated individuals, but it never attracted the masses or formed a community. It was a staff of professors without classes. This sterility must have been due to some inherent vicious principles: and I propose now to consider its chief defects, drawing out the contrast with Christianity at the same time.

Causes of this failure.

1. Its pantheism.

1. The fundamental and invincible error of Stoic philosophy was its theological creed. Though frequently disguised in devout language which the most sincere believer in a personal God might have welcomed as expressing his loftiest aspirations, its theology was nevertheless, as dogmatically expounded by its ablest teachers, nothing better than a pantheistic materialism. This inconsistency between the philosophic doctrine and the religious phraseology of the Stoics is a remarkable feature, which perhaps may be best explained by its mixed origin. The theological language would be derived in great measure from Eastern (I venture to think from Jewish) affinities, while the philosophical dogma was the product of Hellenized thought. Heathen devotion seldom or never soars higher than in the sublime hymn of Cleanthes. 'Thine offspring are we,' so he addresses the Supreme Being, 'therefore will I hymn Thy praises and sing Thy might for ever. Thee all this universe which rolls about the earth obeys, wheresoever Thou dost guide it, and gladly owns Thy sway.' 'No work on earth is wrought apart from Thee, nor through the vast heavenly sphere, nor in the sea, save only the deeds which bad men in their folly do.' 'Unhappy they, who ever craving the possession of good things, yet have no eyes or ears for the universal law of God, by wise

Hymn of Cleanthes.

obedience whereunto they might lead a noble life.' 'Do Thou, Father, banish fell ignorance from our soul, and grant us wisdom, whereon relying Thou rulest all things with justice, that being honoured, we with honour may requite Thee, as beseemeth mortal man: since neither men nor gods have any nobler task than duly to praise the universal law for aye[1].' If these words might be accepted in their first and obvious meaning, we could hardly wish for any more sublime and devout expression of the relations of the creature to his Creator and Father. But a reference to the doctrinal teaching of the school dispels the splendid illusion. Stoic dogma empties Stoic hymnology of half its sublimity and more than half its devoutness. This Father in heaven, we learn, is no personal Being, all righteous and all holy, of whose loving care the purest love of an earthly parent is but a shadowy counterfeit. He—or It—is only another name for nature, for necessity, for fate, for the universe. Just in proportion as the theological doctrine of the school is realised, does its liturgical language appear forced and unnatural. Terms derived from human relationships are confessedly very feeble and inadequate at best to express the person and attributes of God; but only a mind prepared by an artificial training could use such language as I have quoted with the meaning which it is intended to bear. To simple people it would be impossible to address fate or necessity or universal nature, as a Father, or to express towards it feelings of filial obedience and love.

Contradiction between Stoic dogma and Stoic hymnology.

And with the belief in a Personal Being, as has been already remarked, the sense of sin also will stand or fall[2]. Where this belief is absent, error or wrong-doing may be condemned from two points of view, irrespective of its consequences and on grounds of independent morality. It may be regarded as a defiance of the law of our being, or it may be deprecated as a violation of the principles of beauty and propriety implanted in

No consciousness of sin.

---

[1] *Fragm. Philos. Graec.* I. p. 151 (ed. Mullach).   [2] See above, p. 278 sq.

the mind. In other words it may be condemned either from *physical* or from *æsthetic* considerations. The former aspect is especially common with the Stoics, for indeed conformity with nature is the groundwork of Stoical ethics. The latter appears occasionally, though this point of view is characteristic rather of the Academy than of the Porch. These are important subsidiary aids to ethical teaching, and should not be neglected: but the consciousness of sin, as sin, is distinct from both. It is only possible where there is a clear sense of a personal relation to a Personal Being, whom we are bound to love and obey, whose will must be the law of our lives and should be the joy of our hearts. Here again the Stoic's language is treacherous. He can talk of sin, just as he can talk of God his Father. But so long as he is true to his dogma, he uses terms here, as before, in a non-natural sense. Only so far as he deserts the theological standing-ground of his school (and there is much of this happy inconsistency in the great Stoic teachers), does he attain to such an apprehension of the 'exceeding sinfulness of sin' as enables him to probe the depths of the human conscience.

2. Defects in Stoical ethics.

2. When we turn from the theology to the ethics of the Stoical school, we find defects not less vital in its teaching. Here again Stoicism presents in itself a startling and irreconcilable contradiction. The fundamental Stoic maxim of conformity to nature, though involving great difficulties in its practical application, might at all events have afforded a starting-point for a reasonable ethical code. Yet it is hardly too much to say that no system of morals, which the wit of man has ever devised, assumes an attitude so fiercely defiant of nature as this. It is mere folly to maintain that pain and privation are no evils. The paradox must defeat its own ends. True religion, like true philosophy, concedes the point, and sets itself to counteract, to reduce, to minimise them. Our Lord 'divides himself at once from the ascetic and the Stoic. They had said, Make yourselves independent of bodily comforts: he says, Ye have need of these things[1].' Christianity itself also

Defiance of nature.

[1] *Ecce Homo* p. 116.

preaches an αὐτάρκεια, a moral independence, but its preaching starts from a due recognition of the facts of human life.

And, while Stoicism is thus paradoxical towards the individual, its view of the mutual relations between man and man is a still greater outrage on humanity. 'In every age the Christian temper has shivered at the touch of Stoic apathy[1].' Pity, anger, love—all the most powerful social impulses of our nature—are ignored by the Stoic, or at least recognised only to be crushed. There is no attempt to chasten or to guide these affections: they must simply be rooted out. The Stoic ideal is stern, impassive, immovable. As a natural consequence, the genuine Stoic is isolated and selfish: he feels no sympathy with others, and therefore he excites no sympathy in others. Any wide extension of Stoicism was thus rendered impossible by its inherent repulsiveness. It took a firm hold on a few solitary spirits, but it was wholly powerless with the masses. *Want of sympathy.*

Nor indeed can it be said in this respect to have failed in its aim. The true Stoic was too self-contained, too indifferent to the condition of others, to concern himself whether the tenets of his school made many proselytes or few. He wrapped himself up in his self-conceit, declared the world to be mad, and gave himself no more trouble about the matter. His avowal of cosmopolitan principles, his tenet of religious equality, became inoperative, because the springs of sympathy, which alone could make them effective, had been frozen at their source. Where enthusiasm is a weakness and love a delusion, such professions must necessarily be empty verbiage. The temper of Stoicism was essentially aristocratic and exclusive in religion, as it was in politics. While professing the largest comprehension, it was practically the narrowest of all philosophical castes. *Stoicism exclusive and not proselytizing.*

3. Though older philosophers had speculated on the immortality of the soul, and though the belief had been encouraged by some schools of moralists as supplying a most powerful motive for well-doing, yet still it remained for the heathen a *3. No distinct belief in man's immortality.*

---

[1] *Ecce Homo* p. 119.

vague theory, unascertained and unascertainable. To the Christian alone, when he accepted the fact of Christ's resurrection, did it become an established and incontrovertible truth. Stoicism does not escape the vagueness which overclouds all mere philosophical speculation on this subject. On one point alone were the professors of this school agreed. An *eternal* existence of the human soul was out of the question. At the great periodic conflagration, when the universe should be fused and the manifold organizations dissolved into chaos, the souls of men must necessarily be involved in the common destruction[1]. But within this limit much diversity of opinion prevailed.

Diversity of opinion among the Stoics.

Some maintained a longer, some a shorter, duration of the soul. Cleanthes said that all men would continue to exist till the conflagration; Chrysippus confined even this limited immortality to the wise[2]. The language of Seneca on this point is

Seneca's inconsistency and vagueness.

both timid and capricious. 'If there be any sense or feeling after death' is his cautious hypothesis, frequently repeated[3]. 'I was pleasantly engaged,' he writes to his friend Lucilius, 'in enquiring about the eternity of souls, or rather, I should say, in trusting. For I was ready to trust myself to the opinions of great men, who avow rather than prove so very acceptable a thing. I was surrendering myself to this great hope, I was beginning to be weary of myself, to despise the remaining fragments of a broken life, as though I were destined to pass away into that illimitable time, and into the possession of eternity; when I was suddenly aroused by the receipt of your letter, and this beautiful dream vanished[4].' When again he would console the bereaved mourner, he has no better words of comfort to offer than these: 'Why do I waste away with fond regret for one who either is happy or does not exist at all? It

---

[1] See e.g. Seneca *ad Marc.* 26, *ad Polyb.* 1. (20).

[2] Diog. Laert. vii. 157.

[3] *De Brev. Vit.* 18, *ad Polyb.* 5, 9. *Ep. Mor.* xxiv. 18, lxv. 24, lxxi. 16. Tertullian (*de Resurr. Carn.* 1, *de Anim.* 42) quotes Seneca as saying 'Omnia post mortem finiri, etiam ipsam.'

[4] *Ep. Mor.* cii. 2; comp. *Ep. Mor.* cxvii. 6 'Cum animarum aeternitatem disserimus, non leve momentum apud nos habet consensus hominum aut timentium inferos aut colentium.'

is envy to bewail him if he is happy, and madness if he does not exist[1].' 'Bear in mind that no evils affect the dead; that the circumstances which make the lower world terrible to us are an idle story.' 'Death is the release and end of all pains.' 'Death is neither a good nor an evil: for that only can be good or evil which is something.' 'Fortune can retain no hold, where nature has given a release: nor can one be wretched, who does not exist at all[2].' Afterwards indeed he speaks in a more cheerful strain: 'Eternal rest awaits him leaving this murky and troubled (earth) and migrating to the pure and liquid (sky)[3]': but such expressions must be qualified by what has gone before. Again in this same treatise, as in other places[4], he promises after death an enlarged sphere of knowledge and a limitless field of calm and pure contemplation. But the promise which he gives in one sentence is often modified or retracted in the next; and even where the prospects held out are the brightest, it is not always clear whether he contemplates a continuance of conscious individual existence, or merely the absorption into Universal Being and the impersonal participation in its beauty and order[5]. The views of Epictetus and M. Aurelius are even more cloudy and cheerless than those of Seneca. Immortality, properly so called, has no place in their philosophies.

Gibbon, in his well-known chapter on the origin and growth of Christianity, singles out the promise of eternal life as among the chief causes which promoted its diffusion. Overlooking much that is offensive in the tone of his remarks, we need not hesitate to accept the statement as substantially true. It is

Importance of the doctrine to Christianity.

---

[1] *Ad Polyb.* 9.
[2] *Ad Marc.* 19; comp. *Ep. Mor.* xxxvi. 10 'Mors nullum habet incommodum: esse enim debet aliquis, cujus sit incommodum,' with the context.
[3] *Ad Marc.* 24.
[4] Comp. e.g. *Ep. Mor.* lxxix. 12, lxxxvi. 1, cii. 22, 28 sq.
[5] Holzherr *Der Philosoph L. Annæus*

Seneca II. p. 58 sq. (1859) endeavours to show that Seneca is throughout consistent with himself and follows the Platonists rather than the Stoics in his doctrine of the immortality of the soul. I do not see how it is possible, after reading the treatise *ad Marciam*, to acquit him of inconsistency.

indeed more than questionable whether (as Gibbon implies) the growth of the Church was directly due to the inducements of the offer; for (looking only to self-interest) it has a repulsive as well as an attractive side: but without doubt it added enormously to the moral power of the Gospel in commending it to the hearts and consciences of men. Deterring, stimulating, reassuring, purifying and exalting the inward and outward life, 'the power of Christ's resurrection' extends over the whole domain of Christian ethics.

Its indifference to Stoicism.

On the other hand it was a matter of indifference to the Stoic whether he doubted or believed or denied the immortality of man; for the doctrine was wholly external to his creed, and nothing could be lost or gained by the decision. Not life but death was the constant subject of his meditations. His religious director was summoned to his side, not to prepare him for eternity, but to teach him how to die[1]. This defect alone would have rendered Stoicism utterly powerless with the masses of men: for the enormous demands which it made on the faith and self-denial of its adherents could not be sustained without the sanction and support of such a belief. The Epicurean motto, 'Let us eat and drink, for to-morrow we die,' base though it was, had at least this recommendation, that the conclusion did seem to follow from the premises: but the moral teaching of the Stoic was practically summed up in the paralogism, 'Let us neither eat nor drink, for to-morrow we die,' where no wit of man could bridge over the gulf between the premises and the conclusion. A belief in man's immortality might have saved the Stoic from many intellectual paradoxes and much practical perplexity: but then it would have made him other than a Stoic. He had a profound sense of the reign of moral order in the universe. Herein he was right. But the postulate of man's immortality alone reconciles

Consequent paradoxes and perplexities of Stoicism.

---

[1] Socrates (or Plato) said that with true philosophers οὐδὲν ἄλλο αὐτοὶ ἐπιτηδεύουσιν ἢ ἀποθνήσκειν τε καὶ τεθνάναι (*Phædo* 64 A). The Stoic, by accepting the ἀποθνήσκειν and forgetting the τεθνάναι, robbed the saying of its virtue.

this belief with many facts of actual experience; and, refusing to extend his views beyond the present life, he was obliged to misstate or deny these facts in order to save his thesis[1]. He staunchly maintained the inherent quality of actions as good or bad (irrespective of their consequences), and he has deserved the gratitude of mankind as the champion of a morality of principles. But he falsely supposed himself bound in consequence to deny any force to the utilitarian aspect of ethics, as though it were irrreconcilable with his own doctrine; and so he was led into the wildest paradoxes, calling good evil and evil good. The meeting-point of these two distinct lines of view is beyond the grave, and he refused to carry his range of vision so far. It was inconsistent with his tenets to hold out the hope of a future life as an incentive to well-doing and a dissuasive from sin; for he wholly ignored the idea of retribution. So far, there was more substantial truth and greater moral power in the crude and gross conceptions of an afterworld embodied in the popular mythology which was held up to scorn by him, than in the imposing philosophy which he himself had devised to supplant them.

4. Attention was directed above to an instructive parallel which Seneca's language presents to our Lord's image of the vine and the branches[2]. Precepts, writes the philosopher, wither unless they are grafted in a sect. By this confession Seneca virtually abandons the position of self-isolation and self-sufficiency, which the Stoic assumes. He felt vaguely the want of some historical basis, some bond of social union, in short some principle of cohesion, which should give force and vitality to his ethical teaching. No mere abstract philosophy has influenced or can influence permanently large masses of men. A Bible and a Church—a sacred record and a religious

4. Absence of a historical basis.

A sacred record and a religious

---

[1] Butler argues from the fact that 'the divine government which we experience ourselves under in the present state, taken alone, is allowed not to be the perfection of moral government.' The Stoic denied what the Christian philosopher assumes, and contradicted experience by maintaining that it s perfect, taken alone.

[2] See above, p. 267.

community—are primary conditions of extensive and abiding success. An isolated spirit here and there may have dispensed with such aids; but, as a social power, as a continuous agency, mere doctrine, however imposing, will for the most part be ineffective without such a support.

community necessary.

So far we have been speaking of conditions of success which were wanting indeed to Stoicism, but which nevertheless are not peculiar to Christianity. All creeds, which have secured any wide and lasting allegiance, have had their sacred books and their religious organization. But our Lord's language, of which Seneca's image is a partial though unconscious echo, points to the one distinguishing feature of Christianity. It is not a record nor a community, but a Person, whence the sap spreads to the branches and ripens into the rich clusters. I have already alluded to Gibbon's account of the causes which combined to promote the spread of the Church. It will seem strange to any one who has at all felt the spirit of the Gospel, that a writer, enumerating the forces to which the dissemination and predominance of Christianity were due, should omit all mention of the Christ. One might have thought it impossible to study with common attention the records of the Apostles and martyrs of the first ages or of the saints and heroes of the later Church, without seeing that the consciousness of personal union with Him, the belief in His abiding presence, was the mainspring of their actions and the fountain of all their strength. This is not a preconceived theory of what should have happened, but a bare statement of what stands recorded on the pages of history. In all ages and under all circumstances, the Christian life has ever radiated from this central fire. Whether we take St Peter or St Paul, St Francis of Assisi or John Wesley, whether Athanasius or Augustine, Anselm or Luther, whether Boniface or Francis Xavier, here has been the impulse of their activity and the secret of their moral power. Their lives have illustrated the parable of the vine and the branches.

Christianity centres in a Person.

Christ the source of the moral power of Christianity.

It is this which differentiates Christianity from all other

Distinctive fea-

religions, and still more from all abstract systems of philosophy. Those who assume the entire aim and substance of the Gospel to have been the inculcation of moral precepts, and who therefore rest its claims solely or chiefly on the purity of its ethical code, often find themselves sorely perplexed, when they stumble upon some noble and true utterance of Jewish or Heathen antiquity before the coming of Christ. A maxim of a Stoic philosopher or a Rabbinical schoolman, a saying of Plato or Confucius, startles them by its resemblance to the teaching of the Gospel. Such perplexity is founded on a twofold error. On the one hand they have not realised the truth that the same Divine Power was teaching mankind before He was made flesh: while on the other they have failed to see what is involved in this incarnation and its sequel. To those who have felt how much is implied in St John's description of the pre-incarnate Word as the life and light of men; to those who allow the force of Tertullian's appeal to the 'witness of a soul naturally Christian'; to those who have sounded the depths of Augustine's bold saying, that what we now call the Christian religion existed from the dawn of the human race, though it only began to be named Christian when Christ came in the flesh[1]; to those who can respond to the sentiment of the old English poem,

> 'Many man for Cristes love
> Was martired in Romayne,
> Er any Cristendom was knowe there
> Or any cros honoured';

it cannot be a surprise to find such flashes of divine truth in men who lived before the coming of our Lord or were placed beyond the reach of the Gospel. The significance of Christ's moral precepts does not lose but gain by the admission: for we learn to view Him no longer as one wholly apart from our race, but recognising in His teaching old truths which 'in manhood darkly join,' we shall only be the more prompt to

> 'Yield all blessing to the name
> Of Him that made them current coin.'

---

[1] *Retract.* i. 13.

but a principle of life centred in a Person.

But the mere ethical teaching, however important, is the least important, because the least distinctive part of Christianity. If there be any meaning in the saying that Christ appeared to 'bring life and immortality to light,' if the stedfast convictions of St Peter and St Paul and St John were not a delusion, and their lives not built upon a lie, then obviously a deeper principle is involved. The moral teaching and the moral example of our Lord will ever have the highest value in their own province; but the core of the Gospel does not lie here. Its distinctive character is, that in revealing a Person it reveals also a principle of life—the union with God in Christ, apprehended by faith in the present and assured to us hereafter by the Resurrection. This Stoicism could not give; and therefore its dogmas and precepts were barren. Its noblest branches bore neither flowers nor fruit, because there was no parent stem from which they could draw fresh sap.

The Letters of Paul and Seneca.

THE spurious correspondence between the Apostle and the philosopher to which reference is made in the preceding essay, consists of fourteen letters, the 1st, 3rd, 5th, 7th, 9th, 11th, 12th, and 13th written in the name of Seneca, and the 2nd, 4th, 6th, 8th, 10th, and 14th of St Paul. In the address of the 6th the name of Lucilius is added to that of Seneca, and in the same way in the address of the 7th Theophilus is named along with St Paul.

The correspondence described.

I have not thought it worth while to reprint these letters, as they may be read conveniently in the recent edition of Seneca's works by F. Haase (III. p. 476 sq.) included in Teubner's series, and are to be found likewise in several older editions of this author. They have been printed lately also in Fleury's *St Paul et Sénèque* (II. p. 300 sq.) and in Aubertin's *Sénèque et St Paul* (p. 409 sq.), and still more recently in an article by Kraus, entitled *Der Briefwechsel Pauli mit Seneca*, in the *Theologische Quartalschrift* XLIX. p. 601 (1867).

Editions of the letters.

The great popularity of this correspondence in the ages before the Reformation is shown by the large number of extant MSS. Fleury, making use of the common catalogues, has enumerated about sixty; and probably a careful search would largely increase the number. The majority, as is usual in such cases, belong to the thirteenth, fourteenth, and fifteenth centuries, but two at least are as early as the ninth. Haase used some fresh collations, from which however he complains that little was to be got (p. xxii.); and Fleury also collated three MSS from Paris and one from Toulouse. Haase directed attention to the two most ancient, Ambrosianus C. 90 and Argentoratensis C. vi. 5, both belonging to the ninth century (which had not yet been examined), but had no opportunity of collating them himself. Collations from these (together with another later Strassburg MS, Argentoratensis C. vi. 7) were afterwards used by Kraus for his text, which is thus constructed of better materials

The MSS and collations.

than any other. But after all, it remains in an unsatisfactory state, which the worthlessness of the letters themselves may well excuse.

Probable motive of the forgery.

This correspondence was probably forged in the fourth century, either to recommend Seneca to Christian readers or to recommend Christianity to students of Seneca. In favour of this view may be urged the fact that in several MSS these spurious letters precede the genuine works of Seneca[1]. Nor does any other motive seem consistent with the letters themselves; for they have no doctrinal bearing at all, and no historical interest of sufficient importance to account for the forgery. They are made up chiefly of an interchange of compliments between the Apostle and the philosopher; and the only historical thread which can be said to run through them is the endeavour of Seneca to gain the ear of Nero for the writings of St Paul.

Reference to the letters by Jerome,

It is commonly said that St Jerome, who first mentions these letters, had no suspicion that they were spurious. This statement however is exaggerated, for he does not commit himself to any opinion at all about their genuineness. He merely says, that he 'should not have given a place to Seneca in a catalogue of saints, unless challenged to do so by those letters of Paul to Seneca and from Seneca to Paul which are read by very many persons' (*de Vir. Ill.* 12 'nisi me illae epistolae provocarent quae leguntur a plurimis'). When it is remembered how slight an excuse serves to bring other names into his list, such as Philo, Josephus, and Justus Tiberiensis, we cannot lay any stress on the vague language which he uses in this case. The more probable inference is that he did not deliberately accept them as genuine. Indeed, if he had so accepted them, his profound silence about them elsewhere would be wholly inexplicable.

Augustine,

St Augustine, as generally happens in questions of historical criticism, repeats the language of Jerome and perhaps had not seen the letters (*Epist.* cliii. 14 'Seneca cujus quaedam ad Paulum apostolum leguntur epistolae[2]'). Throughout the middle

[1] As for instance Argent. C. vi. 5 described by Kraus. So in Burn. 251 (British Museum), which I have examined, they are included in a collection of genuine and spurious works of Seneca, being themselves preceded by the notice of Jerome and followed by the first of the epistles to Lucilius. It is not uncommon to find them immediately before the genuine epistles.

[2] Another passage quoted *Philippians*, p. 29, note 2, in which Augustine remarks on Seneca's silence about the Christians, is inconsistent with a conviction of the genuineness of these letters.

ages they are mentioned or quoted, most frequently as genuine, but *and later* occasionally with an expression of doubt, until the revival of learning, *writers.* when the light of criticism rapidly dispelled the illusion[1].

As they are now universally allowed to be spurious, it will be *These let-* unnecessary to state at length the grounds of their condemnation. *ters a manifest* It is sufficient to say that the letters are inane and unworthy *forgery.* throughout; that the style of either correspondent is unlike his genuine writings; that the relations between the two, as there represented, are highly improbable; and lastly, that the chronological notices (which however are absent in some important MSS) are wrong in almost every instance. Thus, independently of the unbroken silence of three centuries and a half about this correspondence, internal evidence alone is sufficient to condemn them hopelessly.

Yet the writer is not an ignorant man. He has read part of *Yet the* Seneca and is aware of the philosopher's relations with Lucilius; he *writer is not igno-* is acquainted with the story of Castor and Pollux appearing to one *rant nor* Vatinius (or Vatienus); he can talk glibly of the gardens of Sallust; *wholly careless.* he is acquainted with the character of Caligula whom he properly calls Gaius Cæsar; he is even aware of the Jewish sympathies of the empress Poppæa and makes her regard St Paul as a renegade[2]; and lastly, he seems to have had before him some account of the Neronian fire and persecution[3] which is no longer extant, for he speaks of 'Christians and Jews' being punished as the authors of the conflagration and mentions that 'a hundred and thirty-two houses and six insulæ were burnt in six days.'

Moreover I believe he attempts, though he succeeds ill in the attempt, to make a difference in the styles of Seneca and St Paul, the writing of the latter being more ponderous. Unfortunately he betrays himself by representing Seneca as referring more than once to St Paul's bad style; and in one letter the philosopher mentions sending the Apostle a book *de Copia Verborum*, obviously for the purpose of improving his Latin.

I mention these facts, because they bear upon a theory main- *Theory of* tained by some modern critics[4], that these letters are not the same *some modern critics.*

---

[1] See Fleury I. p. 269 sq. for a catena of references.

[2] *Ep.* 5 'Indignatio dominae, quod a ritu et secta veteri recesseris et [te] aliorsum converteris'; comp. *Ep.* 8, where however the reading is doubtful.

[3] Yet there must be some mistake in the numbers, which appear too small.

[4] An account of these views will be found in Fleury II. p. 225 sq. He himself holds that the letters read by these fathers were not the same with our correspondence, but questions whether those letters were genuine.

with those to which Jerome and Augustine refer; that they had before them a genuine correspondence between St Paul and Seneca, which has since perished; and that the extant epistles were forged later (say about the ninth century), being suggested by the notices in these fathers and invented in consequence to supply their place. The only specious arguments advanced in favour of this view, so far as I know, are these: (1) A man like Jerome could not possibly have believed the extant correspondence to be genuine, for the forgery is transparent; (2) The *de Copia Verborum* is a third title to a work otherwise known as *de Formula Honestae Vitae* or *de Quatuor Virtutibus*, written by Martinus Bragensis or Dumiensis († circ. A. D. 580), but ascribed in many MSS to Seneca. Sufficient time therefore must have elapsed since this date to allow the false title and false ascription to take the place of the true and to be generally circulated and recognised[1].

The arguments for this view stated

To both these arguments a ready answer may be given: (1) There is no reason to suppose that Jerome did believe the correspondence to be genuine, as I have already shown. He would hardly have spoken so vaguely, if he had accepted the letters as genuine or even inclined to this belief. (2) A much better account can be given of the false title and ascription of Martin's treatise, if we suppose that they arose out of the allusion in the letters, than on the converse hypothesis that they were prior to and suggested this allusion. This Martin, whose works appear to have had a very large circulation in the middle ages, wrote on kindred subjects and seems occasionally to have abridged and adapted Seneca's writings. For this reason his works were commonly bound up with those of Seneca, and in some instances came to be ascribed to the Stoic philosopher. This is the case at all events with the *de Moribus*, as well as the *de Quatuor Virtutibus*, and perhaps other spurious treatises bearing the name of Seneca may be assigned to the same author. A copy of the *de Quatuor Virtutibus*, either designedly abridged or accidentally mutilated, and on this account wanting the title, was bound up so as to precede or follow the correspondence of Paul and Seneca[2];

and answered.

Martinus Bragensis.

Account of de Copia Verborum.

---

[1] This argument is urged by Fleury II. p. 267 sq. The *de Formula Honestae Vitae* is printed in Haase's edition of Seneca (III. p. 468) together with other spurious works.

[2] It is found in some extant MSS (e.g. Flor. Pl. xlv. Cod. iv) immediately before the letters, and it may perhaps occur in some others immediately after them. [Since the first edition appeared, in which this conjecture was hazarded, I have found the treatise immediately after the letters, Bodl. *Laud. Misc.* 383, fol. 77 a, where it is anonymous, 1869.]

and, as Seneca in one of these letters mentions sending the *de Copia Verborum*, a later transcriber assumed that the neighbouring treatise must be the work in question, and without reflecting gave it this title[1]. Whether the forger of the correspondence invented an imaginary title, or whether a standard work bearing this name, either by Seneca himself or by some one else, was in general circulation when he wrote, we have no means of deciding; but the motive in the allusion is clearly the improvement of St Paul's Latin, of which Seneca more than once complains. On the other hand the *de Quatuor Virtutibus* is, as its name implies, a treatise on the cardinal virtues. An allusion to this treatise therefore would be meaningless; nor indeed has any reasonable explanation been given, how it got the title *de Copia Verborum*, on the supposition that this title was prior to the allusion in the correspondence and was not

---

[1] The work, when complete, consists of (1) A dedication in Martin's name to Miro king of Gallicia, in which he mentions the title of the book *Formula Vitae Honestae;* (2) A short paragraph enumerating the four cardinal virtues; (3) A discussion of these several virtues and the measure to be observed in each. In the MSS, so far as I have learnt from personal inspection and from notices in other writers, it is found in three different forms; (1) Complete (e.g. Cambridge Univ. Libr. Dd. xv. 21; Bodl. *Laud. Misc.* 444, fol. 146), in which case there is no possibility of mistaking its authorship; (2) Without the dedicatory preface, so that it begins *Quatuor virtutum species* etc. In this form it is generally entitled *de Quatuor Virtutibus* and ascribed to Seneca. So it is for instance in three British Museum MSS, *Burn.* 251 fol. 33 a (XIIIth cent.; the treatise being mutilated at the end and concluding 'In has ergo maculas prudentia immensurata perducet'), *Burn.* 360, fol. 35 a (XIVth cent.?), and *Harl.* 233 (XIIIth or XIVth cent.?; where however the general title is wanting and the treatise has the special heading *Seneca de prudentia*). The transcriber of *Arund.* 249 (XVth cent.) also gives it in this form, but is aware of the true author, for the heading is *Incipit tractatus libri honeste vite editus a Martino episcopo Qui a multis intitulatur de quatuor virtutibus et attribuitur Senece;* but he ends it *Explicit tractatus de quatuor virtutibus Annei Senece Cordubensis*, as he doubtless found it in the copy which he transcribed. In Bodl. *Laud. Lat.* 86, fol. 58 a, where it occurs in this form, it is ascribed to its right author; while again in Bodl. *Laud. Misc.* 280, fol. 117 a, it is anonymous. These MSS I have examined. (3) It occurs without either the dedicatory preface or the general paragraph on the four virtues, and some extraneous matter is added at the end. Only in this form, so far as I can discover, does it bear the strange title *de Verborum Copia*. So in one of the Gale MSS at Trinity College Cambridge (O. 3. 31) it begins '*Senece de quatuor virtutibus primo* (?) *de prudentia. Quisquis prudentiam...*' and ends '... jactura que per negligentiam fit. *Explicit liber Senece de verborum copia*'; and the MS described by Haase (III. p. xxii) belongs to the same type. These facts accord with the account of the title which I have suggested in the text.

itself suggested thereby, for it is wholly alien to the subject of the treatise.

Direct reasons against this theory. But other strong and (as it seems to me) convincing arguments may be brought against this theory: (1) Extant MSS of the correspondence date from the ninth century, and in these the text is already in a corrupt state. (2) The historical knowledge which the letters show could hardly have been possessed, or turned to such account, by a writer later than the fourth or fifth century. (3) Jerome quotes obliquely a passage from the letters, and this passage is found in the extant correspondence. To this it is replied, that the forger, taking the notice of Jerome as his starting-point, would necessarily insert the quotation to give colour to his forgery. But I think it may be assumed in this case that the pseudo-Seneca would have preserved the words of Jerome accurately or nearly so; whereas, though the sense is the same, the difference in form is considerable[1]. It may be added also that the sentiment is in entire keeping with the pervading tone of the letters, and has no appearance of being introduced for a distinct purpose. (4) It is wholly inconceivable that a genuine correspondence of the Apostle could have escaped notice for three centuries and a half; and not less inconceivable that, having once been brought to light at the end of the fourth and beginning of the fifth century, it should again have fallen into oblivion and been suffered to disappear. This theory therefore may be confidently rejected.

[1] The reference in St Jerome is '(Seneca) optare se dicit ejus esse loci apud suos, cujus sit Paulus apud Christianos.' The words stand in the letters (no. 11), '[Uti] nam qui meus, tuus apud te locus, qui tuus, velim ut meus.'

V.

THE ESSENES.

On some points connected with the Essenes..

A.
THE NAME ESSENE.

B.
ORIGIN AND AFFINITY OF THE ESSENES..

C.
ESSENISM AND CHRISTIANITY.

V.

A.

THE NAME ESSENE.

The name is variously written in Greek: *Various forms of the name in Greek.*

1. 'Εσσηνός: Joseph. *Ant.* xiii. 5. 9, xiii. 10. 6, xv. 10. 5, xviii. 1. 2, 5, *B. J.* ii. 8. 2, 13, *Vit.* 2; Plin. *N. H.* v. 15. 17 (Essenus); Dion Chrys. in Synes. *Dion* 3; Hippol. *Haer.* ix. 18, 28 (MS ἐσηνός); Epiphan. *Haer.* p. 28 sq., 127 (ed. Pet.).

2. 'Εσσαῖος: Philo II. pp. 457, 471, 632 (ed. Mang.); Hegesippus in Euseb. *H. E.* iv. 22; Porphyr. *de Abstin.* iv. 11. So too Joseph. *B. J.* ii. 7. 3, ii. 20. 4, iii. 2. 1; *Ant.* xv. 10. 4; though in the immediate context of this last passage he writes 'Εσσηνός, if the common texts may be trusted.

3. 'Οσσαῖος: Epiphan. *Haer.* pp. 40 sq., 125, 462. The common texts very frequently make him write 'Οσσηνός, but see Dindorf's notes, Epiphan. *Op.* I. pp. 380, 425. With Epiphanius the Essenes are a Samaritan, the Ossæans a Judaic sect. He has evidently got his information from two distinct sources, and does not see that the same persons are intended.

4. 'Ιεσσαῖος, Epiphan. *Haer.* p. 117. From the connexion the same sect again seems to be meant: but owing to the form Epiphanius conjectures (οἶμαι) that the name is derived from Jesse, the father of David.

If any certain example could be produced where the name occurs in any early Hebrew or Aramaic writing, the question of its derivation would probably be settled; but in the absence of a single decisive instance a wide field is opened for conjecture, and critics have not been backward in availing themselves of the license. In discussing the claims of the different etymologies proposed we may reject:

First: derivations from the Greek. Thus Philo connects the word with ὅσιος 'holy': *Quod omn. prob.* 12, p. 457 Ἐσσαῖοι...διαλέκτου ἑλληνικῆς παρώνυμοι ὁσιότητος, § 13, p. 459 τῶν Ἐσσαίων ἢ ὁσίων, *Fragm.* p. 632 καλοῦνται μὲν Ἐσσαῖοι, παρὰ τὴν ὁσιότητα, μοὶ δοκῶ [δοκεῖ?], τῆς προσηγορίας ἀξιωθέντες. It is not quite clear whether Philo is here playing with words after the manner of his master Plato, or whether he holds a pre-established harmony to exist among different languages by which similar sounds represent similar things, or whether lastly he seriously means that the name was directly derived from the Greek word ὅσιος. The last supposition is the least probable; but he certainly does not reject this derivation 'as incorrect' (Ginsburg *Essenes* p. 27), nor can παρώνυμοι ὁσιότητος be rendered 'from an incorrect derivation from the Greek homonym *hosiotes*' (ib. p. 32), since the word παρώνυμος never involves the notion of *false* etymology. The amount of truth which probably underlies Philo's statement will be considered hereafter. Another Greek derivation is ἴσος, 'companion, associate,' suggested by Rapoport, *Erech Millin* p. 41. Several others again are suggested by Löwy, s. v. Essäer, e.g. ἔσω from their esoteric doctrine, or αἶσα from their fatalism. All such may be rejected as instances of ingenious trifling, if indeed they deserve to be called ingenious.

Secondly: derivations from proper names whether of persons or of places. Thus the word has been derived from *Jesse* the father of David (Epiphan. l. c.), or from one ישי *Isai*, the disciple of R. Joshua ben Perachia who migrated to Egypt in the time of Alexander Jannæus (Löw in *Ben Chananja* I. p. 352). Again it has been referred to the town *Essa* (a doubtful reading in

Joseph. *Ant.* xiii. 15. 3) beyond the Jordan. And other similar derivations have been suggested.

Thirdly: etymologies from the Hebrew or Aramaic, which do not supply the right consonants, or do not supply them in the right order. Under this head several must be rejected;

אסר *āsar* 'to bind,' Adler *Volkslehrer* VI. p. 50, referred to by Ginsburg *Essenes* p. 29.

חסיד *chāsīd* 'pious,' which is represented by Ἀσιδαῖος (1 Macc. ii. 42 (v. l.), vii. 13, 2 Macc. xiv. 6), and could not possibly assume the form Ἐσσαῖος or Ἐσσηνός. Yet this derivation appears in Josippon ben Gorion (iv. 6, 7, v. 24, pp. 274, 278, 451), who substitutes *Chasidim* in narratives where the Essenes are mentioned in the original of Josephus; and it has been adopted by many more recent writers.

סחא *s'chā* 'to bathe,' from which with an *Aleph* prefixed we might get אסחאי *as'chai* 'bathers' (a word however which does not occur): Grätz *Gesch. der Juden* III. pp. 82, 468.

צנוע *tsanūat* 'retired, modest,' adopted by Frankel (*Zeitschrift* 1846, p. 449, *Monatsschrift* II. p. 32) after a suggestion by Löw.

To this category must be assigned those etymologies which contain a ן as the third consonant of the root; since the comparison of the parallel forms Ἐσσαῖος and Ἐσσηνός shows that in the latter word the ν is only formative. On this ground we must reject:

חסין *chāsīn*; see below under עשין.

חצן *chōtsen* 'a fold' of a garment, and so supposed to signify the περίζωμα or 'apron,' which was given to every neophyte among the Essenes (Joseph. *B. J.* ii. 8. 5, 7): suggested by Jellinek *Ben Chananja* IV. p. 374.

עשין *ɛāshīn* 'strong': see Cohn in Frankel's *Monatsschrift* VII. p. 271. This etymology is suggested to explain Epiphanius *Haer.* p. 40 τοῦτο δὲ τὸ γένος τῶν Ὀσσηνῶν ἑρμηνεύεται διὰ τῆς ἐκδόσεως τοῦ ὀνόματος στιβαρὸν γένος ('a sturdy race'). The name 'Essene' is so interpreted also in Makrisi (de Sacy, *Chrestom. Arab.* I. pp. 114, 306); but, as he himself writes it

(iii) From Hebrew roots not supplying the right consonants,

such as those which make ν part of the root.

328   THE ESSENES.

with *Elif* and not *Ain*, it is plain that he got this interpretation from some one else, probably from Epiphanius. The correct reading however in Epiphanius is Ὀσσαίων, not Ὀσσηνῶν; and it would therefore appear that this father or his informant derived the word from the Hebrew root עשׂה rather than from the Aramaic עשׂן. The Ὀσσαῖοι would then be the עשׂים, and this is so far a possible derivation, that the *n* does not enter into the root. Another word suggested to explain the etymology of Epiphanius is the Hebrew and Aramaic חסין *chasīn* 'powerful, strong' (from חסן); but this is open to the same objections as עשׂין.

Other derivations considered:

When all such derivations are eliminated as untenable or improbable, considerable uncertainty still remains. The 1st and 3rd radicals might be any of the gutturals א, ה, ח, ע; and the Greek σ, as the 2nd radical, might represent any one of several Shemitic sibilants.

Thus we have the choice of the following etymologies, which have found more or less favour.

(1) אסיא 'a physician';

(1) אסא *āsā* 'to heal,' whence אסיא *asyā*, 'a physician.' The Essenes are supposed to be so called because Josephus states (*B. J.* ii. 8. 6) that they paid great attention to the qualities of herbs and minerals 'with a view to the healing of diseases (πρὸς θεραπείαν παθῶν).' This etymology is supported likewise by an appeal to the name θεραπευταί, which Philo gives to an allied sect in Egypt (*de Vit. Cont.* § 1, II. p. 471). It seems highly improbable however, that the ordinary name of the Essenes should have been derived from a pursuit which was merely secondary and incidental; while the supposed analogy of the Therapeutæ rests on a wrong interpretation of the word. Philo indeed (l. c.), bent upon extracting from it as much moral significance as possible, says, θεραπευταὶ καὶ θεραπευτρίδες καλοῦνται, ἤτοι παρ' ὅσον ἰατρικὴν ἐπαγγέλλονται κρείσσονα τῆς κατὰ πόλεις (ἡ μὲν γὰρ σώματα θεραπεύει μόνον, ἐκείνη δὲ καὶ ψυχὰς κ.τ.λ.) ἢ παρ' ὅσον ἐκ φύσεως καὶ τῶν ἱερῶν νόμων ἐπαιδεύθησαν θεραπεύειν τὸ ὂν κ.τ.λ.: but the latter meaning alone accords with the usage of the word; for θεραπευτής, used

absolutely, signifies 'a worshipper, devotee,' not 'a physician, healer.' This etymology of Ἐσσαῖος is ascribed, though wrongly, to Philo by Asaria de' Rossi (*Meor Enayim* 3, fol. 33 *a*) and has been very widely received. Among more recent writers, who have adopted or favoured it, are Bellermann (*Ueber Essäer u. Therapeuten* p. 7), Gfrörer (*Philo* II. p. 341), Dähne (*Ersch. u. Gruber*, s. v.), Baur (*Christl. Kirche der drei erst. Jahrh.* p. 20), Herzfeld (*Gesch. des Judenthums* II. p. 371, 395, 397 sq.), Geiger (*Urschrift* p. 126), Derenbourg (*L'Histoire et la Géographie de la Palestine* pp. 170, 175, notes), Keim (*Jesus von Nazara* I. p. 284 sq.), and Hamburger (*Real-Encyclopädie für Bibel u. Talmud*, s. v.). Several of these writers identify the Essenes with the Baithusians (ביתוסין) of the Talmud, though in the Talmud the Baithusians are connected with the Sadducees. This identification was suggested by Asaria de' Rossi (l. c. fol. 33 *b*), who interprets 'Baithusians' as 'the school of the Essenes' (בית איסיא): while subsequent writers, going a step further, have explained it 'the school of the physicians' (בית אסיא).

(2) חזא *chăzā* 'to see,' whence חזיא *chazyā* 'a seer,' in reference to the prophetic powers which the Essenes claimed, as the result of ascetic contemplation: Joseph. *B. J.* ii. 8. 12 εἰσὶ δὲ ἐν αὐτοῖς οἳ καὶ τὰ μέλλοντα προγινώσκειν ὑπισχνοῦνται κ.τ.λ. For instances of such Essene prophets see *Ant.* xiii. 11. 2, xv. 10. 5, *B. J.* i. 3. 5, ii. 7. 3. Suidas, s. v. Ἐσσαῖοι, says: θεωρίᾳ τὰ πολλὰ παραμένουσιν, ἔνθεν καὶ Ἐσσαῖοι καλοῦνται, τοῦτο δηλοῦντος τοῦ ὀνόματος, τουτέστι, θεωρητικοί. For this derivation, which was suggested by Baumgarten (see Bellermann p. 10) and is adopted by Hilgenfeld (*Jüd. Apocal.* p. 278), there is something to be said: but חזא is rather ὁρᾶν than θεωρεῖν; and thus it must denote the result rather than the process, the *vision* which was the privilege of the few rather than the *contemplation* which was the duty of all. Indeed in a later paper (*Zeitschr.* XI. p. 346, 1868) Hilgenfeld expresses himself doubtfully about this derivation, feeling the difficulty of explaining the σσ from the ז. This is a real objection. In the transliteration of the LXX the ז is persistently represented by ζ,

(2) חזיא 'a seer';

and the צ by σ. The exceptions to this rule, where the manuscript authority is beyond question, are very few, and in every case they seem capable of explanation by peculiar circumstances.

(3) עשה 'to do';

(3) עשה *‛āsāh* 'to do,' so that Ἐσσαῖοι would signify 'the doers, the observers of the law,' thus referring to the strictness of Essene practices: see Oppenheim in Frankel's *Monatsschrift* VII. p. 272 sq. It has been suggested also that, as the Pharisees were especially designated the teachers, the Essenes were called the 'doers' by a sort of antithesis: see an article in Jost's *Annalen* 1839, p. 145. Thus the Talmudic phrase אנשי מעשה, interpreted 'men of practice, of good deeds,' is supposed to refer to the Essenes (see Frankel's *Zeitschrift* III. p. 458, *Monatsschrift* II. p. 70). In some passages indeed (see Surenhuis *Mishna* III. p. 313) it may possibly mean 'workers of miracles' (as ἔργον Joh. v. 20, vii. 21, x. 25, etc.); but in this sense also it might be explained of the thaumaturgic powers claimed by the Essenes. (See below, p. 340.) On the use which has been made of a passage in the *Aboth* of R. Nathan c. 37, as supporting this derivation, I shall have to speak hereafter. Altogether this etymology has little or nothing to recommend it.

I have reserved to the last the two derivations which seem to deserve most consideration.

(4) *chasyo* 'pious';

(4) ܚܣܐ *chasi* (ܚܣܐ *ch'sē*) or ܚܣܝܐ *chasyo*, 'pious,' in Syriac. This derivation, which is also given by de Sacy (*Chrestom. Arab.* I. p. 347), is adopted by Ewald (*Gesch. des V. Isr.* IV. p. 484, ed. 3, 1864, VII. pp. 154, 477, ed. 2, 1859), who abandons in its favour another etymology (חזן *chazzan* 'watcher, worshipper' = θεραπευτής) which he had suggested in an earlier edition of his fourth volume (p. 420). It is recommended by the fact that it resembles not only in sound, but in meaning, the Greek ὅσιος, of which it is a common rendering in the Peshito (Acts ii. 27, xiii. 35, Tit. i. 8). Thus it explains the derivation given by Philo (see above, p. 326), and it also accounts for the tendency to write Ὀσσαῖος for Ἐσσαῖος in Greek. Ewald moreover points out how an Essenizing Sibylline poem

(*Orac. Sib.* iv; see *Colossians*, p. 96) dwells on the Greek equivalents, εὐσεβής, εὐσεβίη, etc. (vv. 26, 35, 42 sq., 148 sq., 162, 165 sq., 178 sq., ed. Alexandre), as if they had a special value for the writer: see *Gesch.* VII. p. 154, *Sibyll. Bücher* p. 46. Lipsius (Schenkel's *Bibel-Lexicon*, s. v.) also considers this the most probable etymology.

(5) חָשָׁא *chāshā* (also חשה) Heb. 'to be silent'; whence חשאים *chashshāīm* 'the silent ones,' who meditate on mysteries. Jost (*Gesch. d. Judenth.* I. p. 207) believes that this was the derivation accepted by Josephus, since he elsewhere (*Ant.* iii. 7. 5, iii. 8. 9) writes out חשן, *chōshen* 'the high-priest's breast-plate' (Exod. xxviii. 15 sq.), ἐσσήν or ἐσσήνης in Greek, and explains it σημαίνει τοῦτο κατὰ τὴν Ἑλλήνων γλῶτταν λογεῖον (i.e. the 'place of oracles' or 'of reason': comp. Philo *de Mon.* ii. § 5, II. p. 226, καλεῖται λογεῖον ἐτύμως, ἐπειδὴ τὰ ἐν οὐρανῷ πάντα λόγοις καὶ ἀναλογίαις δεδημιούργηται κ.τ.λ.), as it is translated in the LXX. Even though modern critics should be right in connecting חשן with the Arab. حسن 'pulcher fuit, ornavit' (see Gesen. *Thes.* p. 535, s. v.), the other derivation may have prevailed in Josephus' time. We may illustrate this derivation by Josephus' description of the Essenes, *B. J.* ii. 8. 5 τοῖς ἔξωθεν ὡς μυστήριόν τι φρικτὸν ἡ τῶν ἔνδον σιωπὴ καταφαίνεται; and perhaps this will also explain the Greek equivalent θεωρητικοί, which Suidas gives for Ἐσσαῖοι. The use of the Hebrew word חשאים in Mishna *Shekalim* v. 6, though we need not suppose that the Essenes are there meant, will serve to show how it might be adopted as the name of the sect. On this word see Levy *Chaldäisches Wörterbuch* p. 287. On the whole this seems the most probable etymology of any, though it has not found so much favour as the last. At all events the rules of transliteration are entirely satisfied, and this can hardly be said of the other derivations which come into competition with it.

(5) חשאים 'silent ones.'

B.

ORIGIN AND AFFINITIES OF THE ESSENES.

The principle of the restoration.

THE ruling principle of the Restoration under Ezra was the isolation of the Jewish people from all influences of the surrounding nations. Only by the rigorous application of this principle was it possible to guard the nationality of the Hebrews, and thus to preserve the sacred deposit of religious truth of which this nationality was the husk. Hence the strictest attention was paid to the Levitical ordinances, and more especially to those which aimed at ceremonial purity. The principle, which was thus distinctly asserted at the period of the national revival, gained force and concentration at a later date from the active antagonism to which the patriotic Jews were driven by the religious and political aggressions of the Syrian kings. During the Maccabæan wars we read of a party or sect called the *Chasidim* or *Asidæans* (Ἀσιδαῖοι), the 'pious' or 'devout,' who zealous in their observance of the ceremonial law stoutly resisted any concession to the practices of Hellenism, and took their place in the van of the struggle with their national enemies, the Antiochene monarchs (1 Macc. ii. 42, vii. 13, 2 Macc. xiv. 6). But, though their names appear now for the first time, they are not mentioned as a newly formed party; and it is probable that they had their origin at a much earlier date.

Rise of the Asidæans.

Pharisaism and

The subsequent history of this tendency to exclusiveness and isolation is wrapt in the same obscurity. At a somewhat later date it is exhibited in the *Pharisees* and the *Essenes*; but whether these were historically connected with the Chasidim as divergent offshoots of the original sect, or whether they represent independent developments of the same principle, we are without the proper data for deciding. The principle itself appears in the name of the Pharisees, which, as denoting 'separation,' points to the avoidance of all foreign and contaminating influences. On the other hand the meaning of the name *Essene* is uncertain, for the attempt to derive it directly from *Chasidim* must be abandoned; but the tendency of the sect is unmistakable. If with the Pharisees ceremonial purity was a principal aim, with the Essenes it was an absorbing passion. It was enforced and guarded moreover by a special organization. While the Pharisees were a sect, the Essenes were an order. Like the Pythagoreans in Magna Græcia and the Buddhists in India before them, like the Christian monks of the Egyptian and Syrian deserts after them, they were formed into a religious brotherhood, fenced about by minute and rigid rules, and carefully guarded from any contamination with the outer world. *[Essenism traced to the same principle.]*

Thus the sect may have arisen in the heart of Judaism. The idea of ceremonial purity was essentially Judaic. But still, when we turn to the representations of Philo and Josephus, it is impossible to overlook other traits which betoken foreign affinities. Whatever the Essenes may have been in their origin, at the Christian era at least and in the Apostolic age they no longer represented the current type of religious thought and practice among the Jews. This foreign element has been derived by some from the Pythagoreans, by others from the Syrians or Persians or even from the farther East; but, whether Greek or Oriental, its existence has until lately been almost universally allowed. *[Foreign elements in Essenism.]*

The investigations of Frankel, published first in 1846 in his *Zeitschrift*, and continued in 1853 in his *Monatsschrift*, have given a different direction to current opinion. Frankel maintains that Essenism was a purely indigenous growth, that it is only Pharisaism in an exaggerated form, and that it has nothing distinctive and owes nothing, or next to nothing, to foreign *[Frankel's theory well received,]* influences. To establish this point, he disparages the representations of Philo and Josephus as coloured to suit the tastes of their heathen readers, while in their place he brings forward as authorities a number of passages from talmudical and rabbinical writings, in which he discovers references to this sect. In this view he is followed implicitly by some later writers, and has largely influenced the opinions of others; while nearly all speak of his investigations as throwing great light on the subject.

but groundless and misleading.

It is perhaps dangerous to dissent from a view which has found so much favour; but nevertheless I am obliged to confess my belief that, whatever value Frankel's investigations may have as contributions to our knowledge of Jewish religious thought and practice, they throw little or no light on the Essenes specially; and that the blind acceptance of his results by later writers has greatly obscured the distinctive features of this sect. I cannot but think that any one, who will investigate Frankel's references and test his results step by step, will arrive at the conclusion to which I myself have been led, that his talmudical researches have left our knowledge of this sect where it was before, and that we must still refer to Josephus and Philo for any precise information respecting them.

His double derivation of the name.

Frankel starts from the etymology of the name. He supposes that Ἐσσαῖος, Ἐσσηνός, represent two different Hebrew words, the former חסיד *chāsīd*, the latter צנוע *tsanūaʿ*, both clothed in suitable Greek dresses[1]. Wherever therefore either of these words occurs, there is, or there may be, a direct reference to the Essenes.

Fatal objections to it.

It is not too much to say that these etymologies are impossible; and this for several reasons. (1) The two words Ἐσσαῖος, Ἐσσηνός, are plainly duplicate forms of the same Hebrew or Aramaic original, like Σαμψαῖος and Σαμψηνός

---

[1] *Zeitschrift* p. 449 'Für *Essäer* liegt, wie schon von anderen Seiten bemerkt wurde, das Hebr. חסיד, für *Essener*, nach einer Bemerkung des Herrn L. Löw im *Orient*, das Hebr. צנוע nahe'; see also pp. 454, 455; *Monatsschrift* p. 32.

(Epiphan. *Haer.* pp. 40, 47, 127, and even Σαμψίτης p. 46), Ναζωραῖος and Ναζαρηνός, Γιτταῖος and Γιττηνός (Steph. Byz. s. v., Hippol. *Haer.* vi. 7), with which we may compare Βοστραῖος and Βοστρηνός, Μελιταῖος and Μελιτηνός, and numberless other examples. (2) Again; when we consider either word singly, the derivation offered is attended with the most serious difficulties. There is no reason why in 'Εσσαῖος the *d* should have disappeared from *chasid*, while it is hardly possible to conceive that *tsanua* should have taken such an incongruous form as 'Εσσηνός. (3) And lastly; the more important of the two words, *chasid*, had already a recognised Greek equivalent in 'Ασιδαῖος; and it seems highly improbable that a form so divergent as 'Εσσαῖος should have taken its place.

Indeed Frankel's derivations are generally, if not universally, abandoned by later writers; and yet these same writers repeat his quotations and accept his results, as if the references were equally valid, though the name of the sect has disappeared. They seem to be satisfied with the stability of the edifice, even when the foundation is undermined. Thus for instance Grätz not only maintains after Frankel that the Essenes 'were properly nothing more than stationary or, more strictly speaking, logically consistent (consequente) *Chasidim*,' and 'that therefore they were not so far removed from the Pharisees that they can be regarded as a separate sect,' and 'accepts entirely these results' which, as he says, 'rest on critical investigation' (III. p. 463), but even boldly translates *chasiduth* 'the Essene mode of life' (ib. 84), though he himself gives a wholly different derivation of the word 'Essene,' making it signify 'washers' or 'baptists' (see above, p. 327). And even those who do not go to this length of inconsistency, yet avail themselves freely of the passages where *chasid* occurs, and interpret it of the Essenes, while distinctly repudiating the etymology[1].

Dependence of the theory on the derivation.

But, although 'Εσσαῖος or 'Εσσηνός is not a Greek form of *The term chasid*

---

[1] e.g. Keim (p. 286) and Derenbourg pp. 166, 461 sq.), who both derive Essene from אסיא 'a physician.'

THE ESSENES.

not applied specially to the Essenes.

chasid, it might still happen that this word was applied to them as an epithet, though not as a proper name. Only in this case the reference ought to be unmistakeable, before any conclusions are based upon it. But in fact, after going through all the passages, which Frankel gives, it is impossible to feel satisfied that in a single instance there is a direct allusion to the Essenes. Sometimes the word seems to refer to the old sect of the *Chasidim* or *Asidæans,* as for instance when Jose ben Joezer, who lived during the Maccabæan war, is called a *chasid*[1]. At all events this R. Jose is known to have been a married man, for he is stated to have disinherited his children (*Baba Bathra* 133 *b*); and therefore he cannot have belonged to the stricter order of Essenes. Sometimes it is employed quite generally to denote pious observers of the ceremonial law, as for instance when it is said that with the death of certain famous teachers the Chasidim ceased[2]. In this latter sense the expression חסידים הראשונים, 'the ancient or primitive Chasidim' (*Monatsschr.* pp. 31, 62), is perhaps used; for these primitive Chasidim again are mentioned as having wives and children[3], and it appears also that they were scrupulously exact in bringing their sacrificial offerings[4]. Thus it is impossible to identify them with the Essenes, as described by Josephus and Philo. Even in those passages of which most has been made, the reference is more than doubtful. Thus great stress is laid on the saying of R. Joshua ben Chananiah in Mishna *Sotah* iii. 4, 'The foolish *chasid* and the clever villain (חסיד שוטה ורשע ערום), etc., are the ruin of the world.' But the connexion points to a much more general meaning of *chasid,* and the rendering in Surenhuis, 'Homo pius qui insipiens, improbus qui astutus,' gives the correct antithesis. So we might say that there is no one more

---

[1] Mishna *Chagigah* ii. 7; *Zeitschr.* p. 454, *Monatsschr.* pp. 33, 62. See Frankel's own account of this R. Jose in an earlier volume, *Monatsschr.* I. p. 405 sq.

[2] *Zeitschr.* p. 457, *Monatsschr.* p. 69 sq.; see below, p. 340.

[3] *Niddah* 38 *a*; see Löwy s.v. Essäer.

[4] Mishna *Kerithuth* vi. 3, *Nedarim* 10 *a*; see *Monatsschr.* p. 65.

mischievous than the wrong-headed conscientious man. It is true that the Gemaras illustrate the expression by examples of those who allow an over-punctilious regard for external forms to stand in the way of deeds of mercy. And perhaps rightly. But there is no reference to any distinctive Essene practices in the illustrations given. Again; the saying in Mishna *Pirke Aboth* v. 10, 'He who says Mine is thine and thine is thine is [a] *chasid* (חסיד שלך ושלך שלך שלי),' is quoted by several writers as though it referred to the Essene community of goods[1]. But in the first place the idea of community of goods would require, 'Mine is thine and thine is mine': and in the second place, the whole context, and especially the clause which immediately follows (and which these writers do not give), 'He who says Thine is mine and mine is mine is wicked (רשע),' show plainly that חסיד must be taken in its general sense 'pious,' and the whole expression implies not reciprocal interchange but individual self-denial.

It might indeed be urged, though this is not Frankel's plea, that supposing the true etymology of the word 'Εσσαῖος, 'Εσσηνός, to be the Syriac ܚܣܐ, ܚܣܝܐ, *ch'sē*, *chasyo* (a possible derivation), *chasid* might have been its Hebrew equivalent as being similar in sound and meaning, and perhaps ultimately connected in derivation, the exactly corresponding

Possible connexion of *chasid* and *chasyo* discussed.

[1] Thus Grätz (III. p. 81) speaking of the community of goods among the Essenes writes, 'From this view springs the proverb; Every Chassid says; *Mine and thine belong to thee* (not *me*)' thus giving a turn to the expression which in its original connexion it does not at all justify. Of the existence of such a proverb I have found no traces. It certainly is not suggested in the passage of *Pirke Aboth*. Later in the volume (p. 467) Grätz tacitly alters the words to make them express, as he supposes, reciprocation or community of goods, substituting 'Thine is mine' for 'Thine is thine' in the second clause; 'The Chassid must have no property of his own, but must treat it as belonging to the Society (שלי שלך שלך שלי חסיד).' At least, as he gives no reference, I suppose that he refers to the same passage. This very expression 'mine is thine and thine is mine' does indeed occur previously in the same section, but it is applied as a formula of disparagement to the *ʿam haarets* (see below, p. 345), who expect to receive again as much as they give. In this loose way Grätz treats the whole subject. Keim (p. 294) quotes the passage correctly, but refers it nevertheless to Essene communism.

triliteral root חסא (comp. חום) not being in use in Hebrew[1]. But before we accept this explanation we have a right to demand some evidence which, if not demonstrative, is at least circumstantial, that *chasid* is used of the Essenes: and this we have seen is not forthcoming. Moreover, if the Essenes had thus inherited the name of the *Chasidim*, we should have expected that its old Greek equivalent Ἀσιδαῖοι, which is still used later than the Maccabæan era, would also have gone with it; rather than that a new Greek word Ἐσσαῖος (or Ἐσσηνός) should have been invented to take its place. But indeed the Syriac Version of the Old Testament furnishes an argument against this convertibility of the Hebrew *chasid* and the Syriac *chasyo*, which must be regarded as almost decisive.

Usage is unfavourable to this view.

The numerous passages in the Psalms, where the expressions 'My *chasidim*,' 'His *chasidim*,' occur (xxx. 5, xxxi. 24, xxxvii. 28, lii. 11, lxxix. 2, lxxxv. 9, xcvii. 10, cxvi. 15, cxxxii. 9, cxlix. 9: comp. xxxii. 6, cxlix. 1, 5), seem to have suggested the assumption of the name to the original Asidæans. But in such passages חסיד is commonly, if not universally, rendered in the Peshito not by ܚܣܝܐ, ܚܣܝܢܐ, but by a wholly different word ܙܕܝܩ *zadīk*. And again, in the Books of Maccabees the Syriac rendering for the name Ἀσιδαῖοι, *Chasidim*, is a word derived from another quite distinct root. These facts show that the Hebrew *chasid* and the Syriac *chasyo* were not practically equivalents, so that the one would suggest the other; and thus all presumption in favour of a connexion between Ἀσιδαῖος and Ἐσσαῖος is removed.

Frankel's second derivation tsanuaʿ considered.

Frankel's other derivation צנוע, *tsanūaʿ*, suggested as an equivalent to Ἐσσηνός, has found no favour with later writers, and indeed is too far removed from the Greek form to be tenable. Nor do the passages quoted by him[2] require or suggest any allusion to this sect. Thus in Mishna *Demai*, vi. 6,

---

[1] This is Hitzig's view (*Geschichte des Volkes Israel* p. 427). He maintains that "they were called '*Hasidim*' by the later Jews because the Syrian Essenes means exactly the same as '*Hasidim*.'"

[2] *Zeitschr.* pp. 455, 457; *Monatsschr.* p. 32.

we are told that the school of Hillel permits a certain license in a particular matter, but it is added, 'The צנוע of the school of Hillel followed the precept of the school of Shammai.' Here, as Frankel himself confesses, the Jerusalem Talmud knows nothing about Essenes, but explains the word by כשרי, i.e. 'upright, worthy[1]'; while elsewhere, as he allows[2], it must have this general sense. Indeed the mention of the 'school of Hillel' here seems to exclude the Essenes. In its comprehensive meaning it will most naturally be taken also in the other passage quoted by Frankel, *Kiddushin* 71 *a*, where it is stated that the pronunciation of the sacred name, which formerly was known to all, is now only to be divulged to the צנועים, i.e. the discreet, among the priests; and in fact it occurs in reference to the communication of the same mystery in the immediate context also, where it could not possibly be treated as a proper name; שצנוע ועניו ועומד בחצי ימיו, 'who is *discreet* and meek and has reached middle age,' etc.

Of other etymologies, which have been suggested, and through which it might be supposed the Essenes are mentioned by name in the Talmud, אסיא *asya*, 'a physician,' is the one which has found most favour. For the reasons given above (p. 328) this derivation seems highly improbable, and the passages quoted are quite insufficient to overcome the objections. Of these the strongest is in the Talm. Jerus. *Yoma* iii. 7, where we are told that a certain physician (אסי) offered to communicate the sacred name to R. Pinchas the son of Chama, and the latter refused on the ground that he ate of the tithes—this being regarded as a disqualification, apparently because it was inconsistent with the highest degree of ceremonial purity[3]. The same story is told with some modifications in Midrash *Qoheleth* iii. 11[4]. Here Frankel, though himself (as we have seen) adopting a different derivation of the word 'Essene,' yet supposes that this particular physician belonged to the sect,

Other supposed etymologies in the Talmud.
(1) *Asya* 'a physician,'

not supported by the passages quoted in its behalf.

---

[1] *Monatsschr.* p. 32.
[2] *Zeitschr.* p. 455.
[3] Frankel *Monatsschr.* p. 71: comp. Derenbourg p. 170 sq.
[4] See Löwy *Krit.-Talm. Lex.* s. v. Essäer.

on the sole ground that ceremonial purity is represented as a qualification for the initiation into the mystery of the Sacred Name. Löwy (l. c.) denies that the allusion to the tithes is rightly interpreted: but even supposing it to be correct, the passage is quite an inadequate basis either for Frankel's conclusion that this particular physician was an Essene, or for the derivation of the word Essene which others maintain. Again, in the statement of Talm. Jerus. *Kethuboth* ii. 3, that correct manuscripts were called books of אסי[1], the word *Asi* is generally taken as a proper name. But even if this interpretation be false, there is absolutely nothing in the context which suggests any allusion to the Essenes[2]. In like manner the passage from *Sanhedrin* 99 *b*, where a physician is mentioned[3], supports no such inference. Indeed, as this last passage relates to the family of the *Asi*, he obviously can have had no connexion with the celibate Essenes.

(2) *asah* 'to do.'

Hitherto our search for the name in the Talmud has been unsuccessful. One possibility however still remains. The talmudical writers speak of certain אנשי מעשה 'men of deeds'; and if (as some suppose) the name Essene is derived from עשה have we not here the mention which we are seeking? Frankel rejects the etymology, but presses the identification[4]. The expression, he urges, is often used in connexion with *chasidim*. It signifies 'miracle workers,' and therefore aptly describes the supernatural powers supposed to be exercised by the Essenes[5]. Thus we are informed in Mishna *Sotah* ix. 15, that 'When R. Chaninah ben Dosa died, the men of deeds ceased; when

---

[1] Urged in favour of this derivation by Herzfeld II. p. 398.

[2] The oath taken by the Essenes (Joseph. *B. J.* ii. 8. 7) συντηρήσειν... τὰ τῆς αἱρέσεως αὐτῶν βιβλία can have nothing to do with accuracy in transcribing copies, as Herzfeld (II. pp. 398, 407) seems to think. The natural meaning of συντηρεῖν, 'to keep safe or close' and so 'not to divulge' (e.g. Polyb. xxxi. 6. 5 οὐκ ἐξέφαινε τὴν ἑαυτῆς γνώμην ἀλλὰ συνετήρει παρ' ἑαυτῇ), is also the meaning suggested here by the context.

[3] The passage is adduced in support of this derivation by Derenbourg p. 175.

[4] See *Zeitschr.* p. 438, *Monatsschr.* pp. 68—70.

[5] See above, p. 330.

R. Jose Ketinta died, the chasidim ceased.' In the Jerusalem Talmud however this mishna is read, 'With the death of R. Chaninah ben Dosa and R. Jose Ketinta the chasidim ceased'; while the Gemara there explains R. Chaninah to have been one of the אנשי מעשה. Thus, Frankel concludes, 'the identity of these with חסידים becomes still more plain.' Now it seems clear that this expression אנשי מעשה in some places cannot refer to miraculous powers, but must mean 'men of practical goodness,' as for instance in *Succah* 51 *a*, 53 *a*; and being a general term expressive of moral excellence, it is naturally connected with *chasidim*, which is likewise a general term expressive of piety and goodness. Nor is there any reason why it should not always be taken in this sense. It is true that stories are told elsewhere of this R. Chaninah, which ascribe miraculous powers to him[1], and hence there is a temptation to translate it 'wonder-worker,' as applied to him. But the reason is quite insufficient. Moreover it must be observed that R. Chaninah's wife is a prominent person in the legends of his miracles reported in *Taanith* 24 *b*; and thus we need hardly stop to discuss the possible meanings of אנשי מעשה, since his claims to being considered an Essene are barred at the outset by this fact[2].

It has been asserted indeed by a recent author, that one very ancient Jewish writer distinctly adopts this derivation, and as distinctly states that the Essenes were a class of Pharisees[3]. If this were the case, Frankel's theory, though not his etymology, would receive a striking confirmation: and it is therefore important to enquire on what foundation the assertion rests.

Dr Ginsburg's authority for this statement is a passage The authority

---

[1] *Taanith* 24 *b*, *Yoma* 53 *b*; see Surenhuis *Mishna* III. p. 313.

[2] In this and similar cases it is unnecessary to consider whether the persons mentioned might have belonged to those looser disciples of Essenism, who married (see *Colossians* p. 83): because the identification is meaningless unless the strict order were intended.

[3] Ginsburg in Kitto's *Cyclopædia* s.v., I. p. 829: comp. *Essenes* pp. 22, 28.

for this derivation traced to an error.

from the *Aboth* of Rabbi Nathan, c. 37, which, as he gives it, appears conclusive; 'There are eight kinds of Pharisees... and those Pharisees who live in celibacy are Essenes.' But what are the facts of the case? *First;* This book was certainly not written by its reputed author, the R. Nathan who was vice-president under the younger Gamaliel about A.D. 140. It may possibly have been founded on an earlier treatise by that famous teacher, though even this is very doubtful: but in its present form it is a comparatively modern work. On this point all or almost all recent writers on Hebrew literature are agreed[1]. *Secondly;* Dr Ginsburg has taken the reading מחופתו עשאני, without even mentioning any alternative. Whether the words so read are capable of the meaning which he has assigned to them, may be highly questionable; but at all events this cannot have been the original reading, as the parallel passages, Babl. *Sotah* fol. 22 b, Jerus. *Sotah* v. 5, Jerus. *Berakhoth*, ix. 5, (quoted by Buxtorf and Levy, s.v. פריש), distinctly prove. In Babl. *Sotah* l. c., the corresponding expression is מה חובתי ואעשנה 'What is my duty, and I will do it,' and the passage in Jerus. *Berakhoth* l. c. is to the same effect. These parallels show that the reading מה חובתי ואעשנה must be taken also in *Aboth* c. 37, so that the passage will be rendered, 'The Pharisee *who says*, What is my duty, and I will do it.' Thus the Essenes and celibacy disappear together. *Lastly;* Inasmuch as Dr Ginsburg himself takes a wholly different view of the name Essene, connecting it either with חצן 'an apron,' or with חסיא 'pious[2],' it is difficult to see how he could translate עשאני 'Essene' (from עשא 'to do') in this passage, except on the supposition that R. Nathan was entirely ignorant of the orthography and derivation of the word Essene. Yet, if such ignorance were conceivable in so ancient a writer, his authority on this question would be absolutely worthless. But indeed

---

[1] e.g. Geiger *Zeitschrift f. Jüdische Theologie* VI. p. 20 sq.; Zunz *Gottesdienstliche Vorträge* p. 108 sq.: comp. Steinschneider *Catal. Heb. Bibl. Bodl.* col. 2032 sq. These two last references are given by Dr Ginsburg himself.

[2] *Essenes* p. 30; comp. Kitto's *Cyclopædia*, s.v. Essenes.

Dr Ginsburg would appear to have adopted this reference to R. Nathan, with the reading of the passage and the interpretation of the name, from some other writer[1]. At all events it is quite inconsistent with his own opinion as expressed previously.

But, though we have not succeeded in finding any direct mention of this sect by name in the Talmud, and all the identifications of the word Essene with diverse expressions occurring there have failed us on examination, it might still happen that allusions to them were so frequent as to leave no doubt about the persons meant. Their organisation or their practices or their tenets might be precisely described, though their name was suppressed. Such allusions Frankel finds scattered up and down the Talmud in great profusion. *Are the Essenes alluded to, though not named, in the Talmud?*

(1) He sees a reference to the Essenes in the חבורא *chăbūra* or 'Society,' which is mentioned several times in talmudical writers[2]. The *chāber* (חבר) or 'Associate' is, he supposes, a member of this brotherhood. He is obliged to confess that the word cannot always have this sense, but still he considers this to be a common designation of the Essenes. The chaber was bound to observe certain rules of ceremonial purity, and a period of probation was imposed upon him before he was admitted. With this fact Frankel connects the passage in Mishna *Chagigah* ii. 5, 6, where several degrees of ceremonial purity are specified. Having done this, he considers that he has the explanation of the statement in Josephus (*B. J.* ii. 8. 7, 10), that the Essenes were divided into four different grades or orders according to the time of their continuance in the ascetic practices demanded by the sect. *(1) The chaber or Associate.*

But in the first place there is no reference direct or indirect to the chaber, or indeed to any organisation of any kind, in the passage of *Chagigah*. It simply contemplates different degrees *A passage in Chagigah considered.*

---

[1] It is given by Landsberg in the *Allgemeine Zeitung des Judenthums* 1862, no. 33, p. 459, a reference pointed out to me by a friend.
[2] *Zeitschr.* p. 450 sq., *Monatsschr.* pp. 31, 70.

of purification as qualifying for the performance of certain Levitical rites in an ascending scale. There is no indication that these lustrations are more than temporary and immediate in their application; and not the faintest hint is given of distinct orders of men, each separated from the other by formal barriers and each demanding a period of probation before admission from the order below, as was the case with the grades of the Essene brotherhood described by Josephus. Moreover the orders in Josephus are four in number[1], while the degrees of ceremonial purity in *Chagigah* are five. Frankel indeed is inclined to maintain that only four degrees are intended in *Chagigah*, though this interpretation is opposed to the plain sense of the passage. But, even if he should be obliged to grant that the number of degrees is five[2], he will not surrender the allusion to the Essenes, but meets the difficulty by supposing (it is a pure hypothesis) that there was a fifth and highest degree of purity among the Essenes, to

---

[1] As the notices in Josephus (*B. J.* ii. 8) relating to this point have been frequently misunderstood, it may be well once for all to explain his meaning. The grades of the Essene order are mentioned in two separate notices, apparently, though not really, discordant. (1) In § 10 he says that they are 'divided into four sections according to the duration of their discipline' (διῄρηνται κατὰ χρόνον τῆς ἀσκήσεως εἰς μοίρας τέσσαρας), adding that the older members are considered to be defiled by contact with the younger, i.e. each superior grade by contact with the inferior. So far his meaning is clear. (2) In § 7 he states that one who is anxious to become a member of the sect undergoes a year's probation, submitting to discipline but 'remaining outside.' Then, 'after he has given evidence of his perseverance (μετὰ τὴν τῆς καρτερίας ἐπίδειξιν), his character is tested for two years more; and, if found worthy, he is accordingly admitted into the society.' A comparison with the other passage shows that these two years comprise the period spent in the second and third grades, each extending over a year. After passing through these three stages in three successive years, he enters upon the fourth and highest grade, thus becoming a perfect member.

It is stated by Dr Ginsburg (*Essenes* p. 12 sq., comp. Kitto's *Cyclopædia* s.v. p. 828) that the Essenes passed through eight stages 'from the beginning of the noviciate to the achievement of the highest spiritual state,' this last stage qualifying them, like Elias, to be forerunners of the Messiah. But it is a pure hypothesis that the Talmudical notices thus combined have anything to do with the Essenes; and, as I shall have occasion to point out afterwards, there is no ground for ascribing to this sect any Messianic expectations whatever.

[2] *Zeitschr.* p. 452, note.

which very few attained, and which, as I understand him, is not mentioned by Josephus on this account. But enough has already been said to show, that this passage in *Chagigah* can have no connexion with the Essenes and gives no countenance to Frankel's views.

As this artificial combination has failed, we are compelled to fall back on the notices relating to the chaber, and to ask whether these suggest any connexion with the account of the Essenes in Josephus. And the facts oblige us to answer this question in the negative. Not only do they not suggest such a connexion, but they are wholly irreconcilable with the account in the Jewish historian. This association or confraternity (if indeed the term is applicable to an organisation so loose and so comprehensive) was maintained for the sake of securing a more accurate study and a better observance of the ceremonial law. Two grades of purity are mentioned in connexion with it, designated by different names and presenting some difficulties[1], into which it is not necessary to enter here. A chaber, it would appear, was one who had entered upon the second or higher stage. For this a period of a year's probation was necessary. The chaber enrolled himself in the presence of three others who were already members of the association. This apparently was all the formality necessary: and in the case of a teacher even this was dispensed with, for being presumably acquainted with the law of things clean and unclean he was regarded as *ex officio* a chaber. The chaber was bound to keep himself from ceremonial defilements, and was thus distinguished from the *ṭam haarets* or common people[2]; but he was under no external

Difference between the chaber and the Essene.

---

[1] The entrance into the lower grade was described as 'taking כנפים' or 'wings.' The meaning of this expression has been the subject of much discussion; see e.g. Herzfeld II. p. 390 sq., Frankel *Monatsschr.* p. 33 sq.

[2] The contempt with which a chaber would look down upon the vulgar herd, the *ṭam haarets*, finds expression in the language of the Pharisees, Joh. vii. 49 ὁ ὄχλος οὗτος ὁ μὴ γινώσκων τὸν νόμον ἐπάρατοί εἰσιν. Again in Acts iv. 13, where the Apostles are described as ἰδιῶται, the expression is equivalent to *ṭam haarets*. See the passages quoted in Buxtorf *Lex.* p. 1626.

surveillance and decided for himself as to his own purity. Moreover he was, or might be a married man: for the doctors disputed whether the wives and children of an associate were not themselves to be regarded as associates[1]. In one passage, *Sanhedrin* 41 *a*, it is even assumed, as a matter of course, that a woman may be an associate (חברה). In another (*Niddah* 33 *b*)[2] there is mention of a Sadducee and even of a Samaritan as a chaber. An organisation so flexible as this has obviously only the most superficial resemblances with the rigid rules of the Essene order; and in many points it presents a direct contrast to the characteristic tenets of that sect.

(2) The Bene hakkeneseth.

(2) Having discussed Frankel's hypothesis respecting the chaber, I need hardly follow his speculations on the *Bĕnē-hakkĕneseth*, בני הכנסת, 'sons of the congregation' (*Zabim* iii. 2), in which expression probably few would discover the reference, which he finds, to the lowest of the Essene orders[3].

(3) The 'holy congregation at Jerusalem'

(3) But mention is also made of a 'holy congregation' or 'assembly' (קהלא קדישא, עדה קדישה) 'in Jerusalem'; and, following Rapoport, Frankel sees in this expression also an allusion to the Essenes[4]. The grounds for this identification are, that in one passage (*Berakhoth* 9 *b*) they are mentioned in connexion with prayer at daybreak, and in another (Midrash *Qoheleth* ix. 9) two persons are stated to belong to this 'holy congregation,' because they divided their day into three parts, devoting one-third to learning, another to prayer, and another to work. The first notice would suit the Essenes very well, though the practice mentioned was not so distinctively Essene as to afford any safe ground for this hypothesis. Of the second it should be observed, that no such division of the day is recorded of the Essenes, and indeed both Josephus (*B. J.* ii. 8. 5) and Philo (*Fragm.* p. 633) describe them as working from morning till night with the

---

[1] All these particulars and others may be gathered from *Bekhoroth* 30 *b*, Mishna *Demai* ii. 2. 3, Jerus. *Demai* ii. 3, v. 1, Tosifta *Demai* 2, *Aboth R. Nathan* c. 41.

[2] See Herzfeld II. p. 386.
[3] *Monatsschr.* p. 35.
[4] *Zeitschr.* pp. 458, 461, *Monatsschr.* pp. 32, 34.

single interruption of their mid-day meal[1]. But in fact the identification is beset with other and more serious difficulties. For this 'holy congregation' at Jerusalem is mentioned long after the second destruction of the city under Hadrian[2], when on Frankel's own showing[3] the Essene society had in all probability ceased to exist. And again certain members of it, e.g. Jose ben Meshullam (Mishna *Bekhoroth* iii. 3, vi. 1), are represented as uttering precepts respecting animals fit for sacrifice, though we have it on the authority of Josephus and Philo that the Essenes avoided the temple sacrifices altogether. The probability therefore seems to be that this 'holy congregation' was an assemblage of devout Jews who were drawn to the neighbourhood of the sanctuary after the destruction of the nation, and whose practices were regarded with peculiar reverence by the later Jews[4].

not an Essene community.

(4) Neither can we with Frankel[5] discern any reference to the Essenes in those ותיקין *Vathikin*, 'pious' or 'learned' men (whatever may be the exact sense of the word), who are mentioned in *Berakhoth* 9 *b* as praying before sunrise; because the word itself seems quite general, and the practice, though enforced among the Essenes, as we know from Josephus (*B. J.* ii. 8. 5), would be common to all devout and earnest Jews. If we are not justified in saying that these ותיקין were not Essenes, we have no sufficient grounds for maintaining that they were.

(4) The Vathikin.

(5) Nor again can we find any such reference in the זקנים הראשונים or 'primitive elders[6].' It may readily be granted that this term is used synonymously, or nearly so, with חסידים הראשונים 'the primitive chasidim'; but, as we failed to see anything more than a general expression in the one, so we are naturally led to take the other in the same sense. The passages

(5) The 'primitive elders.'

---

[1] It is added however in Midrash *Qoheleth* ix. 9 'Some say that they (the holy congregation) devoted the whole of the winter to studying the Scriptures and the summer to work.'

[2] *Monatsschr.* p. 32.
[3] *Ib.* p. 70.
[4] See Derenbourg p. 175.
[5] *Monatsschr.* p. 32.
[6] *Ib.* pp. 32, 68.

where the expression occurs (e.g. *Shabbath* 64 *b*) simply refer to the stricter observances of early times, and do not indicate any reference to a particular society or body of men.

(6) The 'morning bathers.'

(6) Again Frankel finds another reference to this sect in the טובלי שחרית *Tōblē-shachărīth*, or 'morning-bathers,' mentioned in Tosifta *Yadayim* c. 2[1]. The identity of these with the ἡμεροβαπτισταί of Greek writers seems highly probable. The latter however, though they may have had some affinities with Essene practices and tenets, are nevertheless distinguished from this sect wherever they are mentioned[2]. But the point to be observed is that, even though we should identify these Toble-shacharith with the Essenes, the passage in Tosifta *Yadayim*, so far from favouring, is distinctly adverse to Frankel's view which regards the Essenes as only a branch of Pharisees: for the two are here represented as in direct antagonism. The Toble-shacharith say, 'We grieve over you, Pharisees, because you pronounce the (sacred) Name in the morning without having bathed.' The Pharisees retort, 'We grieve over you, Toble-shacharith, because you pronounce the Name from this body in which is impurity.'

(7) The *Banaim*.

(7) In connexion with the Toble-shacharith we may consider another name, *Banāīm* (בנאים), in which also Frankel discovers an allusion to the Essenes[3]. In Mishna *Mikvaoth* ix. 6 the word is opposed to בור *bōr*, 'an ignorant or stupid person'; and this points to its proper meaning 'the builders,' i.e. the edifiers or teachers, according to the common metaphor in Biblical language. The word is discussed in *Shabbath* 114 and explained to mean 'learned.' But, because in *Mikvaoth* it is mentioned in connexion with ceremonial purity, and because in Josephus the Essenes are stated to have carried an 'axe and shovel' (*B. J.* ii. 8. 7, 9), and because moreover the Jewish historian in another place (*Vit.* 2) mentions having spent some time with one Banus a dweller in the wilderness, who lived on

---

[1] *Monatsschr.* p. 67.
[2] See below, p. 391.
[3] *Zeitschr.* p. 455.

vegetables and fruits and bathed often day and night for the sake of purity, and who is generally considered to have been an Essene; therefore Frankel holds these Banaim to have been Essenes. This is a specimen of the misplaced ingenuity which distinguishes Frankel's learned speculations on the Essenes. Josephus does not mention an 'axe *and* shovel,' but an axe only (§ 7 ἀξινάριον), which he afterwards defines more accurately as a spade (§ 9 τῇ σκαλίδι, τοιοῦτον γάρ ἐστι τὸ διδόμενον ὑπ' αὐτῶν ἀξινίδιον τοῖς νεοσυστάτοις) and which, as he distinctly states, was given them for the purpose of burying impurities out of sight (comp. Deut. xxiii. 12—14). Thus it has no connexion whatever with any 'building' implement. And again, it is true that Banus has frequently been regarded as an Essene, but there is absolutely no ground for this supposition. On the contrary the narrative of Josephus in his *Life* seems to exclude it, as I shall have occasion to show hereafter[1]. I should add that Sachs interprets Banaim 'the bathers,' regarding the explanation in *Shabbath* l. c. as a 'later accommodation[2].' This seems to me very improbable; but, if it were conceded, the Banaim would then apparently be connected not with the Essenes, but with the Hemerobaptists.

<small>Josephus misinterpreted.</small>

<small>Another derivation of Banaim.</small>

From the preceding investigation it will have appeared how little Frankel has succeeded in establishing his thesis that 'the talmudical sources are acquainted with the Essenes and make mention of them constantly[3].' We have seen not only that no instance of the name Essene has been produced, but that all those passages which are supposed to refer to them under other designations, or to describe their practices or tenets, fail us on closer examination. In no case can we feel sure that there is any direct reference to this sect, while in most cases such reference seems to be excluded by the language or the attendant circumstances[4]. Thus we are obliged to fall back upon the

<small>Results of this investigation.</small>

---

[1] See below, p. 385.
[2] *Beiträge* II. p. 199. In this derivation he is followed by Grätz (III. p. 82, 468) and Derenbourg (p. 166).
[3] *Monatsschr.* p. 31.
[4] 'The attempt to point out the Essenes in our patristic (i.e. rabbinical) literature,' says Herzfeld truly (II.

representations of Philo and Josephus. Their accounts are penned by eye-witnesses. They are direct and explicit, if not so precise or so full as we could have wished. The writers obviously consider that they are describing a distinct and exceptional phenomenon. And it would be a reversal of all established rules of historical criticism to desert the solid standing-ground of contemporary history for the artificial combinations and shadowy hypotheses which Frankel would substitute in its place.

Philo and Josephus our main authorities.

But here we are confronted with Frankel's depreciation of these ancient writers, which has been echoed by several later critics. They were interested, it is argued, in making their accounts attractive to their heathen contemporaries, and they coloured them highly for this purpose[1]. We may readily allow that they would not be uninfluenced by such a motive, but the concession does not touch the main points at issue. This aim might have led Josephus, for example, to throw into bold relief the coincidences between the Essenes and Pythagoreans; it might even have induced him to give a semi-pagan tinge to the Essene doctrine of the future state of the blessed (*B. J.* ii. 8. 11). But it entirely fails to explain those peculiarities of the sect which marked them off by a sharp line from orthodox Judaism, and which fully justify the term 'separatists' as applied to them by a recent writer. In three main features especially the portrait of the Essenes retains its distinctive character unaffected by this consideration.

Frankel's depreciation of them is unreasonable, and explains nothing.

(i) How, for instance, could this principle of accommodation have led both Philo and Josephus to lay so much stress on their divergence from Judaic orthodoxy in the matter of sacrifices? Yet this is perhaps the most crucial note of heresy which is recorded of the Essenes. What was the law to the orthodox Pharisee without the sacrifices, the temple-worship, the hierarchy? Yet the Essene declined to take any part in

(i) The avoidance of sacrifices is not accounted for.

---

p. 397), 'has led to a splendid hypothesis-hunt (*einer stattlichen Hypothesenjagd*).'

[1] *Monatsschr.* p. 31.

the sacrifices; he had priests of his own independently of the Levitical priesthood. On Frankel's hypothesis that Essenism is merely an exaggeration of pure Pharisaism, no explanation of this abnormal phenomenon can be given. Frankel does indeed attempt to meet the case by some speculations respecting the red heifer[1], which are so obviously inadequate that they have not been repeated by later writers and may safely be passed over in silence here. On this point indeed the language of Josephus is not quite explicit. He says (*Ant.* xviii. 1. 5) that, though they send offerings (ἀναθήματα) to the temple, they perform no sacrifices, and he assigns as the reason their greater strictness as regards ceremonial purity (διαφορότητι ἁγνειῶν ἃς νομίζοιεν), adding that 'for this reason being excluded from the common sanctuary (τεμενίσματος) they perform their sacrifices by themselves (ἐφ' αὑτῶν τὰς θυσίας ἐπιτελοῦσι).' Frankel therefore supposes that their only reason for abstaining from the temple sacrifices was that according to their severe notions the temple itself was profaned and therefore unfit for sacrificial worship. But if so, why should it not vitiate the offerings, as well as the sacrifices, and make them also unlawful? And indeed, where Josephus is vague, Philo is explicit. Philo (II. p. 457) distinctly states that the Essenes being more scrupulous than any in the worship of God (ἐν τοῖς μάλιστα θεραπευταὶ Θεοῦ) do not sacrifice animals (οὐ ζῶα καταθύοντες), but hold it right to dedicate their own hearts as a worthy offering (ἀλλ' ἱεροπρεπεῖς τὰς ἑαυτῶν διανοίας κατασκευάζειν ἀξιοῦντες). Thus the greater strictness, which Josephus ascribes to them, consists in the abstention from shedding blood, as a pollution in itself. And, when he speaks of their substituting private sacrifices, his own qualifications show that he does not mean the word to be taken literally. Their simple meals are their sacrifices; their refectory is their sanctuary; their president is their priest[2]. It should be added also that, though we once hear of an Essene

The notices of Josephus and Philo considered.

---

[1] *Monatsschr.* 64.
[2] *B. J.* ii. 8. 5 καθάπερ εἰς ἅγιόν τι τέμενος παραγίνονται τὸ δειπνητήριον: see also the passages quoted *Colossians* p. 89, note 3.

352   THE ESSENES.

Their statements confirmed by the doctrine of Christian Essenes.

apparently within the temple precincts (*B. J.* i. 3. 5, *Ant.* xiii. 11. 2)[1], no mention is ever made of one offering sacrifices. Thus it is clear that with the Essene it was the sacrifices which polluted the temple, and not the temple which polluted the sacrifices. And this view is further recommended by the fact that it alone will explain the position of their descendants, the Christianized Essenes, who condemned the slaughter of victims on grounds very different from those alleged in the Epistle to the Hebrews, not because they have been superseded by the Atonement, but because they are in their very nature repulsive to God; not because they have ceased to be right, but because they never were right from the beginning.

It may be said indeed, that such a view could not be maintained without impugning the authority, or at least disputing the integrity, of the Old Testament writings. The sacrificial system is so bound up with the Mosaic law, that it can only be rejected by the most arbitrary excision. This violent process however, uncritical as it is, was very likely to have been adopted by the Essenes[2]. As a matter of fact, it did recommend itself to those Judaizing Christians who reproduced many of the Essene tenets, and who both theologically and historically may be regarded as the lineal descendants of this Judaic sect[3].

The Clementine Homilies justify this doctrine by arbitrary excision of the Scriptures.

Thus in the *Clementine Homilies*, an Ebionite work which exhibits many Essene features, the chief spokesman St Peter is represented as laying great stress on the duty of distinguishing the true and the false elements in the current Scriptures (ii. 38, 51, iii. 4, 5, 10, 42, 47, 49, 50, comp. xviii. 19). The saying traditionally ascribed to our Lord, 'Show yourselves approved money-changers' ($\gamma\acute{\iota}\nu\epsilon\sigma\theta\epsilon$ $\tau\rho\alpha\pi\epsilon\zeta\hat{\iota}\tau\alpha\iota$ $\delta\acute{o}\kappa\iota\mu\omicron\iota$), is more than

---

[1] See below, p. 360.

[2] Herzfeld (II. p. 403) is unable to reconcile any rejection of the Old Testament Scriptures with the reverence paid to Moses by the Essenes (*B. J.* ii. 8. 9, 10). The Christian Essenes however did combine both these incongruous tenets by the expedient which is explained in the text. Herzfeld himself suggests that allegorical interpretation may have been employed to justify this abstention from the temple sacrifices.

[3] See *Galatians* p. 322 sq.

once quoted by the Apostle as enforcing this duty (ii. 51, iii. 50, xviii. 20). Among these false elements he places all those passages which represent God as enjoining sacrifices (iii. 45, xviii. 19). It is plain, so he argues, that God did not desire sacrifices, for did He not kill those who lusted after the taste of flesh in the wilderness? and, if the slaughter of animals was thus displeasing to Him, how could He possibly have commanded victims to be offered to Himself (iii. 45)? It is equally clear from other considerations that this was no part of God's genuine law. For instance, Christ declared that He came to fulfil every tittle of the Law; yet Christ abolished sacrifices (iii. 51). And again, the saying 'I will have mercy and not sacrifice' is a condemnation of this practice (iii. 56). The true prophet 'hates sacrifices, bloodshed, libations'; he 'extinguishes the fire of altars' (iii. 26). The frenzy of the lying soothsayer is a mere intoxication produced by the reeking fumes of sacrifice (iii. 13). When in the immediate context of these denunciations we find it reckoned among the highest achievements of man 'to know the *names of angels*, to drive away demons, to endeavour to heal diseases by charms (φαρμακίαις), and to find incantations (ἐπαοιδάς) against venomous serpents' (iii. 36); when again St Peter is made to condemn as false Essene those scriptures which speak of God swearing, and to set against them Christ's command 'Let your yea be yea' (iii. 55); we feel how thoroughly this strange production of Ebionite Christianity is saturated with Essene ideas[1].

features in this work.

---

[1] Epiphanius (*Haer*. xviii. 1, p. 38) again describes, as the account was handed down to him (ὡς ὁ εἰς ἡμᾶς ἐλθὼν περιέχει λόγος), the tenets of a Jewish sect which he calls the Nasareans αὐτὴν δὲ οὐ παρεδέχετο τὴν πεντάτευχον, ἀλλὰ ὡμολόγει μὲν τὸν Μωϋσέα, καὶ ὅτι ἐδέξατο νομοθεσίαν ἐπίστευεν, οὐ ταύτην δέ φησιν, ἀλλ' ἑτέραν. ὅθεν τὰ μὲν πάντα φυλάττουσι τῶν 'Ιουδαίων 'Ιουδαῖοι ὄντες, θυσίαν δὲ οὐκ ἔθυον οὔτε ἐμψύχων μετεῖχον, ἀλλὰ ἀθέμιτον ἦν παρ' αὐτοῖς τὸ κρεῶν μεταλαμβάνειν ἢ θυσιάζειν αὐτοῖς. ἔφασκον γὰρ πεπλάσθαι ταῦτα τὰ βιβλία καὶ μηδὲν τούτων ὑπὸ τῶν πατέρων γεγενῆσθαι. Here we have in combination all the features which we are seeking. The cradle of this sect is placed by him in Gilead and Bashan and 'the regions beyond the Jordan.' He uses similar language also (xxx. 18, p. 142) in describing the Ebionites, whom he places in much the same localities (naming Moab also), and

354   THE ESSENES.

(ii) The Essene worship of the Sun cannot be explained away.

(ii) Nor again is Frankel successful in explaining the Essene prayers to the sun by rabbinical practices[1]. Following Rapoport, he supposes that Josephus and Philo refer to the beautiful hymn of praise for the creation of light and the return of day, which forms part of the morning-prayer of the Jews to the present time[2], and which seems to be enjoined in the Mishna itself[3]; and this view has been adopted by many subsequent writers. But the language of Josephus is not satisfied by this explanation. For he says plainly (*B. J.* ii. 8. 5) that they addressed prayers to the sun[4], and it is difficult to suppose that he has wantonly introduced a dash of paganism into his picture; nor indeed was there any adequate motive for his doing so. Similarly Philo relates of the Therapeutes (*Vit. Cont.* 11, II. p. 485), that they 'stand with their faces and their whole body towards the East, and when they see that the sun is risen, holding out their hands to heaven they pray for a happy day (εὐημερίαν) and for truth and for keen vision of reason (ὀξυωπίαν λογισμοῦ).' And here again it is impossible to overlook the confirmation which these accounts receive from the history of certain Christian heretics deriving their descent from this Judaic sect. Epiphanius (*Haer.* xix. 2, xx. 3, pp. 40 sq., 47) speaks of a sect called the Sampsæans or 'Sun-worshippers[5],' as existing in his own time in Peræa on the borders of Moab and on the shores of the Dead Sea. He describes them as a remnant of the Ossenes (i.e. Essenes), who have accepted a spurious form of Christianity and are neither Jews nor Christians. This debased Christianity which they adopted is embodied, he tells us, in the pretended revelation of the Book of Elchasai, and dates from the time of Trajan[6]. Elsewhere (xxx. 3, p. 127) he seems to use the terms Sampsæan,

The Sampsæans are an Essene sect,

---

whose Essene features are unmistakeable: οὔτε γὰρ δέχονται τὴν πεντάτευχον Μωϋσέως ὅλην ἀλλά τινα ῥήματα ἀποβάλλουσιν. ὅταν δὲ αὐτοῖς εἴπῃς περὶ ἐμψύχων βρώσεως κ.τ.λ. These parallels will speak for themselves.
[1] *Zeitschr.* p. 458.

[2] See Ginsburg *Essenes* p. 69 sq.
[3] *Berakhoth* i. 4; see Derenbourg, p. 169 sq.
[4] See *Colossians* p. 87, note 1.
[5] See *Colossians* p. 88.
[6] See above, p. 80 sq., and below, p. 392.

Ossene, and Elchasaite as synonymous (παρὰ τοῖς Σαμψηνοῖς καὶ Ὀσσηνοῖς καὶ Ἐλκεσσαίοις καλουμένοις). Now we happen to know something of this book of Elchasai, not only from Epiphanius himself (xix. 1 sq., p. 40 sq., xxx. 17, p. 141), but also from Hippolytus (*Haer.* ix. 13 sq.) who describes it at considerable length. From these accounts it appears that the principal feature in the book was the injunction of frequent bathings for the remission of sins (Hipp. *Haer.* ix. 13, 15 sq.). We are likewise told that it 'anathematizes immolations and sacrifices (θυσίας καὶ ἱερουργίας) as being alien to God and certainly not offered to God by tradition from (ἐκ) the fathers and the law,' while at the same time it 'says that men ought to pray there at Jerusalem, where the altar was and the sacrifices (were offered), prohibiting the eating of flesh which exists among the Jews, and the rest (of their customs), and the altar and the fire, as being alien to God' (Epiph. *Haer.* xix. 3, p. 42). Notwithstanding, we are informed that the sect retained the rite of circumcision, the observance of the sabbath, and other practices of the Mosaic law (Hipp. *Haer.* ix. 14; Epiph. *Haer.* xix. 5, p. 43, comp. xxx. 17, p. 141). This inconsistency is explained by a further notice in Epiphanius (l. c.) that they treated the Scriptures in the same way as the Nasaræans[1]; that is, they submitted them to a process of arbitrary excision, as recommended in the Clementine Homilies, and thus rejected as falsifications all statements which did not square with their own theory. Hippolytus also speaks of the Elchasaites as studying astrology and magic, and as practising charms and incantations on the sick and the demoniacs (§ 14). Moreover in two formularies, one of expiation, another of purification, which this father has extracted from the book, invocation is made to 'the holy spirits and the angels of prayer' (§ 15, comp. Epiph. *Haer.* xix. 1). It should be added that the word Elchasai probably signifies the 'hidden power'[2]; while the book

as appears from their sacred book of Elchasai.

Its Essene peculiarities.

---

[1] See above, p. 352, note 2.
[2] See above, p. 81, note 2. For another derivation see below, p. 393, note 1.

itself directed that its mysteries should be guarded as precious pearls, and should not be communicated to the world at large, but only to the faithful few (Hipp. *Haer.* ix. 15, 17). It is hardly necessary to call attention to the number of Essene features which are here combined[1]. I would only remark that the value of the notice is not at all diminished, but rather enhanced, by the uncritical character of Epiphanius' work; for this very fact prevents us from ascribing the coincidences, which here reveal themselves, to this father's own invention.

In this heresy we have plainly the dregs of Essenism, which has only been corrupted from its earlier and nobler type by the admixture of a spurious Christianity. But how came the Essenes to be called Sampsæans? What was the original meaning of this outward reverence which they paid to the sun? Did they regard it merely as the symbol of Divine illumination, just as Philo frequently treats it as a type of God, the centre of all light (e. g. *de Somn.* i. 13 sq., I. p. 631 sq.), and even calls the heavenly bodies 'visible and sensible gods' (*de Mund. Op.* 7, I. p. 6)[2]? Or did they honour the light, as the pure ethereal element in contrast to gross terrestrial matter, according to a suggestion of a recent writer[3]? Whatever may have been the motive of this reverence, it is strangely repugnant to the spirit of orthodox Judaism. In Ezek. viii. 16 it is denounced as an abomination, that men shall turn towards the east and worship the sun; and accordingly in *Berakhoth* 7 *a* a saying of R. Meir is reported to the effect that God is angry when the sun appears and the kings of the East and the West prostrate themselves before this luminary[4]. We cannot fail therefore to recognise

Doubtful bearing of this Sun-worship.

The practice repugnant to Jewish orthodoxy.

---

[1] Celibacy however is not one of these: comp. Epiphan. *Haer.* xix. 1 (p. 40) ἀπεχθάνεται δὲ τῇ παρθενίᾳ, μισεῖ δὲ τὴν ἐγκράτειαν, ἀναγκάζει δὲ γάμον. In this respect they departed from the original principles of Essenism, alleging, as it would appear, a special revelation (ὡς δῆθεν ἀποκαλύψεως) in justification. In like manner marriage is commended in the Clementine Homilies.

[2] The important place which the heavenly bodies held in the system of Philo, who regarded them as animated beings, may be seen from Gfrörer's *Philo* I. p. 349 sq.

[3] Keim I. p. 289.

[4] See Wiesner *Schol. zum Babyl. Talm.* I. pp. 18, 20.

the action of some foreign influence in this Essene practice—whether Greek or Syrian or Persian, it will be time to consider hereafter.

(iii) On the subject of marriage again, talmudical and rabbinical notices contribute nothing towards elucidating the practices of this sect. Least of all do they point to any affinity between the Essenes and the Pharisees. The nearest resemblance, which Frankel can produce, to any approximation in this respect is an injunction in Mishna *Kethuboth* v. 8 respecting the duties of the husband in providing for the wife in case of his separating from her, and this he ascribes to Essene influences[1]; but this mishna does not express any approval of such a separation. The direction seems to be framed entirely in the interests of the wife: nor can I see that it is at all inconsistent, as Frankel urges, with Mishna *Kethuboth* vii. 1 which allows her to claim a divorce under such circumstances. But however this may be, Essene and Pharisaic opinion stand generally in the sharpest contrast to each other with respect to marriage. The talmudic writings teem with passages implying not only the superior sanctity, but even the imperative duty, of marriage. The words 'Be fruitful and multiply' (Gen. i. 28) were regarded not merely as a promise, but as a command which was binding on all. It is a maxim of the Talmud that 'Any Jew who has not a wife is no man' (אינו אדם), *Yebamoth* 63 a. The fact indeed is so patent, that any accumulation of examples would be superfluous, and I shall content myself with referring to *Pesachim* 113 a, b, as fairly illustrating the doctrine of orthodox Judaism on this point[2]. As this question affects the whole framework not only of religious, but also of social life, the

(iii) The depreciation of marriage not accounted for.

---

[1] *Monatsschr.* p. 37.

[2] Justin Martyr more than once taunts the Jewish rabbis with their reckless encouragement of polygamy. See *Dial.* 134, p. 363 D; τοῖς ἀσυνέτοις καὶ τυφλοῖς διδασκάλοις ὑμῶν, οἵτινες καὶ μέχρι νῦν καὶ τέσσαρας καὶ πέντε ἔχειν ὑμᾶς γυναῖκας ἕκαστον συγχωροῦσι· καὶ ἐὰν εὔμορφόν τις ἰδὼν ἐπιθυμήσῃ αὐτῆς κ.τ.λ., *ib.* 141, p. 371 A, B, ὁποῖον πράττουσιν οἱ ἀπὸ τοῦ γένους ὑμῶν ἄνθρωποι, κατὰ πᾶσαν γῆν ἔνθα ἂν ἐπιδημήσωσιν ἢ προσπεμφθῶσιν ἀγόμενοι ὀνόματι γάμου γυναῖκας κ.τ.λ., with Otto's note on the first passage.

358   THE ESSENES.

antagonism between the Essene and the Pharisee in a matter so vital could not be overlooked.

(iv) The Essene practice of magic still a difficulty.

(iv) Nor again is it probable that the magical rites and incantations which are so prominent in the practice of the Essenes would, as a rule, have been received with any favour by the Pharisaic Jew. In Mishna *Pesachim* iv. 9 (comp. *Berakhoth* 10 *b*) it is mentioned with approval that Hezekiah put away a 'book of healings'; where doubtless the author of the tradition had in view some volume of charms ascribed to Solomon, like those which apparently formed part of the esoteric literature of the Essenes[1]. In the same spirit in Mishna *Sanhedrin* xi. 1 R. Akiba shuts out from the hope of eternal life any 'who read profane or foreign (i. e. perhaps, apocryphal) books, and who mutter over a wound' the words of Exod. xv. 26. On this point of difference however no great stress can be laid. Though the nobler teachers among the orthodox Jews set themselves steadfastly against the introduction of magic, they were unable to resist the inpouring tide of superstition. In the middle of the second century Justin Martyr alludes to exorcists and magicians among the Jews, as though they were neither few nor obscure[2]. Whether these were a remnant of Essene Judaism, or whether such practices had by this time spread throughout the whole body, it is impossible to say; but the fact of their existence prevents us from founding an argument on the use of magic, as an absolutely distinctive feature of Essenism.

General result.

Other divergences also have been enumerated[3]; but, as these do not for the most part involve any great principles, and refer only to practical details in which much fluctuation was possible, they cannot under any circumstances be taken as crucial tests, and I have not thought it worth while to discuss them. But the antagonisms on which I have dwelt will tell their own tale. In three respects more especially, in the avoid-

---

[1] See *Colossians* p. 91, note 2.
[2] *Dial.* 85, p. 311 c, ἤδη μέντοι οἱ ἐξ ὑμῶν ἐπορκισταὶ τῇ τέχνῃ, ὥσπερ καὶ τὰ ἔθνη, χρώμενοι ἐξορκίζουσι καὶ θυμιάμασι καὶ καταδέσμοις χρῶνται.
[3] Herzfeld II. p. 392 sq.

ance of marriage, in the abstention from the temple sacrifices, and (if the view which I have adopted be correct) in the outward reverence paid to the sun, we have seen that there is an impassable gulf between the Essenes and the Pharisees. No known influences within the sphere of Judaism proper will serve to account for the position of the Essenes in these respects; and we are obliged to look elsewhere for an explanation.

It was shown above that the investigations of Frankel and others failed to discover in the talmudical writings a single reference to the Essenes, which is at once direct and indisputable. It has now appeared that they have also failed (and this is the really important point) in showing that the ideas and practices generally considered characteristic of the Essenes are recognised and incorporated in these representative books of Jewish orthodoxy; and thus the hypothesis that Essenism was merely a type, though an exaggerated type, of pure Judaism falls to the ground. *Frankel has failed in establishing his point.*

Some affinities indeed have been made out by Frankel and by those who have anticipated or followed him. But these are exactly such as we might have expected. Two distinct features combine to make up the portrait of the Essene. The Judaic element is quite as prominent in this sect as the non-Judaic. It could not be more strongly emphasized than in the description given by Josephus himself. In everything therefore which relates to the strictly Judaic side of their tenets and practices, we should expect to discover not only affinities, but even close affinities, in talmudic and rabbinic authorities. And this is exactly what, as a matter of fact, we do find. The Essene rules respecting the observance of the sabbath, the rites of lustration, and the like, have often very exact parallels in the writings of more orthodox Judaism. But I have not thought it necessary to dwell on these coincidences, because they may well be taken for granted, and my immediate purpose did not require me to emphasize them. *Affinities between Essenes and Pharisees confined to the Judaic side.*

And again; it must be remembered that the separation

The divergence of the Essenes from the Pharisees gradual.

between Pharisee and Essene cannot always have been so great as it appears in the Apostolic age. Both sects apparently arose out of one great movement, of which the motive was the avoidance of pollution[1]. The divergence therefore must have been gradual. At the same time, it does not seem a very profitable task to write a hypothetical history of the growth of Essenism, where the data are wanting; and I shall therefore abstain from the attempt. Frankel indeed has not been deterred by this difficulty; but he has been obliged to assume his data by postulating that such and such a person, of whom notices are preserved, was an Essene, and thence inferring the character of Essenism at the period in question from his recorded sayings or doings. But without attempting any such reconstruction of history, we may fairly allow that there must have been a gradual development; and consequently in the earlier stages of its growth we should not expect to find that sharp antagonism between the two sects, which the principles of the Essenes when fully matured would involve.

Hence the possibility of their appearing in the records of orthodox Judaism.

If therefore it should be shown that the talmudical and rabbinical writings here and there preserve with approval the sayings of certain Essenes, this fact would present no difficulty. At present however no decisive example has been produced; and the discoveries of Jellinek for instance[2], who traces the influence of this sect in almost every page of *Pirke Aboth*, can only be regarded as another illustration of the extravagance with which the whole subject has been treated by a large section of modern Jewish writers. More to the point is a notice of an earlier Essene preserved in Josephus himself. We learn from this historian that one Judas, a member of the sect, who had prophesied the death of Antigonus, saw this prince 'passing by through the temple[3],'

---

[1] See *Colossians* p. 91 sq.

[2] *Orient* 1849, pp. 489, 537, 553.

[3] *B. J.* i. 3. 5 παριόντα διὰ τοῦ ἱεροῦ. In the parallel narrative, *Ant.* xii. 11. 2, the expression is παριόντα τὸ ἱερόν, which does not imply so much; but the less precise notice must be interpreted by the more precise. Even then however it is not directly stated that Judas himself was within the temple area.

when his prophecy was on the point of fulfilment (about B.C. 110). At this moment Judas is represented as sitting in the midst of his disciples, instructing them in the science of prediction. The expression quoted would seem to imply that he was actually teaching within the temple area. Thus he would appear not only as mixing in the ordinary life of the Jews, but also as frequenting the national sanctuary. But even supposing this to be the right explanation of the passage, it will not present any serious difficulty. Even at a later date, when (as we may suppose) the principles of the sect had stiffened, the scruples of the Essene were directed, if I have rightly interpreted the account of Josephus, rather against the sacrifices than against the locality[1]. The temple itself, independently of its accompaniments, would not suggest any offence to his conscience.

Nor again, is it any obstacle to the view which is here maintained, that the Essenes are regarded with so much sympathy by Philo and Josephus themselves. Even though the purity of Judaism might have been somewhat sullied in this sect by the admixture of foreign elements, this fact would attract rather than repel an eclectic like Philo, and a latitudinarian like Josephus. The former, as an Alexandrian, absorbed into his system many and diverse elements of heathen philosophy, Platonic, Stoic, and Pythagorean. The latter, though professedly a Pharisee, lost no opportunity of ingratiating himself with his heathen conquerors, and would not be unwilling to gratify their curiosity respecting a society with whose fame, as we infer from the notice of Pliny, they were already acquainted.

The approbation of Philo and Josephus is no evidence of orthodoxy.

But if Essenism owed the features which distinguished it from Pharisaic Judaism to an alien admixture, whence were these foreign influences derived? From the philosophers of Greece or from the religious mystics of the East? On this point recent writers are divided.

What was the foreign element in Essenism?

[1] See *Colossians* p. 89, and above, p. 350 sq.

THE ESSENES.

Theory of Neopythagorean influence.

Those who trace the distinctive characteristics of the sect to Greece, regard it as an offshoot of the Neopythagorean School grafted on the stem of Judaism. This solution is suggested by the statement of Josephus, that 'they practise the mode of life which among the Greeks was introduced (καταδεδειγμένη) by Pythagoras[1].' It is thought to be confirmed by the strong resemblances which as a matter of fact are found to exist between the institutions and practices of the two.

Statement of the theory by Zeller.

This theory, which is maintained also by other writers, as for instance by Baur and Herzfeld, has found its ablest and most persistent advocate in Zeller, who draws out the parallels with great force and precision. 'The Essenes,' he writes, 'like the Pythagoreans, desire to attain a higher sanctity by an ascetic life; and the abstentions, which they impose on themselves for this end, are the same with both. They reject animal food and bloody sacrifices; they avoid wine, warm baths, and oil for anointing; they set a high value on celibate life: or, so far as they allow marriage, they require that it be restricted to the one object of procreating children. Both wear only white garments and consider linen purer than wool. Washings and purifications are prescribed by both, though for the Essenes they have a yet higher significance as religious acts. Both prohibit oaths and (what is more) on the same grounds. Both find their social ideal in those institutions, which indeed the Essenes alone set themselves to realise—in a corporate life with entire community of goods, in sharply defined orders of rank, in the unconditional submission of all the members to their superiors, in a society carefully barred from without, into which new members are received only after a severe probation of several years, and from which the unworthy are inexorably excluded. Both require a strict initiation, both desire to maintain a traditional doctrine inviolable; both pay the highest respect to the men from whom it was derived, as

---

[1] *Ant.* xv. 10. 4.

instruments of the deity: yet both also love figurative clothing for their doctrines, and treat the old traditions as symbols of deeper truths, which they must extract from them by means of allegorical explanation. In order to prove the later form of teaching original, newly-composed writings were unhesitatingly forged by the one as by the other, and fathered upon illustrious names of the past. Both parties pay honour to divine powers in the elements, both invoke the rising sun, both seek to withdraw everything unclean from his sight, and with this view give special directions, in which they agree as well with each other as with older Greek superstition, in a remarkable way. For both the belief in intermediate beings between God and the world has an importance which is higher in proportion as their own conception of God is purer; both appear not to have disdained magic; yet both regard the gift of prophecy as the highest fruit of wisdom and piety, which they pique themselves on possessing in their most distinguished members. Finally, both agree (along with the dualistic character of their whole conception of the world...) in their tenets respecting the origin of the soul, its relation to the body, and the life after death[1]...'

This array of coincidences is formidable, and thus skilfully marshalled might appear at first sight invincible. But a closer examination detracts from its value. In the first place the two distinctive characteristics of the Pythagorean philosophy are wanting to the Essenes. The Jewish sect did not believe in the transmigration of souls; and the doctrine of numbers, at least so far as our information goes, had no place in their system. Yet these constitute the very essence of the Pythagorean teaching. In the next place several of the coincidences are more apparent than real. Thus for instance the demons who in the Pythagorean system held an intermediate place between the Supreme God and man, and were the result of a compromise between polytheism and philosophy, have no near

Absence of distinctive Pythagorean features in the Essenes.

The coincidences are in some cases only apparent,

---

[1] Zeller *Philosophie der Griechen* Th. III. Abth. 2, p. 281.

relation to the angelology of the Essenes, which arose out of a wholly different motive. Nor again can we find distinct traces among the Pythagoreans of any such reverence for the sun as is ascribed to the Essenes, the only notice which is adduced having no prominence whatever in its own context, and referring to a rule which would be dictated by natural decency and certainly was not peculiar to the Pythagoreans[1]. When these imperfect and (for the purpose) valueless resemblances have been subtracted, the only basis on which the theory of a direct affiliation can rest is withdrawn. All the remaining coincidences are unimportant. Thus the respect paid to founders is not confined to any one sect or any one age. The reverence of the Essenes for Moses, and the reverence of the Pythagoreans for Pythagoras, are indications of a common humanity, but not of a common philosophy. And again the forgery of supposititious documents is unhappily not the badge of any one school. The Solomonian books of the Essenes, so far as we can judge from the extant notices, were about as unlike the tracts ascribed to Pythagoras and his disciples by the Neopythagoreans as two such forgeries could well be. All or nearly all that remains in common to the Greek school and the Jewish sect after these deductions is a certain similarity in the type of life.

and in others do not suggest any historical connexion.

But granted that two bodies of men each held an esoteric teaching of their own, they would secure it independently in a similar way, by a recognised process of initiation, by a solemn form of oath, by a rigid distinction of orders. Granted also, that they both maintained the excellence of an ascetic life, their asceticism would naturally take the same form; they would avoid wine and flesh; they would abstain from anointing themselves with oil; they would depreciate, and perhaps

---

[1] Diog. Laert. viii. 17; see Zeller l. c. p. 282, note 5. The precept in question occurs among a number of insignificant details, and has no special prominence given to it. In the *Life of Apollonius* by Philostratus (e.g. vi. 10) considerable stress is laid on the worship of the sun (Zeller l. c. p. 137, note 6); but the syncretism of this late work detracts from its value as representing Pythagorean doctrine.

altogether prohibit, marriage. Unless therefore the historical conditions are themselves favourable to a direct and immediate connexion between the Pythagoreans and the Essenes, this theory of affiliation has little to recommend it.

And a closer examination must pronounce them to be most unfavourable. Chronology and geography alike present serious obstacles to any solution which derives the peculiarities of the Essenes from the Pythagoreans. *Twofold objection to this theory.*

(i) The priority of time, if it can be pleaded on either side, must be urged in favour of the Essenes. The Pythagoreans as a philosophical school entirely disappear from history before the middle of the fourth century before Christ. The last Pythagoreans were scholars of Philolaus and Eurytus, the contemporaries of Socrates and Plato[1]. For nearly two centuries after their extinction we hear nothing of them. Here and there persons like Diodorus of Aspendus are satirised by the Attic poets of the middle comedy as 'pythagorizers,' in other words, as total abstainers and vegetarians[2]; but the philosophy had wholly died or was fast dying out. This is the universal testimony of ancient writers. It is not till the first century before Christ, that we meet with any distinct traces of a revival. In Alexander Polyhistor[3], a younger contemporary of Sulla, for the first time we find references to certain writings, which would seem to have emanated from this incipient Neopythagoreanism, rather than from the elder school of Pythagoreans. And a little later Cicero commends his friend Nigidius Figulus as one specially raised up to revive the extinct philosophy[4]. *(i) Chronological facts are adverse.*

Disappearance of the Pythagoreans.

---

[1] Zeller l. c. p. 68 (comp. I. p. 242). While disputing Zeller's position, I have freely made use of his references. It is impossible not to admire the mastery of detail and clearness of exposition in this work, even when the conclusions seem questionable.

[2] Athen. iv. p. 161, Diog. Laert. viii. 37. See the index to Meineke *Fragm. Com.* s. vv. πυθαγορικός, etc. The words commonly used by these satirists are πυθαγορίζειν, πυθαγοριστής, πυθαγορισμός. The persons so satirised were probably in many cases not more Pythagoreans than modern teetotallers are Rechabites.

[3] Diog. Laert. viii. 24 sq.; see Zeller l. c. p. 74—78.

[4] Cic. *Tim.* I 'sic judico, post illos nobiles Pythagoreos quorum disci-

But so slow or so chequered was its progress, that a whole century after Seneca can still speak of the school as practically defunct[1]. Yet long before this the Essenes formed a compact, well-organized, numerous society with a peculiar system of doctrine and a definite rule of life. We have seen that Pliny the elder speaks of this celibate society as having existed 'through thousands of ages[2].' This is a gross exaggeration, but it must at least be taken to imply that in Pliny's time the origin of the Essenes was lost in the obscurity of the past, or at least seemed so to those who had not access to special sources of information. If, as I have given reasons for supposing[3], Pliny's authority in this passage is the same Alexander Polyhistor to whom I have just referred, and if this particular statement, however exaggerated in expression, is derived from him, the fact becomes still more significant. But on any showing the priority in time is distinctly in favour of the Essenes as against the Neopythagoreans.

Priority of Essenism to Neopythagoreanism.

And accordingly we find that what is only a tendency in the Neopythagoreans is with the Essenes an avowed principle and a definite rule of life. Such for instance is the case with celibacy, of which Pliny says that it has existed as an institution among the Essenes *per saeculorum millia*, and which is a chief corner-stone of their practical system. The Pythagorean notices (whether truly or not, it is unimportant for my purpose to enquire) speak of Pythagoras as having a wife and a daughter[4]. Only at a late date do we find the attempt to represent their founder in another light; and if virginity is ascribed to Apollonius of Tyana, the great Pythagorean of the

The Essene tenets developed more than the Neopythagorean.

---

plina *extincta est* quodammodo, cum aliquot saecula in Italia Siciliaque viguisset, hunc exstitisse qui illam *renovaret*.'

[1] Sen. *N. Q.* vii. 32 'Pythagorica illa invidiosa turbae schola praeceptorem non invenit.'

[2] *N.H.* v. 15. The passage is quoted *Colossians* p. 85, note 3. The point of time, at which Josephus thinks it necessary to insert an account of the Essenes as already flourishing (*Ant.* xiii. 5. 9), is prior to the revival of the Neopythagorean school. How much earlier the Jewish sect arose, we are without data for determining.

[3] See *Colossians* p. 83, note 1.

[4] Diog. Laert. viii. 42.

first Christian century, in the fictitious biography of Philostratus[1], this representation is plainly due to the general plan of the novelist, whose hero is perhaps intended to rival the Founder of Christianity, and whose work is saturated with Christian ideas. In fact virginity can never be said to have been a Pythagorean principle, though it may have been an exalted ideal of some not very early adherents of the school. And the same remark applies to other resemblances between the Essene and Neopythagorean teaching. The clearness of conception and the definiteness of practice are in almost every instance on the side of the Essenes; so that, looking at the comparative chronology of the two, it will appear almost inconceivable that they can have derived their principles from the Neopythagoreans.

(ii) But the geographical difficulty also, which this theory of affiliation involves, must be added to the chronological. The home of the Essene sect is allowed on all hands to have been on the eastern borders of Palestine, the shores of the Dead Sea, a region least of all exposed to the influences of Greek philosophy. It is true that we find near Alexandria a closely allied school of Jewish recluses, the Therapeutes; and, as Alexandria may have been the home of Neopythagoreanism, a possible link of connexion is here disclosed. But, as Zeller himself has pointed out, it is not among the Therapeutes, but among the Essenes, that the principles in question appear fully developed and consistently carried out[2]; and therefore, if there be a relation of paternity between Essene and Therapeute, the latter must be derived from the former and not conversely. How then can we suppose this influence of Neopythagoreanism brought to bear on a Jewish community in the south-eastern border of Palestine? Zeller's answer is as follows[3]. Judæa was for more than a hundred and fifty years before the Macca-

(ii) Geographical difficulties in the theory.

---

[1] *Vit. Apol.* i. 15 sq. At the same time Philostratus informs us that the conduct of his hero in this respect had been differently represented by others.
[2] l. c. p. 288 sq.
[3] l. c. p. 290 sq.

bean period under the sovereignty first of the Egyptian and then of the Syrian Greeks. We know that at this time Hellenizing influences did infuse themselves largely into Judaism: and what more natural than that among these the Pythagorean philosophy and discipline should have recommended itself to a section of the Jewish people? It may be said in reply, that at all events the special locality of the Essenes is the least favourable to such a solution: but, without pressing this fact, Zeller's hypothesis is open to two serious objections which combined seem fatal to it, unsupported as it is by any historical notice. First, this influence of Pythagoreanism is assumed to have taken place at the very time when the Pythagorean school was practically extinct: and secondly, it is supposed to have acted upon that very section of the Jewish community, which was the most vigorous advocate of national exclusiveness and the most averse to Hellenizing influences.

The foreign element of Essenism to be sought in the East,

It is not therefore to Greek but to Oriental influences that considerations of time and place, as well as of internal character, lead us to look for an explanation of the alien elements in Essene Judaism. And have we not here also the account of any real coincidences which may exist between Essenism and Neopythagoreanism? We should perhaps be hardly more justified in tracing Neopythagoreanism directly to Essenism than conversely (though, if we had no other alternative, this would appear to be the more probable solution of the two): but were not both alike due to substantially the same influences acting in different degrees? I think it will hardly be denied

to which also Pythagoreanism may have been indebted.

that the characteristic features of Pythagoreanism, and especially of Neopythagoreanism, which distinguish it from other schools of Greek philosophy, are much more Oriental in type, than Hellenic. The asceticism, the magic, the mysticism, of the sect all point in the same direction. And history moreover contains indications that such was the case. There seems to be sufficient ground for the statement that Pythagoras himself was indebted to intercourse with the Egyptians, if not with more strictly Oriental nations, for some leading ideas of his system. But, however this may be, the fact that in the legendary accounts, which the Neopythagoreans invented to do honour to the founder of the school, he is represented as taking lessons from the Chaldeans, Persians, Brahmins, and others, may be taken as an evidence that their own philosophy at all events was partially derived from eastern sources[1].

But, if the alien elements of Essenism were borrowed not so much from Greek philosophy as from Oriental mysticism, to what nation or what religion was it chiefly indebted? To this question it is difficult, with our very imperfect knowledge of the East at the Christian era, to reply with any confidence. Yet there is one system to which we naturally look, as furnishing the most probable answer. The Medo-Persian religion supplies just those elements which distinguish the tenets and practices of the Essenes from the normal type of Judaism. (1) First; we have here a very definite form of dualism, which exercised the greatest influence on subsequent Gnostic sects, and of which Manicheism, the most matured development of dualistic doctrine in connexion with Christianity, was the ultimate fruit. For though dualism may not represent the oldest theology of the Zend-Avesta in its unadulterated form, yet long before the era of which we are speaking it had become the fundamental principle of the Persian religion. (2) Again; the Zoroastrian symbolism of light, and consequent worship of the sun as the fountain of light, will explain those anomalous notices of the Essenes in which they are represented as paying reverence to this luminary[a]. (3) Moreover; the 'worship of

Resemblances to Parsism.

(i) Dualism.

(ii) Sun-worship.

(iii) Angelolatry.

---

[1] See the references in Zeller I. p. 218 sq.; comp. III. 2, p. 67.

[a] Keim *Geschichte Jesu von Nazara* I. p. 303) refers to Tac. *Hist.* iii. 24 'Undique clamor; et *orientem solem* (ita in Syria mos est) tertiani salutavere,' as illustrating this Essene practice. The commentators on Tacitus quote a similar notice of the Parthians in Herodian iv. 15 ἅμα δὲ ἡλίῳ ἀνίσχοντι ἐφάνη ᾽Αρτάβανος σὺν μεγίστῳ πλήθει στρατοῦ· ἀσπασάμενοι δὲ τὸν ἥλιον, ὡς ἔθος αὐτοῖς, οἱ βάρβαροι κ.τ.λ.

angels' in the Essene system has a striking parallel in the invocations of spirits, which form a very prominent feature in the ritual of the Zend-Avesta. And altogether their angelology is illustrated, and not improbably was suggested, by the doctrine of intermediate beings concerned in the government of nature and of man, such as the Amshaspands, which is an integral part of the Zoroastrian system[1]. (4) And once more; the magic, which was so attractive to the Essene, may have received its impulse from the priestly caste of Persia, to whose world-wide fame this form of superstition is indebted for its name. (5) If to these parallels I venture also to add the intense striving after purity, which is the noblest feature in the Persian religion, I do so, not because the Essenes might not have derived this impulse from a higher source, but because this feature was very likely to recommend the Zoroastrian system to their favourable notice, and because also the particular form which the zeal for purity took among them was at all events congenial to the teaching of the Zend-Avesta, and may not have been altogether free from its influences.

(iv) Magic.

(v) Striving after purity.

Other coincidences accidental.

I have preferred dwelling on these broader resemblances, because they are much more significant than any mere coincidence of details, which may or may not have been accidental. Thus for instance the magi, like the Essenes, wore white garments, and eschewed gold and ornaments; they practised frequent lustrations; they avoided flesh, living on bread and cheese or on herbs and fruits; they had different orders in their society; and the like[2]. All these, as I have already

---

[1] See e.g. *Vendidad* Farg. xix; and the liturgical portions of the book are largely taken up with invocations of these intermediate beings. Some extracts are given in Davies' *Colossians* p. 146 sq.

[2] Hilgenfeld (*Zeitschrift* x. p. 99 sq.) finds coincidences even more special than these. He is answered by Zeller (III. 2, p. 276), but defends his position again (*Zeitschrift* xi. p. 347 sq.), though with no great success. Among other points of coincidence Hilgenfeld remarks on the axe (Jos. *B. J.* ii. 8. 7) which was given to the novices among the Essenes, and connects it with the ἀξινομαντεία (Plin. *N. H.* xxxvi. 19) of the magi. Zeller con-

remarked, may be the independent out-growth of the same temper and direction of conduct, and need not imply any direct historical connexion. Nor is there any temptation to press such resemblances; for even without their aid the general connexion seems to be sufficiently established[1].

But it is said, that the history of Persia does not favour the hypothesis of such an influence as is here assumed. The destruction of the Persian empire by Alexander, argues Zeller[2], and the subsequent erection of the Parthian domination on its ruins, must have been fatal to the spread of Zoroastrianism. From the middle of the third century before Christ, when the Parthian empire was established, till towards the middle of the third century of our era, when the Persian monarchy and religion were once more restored[3], its influence must have been reduced within the narrowest limits. But does analogy really suggest such an inference? Does not the history of the Jews themselves show that the religious influence of a people on the world at large may begin just where its national life ends? The very dispersion of Zoroastrianism, consequent on the fall of the empire, would impregnate the atmosphere far and wide; and the germs of new religious developments would thus be implanted in alien soils. For in tracing Essenism to Persian influences I have not wished to imply that this Jewish sect consciously

The destruction of the Persian empire not adverse but favourable to the spread of Parsism.

---

tents himself with replying that the use of the axe among the Essenes for purposes of divination is a pure conjecture, not resting on any known fact. He might have answered with much more effect that Josephus elsewhere (§ 9) defines it as a spade or shovel, and assigns to it a very different use. Hilgenfeld has damaged his cause by laying stress on these accidental resemblances. So far as regards minor coincidences, Zeller makes out as good a case for his Pythagoreans, as Hilgenfeld for his magians.

[1] Those who allow any foreign Oriental element in Essenism most commonly ascribe it to Persia: e.g. among the more recent writers, Hilgenfeld (l. c.), and Lipsius *Schenkel's Bibel-Lexikon* s. v. Essäer p. 189.

[2] l. c. p. 275.

[3] See Gibbon *Decline and Fall* c. viii, Milman *History of Christianity* II. p. 247 sq. The latter speaks of this restoration of Zoroastrianism, as 'perhaps the only instance of the vigorous revival of a Pagan religion.' It was far purer and less Pagan than the system which it superseded; and this may account for its renewed life.

24—2

372   THE ESSENES.

incorporated the Zoroastrian philosophy and religion as such, but only that Zoroastrian ideas were infused into its system by more or less direct contact. And, as a matter of fact, it seems quite certain that Persian ideas were widely spread during this very interval, when the Persian nationality was eclipsed. It was then that Hermippus gave to the Greeks the most detailed account of this religion which had ever been laid before them[1]. It was then that its tenets suggested or moulded the speculations of the various Gnostic sects. It was then that the worship of the Persian Mithras spread throughout the Roman Empire. It was then, if not earlier, that the magian system took root in Asia Minor, making for itself (as it were) a second home in Cappadocia[2]. It was then, if not earlier, that the Zoroastrian demonology stamped itself so deeply on the apocryphal literature of the Jews themselves, which borrowed even the names of evil spirits[3] from the Persians. There are indeed abundant indications that Palestine was surrounded by Persian influences during this period, when the Persian empire was in abeyance.

Indications of its influence during this period.

Thus we seem to have ample ground for the view that certain alien features in Essene Judaism were derived from the Zoroastrian religion. But are we justified in going a step further, and attributing other elements in this eclectic system to the more distant East? The monasticism of the Buddhist will naturally occur to our minds, as a precursor of the cenobitic life among the Essenes; and Hilgenfeld accordingly has not hesitated to ascribe this characteristic of Essenism directly to Buddhist influences[4]. But at the outset we are obliged to

Are Buddhist influences also perceptible?

---

[1] See Müller *Fragm. Hist. Graec.* III. p. 53 sq. for this work of Hermippus περὶ Μάγων. He flourished about B.C. 200. See Max Müller *Lectures on the Science of Language* 1st ser. p. 86.

[2] Strabo xv. 3. 15 (p. 733) Ἐν δὲ τῇ Καππαδοκίᾳ (πολὺ γὰρ ἐκεῖ τὸ τῶν Μάγων φῦλον, οἳ καὶ πύραιθοι καλοῦνται. πολλὰ δὲ καὶ τῶν Περσικῶν θεῶν ἱερά) κ.τ.λ.

[3] At least in one instance, Asmodeus (Tob. iii. 17); see M. Müller *Chips from a German Workshop* I. p. 148 sq. For the different dates assigned to the book of Tobit see Dr Westcott's article *Tobit* in Smith's *Dictionary of the Bible* p. 1525.

[4] *Zeitschrift* x. p. 103 sq.; comp.

ask whether history gives any such indication of the presence of Buddhism in the West as this hypothesis requires. Hilgenfeld answers this question in the affirmative. He points confidently to the fact that as early as the middle of the second century before Christ the Buddhist records speak of their faith as flourishing in Alasanda the chief city of the land of Yavana. The place intended, he conceives, can be none other than the great Alexandria, the most famous of the many places bearing the name[1]. In this opinion however he stands quite alone. Neither Köppen[2], who is his authority for this statement, nor any other Indian scholar[3], so far as I am aware, for a moment contemplates this identification. Yavana, or Yona, was the common Indian name for the Græco-Bactrian kingdom and its dependencies[4]; and to this region we naturally turn. The Alasanda or Alasadda therefore, which is here mentioned, will be one of several Eastern cities bearing the name of the great conqueror, most probably *Alexandria ad Caucasum*. But indeed I hardly think that, if Hilgenfeld had referred to the original authority for the statement, the great Buddhist history *Mahawanso*, he would have ventured to lay any stress at all on

Supposed Buddhist establishment at Alexandria.

The authority misinterpreted

---

xi. p. 351. M. Renan also (*Langues Sémitiques* III. iv. 1, *Vie de Jésus* p. 98) suggests that Buddhist influences operated in Palestine.

[1] x. p. 105 'was schon an sich, zumal in dieser Zeit, schwerlich Alexandria ad Caucasum, sondern nur Alexandrien in Aegypten bedeuten kann.' Comp. xi. p. 351, where he repeats the same argument in reply to Zeller. This is a very natural inference from a Western point of view; but, when we place ourselves in the position of a Buddhist writer to whom Bactria was Greece, the relative proportions of things are wholly changed.

[2] *Die Religion des Buddha* I. p. 193.

[3] Comp. e.g. Weber *Die Verbindungen Indiens mit den Ländern im Westen* p. 675 in the *Allgem. Monatsschr.*

f. Wissensch. u. Literatur, Braunschweig 1853; Lassen *Indische Alterthumskunde* II. p. 236; Hardy *Manual of Budhism* p. 516.

[4] For its geographical meaning in older Indian writers see Köppen l. c. Since then it has entirely departed from its original signification, and Yavana is now a common term used by the Hindoos to designate the Mohammedans. Thus the Greek name has come to be applied to a people which of all others is most unlike the Greeks. This change of meaning admirably illustrates the use of Ἕλλην among the Jews, which in like manner, from being the name of an alien nation, became the name of an alien religion, irrespective of nationality; see the note on Gal. ii. 3.

374 THE ESSENES.

and wholly untrustworthy in itself. this notice, as supporting his theory. The historian, or rather fabulist (for such he is in this earlier part of his chronicle), is relating the foundation of the Mahá thúpo, or great tope, at Ruanwelli by the king Dutthagámini in the year B.C. 157. Beyond the fact that this tope was erected by this king the rest is plainly legendary. All the materials for the construction of the building, we are told, appeared spontaneously as by miracle—the bricks, the metals, the precious stones. The dewos, or demons, lent their aid in the erection. In fact

> the fabric huge
> Rose like an exhalation.

Priests gathered in enormous numbers from all the great Buddhist monasteries to do honour to the festival of the foundation. One place alone sent not less than 96,000. Among the rest it is mentioned that 'Maha Dhammarakkito, théro (i.e. senior priest) of Yóna, accompanied by 30,000 priests from the vicinity of Alasaddá, the capital of the Yóna country, attended[1].' It is obvious that no weight can be attached to a statement occurring as part of a story of which the other details are so manifestly false. An establishment of 30,000 Buddhist priests at Alexandria would indeed be a phenomenon of which historians have shown a strange neglect.

General ignorance of Buddhism in the West. Nor is the presence of any Buddhist establishment even on a much smaller scale in this important centre of western civilisation at all reconcilable with the ignorance of this religion, which the Greeks and Romans betray at a much later date[2]. For some centuries after the Christian era we find that the information possessed by western writers was most shadowy and confused; and in almost every instance we are able to trace it to some other cause than the actual presence of *Strabo.* Buddhists in the Roman Empire[3]. Thus Strabo, who wrote

---

[1] *Mahawanso* p. 171, Turnour's translation.

[2] How for instance, if any such establishment had ever existed at Alexandria, could Strabo have used the language which is quoted in the next note?

[3] Consistently with this view, we may allow that single Indians would visit Alexandria from time to time for

THE ESSENES. 375

under Augustus and Tiberius, apparently mentions the Buddhist priests, the *sramanas*, under the designation *sarmanæ* (Σαρμάνας)[1]; but he avowedly obtains his information from

purposes of trade or for other reasons, and not more than this is required by the rhetorical passage in Dion Chrysost. *Or.* xxxii (p. 373) ὁρῶ γὰρ ἔγωγε οὐ μόνον Ἕλληνας παρ' ὑμῖν......ἀλλὰ καὶ Βακτρίους καὶ Σκύθας καὶ Πέρσας καὶ Ἰνδῶν τινάς. The qualifying τινάς shows how very slight was the communication between India and Alexandria. The mission of Pantænus may have been suggested by the presence of such stray visitors. Jerome (*Vir. Ill.* 36) says that he went 'rogatus ab illius gentis legatis.' It must remain doubtful however, whether some other region than Hindostan, such as Æthiopia for instance, is not meant, when Pantænus is said to have gone to India: see Cave's *Lives of the Primitive Fathers* p. 188 sq.

How very slight the communication was between India and the West in the early years of the Christian era, appears from this passage of Strabo (xv. I. 4, p. 686); καὶ οἱ νῦν δὲ ἐξ Αἰγύπτου πλέοντες ἐμπορικοὶ τῷ Νείλῳ καὶ τῷ Ἀραβίῳ κόλπῳ μέχρι τῆς Ἰνδικῆς σπάνιοι μὲν καὶ περιπεπλεύκασι μέχρι τοῦ Γάγγου, καὶ οὗτοι δ' ἰδιῶται καὶ οὐδὲν πρὸς ἱστορίαν τῶν τόπων χρήσιμοι, after which he goes on to say that the only instance of Indian travellers in the West was the embassy sent to Augustus (see below p. 378), which came ἀφ' ἑνὸς τόπου καὶ παρ' ἑνὸς βασιλέως.

The communications between India and the West are investigated by two recent writers, Reinaud *Relations Politiques et Commerciales de l'Empire Romain avec l'Asie Centrale*, Paris 1863, and Priaulx *The Indian Travels of Apollonius of Tyana and the Indian Embassies to Rome*, 1873. The latter work, which is very thorough and satisfactory, would have saved me much labour of independent investigation, if I had seen it in time.

[1] Strabo xv. 1. 59, p. 712. In the MSS it is written Γαρμάνας, but this must be an error either introduced by Strabo's transcribers or found in the copy of Megasthenes which this author used. This is plain not only from the Indian word itself, but also from the parallel passage in Clement of Alexandria (*Strom.* i. 15). From the coincidences of language it is clear that Clement also derived his information from Megasthenes, whose name he mentions just below. The fragments of Megasthenes relating to the Indian philosophers will be found in Müller *Fragm. Hist. Graec.* II. p. 437. They were previously edited by Schwanbeck, *Megasthenis Indica* (Bonnæ 1846).

For Σαρμᾶναι we also find the form Σαμαναῖοι in other writers; e.g. Clem. Alex. l. c., Bardesanes in Porphyr. *de Abstin.* iv. 17, Orig. *c. Cels.* i. 24 (I. p. 342). This divergence is explained by the fact that the Pali word *sammana* corresponds to the Sanskrit *sramana*. See Schwanbeck, l. c. p. 17, quoted by Müller, p. 437.

It should be borne in mind however, that several eminent Indian scholars believe Megasthenes to have meant not Buddhists but Brahmins by his Σαρμᾶναι. So for instance Lassen *Rhein. Mus.* 1833, p. 180 sq., *Ind. Alterth.* II. p. 700: and Prof. Max Müller (Pref. to Rogers's *Translation of Buddhaghosha's Parables*, London 1870, p. lii) says; 'That Lassen is right in taking the Σαρμᾶναι, mentioned by Megasthenes, for Brahmanic, not for Buddhist ascetics, might be proved also by their dress. Dresses

376   THE ESSENES.

Bardesanes. Megasthenes, who travelled in India somewhere about the year 300 B.C. and wrote a book on Indian affairs. Thus too Bardesanes at a much later date gives an account of these Buddhist ascetics, without however naming the founder of the religion; but he was indebted for his knowledge of them to conversations with certain Indian ambassadors who visited Syria on their way westward in the reign of one of the Antonines[1]. *Clement of Alexandria*, Clement of Alexandria, writing in the latest years of the second century or the earliest of the third, for

made of the bark of trees are not Buddhistic.' If this opinion be correct, the earlier notices of Buddhism in Greek writers entirely disappear, and my position is strengthened. But for the following reasons the other view appears to me more probable: (1) The term *sramana* is the common term for the Buddhist ascetic, whereas it is very seldom used of the Brahmin. (2) The Ζάρμανος (another form of *sramana*), mentioned below, p. 378, note 1, appears to have been a Buddhist. This view is taken even by Lassen, *Ind. Alterth.* III. p. 60. (3) The distinction of Βραχμᾶνες and Σαρμᾶναι in Megasthenes or the writers following him corresponds to the distinction of Βραχμᾶνες and Σαμαναῖοι in Bardesanes, Origen, and others; and, as Schwanbeck has shown (l. c.), the account of the Σαρμᾶναι in Megasthenes for the most part is a close parallel to the account of the Σαμαναῖοι in Bardesanes (or at least in Porphyry's report of Bardesanes). It seems more probable therefore that Megasthenes has been guilty of confusion in describing the dress of the Σαρμᾶναι, than that Brahmins are intended by the term.

The Pali form, Σαμαναῖοι, as a designation of the Buddhists, first occurs in Clement of Alexandria or Bardesanes, whichever may be the earlier writer. It is generally ascribed to Alexander Polyhistor, who flourished B.C. 80—60, because his authority is quoted by Cyril of Alexandria (c. *Julian.* iv. p. 133) in the same context in which the Σαμαναῖοι are mentioned. This inference is drawn by Schwanbeck, Max Müller, Lassen, and others. An examination of Cyril's language however shows that the statement for which he quotes the authority of Alexander Polyhistor does not extend to the mention of the Samanæi. Indeed all the facts given in this passage of Cyril (including the reference to Polyhistor) are taken from Clement of Alexandria (*Strom.* i. 15; see below, p. 378 n. 1), whose account Cyril has abridged. It is possible indeed that Clement himself derived the statement from Polyhistor, but nothing in Clement's own language points to this.

[1] The narrative of Bardesanes is given by Porphyry *de Abst.* iv. 17. The Buddhist ascetics are there called Σαμαναῖοι (see the last note). The work of Bardesanes, recounting his conversations with these Indian ambassadors, is quoted again by Porphyry in a fragment preserved by Stobæus *Ecl.* iii. 56 (p. 141). In this last passage the embassy is said to have arrived ἐπὶ τῆς Βασιλείας τῆς 'Αντωνίνου τοῦ ἐξ 'Εμισῶν, by which, if the words be correct, must be meant Elagabalus

THE ESSENES. 377

the first[1] time mentions Buddha by name; and even he betrays a strange ignorance of this Eastern religion[2].

Still later than this, Hippolytus, while he gives a fairly intelligent, though brief, account of the Brahmins[3], says not a word about the Buddhists, though, if he had been acquainted with their teaching, he would assuredly have seen in them a fresh support to his theory of the affinity between Christian

Hippolytus.

(A.D. 218—222), the spurious Antonine (see Hilgenfeld *Bardesanes* p. 12 sq.). Other ancient authorities however place Bardesanes in the reign of one of the older Antonines; and, as the context is somewhat corrupt, we cannot feel quite certain about the date. Bardesanes gives by far the most accurate account of the Buddhists to be found in any ancient Greek writer; but even here the monstrous stories, which the Indian ambassadors related to him, show how little trustworthy such sources of information were.

[1] Except possibly Arrian, *Ind.* viii. 1, who mentions an ancient Indian king, Budyas (Βουδύας) by name; but what he relates of him is quite inconsistent with the history of Buddha, and probably some one else is intended.

[2] In this passage (*Strom.* i. 15, p. 359) Clement apparently mentions these same persons three times, supposing that he is describing three different schools of Oriental philosophers. (1) He speaks of Σαμαναῖοι Βάκτρων (comp. Cyrill. Alex. l. c.); (2) He distinguishes two classes of Indian gymnosophists, whom he calls Σαρμᾶναι and Βραχμᾶναι. These are Buddhists and Brahmins respectively (see p. 375, note 1); (3) He says afterwards εἰσὶ δὲ τῶν Ἰνδῶν οἱ τοῖς Βοῦττα πειθόμενοι παραγγέλμασιν, ὃν δι' ὑπερβολὴν σεμνότητος εἰς [ὡς?] θεὸν τετιμήκασι. Schwanbeck indeed maintains that Clement here intends to describe the same persons whom he has just mentioned as Σαρμᾶναι; but this is not the natural interpretation of his language, which must mean 'There are also among the Indians those who obey the precepts of Buddha.' Probably Schwanbeck is right in identifying the Σαρμᾶναι with the Buddhist ascetics, but Clement appears not to have known this. In fact he has obtained his information from different sources, and so repeated himself without being aware of it. Where he got the first fact it is impossible to say. The second, as we saw, was derived from Megasthenes. The third, relating to Buddha, came, as we may conjecture, either from Pantænus (if indeed Hindostan is really meant by the India of his missionary labours) or from some chance Indian visitor at Alexandria.

In another passage (*Strom.* iii. 7, p. 539) Clement speaks of certain Indian celibates and ascetics, who are called Σεμνοί. As he distinguishes them from the gymnosophists, and mentions the pyramid as a sacred building with them, the identification with the Buddhists can hardly be doubted. Here therefore Σεμνοί is a Grecized form of Σαμαναῖοι; and this modification of the word would occur naturally to Clement, because σεμνοί, σεμνεῖον, were already used of the ascetic life: e.g. Philo *de Vit. Cont.* 3 (p. 475 M.) ἱερὸν δ καλεῖται σεμνεῖον καὶ μοναστήριον ἐν ᾧ μονούμενοι τὰ τοῦ σεμνοῦ βίου μυστήρια τελοῦνται.

[3] *Haer.* i. 24.

A Buddhist at Athens.

heresies and pre-existing heathen philosophies. With one doubtful exception—an Indian fanatic attached to an embassy sent by king Porus to Augustus, who astonished the Greeks and Romans by burning himself alive at Athens[1]—there is

[1] The chief authority is Nicolaus of Damascus in Strabo xv. 1. 73 (p. 720). The incident is mentioned also in Dion Cass. liv. 9. Nicolaus had met these ambassadors at Antioch, and gives an interesting account of the motley company and their strange presents. This fanatic, who was one of the number, immolated himself in the presence of an astonished crowd, and perhaps of the emperor himself, at Athens. He anointed himself and then leapt smiling on the pyre. The inscription on his tomb was Ζαρμανοχηγὰς Ἰνδὸς ἀπὸ Βαργόσης κατὰ τὰ πάτρια Ἰνδῶν ἔθη ἑαυτὸν ἀπαθανατίσας κεῖται. The tomb was visible at least as late as the age of Plutarch, who recording the self-immolation of Calanus before Alexander (Vit. Alex. 69) says, τοῦτο πολλοῖς ἔτεσιν ὕστερον ἄλλος Ἰνδὸς ἐν Ἀθήναις Καίσαρι συνὼν ἐποίησε, καὶ δείκνυται μέχρι νῦν τὸ μνημεῖον Ἰνδοῦ προσαγορευόμενον. Strabo also places the two incidents in conjunction in another passage in which he refers to this person, xv. 1. 4 (p. 686) ὁ κατακαύσας ἑαυτὸν Ἀθήνῃσι σοφιστὴς Ἰνδός, καθάπερ καὶ ὁ Κάλανος κ.τ.λ.

The reasons for supposing this person to have been a Buddhist, rather than a Brahmin, are: (1) The name Ζαρμανοχηγὰς (which appears with some variations in the MSS of Strabo) being apparently the Indian *sramana-karja*, i.e. 'teacher of the ascetics,' in other words, a Buddhist priest; (2) The place Bargosa, i.e. Barygaza, where Buddhism flourished in that age. See Priaulx p. 78 sq. In Dion Cassius it is written Ζάρμαρος.

And have we not here an explanation of 1 Cor. xiii. 3, if ἵνα καυθήσομαι be the right reading? The passage, being written before the fires of the Neronian persecution, requires explanation. Now it is clear from Plutarch that the 'Tomb of the Indian' was one of the sights shown to strangers at Athens: and the Apostle, who observed the altar ΑΓΝΩΣΤΩΙ ΘΕΩΙ, was not likely to overlook the sepulchre with the strange inscription ΕΑΥΤΟΝ ΑΠΑΘΑΝΑΤΙΣΑΣ ΚΕΙΤΑΙ. Indeed the incident would probably be pressed on his notice in his discussions with Stoics and Epicureans, and he would be forced to declare himself as to the value of these Indian self-immolations, when he preached the doctrine of self-sacrifice. We may well imagine therefore that the fate of this poor Buddhist fanatic was present to his mind when he penned the words καὶ ἐὰν παραδῶ τὸ σῶμά μου...ἀγάπην δὲ μὴ ἔχω, οὐδὲν ὠφελοῦμαι. Indeed it would furnish an almost equally good illustration of the text, whether we read ἵνα καυθήσομαι or ἵνα καυχήσωμαι. Dion Cassius (l. c.) suggests that the deed was done ὑπὸ φιλοτιμίας or εἰς ἐπίδειξιν. How much attention these religious suicides of the Indians attracted in the Apostolic age (doubtless because the act of this Buddhist priest had brought the subject vividly before men's minds in the West), we may infer from the speech which Josephus puts in the mouth of Eleazar (B. J. vii. 8. 7), βλέψωμεν εἰς Ἰνδοὺς τοὺς σοφίαν ἀσκεῖν ὑπισχνουμένους...οἱ δὲ...πυρὶ τὸ σῶμα παραδόντες, ὅπως δὴ καὶ καθαρωτάτην ἀποκρίνωσι τοῦ σώματος τὴν ψυχήν, ὑμνούμενοι τελευντῶσι...ἆρ' οὖν οὐκ αἰδούμεθα χεῖρον Ἰνδῶν φρονοῦντες;

apparently no notice in either heathen or Christian writers, which points to the presence of a Buddhist within the limits of the Roman Empire, till long after the Essenes had ceased to exist[1].

And if so, the coincidences must be very precise, before we are justified in attributing any peculiarities of Essenism to Buddhist influences. This however is far from being the case. They both exhibit a well-organized monastic society: but the monasticism of the Buddhist priests, with its systematized mendicancy, has little in common with the monasticism of the Essene recluse, whose life was largely spent in manual labour. They both enjoin celibacy, both prohibit the use of flesh and of wine, both abstain from the slaughter of animals. But, as we have already seen, such resemblances prove nothing, for they may be explained by the independent development of the same religious principles. One coincidence, and one only, is noticed by Hilgenfeld, which at first sight seems more striking and might suggest a historical connexion. He observes that the four orders of the Essene community are derived from the four steps of Buddhism. Against this it might fairly be argued that such coincidences of numbers are often purely accidental, and that in the present instance there is no more reason for connecting the four steps of Buddhism with the four orders of Essenism than there would be for connecting the ten precepts of Buddha with the Ten Commandments of Moses. But indeed a nearer examination will show that the two have nothing whatever in common except the number. The four steps or paths of Buddhism are not four grades of an external order, but four degrees of spiritual progress on the way to nirvana or annihilation, the ultimate goal of the Buddhist's religious aspira-

The alleged coincidences prove nothing.

Monasticism.

Asceticism.

Four orders and four steps.

---

[1] In the reign of Claudius an embassy arrived from Taprobane (Ceylon); and from these ambassadors Pliny derived his information regarding the island, *N. H.* vi. 24. Respecting their religion however he says only two words 'coli Herculem,' by whom probably Rama is meant (Priaulx p. 116). From this and other statements it appears that they were Tamils and not Singalese, and thus belonged to the non-Buddhist part of the island; see Priaulx p. 91 sq.

tions. They are wholly unconnected with the Buddhist monastic system, as an organization. A reference to the Buddhist notices collected in Hardy's *Eastern Monachism* (p. 280 sq.) will at once dispel any suspicion of a resemblance. A man may attain to the highest of these four stages of Buddhist illumination instantaneously. He does not need to have passed through the lower grades, but may even be a layman at the time. Some merit obtained in a previous state of existence may raise him *per saltum* to the elevation of a rahat, when all earthly desires are crushed and no future birth stands between him and nirvana. There remains therefore no coincidence which would suggest any historical connexion between Essenism and Buddhism. Indeed it is not till some centuries later, when Manicheism[1] starts into being, that we find for the first time any traces of the influence of Buddhism on the religions of the West[2].

Buddhist influences seen first in Manicheism.

---

[1] Even its influence on Manicheism however is disputed in a learned article in the *Home and Foreign Review* III. p. 143 sq. (1863), by Mr P. Le Page Renouf (see *Academy* 1873, p. 399).

[2] An extant inscription, containing an edict of the great Buddhist king Asoka and dating about the middle of the 3rd century B.C., was explained by Prinsep as recording a treaty of this monarch with Ptolemy and other successors of Alexander, by which religious freedom was secured for the Buddhists throughout their dominions. If this interpretation had been correct, we must have supposed that, so far as regards Egypt and Western Asia, the treaty remained a dead letter. But later critics have rejected this interpretation of its purport: see Thomas's edition of Prinsep's *Essays on Indian Antiquities* II. p. 18 sq.

C.

ESSENISM AND CHRISTIANITY.

The theory which explains Christianity as an outgrowth of Essenism

IT has become a common practice with a certain class of writers to call Essenism to their aid in accounting for any distinctive features of Christianity, which they are unable to explain in any other way. Wherever some external power is needed to solve a perplexity, here is the *deus ex machina* whose aid they most readily invoke. Constant repetition is sure to produce its effect, and probably not a few persons, who want either the leisure or the opportunity to investigate the subject for themselves, have a lurking suspicion that the Founder of Christianity may have been an Essene, or at all events that Christianity was largely indebted to Essenism for its doctrinal and ethical teaching[1]. Indeed, when very confident and sweeping assertions are made, it is natural to presume that they rest on a substantial basis of fact. Thus for instance we are told by one writer that Christianity is 'Essenism alloyed with foreign elements'[2]: while another, who however approaches the subject in a different spirit, says; 'It will hardly be doubted that our Saviour Himself belonged to this holy brotherhood. This will especially be apparent, when we remember that *the whole Jewish community* at the advent of Christ was divided

---

[1] De Quincey's attempt to prove that the Essenes were actually Christians (*Works* VI. p. 270 sq., IX. p. 253 sq.), who used the machinery of an esoteric society to inculcate their doctrines 'for fear of the Jews,' is conceived in a wholly different spirit from the theories of the writers mentioned in the text; but it is even more untenable and does not deserve serious refutation.

[2] Grätz III. p. 217.

into three parties, the Pharisees, the Sadducees, and the Essenes, and that *every Jew had to belong to one of these sects.* Jesus who in all things conformed to the Jewish law, and who was holy, harmless, undefiled, and separate from sinners, would therefore naturally associate Himself with that order of Judaism which was most congenial to His nature[1].' I purpose testing these strong assertions by an appeal to facts.

tested by facts.

For the statements involved in those words of the last extract which I have italicized, no authority is given by the writer himself; nor have I been able to find confirmation of them in any quarter. On the contrary the frequent allusions which we find to the vulgar herd, the $ἰδιῶται$, the *am haarets*, who are distinguished from the disciples of the schools[2], suggest that a large proportion of the people was unattached to any sect. If it had been otherwise, we might reasonably presume that our Lord, as one who 'in all things conformed to the Jewish law,' would have preferred attaching Himself to the Pharisees who 'sat in Moses' seat' and whose precepts He recommended His disciples to obey[3], rather than to the Essenes who in one important respect at least—the repudiation of the temple sacrifices—acted in flagrant violation of the Mosaic ordinances.

Our Lord need not have belonged to any sect.

This preliminary barrier being removed, we are free to investigate the evidence for their presumed connexion. And here we are met first with a negative argument, which obviously has great weight with many persons. Why, it is asked, does Jesus, who so unsparingly denounces the vices and the falsehoods of Pharisees and Sadducees, never once mention the Essenes by way of condemnation, or indeed mention them by name at all? Why, except that He Himself belonged to this sect and looked favourably on their teaching? This question is best answered by another. How can we explain the fact, that throughout the enormous mass of talmudical and

The argument from the silence of the New Testament answered.

---

[1] Ginsburg *Essenes* p. 24.
[2] See above, p. 345.
[3] Matt. xxiii. 2, 3.

early rabbinical literature this sect is not once mentioned by name, and that even the supposed allusions to them, which have been discovered for the first time in the present century, turn out on investigation to be hypothetical and illusory? The difficulty is much greater in this latter instance; but the answer is the same in both cases. The silence is explained by the comparative insignificance of the sect, their small numbers and their retired habits. Their settlements were far removed from the great centres of political and religious life. Their recluse habits, as a rule, prevented them from interfering in the common business of the world. Philo and Josephus have given prominence to them, because their ascetic practices invested them with the character of philosophers and interested the Greeks and Romans in their history; but in the national life of the Jews they bore a very insignificant part[1]. If the Sadducees, who held the highest offices in the hierarchy, are only mentioned directly on three occasions in the Gospels[2], it can be no surprise that the Essenes are not named at all.

As no stress therefore can be laid on the argument from silence, any hypothesis of connexion between Essenism and Christianity must make good its claims by establishing one or both of these two points; *first*, that there is direct historical evidence of close intercourse between the two; and *secondly*, that the resemblances of doctrine and practice are so striking as to oblige, or at least to warrant, the belief in such a connexion.

The positive arguments for a connexion may be twofold.

---

[1] This fact is fully recognised by several recent writers, who will not be suspected of any undue bias towards traditional views of Christian history. Thus Lipsius writes (p. 190), 'In the general development of Jewish life Essenism occupies a far more subordinate place than is commonly ascribed to it.' And Keim expresses himself to the same effect (I. p. 305). Derenbourg also, after using similar language, adds this wise caution, 'In any case, in the present state of our acquaintance with the Essenes, which is so imperfect and has no chance of being extended, the greatest prudence is required of science, if she prefers to be true rather than adventurous, if she has at heart rather to enlighten than to surprise' (p. 461). Even Grätz in one passage can write soberly on this subject: 'The Essenes had throughout no influence on political movements, from which they held aloof as far as possible' (III. p. 86).

[2] These are (1) Matt. iii. 7; (2) Matt. xvi. 1 sq.; (3) Matt. xxii. 23 sq., Mark xii. 18, Luke xx. 27.

If both these lines of argument fail, the case must be considered to have broken down.

1. Absence of direct historical evidence of a connexion.

1. On the former point it must be premised that the Gospel narrative does not suggest any hint of a connexion. Indeed its general tenor is directly adverse to such a supposition. From first to last Jesus and His disciples move about freely, taking part in the common business, even in the common recreations, of Jewish life. The recluse ascetic brotherhood, which was gathered about the shores of the Dead Sea, does not once appear above the Evangelists' horizon. Of this close society, as such, there is not the faintest indication. But two individuals have been singled out, as holding an important place either in the Evangelical narrative or in the Apostolic Church, who, it is contended, form direct and personal links of communication with this sect. These are John the Baptist and James the Lord's brother. The one is the forerunner of the Gospel, the first herald of the Kingdom; the other is the most prominent figure in the early Church of Jerusalem.

Two individual cases alleged.

(i) John the Baptist

(i) John the Baptist was an ascetic. His abode was the desert; his clothing was rough; his food was spare; he baptized his penitents. Therefore, it is argued, he was an Essene. Between the premisses and the conclusion however there is a broad gulf, which cannot very easily be bridged over. The solitary independent life, which John led, presents a type wholly different from the cenobitic establishments of the Essenes, who had common property, common meals, common hours of labour and of prayer. It may even be questioned whether his food of locusts would have been permitted by the Essenes, if they really ate nothing which had life ($ἔμψυχον$[1]). And again; his baptism as narrated by the Evangelists, and their illustrations as described by Josephus, have nothing in common except the use of water for a religious purpose. When therefore we are told confidently that 'his manner of life was altogether after the Essene pattern[2],' and that 'he without doubt baptized his

not an Essene.

---

[1] See *Colossians* p. 86.   [2] Grätz III. p. 100.

converts into the Essene order,' we know what value to attach to this bold assertion. If positive statements are allowable, it would be more true to fact to say that he could not possibly have been an Essene. The rule of his life was *isolation*; the principle of theirs, *community*[1].

In this mode of life John was not singular. It would appear that not a few devout Jews at this time retired from the world and buried themselves in the wilderness, that they might devote themselves unmolested to ascetic discipline and religious meditation. One such instance at all events we have in Banus the master of Josephus, with whom the Jewish historian, when a youth, spent three years in the desert. This anchorite was clothed in garments made of bark or of leaves; his food was the natural produce of the earth; he bathed day and night in cold water for purposes of purification. To the careless observer doubtless John and Banus would appear to be men of the same stamp. In their outward mode of life there was perhaps not very much difference[2]. The consciousness of a divine mission, the gift of a prophetic insight, in John was the real and all-important distinction between the two. But here also the same mistake is made; and we not uncommonly find Banus described as an Essene. It is not too much to say however, that the whole tenor of Josephus' narrative is opposed to this supposition[3]. He

External resemblances to John in Banus,

who was not an Essene.

---

[1] τὸ κοινωνητικόν, Joseph. *B. J.* ii. 8. 3. See also Philo *Fragm.* 632 ὑπὲρ τοῦ κοινωφελοῦς, and the context.

[2] Ewald (vi. p. 649) regards this Banus as representing an extravagant development of the school of John, and thus supplying a link between the real teaching of the Baptist and the doctrine of the Hemerobaptists professing to be derived from him.

[3] The passage is so important that I give it in full; Joseph. *Vit.* 2 περὶ ἑκκαίδεκα δὲ ἔτη γενόμενος ἐβουλήθην τῶν παρ' ἡμῖν αἱρέσεων ἐμπειρίαν λαβεῖν. τρεῖς δ' εἰσὶν αὗται· Φαρισαίων μὲν ἡ πρώτη, καὶ Σαδδουκαίων ἡ δευτέρα, τρίτη δὲ ἡ Ἐσσηνῶν, καθὼς πολλάκις εἴπαμεν.

οὕτως γὰρ ᾠόμην αἱρήσεσθαι τὴν ἀρίστην, εἰ πάσας καταμάθοιμι. σκληραγωγήσας γοῦν ἐμαυτὸν καὶ πολλὰ πονηθεὶς τὰς τρεῖς διῆλθον. καὶ μηδὲ τὴν ἐντεῦθεν ἐμπειρίαν ἱκανὴν ἐμαυτῷ νομίσας εἶναι, πυθόμενός τινα Βανοῦν ὄνομα κατὰ τὴν ἐρημίαν διατρίβειν, ἐσθῆτι μὲν ἀπὸ δένδρων χρώμενον, τροφὴν δὲ τὴν αὐτομάτως φυομένην προσφερόμενον, ψυχρῷ δὲ ὕδατι τὴν ἡμέραν καὶ τὴν νύκτα πολλάκις λουόμενον πρὸς ἁγνείαν, ζηλωτὴς ἐγενόμην αὐτοῦ. καὶ διατρίψας παρ' αὐτῷ ἐνιαυτοὺς τρεῖς καὶ τὴν ἐπιθυμίαν τελειώσας εἰς τὴν πόλιν ὑπέστρεφον. ἐννεακαίδεκα δ' ἔτη ἔχων ἠρξάμην τε πολιτεύεσθαι τῇ Φαρισαίων αἱρέσει κατακολουθῶν κ.τ.λ.

L.

386   THE ESSENES.

says that when sixteen years old he desired to acquire a knowledge of the three sects of the Jews before making his choice of one; that accordingly he went through (διῆλθον) all the three at the cost of much rough discipline and toil; that he was not satisfied with the experience thus gained, and hearing of this Banus he attached himself to him as his zealous disciple (ζηλωτὴς ἐγενόμην αὐτοῦ); that having remained three years with him he returned to Jerusalem; and that then, being nineteen years old, he gave in his adhesion to the sect of the Pharisees. Thus there is no more reason for connecting this Banus with the Essenes than with the Pharisees. The only natural interpretation of the narrative is that he did not belong to any of the three sects, but represented a distinct type of religious life, of which Josephus was anxious to gain experience. And his hermit life seems to demand this solution, which the sequence of the narrative suggests.

General result. Of John himself therefore no traits are handed down which suggest that he was a member of the Essene community. He was an ascetic, and the Essenes were ascetics; but this is plainly an inadequate basis for any such inference. Nor indeed is the relation of his asceticism to theirs a question of much moment for the matter in hand; since this was the very point in which Christ's mode of life was so essentially different from John's as to provoke criticism and to point a contrast[1]. But the later history of his real or supposed disciples has, or may seem to have, some bearing on this investigation. Towards the close of the first and the beginning of the second century we meet with a body of sectarians called in Greek *Hemerobaptists*[2],

The Hemerobaptists.

---

[1] Matt. ix. 14 sq., xi. 17 sq., Mark ii. 18 sq., Luke v. 33, vii. 31 sq.

[2] The word ἡμεροβαπτισταί is generally taken to mean 'daily bathers,' and this meaning is suggested by *Apost. Const.* vi. 6 οἵτινες, καθ' ἑκάστην ἡμέραν ἐὰν μὴ βαπτίσωνται, οὐκ ἐσθίουσιν, ib. 23 ἀντὶ καθημερινοῦ ἓν μόνον δοὺς βάπτισμα, Epiphan. *Haer.* xvii. 1 (p. 37) εἰ μή τι ἄρα καθ' ἑκάστην ἡμέραν βαπτίζοιτό τις ἐν ὕδατι. But, if the word is intended as a translation of *Toble-shacharith* 'morning-bathers,' as it seems to be, it must signify rather 'day-bathers'; and this is more in accordance with the analogy of other compounds from ἡμέρα, as ἡμερόβιος, ἡμεροδρόμος, ἡμεροσκόπος, etc.

Josephus (*B. J.* ii. 8. 5) represents the Essenes as bathing, not at dawn,

THE ESSENES. 387

in Hebrew *Toble-shacharith*[1], 'day' or 'morning bathers.' What were their relations to John the Baptist on the one hand, and to the Essenes on the other? Owing to the scantiness of our information the whole subject is wrapped in obscurity, and any restoration of their history must be more or less hypothetical; but it will be possible at all events to suggest an account which is not improbable in itself, and which does no violence to the extant notices of the sect.

(*a*) We must not hastily conclude, when we meet with certain persons at Ephesus about the years A.D. 53, 54, who are described as 'knowing only the baptism of John,' or as having been 'baptized unto John's baptism[2],' that we have here some early representatives of the Hemerobaptist sect. These were Christians, though imperfectly informed Christians. Of Apollos, who was more fully instructed by Aquila and Priscilla, this is stated in the most explicit terms[3]. Of the rest, who owed their fuller knowledge of the Gospel to St Paul, the same appears to be implied, though the language is not free from ambiguity[4]. But these notices have an important bearing on our subject; for they show how profoundly the effect of John's preaching was felt in districts as remote as proconsular Asia, even after a lapse of a quarter of a century. With these disciples it was the initial impulse towards Christianity; but to others it represented a widely different form of belief and practice. The Gospel of St John was written, according to all tradition, at Ephesus in the later years of the first century.

(*a*) Their relation to John the Baptist.

John's disciples at Ephesus.

Professed followers at a later date.

---

but at the fifth hour, just before their meal. This is hardly consistent either with the name of the *Toble-shacharith*, or with the Talmudical anecdote of them quoted above, p. 348. Of Banus he reports (*Vit.* 2) that he 'bathed often day and night in cold water.'

[1] See above, p. 348 sq.

[2] The former expression is used of Apollos, Acts xviii. 24; the latter of 'certain disciples,' Acts xix. 1.

[3] This appears from the whole narrative, but is distinctly stated in ver. 25, as correctly read, ἐδίδασκεν ἀκριβῶς τὰ περὶ τοῦ Ἰησοῦ, not τοῦ κυρίου as in the received text.

[4] The πιστεύσαντες in xix. 1 is slightly ambiguous, and some expressions in the passage might suggest the opposite: but μαθητὰς seems decisive, for the word would not be used absolutely except of Christian disciples; comp. vi. 1, 2, 7, ix. 10, 19, 26, 38, and frequently.

Again and again the Evangelist impresses on his readers, either directly by his own comments or indirectly by the course of the narrative, the transient and subordinate character of John's ministry. He was not the light, says the Evangelist, but came to bear witness of the light[1]. He was not the sun in the heavens: he was only the waning lamp, which shines when kindled from without and burns itself away in shining. His light might well gladden the Jews while it lasted, but this was only 'for a season[2].' John himself lost no opportunity of bearing his testimony to the loftier claims of Jesus[3]. From such notices it is plain that in the interval between the preaching of St Paul and the Gospel of St John the memory of the Baptist at Ephesus had assumed a new attitude towards Christianity. His name is no longer the sign of imperfect appreciation, but the watchword of direct antagonism. John had been set up as a rival Messiah to Jesus. In other words, this Gospel indicates the spread of Hemerobaptist principles, if not the presence of a Hemerobaptist community, in proconsular Asia, when it was written. In two respects these Hemerobaptists distorted the facts of history. They perverted John's teaching, and they misrepresented his office. His baptism was no more a single rite, once performed and initiating an amendment of

The facts of history distorted by them.

---

[1] John i. 8.

[2] John v. 35 ἐκεῖνος ἦν ὁ λύχνος ὁ καιόμενος καὶ φαίνων κ.τ.λ. The word καίειν is not only 'to burn,' but not unfrequently also 'to kindle, to set on fire,' as e.g. Xen. *Anab.* iv. 4. 12 οἱ ἄλλοι ἀναστάντες πῦρ ἔκαιον; so that ὁ καιόμενος may mean either 'which burns away' or 'which is lighted.' With the former meaning it would denote the *transitoriness*, with the latter the *derivative character*, of John's ministry. There seems no reason for excluding either idea here. Thus the whole expression would mean 'the lamp which is kindled and burns away, and (only so) gives light.' For an example of two verbs or participles joined together, where the second describes a result conditional upon the first, see 1 Pet. ii. 20 εἰ ἁμαρτάνοντες καὶ κολαφιζόμενοι ὑπομενεῖτε...εἰ ἀγαθοποιοῦντες καὶ πάσχοντες ὑπομενεῖτε, 1 Thess. iv. 1 πῶς δεῖ περιπατεῖν καὶ ἀρέσκειν Θεῷ.

[3] See John i. 15—34, iii. 23—30, v. 33 sq.: comp. x. 41, 42. This aspect of St John's Gospel has been brought out by Ewald *Jahrb. der Bibl. Wissensch.* III. p. 156 sq.; see also *Geschichte* VII. p. 152 sq.; *die Johanneischen Schriften* p. 13. There is perhaps an allusion to these 'disciples of John' in 1 Joh. v. 6 οὐκ ἐν τῷ ὕδατι μόνον, ἀλλ' ἐν τῷ ὕδατι καὶ ἐν τῷ αἵματι· καὶ τὸ πνεῦμα κ.τ.λ.; comp. Acts i. 5, xi. 16, xix. 4.

life; it was a daily recurrence atoning for sin and sanctifying the person[1]. He himself was no longer the forerunner of the Messiah; he was the very Messiah[2]. In the latter half of the first century, it would seem, there was a great movement among large numbers of the Jews in favour of frequent baptism, as the one purificatory rite essential to salvation. Of this superstition we have had an instance already in the anchorite Banus to whom Josephus attached himself as a disciple. Its presence in the western districts of Asia Minor is shown by a Sibylline poem, dating about A.D. 80, which I have already had occasion to quote[3]. Some years earlier these sectarians are mentioned by name as opposing James the Lord's brother and the Twelve at Jerusalem[4]. Nor is there any reason for questioning their existence as a sect in Palestine during the later years of the Apostolic age, though the source from which our information comes is legendary, and the story itself a fabrication. But when or how they first connected themselves with the name of John the Baptist, and whether this assumption was made by all alike or only by one section of them, we do not know. Such a connexion, however false to history, was obvious and natural; nor would it be difficult to accumulate parallels to this false appropriation of an honoured name. Baptism was the fundamental article of their creed; and John was the Baptist of world-wide fame. Nothing more than this was needed for the choice of an eponym. From St John's Gospel it seems clear

Spread of Hemerobaptist principles.

A wrong use made of John's name.

---

[1] *Apost. Const.* vi. 6; comp. § 23. See p. 386, note 2.

[2] *Clem. Recogn.* i. 54 'ex discipulis Johannis, qui...magistrum suum veluti Christum praedicarunt,' *ib.* § 60 'Ecce unus ex discipulis Johannis adfirmabat Christum Johannem fuisse, et non Jesum; in tantum, inquit, ut et ipse Jesus omnibus hominibus et prophetis majorem esse pronuntiaverit Johannem etc.': see also § 63.

[3] See *Colossians*, p. 96.

[4] *Clem. Recogn.* l.c. This portion of the Clementine Recognitions is apparently taken from an older Judaizing romance, the *Ascents of James* (see above, pp. 87, 126). Hegesippus also (in Euseb. *H. E.* iv. 22) mentions the Hemerobaptists in his list of Jewish sects; and it is not improbable that this list was given as an introduction to his account of the labours and martyrdom of St James (see Euseb. *H. E.* ii. 23). If so, it was probably derived from the same source as the notice in the Recognitions.

that this appropriation was already contemplated, if not completed, at Ephesus before the first century had drawn to a close. In the second century the assumption is recognised as a characteristic of these Hemerobaptists, or Baptists, as they are once called[1], alike by those who allow and those who deny its justice[2]. Even in our age the name of 'John's disciples' has been given, though wrongly given, to an obscure sect in Babylonia, the Mandeans, whose doctrine and practice have some affinities to the older sect, and of whom perhaps they are the collateral, if not the direct, descendants[3].

---

[1] They are called Baptists by Justin Mart. *Dial.* 10, p. 307 A. He mentions them among other Jewish sects, without however alluding to John.

[2] By the author of the *Recognitions* (l. c.) who denies the claim; and by the author of the *Homilies* (see below, p. 391, note 3), who allows it.

[3] These Mandeans are a rapidly diminishing sect living in the region about the Tigris and the Euphrates, south of Bagdad. Our most exact knowledge of them is derived from Petermann (*Herzog's Real-Encyklopädie* s. vv. Mendäer, Zabier, and *Deutsche Zeitschrift* 1854 p. 181 sq., 1856 p. 331 sq., 342 sq., 363 sq., 386 sq.) who has had personal intercourse with them; and from Chwolson (*die Ssabier u. der Ssabismus* I. p. 100 sq.) who has investigated the Arabic authorities for their earlier history. The names by which they are known are (1) *Mendeans*, or more properly *Mandāyē*, contracted from מנדא דחייא *Mandā dĕchāyē* 'the word of life.' This is their own name among themselves, and points to their Gnostic pretentions. (2) *Sabeans, Tsabiyun*, possibly from the root צבע 'to dip' on account of their frequent lustrations (Chwolson I. p. 110; but see above, p. 81, note 3), though this is not the derivation of the word which they themselves adopt, and other etymologies have found favour with some recent writers (see Petermann *Herzog's Real-Encykl.* Suppl. XVIII. p. 342 s.v. Zabier). This is the name by which they are known in the Koran and in Arabic writers, and by which they call themselves when speaking to others. (3) *Nasoreans*, נצוריא *Nătsōrāyē*. This term is at present confined to those among them who are distinguished in knowledge or in business. (4) 'Christians of St John, or Disciples of St John' (i.e. the Baptist). This name is not known among themselves, and was incorrectly given to them by European travellers and missionaries. At the same time John the Baptist has a very prominent place in their theological system, as the one true prophet. On the other hand they are not Christians in any sense.

These Mandeans, the true Sabeans, must not be confused with the false Sabeans, polytheists and star-worshippers, whose locality is Northern Mesopotamia. Chwolson (I. p. 139 sq.) has shown that these last adopted the name in the 9th century to escape persecution from the Mohammedans, because in the Koran the Sabeans, as monotheists, are ranged with the Jews and Christians, and viewed in a more favourable light than polytheists. The

THE ESSENES. 391

(b) Of the connexion between this sect and John the Baptist we have been able to give a probable, though necessarily hypothetical account. But when we attempt to determine its relation to the Essenes, we find ourselves entangled in a hopeless mesh of perplexities. The notices are so confused, the affinities so subtle, the ramifications so numerous, that it becomes a desperate task to distinguish and classify these abnormal Jewish and Judaizing heresies. One fact however seems clear that, whatever affinities they may have had originally, and whatever relations they may have contracted afterwards with one another, the Hemerobaptists, properly speaking, were not Essenes. The Sibylline poem which may be regarded as in some respects a Hemerobaptist manifesto contains on examination many traits inconsistent with pure Essenism[1]. In two several accounts, the memoirs of Hegesippus and the Apostolic Constitutions, the Hemerobaptists are expressly distinguished from the Essenes[2]. In an early production of Judaic Christianity, whose Judaism has a strong Essene tinge, the Clementine Homilies, they and their eponym are condemned in the strongest language. The system of syzygies, or pairs of opposites, is a favourite doctrine of this work, and in these John stands contrasted to Jesus, as Simon Magus to Simon Peter, as the false to the true; for according to this author's philosophy of history the manifestation of the false always precedes the manifestation of the true[3]. And again, Epiphanius speaks of

(b) Their relation to the Essenes.

They were at first distinct, if not antagonistic.

name however has generally been applied in modern times to the false rather than to the true Sabeans.

[1] See *Colossians* p. 96 sq.

[2] Hegesipp. in Euseb. *H. E.* iv. 22, *Apost. Const.* vi. 6. So also the Pseudo-Hieronymus in the *Indiculus de Haeresibus* (*Corp. Haeres.* I. p. 283, ed. Oehler).

[3] *Clem. Hom.* ii. 23 Ἰωάννης τις ἐγένετο ἡμεροβαπτιστής, ὃς καὶ τοῦ κυρίου ἡμῶν Ἰησοῦ κατὰ τὸν τῆς συζυγίας λόγον ἐγένετο πρόοδος. It is then stated that, as Christ had twelve leading disciples, so John had thirty. This, it is argued, was a providential dispensation—the one number represents the solar, the other the lunar period; and so they illustrate another point in this writer's theory, that in the syzygies the true and the false are the male and female principle respectively. Among these 30 disciples he places Simon Magus. With this the doctrine of the Mandeans stands in direct opposition. They too have their syzygies,

them as agreeing substantially in their doctrines, not with the Essenes, but with the Scribes and Pharisees[1]. His authority on such a point may be worth very little; but connected with other notices, it should not be passed over in silence. Yet, whatever may have been their differences, the Hemerobaptists and the Essenes had one point of direct contact, their belief in the moral efficacy of lustrations. When the temple and polity were destroyed, the shock vibrated through the whole fabric of Judaism, loosening and breaking up existing societies, and preparing the way for new combinations. More especially the cessation of the sacrificial rites must have produced a profound effect equally on those who, like the Essenes, had condemned them already, and on those who, as possibly was the case with the Hemerobaptists, had hitherto remained true to the orthodox ritual. One grave obstacle to friendly overtures was thus removed; and a fusion, more or less complete, may have been the consequence. At all events the relations of the Jewish sects must have been materially affected by this great national crisis, as indeed we know to have been the case. In the confusion which follows, it is impossible to attain any clear view of their history. At the beginning of the second century however this pseudo-baptist movement received a fresh impulse from the pretended revelation of Elchasai, which came from the farther East[2]. Henceforth Elchasai is the prominent name in the history of those Jewish and Judaizing sects whose proper home is east of the Jordan[3], and who appear to have reproduced, with various modifications derived from Christian and Heathen sources, the Gnostic theology and the pseudo-baptist ritual of their Essene predecessors. It is still preserved in the records of the only extant people who have any claim

---

but John with them represents the true principle.

[1] *Haer.* xvii. 1 (p. 37) ἴσα τῶν γραμματέων καὶ Φαρισαίων φρονοῦσα. But he adds that they resemble the Sadducees 'not only in the matter of the resurrection of the dead, but also in their unbelief and in the other points.'

[2] See above, p. 80 sq., on this Book of Elchasai.

[3] See above, p. 354 sq.

THE ESSENES.

to be regarded as the religious heirs of the Essenes. Elchasai is regarded as the founder of the sect of Mandeans[1].

(ii) But, if great weight has been attached to the supposed connexion of John the Baptist with the Essenes, the case of James the Lord's brother has been alleged with still more confidence. Here, it is said, we have an indisputable Essene connected by the closest family ties with the Founder of Christianity. James is reported to have been holy from his birth; to have drunk no wine nor strong drink; to have eaten no flesh; to have allowed no razor to touch his head, no oil to anoint his body; to have abstained from using the bath; and lastly to have worn no wool, but only fine linen[2]. Here we have a description of Nazarite practices at least and (must it not be granted?) of Essene tendencies also. *(ii) James the Lord's Brother invested with Essene characteristics.)*

But what is our authority for this description? The writer from whom the account is immediately taken, is the Jewish-Christian historian Hegesippus, who flourished about A.D. 170. He cannot therefore have been an eye-witness of the facts which he relates. And his whole narrative betrays its legendary character. Thus his account of James's death, which follows immediately on this description, is highly improbable and melodramatic in itself, and directly contradicts the contemporary notice of Josephus in its main facts[3]. From whatever source therefore Hegesippus may have derived his information, it is wholly untrustworthy. Nor can we doubt that he was indebted to one of those romances with which the Judaizing Christians of Essene tendencies loved to gratify the natural curiosity of their disciples respecting the first founders of the *(But the account comes from untrustworthy sources.)*

---

[1] See Chwolson I. p. 112 sq., II. p. 543 sq. The Arabic writer En-Nedim, who lived towards the close of the tenth century, says that the founder of the Sabeans (i.e. Mandeans) was El-chasaich (الكساسح) who taught the doctrine of two coordinate principles, the male and female. This notice, as far as it goes, agrees with the account of Elchasai or Elxai in Hippolytus (*Haer.* ix. 13 sq.) and Epiphanius (*Haer.* xix. 1 sq.). But the derivation of the name Elchasai given by Epiphanius (*Haer.* xix. 2) δύναμις κεκαλυμμένη (חיל כסי) is different and probably correct (see above, p. 81).

[2] Hegesippus in Euseb. *H. E.* ii. 23.

[3] See above, p. 125 sq.

Church[1]. In like manner Essene portraits are elsewhere preserved of the Apostles Peter[2] and Matthew[3] which represent them as living on a spare diet of herbs and berries. I believe also that I have pointed out already the true source of this description in Hegesippus, and that it is taken from the 'Ascents of James[4],' a Judæo-Christian work stamped, as we happen to know, with the most distinctive Essene features[5]. But if we turn from these religious novels of Judaic Christianity to earlier and more trustworthy sources of information—to the Gospels or the Acts or the Epistles of St Paul—we fail to discover the faintest traces of Essenism in James. 'The historical James,' says a recent writer, 'shows Pharisaic but not Essene sympathies[6].' This is true of James, as it is true of the early disciples in the mother Church of Jerusalem generally. The temple-ritual, the daily sacrifices, suggested no scruples to them. The only distinction of meats, which they recognised, was the distinction of animals clean and unclean as laid down by the Mosaic law. The only sacrificial victims, which they abhorred, were victims offered to idols. They took their part in the religious offices, and mixed freely in the common life, of their fellow-Israelites, distinguished from them only in this, that to their Hebrew inheritance they superadded the knowledge of a higher truth and the joy of a better hope. It was altogether within the sphere of orthodox Judaism that the Jewish element in the Christian brotherhood found its scope. Essene peculiarities are the objects neither of sympathy nor of antipathy. In the history of the infant Church for the first quarter of a century Essenism is as though it were not.

No Essene features in the true portraits of James or of the earliest disciples.

---

[1] See above, p. 80.
[2] *Clem. Hom.* xii. 6, where St Peter is made to say ἄρτῳ μόνῳ καὶ ἐλαίαις χρῶμαι, καὶ σπανίως λαχάνοις; comp. xv. 17 ὕδατος μόνου καὶ ἄρτου.
[3] Clem. Alex. *Paedag.* ii. 1 (p. 174) σπερμάτων καὶ ἀκροδρύων καὶ λαχάνων ἄνευ κρεῶν μετελάμβανεν.
[4] See above, p. 126, note.
[5] Epiphanius (*Haer.* xxx. 16) mentions two points especially, in which the character of this work is shown: (1) It represented James as condemning the sacrifices and the fire on the altar (see above, pp. 350—353): (2) It published the most unfounded calumnies against St Paul.
[6] Lipsius, *Schenkel's Bibel-Lexicon*, p. 191.

But a time came, when all this was changed. Even as early as the year 58, when St Paul wrote to the Romans, we detect practices in the Christian community of the metropolis, which may possibly have been due to Essene influences[1]. Five or six years later, the heretical teaching which threatened the integrity of the Gospel at Colossæ shows that this type of Judaism was already strong enough within the Church to exert a dangerous influence on its doctrinal purity. Then came the great convulsion—the overthrow of the Jewish polity and nation. This was the turning-point in the relations between Essenism and Christianity, at least in Palestine. The Essenes were extreme sufferers in the Roman war of extermination. It seems probable that their organization was entirely broken up. Thus cast adrift, they were free to enter into other combinations, while the shock of the recent catastrophe would naturally turn their thoughts into new channels. At the same time the nearer proximity of the Christians, who had migrated to Peræa during the war, would bring them into close contact with the new faith and subject them to its influences, as they had never been subjected before[2]. But, whatever may be the explanation, the fact seems certain, that after the destruction of Jerusalem the Christian body was largely reinforced from their ranks. The Judaizing tendencies among the Hebrew Christians, which hitherto had been wholly Pharisaic, are henceforth largely Essene.

Essene influences visible before the close of the Apostolic age.

Consequences of the Jewish war.

2. If then history fails to reveal any such external connexion with Essenism in Christ and His Apostles as to justify the opinion that Essene influences contributed largely to the characteristic features of the Gospel, such a view, if tenable at all, must find its support in some striking coincidence between the doctrines and practices of the Essenes and those which its Founder stamped upon Christianity. This indeed is the really important point; for without it the external connexion, even if proved, would be valueless. The question is not whether

2. Do the resemblances favour the theory of a connexion?

---

[1] Rom. xiv. 2, 21.   [2] See above, p. 77 sq.

Christianity arose amid such and such circumstances, but how far it was created and moulded by those circumstances.

(i) Observance of the sabbath.

(i) Now one point which especially strikes us in the Jewish historian's account of the Essenes, is their strict observance of certain points in the Mosaic ceremonial law, more especially the ultra-Pharisaic rigour with which they kept the sabbath. How far their conduct in this respect was consistent with the teaching and practice of Christ may be seen from the passages quoted in the parallel columns which follow:

'Jesus went on the sabbath-day through the corn fields; and his disciples began to pluck the ears of corn and to eat[1].... But when the Pharisees saw it, they said unto him, Behold, thy disciples do that which it is not lawful to do upon the sabbath-day. But he said unto them, Have ye not read what David did...? The sabbath was made for man, and not man for the sabbath. Therefore the Son of Man is Lord even of the sabbath-day...'

'It is lawful to do well on the sabbath-days' (Matt. xii. 1—12; Mark ii. 23—iii. 6; Luke vi. 1—11, xiv. 1—6.

'And they avoid...touching any work (ἐφάπτεσθαι ἔργων) on the sabbath-day more scrupulously than any of the Jews (διαφορώτατα Ἰουδαίων ἁπάν-

---

[1] Grätz (III. p. 233) considers this narrative an interpolation made from a Pauline point of view ('eine paulinistische Tendenz - interpolation'). This theory of interpolation, interposing wherever the evidence is unfavourable, cuts up all argument by the roots. In this instance however Grätz is consistently carrying out a principle which he broadly lays down elsewhere. He regards it as the great merit of Baur and his school, that they explained the origin of the Gospels by the conflict of two opposing camps, the Ebionite and the Pauline. 'By this master-key,' he adds, 'criticism was first put in a position to test what is historical in the Gospels, and what bears the stamp of a polemical tendency (was einen tendentiösen polemischen Charakter hat). Indeed by this means the element of trustworthy history in the Gospels melts down to a minimum' (III. p. 224). In other words the judgment is not to be pronounced upon the evidence, but the evidence must be mutilated to suit the judgment. The method is not new. The sectarians of the second century, whether Judaic or anti-Judaic, had severally their 'master-key.' The master-key of Marcion was a conflict also—the antagonism of the Old and New Testaments. Under his hands the historical element in the New Testament dissolved rapidly. The mas-

See also a similar incident in Luke xiii. 10—17).

'The Jews therefore said unto him that was cured; It is the sabbath-day; it is not lawful for thee to carry thy bed. But he answered them, He that made me whole, the same said unto me, Take up thy bed and walk....Therefore the Jews did persecute Jesus and sought to slay him, because he did these things on the sabbath-day. But Jesus answered them, My Father worketh hitherto, and I work, etc.' (John v. 10—18; comp. vii. 22, 23).

'And it was the sabbath-day when Jesus made the clay, and opened his eyes......Therefore said some of the Pharisees, This man is not of God, because he keepeth not the sabbath-day' (John ix. 14, 16).

των); for they do not venture so much as to move a vessel[1], nor to perform the most necessary offices of life' (*B. J.* ii. 8. 9).

(ii) But there were other points of ceremonial observance, in which the Essenes superadded to the law. Of these the most remarkable was their practice of constant lustrations. In this respect the Pharisee was sufficiently minute and scrupulous in

(ii) Lustrations and other ceremonial observances.

---

ter-key of the anti-Marcionite writer of the Clementine Homilies was likewise a conflict, though of another kind—the conflict of fire and water, of the sacrificial and the baptismal systems. Wherever sacrifice was mentioned with approval, there was a 'Tendenz-interpolation' (see above, p. 352 sq.). In this manner again the genuine element in the Old Testament melted down to a minimum.

[1] Grätz however (III. p. 228) sees a coincidence between Christ's teaching and Essenism in this notice. Not to do him injustice, I will translate his own words (correcting however several misprints in the Greek): 'For the connexion of Jesus with the Essenes compare moreover Mark xi. 16 καὶ οὐκ ἤφιεν

ὁ Ἰησοῦς ἵνα τις διενέγκῃ σκεῦος διὰ τοῦ ἱεροῦ with Josephus *B. J.* ii. 8. 9 ἀλλ' οὐδὲ σκεῦός τι μετακινῆσαι θαρροῦσιν (οἱ Ἐσσαῖοι).' He does not explain what this notice, which refers solely to the scrupulous observance of the sabbath, has to do with the profanation of the temple, with which the passage in the Gospel is alone concerned. I have seen Grätz's history described as a 'masterly' work. The first requisites in a historian are accuracy in stating facts and sobriety in drawing inferences. Without these, it is difficult to see what claims a history can have to this honourable epithet: and in those portions of his work, which I have consulted, I have not found either.

his observances; but with the Essene these ablutions were the predominant feature of his religious ritual. Here again it will be instructive to compare the practice of Christ and His disciples with the practice of the Essenes.

'And when they saw some of his disciples eat bread with defiled (that is to say, unwashen) hands; for the Pharisees and all the Jews, except they wash their hands oft ($\pi\nu\gamma\mu\hat{\eta}$), eat not....The Pharisees and scribes asked him, Why walk not thy disciples according to the tradition of the elders?...But he answered...Ye hypocrites, laying aside the commandment of God, ye hold the tradition of men....'

'Not that which goeth into the mouth defileth the man; but that which cometh out of the mouth, this defileth the man......Let them alone, they be blind leaders of the blind...'

'To eat with unwashen hands defileth not the man' (Matt. xv. 1—20, Mark vii. 1—23).

'And when the Pharisee saw it, he marvelled that he had not first washed before dinner ($\tau o\hat{v}$ $\dot{a}\rho\dot{\iota}\sigma\tau o\nu$). And the Lord said unto him: Now do ye Pharisees make clean the outside of the cup and the platter...Ye fools...behold all things are clean unto you' (Luke xi. 38—41).

'So they wash their whole body ($\dot{a}\pi o\lambda o\dot{v}o\nu\tau a\iota$ $\tau\dot{o}$ $\sigma\hat{\omega}\mu a$) in cold water; and after this purification ($\dot{a}\gamma\nu\epsilon\dot{\iota}a\nu$)... being clean ($\kappa a\theta a\rho o\dot{\iota}$) they come to the refectory (to dine).......And when they have returned (from their day's work) they sup in like manner' (B.J. ii. 8. 5).

'After a year's probation (the novice) is admitted to closer intercourse ($\pi\rho\dot{o}\sigma\epsilon\iota\sigma\iota\nu$ $\ddot{\epsilon}\gamma\gamma\iota o\nu$ $\tau\hat{\eta}$ $\delta\iota a\dot{\iota}\tau\eta$), and the lustral waters in which he participates have a higher degree of purity ($\kappa a\dot{\iota}$ $\kappa a\theta a\rho\omega\tau\dot{\epsilon}\rho\omega\nu$ $\tau\hat{\omega}\nu$ $\pi\rho\dot{o}s$ $\dot{a}\gamma\nu\epsilon\dot{\iota}a\nu$ $\dot{v}\delta\dot{a}\tau\omega\nu$ $\mu\epsilon\tau a\lambda a\mu\beta\dot{a}\nu\epsilon\iota$, § 7).'

'It is a custom to wash after it, as if polluted by it' (§ 9).

'Racked and dislocated, burnt and crushed, and subjected to every instrument of torture...to make them eat strange food ($\tau\iota$ $\tau\hat{\omega}\nu$ $\dot{a}\sigma\upsilon\nu\dot{\eta}\theta\omega\nu$)... they were not induced to submit' (§ 10).

'Exercising themselves in...divers lustrations ($\delta\iota a\phi\dot{o}\rho o\iota s$ $\dot{a}\gamma\nu\epsilon\dot{\iota}a\iota s$...$\dot{\epsilon}\mu\pi a\iota\delta o\tau\rho\iota\beta o\dot{v}\mu\epsilon\nu o\iota$, § 12).'

Avoidance of strangers.

Connected with this idea of external purity is the avoidance of contact with strangers, as persons who would communicate ceremonial defilement. And here too the Essene went much beyond the Pharisee. The Pharisee avoided Gentiles or aliens, or those whose profession or character placed them in the category of 'sinners'; but the Essene shrunk even from the probationers and inferior grades of his own exclusive community. Here again we may profitably compare the sayings and doings of Christ with the principles of this sect.

'And when the scribes and Pharisees saw him eat with the publicans and sinners they said unto the disciples, Why eateth your Master with the publicans and the sinners...' (Mark ii. 15 sq., Matth. ix. 10 sq., Luke v. 30 sq.).

'They say...a friend of publicans and sinners' (Matth. xi. 19).

'The Pharisees and the scribes murmured, saying, This man receiveth sinners and eateth with them' (Luke xv. 2).

'They all murmured saying that he was gone to be a guest with a man that is a sinner' (Luke xix. 7).

'Behold, a woman in the city that was a sinner...began to wash his feet with her tears, and did wipe them with the hairs of her head and kissed his feet......Now when the Pharisee which had bidden him saw it, he spake within himself, saying, This man, if he had been a prophet, would have known who and what manner of woman this is that toucheth him; for she is a sinner' (Luke vii. 37 sq.).

'And after this purification they assemble in a private room, where no person of a different belief (τῶν ἑτεροδόξων, i.e. not an Essene) is permitted to enter; and (so) being by themselves and clean (αὐτοὶ καθαροί) they present themselves at the refectory (δειπνητήριον), as if it were a sacred precinct' (§ 5).

'And they are divided into four grades according to the time passed under the discipline: and the juniors are regarded as so far inferior to the seniors, that, if they touch them, the latter wash their bodies clean (ἀπολούεσθαι), as if they had come in contact with a foreigner (καθάπερ ἀλλοφύλῳ συμφυρέντας, § 10).'

In all these minute scruples relating to ceremonial observances, the denunciations which are hurled against the Pharisees in the Gospels would apply with tenfold force to the Essenes.

(iii) If the lustrations of the Essenes far outstripped the enactments of the Mosaic law, so also did their asceticism. I have elsewhere given reasons for believing that this asceticism was founded on a false principle, which postulates the malignity of matter and is wholly inconsistent with the teaching of the Gospel[1]. But without pressing this point, of which no abso-

(iii) Asceticism.

---

[1] See *Colossians* p. 87.

400   THE ESSENES.

<small>Eating and drinking.</small>

lutely demonstrative proof can be given, it will be sufficient to call attention to the trenchant contrast in practice which Essene habits present to the life of Christ. He who 'came eating and drinking' and was denounced in consequence as 'a glutton and a wine-bibber[1],' He whose first exercise of power is recorded to have been the multiplication of wine at a festive entertainment, and whose last meal was attended with the drinking of wine and the eating of flesh, could only have excited the pity, if not the indignation, of these rigid abstainers. And again, attention should be directed to another kind of abstinence, where the contrast is all the more speaking, because the matter is so trivial and the scruple so minute.

'My head with oil thou didst not anoint' (Luke vii. 46). 'Thou, when thou fastest, anoint thy head' (Matt. vi. 17).	'And they consider oil a pollution (κηλῖδα), and though one is smeared involuntarily, he rubs his body clean (σμήχεται τὸ σῶμα, § 3).'

<small>Celibacy.</small>

And yet it has been stated that 'the Saviour of the world ......showed what is required for a holy life in the Sermon on the Mount by a description of the Essenes[2].'

But much stress has been laid on the celibacy of the Essenes; and our Lord's saying in Matt. xix. 12 is quoted to establish an identity of doctrine. Yet there is nothing special in the language there used. Nor is there any close affinity between the stern invectives against marriage which Josephus and Philo attribute to the Essene, and the gentle concession 'He that is able to receive it, let him receive it.' The best comment on our Lord's meaning here is the advice of St Paul[3], who was educated not in the Essene, but in the Pharisaic school. Moreover this saying must be balanced by the general tenour of the Gospel narrative. When we find Christ discussing the relations of man and wife, gracing the marriage festival by His presence, again and again employing wedding banquets and wedded life as apt symbols of the highest theological truths,

---

[1] Matt. xi. 19; Luke vii. 34.   [3] 1 Cor. vii. 26—31.
[2] Ginsburg *Essenes* p. 14.

without a word of disparagement or rebuke, we see plainly that we are confronted with a spirit very different from the narrow rigour of the Essenes.

(iv) But not only where the Essenes superadded to the ceremonial law, does their teaching present a direct contrast to the phenomena of the Gospel narrative. The same is true also of those points in which they fell short of the Mosaic enactments. I have already discussed at some length the Essene abstention from the temple sacrifices[1]. There can, I think, be little doubt that they objected to the slaughter of sacrificial victims altogether. But for my present purpose it matters nothing whether they avoided the temple on account of the sacrifices, or the sacrifices on account of the temple. Christ did neither. Certainly He could not have regarded the temple as unholy; for His whole time during His sojourns at Jerusalem was spent within its precincts. It was the scene of His miracles, of His ministrations, of His daily teaching[2]. And in like manner it is the common rendezvous of His disciples after Him[3]. Nor again does He evince any abhorrence of the sacrifices. On the contrary He says that the altar consecrates the gifts[4]; He charges the cleansed lepers to go and fulfil the Mosaic ordinance and offer the sacrificial offerings to the priests[5]. And His practice also is conformable to His teaching. He comes to Jerusalem regularly to attend the great festivals, where sacrifices formed the most striking part of the ceremonial, and He himself enjoins preparation to be made for the sacrifice of the Paschal lamb. If He repeats the inspired warning of the older prophets, that mercy is better than sacrifice[6], this very qualification shows approval of the practice in itself. Nor is His silence less eloquent than His utterances or His actions.

(iv) Avoidance of the Temple sacrifices.

Practice of Christ and His disciples.

---

[1] See p. 350 sq.
[2] Matt. xxi. 12 sq., 23 sq., xxiv. 1 sq., xxvi. 55, Mark xi. 11, 15 sq., 27, xii. 35, xiii. 1 sq., xiv. 49, Luke ii. 46, xix. 45, xx. 1 sq., xxi. 37 sq., xxii. 53, John ii. 14 sq., v. 14, vii. 14, viii. 2, 20, 59, x. 23, xi. 56, xviii. 20.
[3] Luke xxiv. 53, Acts ii. 46, iii. 1 sq., v. 20 sq., 42.
[4] Matt. xxiii. 18 sq.: comp. v. 23, 24.
[5] Matt. viii. 4, Mark i. 44, Luke v. 14.
[6] Matt. ix. 13, xii. 7.

Throughout the Gospels there is not one word which can be construed as condemning the sacrificial system or as implying a desire for its cessation until everything is fulfilled.

(v) Denial of the resurrection of the body.
(v) This last contrast refers to the ceremonial law. But not less wide is the divergence on an important point of doctrine. The resurrection of the body is a fundamental article in the belief of the early disciples. This was distinctly denied by the Essenes[1]. However gross and sensuous may have been the conceptions of the Pharisees on this point, still they so far agreed with the teaching of Christianity, as against the Essenes, in that the risen man could not, as they held, be pure soul or spirit, but must necessarily be body and soul conjoint.

Some supposed coincidences considered.
Thus at whatever point we test the teaching and practice of our Lord by the characteristic tenets of Essenism, the theory of affinity fails. There are indeed several coincidences on which much stress has been laid, but they cannot be placed in the category of distinctive features. They are either exemplifications of a higher morality, which may indeed have been honourably illustrated in the Essenes, but is in no sense confined to them, being the natural outgrowth of the moral sense of mankind whenever circumstances are favourable. Or they are more special, but still independent developments, which owe their similarity to the same influences of climate and soil, though they do not spring from the same root. To this latter class belong such manifestations as are due to the social conditions of the age or nation, whether they result from sympathy with, or from repulsion to, those conditions.

Simplicity and brotherly love.
Thus, for instance, much stress has been laid on the aversion to war and warlike pursuits, on the simplicity of living, and on the feeling of brotherhood which distinguished Christians and Essenes alike. But what is gained by all this? It is quite plain that Christ would have approved whatever was pure and lovely in the morality of the Essenes, just as He

---

[1] See *Colossians* p. 88.

approved whatever was true in the doctrine of the Pharisees, if any occasion had presented itself when His approval was called for. But it is the merest assumption to postulate direct obligation on such grounds. It is said however, that the moral resemblances are more particular than this. There is for instance Christ's precept 'Swear not at all...but let your communication be Yea, yea, Nay, nay.' Have we not here, it is urged, the very counterpart to the Essene prohibition of oaths[1]? Yet it would surely be quite as reasonable to say that both alike enforce that simplicity and truthfulness in conversation which is its own credential and does not require the support of adjuration, both having the same reason for laying stress on this duty, because the leaders of religious opinion made artificial distinctions between oath and oath, as regards their binding force, and thus sapped the foundations of public and private honesty[2]. And indeed this avoidance of oaths is anything but a special badge of the Essenes. It was inculcated by Pythagoreans, by Stoics, by philosophers and moralists of all schools[3]. When Josephus and Philo called the attention of Greeks and Romans to this feature in the Essenes, they were simply asking them to admire in these practical philosophers among the 'barbarians' the realisation of an ideal which their own great men had laid down. Even within the circles of

Prohibition of oaths.

---

[1] Jos. B. J. ii. 8. 6 πᾶν τὸ ῥηθὲν ὑπ' αὐτῶν ἰσχυρότερον ὅρκου· τὸ δὲ ὀμνύειν αὐτοῖς περιίσταται, χεῖρόν τι τῆς ἐπιορκίας ὑπολαμβάνοντες· ἤδη γὰρ κατεγνῶσθαι φασὶ τὸν ἀπιστούμενον δίχα Θεοῦ, Philo Omn. prob. lib. 12 (II. p. 458) τοῦ φιλοθέου δείγματα παρέχονται μυρία...τὸ ἀνώμοτον κ.τ.λ. Accordingly Josephus relates (Ant. xv. 10. 4) that Herod the Great excused the Essenes from taking the oath of allegiance to him. Yet they were not altogether true to their principles; for Josephus says (B. J. ii. 8. 7), that on initiation into the sect the members were bound by fearful oaths (ὅρκους φρικώδεις) to fulfil certain conditions; and he twice again in the same passage mentions oaths (ὀμνύουσι, τοιούτοις ὅρκοις) in this connexion.

[2] On the distinctions which the Jewish doctors made between the validity of different kinds of oaths, see the passages quoted in Lightfoot and Schöttgen on Matt. v. 33 sq. The Talmudical tract *Shebhuoth* tells its own tale, and is the best comment on the precepts in the Sermon on the Mount.

[3] See e.g. the passages in Wetstein on Matt. v. 37.

Pharisaism language is occasionally heard, which meets the Essene principle half-way[1].

Community of goods.

And again; attention has been called to the community of goods in the infant Church of Christ, as though this were a legacy of Essenism. But here too the reasonable explanation is, that we have an independent attempt to realise the idea of brotherhood—an attempt which naturally suggested itself without any direct imitation, but which was soon abandoned under the pressure of circumstances. Indeed the communism of the Christians was from the first wholly unlike the communism of the Essenes. The surrender of property with the Christians was not a necessary condition of entrance into an order; it was a purely voluntary act, which might be withheld without foregoing the privileges of the brotherhood[2]. And the common life too was obviously different in kind, at once more free and more sociable, unfettered by rigid ordinances, respecting individual liberty, and altogether unlike a monastic rule.

Prohibition of slavery.

Not less irrelevant is the stress, which has been laid on another point of supposed coincidence in the social doctrines of the two communities. The prohibition of slavery was indeed a highly honourable feature in the Essene order[3], but it affords no indication of a direct connexion with Christianity. It is true that this social institution of antiquity was not less antagonistic to the spirit of the Gospel, than it was abhorrent to the feelings of the Essene; and ultimately the influence of Christianity has triumphed over it. But the immediate treatment of the question was altogether different in the two cases. The Essene brothers proscribed slavery wholly; they produced no appreciable results by the proscription. The Christian Apostles, without attempting an immediate and violent revolution in society, proclaimed the great principle that all men are equal in Christ, and left it to work. It did work, like leaven,

---

[1] *Baba Metsia* 49 a. See also Lightfoot on Matt. v. 34.
[2] Acts v. 4.
[3] Philo *Omn. prob. lib.* § 12 (II. p. 458) δοῦλός τε παρ' αὐτοῖς οὐδὲ εἷς ἐστιν ἀλλ' ἐλεύθεροι πάντες κ.τ.λ., *Fragm.* II. p. 632 οὐκ ἀνδράποδον, Jos. *Ant.* xviii. 1, 5 οὔτε δούλων ἐπιτηδεύουσι κτῆσιν.

silently but surely, till the whole lump was leavened. In the matter of slavery the resemblance to the Stoic is much closer than to the Essene[1]. The Stoic however began and ended in barren declamation, and no practical fruits were reaped from his doctrine.

Moreover prominence has been given to the fact that riches are decried, and a preference is given to the poor, in the teaching of our Lord and His Apostles. Here again, it is urged, we have a distinctly Essene feature. We need not stop to enquire with what limitations this prerogative of poverty, which appears in the Gospels, must be interpreted; but, quite independently of this question, we may fairly decline to lay any stress on such a coincidence, where all other indications of a direct connexion have failed. The Essenes, pursuing a simple and ascetic life, made it their chief aim to reduce their material wants as far as possible, and in doing so they necessarily exalted poverty. Ascetic philosophers in Greece and Rome had done the same. Christianity was entrusted with the mission of proclaiming the equal rights of all men before God, of setting a truer standard of human worth than the outward conventions of the world, of protesting against the tyranny of the strong and the luxury of the rich, of redressing social inequalities, if not always by a present compensation, at least by a future hope. The needy and oppressed were the special charge of its preachers. It was the characteristic feature of the 'Kingdom of Heaven,' as described by the prophet whose words gave the keynote to the Messianic hopes of the nation, that the glad tidings should be preached to the poor[2]. The exaltation of poverty therefore was an absolute condition of the Gospel.

Respect paid to poverty.

The mention of the kingdom of heaven leads to the last point on which it will be necessary to touch before leaving this

The preaching of the Kingdom

---

[1] See for instance the passages from Seneca quoted in *Philippians* p. 307.

[2] Is. lxi. 1, εὐαγγελίσασθαι πτωχοῖς, quoted in Luke iv. 18. There are references to this particular part of the prophecy again in Matt. xi. 5, Luke vii. 22, and probably also in the beatitude μακάριοι οἱ πτωχοί κ.τ.λ., Matt. v. 3, Luke vi. 20.

subject. 'The whole ascetic life of the Essenes,' it has been said, 'aimed only at furthering the *Kingdom of Heaven* and the *Coming Age.*' Thus John the Baptist was the proper representative of this sect. 'From the Essenes went forth the first call that the Messiah must shortly appear, *The kingdom of heaven is at hand*'[1]. 'The announcement of the kingdom of heaven unquestionably went forth from the Essenes'[2]. For this confident assertion there is absolutely no foundation in fact; and, as a conjectural hypothesis, the assumption is highly improbable.

As fortune-tellers or soothsayers, the Essenes might be called prophets; but as preachers of righteousness, as heralds of the kingdom, they had no claim to the title. Throughout the notices in Josephus and Philo we cannot trace the faintest indication of Messianic hopes. Nor indeed was their position at all likely to foster such hopes[3]. The Messianic idea was built on a belief in the resurrection of the body. The Essenes entirely denied this doctrine. The Messianic idea was intimately bound up with the national hopes and sufferings, with the national life, of the Jews. The Essenes had no interest in the Jewish polity; they separated themselves almost entirely from public affairs. The deliverance of the individual in the shipwreck of the whole, it has been well said, was the plain watchword of Essenism[4]. How entirely the conception of a Messiah might be obliterated, where Judaism was regarded only from the side of a mystic philosophy, we see from the case of Philo. Throughout the works of this voluminous writer only one or two faint and doubtful allusions to a personal Messiah are found[5]. The philosophical tenets of the Essenes

---

[1] Grätz *Gesch.* III. p. 219.
[2] *ib.* p. 470.
[3] Lipsius *Schenkel's Bibel-Lexikon* s. v. Essäer p. 190, Keim *Jesus von Nazara* I. p. 305. Both these writers express themselves very decidedly against the view maintained by Grätz. 'The Essene art of soothsaying,' writes Lipsius, 'has absolutely nothing to do with the Messianic prophecy.' 'Of all this,' says Keim, 'there is no trace.'
[4] Keim, *l. c.*
[5] How little can be made out of Philo's Messianic utterances by one who is anxious to make the most possible out of them, may be seen from

no doubt differed widely from those of Philo; but in the substitution of the individual and contemplative aspect of religion for the national and practical they were united; and the effect in obscuring the Messianic idea would be the same. When therefore it is said that the prominence given to the proclamation of the Messiah's kingdom is a main link which connects Essenism and Christianity, we may dismiss the statement as a mere hypothesis, unsupported by evidence and improbable in itself.

Gfrörer's treatment of the subject, *Philo* I. p. 486 sq. The treatises which bear on this topic are the *de Praemiis et Poenis* (I. p. 408, ed. Mangey) and the *de Execrationibus* (I. p. 429). They deserve to be read, if only for the negative results which they yield.

INDICES.

I. INDEX OF SUBJECTS.

II. INDEX OF PASSAGES.

INDEX OF SUBJECTS.

Aaronic priesthood; see *priesthood*
Acts of the Apostles; its scope and character, 104 sq, 117 sq; its relation to St Paul's Epistles, 59 sq, 104 sq, 117 sq
Addai, the Doctrine of, 172
Aelia Capitolina, foundation of, 72; church of, 73, 169
Aelius Publius Julius, 179
Aerius, 197
Africa, the Church of, catholicity of the, 92, 102; episcopacy in, 187; numerous sees in, 187; synods of, 187, 207; sacerdotalism in, 228
Alasanda or Alasadda, 373
Alcibiades of Apamea, 88
Alexander (the Great); his view of his mission, 290; effects of his conquests, 253, 290 sq
Alexander of Alexandria, 195
Alexander of Rome, 183 sq
Alexander Polyhistor, 376
Alexandria, a supposed Buddhist establishment at, 373
Alexandria, the Church of; early foundation of, 92, 187 sq; orthodoxy of, 92; state of religion in, 187 sq; mode of election of the bishop of, 194 sq
Alexandrian Judaism and the Gospel, 286
Alfius, the name, 20
Alphæus, to be identified with Clopas? 8, 19, 44; with Alfius? 20
altar, use of the word, 217, 229, 234
Ambrose (St), on the Lord's brethren, 24, 41

Ambrosiaster; see *Hilary*
Ancient Syriac Documents (Cureton), 104, 172, 183, 228
Ancyra, Council of, 196
Andrew (St) in Asia Minor, 161
Anencletus, 183
angels, of a synagogue, 158; in the Apocalypse, 158 sq
Anicetus, 182, 185
Antidicomarianites, 39
Antioch; foundation of the Church at, 55 sq; the new metropolis of Christendom, 59; bishops of, 170 sq; catholicity of, 92 sq, 131; Judaizers at, 131; see *Paul (St)*
Antioch in Pisidia, St Paul preaches at, 59
Antonius Melissa, 219
Apocalypse; Hebrew in its imagery, 120, 159; but not Ebionite in doctrine, 120; its relation to Christ, and the Law, 120 sq; compared with St John's Gospel and Epistles, 123; angels in the, 158 sq; date of, 159
Apocryphal Gospels, on the Lord's brethren, 12, 26 sq
Apostles; the title not limited to the twelve, 11; not bishops, 153 sq; supervision of churches by, 157; first Council of, 59 sq (passim); evidence for a second Council of, 161
Apostolic congress and decree, 59 sq (passim), 108
Apostolic Constitutions; on the Jameses, 36; sacerdotal language of, 226; untrustworthy, 190

INDEX OF SUBJECTS.

Apostolic delegates, 157 sq
Aratus, 288
Areopagus; see *Paul (St)*
Ariston of Pella, 68 sq
asah, a supposed derivation of Essene, 330, 340
Ascents of James, 29, 87, 118, 126 sq, 389, 393 sq
asceticism, of the Essenes, 393 sq
Asia Minor; apostles settled in, 161; episcopacy in, 172 sq; probably matured there, 161, 166 sq, 172 sq, 190 sq, 244; catholicity of the Church of, 92; sides with Cyprian, 207
Asidæans, 332
asya, a supposed derivation of Essene, 328
Athens; episcopacy at, 178; a Buddhist burnt alive at, 378
Aubertin's (C.) *Sénèque et St Paul*, 258, 275, 282, 317
Augustine (St); on the Lord's brethren, 8, 42 sq; on episcopacy, 193; on pre-Christian Christianity, 315
Augustus, Indian embassy to, 375, 378
Aurelius (M. Antoninus); his character, 282, 303 sq; his modified Stoicism, 303 sq; defects of his teaching, 304; persecution of the Christians by, 304; supposed relations with rabbi Jehuda, 304; notice of Christianity by, 305; on immortality, 311

Bacchyllus, 178
Balaam and Nicolas, 52, 64
Banaim, 348 sq
Banus, 348 sq, 385
Barcochba, rebellion of, 69, 71 sq
Bardesanes; on Buddhists, 376; his date, 377; the *de Fato* by a disciple of, 86
Barnabas, Joseph, not Joses, 20
Barnabas, Epistle of, date and place of writing of, 187
Barsabas, Joseph or Joses, 20
Basil (St), on the Lord's brethren, 38

Basilides; and idol-sacrifices, 65; and Glaucus, 112
Baur (C. F.), 49, 64, 91, 98, 105, 111, 197, 258, 279, 362
Bene-hakkeneseth, 346
bishops; see *episcopate*
Bonosus, 40
Bradshaw, 26
Brahminism, 375 sq
brethren of the Lord, 3 sq (passim)
'brother,' wide use of the term, 7, 12 sq, 42
Buddhism; its assumed influence on Essenism, 372 sq; supposed establishment of, at Alexandria, 373; unknown in the West, 374 sq; four steps of, 379
Buddhist at Athens, 378
Bunsen, 32, 33, 35
burial clubs, Christian brotherhoods first recognized by Roman government as, 152
Burrus and St Paul, 285
Butler (Bp.), 313

Caius or Gaius (St Paul's host), 177
Callistus, 102, 186
Calvin's distinction of lay and teaching elders, 153
Carthage; see *Africa*
Cassiodorus; his translation of Clement of Alexandria, 32
Cassius of Tyre, 169
Catholic Church, 163, 167 sq
Cato the younger, his character, 296
celibacy, 357, 400 sq
chaber, 343 sq
Chagigah, on ceremonial purity, 343 sq
chasha, chashaim, a derivation of Essene, 331
chasid, chasyo, a derivation of Essene, 327, 330
Chasidim, 332, 335 sq; not a proper name for Essene, 327
chasin, chosin, a derivation of Essene, 327
chaza, chazya, a derivation of Essene, 329

INDEX OF SUBJECTS.

chazan, his duties, 147

chorepiscopi, 196

Christ; high priesthood of, 217; the Word, 274, 287, 315; the true vine, 314, 316; membership in, 291 sq; His teaching and practice not Essene, 395 sq; see *Christianity, Church, Resurrection* etc.

Christian, the name, 56

Christian ministry, priesthood etc.; see *ministry, priesthood* etc.

Christianity; distinguishing feature of, 313 sq; its true character, 314 sq; not an outgrowth of Essenism, 381 sq

Christianized Essenes, 352

Christians of St John, 390

Chrysippus, 255 sq, 278, 288, 310

Chrysostom (St), on the Lord's brethren, 8, 38, 43 sq

Church of Christ; ideal of, 137; its practical limitations, 137 sq; influence of this ideal, 139 sq; false ideas prevailing in, 237 sq

circumcision, the question of, 59 sq

citizenship; St Paul's metaphor of the heavenly, 292; rights of Roman, 290 sq

Clarus of Ptolemais, 169

Claudius, embassy from Ceylon in the reign of, 379

Claudius Apollinaris, 174

Cleanthes; character of, 295; hymn of, 288, 306; on immortality, 310; committed suicide, 295

Clement of Alexandria; on the Lord's brethren, 32 sq; on the Nicolaitans, 52; his commentary on the Catholic Epistles, 32; on the ministry, 172, 189, 192, 221 sq; no sacerdotalism in, 221; on Indian philosophers, 375; on Plato, 276; on St Matthew, 80; quotes the 'Preaching of Peter,' 111

Clement of Rome; a Greek, 186; his position in the Church, 95 sq, 99, 179, 183 sq; his Epistle, 95 sq, 116 sq, 164 sq, 177, 215; passages discussed, 162 sq, 164 sq, 215 sq; no sacerdotalism in, 215 sq; use of term

'offerings' in, 230; bishops and presbyters identified in, 165, 179 sq

Clementine Homilies; their scope and complexion, 83 sq, 98 sq; editions and epitomes of, 84; their Roman origin doubtful, 98 sq; their representation of St James, 27, 29, 130, 155 sq, 168; attacks on St Paul, 83 sq; letter of Peter prefixed to, 86; letter of Clement prefixed to, 99; not sacerdotal, 227; on episcopacy, 170, 171, 202; Essene features in, 352 sq; recommend excision of the scriptures, 352 sq, 355; on the Hemerobaptists, 391

Clementine Recognitions; composition of, 36 sq; editions and collations of, 84; 'Ascents of James' incorporated in, 29, 87, 118, 126 sq, 389; arbitrary alteration of Rufinus in, 86 sq; on episcopacy, 170, 171

Cleopas, the name, 19

clergy; distinguished from the laity, 212 sq; origin of the term, 212

Cletus, 183

Clopas, 7 sq, 19 sq, 29 sq; to be identified with Alphæus? 7 sq, 19, 44

clubs, 152

Collyridians, 39

community of goods, 404

compresbyterus, 193

confraternities, 152

congregation, the holy, at Jerusalem, 346

conscientia, 303

Corinth, the Church of; associated with St Peter and St Paul, 117; its catholicity, 117; parties in, 117 sq, 132 sq, 177; Judaizers in, 132 sq; St Paul's dealings with, 157; episcopacy in, 177; see *Clement of Rome*

Corinthians, the Epistles to the; no sacerdotalism in, 211

Cornelius, conversion of, 54 sq

Cornelius, bishop of Rome, 146

Crete, episcopacy in, 178

Cyprian; his mode of addressing presbyters, 193; his view of the episcopate, 204 sq, 208 sq; controversies of, 205 sq; his character and work, 204 sq; genuineness of his letters, 206; sacerdotalism of, 226

Cyril of Alexandria; on the Lord's brethren, 44; source of his account of the Buddhists, 376

Cyril of Jerusalem, on the Lord's brethren, 37

Damascene, John, 219
De Quincey, 381
diaconate; its establishment, 144 sq; its novelty, 146 sq; limitation to seven, 145 sq; its functions, 146 sq; teaching incidental to, 147; extension to gentile churches, 148 sq
deaconesses, 148
deacons; see *diaconate*
Demetrius of Alexandria, 196
Dion Chrysostom, 375
Dionysius of Alexandria, 194
Dionysius the Areopagite, 178
Dionysius of Corinth, 102; his testimony to episcopacy, 175, 177, 185; couples St Peter and St Paul, 117
dispersion, the, 50
Dorotheus Tyrius, the pseudo-, 5, 40
dualism, in Essenism, 369

Eastern Churches, testimony respecting the Jameses from, 44
Ebionites; different classes of, 73 sq, 77 sq (passim); the churches of Palestine not Ebionite, 88 sq; nor other churches, 92 sq; the sect dies out, 103
Ecce Homo quoted, 293, 308, 309
Egnatius the Stoic, 265
Egypt, episcopacy in, 194 sq
Egyptians, Gospel of the; tradition respecting gnosis in, 33 sq
Elchasai, founder of the Mandeans, 393
Elchasai or Elxai, book of, 80 sq, 102, 354 sq, 392 sq
elders, primitive, 347 sq
Eleutherus, 185
Elieser (Rabbi), on the Samaritans, 53 sq

Emesa, 229
Epaphroditus, Nero's freedman, 299
Epictetus; his earnestness and piety, 299 sq; his theology and ethics, 302; modified stoicism of, 305; his places of abode, 300; coincidences with the N. T. in, 281 sq, 299 sq; especially with St Paul, 299 sq, 302; his notice of Christianity, 305; his views on immortality, 311
Epicurus; sayings of, 262, 269, 271; admired by Seneca, 275; his system, 251 sq; its Greek origin, 252; Epicurean ethics basely consistent, 312
Epiphanius; on the Lord's brethren, 4 sq (passim), 39 sq; on the Nazarenes, 75; on the Nasareans, 353
episcopate; bishops not the same as Apostles, 153 sq; episcopate developed from presbytery, 154 sq, 166, 189 sq; preparatory steps towards, 156 sq; causes of development, 160, 165 sq, 198; gradual progress of, 165 sq, 190, 197 sq; first matured in Asia Minor, 161, 166 sq, 172 sq, 190 sq, 244; episcopate of Jerusalem, 155, 168 sq; of other churches, 160, 169 sq; prevalence of episcopacy, 190; ordination confined to bishops, 197; foreign correspondence entrusted to them, 184; their mode of addressing presbyters, 193; they represent the universal Church, 207; their increased power involves no principle, 209 sq; see *synods* etc.
Escha, 12
Essene; meaning of the name, 325 sq; Frankel's theory, 333 sq
Essene Ebionism, 79 sq, 127, 322 (passim)
Essenes; Josephus and Philo chief authorities upon, 350; oath taken by, 340; their grades, 343; origin and affinities, 332 sq; relation to Christianity, 381 sq; to Pharisaism, 333; to Neopythagoreanism, 362 sq; to Hemerobaptists, 386 sq; to Parsism, 369 sq; to Buddhism, 372 sq; avoidance of oaths, 403; fortune-

INDEX OF SUBJECTS. 415

tellers, 406; silence of New Test. about, 382 sq; relation to John the Baptist, 384 sq; to James, the Lord's brother, 393 sq; Christianized Essenes, 352; not sacerdotal, 228

Essenism; compared with Christianity, 395 sq; the sabbath, 396 sq; lustrations, 397 sq; avoidance of strangers, 398 sq; asceticism, celibacy, 399 sq; avoidance of the temple, 401; denial of the resurrection of the body, 402; certain supposed coincidences with Christianity, 402

Ethiopian Eunuch, conversion of, 54

Euarestus, 183, 184

Euodius, 170

Eusebius of Cæsarea; Syriac translation of, 33, 36, 90, 117; a passage of Clement of Alexandria preserved in, 33 sq; on the Lord's brethren, 36; his silence misinterpreted, 103 sq; on the second apostolic council, 162; his list of bishops of Jerusalem, 168 sq; of Rome, 183; of Alexandria, 188

Eutychius, on the mode of appointment of the patriarch of Alexandria, 195

Fleury's *St Paul et Sénèque*, 258, 262, 317, 319 sq

Frankel, on the Essenes, 333 sq

Gaius; see *Caius*

Gallio; St Paul before, 285; Seneca's account of, 285

Gaul, episcopacy in, 186

Gentiles; the Gospel preached to, 49 sq (passim); emancipation and progress of, 56 sq (passim)

Gibbon; on the Lord's brethren, 41; on the spread of Christianity, 311, 314

Ginsburg (Dr), 341 sq, 344, 382, 400

Glaucias, 111

Gnosticism serves to develope episcopacy, 160

Grätz, 70, 327, 337, 381, 383, 396, 397

Gregory Nyssen, on the Lord's brethren, 38

Hadrian; his treatment of Jews and Christians, 72; authenticity of his letter to Servianus, 188; his visit to Egypt, 188

Hananias, 195

Hebrews, Epistle to the; its Alexandrian origin, 187; absence of sacerdotalism in and general argument of, 233 sq

Hebrews, Gospel of the; account of our Lord appearing to James in, 26 sq

Hegesippus; not an Ebionite, 90 sq; on the Lord's brethren, 18 sq, 29 sq; on James the Lord's brother, 80, 125, 168; on heresies in the Church of Jerusalem, 71, 82; on Symeon, 19, 30, 162, 168; on the Corinthian Church, 177; his sojourn in Rome, 89 sq, 102, 182 sq; on the Roman Church and bishops, 182 sq; his acquaintance with Eleutherus, 185; aim of his work, 182, 204

Hellenists, their influence in the early Church, 51 sq, 144 sq

Helvidius, on the Lord's brethren, 4 sq (passim), 40

Helvidius Priscus, 297

Hemerobaptists, 386 sq

Heraclas of Alexandria, 194, 196

heretics, rebaptism of, 207

Hermas, the Shepherd of; its author, 184; his language, 186; its character and teaching, 97; on Church officers, etc. 180 sq; on Clement, 180, 184

Hermippus, 372

Hero of Antioch, 171

Hierapolis, its bishops, 174

high-priests; mitre of, 220; Christians so called, 217 sq, 220, 223 sq; see *Christ*

Hilary (Ambrosiaster); on the Lord's brethren, 37; on the priesthood, 141; on episcopacy, 163, 167, 192; on the Alexandrian episcopate, 194

Hilary of Poitiers, on the Lord's brethren, 24, 37

Hilgenfeld, on the Essenes, 372 sq

Hippolytus; on James the Lord's brother, 33; on the Nicolaitans, 52; on the book of Elchasai, 80 sq, 88, 100; St John illustrated from, 65; use of κλῆρος in, 214; sacerdotal terms in, 223; the pseudo-, on the Lord's brethren, 9, 35
Holzherr, 311
Hyginus, 184

idols, things sacrificed to, 63 sq
Ignatian letters (short Greek); their genuineness, 198, 239 sq, 242 sq; on episcopacy, 173 sq, 200 sq; on presbyters, 201; the language considered, 201 sq; not sacerdotal, 217; use of 'altar' in, 234; a passage misinterpreted (*Philad*. 9), 217
Ignatian letters (Syriac Version); an abridgment, 198, 242; their testimony to episcopacy, 173, 198 sq, 243
Ignatius; his testimony to the Roman Church, 96, 180; on St Peter and St Paul, 116; see *Ignatian letters*
immortality of man, 309 sq
India, communications between the West and, 372 sq, 375 sq
Irenæus; his use of terms 'bishop' and 'presbyter,' 189, 190, 191 sq; of 'oblations,' 231; of κλῆρος, 214; list of Roman bishops in, 182 sq; on episcopacy, 172, 190, 203 sq; on priesthood, 218 sq; on a second Apostolic Council, 162; on the Paschal controversy, 101; Pfaffian fragments of, 164; his relation to Hegesippus, 182
Ischyras, 195

James, the Lord's brother; was he one of the Twelve? 12 sq (passim); our Lord's appearance to him, 17, 26, 124; his position, 123 sq; a bishop, 155, 168; but one of the presbytery, 155 sq; his asceticism, 124 sq, 394; but not an Essene, 393 sq; his relation to the Judaizers, 61, 124 sq, 129 sq (passim); to St Peter and St John, 127 sq; to St Paul (faith and works), 129 sq; his death, 68, 126; account of him in the Hebrew Gospel, 26 sq; in the Clementines, 29; among the Ophites, 33; see also *Ascents of James*
James, the son of Alphæus, 5 sq (passim)
James, the son of Mary, 7 sq (passim)
James, the son of Zebedee, martyrdom of, 58; was he a cousin of our Lord? 15 sq
Jason and Papiscus, 69
Jehuda ha-Nasi, 304
Jerome; his disingenuousness, 31; on the Lord's brethren, 4 sq (passim), 41; on the Nazarenes, 73; on the origin of episcopacy, 166, 193; on Church policy in Alexandria, 194; on episcopal ordination, 197; on Seneca, 249 sq, 276, 318; dates of some of his works, 11
Jerusalem; the fall of, 68 sq; the early Church of, 49 sq; its waning influence, 58 sq (passim); the Council of, 59 sq; outbreak of heresies in, 70 sq; reconstitution of, 72 sq, 88; bishops of, 155, 168 sq; presbytery of, 156; its attitude in the Paschal controversy, 88
Jewish names; exchanged for heathen, 19 sq; abbreviated, 20 sq
Jewish priesthood; see *priesthood*
John (St); was he the Lord's cousin? 15 sq; in Asia Minor, 161, 167; his position in the Church, 118 sq; matures episcopacy, 160, 167, 172 sq, 244; traditions relating to, 121; not claimed by the Ebionites, 118; on idol-sacrifices, 64; Gospel and Epistles of, 123, 387 sq; Apocalypse of, 120 sq
John Damascene, 219
John the Baptist; not an Essene, 384 sq; disciples of, at Ephesus, 387; claimed by the Hemerobaptists, 387
John (St), Christians of, 390
Joseph, a common name, 20; occurrence in our Lord's genealogy, 21; the same as Joses? 20

INDEX OF SUBJECTS. 417

Joseph, the Virgin's husband, early death of, 22
Josephus; on the death of St James, 126; on Essenism, 325 sq, 344 sq; the pseudo-, 68
Joses, the son of Mary, 20
Jovinianus, 40
Judaizers, 59 sq (passim), 66, 73 sq (passim), 107 sq (passim), 131 sq (passim); not sacerdotal, 227
Judas the Apostle and the Lord's brother the same? 8 sq (passim)
Judas, a name of Thomas, 15
Julianus of Apamea, 175
Justin Martyr; not an Ebionite, 88, 89 sq; a fragment wrongly ascribed to, 81 sq; use of 'oblations' in, 231; not sacerdotal, 218
Justus, bishop of Jerusalem, 168
Justus, the name, 125

laity, 212 sq
Lactantius, 277
lapsed, controversy about the, 205 sq
law, our Lord's teaching as regards, 49; zeal for and decline of, 67 sq (passim); relation of St Peter to, 110 sq; of St John to, 121 sq, 128; of St James to, 124 sq, 127 sq; see *St Paul*
Linus, 183
lots, the use of, 213
Lucian, sacerdotal language of, 229
lustrations of the Essenes, 397 sq
Luther uses different language at different times, 108

M. Anneus Paulus Petrus, 284
Macedonia, the church of, episcopacy in, 175 sq
magic among the Essenes, 358
Mandeans, 390
Marcion, parentage of, 175
Marcus, bishop of Jerusalem, 169
Marcus Aurelius; see *Aurelius*
Mark (St); his connexion with Alexandria, 187, 194; a link between St Peter and St Paul, 116
Martinus Bragensis; his relation to Seneca, 320; works of, 320; recensions, titles and MSS. of the *Formula Honestae Vitae* of, 320 sq
Mary, different persons bearing the name, 7 sq, 11 sq, 13 sq, 21 sq, 38, 43
Mary, the Lord's mother; her virginity, 23 sq; commended to the keeping of St John, 24
Matthew (St), his alleged asceticism, 80
Matthias (St), appointment of, 213
Megasthenes, 375 sq
Melcha, 12
Melito, 121, 174
Mill, 3, 26, 35, 36
Milman (Dean), 98, 216, 371
ministry (the Christian), three orders of, 143 sq, 235 sq; not sacerdotal, 141 sq; St Paul on, 141 sq; the temporary and the permanent, 142 sq; views as to the origin of, 143 sq; how far a priesthood, 232 sq; representative, not vicarial, 235 sq; see *sacerdotalism, priesthood, episcopate* etc
Mithras-worship, 372
Mommsen, on Cato, 296
monasticism of the Essenes and Buddhists, 379
Montanism, a reaction, 203
morning-bathers, 348, 386 sq

Narcissus, bishop of Jerusalem, 169
Nasareans, 353
Nazarenes (Nasoreans), 74 sq, 352, 355, 390
Neander, criticism on, 216
Neoplatonism, its conflict with Christianity, 305
Neopythagoreanism and Essenism, 362 sq
Neronian persecution mentioned in the correspondence of St Paul and Seneca, 319
Nicolas and the Nicolaitans, 52
Nicolaus of Damascus, 378
Novatian schism, 206

oblation, offering; see *sacrifice*
Onesimus of Ephesus, 173
Ophites; perhaps referred to in the

Apocalypse, 65; used the Gospel of the Egyptians, 33
ordination; at Alexandria, 194 sq; generally restricted to bishops, 195 sq
Oriental characteristics of Stoicism, 252 sq
Origen; on the Lord's brethren, 34 sq; on the Ebionites, 73, 88; on Gaius, 177; on the priesthood, 224

Palestine, churches of: not Ebionite, 88 sq; sees and bishops of, 169 sq
Palmas, 175
Panætius, 256
Pantænus in India, 375, 377
Pantheism admits no consciousness of sin, 278 sq, 307 sq
papacy, power of the, 209 sq
Papias; bishop of Hierapolis, 174; his use of the word 'presbyter', 192; passage wrongly ascribed to, 25 sq
Papias (the medieval), his *Elementarium*, 25 sq
Parsism; resemblances to, in Essenism, 369 sq; spread by the destruction of the Persian Empire, 371; influence of, 372
Paschal controversy, 88, 101
Pastoral Epistles; date of, 159; no sacerdotalism in, 210 sq
patriarchs; Jewish, 188; Alexandrian, 189, 194 sq
Paul (St); his portrait in the Acts, 104; his qualifications and conversion, 57; his first missionary journey, 59 sq; at the council of Jerusalem, 60 sq; conflict with St Peter at Antioch, 112; his speech on Areopagus, 272, 288; his supposed connexion with Seneca, 284; his trial at Rome, 285; his acquaintance with Stoic diction, etc. 288 sq; on idol-sacrifices, 63; his relation to the Apostles of the circumcision, 46 sq (passim), 108 sq (passim), see *James, Peter, John;* relations to his countrymen, 105 sq; attacks of Judaizers on, see *Judaizers, Clementine Homilies;* on the law, see *law;* recognised in the *Test. xii Patr.* 75 sq, 77
Paul (St), Epistles of; their partial reception in the early Church, 345; questioned by modern critics, 105
Pauli Praedicatio, 111 sq, 162
peccatum, 278 sq, 307 sq
Pelagius, on the Lord's brethren, 42
Pella, Church of, 68 sq, 72 sq
Peter (St); his vision and its effects, 113; at Antioch, 112 sq, 115; at Rome, 94; his character, 114; his position, 59; how regarded by St Paul, 109 sq; how represented in the Clementines, 80, 83 sq, 110 sq; by Basilides etc., 111; coupled with St Paul in early writers, 116 sq; writings ascribed to, 111 sq; bishops traditionally appointed by, 170; styled himself a 'fellow-presbyter,' 157
Peter (St), First Epistle of; its character etc. 114 sq; its resemblance to St Paul, 114 sq
Peter, Gospel of; its docetism, 27; on the Lord's brethren, 27
Peter, Preaching of, not Ebionite, 111 sq
Pfaff, 164
Pharisees, their relation to Essenes, 333 sq, 357, 359
Philip the Apostle, settled at Hierapolis, 161
Philip the deacon, his work, 53
Philip of Gortyna, 178
Philo, on the Essenes, 326, 361
philosophy, later Greek, 251 sq
Piers Ploughman, 315
Pinytus, 178
Pius (I) of Rome, 184, 186
Plato; his portrait of the just man, 275; on preparation for death, 312
Polycarp; a bishop, 170, 173; visits Rome, 101, 185; mentions no bishop of Philippi, 176; has no sacerdotal views, 217
Polycrates of Ephesus; his date and style, 121 sq; his relatives, 174; his testimony to Polycarp, 173;

INDEX OF SUBJECTS. 419

traditions preserved by, 101, 121 sq; other quotations from his writings, 173, 175; notice of St John in, 121 sq, 220; is he sacerdotal? 220

Poppæa; her relations with the Jews, 319; her supposed antagonism to St Paul, 319

Posidonius the Stoic, 295

Pothinus, 187

poverty, respect paid to, by Essenes and by Christ, 405

Praedicatio Pauli, 111 sq, 162

presbyter (elder) among the Jews, 149 sq; 'bishop' a synonyme of, 151 sq; Christian presbyters derived from the synagogue, 149 sq; in the mother Church, 150 sq; in Gentile Churches, 151; their duties, 152 sq; their designations, 152; bishops so called, 191 sq; how addressed by bishops, 193; see *ministry, priests, priesthood* etc

priest; distinguished from presbyter, 143; the two confused in many languages, 143, 212 sq

priesthood; idea common to Jewish and heathen, 138, 233; the Christian, 139 sq, 232 sq; universal, 237; the Jewish, 138 sq; not called κλῆρος, 212 sq; analogous with Christian ministry, 231 sq; see *ministry, priest, sacerdotalism* etc

Primus of Corinth, 177

proselytes, grades of Jewish, 50 sq

Protevangelium, on the Lord's brethren, 28, 35

Publius of Athens, 178

Pythagoreanism; and Essenism, 361 sq; disappearance of, 365

Quadratus, 178
Quinisextine Council, 145, 146

rebaptism of heretics, 207
Renan, 5, 152, 373
Resurrection, power of the, 310 sq, 401 sq
Revelation; see *Apocalypse*
Ritschl; on the early Church, 49, 61, 74, 75, 79; on the Christian ministry, 144, 145

Roman Empire, cosmopolitan idea realised in, 290 sq

Romans, Epistle to the, contrasted with Galatians, 107 sq

Rome, the Church of; its early history, 93 sq; at first Greek, not Latin, 186; transition to a Latin Church, 186; deacons limited to seven in, 145 sq; episcopacy and church government in, 179 sq; succession of bishops, 89 sq, 182 sq; recognition of St Peter and St Paul by, 116 sq; communications with Cyprian, 207 sq; see *Clement of Rome, Hegesippus*

Rothe; on the origin of episcopacy, 144, 160 sq; on the angels of the Apocalypse, 158; on Diotrephes, 158

Rufinus; his translation of Eusebius, 89; of the Clementine Recognitions, 84, 86

Sabbath, observance of, by Essenes, 396

Sabeans, 390

sacerdotalism; the term defined, 210; its absence in the N.T., 137, 139 sq, 210, 232 sq; rapid growth, 211 sq; progress of development, 220 sq; how far innocent, 225; whether due to Jewish or Gentile influences, 226 sq; see *priesthood*

sacrifices, prohibited by the Essenes, 350 sq

Sagaris, 174

Salome, 16

Samanæi, 375 sq

Samaritans; how regarded by the Jews, 53; their conversion, 53

Sampsæans, 354

Sarmanæ, 375 sq

Schliemann, 73 sq, 78

Seneca; possibly of Shemetic race, 257; his personal appearance, 265; relations with Nero, 297 sq; chronology of his writings, 273, 281;

spurious work ascribed to, 317 sq; Haase's edition of, 317, 320; his character, 296 sq; his own confessions of weakness, 298; accounted a Christian, 249; supposed connexion with St Paul, 249, 283 sq; literature on the subject, 258; compared and contrasted with St Paul, 258 sq; coincidence of thought and language with the Bible, 258 sq; nature of God, 259; relation of man to God, 259 sq; guardian angels, 260; an indwelling spirit, 260; universality of sin, 261; the conscience, 262; self-examination, 262; duties towards others, 263; parallels to the Sermon on the Mount and to the Gospels, 264 sq; to the Apostolic Epistles, 268; to St Paul, 269 sq; fallacious inferences therefrom, 272 sq; his obligations to earlier writers, 274; portrait of the wise man, 275; a true Stoic in his theology and ethics, 277 sq; his possible knowledge of Christianity, 283 sq; his cosmopolitanism, 290 sq; his vague ideas on immortality, 310 sq; his sense of the need of a historic basis, 313 sq; see *Stoicism*

Seneca and Paul, the letters of; described, 250, 317 sq; MSS and editions of, 317; motive of the forgery, 318; opinion of St Jerome about them, 250, 318, 320; mentioned by St Augustine and later writers, 318; their spuriousness, 250, 319; a theory respecting them discussed, 319 sq; *de Copia Verborum* mentioned in them, 320

Serapion of Antioch, 171, 174; on the Gospel of Peter, 27

Seres, mythical character of, 81

Servianus, Hadrian's letter to, 188

Seven, appointment of the, 51 sq, 144 sq; they were deacons, 145

Simon, Symeon, different persons called, 9, 18; a common name, 20

sin; see *peccatum*

slavery, prohibited by the Essenes, 404

Socrates, on preparation for death, 312

Sophronius, 9

Soter, 185

Stephanus Gobarus, on Hegesippus, 91

Stephen (St), influence and work of, 52, 56, 58

Stephen of Rome, 207

Stoicism; rise of, 251 sq; Oriental origin and character of, 252 sq, 255, 282 sq, 295, 305 sq; exclusive attention to ethics in, 254; neglect of physics and logic, 254 sq; its prophetic character, 255 sq; its westward progress, 256; the older Stoics, 294 sq; Stoicism at Tarsus, 287 sq; in Rome, 256, 295; native places of its great teachers, 282, 288; its obligations to Judaism, 283; a preparation for the Gospel, 286 sq; wide influence of its vocabulary, 287; contrast to Christianity, 276, 293 sq; its materialistic pantheism, 277, 306 sq; consistent blasphemies, 278, 306 sq; no consciousness of sin, 278 sq, 307 sq; 'sacer spiritus,' 260, 279; faulty ethics of, 278 sq, 308 sq; apathy of, 280, 309; defiance of nature in, 308; inconsistencies of, 281, 307 sq; paradoxes and paralogisms of, 312 sq; its cosmopolitanism, 290 sq; the wise man, 289; diverse and vague ideas about man's immortality, 309 sq; no idea of retribution, 312; want of a historic basis, 313 sq; religious directors, 295; improved theology in Epictetus, 302; improved ethics in M. Aurelius, 303; modifications and decline of, 305 sq; hymnology of, 306; exclusiveness of, 309; meagre results of, 294, 306; causes of failure, 306 sq; see *Epictetus, M. Aurelius, Seneca, Zeno* etc

Strabo, on Buddhism, 374 sq

subdeacons, 145 sq

sun-worship, 229, 354, 364, 369

Symeon, son of Clopas, 18 sq, 29 sq,

INDEX OF SUBJECTS. 421

68, 162, 168; his martyrdom, 71, 168; see *Simon*
synagogues; character and number of, 149 sq; adopted by the Christians, 167; angels of, 158; rulers of, 149; chazan of, 147
synods (episcopal), 175, 187, 207
Syriac translations; of Clement, 216; of the Clementines, 84, 87; of Ignatius, 96, 198, 242; of Eusebius, 33, 36, 90, 117; see *Ancient Syriac Documents*
Syrian Church, 172; sacerdotalism in, 228 sq

Talmud; supposed etymologies of Essene in, 329 sq, 334 sq; supposed allusions to the Essenes in, 343 sq
Tarsus, Stoicism at, 287 sq
Telesphorus, 183, 184
Tertullian; on the Lord's brethren, 4, 10, 31 sq; on episcopacy, 172, 176, 190, 204; on the Church and bishops of Rome, 185 sq; on Praxeas, 102; on Seneca, 249; on natural Christianity, 315; use of 'clerus' in, 214; sacerdotal views of, 222 sq
Testaments of the Twelve Patriarchs, 75 sq; no sacerdotalism in, 227
Thebuthis, 168
Theodoret; on the Lord's brethren, 8, 44; on bishops and Apostles, 153 sq
Theophilus of Antioch, 171
Theophilus of Cæsarea, 169
Theophylact, on the Lord's brethren, 5, 44
Therapeutes, 354
Thomas (St), his name Judas, 15
Thrace, episcopacy in, 179
Thrasea Pætus, 297
Thraseas of Eumenia, 175
Timothy, his position at Ephesus, 157 sq
Titus, his position in Crete, 157 sq

Tours, Council of, 249
Tübingen School, 47 sq, 91, 93, 104 sq, 113, 123, 133; see *Baur*
Tyndale and other versions, rendering of πρεσβύτερος in, 211

Valens, the Philippian, his crime, 176
vathikin, 347
Versions; their testimony respecting the Lord's brethren, 8, 14, 15, 18 sq, 21, 28
Victor of Rome, 90, 93 sq, 101, 175, 186, 192, 207
Victorinus Petavionensis, on the Lord's brethren, 10, 36
Victorinus Philosophus, on the Lord's brethren, 37
vine, parable of the, 314, 316
Vitringa, criticisms on, 145, 147, 158, 167
Vopiscus, 188
Vulgate, rendering of πρεσβύτερος in, 211

Western Services, their testimony respecting the Jameses, 43
Wiclif, rendering of πρεσβύτερος by, 211
Wieseler, 16, 20
Word of God, the; see *Christ*

Xystus, 183, 184; proverbs ascribed to, 184

Yavana or Yona, 373

Zeller on Essenism, 362 sq
Zend Avesta, 369
Zeno; his system compared with that of Epicurus, 251 sq; a Phœnician, 253; his character, 295; his admired polity, 290, 295; see *Stoicism*
Zephyrinus, 102, 186
Zoroastrianism and Essenism, 369 sq
Zoticus, 175

INDEX OF PASSAGES.

		PAGE
Genesis	i 28	357
	xi 29	12
	xiii 8	7
	xxix 15	7
Exodus	xv 26	358
	xxviii 15 sq	331
	xxviii 36	121
Leviticus	xviii 18	61
Numbers	viii 10	139
	xxvi 62	212
Deuteronomy	x 9	212
	xii 12, xiv 27	212
	xvii 12	226
	xviii 1, 2	212
	xx 6	212
	xxiii 1	54
	xxiii 12 sq	349
	xxviii 30	212
Joshua	xiv 3	212
Ruth	i 12	212
1 Chronicles	xxiv 5, 7, 31	213
	xxv 8, 9	213
Job	i 21	272
	vii 1	269
Psalms	xxii 22	11
	xxx 5	338
	xxxi 12	271
	xxxi 24	338
Proverbs	iii 11, 12	274
	xxii 9	271
Isaiah	lvi 3 sq	55
	lviii 7	263
	lx 17	216
	lxi 1	405
Ezekiel	vii 22	212

		PAGE
Ezekiel	viii 16	356
	xviii 7, 16	263
Daniel	ix 27	87
	x 13, 20, 21	159
Haggai	i 13	158
Malachi	i 10, 11	218
	ii 7	158
Tobit	iii 17	372
Ecclus.	vii 29, 31	226
1 Maccabees	ii 42	327, 332
	vii 13	327, 332
2 Maccabees	xiv 6	327, 332
St Matthew	i 15, 16	21
	25	23
	iii 7	383
	v 3	405
	v 8, 21 sq, 29	264
	v 23, 24	401
	v 33, 34	403
	v 39, 44, 45	264
	v 41	302
	vi 3 sq, 10, 16	265
	vi 17	400
	vi 19	266
	vii 3 sq, 12, 16, 26	266
	vii 15	85
	viii 4	401
	ix 10 sq	399
	ix 13	268, 401
	ix 14 sq	386
	x 2 sq, 15 sq	19
	x 18	110
	xi 5	405
	xi 17 sq	386
	xi 19	399, 400

INDEX OF PASSAGES.

		PAGE
St Matthew	xii 1 sq	396
	xii 7	401
	xiii 3 sq, 31 sq	267
	xiii 55	8 sq, 20
	xv 1 sq	398
	xvi 1 sq	383
	xvi 17	86
	xviii 23 sq	267
	xix 12	400
	xx 22, 23	27
	xxi 12 sq, 23 sq	401
	xxii 21	299
	xxii 23 sq	383
	xxiii 2, 3	382
	xxiii 18 sq	401
	xxiii 26, 27	266
	xxiv 1 sq	401
	xxiv 45 sq	302
	xxv 14 sq	267
	xxvi 55	401
	xxvii 56	7, 16, 21
St Mark	i 44	401
	ii 15 sq	399
	ii 18 sq	386
	ii 23 sq	396
	iii 18	15, 19
	v 22	167
	vi 3	8 sq, 20
	vii 1 sq	398
	x 38, 39	27
	xi 11, 15 sq	401
	xi 27	401
	xii 18	383
	xii 35	401
	xiii 1 sq	401
	xiv 36	27
	xiv 49	401
	xv 40 7, 14, 16, 20, 21, 22	
	xv 41	16
	xv 47	20, 21
	xvi 1	16, 22
St Luke	ii 7, 23	23
	ii 33, 41, 43, 48	22
	ii 46	401
	iii 24, 26, 29, 30	21
	iv 18	405
	iv 20	147
	v 14	401

		PAGE
St Luke	v 30 sq	399
	v 33	386
	vi 1 sq	396
	vi 15	19
	vi 16	8 sq, 28
	vi 20	405
	vi 35	265
	vii 22	405
	vii 31 sq	386
	vii 34	400
	vii 37 sq	399
	vii 46	400
	xi 38 sq	398
	xii 16 sq	267
	xii 41 sq	302
	xiii 10 sq	396
	xiv 1 sq	396
	xv 2	399
	xix 7	399
	xix 45	401
	xx 1 sq	401
	xx 27	383
	xxi 3, 4	268
	xxi 37 sq	401
	xxii 42	27
	xxii 53	401
	xxiii 34	268
	xxiv 10	16, 22, 28
	xxiv 18	19
	xxiv 53	401
St John	i 8	388
	i 11	123
	i 15 sq	388
	ii 14 sq	401
	iii 23 sq	388
	iv 9	54
	iv 22	123
	v 10 sq	396
	v 14	401
	v 20	330
	v 35	388
	vii 5	13
	vii 14	401
	vii 21	330
	vii 22, 23	396
	vii 49	345
	viii 2, 20	401
	viii 48	54

INDEX OF PASSAGES.

		PAGE			PAGE
St John	viii 59	401	Acts	xiii 35	330
	ix 14, 16	396		xiv 23	151, 211
	x 16	293		xv 1 sq	59 sq, 127
	x 23	401		xv 2, 4, 6,	151, 211
	x 25	330		xv 4	156
	x 41, 42	388		xv 13 sq	155
	xi 16	15		xv 23	62, 151, 156
	xi 56	401		xv 24	131
	xiv 5	15		xv 26	66
	xiv 22	10		xvi 4	63, 151, 156, 211
	xv 4	266		xvii 23	378
	xviii 20	401		xvii 24 sq	272
	xix 25	7, 10 sq, 16, 18, 19, 28		xvii 28	260, 288, 306
				xviii 7	125
	xix 26, 27	24		xviii 8	167
	xx 17	11		xviii 12 sq	285
	xx 24	15		xviii 17	167
Acts	i 5, 8	388		xviii 24	187, 387
	i 13, 14	8 sq, 13, 19, 28		xix 1	387
	i 17, 25, 26	213		xix 4	388
	i 23	20, 125		xx 17	152, 211
	ii 1 sq	50 sq		xx 28	151, 152
	ii 27	330		xx 35	268
	ii 42, 46	401, 403		xxi 18	124, 125, 155, 156, 211
	iv 13	345			
	iv 36	20		xxi 25	62
	v 4	404		xxii 3	302
	v 6, 10	146		xxiii 4	226
	v 29	31		xxiv 17	229
	v 35	388		xxviii 16	285
	vi 1 sq	51 sq, 144 sq	Romans	i 16	105
	vi 1, 2, 7	387		i 23, 28, 32	270
	vi 9	149		ii 9, 10	105, 123
	viii 5 sq	53 sq		ii 21, 22	271
	viii 14	118		iii 1, 2	105
	viii 26 sq	54		vi 6	122
	ix 3	85		vi 15 sq	129
	ix 10, 19, 26, 38	387		viii 19	302
	ix 20, 22, 26, 29	57		viii 24	271
	x 1 sq	54 sq		ix 1 sq	106
	x 9 sq	113 sq		x 1, 2	106
	xi 16	388		xi 1, 26	106
	xi 19	53		xii 1	229
	xi 20	56		xii 5	292
	xi 30	151, 156, 211		xii 7	148
	xii 17	124, 155, 156		xii 8	152
	xiii 1 sq	59		xii 21	271
	xiii 15	167		xiv 2, 21	395

INDEX OF PASSAGES.

Book	Reference	Page
Romans	xv 16	229
	xv 25, 26	106
	xvi 1	148
1 Corinthians	i 12 sq	132
	ii 9	91 sq
	ii 11	271
	iii 4 sq	110
	iii 22, 23	117, 289
	iv 8, 10	289
	v 1 sq	63, 157
	vi 9 sq	129
	vi 18 sq	63
	vii 20	300
	vii 26 sq	400
	vii 31	271
	vii 35	302
	viii 1 sq	63, 65
	viii 13	64
	ix 1	302
	ix 5	109
	ix 13, 14	234
	ix 20, 22	106
	ix 25	270
	x 7, 8, 14 sq	63, 64
	x 18	234
	x 20, 32	64, 65
	xii 12, 13, 27	292
	xii 28	142
	xiii 3	378
	xv 5, 7	17, 27, 109, 124
	xv 9	110
	xv 32	312
	xvi 1 sq	106
	xvi 12	110
2 Corinthians	ii 6	157
	iii 1	85, 133, 302
	iii 13	52
	iii 17, 18	271
	iv 7	271
	iv 16	122
	vi 8, 9	85
	vi 10	289
	vi 14	271
	viii 23	154
	viii 1 sq	106
	ix 1 sq	106
	ix 7	271
	ix 8, 11	289
2 Corinthians	x 7, 13 sq	132
	xi 5	109
	xi 13, 21 sq	133
	xii 1 sq	133
	xii 11	109
	xii 15	270, 282
Galatians	i 18	108
	i 19	5, 7, 13, 155
	ii 1 sq	60 sq, 66, 108, 112
	ii 9	5, 33, 103, 155
	ii 10	106
	ii 11 sq	85 sq, 112 sq, 119
	ii 12	131, 155
	ii 20	115
	iii 28	292
	v 13 sq	129
Ephesians	ii 6, 19	292
	iii 15	36
	iv 1	300
	iv 11	142, 152
	iv 25	292
	v 16, 28, 29	271
	v 30	292
Philippians	i 1	148, 151
	i 27	292
	ii 17	229
	ii 25	154
	iii 20	292
	iv 11, 13	289
	iv 18	229, 289
	iv 22	284
Colossians	ii 22	271
	iii 11	292
	iv 10, 11	116, 125
1 Thessalonians	iv 1	388
	v 12	152
1 Timothy	i 3	158
	ii 9	272
	iii 1, 2	151, 153
	iii 8 sq	148, 149
	iii 12, 14	158
	iv 8	272
	iv 14	201
	iv 15	302
	v 6	272
	v 17	152, 153, 211

INDEX OF PASSAGES.

		PAGE
1 Timothy	vi 7	272
2 Timothy	i 9	300
	ii 5	302
	ii 18	52
	iii 7	272
	iv 9, 21	158
Titus	i 5 sq 149, 152, 158, 211	
	i 7	151
	i 8	330
	i 9	153
	i 15	270
Hebrews	v 12	302
	x 11, 12	233
	xii 5 sq	274
	xiii 7, 17	152
	xiii 10	229, 230, 234 sq
	xiii 15, 16	229, 230
	xiii 24	152
James	i 1 sq	128 sq
	i 25 sq	128, 129
	ii 2	150
	ii 9 sq	128
	ii 19	130
	ii 26	129
	iv 11	128
	iv 13	269
	v 1 sq	116
	v 14	211
1 Peter	i 1 sq	114 sq
	i 13	269
	ii 9, 12	116
	ii 20	388 sq
	ii 24, 25	115, 151, 152
	iii 4	122
	v 1, 2	152, 157
	v 12, 13	116
1 John	v 6	388
3 John	9	158
Jude	1	9
	17	14
Revelation	i 1 sq	120 sq
	i 6	122, 141
	i 8	120
	ii 6, 15	52
	ii 9	122
	ii 14	64
	ii 17	122, 220
	ii 20	64, 159

		PAGE
Revelation	ii 24	64, 122
	iii 14	120
	v 1 sq	116
	v 9	121
	v 10	122, 141
	v 13	120
	vii 9	122
	xvii 14	121
	xix 10	120
	xix 13	120, 123
	xix 16	121
	xx 6	122, 141
	xxii 13	120

Acta Perp. et Fel. 13	153
Acta Thomae 1	15
Æschylus *Fragm.* 285	36
Aristophanes *Ranae* 708	14
Arrianus *Ind.* viii. 1	377
Ascents of James i. 59	
29, 87, 118, 126, 389	
Athanasius *c. Arianos* 75 (I. p. 152 ed. Ben.)	195
Athenagoras *Suppl.* 33, 34	122
Ambrose *de Inst. Virg.* (II. p. 260 ed. Ben.)	42
Ambrosiaster *in Gal.* i. 19	37
in Eph. iv. 11	154
in Eph. iv. 12	141, 163, 167, 194
in 1 *Tim.* iii. 10	193
Augustinus	
Retract. i. 13 § 3 (I. p. 18 ed. Ben.)	315
Epist. lxxxii. 33 (II. p. 202)	193
Epist. cliii. 14 (II. p. 329)	318
Quaest. XVII. *in Matth.* No. 17 (III. 2. p. 285)	43
in Joh. x. (III. 2, p. 368)	43
in Joh. xxviii. (III. 2, p. 507)	43
in Gal. i. 19 (III. 2, p. 944)	42
Quaest. Vet. et Nov. Test. ci. (III. 2 App. p. 92)	193, 194
Enarr. in Ps. cxxvii. (IV. 2, p. 1443)	43
de Civ. Dei vi. 10 (VII. p. 158)	270
adv. Haer. 53 (VIII. p. 18)	197

INDEX OF PASSAGES. 427

Augustinus	PAGE
adv. Haer. 84 (VIII. p. 24)	39
Aulus Gellius xvii. 19	299
Basilius	
Hom. in Sanct. Christ. Gen.	
II. p. 600 (ed. Garnier)	38
Cassiodorus de Inst. Div. Lit. 8	32
Chrysostomus	
in Matth. i. 25, x. 2, xxvii. 55	43
in Joh. vii. 5	43
in 1 Cor. ix. 4, xv. 7	43
Hom. XIV. in Act.	145
Hom. XI. in 1 Tim. iii. 8	197
Cicero	
pro Balbo 13	291
Brutus XXXI.	296
Orator 25	122
Parad. procem. 2	296
Tim. 1	365
Verr. v. 57, 65	291
Clemens Rom. i.	152
5	116, 117
21	152, 153
34	91
35	230
36	230, 232
40 sq	216
41	230
42	151
44	151, 152, 163 sq, 230
47	117
52	230
61, 64	232
Clemens Alexandrinus	
Paedag. ii. 1 (p. 174 ed. Potter)	80, 127, 394
iii. 4 (p. 269)	122
iii. 12 (p. 309)	189, 190
Strom. i. 15 (p. 359)	375 sq
ii. 20 (p. 491)	52
iii. 1 (p. 509 sq)	122
iii. 4 (p. 522)	52
iii. 5 (p. 529 sq)	33
iii. 7 (p. 539)	377
iii. 12 (p. 552)	189
iii. 12 § 90 (p. 552)	221
iii. 13 (p. 553)	33
v. 5 § 33 sq (p. 665 sq)	222
v. 14 (p. 714)	276

Clemens Alexandrinus	PAGE
Strom. vi. 5 (p. 760)	111
vi. 13 (p. 793)	189, 221
vii. 1 (p. 830)	189, 192
vii. 6 (p. 848)	234
vii. 17 (p. 898)	111
Quis div. salv. § 42 (p. 959)	172, 192, 214
Clementine Homilies	
Epistle of Peter to James	
1, 2	86, 110 sq, 168
Epistle of Clement to James	
1 sq, 15	99, 168, 203
i. 16	99
ii. 1	15
ii. 16	228
ii. 17, 18	80, 82, 85, 87
ii. 23	390, 391
ii. 33	228
ii. 38, 51	352, 353
iii. 4, 5	352
iii. 6 sq	130
iii. 10	352
iii. 13	353
iii. 15	80
iii. 26	353
iii. 36	353
iii. 47, 49 sq, 55 sq	352, 353
iii. 60 sq	202
iii. 62, 66, 68 sq	170, 171, 202
v. 18	295
vii. 5, 8, 12	170, 171
viii. 15	80
xi. 35	29, 84, 168
xi. 36	170, 171
xii. 6	80, 394
xv. 7	80
xv. 17	394
xvii. 19	86
xviii. 19, 20	352, 353
xx. 23	170, 171
Clementine Recognitions	
i. 37	80
i. 43	168
i. 46	228
i. 48	228, 232
i. 54, 60, 63	389, 390
i. 57	118, 126
i. 64	80

INDEX OF PASSAGES.

Clementine Recognitions	PAGE
i. 68	168
i. 70, 71	87
i. 73	168
i. 74	99
iii. 61	80, 86
iii. 65, 66, 74	170, 171
vi. 15	170, 171
viii. 48	81
ix. 19	81
x. 68	170, 171
Constit. Apost. ii. 25, 27, 34, 35	231
ii. 39	91
ii. 53	231
v. 8	168
vi. 6, 23	386, 389, 391
vi. 14	168
vii. 46	157, 170
viii. 28	197
viii. 35, 46	168
Cyprianus *Epist.*	
3	209, 226
4	226
15 § 1, 33 § 1, 41 § 2, 46	208
29	153
38 § 1, 39 § 1, 40	209
43	208, 209, 226
44, 45, 71, 76	193, 209
55	208, 209
59	187, 208, 209, 226
66 esp. § 8	208, 209, 226
67	208, 226
69	226
73	209, 226
de unit. eccles. § 5	208
§ 18	226
Cyrillus Alexandrinus	
Glaphyr. in Gen. vii. (p. 221 ed. Auberti)	44
c. Julian. iv. (p. 133)	376 sq
Cyrillus Hierosolymitanus	
Catech. iv. 28, xiv. 21 (pp. 65, 216 ed. Touttée)	37
Demosthenes *Timocr.* § 157	155
Diog. Laertius	
ii. 114	252
vii. 3, 7, 15, 25, 30	252
vii. 40	254
vii. 160, 179	255

Diog. Laertius	PAGE
vii. 157	310
viii. 17	364
viii. 24 sq, 37	365
viii. 42	366
Dion Cassius liv. 9	378
Dion Chrysostom	
Or. xxxii. (p. 373)	375
Epictetus *Diss.* i. 9. 19, 14. 13 sq, 16. 15 sq, 25. 10, 29. 31, 29. 46 sq, 30. 1; ii. 3. 1, 7. 12, 8. 11 sq, 10. 7, 14. 13, 16. 39, 42, 46, 26. 1; iii. 1. 36 sq, 10. 8, 21. 16, 22. 2 sq, 23, 35, 48, 69; iv. 1. 79, 170	299—302
Diss. iv. 7. 6	305
Epiphanius *Haer.*	
x. (p. 28 sq ed. Petav.)	325
xvii. 1 (p. 37)	386, 392
xviii. 1 (p. 38)	353
xix. 1 sq (p. 40 sq.)	81, 82, 325, 327, 335, 354, 355, 356, 393
xix. 3, 5 (pp. 42, 43)	355
xx. 3 (pp. 46, 47)	335, 354
xxviii. 7 (p. 115)	39
xxix. 1 (p. 117)	325, 326
xxix. 4 (p. 119)	34, 39
xxix. 9 (p. 124)	75
xxx. 1 (p. 125)	325
xxx. 2 (p. 126)	80
xxx. 3 (p. 127)	325, 335, 354
xxx. 16 (p. 140)	82, 83, 87, 394
xxx. 17 (p. 141)	355
xxx. 18 (p. 142)	77, 150, 353
xxx. 23 (p. 147)	118
xxx. 25 (p. 149)	82, 83
li. 10 (p. 432)	39
liii. 1 (p. 462)	325
lxvi. 19 (p. 636)	39
lxxv. 3 (p. 906)	197
lxxviii. (p. 1034 sq)	39 sq
lxxviii. 13 (p. 1045)	118
lxxviii. 14 (p. 1046)	126
Euripides *Electra* 935	36
Eusebius *Hist. Eccl.*	
i. 12 § 4	36
i. 13 § 10	15, 169, 172
ii. 1 §§ 2, 3	36, 168

INDEX OF PASSAGES.

Eusebius *Hist. Eccl.* PAGE
  ii. 23 §§ 4 sq, 18 30, 68, 90
                    125 sq, 168, 389, 393
  ii. 24 188
  ii. 25 § 8 117
  iii. 1 162
  iii. 4 § 6 157
  iii. 5 § 3 68
  iii. 7 § 9 36
  iii. 11 19, 162
  iii. 14 29, 188
  iii. 16 177
  iii. 20 § 1 30
  iii. 27 73
  iii. 30 § 1 34
  iii. 31 §§ 3, 4 161
  iii. 32 30, 71, 72, 82, 204
  iii. 35 72
  iii. 36 §§ 2, 15 171, 174
  iii. 39 §§ 3, 4, 9 161, 192
  iv. 5 72, 125, 168, 169, 257
  iv. 6 § 4 69, 72, 73
  iv. 11 § 7 89
  iv. 20 171
  iv. 21 90
  iv. 22 29, 71, 89, 90 sq, 168
               177, 182, 185, 204, 389, 391
  iv. 23 102, 175, 177, 178, 185
  iv. 25 179
  iv. 26 § 3 174
  v. 1 §§ 10, 26 187, 214
  v. 12 § 2 169
  v. 16 §§ 17, 22 175
  v. 19 174, 179
  v. 20 § 7 192
  v. 22 178
  v. 23 88, 101, 175, 178
  v. 24 88, 101, 121, 173 sq
               184 sq, 192, 220
  v. 25 170
  vi. 11 § 3 169
  vi. 12 § 2 27
  vi. 38 82, 83, 88
  vi. 43 § 11 146
  Quaest. ad Marin. ii. 5 18
  Comm. in Isai. 36
  on the star 36
Eutychius *Annales*
  (I. pp. 331, 2 ed. Pococke) 195, 196

Evangelia Apocrypha PAGE
  Protevangelium Jacobi §§
    9, 17, 25 (pp. 18, 31, 48
    ed. Tisch.). 28, 121
  Ps-Matthaei Ev. § 32 (p.
    104) 18, 28
  Evang. de Nativ. Mar. § 8
    (p. 111) 28
  Historia Joseph. § 2 (p. 116) 28
  Evang. Thomae § 16 (p. 147) 28
  Evang. Inf. Arab. § 35 (p.
    191) 18, 28
Gregorius Nyssenus
  in Christ. Resurr. ii. (III.
    p. 412 ed. Paris) 39
Hieronymus
  Epist. cxii. 13 (I. p. 740 ed.
    Vallarsi) 150
  Epist. cxx. (I. p. 826) 12
  ad evang. (I. p. 1076) 166, 189, 194
  de vir. illustr. 2 (II. p. 815)
               10 sq, 26, 30
    3 (II. p. 819) 74
    12 (II. p. 835) 250, 318
    22 (II. p. 849) 90
    36 (II. p. 861) 375
  adv. Helvidium § 1 sq (II.
    p. 206 sq) 4
    § 13 (II. p. 219) 8
    § 17 (II. p. 225)
               10, 31, 36
    (II. p. 958) 9
  de nomin. Hebr. (III. pp. 89, 98) 8
  Quaest. Hebr. in Gen. (III.
    p. 305) 69
  in Isai. ix. 1 (IV. p. 130) 74
  in Matth. xii. 49 (VII. p. 86)
               10, 11, 28
Hilarius Pictaviensis
  in Matth. i. 1 (p. 671 ed. Ben.) 37
Hermas *Pastor*
  Vis. ii. 2 § 6 152, 181
    ii. 4 § 3 98, 152, 180
    iii. 5 § 1 181
    iii. 8 § 3 97
    iii. 9 § 7 152, 181
  Mand. iv. 4 § 2 97
    viii. § 9 97
    xi. § 12 181

Hermas *Pastor*	PAGE
Sim. v. 3 § 3 sq	97
viii. 7 § 4	181
ix. 12 §§ 1—3, 14 § 5	97
ix. 25 sq	181
Herodianus iv. 15	369
Hippolytus	
Haer. i. 24 (p. 28 ed. Miller)	377
v. 6 (p. 64)	65
v. 7 (p. 95)	33
v. 24, 26, 27 (pp. 149, 153, 158)	91
vi. 7 (p. 161)	335
vi. 24 (p. 180)	91
vii. 34 (p. 257)	73, 78
vii. 36 (p. 258)	52
viii. 19 (p. 275)	91
ix. 7 sq (p. 279)	102
ix. 12 (pp. 287, 288)	186, 214
ix. 13 sq	81, 82, 88, 355, 393
ix. 18 (p. 297)	325
ix. 28 (p. 305)	325
pp. 74, 82 (ed. Lagarde)	164
Horatius *Epod.* 2. 67	20
Satir. i. 3. 124 sq	289
Ignatius	
Ephes. 1	173, 199
2, 3, 6, 20	200
4	201
5	201, 234
Magn. 2	174, 200, 201
3	200
4	201
6, 13	200, 201
7	201, 234
8, 10	96
Trall. 1	174
2, 3	200, 201
7	200, 234
12	201
13	200
Rom. inscr.	96
4	117
Philad. 1	174, 201
3, 7, 8	200, 201
4	200, 234
6	96
9	217, 232
Smyrn. 8	167, 200, 201

Ignatius	PAGE
Smyrn. 9, 12	200
Polyc. inscr.	173
1 sq	199
6	170, 199
8	201
Irenæus	
adv. omnes Haer.	
i. 26. 2	73
i. 26. 3	52, 145
i. 27. 1	214
ii. 22. 5	192
ii. 28. 9	65
ii. 30. 6	91
iii. 2. 2	191
iii. 3. 1	172, 191
iii. 3. 2, 3	182, 184, 185, 191, 204, 214
iii. 3. 4	173, 185
iii. 4. 3	184
iii. 4. 4	185
iii. 12. 10	145
iv. 8. 3	219
iv. 15. 1	145
iv. 17 sq	312
iv. 26. 2 sq	182, 192, 204
iv. 32. 1	204
v. praef.	204
v. 2. 3	231
v. 20. 1, 2	172, 204
v. 34. 3	220
Fragm. 17 (p. 836 sq, ed. Stieren)	76
Fragm. 38 (p. 854)	162, 164, 231
Isidorus Hispalensis	
de vit. et obit. sanct. 81	9
Josephus	
Ant. iii. 7. 5	331
iii. 8. 9	331
xii. 11. 2	360
xiii. 5. 9	325, 366
xiii. 10. 6	325
xiii. 11. 2	329, 352, 360
xiii. 15. 3	327
xv. 10. 4	325, 362, 403
xv. 10. 5	325, 329
xviii. 1. 2, 5	325, 351, 404
xx. 9. 1	126
B. J. i. 3. 5	329, 352, 360

INDEX OF PASSAGES. 431

Josephus	PAGE
B. J. ii. 7. 3	325, 329
ii. 8. 2	325
ii. 8. 3	385, 400, 401
ii. 8. 5	327, 331, 346 sq, 351, 354, 386, 398 sq
ii. 8. 6	80, 328, 403
ii. 8. 7	327, 340, 343 sq, 348 sq, 370, 398, 403
ii. 8. 9	348 sq, 352, 371, 396 sq
ii. 8. 10	343 sq, 352, 398, 399
ii. 8. 11	350
ii. 8. 12	329, 398
ii. 8. 13	325
ii. 20. 4	325
iii. 2. 1	325
vii. 8. 7	378
Vita 2	325, 348, 385, 387

Justinus Martyr
Apol. i. 13	231
i. 31	72
i. 47	69, 72
i. 65—7	231
i. 67	152

Dial. c. Tryph.
10	390
28, 29	231
35	65
41	231
47, 8	73, 89
85	358
110	72
116, 117	218, 220, 228, 231
127	89
134	357
137	167
141	357

Juvenalis *Satir.* iii. 116	265

Lactantius *Div. Inst.*
i. 5, ii. 9, vi. 24	249
vi. 25	272

Lucianus *de morte Peregrini* 11	229
Mart. Ignat. Ant. 3	173
Mart. Polyc. inscr. 8, 19	168 sq
14	27
16	168 sq, 173
Marcus Antonius xi. 3	305
Mela iii. 7	81
Muratorian Canon	161, 172

Nicephorus Callistus	PAGE
H. E. ii. 3	35

Oracula Sibyllina
ii. 96	65
iv. 26, 35, 42 sq, etc.	331

Origen
de Orat. 28 (I. p. 225 ed. Delarue)	224
c. Cels. i. 24 (I. p. 342)	375, 376
i. 47 (I. p. 363)	34
iv. 52 (I. p. 544)	69
v. 61, 65 (I. pp. 625, 628)	73
viii. 69 (I. p. 794)	72
Hom. v. *in Lev.* § 4 (II. p. 208 sq)	225
Hom. ix. *in Lev.* §§ 9, 10 (II. p. 243)	220, 224
Hom. iv. *in Num.* 3 (II. p. 283)	224
Hom. x. *in Num.* §§ 1, 2 (II. p. 302)	225
Hom. xv. *in Josh.* § 6 (II. p. 435)	76
Hom. in Ps. xxxvii. § 6 (II. p. 688)	225
Hom. xii. *in Jerem.* § 3 (p. 196)	225
Hom. in Matth. xiii. 55 (III. p. 462 sq.)	35
Hom. vii. *in Luc.* (III. p. 940)	34
Hom. in Joh. § 3 (IV. p. 3)	220, 224
Hom. in Joh. ii. 12 (*Cat. Corder.* p. 75)	34
Hom. in Rom. xvi. 23 (IV. p. 687)	177

Pelagius in Gal. i. 19	42

Philo
de mundi op. 7 (I. p. 6 ed. Mangey)	356
de agricult. 3 (I. p. 302)	254
de mutat. nomin. 10 (I. p. 589)	254
de somn. i. 13 sq (I. p. 631 sq)	356
de monarch. ii. 5 (II. p. 226)	331
quod omn. prob. 12, 13 (II. pp. 457, 459)	325, 326, 330, 351, 403
de vit. contempl. 1 (II. p. 471)	325, 328
3 (II. p. 475)	377

INDEX OF PASSAGES.

Philo	PAGE
de vit. contempl. 11 (II. p. 485)	354
Fragm. (II. p. 632)	
325, 326, 330,	385
(II. p. 633)	346
Philostratus vita Apollonii i. 15 sq	367
vi. 10	364
Photius Bibliotheca 232	91
Plato Phaedo 64 A	312
Sympos. 173 B	14
Plinius N. H. v. 15	325, 366
v. 17	325
vi. 24	81, 379
xxxvi. 19	370
Plutarchus vit. Anton. 2	122
vit. Alexandr. 69	378
vit. Cat. 4, 10, 16	296
Op. Mor. p. 329	290, 293
Op. Mor. p. 1044	295
Polybius xxxi. 6. 5	340
Polycarpus ad Phil. inscr.	173
4	234
12	232
Porphyrius de abstin. iv. 11	325
iv. 17	375 sq
Praedicatio Pauli	111 sq, 162
Rutilius de Red. i. 63, 66	290
Seneca	
ad Helv. Matrem 5 § 2	299
8	259
8 § 3	277
11 §§ 6, 7	261
16 § 3	272
ad Marciam 4 § 2	310
10 § 2	267
11 § 3	271
19 §§ 4, 5	311
24 § 5	269, 311
26 § 7	310
ad Polybium 1 (20) § 2	310
5 §§ 1, 2	310
7 § 4	270
9 § 2	310
9 § 3	310, 311
11 § 1	261
11 § 3	269
de Beneficiis i. 1	265
i. 1 § 9	259
i. 1 § 13	268

Seneca	PAGE
de Beneficiis i. 6 §§ 3, 4	268
i. 7 § 2	271
i. 10 § 3	260
ii. 1 § 1	266
ii. 10 § 4	265
ii. 29 § 4	259
iii. 18 § 2	292
iv. 7 §§ 1, 2	277
iv. 8 § 3	277
iv. 12 § 2	268
iv. 25, 26	265
iv. 27 § 3	261
v. 1 § 5	264
v. 8 § 1	265
v. 14 § 2	264
v. 17 § 3	268
vii. 1 § 7	262
vii. 3, 4, 6, 10	305
vii. 7 § 3	273
vii. 31 § 1, 2	265, 271
vii. 31 § 4, 5	264, 265
vii. 31, 32	268
de Brevitate Vitae 1 § 3	271
12 § 9	272
14 § 2	280
18 § 5	310
de Clem. i. 8 § 3	277
ii. 2 § 1	270
ii. 5—7	280
de Const. Sap. 8 § 2	278
14 § 3	264
de Ira i. 14 § 1—3	262, 264
ii. 16 § 2	278
ii. 28 § 1 sq	261
ii. 28 § 8	271
iii. 3 passim	280
iii. 36 § 3	263
de Otio 5. 5	261
28 (1) § 1	263
28 (1) § 4	264, 275
29 (2) § 1	275
30 (3) § 5	263
31 (4) § 1	292
de Tranq. Anim. 7 § 3	263
13	269
14 § 9	296
de Vita beata 2 § 2	271
3 § 2	275

INDEX OF PASSAGES. 433

Seneca		PAGE	Seneca		PAGE
de Vita beata	7 § 4	271	Ep. Mor.	xli. 2	260, 261
	8 § 4	277		xlii. 3	261
	13 § 1	275		xlvii. 2, 4, 8	284
	15 § 5	259		xlvii. 15	263, 384
	15 § 7	271		xlvii. 17	263
	15 § 17	259		xlvii. 18	268
	17	299		xlviii. 2	263
	20 § 3	263, 291		li. 6	269
	20 § 5	264		lvii. 3	299
	21 § 4	299		lxiii. 7	272
	24 § 2	266		lxv. 10	259
	24 § 3	292		lxv. 17	261
	27 §§ 3, 4	266		lxv. 18	259, 261, 269
de Providentia	1 § 5	260, 278		lxv. 24	310
	2 § 6	260		lxvii. 14	260
	3 § 3	260		lxviii. 2	291
	4 §§ 1, 7	260		lxxi. 16	310
	5 § 4	270		lxxiii. 12, 13	278
	6 § 4	266		lxxiii. 16	260, 267
	6 § 6	278		lxxiv. 16	269
Ep. Mor.	i. 1	271		lxxiv. 18	271
	ii. 5	275		lxxiv. 20	265
	v. 1, 2	265		lxxvi. 23	260
	vi. 1	271		lxxviii. 16	270
	vi. 6	275		lxxix. 22	311
	vii. 8	263		lxxx. 2	272
	viii. 7	271		lxxxi.	264
	viii. 8	275		lxxxiii. 1	261
	ix.	289		lxxxvi. 1	311
	ix. 10	263		lxxxvii. 2	298
	x. 2	271		lxxxvii. 21	264
	x. 5	261		lxxxvii. 24, 25	266
	xi. 9	263		xcii. 30	261
	xiv. 1	271		xciv. 43	266
	xv. 2, 5	272		xciv. 48	271
	xx. 9	275		xcv. 47	268, 272
	xxiii. 9	272		xcv. 50	259
	xxiv. 18	310		xcv. 51	263
	xxv. 6 sq	263		xcv. 52	268, 291
	xxviii. 9, 10	262		xcv. 59	267
	xxxi. 9	278		xcvi. 5	269
	xxxi. 11	261, 272, 292		xcvii. 1	261
	xxxii. 2	271		xcvii. 14, 15	262
	xxxiii. 9	272		xcviii. 3	270
	xxxvi. 10	311		ci. 1	262
	xxxviii. 2	267		ci. 4, 5	267
	xxxix. 6	271		cii. 2	310
	xli. 1	272		cii. 22	261, 311

L.

INDEX OF PASSAGES.

Seneca	PAGE
Ep. Mor. cii. 23, 24	269
cii. 25	272
cii. 26	261, 269
cii. 28 sq	261, 311
civ. 1	285
cvi. 7 sq	277
cvii. 9	260
cviii. 14	298
cx. 1	259
cx. 18	266
cxv. 5	268
cxvii. 2	277
cxvii. 6	310
cxx. 12	269
cxx. 13	274
cxx. 14, 18	269
cxxii. 3	272
cxxiv. 23	259
Fragm. 14	261
31	270
123	272
Nat. Quaest. pro. § 12	260
ii. 59 § 8	262
iv. praef. § 10	285
Sextus Empiricus	
Pyrrh. iii. 200 sq	295
vii. 17	254
Sophocles *Trachin.* 1105	36
Sozomen *H. E.* vii. 19	146
Spartianus *Ver.* 3	188
Stobæus	
Flor. lxxx. 7	255
Ecl. iii. 56 (p. 141)	376
Strabo	
xiv. 8 (p. 671 ed. Cas.)	288
xiv. 13, 14 (p. 673 sq)	288
xv. 1, 4 (p. 686)	375, 378
xv. (p. 701)	81
xv. 1, 59 (p. 712)	375
xv. 1, 73 (p. 720)	378
xv. 3, 15 (p. 733)	372
Sulpicius Severus *H. S.* ii. 31	72
Tacitus	
Hist. iii. 24	369
Ann. xiii. 3	297
xiv. 53	298
xv. 45, 63	298
xvi. 32	365

Tertullianus	PAGE
de spectaculis 16	223
Scorpiace 13	76
de baptismo 17	222
ad uxorem i. 6, 7	223
de cultu femin. ii. 12	223
de exhort. castit. 7	223, 237
de monogamia 8	32
12	214, 220, 223
de pudicit. 1	186
de jejun. 14	101
de virgin. veland. 9	222
de pallio 4	223
de praescript. haeret.	
30	185, 186
32	173, 186
33	73
36	102, 176, 186
41	222
adv. Marcion. iv. 5	172, 186
iv. 9	223
iv. 19	32
v. 1	76
de carne Christi 7, 23	32
de resurrect. carnis 1	310
de anima 20	249
42	310
adv. Praxean 1	102
adv. Judaeos 14	220, 223
Testamenta xii. Patriarch.	
Reuben 6	76, 227, 232
Simeon 5	76
7	76, 227, 232
Levi 6, 7	77
8	214, 220, 227
13	76
18	227
19	76
Judas 18, 26	76
Dan 5, 6	76
Nephth. 6, 8	76
Gad 3, 8	76
Aser 2, 6, 7	76
Issach. 5	76
Zabul. 10	76
Joseph 11, 19	76
Benj. 10, 11	76, 77, 150
Theodor. Mopsuest. *in* 1 *Tim.* iii. 1	154

INDEX OF PASSAGES. 435

	PAGE		PAGE
Theodoretus *in Gal.* i. 19	8, 44	Vergilius *Æn.* viii. 352	261
in 1 *Tim.* iii. 1	153 sq	Victorinus Philosophus *in Gal.*	
Haer. Fab. ii. 11	103	i. 19	37
Theophylactus *in Matth.* xiii. 55,		Vopiscus *Vit. Saturn.* 8	188
Gal. i. 19	5, 44	Xenophon *Anab.* iv. 4, 12	388
Thucydides vi. 14	155	*Memor.* i. 4, 2	14
Vergilius *Æn.* vi. 726 sq	279		

www.ingramcontent.com/pod-product-compliance
Lightning Source LLC
Chambersburg PA
CBHW052137300426
44115CB00011B/1419